Ninth Edition

java™ SOFTWARE SOLUTIONS

FOUNDATIONS OF PROGRAM DESIGN

JOHN LEWIS
Virginia Tech

•

WILLIAM LOFTUS
Accenture

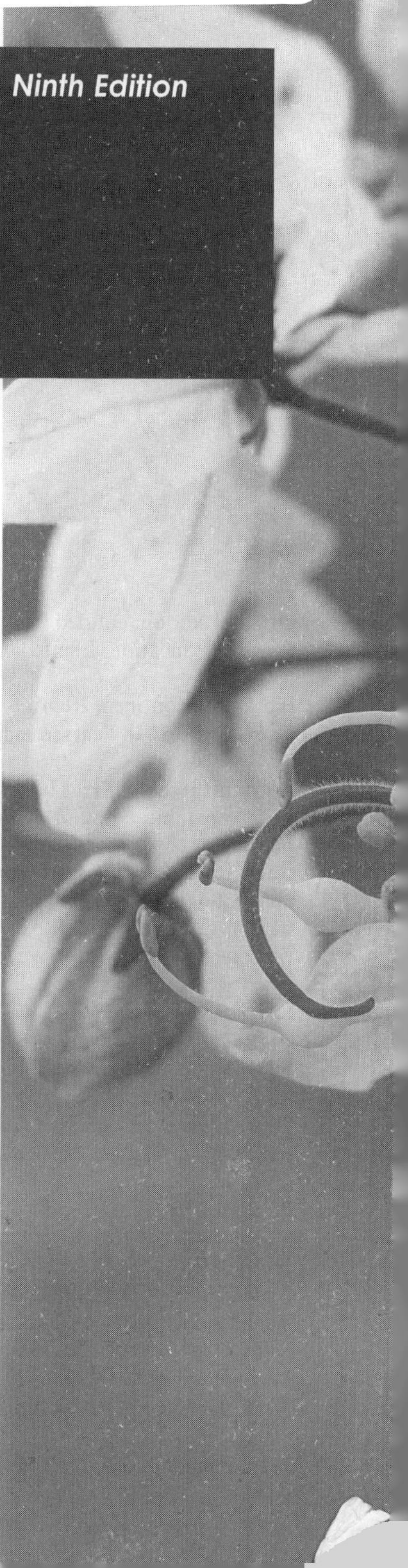

Pearson

Original edition, entitled *Java Software Solutions,* 9th Edition, by Lewis, John; Loftus, William, published by Pearson Education, Limited.

Indian Subcontinent Reprint

ISBN 978-93-530-6361-0

First Impression

Published by Pearson India Education Services Pvt. Ltd, CIN: U72200TN2005PTC057128.

Head Office: 15th Floor, Tower-B, World Trade Tower, Plot No. 1, Block-C, Sector 16, Noida 201 301, Uttar Pradesh, India.
Registered Office: 4th Floor, Software Block, Elnet Software City, TS 140, Block 2 & 9, Rajiv Gandhi Salai, Taramani, Chennai 600 113, Tamil Nadu, India.
Fax: 080-30461003, Phone: 080-30461060
Website: in.pearson.com; Email: companysecretary.india@pearson.com

Printed in India at Saurabh Printers Pvt. Ltd.

This book is dedicated to our families.
Sharon, Justin, Kayla, Nathan, and Samantha Lewis
and
Veena, Isaac, and Dévi Loftus

Preface

Welcome to the Ninth Edition of *Java Software Solutions: Foundations of Program Design*. We are pleased that this book has served the needs of so many students and faculty over the years. This edition has been tailored further to improve the coverage of topics key to introductory computing.

New to This Edition

The biggest change to this edition of Java Software Solutions is a sweeping overhaul of the Graphics Track sections of the book to fully embrace the JavaFX API. Swing is no longer actively supported by Oracle. JavaFX is now the preferred approach for developing graphics and graphical user interfaces (GUIs) in Java, and we make use of it throughout this text.

The changes include the following:

- Coverage of JavaFX graphical shapes.
- Coverage of JavaFX controls, including buttons, text fields, check boxes, radio buttons, choice boxes, color pickers, date pickers, dialog boxes, sliders, and spinners.
- Use of Java 8 method references and lambda expressions to define event handlers.
- An exploration of the JavaFX class hierarchy.
- An explanation of JavaFX properties and property binding.
- Revised end-of-chapter exercises and programming projects.
- A new appendix (Appendix G) that presents an overview of JavaFX layout panes.
- A new appendix (Appendix H) that introduces the JavaFX Scene Builder software.

There are two exciting aspects to embracing JavaFX. First, it provides a much cleaner approach to GUI development than Swing did. Equivalent programs using JavaFX are shorter and more easily understood.

Second, the JavaFX approach embraces core object-oriented principles better than Swing did. For example, all graphic shapes are represented by classes with fundamental data elements, such as a `Circle` class with a radius. Early on (Chapter 3), the shape classes provide a wealth of basic, well-designed classes, just when students need to understand what classes and objects are all about.

The use of Java 8 method references provides an easy-to-understand approach to defining event handlers. The use of the (underlying) lambda expressions is also explored as an alternative approach.

JavaFX layout panes are used and explained as needed in examples, with a full overview of layout panes provided in a new appendix. We think this works better than the way we treated Swing layout managers, as a separate topic in a chapter.

All GUI development in the book is done "by hand" in straight Java code, which is important for beginning students. The JavaFX drag-and-drop Scene Builder is discussed in a new appendix, but it is not used in the book itself.

In addition to the changes related to JavaFX, we also updated examples and discussions in various places throughout the book as needed to bring them up-to-date and improve their pedagogy.

We're excited about the opportunities this new edition of Java Software Solutions provides for both students and instructors. As always, questions and comments are welcome.

Cornerstones of the Text

This text is based on the following basic ideas that we believe make for a sound introductory text:

- *True object-orientation.* A text that really teaches a solid object-oriented approach must use what we call object-speak. That is, all processing should be discussed in object-oriented terms. That does not mean, however, that the first program a student sees must discuss the writing of multiple classes and methods. A student should learn to use objects before learning to write them. This text uses a natural progression that culminates in the ability to design real object-oriented solutions.
- *Sound programming practices.* Students should not be taught how to program; they should be taught how to write good software. There's a difference. Writing software is not a set of cookbook actions, and a good program is more than a collection of statements. This text integrates practices that serve as the foundation of good programming skills. These practices are used in all examples and are reinforced in the discussions. Students learn how to solve problems as well as how to implement solutions. We introduce and integrate basic software engineering techniques throughout the text. The **Software Failure** vignettes reiterate these lessons by demonstrating the perils of not following these sound practices.
- *Examples.* Students learn by example. This text is filled with fully implemented examples that demonstrate specific concepts. We have intertwined small, readily understandable examples with larger, more realistic ones. There is a balance between graphics and nongraphics programs. The **VideoNotes** provide additional examples in a live presentation format.

- *Graphics and GUIs.* Graphics can be a great motivator for students, and their use can serve as excellent examples of object-orientation. As such, we use them throughout the text in a well-defined set of sections that we call the Graphics Track. The book fully embraces the JavaFX API, the preferred and fully-supported approach to Java graphics and GUIs. Students learn to build GUIs in the appropriate way by using a natural progression of topics. The Graphics Track can be avoided entirely for those who do not choose to use graphics.

Chapter Breakdown

Chapter 1 (Introduction) introduces computer systems in general, including basic architecture and hardware, networking, programming, and language translation. Java is introduced in this chapter, and the basics of general program development, as well as object-oriented programming, are discussed. This chapter contains broad introductory material that can be covered while students become familiar with their development environment.

Chapter 2 (Data and Expressions) explores some of the basic types of data used in a Java program and the use of expressions to perform calculations. It discusses the conversion of data from one type to another and how to read input interactively from the user with the help of the standard `Scanner` class.

Chapter 3 (Using Classes and Objects) explores the use of predefined classes and the objects that can be created from them. Classes and objects are used to manipulate character strings, produce random numbers, perform complex calculations, and format output. Enumerated types are also discussed.

Chapter 4 (Writing Classes) explores the basic issues related to writing classes and methods. Topics include instance data, visibility, scope, method parameters, and return types. Encapsulation and constructors are covered as well. Some of the more involved topics are deferred to or revisited in Chapter 6.

Chapter 5 (Conditionals and Loops) covers the use of boolean expressions to make decisions. Then the `if` statement and `while` loop are explored in detail. Once loops are established, the concept of an iterator is introduced and the `Scanner` class is revisited for additional input parsing and the reading of text files. Finally, the `ArrayList` class introduced, which provides the option for managing a large number of objects.

Chapter 6 (More Conditionals and Loops) examines the rest of Java's conditional (`switch`) and loop (`do`, `for`) statements. All related statements for conditionals and loops are discussed, including the enhanced version of the `for` loop. The for-each loop is also used to process iterators and `ArrayList` objects.

Chapter 7 (Object-Oriented Design) reinforces and extends the coverage of issues related to the design of classes. Techniques for identifying the classes and objects needed for a problem and the relationships among them are discussed. This chapter also covers static class members, interfaces, and the design of enumerated type classes. Method design issues and method overloading are also discussed.

Chapter 8 (Arrays) contains extensive coverage of arrays and array processing. The nature of an array as a low-level programming structure is contrasted to the higher-level object management approach. Additional topics include command-line arguments, variable length parameter lists, and multidimensional arrays.

Chapter 9 (Inheritance) covers class derivations and associated concepts such as class hierarchies, overriding, and visibility. Strong emphasis is put on the proper use of inheritance and its role in software design.

Chapter 10 (Polymorphism) explores the concept of binding and how it relates to polymorphism. Then we examine how polymorphic references can be accomplished using either inheritance or interfaces. Sorting is used as an example of polymorphism. Design issues related to polymorphism are examined as well.

Chapter 11 (Exceptions) explores the class hierarchy from the Java standard library used to define exceptions, as well as the ability to define our own exception objects. We also discuss the use of exceptions when dealing with input and output and examine an example that writes a text file.

Chapter 12 (Recursion) covers the concept, implementation, and proper use of recursion. Several examples from various domains are used to demonstrate how recursive techniques make certain types of processing elegant.

Chapter 13 (Collections) introduces the idea of a collection and its underlying data structure. Abstraction is revisited in this context and the classic data structures are explored. Generic types are introduced as well. This chapter serves as an introduction to a CS2 course.

Supplements

Student Online Resources

These student resources can be accessed at the book's Companion Website, "www.pearsoned.co.in/johnlewis"

- Source Code for all the programs in the text
- Links to Java development environments
- VideoNotes: short step-by-step videos demonstrating how to solve problems from design through coding. VideoNotes allow for self-paced instruction with easy navigation including the ability to select, play, rewind, fast-forward, and stop within each VideoNote exercise. Margin icons in your textbook let you know when a VideoNote video is available for a particular concept or homework problem.

Instructor Resources

The following supplements are available to qualified instructors only. Visit the www.pearsoned.co.in/johnlewis for information on how to access them:

- Presentation Slides—in PowerPoint.
- Solutions to end-of-chapter Exercises.
- Solutions to end-of-chapter Programming Projects.

Acknowledgments

I am most grateful to the faculty and students from around the world who have provided their feedback on previous editions of this book. I am pleased to see the depth of the faculty's concern for their students and the students' thirst for knowledge. Your comments and questions are always welcome.

I am particularly thankful for the assistance, insight, and attention to detail of Robert Burton from Brigham Young University. For years, Robert has consistently provided valuable feedback that helps shape and evolve this textbook.

Bradley Richards, at the University of Applied Sciences in Northwestern Switzerland, provided helpful advice and resources during the transition to JavaFX. Brian Fraser of Simon Fraser University also has provided some excellent feedback that helped clarify some issues. Such interaction with computing educators is incredibly valuable.

I also want to thank Dan Joyce from Villanova University, who developed the original Self-Review questions, ensuring that each relevant topic had enough review material, as well as developing the answers to each.

I continue to be amazed at the talent and effort demonstrated by the team at Pearson. Matt Goldstein, our editor, has amazing insight and commitment. His assistant, Kristy Alaura, is a source of consistent and helpful support. Marketing Manager Demetrius Hall makes sure that instructors understand the pedagogical advantages of the text. The cover was designed by the skilled talents of Joyce Wells. Scott Disanno and Carole Snyder led the production effort. Louise Capulli, of Lakeside Editorial Services, was the Project Manager for this edition and a huge help to the author on a daily basis. We thank all of these people for ensuring that this book meets the highest quality standards.

Special thanks go to the following people who provided valuable advice to us about this book via their participation in focus groups, interviews, and reviews. They, as well as many other instructors and friends, have provided valuable feedback. They include:

Elizabeth Adams	James Madison University
Hossein Assadipour	Rutgers University
David Atkins	University of Oregon
Lewis Barnett	University of Richmond
Thomas W. Bennet	Mississippi College
Gian Mario Besana	DePaul University
Hans-Peter Bischof	Rochester Institute of Technology
Don Braffitt	Radford University
Robert Burton	Brigham Young University
John Chandler	Oklahoma State University
Robert Cohen	University of Massachusetts, Boston

Dodi Coreson	Linn Benton Community College
James H. Cross II	Auburn University
Eman El-Sheikh	University of West Florida
Sherif Elfayoumy	University of North Florida
Christopher Eliot	University of Massachusetts, Amherst
Wanda M. Eanes	Macon State College
Stephanie Elzer	Millersville University
Matt Evett	Eastern Michigan University
Marj Feroe	Delaware County Community College, Pennsylvania
John Gauch	University of Kansas
Chris Haynes	Indiana University
James Heliotis	Rochester Institute of Technology
Laurie Hendren	McGill University
Mike Higgs	Austin College
Stephen Hughes	Roanoke College
Daniel Joyce	Villanova University
Saroja Kanchi	Kettering University
Gregory Kapfhammer	Allegheny College
Karen Kluge	Dartmouth College
Jason Levy	University of Hawaii
Peter MacKenzie	McGill University
Jerry Marsh	Oakland University
Blayne Mayfield	Oklahoma State University
Gheorghe Muresan	Rutgers University
Laurie Murphy Pacific	Lutheran University
Dave Musicant	Carleton College
Faye Navabi-Tadayon	Arizona State University
Lawrence Osborne	Lamar University
Barry Pollack	City College of San Francisco
B. Ravikumar	University of Rhode Island
David Riley	University of Wisconsin (La Crosse)
Bob Roos	Allegheny College
Carolyn Rosiene	University of Hartford
Jerry Ross Lane	Community College
Patricia Roth	Southeastern Polytechnic State University
Carolyn Schauble	Colorado State University
Arjit Sengupta	Georgia State University
Bennet Setzer	Kennesaw State University
Vijay Srinivasan	JavaSoft, Sun Microsystems, Inc.
Stuart Steiner	Eastern Washington University
Katherine St. John	Lehman College, CUNY
Alexander Stoytchev	Iowa State University
Ed Timmerman	University of Maryland, University College

Shengru Tu	University of New Orleans
Paul Tymann	Rochester Institute of Technology
John J. Wegis	JavaSoft, Sun Microsystems, Inc.
Ken Williams	North Carolina Agricultural and Technical University
Linda Wilson	Dartmouth College
David Wittenberg	Brandeis University
Wang-Chan Wong	California State University (Dominguez Hills)

Thanks also go to my friends and former colleagues at Villanova University who have provided so much wonderful feedback. They include Bob Beck, Cathy Helwig, Anany Levitin, Najib Nadi, Beth Taddei, and Barbara Zimmerman. Thanks also to Pete DePasquale, formerly of The College of New Jersey and now with SailThru, Inc.

Many other people have helped in various ways. They include Ken Arnold, Mike Czepiel, John Loftus, Sebastian Niezgoda, and Saverio Perugini. Our apologies to anyone we may have omitted.

The ACM Special Interest Group on Computer Science Education (SIGCSE) is a tremendous resource. Their conferences provide an opportunity for educators from all levels and all types of schools to share ideas and materials. If you are an educator in any area of computing and are not involved with SIGCSE, you're missing out.

This Edition Acknowledgments

The publishers would like to thank the following for their contribution to this Edition:

Contributor

Vincent Ramdhanie	School of Business and Computer Science (SBCS)

Reviewers

Muthuraj M.	Samsung
Patricia Moore	Dublin City University
Subrata Sinha	Dibrugarh University

Contents

Preface **5**

Chapter 1 **Introduction** **29**

1.1 **Computer Processing** **30**
Software Categories 31
Digital Computers 33
Binary Numbers 35

1.2 **Hardware Components** **38**
Computer Architecture 39
Input/Output Devices 40
Main Memory and Secondary Memory 41
The Central Processing Unit 45

1.3 **Networks** **47**
Network Connections 48
Local-Area Networks and Wide-Area Networks 49
The Internet 50
The World Wide Web 52
Uniform Resource Locators 53

1.4 **The Java Programming Language** **54**
A Java Program 55
Comments 57
Identifiers and Reserved Words 58
White Space 61

1.5 **Program Development** **63**
Programming Language Levels 64
Editors, Compilers, and Interpreters 66
Development Environments 68
Syntax and Semantics 68
Errors 69

	1.6	**Object-Oriented Programming**	**71**
		Problem Solving	72
		Object-Oriented Software Principles	73
Chapter 2		**Data and Expressions**	**83**
	2.1	**Character Strings**	**84**
		The `print` and `println` Methods	84
		String Concatenation	86
		Escape Sequences	89
	2.2	**Variables and Assignment**	**91**
		Variables	91
		The Assignment Statement	93
		Constants	95
	2.3	**Primitive Data Types**	**97**
		Integers and Floating Points	97
		Characters	99
		Booleans	100
	2.4	**Expressions**	**101**
		Arithmetic Operators	101
		Operator Precedence	102
		Increment and Decrement Operators	106
		Assignment Operators	107
	2.5	**Data Conversion**	**109**
		Conversion Techniques	111
	2.6	**Interactive Programs**	**113**
		The `Scanner` Class	113
	Software Failure:	NASA Mars Climate Orbiter and Polar Lander	124
Chapter 3		**Using Classes and Objects**	**127**
	3.1	**Creating Objects**	**128**
		Aliases	130
	3.2	**The `String` Class**	**132**

	3.3	**Packages**	**136**
		The `import` Declaration	138
	3.4	**The `Random` Class**	**140**
	3.5	**The `Math` Class**	**143**
	3.6	**Formatting Output**	**146**
		The `NumberFormat` Class	146
		The `DecimalFormat` Class	148
		The `printf` Method	149
	3.7	**Enumerated Types**	**152**
	3.8	**Wrapper Classes**	**155**
		Autoboxing	157
	3.9	**Introduction to JavaFX**	**157**
	3.10	**Basic Shapes**	**161**
	3.11	**Representing Colors**	**168**
Chapter 4		**Writing Classes**	**175**
	4.1	**Classes and Objects Revisited**	**176**
	4.2	**Anatomy of a Class**	**178**
		Instance Data	183
		UML Class Diagrams	183
	4.3	**Encapsulation**	**185**
		Visibility Modifiers	186
		Accessors and Mutators	187
	4.4	**Anatomy of a Method**	**188**
		The `return` Statement	190
		Parameters	191
		Local Data	191
		Bank Account Example	192
	4.5	**Constructors Revisited**	**197**
	4.6	**Arcs**	**198**
	4.7	**Images**	**201**
		Viewports	203

	4.8	**Graphical User Interfaces**	**204**
		Alternate Ways to Specify Event Handlers	207
	4.9	**Text Fields**	**208**
	Software Failure:		
		Denver Airport Baggage Handling System	217
Chapter 5	**Conditionals and Loops**		**219**
	5.1	**Boolean Expressions**	**220**
		Equality and Relational Operators	221
		Logical Operators	222
	5.2	**The `if` Statement**	**225**
		The `if-else` Statement	228
		Using Block Statements	231
		Nested `if` Statements	235
	5.3	**Comparing Data**	**238**
		Comparing Floats	238
		Comparing Characters	239
		Comparing Objects	240
	5.4	**The `while` Statement**	**242**
		Infinite Loops	246
		Nested Loops	248
		The `break` and `continue` Statements	251
	5.5	**Iterators**	**253**
		Reading Text Files	254
	5.6	**The `ArrayList` Class**	**257**
	5.7	**Determining Event Sources**	**260**
	5.8	**Managing Fonts**	**262**
	5.9	**Check Boxes**	**265**
	5.10	**Radio Buttons**	**269**
	Software Failure:		
		Therac-25	281

Chapter 6 More Conditionals and Loops 283

6.1 **The switch Statement** 284

6.2 **The Conditional Operator** 288

6.3 **The do Statement** 289

6.4 **The `for` Statement** 293
The for-each Loop 296
Comparing Loops 298

6.5 **Using Loops and Conditionals with Graphics** 299

6.6 **Graphic Transformations** 304
Translation 304
Scaling 304
Rotation 305
Shearing 306
Applying Transformations on Groups 307

Chapter 7 Object-Oriented Design 317

7.1 **Software Development Activities** 318

7.2 **Identifying Classes and Objects** 319
Assigning Responsibilities 321

7.3 **Static Class Members** 321
Static Variables 322
Static Methods 322

7.4 **Class Relationships** 326
Dependency 326
Dependencies Among Objects of the Same Class 326
Aggregation 332
The `this` Reference 336

7.5 **Interfaces** 338
The `Comparable` Interface 343
The `Iterator` Interface 344

7.6	**Enumerated Types Revisited**	**345**
7.7	**Method Design**	**348**
	Method Decomposition	349
	Method Parameters Revisited	354
7.8	**Method Overloading**	**359**
7.9	**Testing**	**361**
	Reviews	362
	Defect Testing	362
7.10	**GUI Design**	**365**
7.11	**Mouse Events**	**366**
7.12	**Key Events**	**371**
Software Failure:	2003 Northeast Blackout	380

Chapter 8 Arrays 383

8.1	**Array Elements**	**384**
8.2	**Declaring and Using Arrays**	**385**
	Bounds Checking	388
	Alternate Array Syntax	393
	Initializer Lists	393
	Arrays as Parameters	394
8.3	**Arrays of Objects**	**396**
8.4	**Command-Line Arguments**	**406**
8.5	**Variable Length Parameter Lists**	**408**
8.6	**Two-Dimensional Arrays**	**412**
	Multidimensional Arrays	416
8.7	**Polygons and Polylines**	**417**
8.8	**An Array of Color Objects**	**420**
8.9	**Choice Boxes**	**423**
Software Failure:	LA Air Traffic Control	433

Chapter 9 Inheritance 435

9.1 Creating Subclasses 436
The `protected` Modifier 439
The `super` Reference 442
Multiple Inheritance 445

9.2 Overriding Methods 447
Shadowing Variables 449

9.3 Class Hierarchies 450
The `Object` Class 452
Abstract Classes 453
Interface Hierarchies 455

9.4 Visibility 455

9.5 Designing for Inheritance 458
Restricting Inheritance 459

9.6 Inheritance in JavaFX 460

9.7 Color and Date Pickers 462

9.8 Dialog Boxes 466
File Choosers 469

Software Failure:
Ariane 5 Flight 501 477

Chapter 10 Polymorphism 479

10.1 Late Binding 480

10.2 Polymorphism via Inheritance 481

10.3 Polymorphism via Interfaces 494

10.4 Sorting 496
Selection Sort 497
Insertion Sort 503
Comparing Sorts 504

10.5 **Searching** **505**
Linear Search 505
Binary Search 507
Comparing Searches 511

10.6 **Designing for Polymorphism** **511**

10.7 **Properties** **513**
Change Listeners 516

10.8 **Sliders** **519**

10.9 **Spinners** **521**

Chapter 11 Exceptions 529

11.1 **Exception Handling** **530**

11.2 **Uncaught Exceptions** **531**

11.3 **The `try-catch` Statement** **532**
The `finally` Clause 536

11.4 **Exception Propagation** **537**

11.5 **The Exception Class Hierarchy** **541**
Checked and Unchecked Exceptions 544

11.6 **I/O Exceptions** **545**

11.7 **Tool Tips and Disabling Controls** **549**

11.8 **Scroll Panes** **553**

11.9 **Split Panes and List Views** **556**

Chapter 12 Recursion 565

12.1 **Recursive Thinking** **566**
Infinite Recursion 566
Recursion in Math 567

12.2 **Recursive Programming** **568**
Recursion vs. Iteration 571
Direct vs. Indirect Recursion 571

	12.3	**Using Recursion**	**572**
		Traversing a Maze	573
		The Towers of Hanoi	578
	12.4	**Tiled Images**	**583**
	12.5	**Fractals**	**587**
Chapter 13		**Collections**	**601**
	13.1	**Collections and Data Structures**	**602**
		Separating Interface from Implementation	602
	13.2	**Dynamic Representations**	**603**
		Dynamic Structures	603
		A Dynamically Linked List	604
		Other Dynamic List Representations	609
	13.3	**Linear Collections**	**611**
		Queues	611
		Stacks	612
	13.4	**Non-Linear Data Structures**	**615**
		Trees	615
		Graphs	616
	13.5	**The Java Collections API**	**618**
		Generics	618
Appendix A		**Glossary**	**625**
Appendix B		**Number Systems**	**649**
Appendix C		**The Unicode Character Set**	**657**
Appendix D		**Java Operators**	**661**
Appendix E		**Java Modifiers**	**667**
Appendix F		**Java Coding Guidelines**	**671**

Appendix G JavaFX Layout Panes 677

Appendix H JavaFX Scene Builder 687

Appendix I Regular Expressions 697

Appendix J Javadoc Documentation Generator 699

Appendix K Java Syntax 705

Appendix L Answers to Self-Review Questions 719

Index 773

VideoNote

Overview of program elements. 56
Comparison of Java IDEs. 68
Examples of various error types. 70
Developing a solution for PP 1.2. 81
Example using strings and escape sequences. 89
Review of primitive data and expressions. 102
Example using the `Scanner` class. 117
Developing a solution of PP 2.10. 122
Creating objects. 129
Example using the `Random` and `Math` classes. 143
Developing a solution of PP 3.6. 173
Dissecting the `Die` class. 180
Discussion of the `Account` class. 194
Developing a solution of PP 4.2. 214
Examples using conditionals. 233
Examples using `while` loops. 245
Developing a solution of PP 5.4. 278
Examples using `for` loops. 294
Developing a solution of PP 6.2. 313
Exploring the `static` modifier. 321
Examples of method overloading. 360
Developing a solution of PP 7.1. 377
Overview of arrays. 387
Discussion of the `LetterCount` example. 392
Developing a solution of PP 8.5. 431
Overview of inheritance. 441
Example using a class hierarchy. 453
Exploring the Firm program. 482

Sorting `Comparable` objects. 502
Developing a solution of PP 10.1. 526
Proper exception handling. 537
Developing a solution of PP 11.1. 562
Tracing the `MazeSearch` program. 576
Exploring the Towers of Hanoi. 579
Developing a solution of PP 12.1. 597
Example using a linked list. 604
Implementing a queue. 612
Developing a solution of PP 13.3. 622

Credits

Figure 2.1: NASA EOS Earth Observing System
Figure 4.2: Susan Van Etten/PhotoEdit
Figure 5.1: David Joel/The Image Bank/Getty Images
Figures 4.1a, 4.1b, 6.1a, 6.1b, 6.2, 11.3, 11.8, 11.9, 11.10, 12.5, APG.1a, APG.1b: Pixabay
Figures 7.1a and 7.1b: Anarres/Openclipart
Figures 7.2a and 7.2b: National Oceanic and Atmospheric Administration
Figure 8.1: Matthew McVay/The Image Bank/Getty Images
Figure 9.1: Mario Fourmy/Redux Pictures
Figure H.1: NASA

1 Introduction

CHAPTER OBJECTIVES

- Describe the relationship between hardware and software.
- Define various types of software and how they are used.
- Identify the core hardware components of a computer and explain their roles.
- Explain how the hardware components interact to execute programs and manage data.
- Describe how computers are connected into networks to share information.
- Introduce the Java programming language.
- Describe the steps involved in program compilation and execution.
- Present an overview of object-oriented principles.

This book is about writing well-designed software. To understand software, we must first have a fundamental understanding of its role in a computer system. Hardware and software cooperate in a computer system to accomplish complex tasks. The purpose of various hardware components and the way those components are connected into networks are important prerequisites to the study of software development. This chapter first discusses basic computer processing and then begins our exploration of software development by introducing the Java programming language and the principles of object-oriented programming.

1.1 Computer Processing

All computer systems, whether it's a desktop, laptop, tablet, smartphone, gaming console, or a special-purpose device such as a car's navigation system, share certain characteristics. The details vary, but they all process data in similar ways. While the majority of this book deals with the development of software, we'll begin with an overview of computer processing to set the context. It's important to establish some fundamental terminology and see how key pieces of a computer system interact.

A computer system is made up of hardware and software. The *hardware* components of a computer system are the physical, tangible pieces that support the computing effort. They include chips, boxes, wires, keyboards, speakers, disks, memory cards, universal serial bus (USB) flash drives (also called jump drives), cables, plugs, printers, mice, monitors, routers, and so on. If you can physically touch it and it can be considered part of a computer system, then it is computer hardware.

KEY CONCEPT
A computer system consists of hardware and software that work in concert to help us solve problems.

The hardware components of a computer are essentially useless without instructions to tell them what to do. A *program* is a series of instructions that the hardware executes one after another. *Software* consists of programs and the data that programs use. Software is the intangible counterpart to the physical hardware components. Together they form a tool that we can use to help solve problems.

The key hardware components in a computer system are

- central processing unit (CPU)
- input/output (I/O) devices
- main memory
- secondary memory devices

Each of these hardware components is described in detail in the next section. For now, let's simply examine their basic roles. The *central processing unit (CPU)* is a device that executes the individual commands of a program. *Input/output (I/O) devices*, such as the keyboard, mouse, trackpad, and monitor, allow a human being to interact with the computer.

Programs and data are held in storage devices called memory, which fall into two categories: main memory and secondary memory. *Main memory* is the storage device that holds the software while it is being processed by the CPU. *Secondary memory* devices store software in a relatively permanent manner. The most important secondary memory device of a typical computer system is the hard disk that resides inside the main computer box. A USB flash drive is also an important secondary memory device. A typical USB flash drive cannot store nearly as much information as a hard disk. USB flash drives have the advantage of portability; they can be removed temporarily or moved from computer to computer as needed.

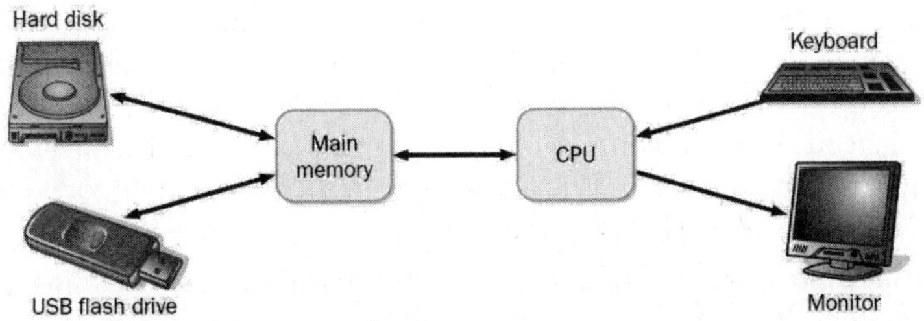

FIGURE 1.1 A simplified view of a computer system

Figure 1.1 shows how information moves among the basic hardware components of a computer. Suppose you have an executable program you wish to run. The program is stored on some secondary memory device, such as a hard disk. When you instruct the computer to execute your program, a copy of the program is brought in from secondary memory and stored in main memory. The CPU reads the individual program instructions from main memory. The CPU then executes the instructions one at a time until the program ends. The data that the instructions use, such as two numbers that will be added together, also are stored in main memory. They are either brought in from secondary memory or read from an input device such as the keyboard. During execution, the program may display information to an output device such as a monitor.

> **KEY CONCEPT**
> The CPU reads the program instructions from main memory, executing them one at a time until the program ends.

The process of executing a program is fundamental to the operation of a computer. All computer systems basically work in the same way.

Software Categories

Software can be classified into many categories using various criteria. At this point, we will simply differentiate between system programs and application programs.

The *operating system* is the core software of a computer. It performs two important functions. First, it provides a *user interface* that allows the user to interact with the machine. Second, the operating system manages computer resources such as the CPU and main memory. It determines when programs are allowed to run, where they are loaded into memory, and how hardware devices communicate. It is the operating system's job to make the computer easy to use and to ensure that it runs efficiently.

> **KEY CONCEPT**
> The operating system provides a user interface and manages computer resources.

Several popular operating systems are in use today. The Windows operating system was developed for personal computers by Microsoft, which has captured the lion's share of the operating systems market.

Various versions of the Unix operating system are also quite popular, especially in larger computer systems. A version of Unix called Linux was developed as an open-source project, which means that many people contributed to its development and its code is freely available. Because of that Linux has become a particular favorite among some users. Mac OS is an operating system used for computing systems developed by Apple Computers.

Operating systems are often specialized for mobile devices such as smartphones and tablets. The iOS operating system from Apple is used on the iPhone, iPad, and iPod. It is similar in functionality and appearance to the desktop Mac OS, but tailored for the smaller devices. The Android operating system developed by Google currently dominates the smartphone market.

An *application* (often shortened in conversation to "app") is a generic term for just about any software other than the operating system. Word processors, missile control systems, database managers, Web browsers, and games all can be considered application programs. Each application program has its own user interface that allows the user to interact with that particular program.

The user interface for most modern operating systems and applications is a *graphical user interface (GUI*, pronounced "gooey"), which, as the name implies, makes use of graphical screen elements. Among many others, these elements include

- *windows*, which are used to separate the screen into distinct work areas
- *icons*, which are small images that represent computer resources, such as a file
- *menus, checkboxes, and radio buttons*, which provide the user with selectable options
- *sliders*, which allow the user to select from a range of values
- *buttons*, which can be "pushed" with a mouse click to indicate a user selection

A mouse or trackpad is the primary input device used with GUIs; thus, GUIs are sometimes called *point-and-click interfaces*. The screenshot in Figure 1.2 shows an example of a GUI.

KEY CONCEPT
As far as the user is concerned, the interface is the program.

The interface to an application or operating system is an important part of the software because it is the only part of the program with which the user interacts directly. To the user, the interface *is* the program. Throughout this book, we discuss the design and implementation of graphical user interfaces.

The focus of this book is the development of high-quality application programs. We explore how to design and write software that will perform calculations, make decisions, and present results textually or graphically. We use the Java programming language throughout the text to demonstrate various computing concepts.

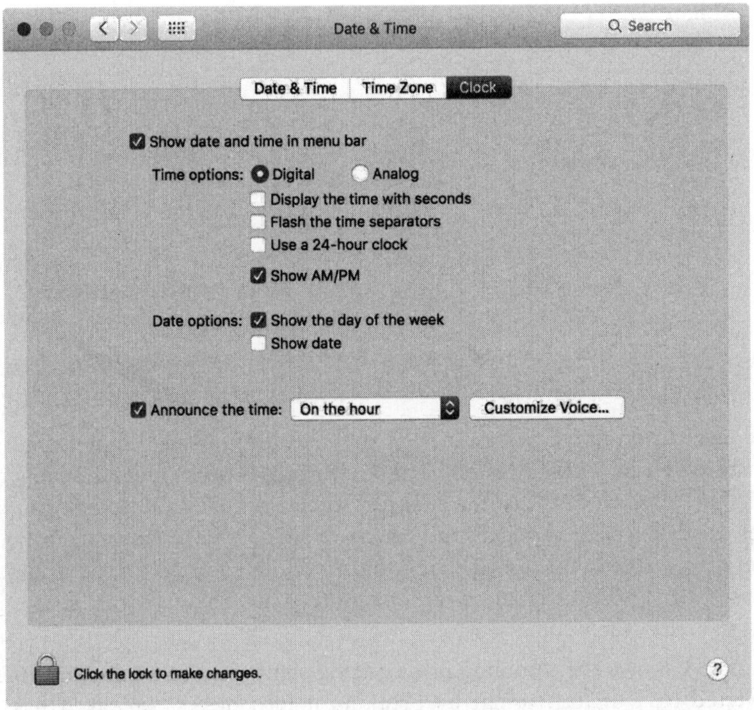

FIGURE 1.2 An example of a graphical user interface (GUI)

Digital Computers

Two fundamental techniques are used to store and manage information: analog and digital. *Analog* information is continuous, in direct proportion to the source of the information. For example, an alcohol thermometer is an analog device for measuring temperature. The alcohol rises in a tube in direct proportion to the temperature outside the tube. Another example of analog information is an electronic signal used to represent the vibrations of a sound wave. The signal's voltage varies in direct proportion to the original sound wave. A stereo amplifier sends this kind of electronic signal to its speakers, which vibrate to reproduce the sound. We use the term *analog* because the signal is directly analogous to the information it represents. Figure 1.3 graphically depicts a sound wave captured by a microphone and represented as an electronic signal.

KEY CONCEPT
Digital computers store information by breaking it into pieces and representing each piece as a number.

Digital technology breaks information into discrete pieces and represents those pieces as numbers. The music on a compact disc is stored digitally, as a series of numbers. Each number represents the

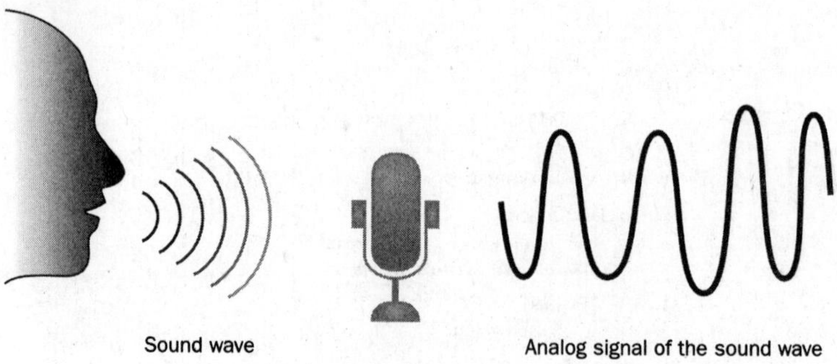

FIGURE 1.3 A sound wave and an electronic analog signal that represents the wave

voltage level of one specific instance of the recording. Many of these measurements are taken in a short period of time, perhaps 44,000 measurements every second. The number of measurements per second is called the *sampling rate*. If samples are taken often enough, the discrete voltage measurements can be used to generate a continuous analog signal that is "close enough" to the original. In most cases, the goal is to create a reproduction of the original signal that is good enough to satisfy the human senses.

Figure 1.4 shows the sampling of an analog signal. When analog information is converted to a digital format by breaking it into pieces, we say it has been

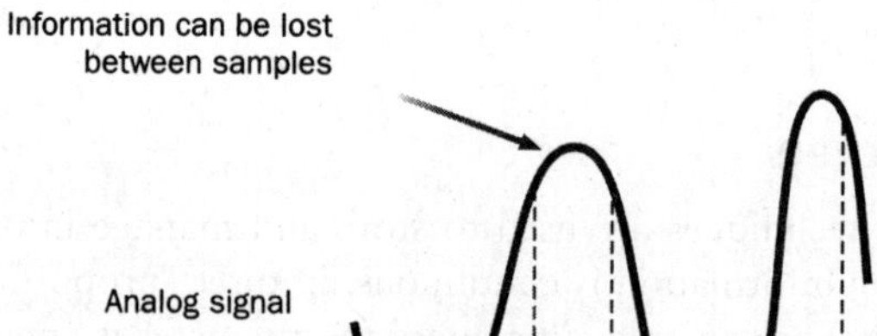

FIGURE 1.4 Digitizing an analog signal by sampling

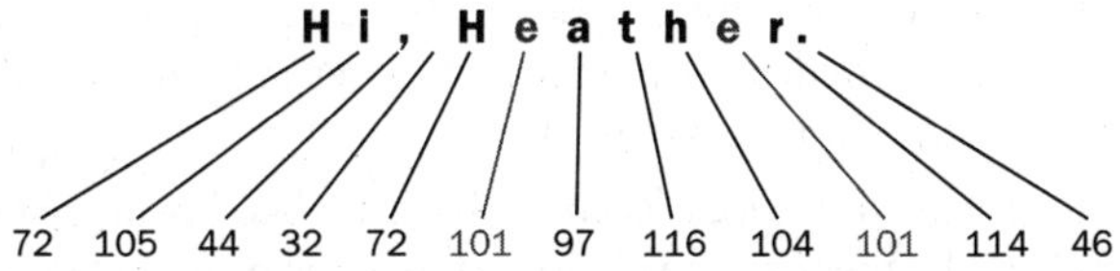

FIGURE 1.5 Text is stored by mapping each character to a number

digitized. Because the changes that occur in a signal between samples are lost, the sampling rate must be sufficiently fast.

Sampling is only one way to digitize information. For example, a sentence of text is stored on a computer as a series of numbers, where each number represents a single character in the sentence. Every letter, digit, and punctuation symbol has been assigned a number. Even the space character is assigned a number. Consider the following sentence:

Hi, Heather.

The characters of the sentence are represented as a series of 12 numbers, as shown in Figure 1.5. When a character is repeated, such as the uppercase `'H'`, the same representation number is used. Note that the uppercase version of a letter is stored as a different number from the lowercase version, such as the `'H'` and `'h'` in the word Heather. They are considered distinct characters.

Modern electronic computers are digital. Every kind of information, including text, images, numbers, audio, video, and even program instructions, is broken into pieces. Each piece is represented as a number. The information is stored by storing those numbers.

Binary Numbers

A digital computer stores information as numbers, but those numbers are not stored as *decimal* values. All information in a computer is stored and managed as *binary* values. Unlike the decimal system, which has 10 digits (0 through 9), the binary number system has only two digits (0 and 1). A single binary digit is called a *bit*.

All number systems work according to the same rules. The *base value* of a number system dictates how many digits we have to work with and indicates the place value of each digit in a number. The decimal number system is base 10, whereas the binary number system is base 2. Appendix B contains a detailed discussion of number systems.

KEY CONCEPT

Binary is used to store and move information in a computer because the devices that store and manipulate binary data are inexpensive and reliable.

Modern computers use binary numbers because the devices that store and move information are less expensive and more reliable if they have to represent only one of two possible values. Other than this characteristic, there is nothing special about the binary number system. Computers have been created that use other number systems to store and move information, but they aren't as convenient.

Some computer memory devices, such as hard drives, are magnetic in nature. Magnetic material can be polarized easily to one extreme or the other, but intermediate levels are difficult to distinguish. Therefore, magnetic devices can be used to represent binary values quite effectively—a magnetized area represents a binary 1 and a demagnetized area represents a binary 0. Other computer memory devices are made up of tiny electrical circuits. These devices are easier to create and are less likely to fail if they have to switch between only two states. We're better off reproducing millions of these simple devices than creating fewer, more complicated ones.

Binary values and digital electronic signals go hand in hand. They improve our ability to transmit information reliably along a wire. As we've seen, an analog signal has continuously varying voltage with infinitely many states, but a digital signal is *discrete*, which means the voltage changes dramatically between one extreme (such as +5 volts) and the other (such as –5 volts). At any point, the voltage of a digital signal is considered to be either "high," which represents a binary 1, or "low," which represents a binary 0. Figure 1.6 compares these two types of signals.

As a signal moves down a wire, it gets weaker and degrades due to environmental conditions. That is, the voltage levels of the original signal change slightly. The trouble with an analog signal is that as it fluctuates, it loses its original information. Since the information is directly analogous to the signal, any change in the signal changes the information. The changes in an analog signal cannot be recovered because the degraded signal is just as valid as the original. A digital signal degrades just as an analog signal does, but because the digital signal is originally at one of two extremes, it can be reinforced before any information is lost. The voltage may change slightly from its original value, but it still can be interpreted correctly as either high or low.

The number of bits we use in any given situation determines the number of unique items we can represent. A single bit has two possible values, 0 and 1, and

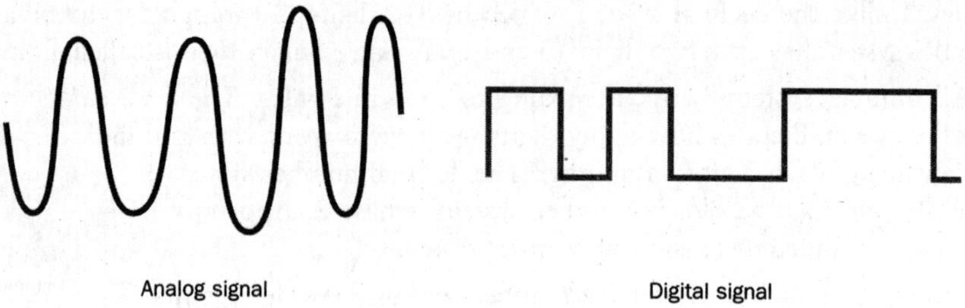

FIGURE 1.6 An analog signal vs. a digital signal

therefore can represent two possible items or situations. If we want to represent the state of a light bulb (off or on), one bit will suffice, because we can interpret 0 as the light bulb being off and 1 as the light bulb being on. If we want to represent more than two things, we need more than one bit.

Two bits, taken together, can represent four possible items because there are exactly four permutations of two bits: 00, 01, 10, and 11. Suppose we want to represent the gear that a car is in (park, drive, reverse, or neutral). We would need only two bits, and could set up a mapping between the bit permutations and the gears. For instance, we could say that 00 represents park, 01 represents drive, 10 represents reverse, and 11 represents neutral. In this case, it wouldn't matter if we switched that mapping around, though in some cases the relationships between the bit permutations and what they represent are important.

Three bits can represent eight unique items, because there are eight permutations of three bits. Similarly, four bits can represent 16 items, five bits can represent 32 items, and so on. Figure 1.7 shows the relationship between the number of bits used and the number of items they can represent. In general, N bits can represent 2^N unique items. For every bit added, the number of items that can be represented doubles.

KEY CONCEPT
There are exactly 2^N permutations of N bits. Therefore, N bits can represent up to 2^N unique items.

1 bit 2 items	2 bits 4 items	3 bits 8 items	4 bits 16 items	5 bits 32 items	
0	00	000	0000	00000	10000
1	01	001	0001	00001	10001
	10	010	0010	00010	10010
	11	011	0011	00011	10011
		100	0100	00100	10100
		101	0101	00101	10101
		110	0110	00110	10110
		111	0111	00111	10111
			1000	01000	11000
			1001	01001	11001
			1010	01010	11010
			1011	01011	11011
			1100	01100	11100
			1101	01101	11101
			1110	01110	11110
			1111	01111	11111

FIGURE 1.7 The number of bits used determines the number of items that can be represented

We've seen how a sentence of text is stored on a computer by mapping characters to numeric values. Those numeric values are stored as binary numbers. Suppose we want to represent character strings in a language that contains 256 characters and symbols. We would need to use eight bits to store each character because there are 256 unique permutations of eight bits (2^8 equals 256). Each bit permutation, or binary value, is mapped to a specific character.

How many bits would be needed to represent 195 countries of the world? Seven wouldn't be enough, because 2^7 equals 128. Eight bits would be enough, but some of the 256 permutations would not be mapped to a country.

Ultimately, representing information on a computer boils down to the number of items there are to represent and determining the way those items are mapped to binary values.

SELF-REVIEW QUESTIONS *(see answers in Appendix L)*

SR 1.1 What is hardware? What is software?

SR 1.2 What are the two primary functions of an operating system?

SR 1.3 The music on a CD is created using a sampling rate of 44,000 measurements per second. Each measurement is stored as a number that represents a specific voltage level. How many such numbers are used to store a three-minute long song? How many such numbers does it take to represent one hour of music?

SR 1.4 What happens to information when it is stored digitally?

SR 1.5 How many unique items can be represented with the following?

a. 2 bits
b. 4 bits
c. 5 bits
d. 7 bits

SR 1.6 Suppose you want to represent each of the 50 states of the United States using a unique permutation of bits. How many bits would be needed to store each state representation? Why?

1.2 Hardware Components

Let's examine the hardware components of a computer system in more detail. Consider the desktop computer described in Figure 1.8. What does it all mean? Is the system capable of running the software you want it to? How does it compare with other systems? These terms are explained throughout this section.

Intel Dual-Core i7 processor

4 GB memory

750 GB hard drive

15.6" High Definition display
with 1366 x 768 resolution

802.11 wireless card

FIGURE 1.8 The hardware specification of a particular computer

Computer Architecture

The architecture of a house defines its structure. Similarly, we use the term *computer architecture* to describe how the hardware components of a computer are put together. Figure 1.9 illustrates the basic architecture of a generic computer system. Information travels between components across a group of wires called a *bus*.

The CPU and the main memory make up the core of a computer. As we mentioned earlier, main memory stores programs and data that are in active use, and the CPU methodically executes program instructions one at a time. The CPU in the computer described in Figure 1.8 is manufactured by the Intel Corporation, which supplies processors for many computer systems.

KEY CONCEPT
The core of a computer is made up of main memory, which stores programs and data, and the CPU, which executes program instructions one at a time.

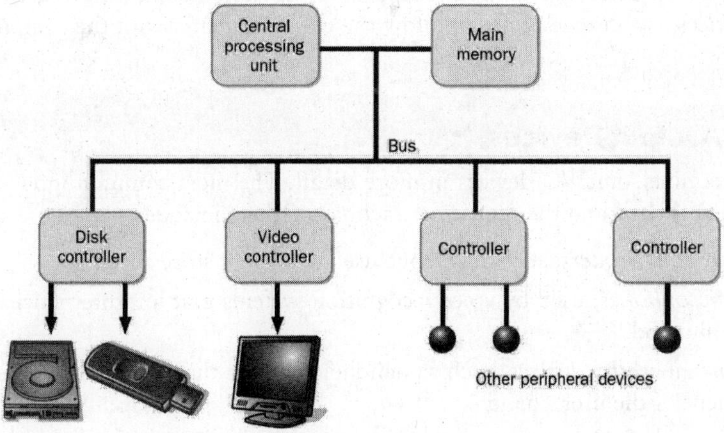

FIGURE 1.9 Basic computer architecture

Suppose we have a program that computes the average of a list of numbers. The program and the numbers must reside in main memory while the program runs. The CPU reads one program instruction from main memory and executes it. If an instruction needs data, such as a number in the list, to perform its task, the CPU reads that information as well. This process repeats until the program ends. The average, when computed, is stored in main memory to await further processing or long-term storage in secondary memory.

Almost all devices in a computer system other than the CPU and main memory are called *peripherals*; they operate at the periphery, or outer edges, of the system (although they may be in the same box). Users don't interact directly with the CPU or main memory. Although they form the essence of the machine, the CPU and main memory would not be useful without peripheral devices.

Controllers are devices that coordinate the activities of specific peripherals. Every device has its own particular way of formatting and communicating data, and part of the controller's role is to handle these idiosyncrasies and isolate them from the rest of the computer hardware. Furthermore, the controller often handles much of the actual transmission of information, allowing the CPU to focus on other activities.

Input/output (I/O) devices and secondary memory devices are considered peripherals. Another category of peripherals consists of *data transfer devices*, which allow information to be sent and received between computers. The computer specified in Figure 1.8 includes a network card that uses the 802.11 standard for wireless radio communication (or WiFi) to a computer network.

In some ways, secondary memory devices and data transfer devices can be thought of as I/O devices because they represent a source of information (input) and a place to send information (output). For our discussion, however, we define I/O devices as those devices that allow the user to interact with the computer.

Input/Output Devices

Let's examine some I/O devices in more detail. The most common input devices are the keyboard and the mouse or trackpad. Others include

- *bar code readers*, such as the one used at a retail store checkout
- *microphones*, used by voice recognition systems that interpret voice commands
- *virtual reality devices*, such as handheld devices that interpret the movement of the user's hand
- *scanners*, which convert text, photographs, and graphics into machine-readable form

- *cameras*, which capture still pictures and video, and can also be used to process special input such as QR codes

Monitors and printers are the most common output devices. Others include

- *plotters*, which move pens across large sheets of paper (or vice versa)
- *speakers*, for audio output
- *goggles*, for virtual reality display

Some devices can provide both input and output capabilities. A *touch screen* system can detect the user touching the screen at a particular place. Software can then use the screen to display text and graphics in response to the user's touch. Touch screens have become commonplace for handheld devices.

The computer described in Figure 1.8 includes a monitor with a 15.6-inch display area (measured diagonally). A picture is represented in a computer by breaking it up into separate picture elements, or *pixels*. This monitor can display a grid of 1366 by 768 pixels.

Main Memory and Secondary Memory

Main memory is made up of a series of small, consecutive *memory locations*, as shown in Figure 1.10. Associated with each memory location is a unique number called an *address*.

KEY CONCEPT
An address is a unique number associated with a memory location.

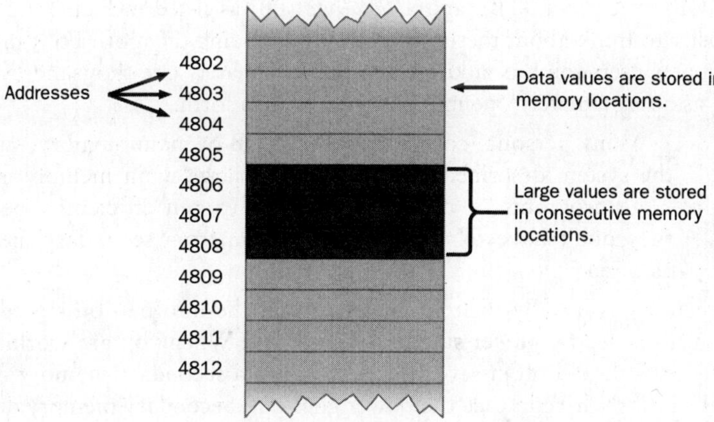

FIGURE 1.10 Memory locations

Unit	Symbol	Number of Bytes
byte		$2^0 = 1$
kilobyte	KB	$2^{10} = 1024$
megabyte	MB	$2^{20} = 1,048,576$
gigabyte	GB	$2^{30} = 1,073,741,824$
terabyte	TB	$2^{40} = 1,099,511,627,776$
petabyte	PB	$2^{50} = 1,125,899,906,842,624$

FIGURE 1.11 Units of binary storage

When data is stored in a memory location, it overwrites and destroys any information that was previously stored at that location. However, the process of reading data from a memory location does not affect it.

On many computers, each memory location consists of eight bits, or one *byte*, of information. If we need to store a value that cannot be represented in a single byte, such as a large number, then multiple, consecutive bytes are used to store the data.

The *storage capacity* of a device such as main memory is the total number of bytes it can hold. Devices can store thousands or millions of bytes, so you should become familiar with larger units of measure. Because computer memory is based on the binary number system, all units of storage are powers of two. A *kilobyte* (KB) is 1024, or 2^{10}, bytes. Some larger units of storage are a *megabyte* (MB), a *gigabyte* (GB), a *terabyte* (TB), and a *petabyte* (PB) as listed in Figure 1.11. It's usually easier to think about these capacities by rounding them off. For example, most computer users think of a kilobyte as approximately one thousand bytes, a megabyte as approximately one million bytes, and so forth.

KEY CONCEPT

Main memory is volatile, meaning the stored information is maintained only as long as electric power is supplied.

Many personal computers have 4 GB of main memory, such as the system described in Figure 1.8. A large main memory allows large programs or multiple programs to run efficiently, because they don't have to retrieve information from secondary memory as often.

Main memory is usually *volatile*, meaning that the information stored in it will be lost if its electric power supply is turned off. When you are working on a computer, you should often save your work onto a secondary memory device such as a USB flash drive in case the power goes out. Secondary memory devices are usually *nonvolatile*; the information is retained even if the power supply is turned off.

The *cache* is used by the CPU to reduce the average access time to instructions and data. The cache is a small, fast memory that stores the contents of the most frequently used main memory locations. Contemporary CPUs include an instruction cache to speed up the fetching of executable instructions and a data cache to speed up the fetching and storing of data.

The most common secondary storage devices are *hard disks* and USB *flash drives*. A typical USB flash drive stores between 1 and 256 GB of information. The storage capacities of hard drives vary, but on personal computers, capacities typically range between 500 and 750 GB, such as in the system described in Figure 1.8. Some hard disks can store much more.

A USB flash drive consists of a small printed circuit board carrying the circuit elements and a USB connector, insulated electrically and protected inside a plastic, metal, or rubberized case, which can be carried in a pocket or on a key chain, for example.

A disk is a magnetic medium on which bits are represented as magnetized particles. A read/write head passes over the spinning disk, reading or writing information as appropriate. A hard disk drive might actually contain several disks in a vertical column with several read/write heads, such as the one shown in Figure 1.12.

Before disk drives were common, magnetic tapes were used as secondary storage. Tapes are considerably slower than hard disk and USB flash drives because of the way information is accessed. A hard disk is a *direct access device* since the read/write head can move, in general, directly to the information needed. A USB flash drive is also a direct access device, but nothing moves mechanically. The

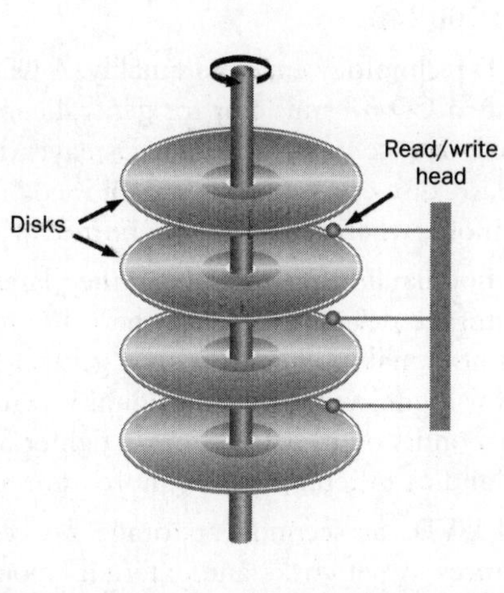

FIGURE 1.12 A hard disk drive with multiple disks and read/write heads

terms *direct access* and *random access* are often used interchangeably. However, information on a tape can be accessed only after first getting past the intervening data. A tape must be rewound or fast-forwarded to get to the appropriate position. A tape is therefore considered a *sequential access device*. For these reasons, tapes are no longer used as a computing storage device, just as audio cassettes were supplanted by compact discs.

Two other terms are used to describe memory devices: *random access memory* (RAM) and *read-only memory* (ROM). It's important to understand these terms because they are used often and their names can be misleading. The terms RAM and main memory are basically interchangeable, describing the memory where active programs and data are stored. *ROM* can refer to chips on the computer motherboard or to portable storage such as a compact disc. ROM chips typically store software called BIOS (basic input/output system) that provide the preliminary instructions needed when the computer is turned on initially. After information is stored on ROM, generally it is not altered (as the term *read-only* implies) during typical computer use. Both RAM and ROM are direct (or random) access devices.

KEY CONCEPT

The surface of a CD has both smooth areas and small pits. A pit represents a binary 1 and a smooth area represents a binary 0.

A *CD-ROM* is a portable secondary memory device. CD stands for compact disc. It is called ROM because information is stored permanently when the CD is created and cannot be changed. Like its musical CD counterpart, a CD-ROM stores information in binary format. When the CD is initially created, a microscopic pit is pressed into the disc to represent a binary 1, and the disc is left smooth to represent a binary 0. The bits are read by shining a low-intensity laser beam onto the spinning disc. The laser beam reflects strongly from a smooth area on the disc but weakly from a pitted area. A sensor receiving the reflection determines whether each bit is a 1 or a 0 accordingly. A typical CD-ROM's storage capacity ranges between 650 and 900 MB.

Variations on basic CD technology emerged quickly. A CD-Recordable (CD-R) disk can be used to create a CD for music or for general computer storage. Once created, you can use a CD-R disc in a standard CD player, but you can't change the information on a CD-R disc once it has been "burned." Music CDs that you buy are pressed from a mold, whereas CD-Rs are burned with a laser.

CDs were initially a popular format for music; they later evolved to be used as a general computer storage device. Similarly, the *DVD* format was originally created for video and is now making headway as a general format for computer data. DVD once stood for digital video disc or digital versatile disc, but now the acronym generally stands on its own. A DVD has a tighter format (more bits per square inch) than a CD and can therefore store more information.

The use of CDs and DVDs as secondary storage devices for computers has declined greatly as advances in networks and external "cloud" storage provided better options.

The capacity of storage devices changes continually as technology improves. A general rule in the computer industry suggests that storage capacity approximately doubles every 18 months. However, this progress eventually will slow down as capacities approach absolute physical limits.

The Central Processing Unit

The CPU interacts with main memory to perform all fundamental processing in a computer. The CPU interprets and executes instructions, one after another, in a continuous cycle. It is made up of three important components, as shown in Figure 1.13. The *control unit* coordinates the processing steps, the *registers* provide a small amount of storage space in the CPU itself, and the *arithmetic/logic unit* performs calculations and makes decisions. The registers are the smallest, fastest cache in the system.

The control unit coordinates the transfer of data and instructions between main memory and the registers in the CPU. It also coordinates the execution of the circuitry in the arithmetic/logic unit to perform operations on data stored in particular registers.

In most CPUs, some registers are reserved for special purposes. For example, the *instruction register* holds the current instruction being executed. The *program counter* is a register that holds the address of the next instruction to be executed. In addition to these and other special-purpose registers, the CPU also contains a set of general-purpose registers that are used for temporary storage of values as needed.

The concept of storing both program instructions and data together in main memory is the underlying principle of the *von Neumann architecture* of computer design, named after John von Neumann, a Hungarian-American mathematician who first advanced this programming concept in 1945. These computers continually follow the *fetch–decode–execute* cycle depicted in Figure 1.14. An instruction is fetched

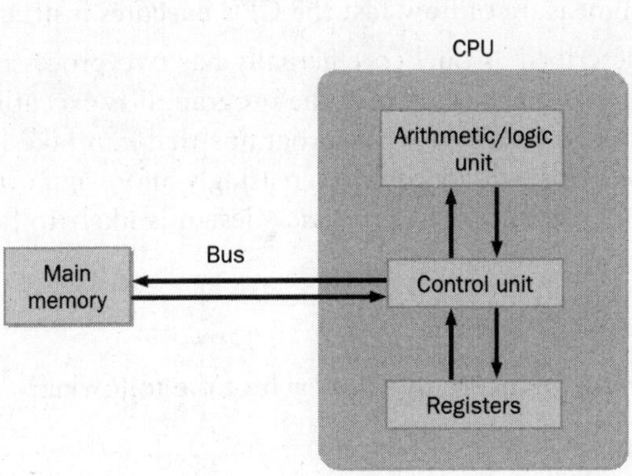

FIGURE 1.13 CPU components and main memory

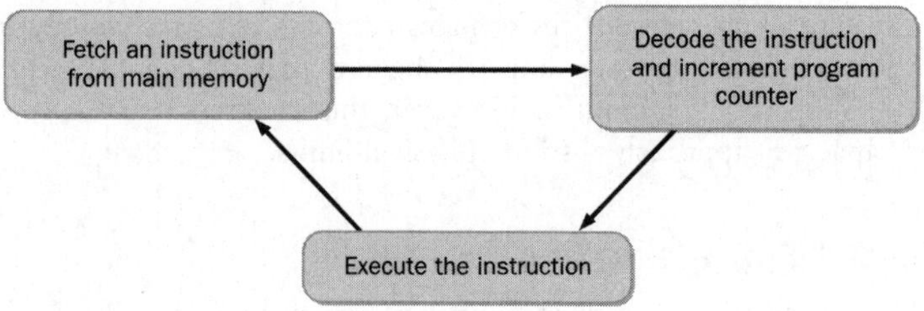

FIGURE 1.14 The continuous fetch–decode–execute cycle

KEY CONCEPT
The fetch-decode-execute cycle forms the foundation of computer processing.

from main memory at the address stored in the program counter and is put into the instruction register. The program counter is incremented at this point to prepare for the next cycle. Then, the instruction is decoded electronically to determine which operation to carry out. Finally, the control unit activates the correct circuitry to carry out the instruction, which may load a data value into a register or add two values together, for example.

The CPU is constructed on a chip called a *microprocessor*, a device that is part of the main circuit board of the computer. This board also contains ROM chips and communication sockets to which device controllers, such as the controller that manages the video display, can be connected.

Another crucial component of the main circuit board is the *system clock*. The clock generates an electronic pulse at regular intervals, which synchronizes the events of the CPU. The rate at which the pulses occur is called the *clock speed*, and it varies depending on the processor. The computer described in Figure 1.8 includes an Intel Dual Core i7 processor that runs at a clock speed of 3.1 GHz, or approximately 3.1 billion pulses per second. The speed of the system clock provides a rough measure of how fast the CPU executes instructions.

A processor described as duel-core actually has two processors built onto one chip, and can do two things at once if the program it is executing is designed for that. However, it is difficult to write programs that can take advantage of that second processor. This will become increasingly more important for software developers, because the future of processor design is likely to be more cores, not single cores that run at faster speeds.

SELF-REVIEW QUESTIONS *(see answers in Appendix L)*

SR 1.7 How many bytes are there in each of the following?

a. 3 KB
b. 2 MB
c. 4 GB

SR 1.8 How many bits are there in each of the following?

a. 8 bytes
b. 2 KB
c. 4 MB

SR 1.9 The music on a CD is created using a sampling rate of 44,000 measurements per second. Each measurement is stored as a number that represents a specific voltage level. Suppose each of these numbers requires two bytes of storage space. How many MB does it take to represent one hour of music?

SR 1.10 What are the two primary hardware components in a computer? How do they interact?

SR 1.11 What is a memory address?

SR 1.12 What does volatile mean? Which memory devices are volatile and which are nonvolatile?

SR 1.13 Select the word from the following list that best matches each of the following phrases:

controller, CPU, main, network card, peripheral, RAM, register, ROM, secondary

a. Almost all devices in a computer system, other than the CPU and the main memory, are categorized as this.
b. A device that coordinates the activities of a peripheral device.
c. Allows information to be sent and received.
d. This type of memory is usually volatile.
e. This type of memory is usually nonvolatile.
f. This term basically is interchangeable with the term "main memory."
g. Where the fundamental processing of a computer takes place.

1.3 Networks

A *network* consists of two or more computers connected together so they can exchange information. Using networks has become the normal mode of commercial computer operation. New technologies are emerging every day to capitalize on the connected environments of modern computer systems.

KEY CONCEPT
A network consists of two or more computers connected together so that they can exchange information.

Figure 1.15 shows a simple computer network. One of the devices on the network is a printer, which allows any computer connected

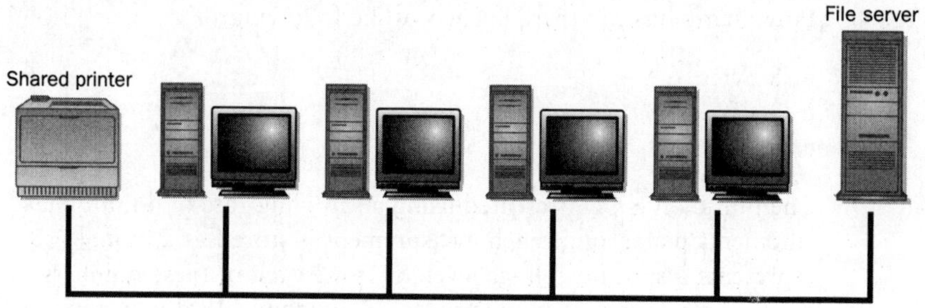

FIGURE 1.15 A simple computer network

to the network to print a document on that printer. One of the computers on the network is designated as a *file server*, which is dedicated to storing programs and data that are needed by many network users. A file server usually has a large amount of secondary memory. When a network has a file server, each individual computer doesn't need its own copy of a program.

Network Connections

If two computers are directly connected, they can communicate in basically the same way that information moves across wires inside a single machine. When connecting two geographically close computers, this solution works well and is called a *point-to-point connection*. However, consider the task of connecting many computers together across large distances. If point-to-point connections are used, every computer is directly connected by a wire to every other computer in the network. A separate wire for each connection is not a workable solution because every time a new computer is added to the network, a new communication line will have to be installed for each computer already in the network. Furthermore, a single computer can handle only a small number of direct connections.

Figure 1.16 shows multiple point-to-point connections. Consider the number of communication lines that would be needed if two or three additional computers were added to the network. These days, local networks, such as those within a single building, often use wireless connections, minimizing the need for running wires.

Compare the diagrams in Figures 1.15 and 1.16. All of the computers shown in Figure 1.15 share a single communication line. Each computer on the network has its own *network address*, which uniquely identifies it. These addresses are similar in concept to the addresses in main memory except that they identify individual computers on a network instead of individual memory locations inside a single

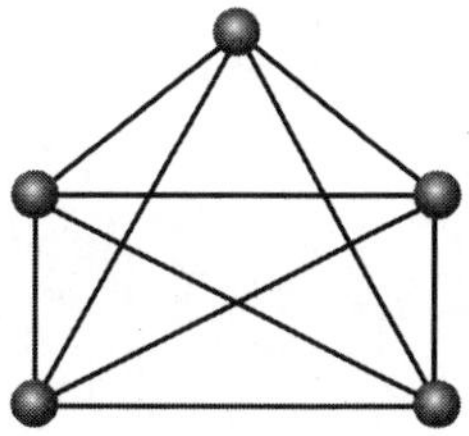

FIGURE 1.16 Point-to-point connections

computer. A message is sent across the line from one computer to another by specifying the network address of the computer for which it is intended.

Sharing a communication line is cost effective and makes adding new computers to the network relatively easy. However, a shared line introduces delays. The computers on the network cannot use the communication line at the same time. They have to take turns sending information, which means they have to wait when the line is busy.

KEY CONCEPT
Sharing a communication line creates delays, but it is cost effective and simplifies adding new computers to the network.

One technique to improve network delays is to divide large messages into segments, called *packets*, and then send the individual packets across the network intermixed with pieces of other messages sent by other users. The packets are collected at the destination and reassembled into the original message. This situation is similar to a group of people using a conveyor belt to move a set of boxes from one place to another. If only one person were allowed to use the conveyor belt at a time, and that person had a large number of boxes to move, the others would be waiting a long time before they could use it. By taking turns, each person can put one box on at a time, and they all can get their work done. It's not as fast as having a conveyor belt of your own, but it's not as slow as having to wait until everyone else is finished.

Local-Area Networks and Wide-Area Networks

A *local-area network* (LAN) is designed to span short distances and connect a relatively small number of computers. Usually, a LAN connects the machines in only one building or in a single room. LANs are convenient to install and manage and are highly reliable. As computers became increasingly small and versatile, LANs provided an inexpensive way to share information throughout an organization. However, having a LAN is like having a telephone system that allows you to call only the people in your own town. We need to be able to share information across longer distances.

KEY CONCEPT
A local-area network (LAN) is an effective way to share information and resources throughout an organization.

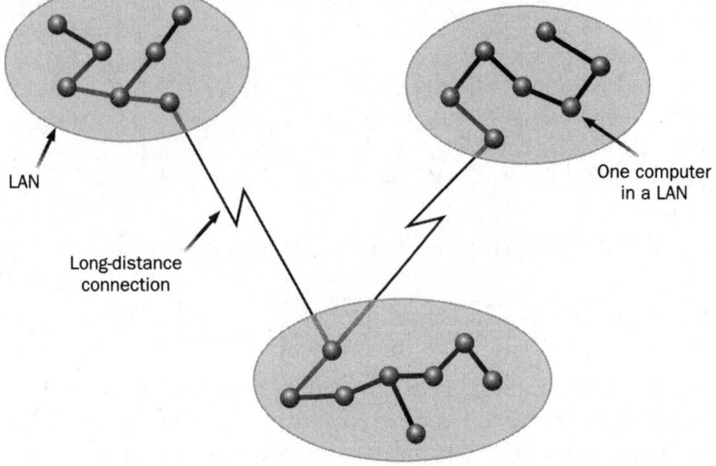

FIGURE 1.17 LANs connected into a WAN

A *wide-area network* (WAN) connects two or more LANs, often across long distances. Usually one computer on each LAN is dedicated to handling the communication across a WAN. This technique relieves the other computers in a LAN from having to perform the details of long-distance communication. Figure 1.17 shows several LANs connected into a WAN. The LANs connected by a WAN are often owned by different companies or organizations and might even be located in different countries.

The Internet

Throughout the 1970s, an agency in the Department of Defense known as the Advanced Research Projects Agency (ARPA) funded several projects to explore network technology. One result of these efforts was the ARPANET, a wide-area network that eventually became known as the Internet. The *Internet* is a network of networks. The term *Internet* comes from the WAN concept of *internetworking*—connecting many smaller networks together.

KEY CONCEPT
The Internet is a wide-area network (WAN) that spans the globe.

In 1983, there were fewer than 600 computers connected to the Internet. At the present time, the Internet serves billions of users worldwide. As more and more computers connected to the Internet, the task of keeping up with the larger number of users and heavier traffic became difficult. New technologies have replaced the ARPANET several times since the initial development, each time providing more capacity and faster processing.

A *protocol* is a set of rules that governs how two things communicate. The software that controls the movement of messages across the Internet must conform to a set of protocols called *TCP/IP* (pronounced by spelling out the letters, T-C-P-I-P). TCP stands for *Transmission Control Protocol*, and IP stands for *Internet Protocol*. The IP software defines how information is formatted and transferred from the source to the destination. The TCP software handles problems such as pieces of information arriving out of their original order or information getting lost, which can happen if too much information converges at one location at the same time.

Every computer connected to the Internet has an *IP address* that uniquely identifies it among all other computers on the Internet. An example of an IP address is 204.192.116.2. Fortunately, the users of the Internet rarely have to deal with IP addresses. The Internet allows each computer to be given a name. Like IP addresses, the names must be unique. The Internet name of a computer is often referred to as its *Internet address*. An example of Internet address is `hector.vt.edu`.

KEY CONCEPT

Every computer connected to the Internet has an IP address that uniquely identifies it.

The first part of an Internet address is the local name of a specific computer. The rest of the address is the *domain name*, which indicates the organization to which the computer belongs. For example, `vt.edu` is the domain name for the network of computers at Virginia Tech, and `hector` is the name of a particular computer on that campus. Because the domain names are unique, many organizations can have a computer named `hector` without confusion. Individual departments might be assigned *subdomains* that are added to the basic domain name to uniquely distinguish their set of computers within the larger organization. For example, the cs.vt.edu subdomain is devoted to the Department of Computer Science at Virginia Tech.

The last part of each domain name, called a *top-level domain* (TLD), usually indicates the type of organization to which the computer belongs. The TLD `edu` indicates an educational institution. The TLD `com` usually refers to a commercial business. Another common TLD is `org`, used by nonprofit organizations. Other top-level domains include `biz`, `info`, `jobs`, and `name`. Many computers, especially those outside of the United States, use a country-code top-level domain that denotes the country of origin, such as `uk` for the United Kingdom or `au` for Australia.

When an Internet address is referenced, it gets translated to its corresponding IP address, which is used from that point on. The software that does this translation is called the *Domain Name System* (DNS). Each organization connected to the Internet operates a *domain server* that maintains a list of all computers at that organization and their IP addresses. You provide the name, and the domain server gives back a number. If the local domain server does not have the IP address for the name, it contacts another domain server that does.

Initially, the primary use of interconnected computers was to send electronic mail, but Internet capabilities grew quickly. One of the most significant uses of the Internet today is the World Wide Web.

The World Wide Web

The Internet gives us the capability to exchange information. The *World Wide Web* (also known as WWW or simply the Web) makes the exchange of information easy for humans. Web software provides a common user interface through which many different types of information can be accessed with the click of a mouse.

KEY CONCEPT
The World Wide Web is software that makes sharing information across a network easy for humans.

The Web is based on the concepts of hypertext and hypermedia. The term *hypertext* was coined in 1965 by Ted Nelson. It describes a way to organize information so that the flow of ideas was not constrained to a linear progression. Paul Otlet (1868–1944), considered by some to be the father of information science, envisioned that concept as a way to manage large amounts of information. The underlying idea is that documents can be linked at various points according to natural relationships so that the reader can jump from one document to another, following the appropriate path for that reader's needs. When other media components are incorporated, such as graphics, sound, animations, and video, the resulting organization is called *hypermedia*.

The terms Internet and World Wide Web are sometimes used interchangeably, but there are important differences between the two. The Internet makes it possible to communicate via computers around the world. The Web makes that communication a straightforward and enjoyable activity. The Web is essentially a distributed information service based on a set of software applications.

A *browser* is a software tool that loads and formats Web documents for viewing. *Mosaic*, the first graphical interface browser for the Web, was released in 1993. The designer of a Web document refers to other Web information that might be anywhere on the Internet. Popular browsers include Google Chrome, Apple Safari, Mozilla Firefox, and Opera. The use of Internet Explorer, from Microsoft, has recently declined with the rise of alternatives. The Microsoft Edge browser has recently replaced Internet Explorer.

A computer dedicated to providing access to Web documents is called a *Web server*. Browsers load and interpret documents provided by a Web server. Many such documents are formatted using the *HyperText Markup Language* (HTML). The Java programming language has an intimate relationship with Web processing, because links to Java programs can be embedded in HTML documents and executed through Web browsers.

Uniform Resource Locators

Information on the Web is found by identifying a *Uniform Resource Locator* (URL, pronounced by spelling out the letters U-R-L). A *URL* uniquely specifies documents and other information for a browser to obtain and display. The following is an example URL:

```
http://www.google.com
```

The Web site at this particular URL is the home of the well-known Google *search engine*, which enables you to search the Web for information using particular words or phrases.

A URL contains several pieces of information. The first piece is a protocol, which determines the way the browser transmits and processes information. The second piece is the Internet address of the machine on which the document is stored. The third piece of information is the file name or resource of interest. If no file name is given, as is the case with the Google URL, the Web server usually provides a default page.

KEY CONCEPT
A URL uniquely specifies documents and other information found on the Web for a browser to obtain and display.

Let's look at another example URL:

```
https://www.whitehouse.gov/issues/education
```

In this URL, the protocol is https, which stands for a secure version of the *HyperText Transfer Protocol*. The machine referenced is `www` (a typical reference to a Web server), found at domain `whitehouse.gov`. Finally, `issues/education` represents a file (or a reference that generates a file) to be transferred to the browser for viewing. Many other forms for URLs exist, but this form is the most common.

SELF-REVIEW QUESTIONS *(see answers in Appendix L)*

SR 1.14 What is a file server?

SR 1.15 What is the total number of communication lines needed for a fully connected point-to-point network of five computers? Six computers?

SR 1.16 Describe a benefit of having computers on a network share a communication line. Describe a cost/drawback of sharing a communication line.

SR 1.17 What is the etymology of the word Internet?

SR 1.18 The TCP/IP set of protocols describes communication rules for software that uses the Internet. What does TCP stand for? What does IP stand for?

SR 1.19 Explain the parts of the following URLs:

a. duke.csc.villanova.edu/jss/examples.html
b. java.sun.com/products/index.html

1.4 The Java Programming Language

Let's now turn our attention to the software that makes a computer system useful. A program is written in a particular *programming language* that uses specific words and symbols to express the problem solution. A programming language defines a set of rules that determines exactly how a programmer can combine the words and symbols of the language into *programming statements*, which are the instructions that are carried out when the program is executed.

Since the inception of computers, many programming languages have been created. We use the Java language in this book to demonstrate various programming concepts and techniques. Although our main goal is to learn these underlying software development principles, an important side effect will be to become proficient in the development of Java programs specifically.

The development of the Java programming language began in 1991 by James Gosling at Sun Microsystems. The language initially was called Oak, then Green, and ultimately Java. Java was introduced to the public in 1995 and has gained tremendous popularity since. In 2010, Sun Microsystems was purchased by Oracle.

There are variations of the Java Platform, including the Standard Edition, which is the mainstream version of the language; the Enterprise Edition, which includes extra libraries to support large-scale system development; and the Micro Edition, which is specifically for developing software for portable devices such as cell phones. This book focuses on the Standard Edition.

Furthermore, the Java Standard Edition has gone through several revisions over the years, extending its capabilities and making changes to certain aspects of it. The table below lists the versions and some of the new features. Note that they changed the numbering technique with version 5. Readers of this book should be using version 6 or later.

Version	Year	New Features
1.0	1996	Initial deployment
1.1	1997	Inner classes
1.2	1998	Collections framework, Swing graphics
1.3	2000	Sound framework
1.4	2002	Assertions, XML support, regular expressions
5	2004	Generics, for-each loop, autoboxing, enumerations, annotations, variable-length parameter lists
6	2006	GUI improvements, various library updates
7	2011	Use of strings in a switch, other language changes
8	2014	JavaFX, lambda expressions, date and time API

Some parts of early Java technologies have been *deprecated*, which means they are considered old-fashioned and should not be used. When it is important, we point out deprecated elements and discuss their preferred alternatives.

One reason Java attracted some initial attention was because it was the first programming language to deliberately embrace the concept of writing programs (called applets) that can be executed using the Web. Since then, the techniques for creating a Web page that has dynamic, functional capabilities have expanded dramatically.

Java is an *object-oriented programming language*. Objects are the fundamental elements that make up a program. The principles of object-oriented software development are the cornerstone of this book. We explore object-oriented programming concepts later in this chapter and throughout the rest of the book.

KEY CONCEPT
This book focuses on the principles of object-oriented programming.

The Java language is accompanied by a library of extra software that we can use when developing programs. This software is referred to as the *Java API*, which stands for Application Programmer Interface, or simply the *standard class library*. The Java API provides the ability to create graphics, communicate over networks, and interact with databases, among many other features. The Java API is huge and quite versatile. We won't be able to cover all aspects of the library, though we will explore several of them.

Java is used in commercial environments all over the world. It is one of the fastest growing programming technologies of all time. So not only is it a good language in which to learn programming concepts, it is also a practical language that will serve you well in the future.

A Java Program

Let's look at a simple but complete Java program. The program in Listing 1.1 prints two sentences to the screen. This particular program prints a quote by Abraham Lincoln. The output is shown below the program listing.

All Java applications have a similar basic structure. Despite its small size and simple purpose, this program contains several important features. Let's carefully dissect it and examine its pieces.

The first few lines of the program are comments, which start with the // symbols and continue to the end of the line. Comments don't affect what the program does but are included to make the program easier to understand by humans. Programmers can and should include comments as needed throughout a program to clearly identify the purpose of the program and describe any special processing. Any written comments or documents, including a user's guide and technical references, are called *documentation*. Comments included in a program are called *inline documentation*.

KEY CONCEPT
Comments do not affect a program's processing; instead, they serve to facilitate human comprehension.

LISTING 1.1

```
//********************************************************************
//  Lincoln.java       Author: Lewis/Loftus
//
//  Demonstrates the basic structure of a Java application.
//********************************************************************

public class Lincoln
{
   //-----------------------------------------------------------------
   //  Prints a presidential quote.
   //-----------------------------------------------------------------
   public static void main(String[] args)
   {
      System.out.println("A quote by Abraham Lincoln:");

      System.out.println("Whatever you are, be a good one.");
   }
}
```

OUTPUT

```
A quote by Abraham Lincoln:
Whatever you are, be a good one.
```

VideoNote
Overview of program elements.

The rest of the program is a *class definition*. This class is called `Lincoln`, though we could have named it just about anything we wished. The class definition runs from the first opening brace (`{`) to the final closing brace (`}`) on the last line of the program. All Java programs are defined using class definitions.

Inside the class definition are some more comments describing the purpose of the `main` method, which is defined directly below the comments. A *method* is a group of programming statements that is given a name. In this case, the name of the method is `main` and it contains only two programming statements. Like a class definition, a method is also delimited by braces.

All Java applications have a `main` method, which is where processing begins. Each programming statement in the `main` method is executed, one at a time in order, until the end of the method is reached. Then the program ends, or *terminates*. The `main` method definition in a Java program is always preceded by the words `public`, `static`, and `void`, which we examine later in the text. The use of `String` and `args` does not come into play in this particular program. We describe these later also.

The two lines of code in the `main` method invoke another method called `println` (pronounced print line). We *invoke*, or *call*, a method when we want it to execute. The `println` method prints the specified characters to the screen. The characters to be printed are represented as a *character string*, enclosed in double quote characters ("). When the program is executed, it calls the `println` method to print the first statement, calls it again to print the second statement, and then, because that is the last line in the `main` method, the program terminates.

The code executed when the `println` method is invoked is not defined in this program. The `println` method is part of the `System.out` object, which is part of the Java standard class library. It's not technically part of the Java language, but is always available for use in any Java program. We explore the `println` method in more detail in Chapter 2.

Comments

Let's examine comments in more detail. *Comments* are the only language feature that allows programmers to compose and communicate their thoughts independent of the code. Comments should provide insight into the programmer's original intent. A program is often used for many years, and often many modifications are made to it over time. The original programmer often will not remember the details of a particular program when, at some point in the future, modifications are required. Furthermore, the original programmer is not always available to make the changes; thus, someone completely unfamiliar with the program will need to understand it. Good documentation is therefore essential.

As far as the Java programming language is concerned, the content of comments can be any text whatsoever. Comments are ignored by the computer; they do not affect how the program executes.

The comments in the `Lincoln` program represent one of two types of comments allowed in Java. The comments in `Lincoln` take the following form:

```
// This is a comment.
```

This type of comment begins with a double slash (//) and continues to the end of the line. You cannot have any characters between the two slashes. The computer ignores any text after the double slash to the end of the line. A comment can follow code on the same line to document that particular line, as in the following example:

```
System.out.println("Monthly Report");  // always use this title
```

The second form a Java comment may have is the following:

```
/* This is another comment. */
```

This comment type does not use the end of a line to indicate the end of the comment. Anything between the initiating slash-asterisk (/*) and the terminating asterisk-slash (*/) is part of the comment, including the invisible *newline* character that represents the end of a line. Therefore, this type of comment can extend over multiple lines. No space can be between the slash and the asterisk.

If there is a second asterisk following the /* at the beginning of a comment, the content of the comment can be used to automatically generate external documentation about your program by using a tool called *javadoc*. More information about javadoc is given in Appendix I.

The two basic comment types can be used to create various documentation styles, such as the following:

```
// This is a comment on a single line.

//------------------------------------------------------------
// Some comments such as those above methods or classes
// deserve to be blocked off to focus special attention
// on a particular aspect of your code. Note that each of
// these lines is technically a separate comment.
//------------------------------------------------------------

/*
   This is one comment
   that spans several lines.
*/
```

Programmers often concentrate so much on writing code that they focus too little on documentation. You should develop good commenting practices and follow them habitually. Comments should be well written, often in complete sentences. They should not belabor the obvious but should provide appropriate insight into the intent of the code. The following examples are *not* good comments:

```
System.out.println("hello");     // prints hello
System.out.println("test");      // change this later
```

KEY CONCEPT
Inline documentation should provide insight into your code. It should not be ambiguous or belabor the obvious.

The first comment paraphrases the obvious purpose of the line and does not add any value to the statement. It is better to have no comment than a useless one. The second comment is ambiguous. What should be changed later? When is later? Why should it be changed?

Identifiers and Reserved Words

The various words used when writing programs are called *identifiers*. The identifiers in the Lincoln program are class, Lincoln, public, static, void, main, String, args, System, out, and println. These fall into three categories:

- words that we make up when writing a program (`Lincoln` and `args`)
- words that another programmer chose (`String`, `System`, `out`, `println`, and `main`)
- words that are reserved for special purposes in the language (`class`, `public`, `static`, and `void`)

While writing the program, we simply chose to name the class `Lincoln`, but we could have used one of many other possibilities. For example, we could have called it `Quote`, or `Abe`, or `GoodOne`. The identifier `args` (which is short for arguments) is often used in the way we use it in `Lincoln`, but we could have used just about any other identifier in its place.

The identifiers `String`, `System`, `out`, and `println` were chosen by other programmers. These words are not part of the Java language. They are part of the Java standard library of predefined code, a set of classes and methods that someone has already written for us. The authors of that code chose the identifiers in that code—we're just making use of them.

Reserved words are identifiers that have a special meaning in a programming language and can only be used in predefined ways. A reserved word cannot be used for any other purpose, such as naming a class or method. In the `Lincoln` program, the reserved words used are `class`, `public`, `static`, and `void`. Throughout the book, we show Java reserved words in blue type. Figure 1.18 lists all of the Java reserved words in alphabetical order. The words marked with an asterisk have been reserved, but currently have no meaning in Java.

An identifier that we make up for use in a program can be composed of any combination of letters, digits, the underscore character (_), and the dollar sign (`$`), but it cannot begin with a digit. Identifiers may be of any length. Therefore,

abstract	default	goto*	package	this
assert	do	if	private	throw
boolean	double	implements	protected	throws
break	else	import	public	transient
byte	enum	instanceof	return	true
case	extends	int	short	try
catch	false	interface	static	void
char	final	long	strictfp	volatile
class	finally	native	super	while
const*	float	new	switch	
continue	for	null	synchronized	

FIGURE 1.18 Java reserved words

Identifier

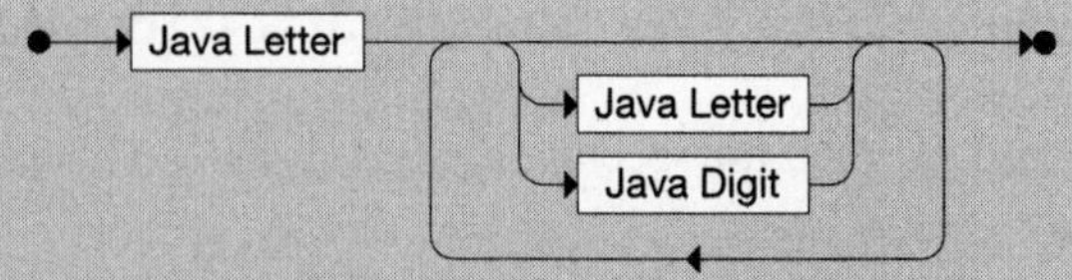

An identifier is a letter followed by zero or more letters and digits. A Java Letter includes the 26 English alphabetic characters in both uppercase and lowercase, the `$` and _ (underscore) characters, as well as alphabetic characters from other languages. A Java Digit includes the digits `0` through `9`.

Examples:

```
total
MAX_HEIGHT
num1
Keyboard
System
```

`total`, `label7`, `nextStockItem`, `NUM_BOXES`, and `$amount` are all valid identifiers, but `4th_word` and `coin#value` are not valid.

Both uppercase and lowercase letters can be used in an identifier, and the difference is important. Java is *case sensitive*, which means that two identifier names that differ only in the case of their letters are considered to be different identifiers. Therefore, `total`, `Total`, `ToTaL`, and `TOTAL` are all different identifiers. As you can imagine, it is not a good idea to use multiple identifiers that differ only in their case, because they can be easily confused.

KEY CONCEPT

Java is case sensitive. The uppercase and lowercase versions of a letter are distinct.

Although the Java language doesn't require it, using a consistent case format for each kind of identifier makes your identifiers easier to understand. There are various Java conventions regarding identifiers that should be followed, though technically they don't have to be. For example, we use *title case* (uppercase for the first letter of each word) for class names. Throughout the text, we describe the preferred case style for each type of identifier when it is first encountered.

While an identifier can be of any length, you should choose your names carefully. They should be descriptive but not verbose. You should avoid meaningless names such as `a` or `x`. An exception to this rule can be made if the short name is actually descriptive, such as using `x` and `y` to represent (x, y) coordinates on a two-dimensional grid. Likewise, you should not use unnecessarily long names, such as the identifier `theCurrentItemBeingProcessed`. The name `currentItem` would serve just as well. As you might imagine, the use of identifiers that are verbose is a much less prevalent problem than the use of names that are not descriptive.

You should always strive to make your programs as readable as possible. Therefore, you should always be careful when abbreviating words. You might think `curStVal` is a good name to represent the current stock value, but another person trying to understand the code may have trouble figuring out what you meant. It might not even be clear to you two months after writing it.

KEY CONCEPT
Identifier names should be descriptive and readable.

White Space

All Java programs use *white space* to separate the words and symbols used in a program. *White space* consists of blanks, tabs, and newline characters. The phrase "white space" refers to the fact that, on a white sheet of paper with black printing, the space between the words and symbols is white. The way a programmer uses white space is important because it can be used to emphasize parts of the code and can make a program easier to read.

Except when it's used to separate words, the computer ignores white space. It does not affect the execution of a program. This fact gives programmers a great deal of flexibility in how they format a program. The lines of a program should be divided in logical places, and certain lines should be indented and aligned so that the program's underlying structure is clear.

KEY CONCEPT
Appropriate use of white space makes a program easier to read and understand.

Because white space is ignored, we can write a program in many different ways. For example, taking white space to one extreme, we could put as many words as possible on each line. The code in Listing 1.2, the `Lincoln2` program, is formatted quite differently from `Lincoln` but prints the same message.

LISTING 1.2

```
//********************************************************************
//  Lincoln2.java       Author: Lewis/Loftus
//
//  Demonstrates a poorly formatted, though valid, program.
//********************************************************************

public class Lincoln2{public static void main(String[]args){
System.out.println("A quote by Abraham Lincoln:");
System.out.println("Whatever you are, be a good one.");}}
```

OUTPUT

```
A quote by Abraham Lincoln:
Whatever you are, be a good one.
```

LISTING 1.3

```
//********************************************************************
//  Lincoln3.java       Author: Lewis/Loftus
//
//  Demonstrates another valid program that is poorly formatted.
//********************************************************************
          public       class
     Lincoln3
   {
                 public
   static
      void
  main
        (
String
           []
    args                          )
  {
  System.out.println     (
"A quote by Abraham Lincoln:"           )
   ;         System.out.println
               (
       "Whatever you are, be a good one."
      )
   ;
}
          }
```

OUTPUT

```
A quote by Abraham Lincoln:
Whatever you are, be a good one.
```

KEY CONCEPT
You should adhere to a set of guidelines that establish the way you format and document your programs.

Taking white space to the other extreme, we could write almost every word and symbol on a different line with varying amounts of spaces, such as `Lincoln3`, shown in Listing 1.3.

All three versions of `Lincoln` are technically valid and will execute in the same way, but they are radically different from a reader's point of view. Both the latter examples show poor style and make the program difficult to understand. You may be asked to adhere to particular guidelines when you write your programs. A software development company often has a programming style policy that it requires its programmers to follow.

In any case, you should adopt and consistently use a set of style guidelines that increase the readability of your code.

SELF-REVIEW QUESTIONS *(see answers in Appendix L)*

SR 1.20 When was the Java programming language developed? By whom? When was it introduced to the public?

SR 1.21 Where does processing begin in a Java application?

SR 1.22 What do you predict would be the result of the following line in a Java program?

```
System.out.println("Hello");  // prints hello
```

SR 1.23 What do you predict would be the result of the following line in a Java program?

```
// prints hello System.out.println("Hello");
```

SR 1.24 Which of the following are not valid Java identifiers? Why?

a. `RESULT`
b. `result`
c. `12345`
d. `x12345y`
e. `black&white`
f. `answer_7`

SR 1.25 Suppose a program requires an identifier to represent the sum of the test scores of a class of students. For each of the following names, state whether or not each is a good name to use for the identifier. Explain your answers.

a. `x`
b. `scoreSum`
c. `sumOfTheTestScoresOfTheStudents`
d. `smTstScr`

SR 1.26 What is white space? How does it affect program execution? How does it affect program readability?

1.5 Program Development

The process of getting a program running involves various activities. The program has to be written in the appropriate programming language, such as Java. That program has to be translated into a form that the computer can execute. Errors can occur at various stages of this process and must be fixed. Various software tools can be used to help with all parts of the development process as well. Let's explore these issues in more detail.

Programming Language Levels

Suppose a particular person is giving travel directions to a friend. That person might explain those directions in any one of several languages, such as English, Russian, or Italian. The directions are the same no matter which language is used to explain them, but the manner in which the directions are expressed is different. The friend must be able to understand the language being used in order to follow the directions.

Similarly, a problem can be solved by writing a program in one of many programming languages, such as Java, Ada, C, C++, C#, Pascal, and Smalltalk. The purpose of the program is essentially the same no matter which language is used, but the particular statements used to express the instructions, and the overall organization of those instructions, vary with each language. A computer must be able to understand the instructions in order to carry them out.

Programming languages can be categorized into the following four groups. These groups basically reflect the historical development of computer languages.

- machine language
- assembly language
- high-level languages
- fourth-generation languages

In order for a program to run on a computer, it must be expressed in that computer's *machine language*. Each type of CPU has its own language.

KEY CONCEPT
All programs must be translated to a particular CPU's machine language in order to be executed.

Each machine language instruction can accomplish only a simple task. For example, a single machine language instruction might copy a value into a register or compare a value to zero. It might take four separate machine language instructions to add two numbers together and to store the result. However, a computer can do millions of these instructions in a second, and therefore many simple commands can be executed quickly to accomplish complex tasks.

Machine language code is expressed as a series of binary digits and is extremely difficult for humans to read and write. Originally, programs were entered into the computer by using switches or some similarly tedious method. Early programmers found these techniques to be time consuming and error prone.

These problems gave rise to the use of *assembly language*, which replaced binary digits with *mnemonics*, short English-like words that represent commands

High-Level Language	Assembly Language	Machine Language
a + b	ld [%fp-20], %o0	...
	ld [%fp-24], %o1	1101 0000 0000 0111
	add %o0, %o1, %o0	1011 1111 1110 1000
		1101 0010 0000 0111
		1011 1111 1110 1000
		1001 0000 0000 0000
		...

FIGURE 1.19 A high-level expression and its assembly language and machine language equivalent

or data. It is much easier for programmers to deal with words than with binary digits. However, an assembly language program cannot be executed directly on a computer. It must first be translated into machine language.

Generally, each assembly language instruction corresponds to an equivalent machine language instruction. Therefore, similar to machine language, each assembly language instruction accomplishes only a simple operation. Although assembly language is an improvement over machine code from a programmer's perspective, it is still tedious to use. Both assembly language and machine language are considered *low-level languages.*

> **KEY CONCEPT**
> High-level languages allow a programmer to ignore the underlying details of machine language.

Today, most programmers use a *high-level language* to write software. A high-level language is expressed in English-like phrases, and thus is easier for programmers to read and write. A single high-level language programming statement can accomplish the equivalent of many—perhaps hundreds—of machine language instructions. The term *high-level* refers to the fact that the programming statements are expressed in a way that is far removed from the machine language that is ultimately executed. Java is a high-level language, as are Ada, C++, Smalltalk, and many others.

Figure 1.19 shows equivalent expressions in a high-level language, assembly language, and machine language. The expressions add two numbers together. The assembly language and machine language in this example are specific to a Sparc processor.

The high-level language expression in Figure 1.19 is readable and intuitive for programmers. It is similar to an algebraic expression. The equivalent assembly language code is somewhat readable, but it is more verbose and less intuitive. The machine language is basically unreadable and much longer. In fact, only a small portion of the binary machine code to add two numbers together is shown in Figure 1.19. The complete machine language code for this particular expression is over 400 bits long.

A high-level language insulates programmers from needing to know the underlying machine language for the processor on which they are working. But high-level language code must be translated into machine language in order to be executed.

Some programming languages are considered to operate at an even higher level than high-level languages. They might include special facilities for automatic report generation or interaction with a database. These languages are called *fourth-generation languages*, or simply 4GLs, because they followed the first three generations of computer programming: machine, assembly, and high-level.

Editors, Compilers, and Interpreters

Several special-purpose programs are needed to help with the process of developing new programs. They are sometimes called software tools because they are used to build programs. Examples of basic software tools include an editor, a compiler, and an interpreter.

Initially, you use an *editor* as you type a program into a computer and store it in a file. There are many different editors with many different features. You should become familiar with the editor you will use regularly because it can dramatically affect the speed at which you enter and modify your programs.

Figure 1.20 shows a very basic view of the program development process. After editing and saving your program, you attempt to translate it from high-level code into a form that can be executed. That translation may result in errors, in which case you return to the editor to make changes to the code to fix the problems. Once the translation occurs successfully, you can execute the program and evaluate the results. If the results are not what you want, or if you want to enhance your existing program, you again return to the editor to make changes.

The translation of source code into (ultimately) machine language for a particular type of CPU can occur in a variety of ways. A *compiler* is a program that

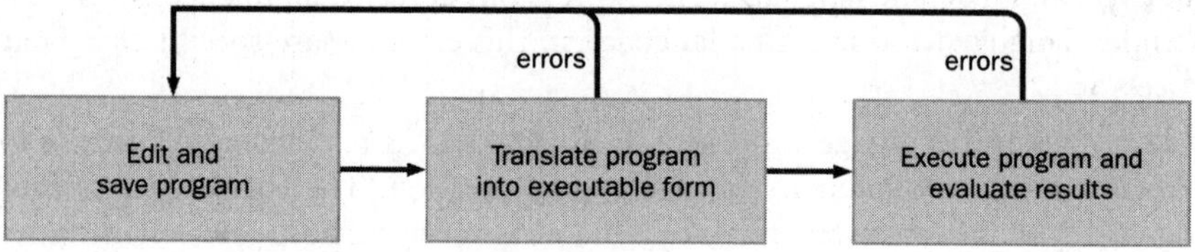

FIGURE 1.20 Editing and running a program

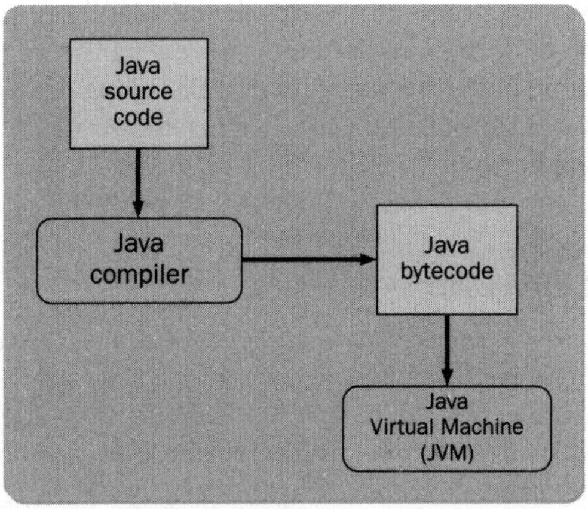

FIGURE 1.21 The Java translation and execution process

translates code in one language to equivalent code in another language. The original code is called *source code*, and the language into which it is translated is called the *target language*. For many traditional compilers, the source code is translated directly into a particular machine language. In that case, the translation process occurs once and the resulting executable program can be run whenever needed on any computer using that type of CPU.

An *interpreter* is similar to a compiler but has an important difference. An interpreter interweaves the translation and execution activities. A small part of the source code, such as one statement, is translated and executed. Then another statement is translated and executed, and so on. One advantage of this technique is that it eliminates the need for a separate compilation phase. However, the program generally runs more slowly because the translation process occurs during each execution.

KEY CONCEPT
A Java compiler translates Java source code into Java bytecode, a low-level, architecture-neutral representation of the program.

The process generally used to translate and execute Java programs combines the use of a compiler and an interpreter. This process is pictured in Figure 1.21. The Java compiler translates Java source code into Java *bytecode*, which is a representation of the program in a low-level form similar to machine language code. A Java interpreter called the *Java Virtual Machine* (JVM) executes the Java bytecode.

The difference between Java bytecode and true machine language code is that Java bytecode is not tied to any particular processor type. This approach has the distinct advantage of making Java *architecture neutral*, and therefore easily portable from one machine type to another. The only restriction is that there must be a JVM on each machine.

Since the compilation process translates the high-level Java source code into a low-level representation, the interpretation process by the JVM is far more efficient than interpreting high-level code directly. Executing a program by interpreting its bytecode is still slower than executing machine code directly, but it is fast enough for most applications.

Development Environments

A software *development environment* is the set of tools used to create, test, and modify a program. Some development environments are available for free while others, which may have advanced features, must be purchased. Some environments are referred to as *integrated development environments* (IDEs) because they integrate various tools into one software program and provide a convenient graphical user interface.

Any development environment will contain certain key tools, such as a Java compiler and interpreter. Some will include a *debugger*, which helps you find errors in a program. Other tools that may be included are documentation generators, archiving tools, and tools that help you visualize your program structure.

VideoNote
Comparison of Java IDEs.

Included in the download of the Java Standard Edition is the Java *Software Development Kit* (SDK), which is sometimes referred to simply as the *Java Development Kit* (JDK). The Java SDK contains the core development tools needed to get a Java program up and running, but it is not an integrated environment. The commands for compilation and interpretation are executed on the command line. That is, the SDK does not have a GUI. It also does not include an editor, although any editor that can save a document as simple text can be used.

One of the most popular Java IDEs is called Eclipse (see www.eclipse.org). Eclipse is an *open-source* project, meaning that it is developed by a wide collection of programmers and is available for free. Other popular Java IDEs include jEdit (www.jedit.org), DrJava (drjava.sourceforge.net), jGRASP (www.jgrasp.com), and BlueJ (www.bluej.org).

KEY CONCEPT
Many different development environments exist to help you create and modify Java programs.

Various other Java development environments are available. A Web search will unveil dozens of them. The choice of which development environment to use is important. The more you know about the capabilities of your environment, the more productive you can be during program development.

Syntax and Semantics

Each programming language has its own unique *syntax*. The *syntax rules* of a language dictate exactly how the vocabulary elements of the language can be combined to form statements. These rules must be followed in order to create a program. We've already discussed several Java syntax rules. For instance, the fact that an identifier cannot begin with a digit is a syntax rule. The fact that braces are used to begin and end classes and methods is also a syntax rule. Appendix L formally defines the basic syntax rules for the Java programming language, and specific rules are highlighted throughout the text.

During compilation, all syntax rules are checked. If a program is not syntactically correct, the compiler will issue error messages and will not produce bytecode. Java has a similar syntax to the programming languages C and C++, and therefore the look and feel of the code is familiar to people with a background in those languages.

The *semantics* of a statement in a programming language define what will happen when that statement is executed. Programming languages are generally unambiguous, which means the semantics of a program are well defined. That is, there is one and only one interpretation for each statement. On the other hand, the *natural languages* that humans use to communicate, such as English and Italian, are full of ambiguities. A sentence can often have two or more different meanings. For example, consider the following sentence:

```
Time flies like an arrow.
```

> **KEY CONCEPT**
> Syntax rules dictate the form of a program. Semantics dictate the meaning of the program statements.

The average human is likely to interpret this sentence as a general observation: that time moves quickly in the same way that an arrow moves quickly. However, if we interpret the word *time* as a verb (as in "run the 50-yard dash and I'll time you") and the word *flies* as a noun (the plural of fly), the interpretation changes completely. We know that arrows don't time things, so we wouldn't normally interpret the sentence that way, but it is a valid interpretation of the words in the sentence. A computer would have a difficult time trying to determine which meaning is intended. Moreover, this sentence could describe the preferences of an unusual insect known as a "time fly," which might be found near an archery range. After all, fruit flies like a banana.

The point is that one specific English sentence can have multiple valid meanings. A computer language cannot allow such ambiguities to exist. If a programming language instruction could have two different meanings, a computer would not be able to determine which one should be carried out.

Errors

Several different kinds of problems can occur in software, particularly during program development. The term *computer error* is often misused and varies in meaning depending on the situation. From a user's point of view, anything that goes awry when interacting with a machine can be called a computer error. For example, suppose you charged a $23 item to your credit card, but when you received the bill, the item was listed at $230. After you have the problem fixed, the credit card company apologizes for the "computer error." Did the computer arbitrarily add a zero to the end of the number, or did it perhaps multiply the value by 10? Of course not. A computer follows the commands we give it and operates on the data we provide. If our programs are wrong or our data inaccurate, then we cannot expect the results to be correct. A common phrase used to describe this situation is "garbage in, garbage out."

KEY CONCEPT
The programmer is responsible for the accuracy and reliability of a program.

You will encounter three kinds of errors as you develop programs:

- compile-time error
- run-time error
- logical error

KEY CONCEPT
A Java program must be syntactically correct or the compiler will not produce bytecode.

The compiler checks to make sure you are using the correct syntax. If you have any statements that do not conform to the syntactic rules of the language, the compiler will produce a *syntax error*. The compiler also tries to find other problems, such as the use of incompatible types of data. The syntax might be technically correct, but you may be attempting to do something that the language doesn't semantically allow. Any error identified by the compiler is called a *compile-time error*. If a compile-time error occurs, an executable version of the program is not created.

The second kind of problem occurs during program execution. It is called a *run-time error* and causes the program to terminate abnormally. For example, if we attempt to divide by zero, the program will "crash" and halt execution at that point. Because the requested operation is undefined, the system simply abandons its attempt to continue processing your program. The best programs are *robust*; that is, they avoid as many run-time errors as possible. For example, the program code could guard against the possibility of dividing by zero and handle the situation appropriately if it arises. In Java, many run-time problems are called *exceptions* that can be caught and dealt with accordingly.

VideoNote
Examples of various error types.

The third kind of software problem is a *logical error*. In this case, the software compiles and executes without complaint, but it produces incorrect results. For example, a logical error occurs when a value is calculated incorrectly or when a graphical button does not appear in the correct place. A programmer must test the program thoroughly, comparing the expected results to those that actually occur. When defects are found, they must be traced back to the source of the problem in the code and corrected. The process of finding and correcting defects in a program is called *debugging*. Logical errors can manifest themselves in many ways, and the actual root cause might be difficult to discover.

SELF-REVIEW QUESTIONS *(see answers in Appendix L)*

SR 1.27 We all know that computers are used to perform complex jobs. In this section, you learned that a computer's instructions can do only simple tasks. Explain this apparent contradiction.

SR 1.28 What is the relationship between a high-level language and a machine language?

SR 1.29 What is Java bytecode?

SR 1.30 Select the word from the following list that best matches each of the following phrases:

assembly, compiler, high-level, IDE, interpreter, Java, low-level, machine

a. A program written in this type of language can run directly on a computer.
b. Generally, each language instruction in this type of language corresponds to an equivalent machine language instruction.
c. Most programmers write their programs using this type of language.
d. Java is an example of this type of language.
e. This type of program translates code in one language to code in another language.
f. This type of program interweaves the translation of code and the execution of the code.

SR 1.31 What do we mean by the syntax and semantics of a programming language?

SR 1.32 Categorize each of the following situations as a compile-time error, run-time error, or logical error.

a. Misspelling a Java reserved word.
b. Calculating the average of an empty list of numbers by dividing the sum of the numbers on the list (which is zero) by the size of the list (which is also zero).
c. Printing a student's high test grade when the student's average test grade should have been output.

1.6 Object-Oriented Programming

As we stated earlier in this chapter, Java is an object-oriented (OO) language. As the name implies, an *object* is a fundamental entity in a Java program. This book is focused on the idea of developing software by defining objects that interact with each other.

The principles of object-oriented software development have been around for many years, essentially as long as high-level programming languages have been used. The programming language Simula, developed in the 1960s, had many characteristics that define the modern OO approach to software development. In the 1980s and 1990s, object-oriented programming became wildly popular, due in large part to the development of programming languages such as C++ and Java. It is now the dominant approach used in commercial software development.

One of the most attractive characteristics of the object-oriented approach is the fact that objects can be used quite effectively to represent real-world entities. We can use a software object to represent an employee in a company, for instance. We'd create one object per employee, each with behaviors and characteristics that we need to represent. In this way, object-oriented programming allows us to map our programs to the real situations that the programs represent. That is, the object-oriented approach makes it easier to solve problems, which is the point of writing a program in the first place.

KEY CONCEPT

Object-oriented programming helps us solve problems, which is the purpose of writing a program.

Let's discuss the general issues related to problem solving, and then explore the specific characteristics of the object-oriented approach that helps us solve those problems.

Problem Solving

In general, problem solving consists of multiple steps:

1. Understanding the problem.
2. Designing a solution.
3. Considering alternatives to the solution and refining the solution.
4. Implementing the solution.
5. Testing the solution and fixing any problems that exist.

Although this approach applies to any kind of problem solving, it works particularly well when developing software. These steps aren't purely linear. That is, some of the activities will overlap others. But at some point, all of these steps should be carefully addressed.

The first step, understanding the problem, may sound obvious, but a lack of attention to this step has been the cause of many misguided software development efforts. If we attempt to solve a problem we don't completely understand, we often end up solving the wrong problem or at least going off on improper tangents. Each problem has a *problem domain*, the real-world issues that are key to our solution. For example, if we are going to write a program to score a bowling match, then the problem domain includes the rules of bowling. To develop a good solution, we must thoroughly understand the problem domain.

The key to designing a problem solution is breaking it down into manageable pieces. A solution to any problem can rarely be expressed as one big task. Instead, it is a series of small cooperating tasks that interact to perform a larger task. When developing software, we don't write one big program. We design separate pieces that are responsible for certain parts of the solution, and then integrate them with the other parts.

KEY CONCEPT
Program design involves breaking a solution down into manageable pieces.

Our first inclination toward a solution may not be the best one. We must always consider alternatives and refine the solution as necessary. The earlier we consider alternatives, the easier it is to modify our approach.

Implementing the solution is the act of taking the design and putting it in a usable form. When developing a software solution to a problem, the implementation stage is the process of actually writing the program. Too often programming is thought of as writing code. But in most cases, the act of designing the program should be far more interesting and creative than the process of implementing the design in a particular programming language.

At many points in the development process, we should test our solution to find any errors that exist so that we can fix them. Testing cannot guarantee that there aren't still problems yet to be discovered, but it can raise our confidence that we have a viable solution.

Throughout this text, we explore techniques that allow us to design and implement elegant programs. Although we will often get immersed in these details, we should never forget that our primary goal is to solve problems.

Object-Oriented Software Principles

Object-oriented programming ultimately requires a solid understanding of the following terms:

- object
- attribute
- method
- class
- encapsulation
- inheritance
- polymorphism

In addition to these terms, there are many associated concepts that allow us to tailor our solutions in innumerable ways. This book is designed to help you evolve your understanding of these concepts gradually and naturally. This section provides an overview of these ideas at a high level to establish some terminology and provide the big picture.

We mentioned earlier that an *object* is a fundamental element in a program. A software object often represents a real object in our problem domain, such as a bank account. Every object has a *state* and a set of *behaviors*. By "state" we mean state of being—fundamental characteristics that currently define the object. For example, part of a bank account's state is its current balance. The behaviors of an object are the activities associated with the object. Behaviors associated with a bank account probably include the ability to make deposits and withdrawals.

In addition to objects, a Java program also manages primitive data. *Primitive data* includes fundamental values such as numbers and characters. Objects usually represent more interesting or complex entities.

KEY CONCEPT

Each object has a state, defined by its attributes, and a set of behaviors, defined by its methods.

An object's *attributes* are the values it stores internally, which may be represented as primitive data or as other objects. For example, a bank account object may store a floating point number (a primitive value) that represents the balance of the account. It may contain other attributes, such as the name of the account owner. Collectively, the values of an object's attributes define its current state.

As mentioned earlier in this chapter, a *method* is a group of programming statements that is given a name. When a method is invoked, its statements are executed. A set of methods is associated with an object. The methods of an object define its potential behaviors. To define the ability to make a deposit into a bank account, we define a method containing programming statements that will update the account balance accordingly.

An object is defined by a *class*. A class is the model or blueprint from which an object is created. Consider the blueprint created by an architect when designing a house. The blueprint defines the important characteristics of the house—its walls, windows, doors, electrical outlets, and so on. Once the blueprint is created, several houses can be built using it, as depicted in Figure 1.22.

In one sense, the houses built from the blueprint are different. They are in different locations, have different addresses, contain different furniture, and are inhabited by different people. Yet in many ways they are the "same" house. The layout of the rooms and other crucial characteristics are the same in each. To create a different house, we would need a different blueprint.

A class is a blueprint of an object. It establishes the kind of data an object of that type will hold and defines the methods that represent the behavior of such objects. However, a class is not an object any more than a blueprint is a house. In general, a class contains no space to store data. Each object has space for its own data, which is why each object can have its own state.

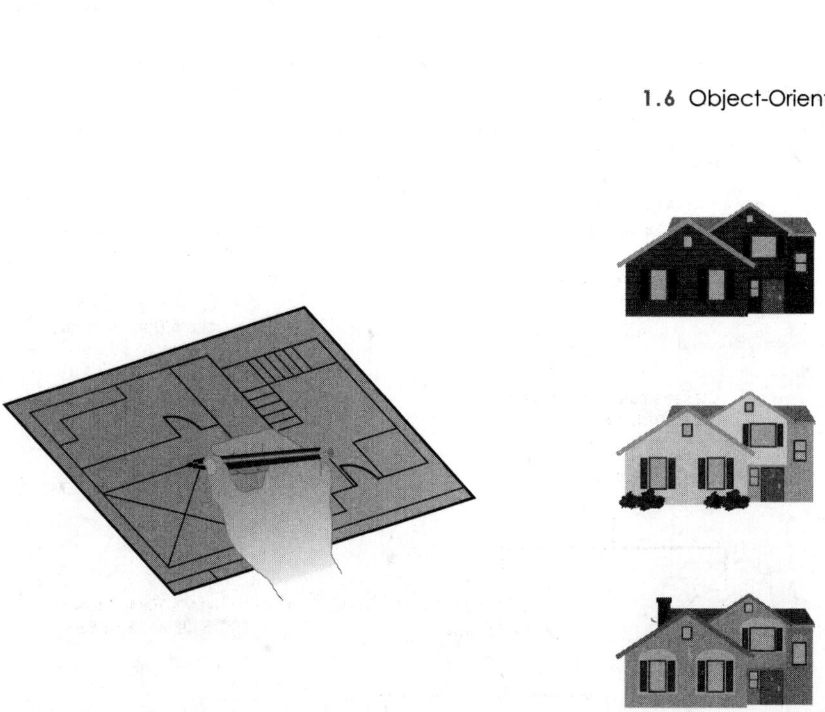

FIGURE 1.22 A class is used to create objects just as a house blueprint is used to create different, but similar, houses

Once a class has been defined, multiple objects can be created from that class. For example, once we define a class to represent the concept of a bank account, we can create multiple objects that represent specific, individual bank accounts. Each bank account object would keep track of its own balance.

KEY CONCEPT

A class is a blueprint of an object. Multiple objects can be created from one class definition.

An object should be *encapsulated*, which means it protects and manages its own information. That is, an object should be self-governing. The only changes made to the state of the object should be accomplished by that object's methods. We should design objects so that other objects cannot "reach in" and change their states.

Classes can be created from other classes by using *inheritance*. That is, the definition of one class can be based on another class that already exists. Inheritance is a form of *software reuse*, capitalizing on the similarities between various kinds of classes that we may want to create. One class can be used to derive several new classes. Derived classes can then be used to derive even more classes. This creates a hierarchy of classes, where the attributes and methods defined in one class are inherited by its children, which in turn pass them on to their children, and so on. For example, we might create a hierarchy of classes that represent various types of accounts. Common characteristics are defined in high-level classes, and specific differences are defined in derived classes.

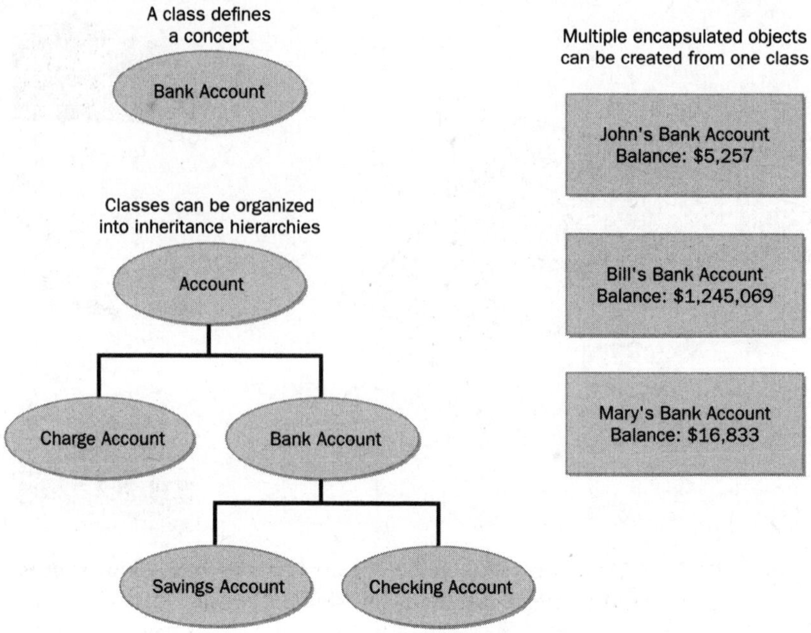

FIGURE 1.23 Various aspects of object-oriented software

Polymorphism is the idea that we can refer to multiple types of related objects over time in consistent ways. It gives us the ability to design powerful and elegant solutions to problems that deal with multiple objects.

Some of the core object-oriented concepts are depicted in Figure 1.23. We don't expect you to understand these ideas fully at this point. Most of this book is designed to flesh out these ideas. This overview is intended only to set the stage.

SELF-REVIEW QUESTIONS *(see answers in Appendix L)*

SR 1.33 List the five general steps required to solve a problem.

SR 1.34 Why is it important to consider more than one approach to solving a problem? Why is it important to consider alternatives early in the process of solving a problem?

SR 1.35 What are the primary concepts that support object-oriented programming?

Summary of Key Concepts

- A computer system consists of hardware and software that work in concert to help us solve problems.
- The CPU reads the program instructions from main memory, executing them one at a time until the program ends.
- The operating system provides a user interface and manages computer resources.
- As far as the user is concerned, the interface *is* the program.
- Digital computers store information by breaking it into pieces and representing each piece as a number.
- Binary is used to store and move information in a computer because the devices that store and manipulate binary data are inexpensive and reliable.
- There are exactly 2^N permutations of N bits. Therefore, N bits can represent up to 2^N unique items.
- The core of a computer is made up of main memory, which stores programs and data, and the CPU, which executes program instructions one at a time.
- An address is a unique number associated with a memory location.
- Main memory is volatile, meaning the stored information is maintained only as long as electric power is supplied.
- The surface of a CD has both smooth areas and small pits. A pit represents a binary 1 and a smooth area represents a binary 0.
- The fetch–decode–execute cycle forms the foundation of computer processing.
- A network consists of two or more computers connected together so that they can exchange information.
- Sharing a communication line creates delays, but it is cost effective and simplifies adding new computers to the network.
- A local-area network (LAN) is an effective way to share information and resources throughout an organization.
- The Internet is a wide-area network (WAN) that spans the globe.
- Every computer connected to the Internet has an IP address that uniquely identifies it.
- The World Wide Web is software that makes sharing information across a network easy for humans.

- A URL uniquely specifies documents and other information found on the Web for a browser to obtain and display.
- This book focuses on the principles of object-oriented programming.
- Comments do not affect a program's processing; instead, they serve to facilitate human comprehension.
- Inline documentation should provide insight into your code. It should not be ambiguous or belabor the obvious.
- Java is case sensitive. The uppercase and lowercase versions of a letter are distinct.
- Identifier names should be descriptive and readable.
- Appropriate use of white space makes a program easier to read and understand.
- You should adhere to a set of guidelines that establish the way you format and document your programs.
- All programs must be translated to a particular CPU's machine language in order to be executed.
- High-level languages allow a programmer to ignore the underlying details of machine language.
- A Java compiler translates Java source code into Java bytecode, a low-level, architecture-neutral representation of the program.
- Many different development environments exist to help you create and modify Java programs.
- Syntax rules dictate the form of a program. Semantics dictate the meaning of the program statements.
- The programmer is responsible for the accuracy and reliability of a program.
- A Java program must be syntactically correct or the compiler will not produce bytecode.
- Object-oriented programming helps us solve problems, which is the purpose of writing a program.
- Program design involves breaking a solution down into manageable pieces.
- Each object has a state, defined by its attributes, and a set of behaviors, defined by its methods.
- A class is a blueprint of an object. Multiple objects can be created from one class definition.

Exercises

EX 1.1 Describe the hardware components of your personal computer or of a computer in a lab to which you have access. Include the processor type and speed, storage capacities of main and secondary memory, and types of I/O devices. Explain how you determined your answers.

EX 1.2 Why do we use the binary number system to store information on a computer?

EX 1.3 How many unique items can be represented with each of the following?

a. 4 bits

b. 7 bits

c. 12 bits

d. 15 bits

e. 24 bits

f. 32 bits

EX 1.4 If a picture is made up of 128 possible colors, how many bits would be needed to store each pixel of the picture? Why?

EX 1.5 If a language uses 50,000 unique characters, how many bits would be needed to store each character of a document? Why?

EX 1.6 How many bits are there in each of the following? How many bytes are there in each?

a. 100 KB

b. 10 MB

c. 5 GB

d. 1.5 TB

EX 1.7 Explain the difference between random access memory (RAM) and read-only memory (ROM).

EX 1.8 A disk is a random access device but it is not RAM (random access memory). Explain.

EX 1.9 Determine how your computer, or a computer in a lab to which you have access, is connected to others across a network. Is it linked to the Internet? Draw a diagram to show the basic connections in your environment.

EX 1.10 Explain the differences between a local-area network (LAN) and a wide-area network (WAN). What is the relationship between them?

EX 1.11 What is the total number of communication lines needed for a fully connected point-to-point network of eight computers? Nine computers? Ten computers? What is a general formula for determining this result?

EX 1.12 Explain the difference between the Internet and the World Wide Web.

EX 1.13 List and explain the parts of the URLs for

a. your school

b. the Computer Science department of your school

c. your instructor's Web page

EX 1.14 Give examples of the two types of Java comments and explain the differences between them.

EX 1.15 Which of the following are not valid Java identifiers? Why?

a. `Fraction`

b. `theSumOfTheSquaresOnTheOtherTwoSides`

c. `1direction`

d. `direction1`

e. `NUMBER_OF_STARS`

f. `high&low`

g. `power$`

EX 1.16 Why are the following valid Java identifiers not considered good identifiers?

a. `q`

b. `studNum`

c. `theNumberOfTheStudent`

EX 1.17 Java is case sensitive. What does that mean?

EX 1.18 What is a Java Virtual Machine? Explain its role.

EX 1.19 What do we mean when we say that the English language is ambiguous? Give two examples of English ambiguity (other than the example used in this chapter) and explain the ambiguity. Why is ambiguity a problem for programming languages?

EX 1.20 Categorize each of the following situations as a compile-time error, run-time error, or logical error.

a. dividing by 10 when you meant to divide by 100

b. using a zero as the denominator of a fraction in a calculation

c. forgetting a } at the end of a program

d. producing the results of a program on a single line when you meant to produce them on separate lines

e. using [] instead of {}

f. producing inaccurate results in calculating the area of a circle

Programming Projects

PP 1.1 Enter, compile, and run the following program:

```
public class Test
{
    public static void main(String[] args)
    {
        System.out.println("An Emergency Broadcast");
    }
}
```

PP 1.2 Introduce the following errors, one at a time, to the program from PP 1.1. Record any error messages that the compiler produces. Fix the previous error each time before you introduce a new one. If no error messages are produced, explain why. Try to predict what will happen before you make each change.

VideoNote
Developing a solution for PP 1.2.

a. change `Test` to `test`

b. change `Emergency` to `emergency`

c. remove the first quotation mark in the string

d. remove the last quotation mark in the string

e. change `main` to `man`

f. change `println` to `bogus`

g. remove the semicolon at the end of the `println` statement

h. remove the last brace in the program

PP 1.3 Write a program that prints, on separate lines, your name, your birthday, your hobbies, your favorite book, and your favorite movie. Label each piece of information in the output.

PP 1.4 Write a program that prints a list of at least five of your favorite movies. Print the title and a short synopsis of each movie.

PP 1.5 Write a program that prints the first few verses of a song (your choice). Label the chorus.

PP 1.6 Write a program that prints the outline of a house with a door and a window using asterisk (*) characters.

PP 1.7 Write a program that prints a paragraph from a novel of your choice.

PP 1.8 Write a program that prints the phrase `Deeds not Words`:

a. on one line

b. on three lines, one word per line, with the words centered relative to each other

c. inside a box made up of the characters - and |

PP 1.9 Write a program that prints the following diamond shape. Don't print any unneeded characters. (That is, don't make any character string longer than it has to be.)

```
    *
   ***
  *****
 *******
*********
 *******
  *****
   ***
    *
```

PP 1.10 Write a program that displays your initials in large block letters. Make each large letter out of the corresponding regular character. For example:

```
JJJJJJJJJJJJJJJ   AAAAAAAAA     LLLL
JJJJJJJJJJJJJJJ  AAAAAAAAAAA    LLLL
          JJJJ   AAA     AAA    LLLL
          JJJJ   AAA     AAA    LLLL
          JJJJ   AAAAAAAAAAA    LLLL
J         JJJJ   AAAAAAAAAAA    LLLL
JJ        JJJJ   AAA     AAA    LLLL
 JJJJJJJJJJJ     AAA     AAA    LLLLLLLLLLLLLL
 JJJJJJJJJ       AAA     AAA    LLLLLLLLLLLLLL
```

2 Data and Expressions

CHAPTER OBJECTIVES

- Discuss the use of character strings, concatenation, and escape sequences.
- Explore the declaration and use of variables.
- Describe the Java primitive data types.
- Discuss the syntax and processing of expressions.
- Define the types of data conversions and the mechanisms for accomplishing them.
- Introduce the Scanner class to create interactive programs.

This chapter explores some of the basic types of data used in a Java program and the use of expressions to perform calculations. It discusses the conversion of data from one type to another and how to read input interactively from the user running a program.

2.1 Character Strings

In Chapter 1, we discussed the basic structure of a Java program, including the use of comments, identifiers, and white space, using the `Lincoln` program as an example. Chapter 1 also included an overview of the various concepts involved in object-oriented programming, such as objects, classes, and methods. Take a moment to review these ideas if necessary.

A character string is an object in Java, defined by the class `String`. Because strings are so fundamental to computer programming, Java provides the ability to use a *string literal*, delimited by double quotation characters, as we've seen in previous examples. We explore the `String` class and its methods in more detail in Chapter 3. For now, let's explore the use of string literals in more detail.

The following are all examples of valid string literals:

```
"The quick brown fox jumped over the lazy dog."
"602 Greenbriar Court, Chalfont PA 18914"
"x"
""
```

A string literal can contain any valid characters, including numeric digits, punctuation, and other special characters. The last example in the list above contains no characters at all.

The `print` and `println` Methods

In the `Lincoln` program in Chapter 1, we invoked the `println` method as follows:

```
System.out.println("Whatever you are, be a good one.");
```

This statement demonstrates the use of objects. The `System.out` object represents an output device or file, which by default is the monitor screen. To be more precise, the object's name is `out` and it is stored in the `System` class. We explore that relationship in more detail at the appropriate point in the text.

The `println` method is a service that the `System.out` object performs for us. Whenever we request it, the object will print a character string to the screen. We can say that we send the `println` message to the `System.out` object to request that some text be printed.

Each piece of data that we send to a method is called a *parameter*. In this case, the `println` method takes only one parameter: the string of characters to be printed.

The `System.out` object also provides another service we can use: the `print` method. The difference between `print` and `println` is small but important. The `println` method prints the information sent to it, then moves to the beginning of the next line. The `print` method is similar to `println` but does not advance to the next line when completed.

KEY CONCEPT

The `print` and `println` methods represent two services provided by the `System.out` object.

The program shown in Listing 2.1 is called `Countdown`, and it invokes both the `print` and `println` methods.

Carefully compare the output of the `Countdown` program, shown at the bottom of the program listing, to the program code. Note that the word `Liftoff` is printed on the same line as the first few words, even though it is printed using the `println` method. Remember that the `println` method moves to the beginning of the next line *after* the information passed to it has been printed.

LISTING 2.1

```
//********************************************************************
//  Countdown.java       Author: Lewis/Loftus
//
//  Demonstrates the difference between print and println.
//********************************************************************
public class Countdown
{
   //-----------------------------------------------------------------
   //  Prints two lines of output representing a rocket countdown.
   //-----------------------------------------------------------------
   public static void main(String[] args)
   {
      System.out.print("Three... ");
      System.out.print("Two... ");
      System.out.print("One... ");
      System.out.print("Zero... ");
      System.out.println("Liftoff!");  // appears on first output line
      System.out.println("Houston, we have a problem.");
   }
}
```

OUTPUT

```
Three... Two... One... Zero... Liftoff!
Houston, we have a problem.
```

String Concatenation

A string literal cannot span multiple lines in a program. The following program statement is improper syntax and would produce an error when attempting to compile:

```
// The following statement will not compile
System.out.println("The only stupid question is
the one that is not asked.");
```

When we want to print a string that is too long to fit on one line in a program, we can rely on *string concatenation* to append one string to the end of another. The string concatenation operator is the plus sign (+). The following expression concatenates one character string to another, producing one long string:

```
"The only stupid question is " + "the one that is not asked."
```

The program called `Facts` shown in Listing 2.2 contains several `println` statements. The first one prints a sentence that is somewhat long and will not fit on one line of the program. Since a character literal cannot span two lines in a program, we split the string into two and use string concatenation to append them. Therefore, the string concatenation operation in the first `println` statement results in one large string that is passed to the method to be printed.

Note that we don't have to pass any information to the `println` method, as shown in the second line of the `Facts` program. This call does not print any visible characters, but it does move to the next line of output. So in this case, calling `println` with no parameters has the effect of printing a blank line.

The last three calls to `println` in the `Facts` program demonstrate another interesting thing about string concatenation: Strings can be concatenated with numbers. Note that the numbers in those lines are not enclosed in double quotes and are therefore not character strings. In these cases, the number is automatically converted to a string, and then the two strings are concatenated.

Because we are printing particular values, we simply could have included the numeric value as part of the string literal, such as

```
"Speed of ketchup: 40 km per year"
```

Digits are characters and can be included in strings as needed. We separate them in the `Facts` program to demonstrate the ability to concatenate a string and a number. This technique will be useful in upcoming examples.

As you can imagine, the + operator is also used for arithmetic addition. Therefore, what the + operator does depends on the types of data on which it

LISTING 2.2

```
//********************************************************************
//  Facts.java       Author: Lewis/Loftus
//
//  Demonstrates the use of the string concatenation operator and the
//  automatic conversion of an integer to a string.
//********************************************************************

public class Facts
{
   //-----------------------------------------------------------------
   //  Prints various facts.
   //-----------------------------------------------------------------
   public static void main(String[] args)
   {
      // Strings can be concatenated into one long string
      System.out.println("We present the following facts for your "
                         + "extracurricular edification:");

      System.out.println();

      // A string can contain numeric digits
      System.out.println("Letters in the Hawaiian alphabet: 12");

      // A numeric value can be concatenated to a string
      System.out.println("Dialing code for Antarctica: " + 672);

      System.out.println("Year in which Leonardo da Vinci invented "
                         + "the parachute: " + 1515);

      System.out.println("Speed of ketchup: " + 40 + " km per year");
   }
}
```

OUTPUT

```
We present the following facts for your extracurricular edification:

Letters in the Hawaiian alphabet: 12
Dialing code for Antarctica: 672
Year in which Leonardo da Vinci invented the parachute: 1515
Speed of ketchup: 40 km per year
```

operates. If either or both of the operands of the + operator are strings, then string concatenation is performed.

The `Addition` program shown in Listing 2.3 demonstrates the distinction between string concatenation and arithmetic addition. The `Addition` program uses the + operator four times. In the first call to `println`, both + operations perform string concatenation because the operators are executed left to right. The first operator concatenates the string with the first number (`24`), creating a larger string. Then that string is concatenated with the second number (`45`), creating an even larger string, which gets printed.

In the second call to `println`, we use parentheses to group the + operation with the two numeric operands. This forces that operation to happen first. Because both operands are numbers, the numbers are added in the arithmetic

LISTING 2.3

```
//********************************************************************
//  Addition.java       Author: Lewis/Loftus
//
//  Demonstrates the difference between the addition and string
//  concatenation operators.
//********************************************************************

public class Addition
{
   //-----------------------------------------------------------------
   //  Concatenates and adds two numbers and prints the results.
   //-----------------------------------------------------------------
   public static void main(String[] args)
   {
      System.out.println("24 and 45 concatenated: " + 24 + 45);

      System.out.println("24 and 45 added: " + (24 + 45));
   }
}
```

OUTPUT

```
24 and 45 concatenated: 2445
24 and 45 added: 69
```

sense, producing the result 69. That number is then concatenated with the string, producing a larger string that gets printed.

We revisit this type of situation later in this chapter when we formalize the precedence rules that define the order in which operators get evaluated.

Escape Sequences

Because the double quotation character (") is used in the Java language to indicate the beginning and end of a string, we must use a special technique to print the quotation character. If we simply put it in a string ("""), the compiler gets confused because it thinks the second quotation character is the end of the string and doesn't know what to do with the third one. This results in a compile-time error.

VideoNote
Example using strings and escape sequences.

To overcome this problem, Java defines several *escape sequences* to represent special characters. An escape sequence begins with the backslash character (\), which indicates that the character or characters that follow should be interpreted in a special way. Figure 2.1 lists the Java escape sequences.

KEY CONCEPT
An escape sequence can be used to represent a character that would otherwise cause compilation problems.

The program in Listing 2.4, called Roses, prints some text resembling a poem. It uses only one println statement to do so, despite the fact that the poem is several lines long. Note the escape sequences used throughout the string. The \n escape sequence forces the output to a new line, and the \t escape sequence represents a tab character. The \" escape sequence ensures that the quote character is treated as part of the string, not the termination of it, which enables it to be printed as part of the output.

Escape Sequence	Meaning
\b	backspace
\t	tab
\n	newline
\r	carriage return
\"	double quote
\'	single quote
\\	backslash

FIGURE 2.1 Java escape sequences

LISTING 2.4

```
//********************************************************************
//  Roses.java       Author: Lewis/Loftus
//
//  Demonstrates the use of escape sequences.
//********************************************************************

public class Roses
{
   //-----------------------------------------------------------------
   //  Prints a poem (of sorts) on multiple lines.
   //-----------------------------------------------------------------
   public static void main(String[] args)
   {
      System.out.println("Roses are red,\n\tViolets are blue,\n" +
         "Sugar is sweet,\n\tBut I have \"commitment issues\",\n\t" +
         "So I'd rather just be friends\n\tAt this point in our " +
         "relationship.");
   }
}
```

OUTPUT

```
Roses are red,
        Violets are blue,
Sugar is sweet,
        But I have "commitment issues",
        So I'd rather just be friends
        At this point in our relationship.
```

SELF-REVIEW QUESTIONS *(see answers in Appendix L)*

SR 2.1 What is a string literal?

SR 2.2 What is the difference between the `print` and `println` methods?

SR 2.3 What is a parameter?

SR 2.4 What output is produced by the following code fragment?

```
System.out.println("One ");
System.out.print("Two ");
System.out.println("Three ");
```

SR 2.5 What output is produced by the following code fragment?

```
System.out.print("Ready ");
System.out.println();
System.out.println("Set ");
System.out.println();
System.out.println("Go ");
```

SR 2.6 What output is produced by the following statement? What is produced if the inner parentheses are removed?

```
System.out.println("It is good to be " + (5 + 5));
```

SR 2.7 What is an escape sequence? Give some examples.

SR 2.8 Write a single `println` statement that will output the following exactly as shown (including line breaks and quotation marks).

> "I made this letter longer than usual because I lack the time to make it short."
> Blaise Pascal

2.2 Variables and Assignment

Most of the information we manage in a program is represented by variables. Let's examine how we declare and use them in a program.

Variables

A *variable* is a name for a location in memory used to hold a data value. A variable declaration instructs the compiler to reserve a portion of main memory space large enough to hold a particular type of value and indicates the name by which we refer to that location.

> **KEY CONCEPT**
> A variable is a name for a memory location used to hold a value of a particular data type.

Consider the program `PianoKeys`, shown in Listing 2.5. The first line of the `main` method is the declaration of a variable named `keys` that holds an integer (`int`) value. The declaration also gives `keys` an initial value of 88. If an initial value is not specified for a variable, the value is undefined. Most Java compilers give errors or warnings if you attempt to use a variable before you've explicitly given it a value.

The `keys` variable, with its value, could be pictured as follows:

Local Variable Declaration

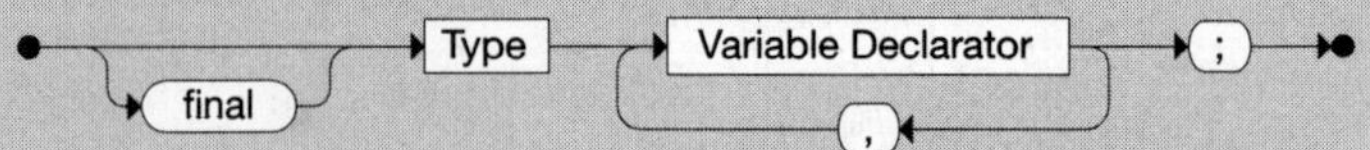

Variable Declarator

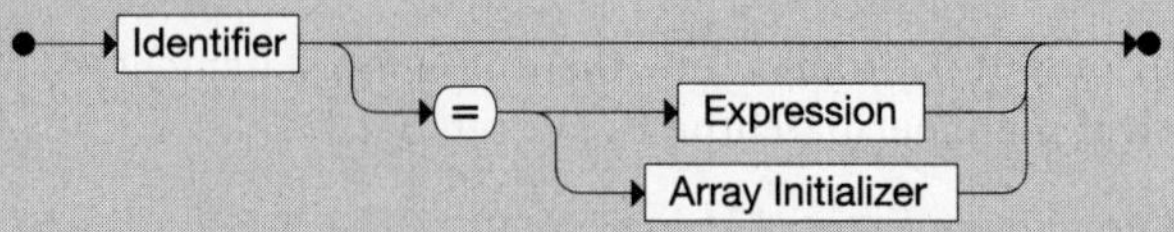

A variable declaration consists of a Type followed by a list of variables. Each variable can be initialized in the declaration to the value of the specified Expression. If the final modifier precedes the declaration, the identifiers are declared as named constants whose values cannot be changed once set.

Examples:

```
int total;
double num1, num2 = 4.356, num3;
char letter = 'A', digit = '7';
final int MAX = 45;
```

LISTING 2.5

```
//********************************************************************
//  PianoKeys.java       Author: Lewis/Loftus
//
//  Demonstrates the declaration, initialization, and use of an
//  integer variable.
//********************************************************************

public class PianoKeys
{
   //-----------------------------------------------------------------
   //  Prints the number of keys on a piano.
   //-----------------------------------------------------------------
   public static void main(String[] args)
```

LISTING 2.5 *continued*

```
    {
       int keys = 88;
       System.out.println("A piano has " + keys + " keys.");
    }
}
```

OUTPUT

```
A piano has 88 keys.
```

In the PianoKeys program, two pieces of information are used in the call to the println method. The first is a string and the second is the variable keys. When a variable is referenced, the value currently stored in it is used. Therefore, when the call to println is executed, the value of keys, which is 88, is obtained. Because that value is an integer, it is automatically converted to a string and concatenated with the initial string. The concatenated string is passed to println and printed.

A variable declaration can have multiple variables of the same type declared on one line. Each variable on the line can be declared with or without an initializing value. For example:

```
int count, minimum = 0, result;
```

The Assignment Statement

Let's examine a program that changes the value of a variable. Listing 2.6 shows a program called Geometry. This program first declares an integer variable called sides and initializes it to 7. It then prints out the current value of sides.

The next line in main changes the value stored in the variable sides:

```
sides = 10;
```

This is called an *assignment statement* because it assigns a value to a variable. When executed, the expression on the right-hand side of the assignment operator (=) is evaluated, and the result is stored in the memory location indicated by the variable on the left-hand side. In this example, the expression is simply a number, 10. We discuss expressions that are more involved than this in the next section.

LISTING 2.6

```
//********************************************************************
//  Geometry.java       Author: Lewis/Loftus
//
//  Demonstrates the use of an assignment statement to change the
//  value stored in a variable.
//********************************************************************

public class Geometry
{
   //-----------------------------------------------------------------
   //  Prints the number of sides of several geometric shapes.
   //-----------------------------------------------------------------
   public static void main(String[] args)
   {
      int sides = 7;   // declaration with initialization
      System.out.println("A heptagon has " + sides + " sides.");

      sides = 10;   // assignment statement
      System.out.println("A decagon has " + sides + " sides.");

      sides = 12;
      System.out.println("A dodecagon has " + sides + " sides.");
   }
}
```

OUTPUT

```
A heptagon has 7 sides.
A decagon has 10 sides.
A dodecagon has 12 sides.
```

KEY CONCEPT
Accessing data leaves it intact in memory, but an assignment statement overwrites the old data.

A variable can store only one value of its declared type. A new value overwrites the old one. In this case, when the value `10` is assigned to `sides`, the original value `7` is overwritten and lost forever, as follows:

After initialization:	`sides`	7
After first assignment:	`sides`	10

Basic Assignment

The basic assignment statement uses the assignment operator (=) to store the result of the Expression into the specified Identifier, usually a variable.

Examples:

```
total = 57;
count = count + 1;
value = (min / 2) * lastValue;
```

When a reference is made to a variable, such as when it is printed, the value of the variable is not changed. This is the nature of computer memory: Accessing (reading) data leaves the values in memory intact, but writing data replaces the old data with the new.

The Java language is *strongly typed*, meaning that we are not allowed to assign a value to a variable that is inconsistent with its declared type. Trying to combine incompatible types will generate an error when you attempt to compile the program. Therefore, the expression on the right-hand side of an assignment statement must evaluate to a value compatible with the type of the variable on the left-hand side.

KEY CONCEPT
We cannot assign a value of one type to a variable of an incompatible type.

Constants

Sometimes we use data that is constant throughout a program. For instance, we might write a program that deals with a theater that can hold no more than 427 people. It is often helpful to give a constant value a name, such as `MAX_OCCUPANCY`, instead of using a literal value, such as `427`, throughout the code. The purpose and meaning of literal values such as `427` is often confusing to someone reading the code. By giving the value a name, you help explain its role in the program.

Constants are identifiers and are similar to variables except that they hold a particular value for the duration of their existence. Constants are, to use the English meaning of the words, not variable. Their value doesn't change.

KEY CONCEPT
Constants hold a particular value for the duration of their existence.

In Java, if you precede a declaration with the reserved word `final`, the identifier is made a constant. By convention, uppercase letters are used when naming constants to distinguish them from regular variables, and individual words are separated using the underscore character. For example, the constant describing the maximum occupancy of a theater could be declared as follows:

```
final int MAX_OCCUPANCY = 427;
```

The compiler will produce an error message if you attempt to change the value of a constant once it has been given its initial value. This is another good reason to use constants. Constants prevent inadvertent coding errors because the only valid place to change their value is in the initial assignment.

There is a third good reason to use constants. If a constant is used throughout a program and its value needs to be modified, then you have to change it in only one place. For example, if the capacity of the theater changes (because of a renovation) from 427 to 535, then you have to change only one declaration, and all uses of `MAX_OCCUPANCY` automatically reflect the change. If the literal `427` had been used throughout the code, each use would have to be found and changed. If you were to miss any uses of the literal value, problems would surely arise.

SELF-REVIEW QUESTIONS *(see answers in Appendix L)*

SR 2.9 What is a variable declaration?

SR 2.10 Given the following variable declarations, answer each question.

```
int count = 0, value, total;
final int MAX_VALUE = 100;
int myValue = 50;
```

a. How many variables are declared?
b. What is the type of these declared variables?
c. Which of the variables are given an initial value?
d. Based on the above declarations, is the following assignment statement valid? Explain.

```
myValue = 100;
```

e. Based on the above declarations, is the following assignment statement valid? Explain.

```
MAX_VALUE = 50;
```

SR 2.11 Your program needs a variable of type `int` to hold the number of CDs in a music collection. The initial value should be zero. Write a declaration statement for the variable.

SR 2.12 Your program needs a variable of type `int` to hold the number of feet in a mile (5280). Write a declaration statement for the variable.

SR 2.13 Briefly describe three reasons for using a constant in a program instead of a literal value.

2.3 Primitive Data Types

There are eight *primitive data types* in Java: four types of integers, two types of floating point numbers, a character data type, and a boolean data type. Everything else is represented using objects. Let's examine these eight primitive data types in detail.

Integers and Floating Points

Java has two basic kinds of numeric values: integers, which have no fractional part, and floating points, which do. There are four integer data types (`byte`, `short`, `int`, and `long`) and two floating point data types (`float` and `double`). All of the numeric types differ by the amount of memory space used to store a value of that type, which determines the range of values that can be represented. The size of each data type is the same for all hardware platforms. All numeric types are *signed*, meaning that both positive and negative values can be stored in them. Figure 2.2 summarizes the numeric primitive types.

KEY CONCEPT
Java has two kinds of numeric values: integer and floating point. There are four integer data types and two floating point data types.

Recall from our discussion in Chapter 1 that a bit can be either a 1 or a 0. Because each bit can represent two different states, a string of N bits can be used to represent 2^N different values. Appendix B describes number systems and these kinds of relationships in more detail.

When designing programs, we occasionally need to be careful about picking variables of appropriate size so that memory space is not wasted. For example, if the value of a particular variable will not vary outside of a range of 1–1000, then a two-byte integer (`short`) is large enough to accommodate it. On the other

Type	Storage	Min Value	Max Value
`byte`	8 bits	−128	127
`short`	16 bits	−32,768	32,767
`int`	32 bits	−2,147,483,648	2,147,483,647
`long`	64 bits	−9,223,372,036,854,775,808	9,223,372,036,854,775,807
`float`	32 bits	Approximately −3.4E+38 with 7 significant digits	Approximately 3.4E+38 with 7 significant digits
`double`	64 bits	Approximately −1.7E+308 with 15 significant digits	Approximately 1.7E+308 with 15 significant digits

FIGURE 2.2 The Java numeric primitive types

hand, when it's not clear what the range of a particular variable will be, we should provide a reasonable, even generous, amount of space. In most situations, memory space is not a serious restriction, and we can usually afford generous assumptions.

Note that even though a `float` value supports very large (and very small) numbers, it has only seven significant digits. Therefore, if it is important to accurately maintain a value such as 50341.2077, we need to use a `double`.

As we've already discussed, a *literal* is an explicit data value used in a program. The various numbers used in programs such as `Facts` and `Addition` and `PianoKeys` are all *integer literals*. Java assumes all integer literals are of type `int`, unless an `L` or `l` is appended to the end of the value to indicate that it should be considered a literal of type `long`, such as `45L`.

Likewise, Java assumes that all *floating point literals* are of type `double`. If we need to treat a floating point literal as a `float`, we append an `F` or `f` to the end of the value, as in `2.718F` or `123.45f`. Numeric literals of type `double` can be followed by a `D` or `d` if desired.

Decimal Integer Literal

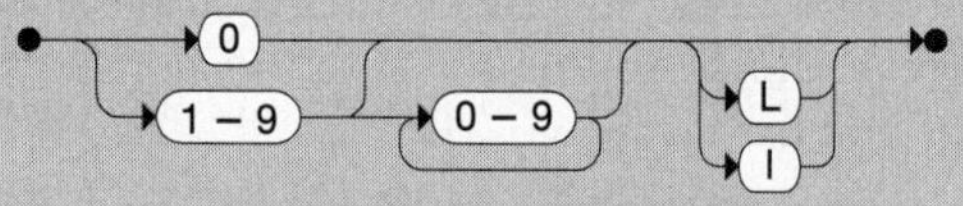

An integer literal is composed of a series of digits followed by an optional suffix to indicate that it should be considered an integer. Negation of a literal is considered a separate operation.

Examples:

```
5
2594
4920328L
```

The following are examples of numeric variable declarations in Java:

```
int answer = 42;
byte smallNumber1, smallNumber2;
long countedStars = 86827263927L;
float ratio = 0.2363F;
double delta = 453.523311903;
```

Characters

Characters are another fundamental type of data used and managed on a computer. Individual characters can be treated as separate data items, and, as we've seen in several examples, they can be combined to form character strings.

A *character literal* is expressed in a Java program with single quotes, such as `'b'` or `'J'` or `';'`. You will recall that *string literals* are delineated using double quotation marks, and that the `String` type is not a primitive data type in Java; it is a class name. We discuss the `String` class in detail in Chapter 3.

Note the difference between a digit as a character (or part of a string) and a digit as a number (or part of a larger number). The number `602` is a numeric value that can be used in an arithmetic calculation. But in the string `"602 Greenbriar Court"` the `6`, `0`, and `2` are characters, just like the rest of the characters that make up the string.

The characters we can manage are defined by a *character set*, which is simply a list of characters in a particular order. Each programming language supports a particular character set that defines the valid values for a character variable in that language. Several character sets have been proposed, but only a few have been used regularly over the years. The *ASCII character set* is a popular choice. ASCII stands for the American Standard Code for Information Interchange. The basic ASCII set uses seven bits per character, providing room to support 128 different characters, including:

- uppercase letters, such as `'A'`, `'B'`, and `'C'`
- lowercase letters, such as `'a'`, `'b'`, and `'c'`
- punctuation, such as the period (`'.'`), semicolon (`';'`), and comma (`','`)
- the digits `'0'` through `'9'`
- the space character, `' '`
- special symbols, such as the ampersand (`'&'`), vertical bar (`'|'`), and backslash (`'\'`)
- control characters, such as the carriage return, null, and end-of-text marks

The *control characters* are sometimes called nonprinting or invisible characters because they do not have a specific symbol that represents them. Yet they are as valid as any other character and can be stored and used in the same ways. Many control characters have special meaning to certain software applications.

As computing became a worldwide endeavor, users demanded a more flexible character set containing other language alphabets. ASCII was extended to use eight bits per character, and the number of characters in the set doubled to 256. The extended ASCII contains many accented and diacritical characters used in languages other than English.

KEY CONCEPT

Java uses the 16-bit Unicode character set to represent character data.

However, even with 256 characters, the ASCII character set cannot represent the world's alphabets, especially given the various Asian alphabets and their many thousands of ideograms. Therefore, the developers of the Java programming language chose the *Unicode character set*, which uses 16 bits per character, supporting 65,536 unique characters (and techniques that allow even more characters to be represented using multiple bytes). The characters and symbols from many languages are included in the Unicode definition. ASCII is a subset of the Unicode character set, comprising the first 256 characters. Appendix C discusses the Unicode character set in more detail.

A character set assigns a particular number to each character, so by definition the characters are in a particular order. This is referred to as lexicographic order. In the ASCII and Unicode ordering, the digit characters '0' through '9' are continuous (no other characters intervene) and in order. Similarly, the lowercase alphabetic characters 'a' through 'z' are continuous and in order, as are the uppercase alphabetic characters 'A' through 'Z'. These characteristics make it relatively easy to keep things in alphabetical order.

In Java, the data type char represents a single character. The following are some examples of character variable declarations in Java:

```
char topGrade = 'A';
char symbol1, symbol2, symbol3;
char terminator = ';', separator = ' ';
```

Booleans

A boolean value, defined in Java using the reserved word boolean, has only two valid values: true and false. A boolean variable is usually used to indicate whether a particular condition is true, but it can also be used to represent any situation that has two states, such as a light bulb being on or off.

A boolean value cannot be converted to any other data type, nor can any other data type be converted to a boolean value. The words true and false are reserved in Java as *boolean literals* and cannot be used outside of this context.

The following are some examples of boolean variable declarations in Java:

```
boolean flag = true;
boolean tooHigh, tooSmall, tooRough;
boolean done = false;
```

SELF-REVIEW QUESTIONS *(see answers in Appendix L)*

SR 2.14 What is primitive data? How are primitive data types different from objects?

SR 2.15 How many values can be stored in an integer variable?

SR 2.16 What are the four integer data types in Java? How are they different?

SR 2.17 What type does Java automatically assign to an integer literal? How can you indicate that an integer literal should be considered a different type?

SR 2.18 What type does Java automatically assign to a floating point literal? How can you indicate that a floating point literal should be considered a different type?

SR 2.19 What is a character set?

SR 2.20 How many characters are supported by the ASCII character set, the extended ASCII character set, and the Unicode character set?

2.4 Expressions

An *expression* is a combination of one or more operators and operands that usually perform a calculation. The value calculated does not have to be a number, but it often is. The operands used in the operations might be literals, constants, variables, or other sources of data. The manner in which expressions are evaluated and used is fundamental to programming. For now, we will focus on arithmetic expressions that use numeric operands and produce numeric results.

KEY CONCEPT
Expressions are combinations of operators and operands used to perform a calculation.

Arithmetic Operators

The usual arithmetic operations are defined for both integer and floating point numeric types, including addition (+), subtraction (–), multiplication (*), and division (/). Java also has another arithmetic operation: The *remainder operator* (%) returns the remainder after dividing the second operand into the first. The remainder operator is sometimes called the *modulus operator*. The sign of the result of a remainder operation is the sign of the numerator. Therefore,

Operation	Result
17 % 4	1
−20 % 3	−2
10 % −5	0
3 % 8	3

VideoNote
Review of primitive data and expressions.

As you might expect, if either or both operands to any numeric operator are floating point values, the result is a floating point value. However, the division operator produces results that are less intuitive, depending on the types of the operands. If both operands are integers, the / operator performs *integer division*, meaning that any fractional part of the result is discarded. If one or the other or both operands are floating point values, the / operator performs *floating point division*, and the fractional part of the result is kept. For example, the result of `10/4` is 2, but the results of `10.0/4` and `10/4.0` and `10.0/4.0` are all 2.5.

A *unary operator* has only one operand, while a *binary operator* has two. The + and – arithmetic operators can be either unary or binary. The binary versions accomplish addition and subtraction, and the unary versions represent positive and negative numbers. For example, –1 is an example of using the unary negation operator to make the value negative. The unary + operator is rarely used.

Java does not have a built-in operator for raising a value to an exponent. However, the `Math` class provides methods that perform exponentiation and many other mathematical functions. The `Math` class is discussed in Chapter 3.

Operator Precedence

Operators can be combined to create more complex expressions. For example, consider the following assignment statement:

```
result = 14 + 8 / 2;
```

KEY CONCEPT
Java follows a well-defined set of precedence rules that governs the order in which operators will be evaluated in an expression.

The entire right-hand side of the assignment is evaluated, and then the result is stored in the variable. But what is the result? If the addition is performed first, the result is `11`; if the division operation is performed first, the result is `18`. The order of operator evaluation makes a big difference. In this case, the division is performed before the addition, yielding a result of `18`.

Note that in this and subsequent examples, we use literal values rather than variables to simplify the expression. The order of operator evaluation is the same if the operands are variables or any other source of data.

All expressions are evaluated according to an *operator precedence hierarchy* that establishes the rules that govern the order in which operations are evaluated. The arithmetic operators generally follow the same rules you learned in algebra. Multiplication, division, and the remainder operator all have equal precedence and are performed before (have higher precedence than) addition and subtraction. Addition and subtraction have equal precedence.

Any arithmetic operators at the same level of precedence are performed left to right. Therefore, we say the arithmetic operators have a *left-to-right association*.

Precedence, however, can be forced in an expression by using parentheses. For instance, if we really wanted the addition to be performed first in the previous example, we could write the expression as follows:

```
result = (14 + 8) / 2;
```

Any expression in parentheses is evaluated first. In complicated expressions, it is good practice to use parentheses, even when it is not strictly necessary, to make it clear how the expression is evaluated.

Parentheses can be nested, and the innermost nested expressions are evaluated first. Consider the following expression:

```
result = 3 * ((18 - 4) / 2);
```

In this example, the result is 21. First, the subtraction is performed, forced by the inner parentheses. Then, even though multiplication and division are at the same level of precedence and usually would be evaluated left to right, the division is performed first because of the outer parentheses. Finally, the multiplication is performed.

After the arithmetic operations are complete, the computed result is stored in the variable on the left-hand side of the assignment operator (=). In other words, the assignment operator has a lower precedence than any of the arithmetic operators.

The evaluation of a particular expression can be shown using an *expression tree*, such as the one in Figure 2.3. The operators are executed from the bottom up, creating values that are used in the rest of the expression. Therefore, the operations lower in the tree have a higher precedence than those above, or they are forced to be executed earlier using parentheses.

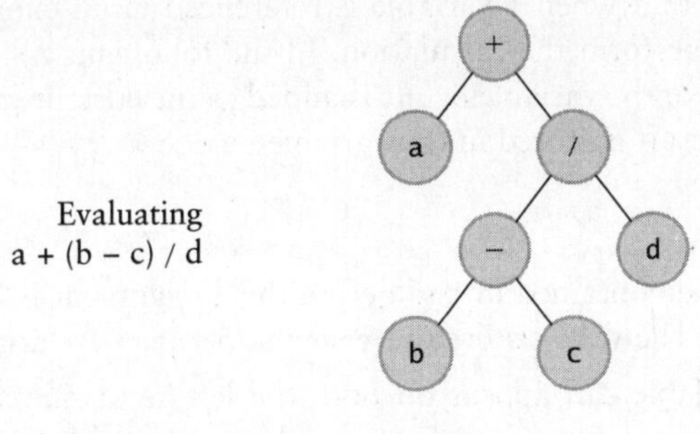

FIGURE 2.3 An expression tree

Precedence Level	Operator	Operation	Associates
1	+	unary plus	R to L
	–	unary minus	
2	*	multiplication	L to R
	/	division	
	%	remainder	
3	+	addition	L to R
	–	subtraction	
	+	string concatenation	
4	=	assignment	R to L

FIGURE 2.4 Precedence among some of the Java operators

The parentheses used in expressions are actually operators themselves. Parentheses have a higher precedence than almost any other operator. Figure 2.4 shows a precedence table with the relationships between the arithmetic operators, parentheses, and the assignment operator. Appendix D includes a full precedence table showing all Java operators.

For an expression to be syntactically correct, the number of left parentheses must match the number of right parentheses and they must be properly nested. The following examples are *not* valid expressions:

```
result = ((19 + 8) % 3) - 4);    // not valid
result = (19 (+ 8 %) 3 - 4);     // not valid
```

Keep in mind that when a variable is referenced in an expression, its current value is used to perform the calculation. In the following assignment statement, the current value of the variable `count` is added to the current value of the variable `total`, and the result is stored in the variable `sum`:

```
sum = count + total;
```

The original value contained in `sum` before this assignment is overwritten by the calculated value. The values stored in `count` and `total` are not changed.

The same variable can appear on both the left-hand side and the right-hand side of an assignment statement. Suppose the current value of a variable called `count` is 15 when the following assignment statement is executed:

```
count = count + 1;
```

Because the right-hand expression is evaluated first, the original value of `count` is obtained and the value 1 is added to it, producing the result 16. That result is then stored in the variable `count`, overwriting the original value of 15 with the new value of 16. Therefore, this assignment statement *increments*, or adds 1 to, the variable `count`.

Let's look at another example of expression processing. The program in Listing 2.7, called `TempConverter`, converts a particular Celsius temperature value to its equivalent Fahrenheit value using an expression that computes the following formula:

$$\text{Fahrenheit} = \frac{9}{5}\,\text{Celsius} + 32$$

LISTING 2.7

```
//********************************************************************
//  TempConverter.java       Author: Lewis/Loftus
//
//  Demonstrates the use of primitive data types and arithmetic
//  expressions.
//********************************************************************

public class TempConverter
{
   //-----------------------------------------------------------------
   //  Computes the Fahrenheit equivalent of a specific Celsius
   //  value using the formula F = (9/5)C + 32.
   //-----------------------------------------------------------------
   public static void main(String[] args)
   {
      final int BASE = 32;
      final double CONVERSION_FACTOR = 9.0 / 5.0;

      double fahrenheitTemp;
      int celsiusTemp = 24;   // value to convert

      fahrenheitTemp = celsiusTemp * CONVERSION_FACTOR + BASE;

      System.out.println("Celsius Temperature: " + celsiusTemp);
      System.out.println("Fahrenheit Equivalent: " + fahrenheitTemp);
   }
}
```

OUTPUT

```
Celsius Temperature: 24
Fahrenheit Equivalent: 75.2
```

Note that in the temperature conversion program, the operands to the division operation are floating point literals to ensure that the fractional part of the number is kept. The precedence rules dictate that the multiplication happens before the addition in the final conversion computation.

The `TempConverter` program is not very useful because it converts only one data value that we included in the program as a constant (24 degrees Celsius). Every time the program is run it produces the same result. A far more useful version of the program would obtain the value to be converted from the user each time the program is executed. Interactive programs that read user input are discussed later in this chapter.

Increment and Decrement Operators

There are two other useful arithmetic operators. The *increment operator* (++) adds 1 to any integer or floating point value. The two plus signs that make up the operator cannot be separated by white space. The *decrement operator* (−−) is similar except that it subtracts 1 from the value. They are both unary operators because they operate on only one operand. The following statement causes the value of `count` to be incremented:

```
count++;
```

The result is stored back into the variable `count`. Therefore, it is functionally equivalent to the following statement, which we discussed in the previous section:

```
count = count + 1;
```

The increment and decrement operators can be applied after the variable (such as `count++` or `count--`), creating what is called the *postfix form* of the operator. They can also be applied before the variable (such as `++count` or `--count`), in what is called the *prefix form*. When used alone in a statement, the prefix and postfix forms are functionally equivalent. That is, it doesn't matter if you write

```
count++;
```

or

```
++count;
```

However, when such a form is written as a statement by itself, it is usually written in its postfix form.

When the increment or decrement operator is used in a larger expression, it can yield different results depending on the form used. For example, if the variable count currently contains the value 15, the following statement assigns the value 15 to total and the value 16 to count:

```
total = count++;
```

However, the following statement assigns the value 16 to both total and count:

```
total = ++count;
```

The value of count is incremented in both situations, but the value used in the larger expression depends on whether a prefix or postfix form of the increment operator is used.

Because of the subtle differences between the prefix and postfix forms of the increment and decrement operators, they should be used with care. As always, favor the side of readability.

Assignment Operators

As a convenience, several *assignment operators* have been defined in Java that combine a basic operation with assignment. For example, the += operator can be used as follows:

```
total += 5;
```

This performs the same operation as the following statement:

```
total = total + 5;
```

The right-hand side of the assignment operator can be a full expression. The expression on the right-hand side of the operator is evaluated, then that result is added to the current value of the variable on the left-hand side, and that value is stored in the variable. Therefore, the following statement:

```
total += (sum - 12) / count;
```

is equivalent to:

```
total = total + ((sum - 12) / count);
```

Many similar assignment operators are defined in Java, including those that perform subtraction (-=), multiplication (*=), division (/=), and remainder (%=). The entire set of Java operators is discussed in Appendix D.

All of the assignment operators evaluate the entire expression on the right-hand side first, then use the result as the right operand of the other operation. Therefore, the following statement:

```
result *= count1 + count2;
```

is equivalent to:

```
result = result * (count1 + count2);
```

Likewise, the following statement:

```
result %= (highest - 40) / 2;
```

is equivalent to:

```
result = result % ((highest - 40) / 2);
```

Some assignment operators perform particular functions depending on the types of the operands, just as their corresponding regular operators do. For example, if the operands to the += operator are strings, then the assignment operator performs string concatenation.

SELF-REVIEW QUESTIONS *(see answers in Appendix L)*

SR 2.21 What is the result of `19%5` when evaluated in a Java expression? Explain.

SR 2.22 What is the result of `13/4` when evaluated in a Java expression? Explain.

SR 2.23 If an integer variable `diameter` currently holds the value 5, what is its value after the following statement is executed? Explain.

```
diameter = diameter * 4;
```

SR 2.24 What is operator precedence?

SR 2.25 What is the value of each of the following expressions?

a. `15 + 7 * 3`
b. `(15 + 7) * 3`
c. `3 * 6 + 10 / 5 + 5`
d. `27 % 5 + 7 % 3`
e. `100 / 2 / 2 / 2`
f. `100 / ( 2 / 2) / 2`

SR 2.26 For each of the following expressions state whether they are valid or invalid. If invalid, explain why.

a. `result = ( 5 + 2 );`
b. `result = ( 5 + 2 * ( 15 - 3 );`
c. `result = ( 5 + 2 (;`
d. `result = ( 5 + 2 ( 4 ) );`

SR 2.27 What value is contained in the integer variable `result` after the following sequence of statements is executed?

```
result = 27;
result = result + 3;
result = result / 7;
result = result * 2;
```

SR 2.28 What value is contained in the integer variable `result` after the following sequence of statements is executed?

```
int base;
int result;
base = 5;
result = base + 3;
base = 7;
```

SR 2.29 What is an assignment operator?

SR 2.30 If an integer variable `weight` currently holds the value 100, what is its value after the following statement is executed? Explain.

```
weight -= 17;
```

2.5 Data Conversion

Because Java is a strongly typed language, each data value is associated with a particular type. It is sometimes helpful or necessary to convert a data value of one type to another type, but we must be careful that we don't lose important information in the process. For example, suppose a `short` variable that holds the number 1000 is converted to a `byte` value. Because a `byte` does not have enough bits to represent the value 1000, some bits would be lost in the conversion, and the number represented in the `byte` would not keep its original value.

A conversion between one primitive type and another falls into one of two categories: widening conversions and narrowing conversions. *Widening conversions* are the safest because they usually do not lose information. They are called widening conversions because they go from one data type to another type that uses an equal or greater amount of space to store the value. Figure 2.5 lists the Java widening conversions.

For example, it is safe to convert from a `byte` to a `short` because a `byte` is stored in 8 bits and a `short` is stored in 16 bits. There is no loss of information. All widening conversions that go from an integer type to another integer type, or from a floating point type to another floating point type, preserve the numeric value exactly.

From	To
byte	short, int, long, float, or double
short	int, long, float, or double
char	int, long, float, or double
int	long, float, or double
long	float or double
float	double

FIGURE 2.5 Java widening conversions

KEY CONCEPT
Narrowing conversions should be avoided because they can lose information.

Although widening conversions do not lose any information about the magnitude of a value, the widening conversions that result in a floating point value can lose precision. When converting from an `int` or a `long` to a `float`, or from a `long` to a `double`, some of the least significant digits may be lost. In this case, the resulting floating point value will be a rounded version of the integer value, following the rounding techniques defined in the IEEE 754 floating point standard.

Narrowing conversions are more likely to lose information than widening conversions are. They often go from one type to a type that uses less space to store a value, and therefore some of the information may be compromised. Narrowing conversions can lose both numeric magnitude and precision. Therefore, in general, they should be avoided. Figure 2.6 lists the Java narrowing conversions.

An exception to the space-shrinking situation in narrowing conversions is when we convert a `byte` (8 bits) or `short` (16 bits) to a `char` (16 bits). These are still

From	To
byte	char
short	byte or char
char	byte or short
int	byte, short, or char
long	byte, short, char, or int
float	byte, short, char, int, or long
double	byte, short, char, int, long, or float

FIGURE 2.6 Java narrowing conversions

considered narrowing conversions because the sign bit is incorporated into the new character value. Since a character value is unsigned, a negative integer will be converted into a character that has no particular relationship to the numeric value of the original integer.

Note that `boolean` values are not mentioned in either widening or narrowing conversions. A `boolean` value cannot be converted to any other primitive type and vice versa.

Conversion Techniques

In Java, conversions can occur in three ways:

- assignment conversion
- promotion
- casting

Assignment conversion occurs when a value of one type is assigned to a variable of another type during which the value is converted to the new type. Only widening conversions can be accomplished through assignment. For example, if `money` is a `float` variable and `dollars` is an `int` variable, then the following assignment statement automatically converts the value in `dollars` to a `float`:

```
money = dollars;
```

Therefore, if `dollars` contains the value `25`, after the assignment, `money` contains the value `25.0`. However, if we attempt to assign `money` to `dollars`, the compiler will issue an error message alerting us to the fact that we are attempting a narrowing conversion that could lose information. If we really want to do this assignment, we have to make the conversion explicit by using a cast.

Conversion via *promotion* occurs automatically when certain operators need to modify their operands in order to perform the operation. For example, when a floating point value called `sum` is divided by an integer value called `count`, the value of `count` is promoted to a floating point value automatically, before the division takes place, producing a floating point result:

```
result = sum / count;
```

A similar conversion is taking place when a number is concatenated with a string. The number is first converted (promoted) to a string, then the two strings are concatenated.

Casting is the most general form of conversion in Java. If a conversion can be accomplished at all in a Java program, it can be accomplished using a cast. A cast is a Java operator that is specified by a type name in parentheses. It is placed in front of the value to be converted. For example, to convert `money` to an integer value, we could put a cast in front of it:

```
dollars = (int) money;
```

The cast returns the value in `money`, truncating any fractional part. If `money` contained the value `84.69`, then after the assignment, `dollars` would contain the value `84`. Note, however, that the cast does not change the value in `money`. After the assignment operation is complete, `money` still contains the value `84.69`.

Casts are helpful in many situations where we need to treat a value temporarily as another type. For example, if we want to divide the integer value `total` by the integer value `count` and get a floating point result, we could do it as follows:

```
result = (float) total / count;
```

First, the cast operator returns a floating point version of the value in `total`. This operation does not change the value in `total`. Then, `count` is treated as a floating point value via arithmetic promotion. Now, the division operator will perform floating point division and produce the intended result. If the cast had not been included, the operation would have performed integer division and truncated the answer before assigning it to `result`. Also note that because the cast operator has a higher precedence than the division operator, the cast operates on the value of `total`, not on the result of the division.

SELF-REVIEW QUESTIONS *(see answers in Appendix L)*

SR 2.31 Why are widening conversions safer than narrowing conversions?

SR 2.32 Identify each of the following conversions as either a widening conversion or a narrowing conversion.

a. `int` to `long`
b. `int` to `byte`
c. `byte` to `short`
d. `byte` to `char`
e. `short` to `double`

SR 2.33 Assuming `result` is a `float` variable and `value` is an `int` variable, what type of variable will `value` be after the following assignment statement is executed? Explain.

```
result = value;
```

SR 2.34 Assuming `result` is a `float` variable that contains the value 27.32 and `value` is an `int` variable that contains the `value` 15, what are the values of each of the variables after the following assignment statement is executed? Explain.

```
value = (int) result;
```

SR 2.35 Given the following declarations, what result is stored by each of the following assignment statements?

```
int iResult, num1 = 17, num2 = 5;
double fResult, val1 = 12.0, val2 = 2.34;
```

a. `iResult = num1 / num2;`
b. `fResult = num1 / num2;`
c. `fResult = val1 / num2;`
d. `fResult = (double) num1 / num2;`
e. `iResult = (int) val1 / num2;`

2.6 Interactive Programs

It is often useful to design a program to read data from the user interactively during execution. That way, new results can be computed each time the program is run, depending on the data that is entered.

The Scanner Class

The `Scanner` class, which is part of the Java API, provides convenient methods for reading input values of various types. The input could come from various sources, including data typed interactively by the user or data stored in a file. The `Scanner` class can also be used to parse a character string into separate pieces. Figure 2.7 lists some of the methods provided by the `Scanner` class.

> **KEY CONCEPT**
> The `Scanner` class provides methods for reading input of various types from various sources.

We must first create a `Scanner` object in order to invoke its methods. Objects in Java are created using the `new` operator. The following declaration creates a `Scanner` object that reads input from the keyboard:

```
Scanner scan = new Scanner(System.in);
```

This declaration creates a variable called scan that represents a `Scanner` object. The object itself is created by the `new` operator and a call to a special method called a *constructor* to set up the object. The `Scanner` constructor accepts a

`Scanner(InputStream source)`
`Scanner(File source)`
`Scanner(String source)`
Constructors: sets up the new scanner to scan values from the specified source.

`String next()`
Returns the next input token as a character string.

`String nextLine()`
Returns all input remaining on the current line as a character string.

`boolean nextBoolean()`
`byte nextByte()`
`double nextDouble()`
`float nextFloat()`
`int nextInt()`
`long nextLong()`
`short nextShort()`
Returns the next input token as the indicated type. Throws `InputMismatchException` if the next token is inconsistent with the type.

`boolean hasNext()`
Returns true if the scanner has another token in its input.

`Scanner useDelimiter(String pattern)`
`Scanner useDelimiter(Pattern pattern)`
Sets the scanner's delimiting pattern.

`Pattern delimiter()`
Returns the pattern the scanner is currently using to match delimiters.

`String findInLine(String pattern)`
`String findInLine(Pattern pattern)`
Attempts to find the next occurrence of the specified pattern, ignoring delimiters.

FIGURE 2.7 Some methods of the `Scanner` class

parameter that indicates the source of the input. The `System.in` object represents the *standard input stream*, which by default is the keyboard. Creating objects using the `new` operator is discussed further in Chapter 3.

Unless specified otherwise, a `Scanner` object assumes that white space characters (space characters, tabs, and new lines) are used to separate the elements of the input, called *tokens*, from each other. These characters are called the input *delimiters*. The set of delimiters can be changed if the input tokens are separated by characters other than white space.

The `next` method of the `Scanner` class reads the next input token as a string and returns it. Therefore, if the input consisted of a series of words separated by spaces, each call to `next` would return the next word. The `nextLine` method reads all of the input until the end of the line is found, and returns it as one string.

The program `Echo`, shown in Listing 2.8, simply reads a line of text typed by the user, stores it in a variable that holds a character string, then echoes it back to the screen.

The `import` statement above the definition of the `Echo` class tells the program that we will be using the `Scanner` class in this program. The `Scanner` class is part of the `java.util` class library. The use of the `import` statement is discussed further in Chapter 3.

Various `Scanner` methods such as `nextInt` and `nextDouble` are provided to read data of particular types. The `GasMileage` program, shown in Listing 2.9, reads the number of miles traveled as an integer, and the number of gallons of fuel consumed as a double, then computes the gas mileage.

LISTING 2.8

```
//********************************************************************
//  Echo.java       Author: Lewis/Loftus
//
//  Demonstrates the use of the nextLine method of the Scanner class
//  to read a string from the user.
//********************************************************************

import java.util.Scanner;

public class Echo
{
   //-----------------------------------------------------------------
   //  Reads a character string from the user and prints it.
   //-----------------------------------------------------------------
   public static void main(String[] args)
```

LISTING 2.8 *continued*

```
   {
      String message;
      Scanner scan = new Scanner(System.in);

      System.out.println("Enter a line of text:");

      message = scan.nextLine();

      System.out.println("You entered: \"" + message + "\"");
   }
}
```

OUTPUT

```
Enter a line of text:
Set your laser printer on stun!
You entered: "Set your laser printer on stun!"
```

As you can see by the output of the `GasMileage` program, the calculation produces a floating point result that is accurate to several decimal places. In Chapter 3, we discuss classes that help us format our output in various ways, including rounding a floating point value to a particular number of decimal places.

LISTING 2.9

```
//********************************************************************
//  GasMileage.java       Author: Lewis/Loftus
//
//  Demonstrates the use of the Scanner class to read numeric data.
//********************************************************************

import java.util.Scanner;

public class GasMileage
{
   //-----------------------------------------------------------------
   //  Calculates fuel efficiency based on values entered by the
   //  user.
   //-----------------------------------------------------------------
   public static void main(String[] args)
```

LISTING 2.9 *continued*

```
   {
      int miles;
      double gallons, mpg;

      Scanner scan = new Scanner(System.in);

      System.out.print("Enter the number of miles: ");
      miles = scan.nextInt();

      System.out.print("Enter the gallons of fuel used: ");
      gallons = scan.nextDouble();

      mpg = miles / gallons;

      System.out.println("Miles Per Gallon: " + mpg);
   }
}
```

OUTPUT

```
Enter the number of miles:  328
Enter the gallons of fuel used:  11.2
Miles Per Gallon: 29.28571428571429
```

A `Scanner` object processes the input one token at a time, based on the methods used to read the data and the delimiters used to separate the input values. Therefore, multiple values can be put on the same line of input or can be separated over multiple lines, as appropriate for the situation.

VideoNote
Example using the `Scanner` class.

In Chapter 5, we use the `Scanner` class to read input from a data file and modify the delimiters it uses to parse the data. Appendix H explores how to use the `Scanner` class to analyze its input using patterns called *regular expressions*.

SELF-REVIEW QUESTIONS *(see answers in Appendix L)*

SR 2.36 Identify which line of the `GasMileage` program does each of the following.

a. Tells the program that we will be using the `Scanner` class.
b. Creates a `Scanner` object.
c. Sets up the `Scanner` object `scan` to read from the standard input stream.
d. Reads an integer from the standard input stream.

SR 2.37 Assume you already have instantiated a `Scanner` object named `myScanner` and an `int` variable named `value` as follows in your program:

```
Scanner myScanner = new Scanner(System.in);
int value = 0;
```

Write program statements that will ask the user to enter their age, and store their response in `value`.

Summary of Key Concepts

- The `print` and `println` methods represent two services provided by the `System.out` object.
- An escape sequence can be used to represent a character that would otherwise cause compilation problems.
- A variable is a name for a memory location used to hold a value of a particular data type.
- Accessing data leaves it intact in memory, but an assignment statement overwrites the old data.
- We cannot assign a value of one type to a variable of an incompatible type.
- Constants hold a particular value for the duration of their existence.
- Java has two kinds of numeric values: integer and floating point. There are four integer data types and two floating point data types.
- Java uses the 16-bit Unicode character set to represent character data.
- Expressions are combinations of operators and operands used to perform a calculation.
- Java follows a well-defined set of precedence rules that governs the order in which operators will be evaluated in an expression.
- Narrowing conversions should be avoided because they can lose information.
- The `Scanner` class provides methods for reading input of various types from various sources.

Exercises

EX 2.1 What is the difference between the literals 4, 4.0, '4', and "4"?

EX 2.2 Explain the following programming statement in terms of objects and the services they provide:

```
System.out.println("I gotta be me!");
```

EX 2.3 What output is produced by the following code fragment? Explain.

```
System.out.print("Name: ");
System.out.println("Sol");
System.out.print("Distance to Earth:");
System.out.println(" 92.96 million miles");
System.out.print("Surface Temperature: ");
System.out.println("5,778 K");
System.out.println ();
System.out.println("------------------------------");
```

EX 2.4 What is wrong with the following program statement? How can it be fixed?

```
System.out.println("To be or not to be, that
is the question.");
```

EX 2.5 What output is produced by the following statement? Explain.

```
System.out.println("50 plus 25 is " + 50 + 25);
```

EX 2.6 What is the output produced by the following statement? Explain.

```
System.out.println("Bill\n\tMacaroni:\t$ t$1.90\n\
tBleu Cheese:\t$0.50\n\tGrape" + "Juice:\t$1.00\
n============================\nTotal \"
less tax\":\t$3.40");
```

EX 2.7 What value is contained in the integer variable `size` after the following statements are executed?

```
size = 18;
size = size + 12;
size = size * 2;
size = size / 4;
```

EX 2.8 What value is contained in the floating point variable `temperature` after the following statements are executed?

```
temperature = 36.0;
temperature = 30.0 + temperature / 4;
temperature = temperature * 2;
```

EX 2.9 What value is contained in the integer variable `count` after the following statements are executed?

```
int count = 0;
count++;
count += 1;
count = count + 1;
++count;
```

EX 2.10 Write four different program statements that increment the value of an integer variable `total`.

EX 2.11 Given the following declarations, what result is stored in each of the listed assignment statements?

```
int iResult, num1 = 25, num2 = 40, num3 = 17, num4 = 5;
double fResult, val1 = 17.0, val2 = 12.78;
```

a. `iResult = num1 / num4;`

b. `fResult = num1 / num4;`

```
c. iResult = num3 / num4;
d. fResult = num3 / num4;
e. fResult = val1 / num4;
f. fResult = val1 / val2;
g. iResult = num1 / num2;
h. fResult = (double) num1 / num2;
i. fResult = num1 / (double) num2;
j. fResult = (double) (num1 / num2);
k. iResult = (int) (val1 / num4);
l. fResult = (int) (val1 / num4);
m. fResult = (int) ((double) num1 / num2);
n. iResult = num3 % num4;
o. iResult = num2 % num3;
p. iResult = num3 % num2;
q. iResult = num2 % num4;
```

EX 2.12 For each of the following expressions, indicate the order in which the operators will be evaluated by writing a number beneath each operator.

```
a. a - b - c - d
b. a - b + c - d
c. a + b / c / d
d. a + b / c * d
e. a / b * c * d
f. a % b / c * d
g. a % b % c % d
h. a - (b - c) - d
i. (a - (b - c)) - d
j. a - ((b - c) - d)
k. a % (b % c) * d * e
l. a + (b - c) * d - e
m. (a + b) * c + d * e
n. (a + b) * (c / d) % e
```

Programming Projects

PP 2.1 Create a revised version of the `Lincoln` program from Chapter 1 such that quotes appear around the quotation.

PP 2.2 Write a program that reads three integers and prints their average.

PP 2.3 Write a program that reads two floating point numbers and prints their sum, difference, and product.

PP 2.4 Write a program that prompts for and reads a person's name, age, college, and pet's name. Then print the following paragraph, inserting the appropriate data:

Hello, my name is ***name*** and I am ***age*** years
old. I'm enjoying my time at ***college***, though
I miss my pet ***petname*** very much!

PP 2.5 Create a version of the `TempConverter` application to convert from Fahrenheit to Celsius. Read the Fahrenheit temperature from the user.

PP 2.6 Write a program that converts miles to kilometers. (One mile equals 1.60935 kilometers.) Read the miles value from the user as a floating point value.

PP 2.7 Write a program that prompts for and reads integer values for speed and distance traveled, then prints the time required for the trip as a floating point result.

PP 2.8 Write a program that reads values representing a distance in kilometers, meters, and centimeters and then prints the equivalent total number of centimeters. (For example, 10 kilometers, 50 meters, and 20 centimeters is equivalent to 1,005,020 centimeters.)

PP 2.9 Create a version of the previous project that reverses the computation. That is, read a value representing a number of centimeters, then print the equivalent distance as a combination of kilometers, meters, and centimeters. (For example, 1,005,020 centimeters is equivalent to 10 kilometers, 50 meters, and 20 centimeters.)

VideoNote
Developing a solution of PP 2.10.

PP 2.10 Write a program that determines the value of the coins in a jar and prints the total in dollars and cents. Read integer values that represent the number of quarters, dimes, nickels, and pennies.

PP 2.11 Suppose that astronauts on a space station need to install exhaust pipes at various places around the station. The pipes come in specific lengths, and these lengths are 10 meters, 5 meters, 1 meter, 25 centimeters, 10 centimeters, 5 centimeters, and 1 centimeter. Write a program that prompts for and reads a `double` value representing the distance to be covered in meters. Then determine the fewest number of pipes needed to cover the distance. For example, to cover 37.72 meters, the program should print:

```
3 ten meter lengths
1 five meter lengths
2 one meter lengths
2 twenty-five centimeter lengths
```

```
2 ten centimeter lengths
0 five centimeter lengths
2 one centimeter lengths
Total: 12 lengths of pipes
```

PP 2.12 Write a program that prompts for and reads an integer representing the length of a square's side, then prints the square's perimeter and area.

PP 2.13 Write a program that prompts for and reads the numerator and denominator of a fraction as integers, then prints the decimal equivalent of the fraction.

SOFTWARE FAILURE

NASA Mars Climate Orbiter and Polar Lander

What Happened?

■ Artist's conception of the Mars Climate Orbiter

As part of a series of missions exploring Mars, NASA launched the Mars Climate Orbiter in December, 1998, and the Mars Polar Lander in January, 1999. The two-spacecraft mission was designed to observe the atmospheric conditions on Mars through each of its seasons. The orbiter and the lander would have collected data about temperature, dust, water vapor, clouds, and the amount of carbon dioxide (CO_2) added and removed from the Martian pole regions.

After its nine-month journey, the orbiter arrived at Mars in September, 1999, and fired its main engines to establish an orbit. The orbiter passed behind the planet (from Earth's perspective) five minutes later as planned, but NASA could not reestablish contact with it after expecting it to emerge. Review of the data showed that the altitude of the orbiter when it was entering orbit was only 57 kilometers, whereas the planned altitude was 140 km. The minimum survivable altitude was between 85 and 100 km. NASA concluded that the orbiter was destroyed by atmospheric friction.

The polar lander arrived at Mars in December, 1999, and all of the data indicated it was on target to make a successful soft landing within 10 kilometers of the target landing site on the Martian south pole. However, NASA lost contact with the lander just after it entered the atmosphere. Multiple attempts to reestablish contact with it over the following weeks and months were unsuccessful.

The total project cost for the orbiter and lander was $327.6 million.

What Caused It?

The root cause of the orbiter's problem was an embarrassing communication issue. The software that guided the navigation of the spacecraft used imperial units of measure (pound-force), while the spacecraft itself expected the data in metric units (newtons). Therefore, the desired navigation changes and the actual effects were off by a factor of 4.45. This mismatch resulted, in part, because one team based in Colorado lead the efforts on the spacecraft, while a California-based team managed issues of navigation.

The cause of the lander's communication problem is unresolved but is not believed to be related to the orbiter's problem. The investigation concluded that the most likely cause was a software error that mistook the vibration caused by the deployment of the lander's legs for the vibration caused by actually landing on the planet's surface. That mistake would have caused the lander's descent engines to cut off while it was still 40 m above the ground. Other problem scenarios are possible, however.

Lessons Learned

The mismatch of units in the Mars Climate Orbiter shows that seemingly obvious problems can be overlooked in a highly complex system. Mistakes are inevitable, but processes must be in place to catch them before they become critical. The investigation concluded that, in this case, the system for tracking and double-checking interconnected elements between subsystems was not robust enough. There was also inconsistent training of and communication with new members of the team, and some communication lines were too informal. In short, the mission lacked a rigorous total-system view that would have led to the discovery of the mismatched units problem before it was too late.

It's difficult to draw strong conclusions from the lander's problem given that the cause is not clearly understood. The fact that it remains an open question underscores the need for more evaluation, simulation, and testing in situations where critical resources are at stake.

Source: nasa.gov

3 Using Classes and Objects

CHAPTER OBJECTIVES

- Discuss the creation of objects and the use of object reference variables.
- Explore the services provided by the `String` class.
- Explore the services provided by the `Random` and `Math` classes.
- Discuss ways to format output.
- Introduce enumerated types.
- Discuss wrapper classes and the concept of autoboxing.
- Introduce the JavaFX API.
- Explore classes used to represent shapes.

This chapter further explores the use of predefined classes and the objects we can create from them. Using classes and objects for the services they provide is a fundamental part of object-oriented software and sets the stage for writing classes of our own. In this chapter, we use classes and objects to manipulate character strings, produce random numbers, perform complex calculations, and format output. This chapter also introduces the concept of an enumerated type, which is a special kind of class in Java, and discusses the concept of a wrapper class. This chapter also begins the Graphics Track for the book, in which we explore the concepts of graphical programming.

3.1 Creating Objects

At the end of Chapter 1, we presented an overview of object-oriented concepts, including the basic relationship between classes and objects. Then in Chapter 2, in addition to discussing primitive data, we provided some examples of using objects for the services they provide. This chapter explores these ideas further.

In previous examples, we've used the `println` method many times. As we mentioned in Chapter 2, the `println` method is a service provided by the `System.out` object, which represents the standard output stream. To be more precise, the identifier `out` is an object variable that is stored in the `System` class. It has been predefined and set up for us as part of the Java standard class library. We can simply use it.

In Chapter 2 we also used the `Scanner` class, which represents an object that allows us to read input from the keyboard or a file. We created a `Scanner` object using the `new` operator. Once the object was created, we were able to use it for the various services it provides. That is, we were able to invoke its methods.

Let's carefully examine the idea of creating an object. In Java, a variable name represents either a primitive value or an object. Like variables that hold primitive types, a variable that refers to an object must be declared. The class used to define an object can be thought of as the type of an object. The declarations of object variables have a similar structure to the declarations of primitive variables.

Consider the following two declarations:

```
int num;
String name;
```

The first declaration creates a variable that holds an integer value, as we've seen many times before. The second declaration creates a `String` variable that holds a *reference* to a `String` object. An object variable doesn't hold an object itself, it holds the address of an object.

Initially, the two variables declared above don't contain any data. We say they are *uninitialized*, which can be depicted as follows:

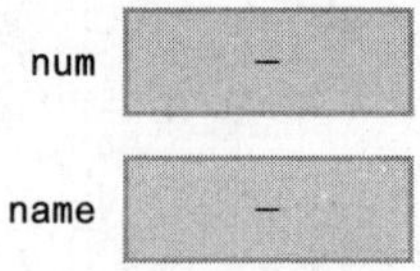

As we pointed out in Chapter 2, it is always important to make sure a variable is initialized before using it. For an object variable, that means we must make sure it refers to a valid object prior to using it. In most situations, the compiler will issue an error if you attempt to use a variable before initializing it.

An object variable can also be set to `null`, which is a reserved word in Java. A null reference specifically indicates that a variable does not refer to an object.

Note that, although we've declared a `String` reference variable, no `String` object actually exists yet. The act of creating an object using the `new` operator is called *instantiation*. An object is said to be an *instance* of a particular class. To instantiate an object, we can use the `new` operator, which returns the address of the new object. The following two assignment statements give values to the two variables declared above:

```
num = 42;
name = new String("James Gosling");
```

After the `new` operator creates the object, a *constructor* is invoked to help set it up initially. A constructor is a special method that has the same name as the class. In this example, the parameter to the constructor is a string literal that specifies the characters that the string object will hold. After these assignments are executed, the variables can be depicted as:

KEY CONCEPT

The `new` operator returns a reference to a newly created object.

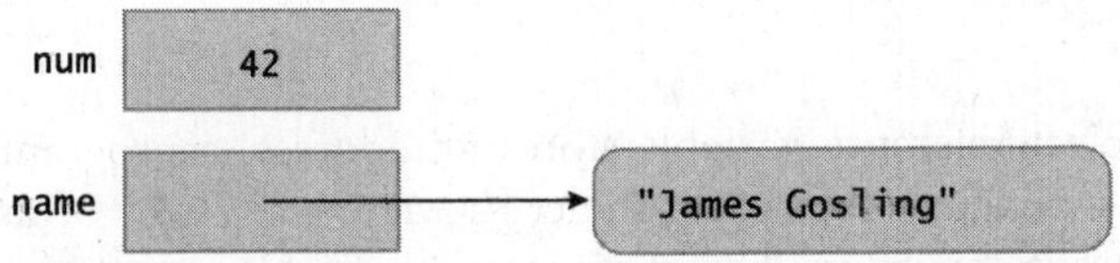

Since an object reference variable holds the address of the object, it can be thought of as a *pointer* to the location in memory where the object is held. We could show the numeric address, but the actual address value is irrelevant—what's important is that the variable refers to a particular object.

VideoNote
Creating objects.

After an object has been instantiated, we use the *dot operator* to access its methods. We've used the dot operator many times already, such as in calls to `System.out.println`. The dot operator is appended directly after the object reference, followed by the method being invoked. For example, to invoke the `length` method defined in the `String` class, we can use the dot operator on the `name` reference variable:

```
count = name.length()
```

The `length` method does not take any parameters, but the parentheses are still necessary to indicate that a method is being invoked. Some methods produce a value that is *returned* when the method completes. The purpose of the `length` method of the `String` class is to determine and return the length of the string (the number of characters it contains). In this example, the returned value is assigned to the variable `count`. For the string `"James Gosling"`, the `length` method returns `13`, which includes the space between the first and last names. Some methods do not return a value. Other `String` methods are discussed in the next section.

The act of declaring the object reference variable and creating the object itself can be combined into one step by initializing the variable in the declaration, just as we do with primitive types:

```
String title = new String("Java Software Solutions");
```

Even though they are not primitive types, character strings are so fundamental and so often used that Java defines string literals delimited by double quotation marks, as we've seen in various examples. This is a shortcut notation. Whenever a string literal appears, a `String` object is created automatically. Therefore, the following declaration is valid:

```
String city = "London";
```

That is, for `String` objects, the explicit use of the `new` operator and the call to the constructor can be eliminated. In most cases, we will use this simplified syntax.

Aliases

Because an object reference variable stores an address, a programmer must be careful when managing objects. First, let's review the effect of assignment on primitive values. Suppose we have two integer variables, `num1`, initialized to 5, and `num2`, initialized to 12:

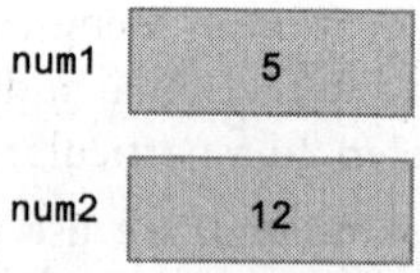

In the following assignment statement, a copy of the value that is stored in `num1` is stored in `num2`:

```
num2 = num1;
```

The original value of 12 in `num2` is overwritten by the value 5. The variables `num1` and `num2` still refer to different locations in memory, and both of those locations now contain the value 5:

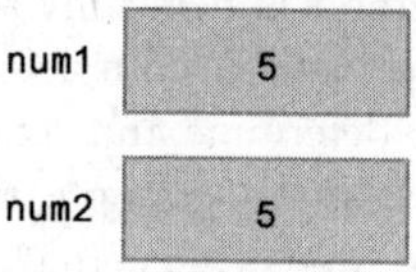

Now consider the following object declarations:

```
String name1 = "Ada, Countess of Lovelace";
String name2 = "Grace Murray Hopper";
```

Initially, the references name1 and name2 refer to two different String objects:

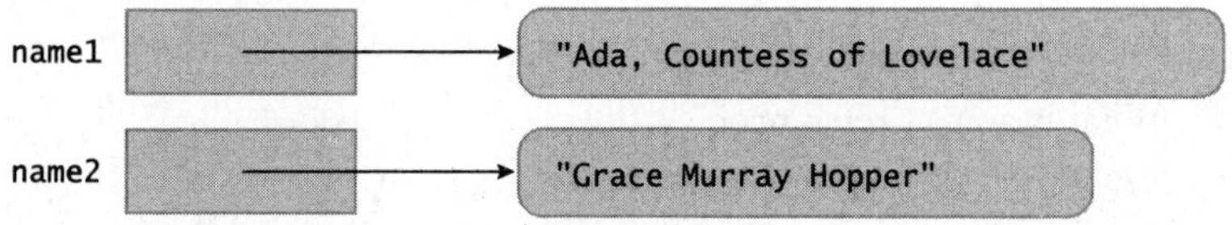

Now suppose the following assignment statement is executed, copying the value in name1 into name2:

```
name2 = name1;
```

This assignment works the same as the integer assignment—a copy of the value of name1 is stored in name2. But remember, object variables hold the address of an object, and it is the address that gets copied. Originally, the two references referred to different objects. After the assignment, both name1 and name2 contain the same address and therefore refer to the same object:

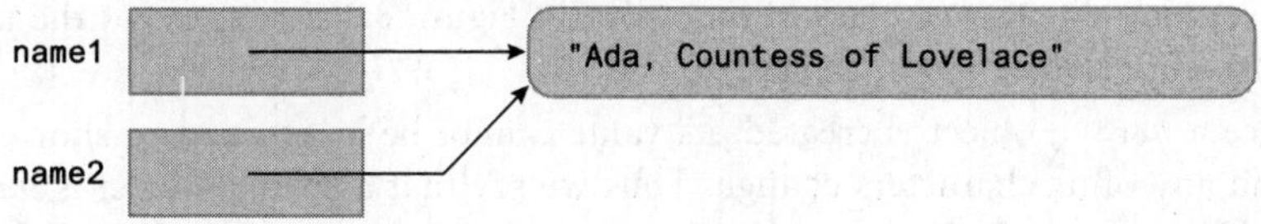

The name1 and name2 reference variables are now *aliases* of each other because they are two names that refer to the same object. All references to the object originally referenced by name2 are now gone; that object cannot be used again in the program.

KEY CONCEPT
Multiple reference variables can refer to the same object.

One important implication of aliases is that when we use one reference to change an object, it is also changed for the other reference because there is really only one object. Aliases can produce undesirable effects unless they are managed carefully.

All interaction with an object occurs through a reference variable, so we can use an object only if we have a reference to it. When all references to an object are lost (perhaps by reassignment), that object can no longer contribute to the program. The program can no longer invoke its methods or use its variables. At this point the object is called *garbage* because it serves no useful purpose.

Java performs *automatic garbage collection*. When the last reference to an object is lost, the object becomes a candidate for garbage collection. Occasionally, behind the scenes, the Java environment executes a method that "collects" all the objects marked for garbage collection and returns their memory to the system for future use. The programmer does not have to worry about explicitly reclaiming memory that has become garbage.

SELF-REVIEW QUESTIONS *(see answers in Appendix L)*

SR 3.1 What is a `null` reference?

SR 3.2 What does the `new` operator accomplish?

SR 3.3 Write a `declaration` for a `String` variable called `author`, and initialize it to the string `"Fred Brooks"`. Draw a graphic representation of the variable and its value.

SR 3.4 Write a code statement that sets the value of an integer variable called `size` to the length of a `String` object called `name`.

SR 3.5 What is an alias? How does it relate to garbage collection?

3.2 The `String` Class

Let's examine the `String` class in more detail. Figure 3.1 lists some of the more useful methods of the `String` class.

Once a `String` object is created, its value cannot be lengthened or shortened, nor can any of its characters change. Thus we say that a `String` object is *immutable*. However, several methods in the `String` class return new `String` objects that are the result of modifying the original string's value.

Note that some of the `String` methods refer to the *index* of a particular character. A character in a string can be specified by its position, or index, in the string. The index of the first character in a string is zero, the index of the next character is one, and so on. Therefore, in the string `"Hello"`, the index of the character `'H'` is zero and the character at index four is `'o'`.

Several `String` methods are exercised in the program shown in Listing 3.1.

As you examine the `StringMutation` program, keep in mind that this is not a single `String` object that changes its data; this program creates five separate `String` objects using various methods of the `String` class. Originally, the `phrase` object is set up:

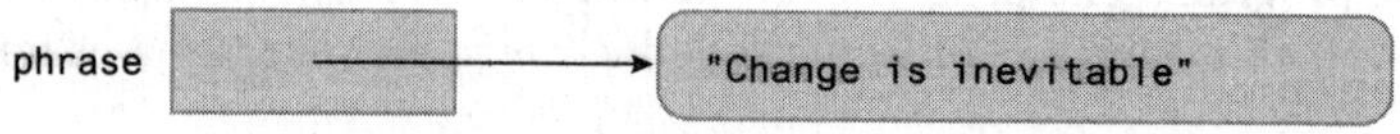

`String(String str)`
Constructor: creates a new string object with the same characters as `str`.

`char charAt(int index)`
Returns the character at the specified `index`.

`int compareTo(String str)`
Returns an integer indicating if this string is lexically before (a negative return value), equal to (a zero return value), or lexically after (a positive return value), the string `str`.

`String concat(String str)`
Returns a new string consisting of this string concatenated with `str`.

`boolean equals(String str)`
Returns true if this string contains the same characters as `str` (including case) and false otherwise.

`boolean equalsIgnoreCase(String str)`
Returns true if this string contains the same characters as `str` (without regard to case) and false otherwise.

`int length()`
Returns the number of characters in this string.

`String replace(char oldChar, char newChar)`
Returns a new string that is identical with this string except that every occurrence of `oldChar` is replaced by `newChar`.

`String substring(int offset, int endIndex)`
Returns a new string that is a subset of this string starting at index `offset` and extending through `endIndex-1`.

`String toLowerCase()`
Returns a new string identical to this string except all uppercase letters are converted to their lowercase equivalent.

`String toUpperCase()`
Returns a new string identical to this string except all lowercase letters are converted to their uppercase equivalent.

FIGURE 3.1 Some methods of the `String` class

LISTING 3.1

```
//********************************************************************
//  StringMutation.java       Author: Lewis/Loftus
//
//  Demonstrates the use of the String class and its methods.
//********************************************************************

public class StringMutation
{
   //-----------------------------------------------------------------
   // Prints a string and various mutations of it.
   //-----------------------------------------------------------------
   public static void main(String[] args)
   {
      String phrase = "Change is inevitable";
      String mutation1, mutation2, mutation3, mutation4;

      System.out.println("Original string: \"" + phrase + "\"");
      System.out.println("Length of string: " + phrase.length());

      mutation1 = phrase.concat(", except from vending machines.");
      mutation2 = mutation1.toUpperCase();
      mutation3 = mutation2.replace('E', 'X');
      mutation4 = mutation3.substring(3, 30);

      // Print each mutated string
      System.out.println("Mutation #1: " + mutation1);
      System.out.println("Mutation #2: " + mutation2);
      System.out.println("Mutation #3: " + mutation3);
      System.out.println("Mutation #4: " + mutation4);

      System.out.println("Mutated length: " + mutation4.length());
   }
}
```

OUTPUT

```
Original string: "Change is inevitable"
Length of string: 20
Mutation #1: Change is inevitable, except from vending machines.
Mutation #2: CHANGE IS INEVITABLE, EXCEPT FROM VENDING MACHINES.
Mutation #3: CHANGX IS INXVITABLX, XXCXPT FROM VXNDING MACHINXS.
Mutation #4: NGX IS INXVITABLX, XXCXPT F
Mutated length: 27
```

After printing the original phrase and its length, the `concat` method is executed to create a new string object referenced by the variable `mutation1`:

Then the `toUpperCase` method is executed on the `mutation1` object, and the resulting string is stored in `mutation2`:

KEY CONCEPT
Usually, a method is executed on a particular object, which affects the results.

Notice that the `length` and `concat` methods are executed on the `phrase` object, but the `toUpperCase` method is executed on the `mutation1` object. Any method of the `String` class can be executed on any `String` object, but for any given invocation, a method is executed on a particular object. The results of executing `toUpperCase` on `mutation1` would be very different from the results of executing `toUpperCase` on `phrase`. Remember, each object has its own state, which often affects the results of method calls.

Finally, the `String` object variables `mutation3` and `mutation4` are initialized by the calls to `mutation2.replace` and `mutation3.substring`, respectively:

SELF-REVIEW QUESTIONS *(see answers in Appendix L)*

SR 3.6 Assume `s1`, `s2`, and `s3` are `String` variables initialized to `"Amanda"`, `"Bobby"`, and `"Chris"`, respectively. Which `String` variable or variables are changed by each of the following statements?

a. `System.out.println(s1);`
b. `s1 = s3.toLowerCase();`
c. `System.out.println(s2.replace('B', 'M'));`
d. `s3 = s2.concat(s1);`

SR 3.7 What output is produced by the following code fragment?

```
String s1 = "Foundations";
String s2;
System.out.println(s1.charAt(1));
s2 = s1.substring(0, 5);
System.out.println(s2);
```

```
System.out.println(s1.length());
System.out.println(s2.length());
```

SR 3.8 Write a statement that prints the value of a `String` object called `title` in all uppercase letters.

SR 3.9 Write a declaration for a `String` variable called `front`, and initialize it to the first 10 characters of another `String` object called `description`.

3.3 Packages

We mentioned earlier that the Java language is supported by a standard class library called the Java API that we can make use of as needed. Let's examine that idea further.

KEY CONCEPT
A class library provides useful support when developing programs.

A *class library* is a set of classes that supports the development of programs. A compiler or development environment often comes with a class library. Class libraries can also be obtained separately through third-party vendors. The classes in a class library contain methods that are often valuable to a programmer because of the special functionality they offer. In fact, programmers often become dependent on the methods in a class library and begin to think of them as part of the language. However, technically, they are not in the language itself.

The `String` class, for instance, is not an inherent part of the Java language. It is part of the Java standard class library that can be found in any Java development environment. The classes that make up the library were created by employees at Sun Microsystems, the people who created the Java language.

The class library is made up of several clusters of related classes, which are often referred to as the Java APIs, which stands for *application programming interfaces*. For example, we may refer to the Java Database API when we're talking about the set of classes that helps us write programs that interact with a database. Another example of an API is the JavaFX API, which refers to a set of classes that defines special graphical components used in a graphical user interface (GUI). Often the entire standard library is referred to generically as the Java API.

KEY CONCEPT
The Java standard class library is organized into packages.

The classes of the Java standard class library are also grouped into *packages*. Each class is part of a particular package. The `String` class, for example, is part of the `java.lang` package. The `System` class is part of the `java.lang` package as well. We mentioned in Chapter 2 that the `Scanner` class is part of the `java.util` package.

The package organization is more fundamental and language based than the API names. Though there is a general correspondence between package and API names, the groups of classes that make up a given API might cross packages.

Package	Provides Support to
java.awt	Draw graphics and create graphical user interfaces; AWT stands for Abstract Windowing Toolkit.
java.beans	Define software components that can be easily combined into applications.
java.io	Perform a wide variety of input and output functions.
java.lang	General support; it is automatically imported into all Java programs.
java.math	Perform calculations with arbitrarily high precision.
java.net	Communicate across a network.
java.rmi	Create programs that can be distributed across multiple computers; RMI stands for Remote Method Invocation.
java.security	Enforce security restrictions.
java.sql	Interact with databases; SQL stands for Structured Query Language.
java.text	Format text for output.
java.util	General utilities.
javafx.scene.shape	Represent shapes such as circles and rectangles.
javafx.scene.control	Display graphical controls such as buttons and sliders.

FIGURE 3.2 Some packages in the Java API

Figure 3.2 describes some of the packages that are part of the Java API. These packages are available on any platform that supports Java software development. Some of these packages support highly specific programming techniques and will not come into play in the development of basic programs.

Various classes of the Java API are discussed throughout this book. For convenience, we include in the book some documentation on the classes used (such as the information about the `String` methods in Figure 3.1) but it's also very important for you to know how to get more information about the Java API classes. The *online Java API documentation* is an invaluable resource for any Java programmer. It is a Web site that contains pages on each class in the standard Java API, listing and describing the methods in each one.

Figure 3.3 shows one page of this documentation. Links on the side allow you to examine particular packages and jump to particular classes. Take some time to get comfortable navigating this site and learning how the information is

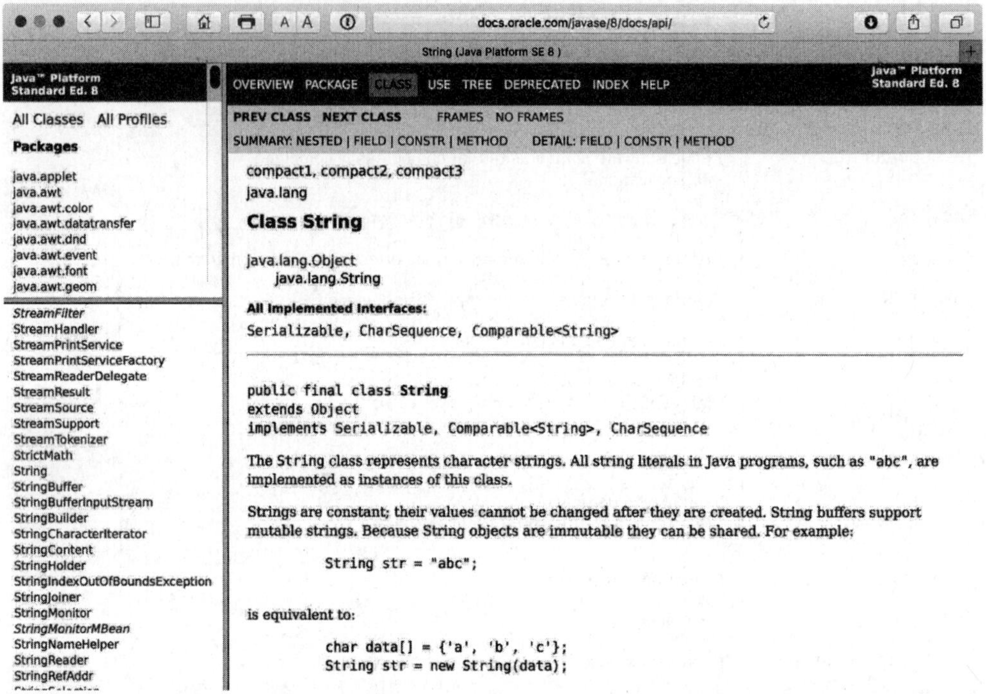

FIGURE 3.3 A page from the online Java API documentation

organized. The entire set of Java API documentation can be downloaded so that you have a local copy always available, or you can rely on the online version.

The `import` Declaration

The classes of the `java.lang` package are automatically available for use when writing a Java program. To use classes from any other package, however, we must either *fully qualify* the reference or use an *import declaration*. Recall that the example programs in Chapter 2 that use the `Scanner` class include an `import` declaration.

When you want to use a class from a class library in a program, you could use its fully qualified name, including the package name, every time it is referenced. For example, every time you want to refer to the `Scanner` class that is defined in the `java.util` package, you could write `java.util.Scanner`. However, completely specifying the package and class name every time it is needed quickly becomes tiring. Java provides the `import` declaration to simplify these references.

The `import` declaration specifies the packages and classes that will be used in a program so that the fully qualified name is not necessary with each reference. As we've seen, the following is an example of an `import` declaration:

```
import java.util.Scanner;
```

This declaration asserts that the `Scanner` class of the `java.util` package may be used in the program. Once this `import` declaration is made, it is sufficient to use the simple name `Scanner` when referring to that class in the program.

If two classes from two different packages have the same name, `import` declarations will not suffice because the compiler won't be able to figure out which class is being referenced in the flow of the code. When such situations arise, which is rare, the fully qualified names should be used in the code.

Another form of the `import` declaration uses an asterisk (*) to indicate that any class inside the package might be used in the program. Therefore, the following declaration allows all classes in the `java.util` package to be referenced in the program without qualifying each reference:

```
import  java.util.*;
```

If only one class of a particular package will be used in a program, it is usually better to name the class specifically in the `import` declaration. However, if two or more will be used, the * notation is usually fine.

The classes of the `java.lang` package are automatically imported because they are fundamental and can be thought of as basic extensions to the language. Therefore, any class in the `java.lang` package, such as `System` and `String`, can be used without an explicit `import` declaration. It's as if all program files automatically contain the following declaration:

KEY CONCEPT

All classes of the `java.lang` package are automatically imported for every program.

```
import java.lang.*;
```

SELF-REVIEW QUESTIONS *(see answers in Appendix L)*

SR 3.10 What is a Java package?

SR 3.11 What does the `java.net` package contain? The `javafx.scene.shape` package?

SR 3.12 What package contains the `Scanner` class? The `String` class? The `Random` class? The `Math` class?

SR 3.13 Using the online Java API documentation, describe the `Point` class.

SR 3.14 What does an `import` statement accomplish?

SR 3.15 Why doesn't the `String` class have to be specifically imported into our programs?

3.4 The Random Class

The need for random numbers occurs frequently when writing software. Games often use a random number to represent the roll of a die or the shuffle of a deck of cards. A flight simulator may use random numbers to determine how often a simulated flight has engine trouble. A program designed to help students prepare for standardized tests may use random numbers to choose the next question to ask.

The `Random` class, which is part of the `java.util` class, represents a *pseudorandom number generator*. A random number generator picks a number at random out of a range of values. A program that serves this role is technically pseudorandom, because a program has no means to actually pick a number randomly. A pseudorandom number generator performs a series of complicated calculations, based on an initial *seed value*, and produces a number. Though they are technically not random (because they are calculated), the values produced by a pseudorandom number generator usually appear random, at least random enough for most situations.

KEY CONCEPT
A pseudorandom number generator performs a complex calculation to create the illusion of randomness.

Figure 3.4 lists some of the methods of the `Random` class. The `nextInt` method can be called with no parameters, or we can pass it a single integer value. The version that takes no parameters generates a random number across the entire range of `int` values, including negative numbers. Usually, though, we need a random number within a more specific range. For instance, to simulate the roll of a die, we might want a random number in the range of 1–6. The `nextInt` method returns a value that's in the range from 0 to 1 less than its parameter. For example, if we pass in 100, we'll get a return value that is greater than or equal to 0 and less than or equal to 99.

`Random()`
Constructor: creates a new pseudorandom number generator.

`float nextFloat()`
Returns a random number between 0.0 (inclusive) and 1.0 (exclusive).

`int nextInt()`
Returns a random number that ranges over all possible `int` values (positive and negative).

`int nextInt(int num)`
Returns a random number in the range 0 to `num-1`.

FIGURE 3.4 Some methods of the `Random` class

Note that the value we pass to the `nextInt` method is also the number of possible values we can get in return. We can shift the range as needed by adding or subtracting the proper amount. To get a random number in the range 1–6, we can call `nextInt(6)` to get a value from 0 to 5, and then add 1.

The `nextFloat` method of the `Random` class returns a `float` value that is greater than or equal to 0 and less than 1. If desired, we can use multiplication to scale the result, cast it into an `int` value to truncate the fractional part, and then shift the range as we do with integers.

The program shown in Listing 3.2 produces several random numbers in various ranges.

LISTING 3.2

```
//********************************************************************
//  RandomNumbers.java       Author: Lewis/Loftus
//
//  Demonstrates the creation of pseudo-random numbers using the
//  Random class.
//********************************************************************

import java.util.Random;

public class RandomNumbers
{
   //-----------------------------------------------------------------
   //  Generates random numbers in various ranges.
   //-----------------------------------------------------------------
   public static void main(String[] args)
   {
      Random generator = new Random();
      int num1;
      float num2;

      num1 = generator.nextInt();
      System.out.println("A random integer: " + num1);

      num1 = generator.nextInt(10);
      System.out.println("From 0 to 9: " + num1);

      num1 = generator.nextInt(10) + 1;
      System.out.println("From 1 to 10: " + num1);
```

LISTING 3.2 *continued*

```
        num1 = generator.nextInt(15) + 20;
        System.out.println("From 20 to 34: " + num1);

        num1 = generator.nextInt(20) - 10;
        System.out.println("From -10 to 9: " + num1);

        num2 = generator.nextFloat();
        System.out.println("A random float (between 0-1): " + num2);

        num2 = generator.nextFloat() * 6;   // 0.0 to 5.999999
        num1 = (int)num2 + 1;
        System.out.println("From 1 to 6: " + num1);
    }
}
```

OUTPUT

```
A random integer: 1773351873
From 0 to 9: 8
From 1 to 10: 6
From 20 to 34: 20
From -10 to 9: -6
A random float (between 0-1): 0.71058085
From 1 to 6: 3
```

SELF-REVIEW QUESTIONS *(see answers in Appendix L)*

SR 3.16 Given a `Random` object called `rand`, what does the call `rand.nextInt()` return?

SR 3.17 Given a `Random` object called `rand`, what does the call `rand.nextInt(20)` return?

SR 3.18 Assuming that a `Random` object has been created called `generator`, what is the range of the result of each of the following expressions?

a. `generator.nextInt(50)`
b. `generator.nextInt(5) + 10`
c. `generator.nextInt(10) + 5`
d. `generator.nextInt(50) - 25`

SR 3.19 Assuming that a `Random` object has been created called `generator`, write expressions that generate each of the following ranges of integers, including the endpoints. Use the version of the `nextInt` method that accepts a single integer parameter.

a. 0 to 30
b. 10 to 19
c. –5 to 5

3.5 The Math Class

The `Math` class provides a large number of basic mathematical functions that are often helpful in making calculations. The `Math` class is defined in the `java.lang` package of the Java standard class library. Figure 3.5 lists several of its methods.

All the methods in the `Math` class are *static methods* (also called *class methods*), which means they can be invoked through the name of the class in which they are defined, without having to instantiate an object of the class first. Static methods are discussed further in Chapter 6.

The methods of the `Math` class return values, which can be used in expressions as needed. For example, the following statement computes the absolute value of the number stored in `total`, adds it to the value of `count` raised to the fourth power, and stores the result in the variable `value`:

KEY CONCEPT

All methods of the `Math` class are static, meaning they are invoked through the class name.

```
value = Math.abs(total) + Math.pow(count, 4);
```

Note that you can pass an integer value to a method that accepts a `double` parameter. This is a form of assignment conversion, which was discussed in Chapter 2.

The `Quadratic` program, shown in Listing 3.3, uses the `Math` class to compute the roots of a quadratic equation. Recall that a quadratic equation has the following general form:

$$ax^2 + bx + c$$

The `Quadratic` program reads values that represent the coefficients in a quadratic equation (a, b, and c), and then evaluates the quadratic formula to determine the roots of the equation. The quadratic formula is

VideoNote

Example using the `Random` and `Math` classes.

$$\text{roots} = \frac{-b \pm \sqrt{b^2 - 4ac}}{2a}$$

`static int abs(int num)`
Returns the absolute value of num.

`static double acos(double num)`

`static double asin(double num)`

`static double atan(double num)`
Returns the arc cosine, arc sine, or arc tangent of num.

`static double cos(double angle)`

`static double sin(double angle)`

`static double tan(double angle)`
Returns the angle cosine, sine, or tangent of angle, which is measured in radians.

`static double ceil(double num)`
Returns the ceiling of num, which is the smallest whole number greater than or equal to num.

`static double exp(double power)`
Returns the value e raised to the specified power.

`static double floor(double num)`
Returns the floor of num, which is the largest whole number less than or equal to num.

`static double pow(double num, double power)`
Returns the value num raised to the specified power.

`static double random()`
Returns a random number between 0.0 (inclusive) and 1.0 (exclusive).

`static double sqrt(double num)`
Returns the square root of num, which must be positive.

FIGURE 3.5 Some methods of the `Math` class

Note that this program assumes that the discriminant (the value under the square root) is negative. If it's not negative, the results will not be a valid number, which Java represents as `NAN`, which stands for Not A Number. In Chapter 5, we will see how we can handle this type of situation gracefully.

LISTING 3.3

```
//********************************************************************
//  Quadratic.java       Author: Lewis/Loftus
//
//  Demonstrates the use of the Math class to perform a calculation
//  based on user input.
//********************************************************************

import java.util.Scanner;

public class Quadratic
{
   //-----------------------------------------------------------------
   //  Determines the roots of a quadratic equation.
   //-----------------------------------------------------------------
   public static void main(String[] args)
   {
      int a, b, c;   // ax^2 + bx + c
      double discriminant, root1, root2;

      Scanner scan = new Scanner(System.in);

      System.out.print("Enter the coefficient of x squared: ");
      a = scan.nextInt();

      System.out.print("Enter the coefficient of x: ");
      b = scan.nextInt();

      System.out.print("Enter the constant: ");
      c = scan.nextInt();

      // Use the quadratic formula to compute the roots.
      // Assumes a positive discriminant.

      discriminant = Math.pow(b, 2) - (4 * a * c);
      root1 = ((-1 * b) + Math.sqrt(discriminant)) / (2 * a);
      root2 = ((-1 * b) - Math.sqrt(discriminant)) / (2 * a);

      System.out.println("Root #1: " + root1);
      System.out.println("Root #2: " + root2);
   }
}
```

LISTING 3.3 *continued*

OUTPUT

```
Enter the coefficient of x squared:  3
Enter the coefficient of x:  8
Enter the constant:  4
Root #1: -0.6666666666666666
Root #2: -2.0
```

SELF-REVIEW QUESTIONS *(see answers in Appendix L)*

SR 3.20 What is a class method (also called a static method)?

SR 3.21 What is the value of each of the following expressions?

a. `Math.abs(10) + Math.abs(-10)`
b. `Math.pow(2, 4)`
c. `Math.pow(4, 2)`
d. `Math.pow(3, 5)`
e. `Math.pow(5, 3)`
f. `Math.sqrt(16)`

SR 3.22 Write a statement that prints the sine of an angle measuring 1.23 radians.

SR 3.23 Write a declaration for a `double` variable called `result` and initialize it to 5 raised to the power 2.5.

SR 3.24 Using the online Java API documentation, list three methods of the `Math` class that are not included in Figure 3.5.

3.6 Formatting Output

The `NumberFormat` class and the `DecimalFormat` class are used to format information so that it looks appropriate when printed or displayed. They are both part of the Java standard class library and are defined in the `java.text` package.

The `NumberFormat` Class

The `NumberFormat` class provides generic formatting capabilities for numbers. You don't instantiate a `NumberFormat` object by using the `new` operator. Instead,

```
String format(double number)
    Returns a string containing the specified number formatted according to this
    object's pattern.

static NumberFormat getCurrencyInstance()
    Returns a NumberFormat object that represents a currency format for the
    current locale.

static NumberFormat getPercentInstance()
    Returns a NumberFormat object that represents a percentage format for the
    current locale.
```

FIGURE 3.6 Some methods of the `NumberFormat` class

you request an object from one of the static methods that you invoke through the class name itself. Figure 3.6 lists some of the methods of the `NumberFormat` class.

Two of the methods in the `NumberFormat` class, `getCurrencyInstance` and `getPercentInstance`, return an object that is used to format numbers. The `getCurrencyInstance` method returns a formatter for monetary values, and the `getPercentInstance` method returns an object that formats a percentage. The `format` method is invoked through a formatter object and returns a `String` that contains the number formatted in the appropriate manner.

The `Purchase` program shown in Listing 3.4 uses both types of formatters. It reads in a sales transaction and computes the final price, including tax.

LISTING 3.4

```
//********************************************************************
//  Purchase.java       Author: Lewis/Loftus
//
//  Demonstrates the use of the NumberFormat class to format output.
//********************************************************************

import java.util.Scanner;
import java.text.NumberFormat;

public class Purchase
{
   //-----------------------------------------------------------------
   //  Calculates the final price of a purchased item using values
   //  entered by the user.
   //-----------------------------------------------------------------
   public static void main(String[] args)
```

LISTING 3.4 *continued*

```
   {
      final double TAX_RATE = 0.06;    // 6% sales tax

      int quantity;
      double subtotal, tax, totalCost, unitPrice;

      Scanner scan = new Scanner(System.in);

      NumberFormat fmt1 = NumberFormat.getCurrencyInstance();
      NumberFormat fmt2 = NumberFormat.getPercentInstance();

      System.out.print("Enter the quantity: ");
      quantity = scan.nextInt();

      System.out.print("Enter the unit price: ");
      unitPrice = scan.nextDouble();

      subtotal = quantity * unitPrice;
      tax = subtotal * TAX_RATE;
      totalCost = subtotal + tax;

      // Print output with appropriate formatting
      System.out.println("Subtotal: " + fmt1.format(subtotal));
      System.out.println("Tax: " + fmt1.format(tax) + " at "
                         + fmt2.format(TAX_RATE));
      System.out.println("Total: " + fmt1.format(totalCost));
   }
}
```

OUTPUT

```
Enter the quantity:  5
Enter the unit price:  3.87
Subtotal: $19.35
Tax: $1.16 at 6%
Total: $20.51
```

The `DecimalFormat` Class

Unlike the `NumberFormat` class, the `DecimalFormat` class is instantiated in the traditional way using the `new` operator. Its constructor takes a string that represents the pattern that will guide the formatting process. We can then use the `format`

`DecimalFormat(String pattern)`
Constructor:, creates a new DecimalFormat object with the specified pattern.

`void applyPattern(String pattern)`
Applies the specified pattern to this DecimalFormat object.

`String format(double number)`
Returns a string containing the specified number formatted according to the current pattern.

FIGURE 3.7 Some methods of the `DecimalFormat` class

method to format a particular value. At a later point, if we want to change the pattern that the formatter object uses, we can invoke the `applyPattern` method. Figure 3.7 describes these methods.

The pattern defined by the string that is passed to the `DecimalFormat` constructor can get fairly elaborate. Various symbols are used to represent particular formatting guidelines. The pattern defined by the string `"0.###"`, for example, indicates that at least one digit should be printed to the left of the decimal point and should be a zero if the integer portion of the value is zero. It also indicates that the fractional portion of the value should be rounded to three digits.

This pattern is used in the `CircleStats` program, shown in Listing 3.5, which reads the radius of a circle from the user and computes its area and circumference. Trailing zeros, such as in the circle's area of 78.540, are not printed.

The `printf` Method

In addition to `print` and `println`, the `System` class has another output method called `printf`, which allows the user to print a formatted string containing data values. The first parameter to the method represents the format string, and the remaining parameters specify the values that are inserted into the format string.

For example, the following line of code prints an ID number and a name:

```
System.out.printf("ID: %5d\tName: %s", id, name);
```

The first parameter specifies the format of the output and includes literal characters that label the output values as well as escape characters such as `\t`. The pattern `%5d` indicates that the corresponding numeric value (`id`) should be printed in a field of five characters. The pattern `%s` matches the string parameter

LISTING 3.5

```
//********************************************************************
//  CircleStats.java       Author: Lewis/Loftus
//
//  Demonstrates the formatting of decimal values using the
//  DecimalFormat class.
//********************************************************************

import java.util.Scanner;
import java.text.DecimalFormat;

public class CircleStats
{
   //-----------------------------------------------------------------
   //  Calculates the area and circumference of a circle given its
   //  radius.
   //-----------------------------------------------------------------
   public static void main(String[] args)
   {
      int radius;
      double area, circumference;

      Scanner scan = new Scanner(System.in);

      System.out.print("Enter the circle's radius: ");
      radius = scan.nextInt();

      area = Math.PI * Math.pow(radius, 2);
      circumference = 2 * Math.PI * radius;

      // Round the output to three decimal places
      DecimalFormat fmt = new DecimalFormat("0.###");

      System.out.println("The circle's area: " + fmt.format(area));
      System.out.println("The circle's circumference: "
                         + fmt.format(circumference));
   }
}
```

OUTPUT

```
Enter the circle's radius:  5
The circle's area: 78.54
The circle's circumference: 31.416
```

name. The values of id and name are inserted into the string, producing a result as follows:

```
ID: 24036   Name: Larry Flagelhopper
```

The printf method was added to Java to mirror a similar function used in programs written in the C programming language. It makes it easier for a programmer to translate (or *migrate*) an existing C program into Java.

Older software that still has value is called a *legacy system.* Maintaining a legacy system is often a costly effort because, among other things, it is based on older technologies. But in many cases, maintaining a legacy system is still more cost-effective than migrating it to new technology, such as writing it in a newer language. Adding the printf method is an attempt to make such migrations easier, and therefore less costly, by providing the same kind of output statement that C programmers have come to rely on.

KEY CONCEPT

The printf method was added to Java to support the migration of legacy systems.

However, using the printf method is not a particularly clean object-oriented solution to the problem of formatting output, so we avoid its use in this book.

SELF-REVIEW QUESTIONS *(see answers in Appendix L)*

SR 3.25 Describe how you request a NumberFormat object for use within a program.

SR 3.26 Suppose that in your program you have a double variable named cost. You want to output the value stored in cost formatted as the currency of the current locale.

a. Write a code statement that declares and requests a NumberFormat object named moneyFormat that can be used to represent currency in the format of the current locale.
b. Write a code statement that uses the moneyFormat object and prints the value of cost, formatted as the currency of the current locale.
c. What would be the output from the statement you wrote in part (b) if the value in cost is 54.89 and your computer's locale is set to the United States? What if your computer's locale is set to the United Kingdom?

SR 3.27 What are the steps to output a floating point value as a percentage using Java's formatting classes?

SR 3.28 Write code statements that prompt for and read in a double value from the user, and then print the result of taking the square root of the absolute value of the input value. Output the result to two decimal places.

3.7 Enumerated Types

Java provides the ability to define an *enumerated type*, which can then be used as the type of a variable when it is declared. An enumerated type establishes all possible values of a variable of that type by listing, or enumerating, them. The values are identifiers and can be anything desired.

For example, the following declaration defines an enumerated type called `Season`, whose possible values are `winter`, `spring`, `summer`, and `fall`:

```
enum Season {winter, spring, summer, fall}
```

There is no limit to the number of values that you can list for an enumerated type. Once the type is defined, a variable can be declared of that type:

```
Season time;
```

KEY CONCEPT

Enumerated types are type-safe, ensuring that invalid values will not be used.

The variable `time` is now restricted in the values it can take on. It can hold one of the four `Season` values, but nothing else. Java enumerated types are considered to be *type-safe*, meaning that any attempt to use a value other than one of the enumerated values will result in a compile-time error.

The values are accessed through the name of the type. For example:

```
time = Season.spring;
```

Enumerated types can be quite helpful in situations in which you have a relatively small number of distinct values that a variable can assume. For example, suppose we wanted to represent the various letter grades a student could earn. We might declare the following enumerated type:

```
enum Grade {A, B, C, D, F}
```

Any initialized variable that holds a `Grade` is guaranteed to have one of those valid grades. That's better than using a simple character or string variable to represent the grade, which could take on any value.

Suppose we also wanted to represent plus and minus grades, such as A– and B+. We couldn't use A– or B+ as values, because they are not valid identifiers (the characters '–' and '+' cannot be part of an identifier in Java). However, the same values could be represented using the identifiers `Aminus`, `Bplus`, etc.

Internally, each value in an enumerated type is stored as an integer, which is referred to as its *ordinal value*. The first value in an enumerated type has an ordinal value of 0, the second one has an ordinal value of 1, the third one 2, and so on. The ordinal values are used internally only. You cannot assign a numeric value to an enumerated type, even if it corresponds to a valid ordinal value.

An enumerated type is a special kind of class, and the variables of an enumerated type are object variables. As such, there are a few methods associated with all enumerated types. The `ordinal` method returns the numeric value associated with a particular enumerated type value. The `name` method returns the name of the value, which is the same as the identifier that defines the value.

Listing 3.6 shows a program called `IceCream` that declares an enumerated type and exercises some of its methods. Because enumerated types are special types of classes, they are not defined within a method. They can be defined either at the class level (within the class but outside a method), as in this example, or at the outermost level.

We explore enumerated types further in Chapter 6.

LISTING 3.6

```
//********************************************************************
//  IceCream.java       Author: Lewis/Loftus
//
//  Demonstrates the use of enumerated types.
//********************************************************************

public class IceCream
{
   enum Flavor {vanilla, chocolate, strawberry, fudgeRipple, coffee,
             rockyRoad, mintChocolateChip, cookieDough}

   //-----------------------------------------------------------------
   //  Creates and uses variables of the Flavor type.
   //-----------------------------------------------------------------
   public static void main(String[] args)
   {
      Flavor cone1, cone2, cone3;

      cone1 = Flavor.rockyRoad;
      cone2 = Flavor.chocolate;

      System.out.println("cone1 value: " + cone1);
      System.out.println("cone1 ordinal: " + cone1.ordinal());
      System.out.println("cone1 name: " + cone1.name());

      System.out.println();
      System.out.println("cone2 value: " + cone2);
      System.out.println("cone2 ordinal: " + cone2.ordinal());
      System.out.println("cone2 name: " + cone2.name());
```

LISTING 3.6 *continued*

```
        cone3 = cone1;

        System.out.println();
        System.out.println("cone3 value: " + cone3);
        System.out.println("cone3 ordinal: " + cone3.ordinal());
        System.out.println("cone3 name: " + cone3.name());
    }
}
```

OUTPUT

```
cone1 value: rockyRoad
cone1 ordinal: 5
cone1 name: rockyRoad

cone2 value: chocolate
cone2 ordinal: 1
cone2 name: chocolate

cone3 value: rockyRoad
cone3 ordinal: 5
cone3 name: rockyRoad
```

SELF-REVIEW QUESTIONS *(see answers in Appendix L)*

SR 3.29 Write the declaration of an enumerated type that represents movie ratings.

SR 3.30 Suppose that an enumerated type called `CardSuit` has been defined as follows:

```
enum CardSuit {clubs, diamonds, hearts, spades}
```

What is the output of the following code sequence?

```
CardSuit card1, card2;
card1 = CardSuit.clubs;
card2 = CardSuit.hearts;
System.out.println(card1);
System.out.println(card2.name());
System.out.println(card1.ordinal());
System.out.println(card2.ordinal());
```

SR 3.31 Why use an enumerated type such as `CardSuit` defined in the previous question? Why not just use `String` variables and assign them values such as `"hearts"`?

3.8 Wrapper Classes

As we've discussed previously, Java represents data by using primitive types (such as `int`, `double`, `char`, and `boolean`) in addition to classes and objects. Having two categories of data to manage (primitive values and object references) can present a challenge in some circumstances. For example, we might create an object that serves as a container to hold various types of other objects. However, in a specific situation, we may want it to hold a simple integer value. In these cases we need to "wrap" a primitive value into an object.

A *wrapper class* represents a particular primitive type. For instance, the `Integer` class represents a simple integer value. An object created from the `Integer` class stores a single `int` value. The constructors of the wrapper classes accept the primitive value to store. For example:

```
Integer ageObj = new Integer(40);
```

Once the declaration and instantiation are performed, the `ageObj` object effectively represents the integer 40 as an object. It can be used wherever an object is needed in a program rather than a primitive type.

KEY CONCEPT
A wrapper class allows a primitive value to be managed as an object.

For each primitive type in Java, there exists a corresponding wrapper class in the Java class library. All wrapper classes are defined in the `java.lang` package. Figure 3.8 shows the wrapper class that corresponds to each primitive type.

Note that there is even a wrapper class that represents the type `void`. However, unlike the other wrapper classes, the `Void` class cannot be instantiated. It simply represents the concept of a void reference.

Primitive Type	Wrapper Class
byte	Byte
short	Short
int	Integer
long	Long
float	Float
double	Double
char	Character
boolean	Boolean
void	Void

FIGURE 3.8 Wrapper classes in the Java API

```
Integer(int value)
   Constructor: creates a new Integer object storing the specified value.

byte byteValue()
double doubleValue()
float floatValue()
int intValue()
long longValue()
   Return the value of this Integer as the corresponding primitive type.

static int parseInt(String str)
   Returns the int corresponding to the value stored in the
   specified string.

static String toBinaryString(int num)
static String tohexString(int num)
static String toOctalString(int num)
   Returns a string representation of the specified integer value in the
   corresponding base.
```

FIGURE 3.9 Some methods of the `Integer` class

Wrapper classes also provide various methods related to the management of the associated primitive type. For example, the `Integer` class contains methods that return the `int` value stored in the object and that convert the stored value to other primitive types. Figure 3.9 lists some of the methods found in the `Integer` class. The other wrapper classes have similar methods.

Note that the wrapper classes also contain static methods that can be invoked independent of any instantiated object. For example, the `Integer` class contains a static method called `parseInt` to convert an integer that is stored in a `String` to its corresponding `int` value. If the `String` object `str` holds the string `"987"`, the following line of code converts the string into the integer value `987` and stores that value in the `int` variable `num`:

```
num = Integer.parseInt(str);
```

The Java wrapper classes often contain static constants that are helpful as well. For example, the `Integer` class contains two constants, `MIN_VALUE` and `MAX_VALUE`, that hold the smallest and largest `int` values, respectively. The other wrapper classes contain similar constants for their types.

Autoboxing

Autoboxing is the automatic conversion between a primitive value and a corresponding wrapper object. For example, in the following code, an `int` value is assigned to an `Integer` object reference variable:

```
Integer obj1;
int num1 = 69;
obj1 = num1;     // automatically creates an Integer object
```

The reverse conversion, called unboxing, also occurs automatically when needed. For example:

```
Integer obj2 = new Integer(69);
int num2;
num2 = obj2;     // automatically extracts the int value
```

Assignments between primitive types and object types are generally incompatible. The ability to autobox occurs only between primitive types and corresponding wrapper classes. In any other case, attempting to assign a primitive value to an object reference variable, or vice versa, will cause a compile-time error.

KEY CONCEPT

Autoboxing provides automatic conversions between primitive values and corresponding wrapper objects.

SELF-REVIEW QUESTIONS *(see answers in Appendix L)*

SR 3.32 How can we represent a primitive value as an object?

SR 3.33 What wrapper classes correspond to each of the following primitive types: `byte`, `int`, `double`, `char`, and `boolean`?

SR 3.34 Suppose that an `int` variable named `number` has been declared and initialized and an `Integer` variable named `holdNumber` has been declared. Show two approaches in Java for having `holdNumber` represent the value stored in `number`.

SR 3.35 Write a statement that prints out the largest possible `int` value.

3.9 Introduction to JavaFX

This section marks the beginning of the *Graphics Track* through the book. From this point on, the last few sections of each chapter are devoted to topics related to generating graphics and GUIs. These sections can be covered as they are encountered in the chapters, explored as a group, or skipped altogether without affecting the coverage of nongraphics topics.

Java's support of graphics and GUIs has evolved in various ways over the years. When the language was first introduced, it used a set of classes called the AWT, which stands for Abstract Windowing Toolkit. Later, the Swing API was introduced, which replaced the GUI components of the AWT with more versatile versions. However, the Swing API was most appropriate for desktop applications; other technologies were used to develop Java programs that ran in a Web browser.

The JavaFX API has now replaced the AWT and Swing for developing graphical programs. JavaFX combines the best aspects of the previous approaches and adds many additional features. It also creates applications that can be run on the Web. Oracle, the company that manages the Java language, no longer supports those older technologies.

KEY CONCEPT

JavaFX is now the preferred approach for developing Java programs that use graphics and GUIs.

Listing 3.7 shows a small JavaFX program in a class called `HelloJavaFX`. This program displays a window containing two text elements.

The first thing to note is that the `HelloJavaFX` class extends the JavaFX `Application` class. This process is making use of the object-oriented concept of inheritance, which we introduced in Chapter 1 and explore in more detail later in the book. All JavaFX programs extend the `Application` class.

Note that there are two methods in the `HelloJavaFX` class: a `main` method, as we've seen in other programs, and the `start` method. The `main` method is used

LISTING 3.7

```
//********************************************************************
//  HelloJavaFX.java       Author: Lewis/Loftus
//
//  Demonstrates a basic JavaFX application.
//********************************************************************

import javafx.application.Application;
import javafx.scene.Group;
import javafx.scene.Scene;
import javafx.scene.paint.Color;
import javafx.scene.text.Text;
import javafx.stage.Stage;

public class HelloJavaFX extends Application
{
   //-----------------------------------------------------------------
   //  Creates and displays two Text objects in a JavaFX window.
   //-----------------------------------------------------------------
   public void start(Stage primaryStage)
   {
```

LISTING 3.7 *continued*

```
        Text hello = new Text(50, 50, "Hello, JavaFX!");
        Text question = new Text(120, 80, "How's it going?");

        Group root = new Group(hello, question);
        Scene scene = new Scene(root, 300, 120, Color.LIGHTGREEN);

        primaryStage.setTitle("A JavaFX Program");
        primaryStage.setScene(scene);
        primaryStage.show();
    }

    //--------------------------------------------------------------------
    //  Launches the JavaFX application. This method is not required
    //  in IDEs that launch JavaFX applications automatically.
    //--------------------------------------------------------------------
    public static void main(String[] args)
    {
        launch(args);
    }
}
```

DISPLAY

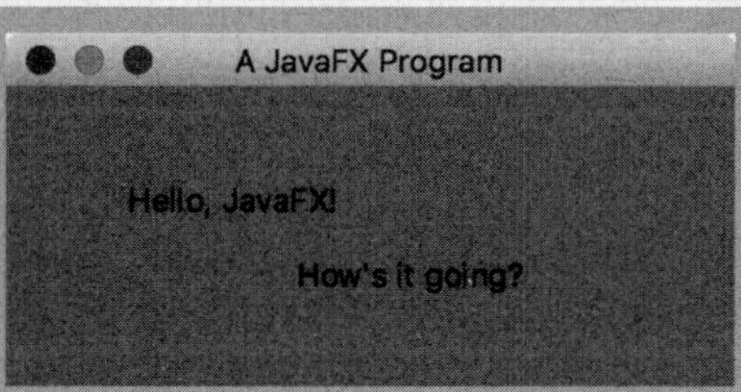

to call the `launch` method of the `Application` class. After performing some background setup, the `launch` method calls the `start` method. You'll typically use the `start` method to set up and display the primary window of the app.

In a development environment that fully supports JavaFX, the `launch` method is called automatically. Therefore, if you are using such an IDE (Integrated Development Environment), you do not need to write the `main` method. We will typically leave the `main` method out of our examples, though you may need to include it.

In this example, the `start` method creates two `Text` objects, adds them to a `Group`, which is then added to a `Scene`. The scene is displayed in the primary

`Stage`. While that may seem like a lot of moving parts, there's a pattern to the organization that you'll quickly get used to.

JavaFX embraces a theatre metaphor. A `Stage` is a window. A program can make use of multiple stages if desired. The primary `Stage` object is created automatically and passed into the `start` method. In this example, the last three lines of the `start` method set the title that is displayed in the window's title bar, set the scene to be displayed in the window, and then call the `show` method to display the window on the monitor.

KEY CONCEPT
JavaFX uses a theatre metaphor to present a scene on a stage.

A scene displays a single element, often referred to as the *root node*. The root node may contain other nodes, which may contain other nodes, and so on, creating a hierarchy of elements that make up the scene. In this example, the root node is a `Group` object, though there are other possibilities. The group contains two `Text` objects, each of which represents a character string and the location at which the text should be displayed.

The constructor of the `Scene` class accepts four parameters: the root node to be displayed, the preferred width and height of the scene, and its background color. In this example, the root element is a `Group` object, which is to be displayed in an area that is 300 pixels wide and 120 pixels high. The background is specified using a `Color` object that represents a light green.

KEY CONCEPT
The origin in Java's coordinate system is in the upper-left corner. All visible coordinates are positive.

Unlike a traditional two-dimensional coordinate system, the origin point (0, 0) of the Java coordinate system is in the upper-left corner of a graphical component. The x-axis coordinates get larger as you move to the right and the y-axis coordinates get larger as you move down. Figure 3.10 compares the two coordinate systems.

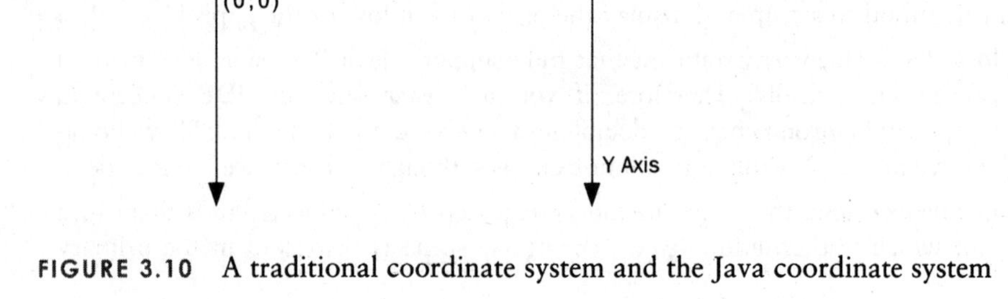

FIGURE 3.10 A traditional coordinate system and the Java coordinate system

The display point of the first `Text` object in this example is (50, 50). So, the first character of the string `"Hello JavaFX!"` is displayed 50 pixels to the right and 50 pixels down from the top-left corner of the window. The second `Text` object is 120 pixels to the right and 80 pixels down from the origin.

The next section presents other JavaFX examples that include various geometric shapes.

SELF-REVIEW QUESTIONS *(see answers in Appendix L)*

SR 3.36 In what situation might you omit the `main` method in a JavaFX application?

SR 3.37 What is a stage in the JavaFX theatre metaphor?

SR 3.38 What does the root node of a scene contain?

SR 3.39 Describe where the point (20, 50) is in the Java coordinate system.

3.10 Basic Shapes

Shapes in JavaFX are represented by classes in the `javafx.scene.shape` package. Objects created from those classes can be added to a scene to be displayed.

Figure 3.11 shows example constructor calls for creating shapes. The constructor parameters specify the position and size of the shape. For example, the `Line` constructor accepts four integer parameters, representing the two end points of a line segment. It doesn't matter which point is specified as the start or end point.

`Line(startX, startY, endX, endY)`
To make a line that runs from point (10, 20) to point (300, 80):
`Line myLine = new Line(10, 20, 300, 80);`

`Rectangle(x, y, width, height)`
To make a 200 x 70 rectangle whose upper-left corner is at point (30, 50):
`Rectangle myRect = new Rectangle(30, 50, 200, 70);`

`Circle(centerX, centerY, radius)`
To make a circle with radius 40 and a center point of (100, 150):
`Circle myCircle = new Circle(100, 150, 40);`

`Ellipse(centerX, centerY, radiusX, radiusY)`
To make an ellipse centered at (100, 50) with a horizontal radius of 80 and a vertical radius of 30:
`Ellipse myEllipse = new Ellipse(100, 50, 80, 30);`

FIGURE 3.11 Constructors for some JavaFX shape classes

The first two parameters of the Rectangle constructor specify the location of the upper-left corner of the rectangle and the other two parameters specify the rectangle's width and height.

The first two parameters of the Circle and Ellipse constructors specify the center point of the shape. A circle also has a single radius value. The shape of an ellipse is based on two radius values: one along the horizontal, or x-axis, and one along the vertical, or y-axis.

Listing 3.8 shows a JavaFX application that displays a variety of shapes and a quote from Albert Einstein. Like the HelloJavaFX example in the last section, the displayed elements are added to a Group object that serves as the root node of the Scene, which is displayed on the primary Stage.

KEY CONCEPT

Shapes are drawn in the order in which they are added to a group, making one appear in front of another.

Shapes are drawn in the order in which they are added to the group (the order in which they are listed in the Group constructor parameters). So, in this example the blue circle is drawn in front of the rectangle and ellipse.

A shape's outline is called the *stroke* and its interior is called the *fill*. The color of the stroke and fill can be set using calls to the setStroke and setFill methods, respectively. The width of the stroke can be set using a call to the setStrokeWidth method, as was done with the rectangle in the Einstein example. The rectangle's

LISTING 3.8

```
//********************************************************************
//  Einstein.java       Author: Lewis/Loftus
//
//  Demonstrates the use of various shape classes.
//********************************************************************

import javafx.application.Application;
import javafx.scene.Group;
import javafx.scene.Scene;
import javafx.scene.paint.Color;
import javafx.scene.shape.*;
import javafx.scene.text.Text;
import javafx.stage.Stage;

public class Einstein extends Application
{
   //-----------------------------------------------------------------
   //  Creates and displays several shapes.
   //-----------------------------------------------------------------
   public void start(Stage primaryStage)
   {
      Line line = new Line(35, 60, 150, 170);
```

LISTING 3.8 *continued*

```
        Circle circle = new Circle(100, 65, 20);
        circle.setFill(Color.BLUE);

        Rectangle rect = new Rectangle(60, 70, 250, 60);
        rect.setStroke(Color.RED);
        rect.setStrokeWidth(2);
        rect.setFill(null);

        Ellipse ellipse = new Ellipse(200, 100, 150, 50);
        ellipse.setFill(Color.PALEGREEN);

        Text quote = new Text(120, 100, "Out of clutter, find " +
            "simplicity.\n— Albert Einstein");

        Group root = new Group(ellipse, rect, circle, line, quote);
        Scene scene = new Scene(root, 400, 200);

        primaryStage.setTitle("Einstein");
        primaryStage.setScene(scene);
        primaryStage.show();
    }
}
```

DISPLAY

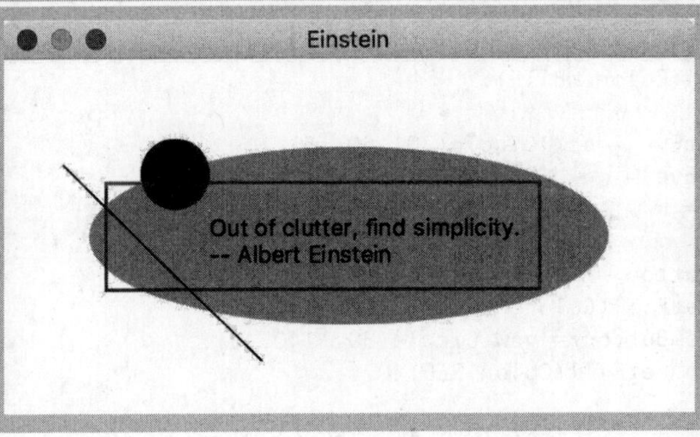

fill color is set to `null`, which removes the fill completely—anything behind the shape will show through.

Note also that the character string in the `Text` object contains a newline character (`\n`), which causes a line break at that point when displayed.

Let's look at another example that works with shapes. Listing 3.9 shows a program that displays a snowman scene.

LISTING 3.9

```
//********************************************************************
//  Snowman.java       Author: Lewis/Loftus
//
//  Demonstrates the translation of a set of shapes.
//********************************************************************

import javafx.application.Application;
import javafx.stage.Stage;
import javafx.scene.Group;
import javafx.scene.Scene;
import javafx.scene.paint.Color;
import javafx.scene.shape.*;

public class Snowman extends Application
{
   //-----------------------------------------------------------------
   //  Presents a snowman scene.
   //-----------------------------------------------------------------
   public void start(Stage primaryStage)
   {
      Ellipse base = new Ellipse(80, 210, 80, 60);
      base.setFill(Color.WHITE);

      Ellipse middle = new Ellipse(80, 130, 50, 40);
      middle.setFill(Color.WHITE);

      Circle head = new Circle(80, 70, 30);
      head.setFill(Color.WHITE);

      Circle rightEye = new Circle(70, 60, 5);
      Circle leftEye = new Circle(90, 60, 5);
      Line mouth = new Line(70, 80, 90, 80);

      Circle topButton = new Circle(80, 120, 6);
      topButton.setFill(Color.RED);
      Circle bottomButton = new Circle(80, 140, 6);
      bottomButton.setFill(Color.RED);

      Line leftArm = new Line(110, 130, 160, 130);
      leftArm.setStrokeWidth(3);
      Line rightArm = new Line(50, 130, 0, 100);
      rightArm.setStrokeWidth(3);

      Rectangle stovepipe = new Rectangle(60, 0, 40, 50);
      Rectangle brim = new Rectangle(50, 45, 60, 5);
```

LISTING 3.9 *continued*

```
        Group hat = new Group(stovepipe, brim);
        hat.setTranslateX(10);
        hat.setRotate(15);

        Group snowman = new Group(base, middle, head, leftEye, rightEye,
            mouth, topButton, bottomButton, leftArm, rightArm, hat);
        snowman.setTranslateX(170);
        snowman.setTranslateY(50);

        Circle sun = new Circle(50, 50, 30);
        sun.setFill(Color.GOLD);

        Rectangle ground = new Rectangle(0, 250, 500, 100);
        ground.setFill(Color.STEELBLUE);

        Group root = new Group(ground, sun, snowman);
        Scene scene = new Scene(root, 500, 350, Color.LIGHTBLUE);

        primaryStage.setTitle("Snowman");
        primaryStage.setScene(scene);
        primaryStage.show();
    }
}
```

DISPLAY

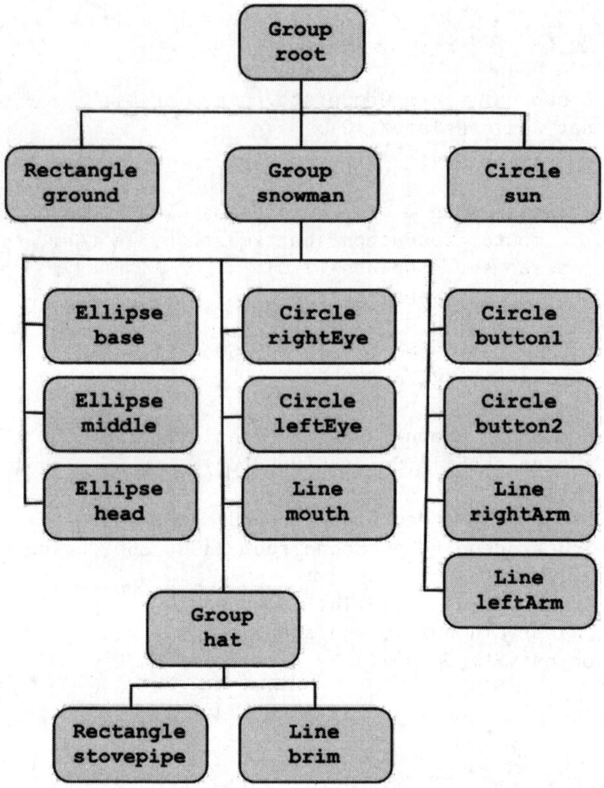

FIGURE 3.12 Hierarchy of `Snowman` scene elements

The `Snowman` example groups elements in various ways so that their properties can be adjusted appropriately. As in previous examples, the root node of the scene is a `Group` object, which contains the ground, the sun, and the snowman. The snowman is itself a group, made up of elements such as body sections, eyes, buttons, arms, and hat. The hat is another group, made up of the stovepipe and brim parts. The element hierarchy of this scene is shown in Figure 3.12.

If you call `setTranslateX` on a shape or group, it translates (shifts) the position of the shape along the x-axis. Likewise, a call to `setTranslateY` shifts the shape along the y-axis. If you scrutinize the values used to position the elements of the snowman, you discover that it would be drawn in the upper-left corner of the scene. It is moved into its final position with the appropriate method calls. Figure 3.13 shows the snowman scene as it would be displayed without shifting the snowman's position.

FIGURE 3.13 Without translating (shifting) the snowman's position

Defining a complex element like the snowman as a `Group` object allows you to perform operations such as shifting on the entire group. To move the snowman further to the right, for instance, you'd only need to change the value passed to one method. If it wasn't grouped, the position of each element would have to be changed.

Similarly, a call to `setRotate` will rotate a shape or group around its center point a specified number of degrees. In the `Snowman` example, the hat is shifted and then rotated 15 degrees clockwise so that it sits jauntily on the snowman's head. If the value passed to the `setRotate` method is negative, the rotation will be in a counterclockwise direction.

KEY CONCEPT
Shapes and groups can be shifted and rotated as needed.

SELF-REVIEW QUESTIONS *(see answers in Appendix L)*

SR 3.40 How do you make one shape appear in front of another?

SR 3.41 Write a declaration for a `Rectangle` that is 100 pixels wide, 200 pixels high, with its upper-left corner positioned at point (30, 20).

SR 3.42 Is the ellipse defined in the following statement wider than it is tall or taller than it is wide?

```
Ellipse ellipse = new Ellipse(100, 150, 70, 90);
```

SR 3.43 What is the effect of calling `setFill` on a `Circle` object, passing it a parameter of `null`?

SR 3.44 What is the advantage of grouping particular elements in a scene?

3.11 Representing Colors

A color in Java is defined by three numbers that are collectively referred to as an *RGB value*. RGB stands for Red–Green–Blue. Each number represents the contribution of the corresponding color. This approach mirrors the way the human eye combines the wavelengths of light corresponding to red, green, and blue.

KEY CONCEPT
Java represents colors using RGB values.

Typically, each number in an RGB value is in the range of 0–255. For example, a color with an RGB value of 255, 255, 0 has a full contribution of red and green and no contribution of blue. This results in the color yellow. A pink color can be defined with an RGB value of 255, 175, 175 (full red and partial green and blue). Any variation in the RGB numbers changes the color, although small changes might not be able to be perceived.

In Java, a color is represented by a `Color` object. The `Color` class has a static method called `rgb` that returns a `Color` object with the RGB value specified by the parameters:

```
Color purple = Color.rgb(183, 44, 150);
```

Color	Object	RGB Value
	`Color.BLACK`	0, 0, 0
	`Color.WHITE`	255, 255, 255
	`Color.GRAY`	128, 128, 128
	`Color.RED`	255, 0, 0
	`Color.MAROON`	128, 0, 0
	`Color.LIME`	0, 255, 0
	`Color.GREEN`	0, 128, 0
	`Color.BLUE`	0, 0, 255
	`Color.NAVY`	0, 0, 128
	`Color.YELLOW`	255, 255, 0
	`Color.MAGENTA`	255, 0, 255
	`Color.CYAN`	0, 255, 255
	`Color.PINK`	255, 192, 203
	`Color.ORANGE`	255, 165, 0

FIGURE 3.14 Some of the predefined colors in the `Color` class

The `Color` class has another static method called `color` that allows you to specify the RGB value as a set of percentages. The following call creates a maroon color based on 60% red, 10% green, and 0% blue:

```
Color maroon = Color.color(0.6, 0.1, 0.0);
```

Using these methods, any color can be defined. However, for convenience, a large set of `Color` objects have been predefined—Figure 3.14 lists only a few of them. See the online documentation of the `Color` class for a full list of predefined colors. The previous JavaFX examples in this chapter make use of several predefined colors.

SELF-REVIEW QUESTIONS *(see answers in Appendix L)*

SR 3.45 What is an RGB value?

SR 3.46 Write a statement to create a `Color` object equivalent to `Color.PINK` using the `rgb` method.

SR 3.47 Write a statement to create a `Color` object equivalent to `Color.YELLOW` using the `color` method.

Summary of Key Concepts

- The `new` operator returns a reference to a newly created object.
- Multiple reference variables can refer to the same object.
- Usually, a method is executed on a particular object, which affects the results.
- A class library provides useful support when developing programs.
- The Java standard class library is organized into packages.
- All classes of the `java.lang` package are automatically imported for every program.
- A pseudorandom number generator performs a complex calculation to create the illusion of randomness.
- All methods of the `Math` class are static, meaning they are invoked through the class name.
- The `printf` method was added to Java to support the migration of legacy systems.
- Enumerated types are type-safe, ensuring that invalid values will not be used.
- A wrapper class allows a primitive value to be managed as an object.
- Autoboxing provides automatic conversions between primitive values and corresponding wrapper objects.
- JavaFX is now the preferred approach for developing Java programs that use graphics and GUIs.
- JavaFX uses a theatre metaphor to present a scene on a stage.
- The origin in Java's coordinate system is in the upper-left corner. All visible coordinates are positive.
- Shapes are drawn in the order in which they are added to a group, making one appear in front of another.
- Shapes and groups can be shifted and rotated as needed.
- Java represents colors using RGB values.

Exercises

EX 3.1 Write a statement that prints the number of characters in a `String` object called `overview`.

EX 3.2 Write a statement that prints the 8th character of a `String` object called `introduction`.

EX 3.3 Declare a `String` variable named `str` and initialize it to contain the same characters as a `String` object called `name`, except in all uppercase characters.

EX 3.4 Write a line of code that changes all commas (,) in a `String` named `sentence` into colons (:). Store the modified `String` in a new variable named `corrected`.

EX 3.5 What output is produced by the following code fragment?

```
String s = "I find that the harder I work, the more
luck I seem to have.";
String s1 = s.substring(16, 20);
String s2 = s.substring(24, 29);
String s3 = s1 + s2;
System.out.println(s3.toUpperCase() + "!");
```

EX 3.6 What is the effect of the following import statement?

```
import java.awt.*;
```

EX 3.7 Assuming that a `Random` object has been created called `generator`, what is the range of the result of each of the following expressions?

a. `generator.nextInt(20)`

b. `generator.nextInt(8) + 1`

c. `generator.nextInt(12) + 2`

d. `generator.nextInt(35) + 10`

e. `generator.nextInt(100) - 50`

EX 3.8 Write code to declare and instantiate an object of the `Random` class (call the object reference variable `rand`). Then write a list of expressions using the `nextInt` or `nextFloat` method that generates random numbers in the following specified ranges.

a. 0.0 to 100.0

b. 1000 to 5000

c. 1 to 6

d. –40.0 to 40.0

e. 2.5 to 3.5

f. 0 to 500

EX 3.9 Write an assignment statement that computes the square root of the sum of `num1` and `num2` and assigns the result to `num3`.

EX 3.10 Write a single statement that computes and prints the absolute value of `total`.

EX 3.11 Write code statements to create a `DecimalFormat` object that will round a formatted value to four decimal places. Then write a statement that uses that object to print the value of `result`, properly formatted.

EX 3.12 Write code statements that prompt for and read a `double` value from the user, and then print the result of raising that value to the fourth power. Output the results to three decimal places.

EX 3.13 Write a declaration for an enumerated type that represents the days of the week.

EX 3.14 Compare and contrast a traditional coordinate system and the coordinate system used by Java graphical components.

EX 3.15 Write a declaration for each of the following:

a. A line that extends from point (60, 100) to point (30, 90).

b. A rectangle that is 20 pixels wide, 100 pixels high, and has its upper-left corner at point (10, 10).

c. A circle that is centered at point (50, 75) and has a radius of 30.

d. An ellipse that is centered at point (150, 180) and is 100 pixels wide and 80 pixels high.

EX 3.16 Do the following lines make a square?

a. `new Line(20, 20, 80, 20)`

b. `new Line(20, 80, 80, 80)`

c. `new Line(20, 20, 20, 80)`

d. `new Line(80, 20, 80, 80)`

EX 3.17 Is each of the following ellipses wider than it is tall or taller than it is wide?

a. `new Ellipse(300, 100, 50, 10)`

b. `new Ellipse(100, 200, 20, 40)`

c. `new Ellipse(150, 220, 60, 30)`

EX 3.18 How do you make a shape that has no fill color, so that you can see the elements behind it?

EX 3.19 Write two lines of code that move a `Group` object named `myGroup` 100 pixels to the right and 20 pixels higher on the screen.

Programming Projects

PP 3.1 Write a program that prompts for and reads the user's first and last name (separately). Then print a string composed of the first letter of the user's first name, followed by the first five characters of the user's last name, followed by a random number in the range 10 to 99. Assume that the last name is at least five letters long. Similar algorithms are sometimes used to generate usernames for new computer accounts.

PP 3.2 Write a program that prints the sum of cubes. Prompt for and read two integer values and print the sum of each value raised to the third power.

PP 3.3 Write a program that generates a random password that meets certain criteria. The password should start with 7 or 8 or 9, and the next five digits can be any digit from 0 to 9. This should be followed by a dash (-) and then three random uppercase letters. *Hint:* The integers from 65 to 90 represent the uppercase letters from A to Z. You can cast an integer to a `char` type like this: `(char)65 is 'A' and (char)66 is 'B'`.

PP 3.4 Write a program that reads a floating point value (`double`) and prints the closest whole numbers less than and greater than that value. For example, if the number is 28.466, the program would print 28 and 29.

PP 3.5 Write a program that reads the (`x, y`) coordinates for two points. Compute the distance between the two points using the following formula:

$$\text{Distance} = \sqrt{(x_2 - x_1)^2 - (y_2 - y_1)^2}$$

PP 3.6 Write a program that reads the radius of a sphere and prints its volume and surface area. Use the following formulas. Print the output to four decimal places. r represents the radius.

VideoNote
Developing a solution of PP 3.6.

$$\text{Volume} = \frac{4}{3}\pi r^3$$

$$\text{Surface Area} = 4\pi r^2$$

PP 3.7 A geometric series is a series of numbers with a constant ratio between successive terms. In order to know the nth term in this series, the formula that can be used is:

$$a_n = a_1 \cdot r^{n-1}$$

Here, a_n is the nth term, a_1 is the first term, and r is the common ratio. Write a program that accepts the first term, the common ratio, and the value n from the user, and calculates the nth term of the series.

PP 3.8 Write a program that generates a random integer in the range 20 to 40, inclusive, and displays the sine, cosine, and tangent of that number.

PP 3.9 Write a program that generates a random integer radius (r) and height (h) for a cylinder in the range 1 to 20, inclusive, and then computes the volume and surface area of the cylinder.

$$\text{Volume} = \pi r^2 h$$

$$\text{Surface Area} = 2\pi r h$$

PP 3.10 Revise the `Snowman` application in the following ways:

- Add a third button.
- Move the sun to the upper-right side of the picture.
- Display your name in the upper-left corner of the picture.
- Shift the entire snowman 40 pixels to the right.

PP 3.11 Write a JavaFX application that displays a target with three red circles and two white circles in a 500 × 500 pixels window.

PP 3.12 Write a JavaFX application that draws a city skyline at night. Show some lighted windows in the buildings and include at least three different shapes for building tops. Add a large rising full moon behind the buildings.

PP 3.13 Write a JavaFX application that draws a circle centered at point (200, 200) with a random radius in the range 50 to 150. Each time the program is run it will draw a different circle.

PP 3.14 Write a JavaFX application that displays your name rotated at a random angle (0 to 360). Each time the program is run it will draw your name at a different angle.

PP 3.15 Write a JavaFX application that displays a rectangle filled with a random color created using the `rgb` method of the `Color` class. Each time the program is run it will display a rectangle with a different color.

PP 3.16 Write a JavaFX application that displays a depiction of a solar system with a sun and three planets. Use ellipses to show the orbits of the planets around the sun.

Writing Classes

4

CHAPTER OBJECTIVES

- Discuss the structure and content of a class definition.
- Establish the concept of object state using instance data.
- Describe the effect of visibility modifiers on methods and data.
- Explore the structure of a method definition, including parameters and return values.
- Discuss the structure and purpose of a constructor.
- Define and display arc shapes.
- Load and display images.
- Introduce the concepts needed to create an interactive graphical user interface.
- Explore some basic GUI controls and event processing.

In Chapter 3, we used classes and objects for the various services they provide. That is, we used the predefined classes in the Java API that are provided to us to make the process of writing programs easier. In this chapter, we address the heart of object-oriented programming: writing our own classes to define our own objects. This chapter explores the basics of class definitions, including the structure of methods and the scope and encapsulation of data. The Graphics Track sections of this chapter discuss how to represent arcs and images, and introduce the issues necessary to create a truly interactive graphical user interface.

4.1 Classes and Objects Revisited

In Chapter 1, we introduced basic object-oriented concepts, including a brief overview of objects and classes. In Chapter 3, we used several predefined classes from the Java standard class library to create objects and use them for the particular functionality they provided.

In this chapter, we turn our attention to writing our own classes. Although existing class libraries provide many useful classes, the essence of object-oriented program development is the process of designing and implementing our own classes to suit our specific needs.

Recall the basic relationship between an object and a class: a class is a blueprint of an object. The class represents the concept of an object, and any object created from that class is a realization of that concept.

For example, from Chapter 3 we know that the `String` class represents a concept of a character string, and that each `String` object represents a particular string that contains specific characters.

Let's consider another example. Suppose a class called `Student` represents a student at a university. An object created from the `Student` class would represent a particular student. The `Student` class represents the general concept of a student, and every object created from that class represents an actual student attending the school. In a system that helps manage the business of a university, we would have one `Student` class and thousands of `Student` objects.

Recall that an object has a *state*, which is defined by the values of the *attributes* associated with that object. The attributes of a student may include the student's name, address, major, and grade point average. The `Student` class establishes that each student has these attributes. Each `Student` object stores the values of these attributes for a particular student. In Java, an object's attributes are defined by variables declared within a class.

An object also has *behaviors*, which are defined by the *operations* associated with that object. The operations of a student would include the ability to update that student's address and compute that student's current grade point average. The `Student` class defines the operations, such as the details of how a grade point average is computed. These operations can then be executed on (or by) a particular `Student` object. Note that the behaviors of an object may modify the state of that object. In Java, an object's operations are defined by methods declared within a class.

Figure 4.1 lists some examples of classes, with some attributes and operations that might be defined for objects of those classes. It's up to the program designer to determine what attributes and operations are needed, which depends on the purpose of the program and the role a particular object plays in that purpose. Consider other attributes and operations you might include for these examples.

Class	Attributes	Operations
Student	Name Address Major Grade point average	Set address Set major Compute grade point average
Rectangle	Length Width Color	Set length Set width Set color
Aquarium	Material Length Width Height	Set material Set length Set width Set height Compute volume Compute filled weight
Flight	Airline Flight number Origin city Destination city Current status	Set airline Set flight number Determine status
Employee	Name Department Title Salary	Set department Set title Set salary Compute wages Compute bonus Compute taxes

FIGURE 4.1 Examples of classes and some possible attributes and operations

SELF-REVIEW QUESTIONS *(see answers in Appendix L)*

SR 4.1 What is an attribute?

SR 4.2 What is an operation?

SR 4.3 List some attributes and operations that might be defined for a class called `Book` that represents a book in a library.

SR 4.4 True or False? Explain.

a. We should use only classes from the Java standard class library when writing our programs—there is no need to define or use other classes.
b. An operation on an object can change the state of an object.
c. The current state of an object can affect the result of an operation on that object.
d. In Java, the state of an object is represented by its methods.

4.2 Anatomy of a Class

In all of our previous examples, we've written a single class containing a single main method. These classes represent small but complete programs. These programs often instantiated objects using predefined classes from the Java class library and used those objects for the services they provide. Those predefined classes are part of the program too, but we never really concern ourselves with them other than to know how to interact with them. We simply trust them to provide the services they promise.

The RollingDice class shown in Listing 4.1 contains a main method that instantiates two Die objects (as in the singular of dice). It then rolls the dice and prints the results. It also calls several other methods provided by the Die class, such as the ability to explicitly set and get the current face value of a die.

LISTING 4.1

```
//********************************************************************
//  RollingDice.java       Author: Lewis/Loftus
//
//  Demonstrates the creation and use of a user-defined class.
//********************************************************************

public class RollingDice
{
   //-----------------------------------------------------------------
   //  Creates two Die objects and rolls them several times.
   //-----------------------------------------------------------------
   public static void main(String[] args)
   {
      Die die1, die2;
      int sum;

      die1 = new Die();
      die2 = new Die();

      die1.roll();
      die2.roll();
      System.out.println("Die One: " + die1 + ", Die Two: " + die2);

      die1.roll();
      die2.setFaceValue(4);
```

LISTING 4.1 *continued*

```
        System.out.println("Die One: " + die1 + ", Die Two: " + die2);

        sum = die1.getFaceValue() + die2.getFaceValue();
        System.out.println("Sum: " + sum);

        sum = die1.roll() + die2.roll();
        System.out.println("Die One: " + die1 + ", Die Two: " + die2);
        System.out.println("New sum: " + sum);
    }
}
```

OUTPUT

```
Die One: 5, Die Two: 2
Die One: 1, Die Two: 4
Sum: 5
Die One: 4, Die Two: 2
New sum: 6
```

The primary difference between this example and previous examples is that the `Die` class is not a predefined part of the Java class library. We have to write the `Die` class ourselves, defining the services we want `Die` objects to perform, if this program is to compile and run.

Every class can contain data declarations and method declarations, as depicted in Figure 4.2. The data declarations represent the data that will be stored in each object of the class. The method declarations define the services that those objects will provide. Collectively, the data and methods of a class are called the *members* of a class.

The classes we've written in previous examples follow this model as well, but contain no data at the class level and contain only one method (the `main` method). We'll continue to define classes like this, such as the `RollingDice` class, to define the starting point of a program.

True object-oriented programming, however, comes from defining classes that represent objects with well-defined state and behavior. For example, at any given moment a `Die` object is showing a particular face value, which we could refer to as the state of the die. A `Die` object also has various methods we can invoke on it, such as the ability to roll the die or get its face value. These methods represent the behavior of a die.

KEY CONCEPT
The heart of object-oriented programming is defining classes that represent objects with well-defined state and behavior.

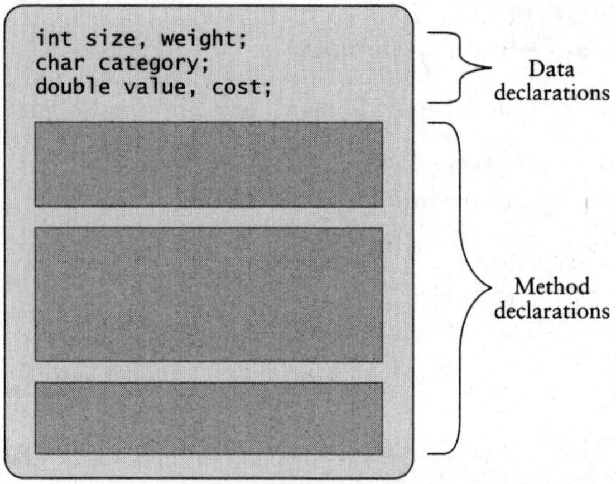

FIGURE 4.2 The members of a class: data and method declarations

The `Die` class is shown in Listing 4.2. It contains two data values: an integer constant (`MAX`) that represents the maximum face value of the die and an integer variable (`faceValue`) that represents the current face value of the die. It also contains a constructor called `Die` and four regular methods: `roll`, `setFaceValue`, `getFaceValue`, and `toString`.

You will recall from Chapters 2 and 3 that constructors are special methods that have the same name as the class. The `Die` constructor gets called when the `new` operator is used to create a new instance of the `Die` class. The rest of the methods in the `Die` class define the various services provided by `Die` objects.

VideoNote
Dissecting the `Die` class.

We use a header block of documentation to explain the purpose of each method in the class. This practice is not only crucial for anyone trying to understand the software, it also separates the code visually so that it's easy for the eye to jump from one method to the next while reading the code.

Figure 4.3 lists the methods of the `Die` class. From this point of view, it looks no different from any other class that we've used in previous examples. The only important difference is that the `Die` class was not provided for us by the Java API. We wrote it ourselves.

The methods of the `Die` class include the ability to roll the die, producing a new random face value. The `roll` method returns the new face value to the calling method, but you can also get the current face value at any time using the `getFaceValue` method. The `setFaceValue` method sets the face value explicitly, as if you had reached over and turned the die to whatever face you wanted. The `toString` method of any object gets called automatically whenever you pass the object to a `print` or `println` method to obtain a string description of the object

LISTING 4.2

```
//********************************************************************
//  Die.java       Author: Lewis/Loftus
//
//  Represents one die (singular of dice) with faces showing values
//  between 1 and 6.
//********************************************************************

public class Die
{
   private final int MAX = 6;   // maximum face value

   private int faceValue;   // current value showing on the die

   //-----------------------------------------------------------------
   //  Constructor: Sets the initial face value.
   //-----------------------------------------------------------------
   public Die()
   {
      faceValue = 1;
   }

   //-----------------------------------------------------------------
   //  Rolls the die and returns the result.
   //-----------------------------------------------------------------
   public int roll()
   {
      faceValue = (int)(Math.random() * MAX) + 1;

      return faceValue;
   }

   //-----------------------------------------------------------------
   //  Face value mutator.
   //-----------------------------------------------------------------
   public void setFaceValue(int value)
   {
      faceValue = value;
   }

   //-----------------------------------------------------------------
   //  Face value accessor.
   //-----------------------------------------------------------------
   public int getFaceValue()
```

LISTING 4.2 *continued*

```
   {
      return faceValue;
   }

   //-----------------------------------------------------------------
   //  Returns a string representation of this die.
   //-----------------------------------------------------------------
   public String toString()
   {
      String result = Integer.toString(faceValue);

      return result;
   }
}
```

to print. Therefore, it's usually a good idea to define a `toString` method for most classes. The definitions of these methods have various parts, and we'll dissect them as we proceed through this chapter.

For the examples in this book, we usually store each class in its own file. Java allows multiple classes to be stored in one file. If a file contains multiple classes, only one of those classes can be declared using the reserved word `public`. Furthermore, the name of the public class must correspond to the name of the file. For instance, class `Die` is stored in a file called `Die.java`.

`Die()`
Constructor: Sets the initial face value of the die to 1.

`int roll()`
Rolls the die by setting the face value to a random number in the appropriate range.

`void setFaceValue(int value)`
Sets the face value of the die to the specified value.

`int getFaceValue()`
Returns the current face value of the die.

`String toString()`
Returns a string representation of the die indicating its current face value.

FIGURE 4.3 Some methods of the `Die` class

Instance Data

Note that in the `Die` class, the constant `MAX` and the variable `faceValue` are declared inside the class but not inside any method. The location at which a variable is declared defines its *scope,* which is the area within a program in which that variable can be referenced. By being declared at the class level (not within a method), these variables and constants can be referenced in any method of the class.

Attributes such as the variable `faceValue` are called *instance data* because new memory space is reserved for that variable every time an instance of the class is created. Each `Die` object has its own `faceValue` variable with its own data space. That's how each `Die` object can have its own state. We see that in the output of the `RollingDice` program: one die has a face value of 5 and the other has a face value of 2. That's possible only because the memory space for the `faceValue` variable is created for each `Die` object.

KEY CONCEPT

The scope of a variable, which determines where it can be referenced, depends on where it is declared.

We can depict this situation as follows:

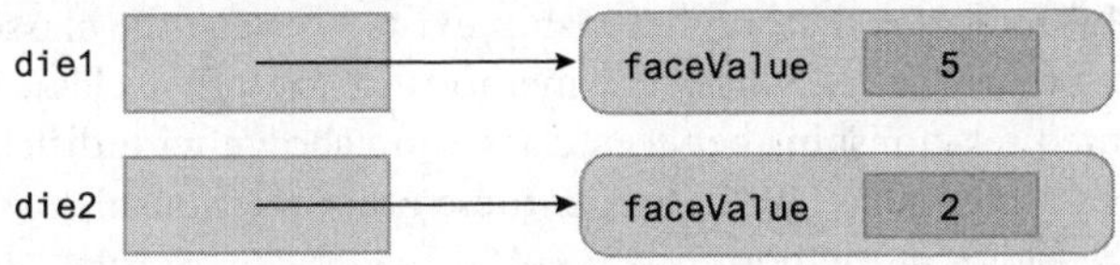

The `die1` and `die2` reference variables point to (that is, contain the address of) their respective `Die` objects. Each object contains a `faceValue` variable with its own memory space. Thus each object can store different values for its instance data.

Java automatically initializes any variables declared at the class level. For example, all variables of numeric types such as `int` and `double` are initialized to zero. However, despite the fact that the language performs this automatic initialization, it is good practice to initialize variables explicitly (usually in a constructor) so that anyone reading the code will clearly understand the intent.

UML Class Diagrams

Throughout this book, we use *UML diagrams* to visualize relationships among classes and objects. UML stands for the *Unified Modeling Language,* which has become the most popular notation for representing the design of an object-oriented program.

Several types of UML diagrams exist, each designed to show specific aspects of object-oriented programs. We focus primarily on UML *class diagrams* in this book to show the contents of classes and the relationships among them.

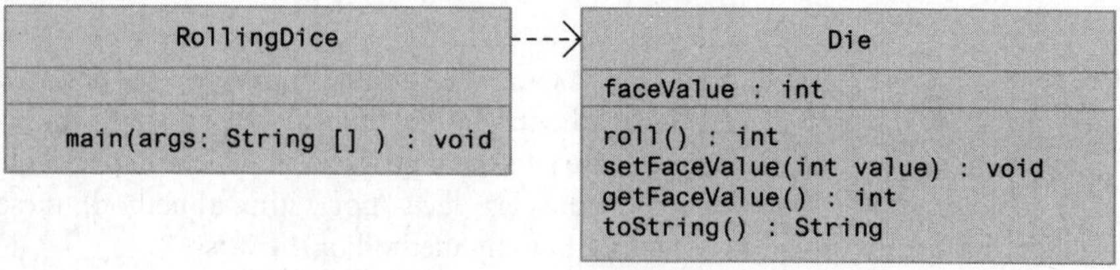

FIGURE 4.4 A UML class diagram showing the classes involved in the `RollingDice` program

KEY CONCEPT
A UML class diagram helps us visualize the contents of and relationships among the classes of a program.

In a UML diagram, each class is represented as a rectangle, possibly containing three sections to show the class name, its attributes (data), and its operations (methods). Figure 4.4 shows a class diagram containing the classes of the `RollingDice` program.

The arrow connecting the `RollingDice` and `Die` classes in Figure 4.4 indicates that a relationship exists between the classes. A dotted arrow indicates that one class *uses* the methods of the other class. Other types of object-oriented relationships between classes are shown with different types of connecting lines and arrows. We'll discuss these other relationships as we explore the appropriate topics in the book.

Keep in mind that UML is not designed specifically for Java programmers. It is intended to be language independent. Therefore, the syntax used in a UML diagram is not necessarily the same as Java. For example, the type of a variable is shown after the variable name, separated by a colon. Return types of methods are shown the same way.

UML diagrams are versatile. We can include whatever appropriate information is desired, depending on the goal of a particular diagram. We might leave out the data and method sections of a class, for instance, if those details aren't relevant for a particular diagram.

UML diagrams allow you to visualize a program's design. As our programs get larger, made up of more and more classes, these visualizations become increasingly helpful. We will explore new aspects of UML diagrams as the situation dictates.

SELF-REVIEW QUESTIONS *(see answers in Appendix L)*

SR 4.5 What is the difference between an object and a class?

SR 4.6 Describe the instance data of the `Die` class.

SR 4.7 Which of the methods defined for the `Die` class can change the state of a `Die` object—that is, which of the methods assign values to the instance data?

SR 4.8 What happens when you pass an object to a `print` or `println` method?

SR 4.9 What is the scope of a variable?

SR 4.10 What are UML diagrams designed to do?

4.3 Encapsulation

We mentioned in our overview of object-oriented concepts in Chapter 1 that an object should be *self-governing*. That is, the instance data of an object should be modified only by that object. For example, the methods of the `Die` class should be solely responsible for changing the value of the `faceValue` variable. We should make it difficult, if not impossible, for code outside of a class to "reach in" and change the value of a variable that is declared inside that class. This characteristic is called *encapsulation*.

An object should be encapsulated from the rest of the system. It should interact with other parts of a program only through the specific set of methods that define the services that that object provides. These methods define the *interface* between that object and the program that uses it.

KEY CONCEPT

An object should be encapsulated, guarding its data from inappropriate access.

Encapsulation is depicted graphically in Figure 4.5. The code that uses an object, sometimes called the *client* of an object, should not be allowed to access variables directly. The client should call an object's methods, and those methods then interact with the data encapsulated within the object. For example, the `main` method in the `RollingDice` program calls the `roll` method of the `Die` objects. The `main` method should not (and in fact cannot) access the `faceValue` variable directly.

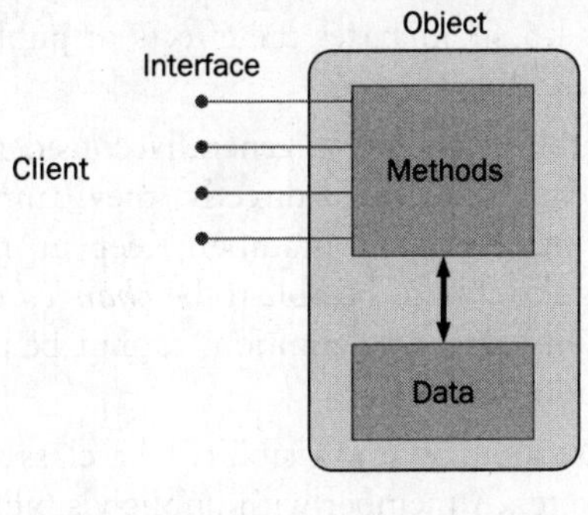

FIGURE 4.5 A client interacting with the methods of an object

In Java, we accomplish object encapsulation using *modifiers*. A *modifier* is a Java reserved word that is used to specify particular characteristics of a programming language construct. In Chapter 2, we discussed the `final` modifier, which is used to declare a constant. Java has several modifiers that can be used in various ways. Some modifiers can be used together, but some combinations are invalid. We discuss various Java modifiers at appropriate points throughout this book, and all of them are summarized in Appendix E.

Visibility Modifiers

Some of the Java modifiers are called *visibility modifiers* because they control access to the members of a class. The reserved words `public` and `private` are visibility modifiers that can be applied to the variables and methods of a class. If a member of a class has *public visibility,* it can be directly referenced from outside of the object. If a member of a class has *private visibility,* it can be used anywhere inside the class definition but cannot be referenced externally. A third visibility modifier, `protected`, is relevant only in the context of inheritance. We discuss it in Chapter 9.

KEY CONCEPT

Instance variables should be declared with private visibility to promote encapsulation.

Public variables violate encapsulation. They allow code external to the class in which the data is defined to reach in and access or modify the value of the data. Therefore, instance data should be defined with private visibility. Data that is declared as `private` can be accessed only by the methods of the class.

The visibility we apply to a method depends on the purpose of that method. Methods that provide services to the client must be declared with public visibility so that they can be invoked by the client. These methods are sometimes referred to as *service methods*. A `private` method cannot be invoked from outside the class. The only purpose of a `private` method is to help the other methods of the class do their job. Therefore, they are sometimes referred to as *support methods.*

The table in Figure 4.6 summarizes the effects of public and private visibility on both variables and methods.

Giving constants public visibility is generally considered acceptable because, although their values can be accessed directly, they cannot be changed because they were declared using the `final` modifier. Keep in mind that encapsulation means that data values should not be able to be *changed* directly by another part of the code. Because constants, by definition, cannot be changed, the encapsulation issue is largely moot.

UML class diagrams can show the visibility of a class member by preceding it with a particular character. A member with public visibility is preceded by a plus sign (+), and a member with private visibility is preceded by a minus sign (–).

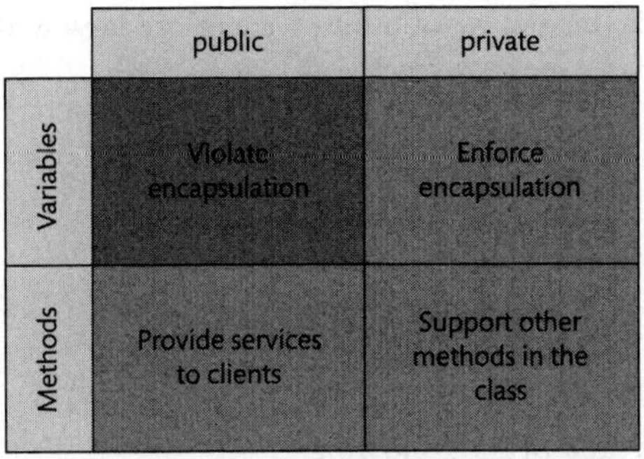

FIGURE 4.6 The effects of public and private visibility

Accessors and Mutators

Because instance data is generally declared with private visibility, a class usually provides services to access and modify data values. A method such as `getFaceValue` is called an *accessor method* because it provides read-only access to a particular value. Likewise, a method such as `setFaceValue` is called a *mutator method* because it changes a particular value.

KEY CONCEPT
Most objects contain accessor and mutator methods to allow the client to manage data in a controlled manner.

Often, accessor method names have the form `getX`, where `X` is the value to which it provides access. Likewise, mutator method names have the form `setX`, where `X` is the value they are setting. Therefore, these types of methods are sometimes referred to as "getters" and "setters."

For example, if a class contains the instance variable `height`, it might also contain the methods `getHeight` and `setHeight`. Note that this naming convention capitalizes the first letter of the variable when used in the method names, which is consistent with how method names are written in general.

Some methods may provide accessor and/or mutator capabilities as a side effect of their primary purpose. For example, the `roll` method of the `Die` class changes the `faceValue` of the die and returns that new value as well. Therefore, `roll` is also a mutator method.

Note that the code of the `roll` method is careful to keep the face value of the die in the valid range (1 to `MAX`). Service methods must be carefully designed to permit only appropriate access and valid changes. This points out a flaw in the design of the `Die` class: there is no restriction on the `setFaceValue` method—a client could use it to set the die value to a number such as 20, which is outside the valid range. The code of the `setFaceValue` method should allow only valid modifications to the face value of a die. We explore how that kind of control can be accomplished in the next chapter.

SELF-REVIEW QUESTIONS *(see answers in Appendix L)*

SR 4.11 Objects should be self-governing. Explain.

SR 4.12 What is the interface to an object?

SR 4.13 What is a modifier?

SR 4.14 Why might a constant be given public visibility?

SR 4.15 Describe each of the following:

a. public method
b. private method
c. public variable
d. private variable

4.4 Anatomy of a Method

We've seen that a class is composed of data declarations and method declarations. Let's examine method declarations in more detail.

As we stated in Chapter 1, a method is a group of programming language statements that is given a name. A *method declaration* specifies the code that is executed when the method is invoked. Every method in a Java program is part of a particular class.

When a method is called, the flow of control transfers to that method. One by one, the statements of that method are executed. When that method is done, control returns to the location where the call was made and execution continues.

The *called method* (the one that is invoked) might be part of the same class as the *calling method* that invoked it. If the called method is part of the same class, only the method name is needed to invoke it. If it is part of a different class, it is invoked through the name of an object of that other class, as we've seen many times. Figure 4.7 shows the flow of execution as methods are called.

We've defined the `main` method of a program many times in previous examples. Its definition follows the same syntax as all methods. The header of a method includes the type of the return value, the method name, and a list of parameters that the method accepts. The statements that make up the body of the method are defined in a block delimited by braces. The rest of this section discusses issues related to method declarations in more detail.

Method Declaration

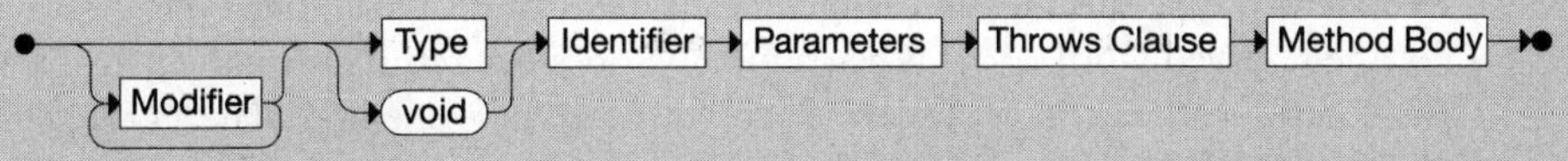

Parameters

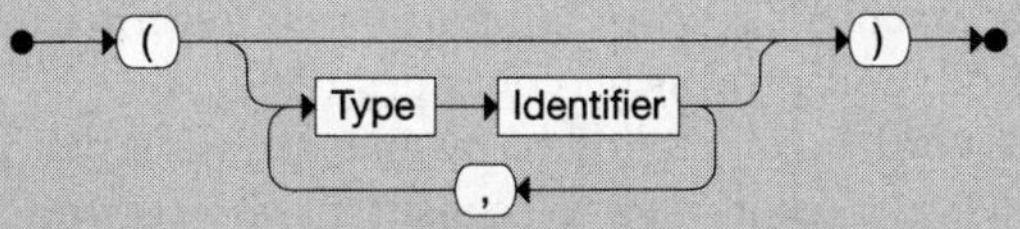

A method is defined by optional modifiers, followed by a return Type, followed by an Identifier that determines the method name, followed by a list of Parameters, followed by the Method Body. The return Type indicates the type of value that will be returned by the method, which may be `void`. The Method Body is a block of statements that executes when the method is invoked. The Throws Clause is optional and indicates the exceptions that may be thrown by this method.

Example:

```
public void instructions(int count)
{
   System.out.println("Follow all instructions.");
   System.out.println("Use no more than " + count +
                      " turns.");
}
```

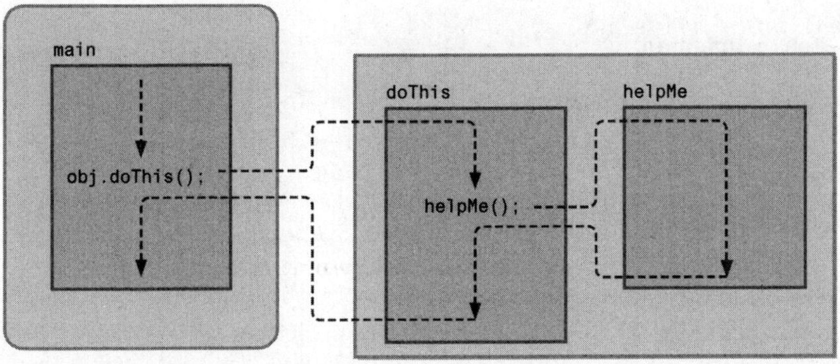

FIGURE 4.7 The flow of control following method invocations

The `return` Statement

The return type specified in the method header can be a primitive type, class name, or the reserved word `void`. When a method does not return any value, `void` is used as the return type, as is always done with the `main` method. The `setFaceValue` method of the `Die` class also has a return type of `void`.

A method that returns a value must have a *return statement*. When a `return` statement is executed, control is immediately returned to the statement in the calling method, and processing continues there. A `return` statement consists of the reserved word `return` followed by an expression that dictates the value to be returned. The expression must be consistent with the return type in the method header.

The `getFaceValue` method of the `Die` class returns an `int` value that represents the current value of the die. The `roll` method does the same, returning the new value to which `faceValue` was just randomly set. The `toString` method returns a `String` object.

KEY CONCEPT
The value returned from a method must be consistent with the return type specified in the method header.

A method that does not return a value does not usually contain a `return` statement. The method automatically returns to the calling method when the end of the method is reached. Such methods may contain a `return` statement without an expression.

It is usually not good practice to use more than one `return` statement in a method, even though it is possible to do so. In general, a method should have one `return` statement as the last line of the method body, unless that makes the method overly complex.

The value that is returned from a method can be ignored in the calling method. For example, in the `main` method of the `RollingDice` class, the value that is

Return Statement

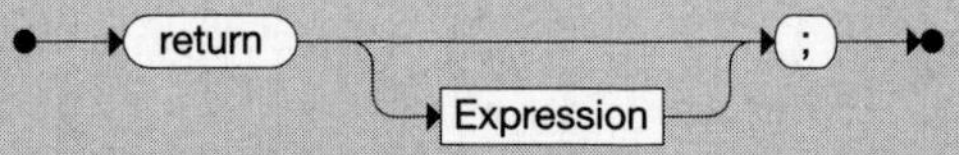

A `return` statement consists of the `return` reserved word followed by an optional Expression. When executed, control is immediately returned to the calling method, returning the value defined by Expression.

Examples:

```
return;
return distance * 4;
```

returned from the `roll` method is ignored in several calls, while in others the return value is used in a calculation.

Constructors do not have a return type (not even `void`) and therefore cannot return a value. We discuss constructors in more detail later in this chapter.

Parameters

As we defined in Chapter 2, a parameter is a value that is passed into a method when it is invoked. The *parameter list* in the header of a method specifies the types of the values that are passed and the names by which the called method will refer to those values.

The names of the parameters in the header of the method declaration are called *formal parameters.* In an invocation, the values passed into a method are called *actual parameters.* The actual parameters are also called the *arguments* to the method.

A method invocation and definition always give the parameter list in parentheses after the method name. If there are no parameters, an empty set of parentheses is used, as is the case in the `roll` and `getFaceValue` methods. The `Die` constructor also takes no parameters, although constructors often do.

The formal parameters are identifiers that serve as variables inside the method and whose initial values come from the actual parameters in the invocation. When a method is called, the value in each actual parameter is copied and stored in the corresponding formal parameter. Actual parameters can be literals, variables, or full expressions. If an expression is used as an actual parameter, it is fully evaluated before the method call and the result is passed as the parameter.

KEY CONCEPT
When a method is called, the actual parameters are copied into the formal parameters.

The only method in the `Die` class that accepts any parameters is the `setFaceValue` method, which accepts a single `int` parameter. The formal parameter name is `value`. In the `main` method, the value of 4 is passed into it as the actual parameter.

The parameter lists in the invocation and the method declaration must match up. That is, the value of the first actual parameter is copied into the first formal parameter, the second actual parameter into the second formal parameter, and so on, as shown in Figure 4.8. The types of the actual parameters must be consistent with the specified types of the formal parameters.

Other details regarding parameter passing are discussed in Chapter 7.

Local Data

As we described earlier in this chapter, the scope of a variable or constant is the part of a program in which a valid reference to that variable can be made.

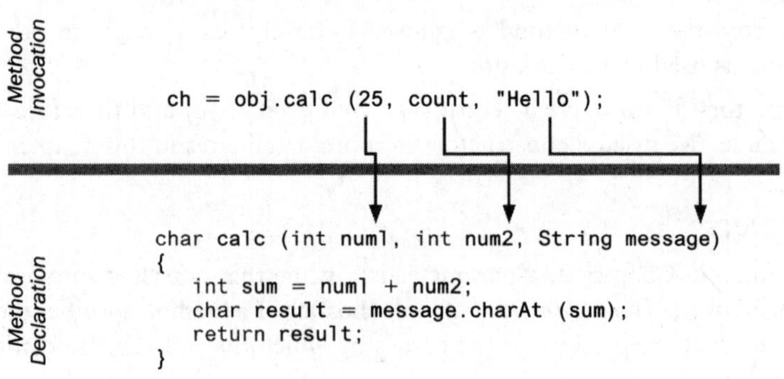

FIGURE 4.8 Passing parameters from the method invocation to the declaration

A variable can be declared inside a method, making it *local data* as opposed to instance data. Recall that instance data is declared in a class but not inside any particular method.

> **KEY CONCEPT**
> A variable declared in a method is local to that method and cannot be used outside of it.

Local data has scope limited to only the method in which it is declared. The variable `result` declared in the `toString` method of the `Die` class is local data. Any reference to `result` in any other method of the `Die` class would have caused the compiler to issue an error message. A local variable simply does not exist outside of the method in which it is declared. On the other hand, instance data, declared at the class level, has a scope of the entire class; any method of the class can refer to it.

Because local data and instance data operate at different levels of scope, it's possible to declare a local variable inside a method with the same name as an instance variable declared at the class level. Referring to that name in the method will reference the local version of the variable. This naming practice obviously has the potential to confuse anyone reading the code, so it should be avoided.

The formal parameter names in a method header serve as local data for that method. They don't exist until the method is called, and they cease to exist when the method is exited. For example, the formal parameter `value` in the `setFaceValue` method comes into existence when the method is called and goes out of existence when the method finishes executing.

Bank Account Example

Let's look at another example of a class and its use. The `Transactions` class shown in Listing 4.3 contains a `main` method that creates a few `Account` objects and invokes their services.

LISTING 4.3

```
//********************************************************************
//  Transactions.java       Author: Lewis/Loftus
//
//  Demonstrates the creation and use of multiple Account objects.
//********************************************************************

public class Transactions
{
   //-----------------------------------------------------------------
   //  Creates some bank accounts and requests various services.
   //-----------------------------------------------------------------
   public static void main(String[] args)
   {
      Account acct1 = new Account("Ted Murphy", 72354, 102.56);
      Account acct2 = new Account("Jane Smith", 69713, 40.00);
      Account acct3 = new Account("Edward Demsey", 93757, 759.32);

      acct1.deposit(25.85);

      double smithBalance = acct2.deposit(500.00);
      System.out.println("Smith balance after deposit: " +
                         smithBalance);

      System.out.println("Smith balance after withdrawal: " +
                         acct2.withdraw (430.75, 1.50));

      acct1.addInterest();
      acct2.addInterest();
      acct3.addInterest();

      System.out.println();
      System.out.println(acct1);
      System.out.println(acct2);
      System.out.println(acct3);
   }
}
```

OUTPUT

```
Smith balance after deposit: 540.0
Smith balance after withdrawal: 107.75

72354   Ted Murphy       $132.90
69713   Jane Smith       $111.52
93757   Edward Demsey    $785.90
```

VideoNote
Discussion of the `Account` class.

The `Account` class, shown in Listing 4.4, represents a basic bank account. It contains instance data representing the account number, the account's current balance, and the name of the account's owner. Note that instance data can be an object reference variable (not just a primitive type), such as the account owner's name, which is a reference to a `String` object. The interest rate for the account is stored as a constant.

The constructor of the `Account` class accepts three parameters that are used to initialize the instance data. The `deposit` and `withdraw` methods perform the basic

LISTING 4.4

```
//********************************************************************
//  Account.java       Author: Lewis/Loftus
//
//  Represents a bank account with basic services such as deposit
//  and withdraw.
//********************************************************************

import java.text.NumberFormat;

public class Account
{
   private final double RATE = 0.035;   // interest rate of 3.5%

   private long acctNumber;
   private double balance;
   private String name;

   //-----------------------------------------------------------------
   // Sets up the account by defining its owner, account number,
   // and initial balance.
   //-----------------------------------------------------------------
   public Account(String owner, long account, double initial)
   {
      name = owner;
      acctNumber = account;
      balance = initial;
   }

   //-----------------------------------------------------------------
   //  Deposits the specified amount into the account. Returns the
   //  new balance.
   //-----------------------------------------------------------------
   public double deposit(double amount)
```

LISTING 4.4 *continued*

```
   {
      balance = balance + amount;
      return balance;
   }

   //-----------------------------------------------------------------
   //  Withdraws the specified amount from the account and applies
   //  the fee. Returns the new balance.
   //-----------------------------------------------------------------
   public double withdraw(double amount, double fee)
   {
      balance = balance - amount - fee;

      return balance;
   }

   //-----------------------------------------------------------------
   //  Adds interest to the account and returns the new balance.
   //-----------------------------------------------------------------
   public double addInterest()
   {
      balance += (balance * RATE);
      return balance;
   }

   //-----------------------------------------------------------------
   //  Returns the current balance of the account.
   //-----------------------------------------------------------------
   public double getBalance()
   {
      return balance;
   }
   //-----------------------------------------------------------------
   //  Returns a one-line description of the account as a string.
   //-----------------------------------------------------------------
   public String toString()
   {
      NumberFormat fmt = NumberFormat.getCurrencyInstance();
      return acctNumber + "\t" + name + "\t" + fmt.format(balance);
   }
}
```

transactions on the account, adjusting the balance based on the parameters. There is also an `addInterest` method that updates the balance by adding in the interest earned. These methods represent valid ways to change the balance, so a classic mutator such as `setBalance` is not provided.

The status of the three `Account` objects just after they were created in the `Transactions` program could be depicted as follows:

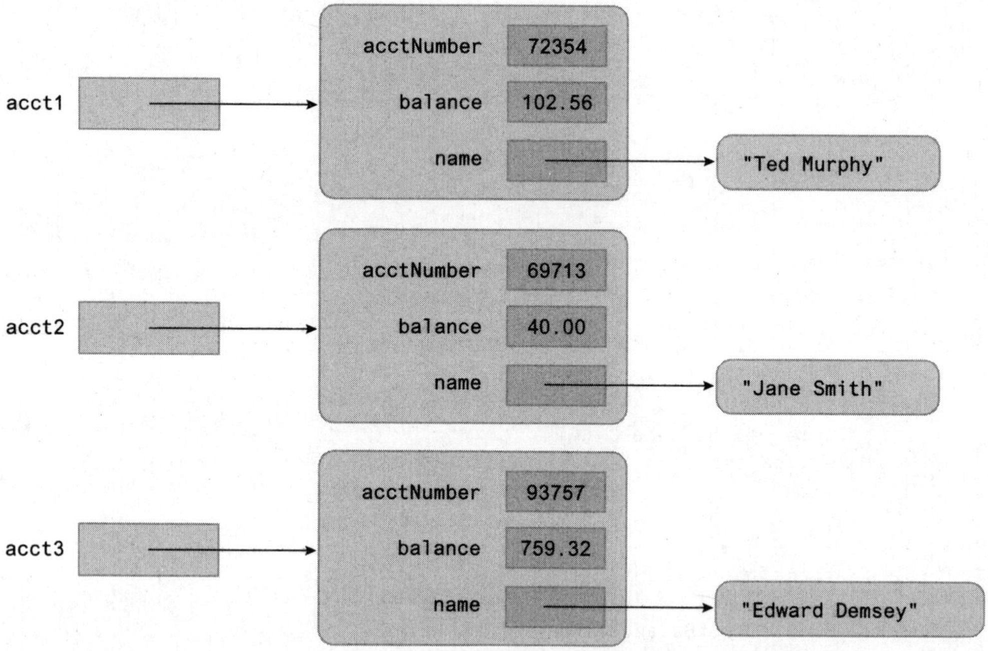

The various methods that update the balance of the account could be more rigorously designed. Checks should be made to ensure that the parameter values are valid, such as preventing the withdrawal of a negative amount (which would essentially be a deposit). This processing is discussed in the next chapter.

SELF-REVIEW QUESTIONS *(see answers in Appendix L)*

SR 4.16 Why is a method invoked through (or on) a particular object? What is the exception to that rule?

SR 4.17 What does it mean for a method to return a value?

SR 4.18 What does the `return` statement do?

SR 4.19 Is a `return` statement required?

SR 4.20 Explain the difference between an actual parameter and a formal parameter.

SR 4.21 Write a method called `getFaceDown` for the `Die` class that returns the current "face down" value of the die. *Hint:* On a standard die, the sum of any two opposite faces is seven.

SR 4.22 In the `Transactions` program:

a. How many `Account` objects are created?
b. How many arguments (actual parameters) are passed to the `withdraw` method when it is invoked on the `acct2` object?
c. How many arguments (actual parameters) are passed to the `addInterest` method when it is invoked on the `acct3` object?

SR 4.23 Which of the `Account` class methods would you classify as accessor methods? As mutator methods? As service methods?

4.5 Constructors Revisited

As we stated in Chapter 2, a constructor is similar to a method that is invoked when an object is instantiated. When we define a class, we usually define a constructor to help us set up the class. In particular, we often use a constructor to initialize the variables associated with each object.

A constructor differs from a regular method in two ways. First, the name of a constructor is the same name as the class. Therefore, the name of the constructor in the `Die` class is `Die`, and the name of the constructor in the `Account` class is `Account`. Second, a constructor cannot return a value and does not have a return type specified in the method header.

KEY CONCEPT
A constructor cannot have any return type, even `void`.

A common mistake made by programmers is to put a `void` return type on a constructor. As far as the compiler is concerned, putting any return type on a constructor, even `void`, turns it into a regular method that happens to have the same name as the class. As such, it cannot be invoked as a constructor. This leads to error messages that are sometimes difficult to decipher.

Generally, a constructor is used to initialize the newly instantiated object. For instance, the constructor of the `Die` class sets the face value of the die to 1 initially. The constructor of the `Account` class sets the values of the instance variables to the values passed in as parameters to the constructor.

We don't have to define a constructor for every class. Each class has a *default constructor* that takes no parameters. The default constructor is used if we don't provide our own. This default constructor generally has no effect on the newly created object.

SELF-REVIEW QUESTIONS *(see answers in Appendix L)*

SR 4.24 What are constructors used for?

SR 4.25 How are constructors defined?

4.6 Arcs

In Chapter 3, we explored how to define and display basic shapes such as lines, rectangles, circles, and ellipses. Let's add arcs to this list.

In JavaFX, an arc can be thought of as a portion of an ellipse. The constructor of the `Arc` class can take six parameters. The first four match the parameters of an ellipse, specifying the center (x, y) point of the ellipse, and the radius lengths along the x and y axes, which give the ellipse (and thus the arc) its shape.

KEY CONCEPT
An arc is defined as a portion of an ellipse.

The last two parameters of the `Arc` constructor specify the *start angle* of the arc (where it begins relative to the horizontal) and the *arc length*. Both the start angle and arc length are measured in degrees.

For example:

```
Arc myArc = new Arc(150, 100, 70, 30, 45, 90);
```

That line of code creates an arc whose underlying ellipse is centered at (150, 100), has a horizontal radius of 70 and a vertical radius of 30, begins at 45 degrees, and continues for another 90 degrees (counterclockwise):

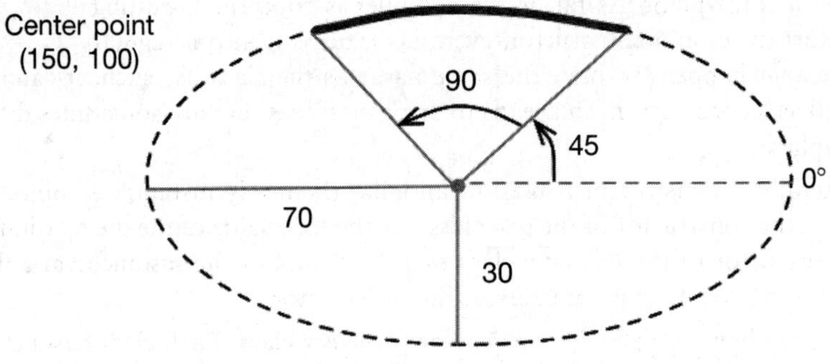

Arc Type	Description
ArcType.OPEN	The curve formed by the specified portion of the ellipse.
ArcType.CHORD	An arc whose end points are connected by a straight line.
ArcType.ROUND	An arc whose end points are connected to the center point of the specified ellipse, forming a "pie" shape with a rounded edge.

FIGURE 4.9 JavaFX arc types

An arc also has an *arc type*, as defined by values of the `ArcType` enumerated type, listed in Figure 4.9.

Listing 4.5 shows a JavaFX program that creates and displays three arcs, one of each type, all defined using the same underlying ellipse.

LISTING 4.5

```
import javafx.application.Application;
import javafx.scene.Scene;
import javafx.scene.Group;
import javafx.scene.paint.Color;
import javafx.scene.shape.Arc;
import javafx.scene.shape.ArcType;
import javafx.scene.shape.Ellipse;
import javafx.stage.Stage;

//************************************************************************
//  ArcDisplay.java       Author: Lewis/Loftus
//
//  Demonstrates the use of the JavaFX Arc class.
//************************************************************************

public class ArcDisplay extends Application
{
    //--------------------------------------------------------------------
    //  Draws three arcs based on the same underlying ellipse.
    //--------------------------------------------------------------------
    public void start(Stage primaryStage)
    {
        Ellipse backgroundEllipse = new Ellipse(250, 150, 170, 100);
        backgroundEllipse.setFill(null);
        backgroundEllipse.setStroke(Color.GRAY);
        backgroundEllipse.getStrokeDashArray().addAll(5.0, 5.0);
```

LISTING 4.5 *continued*

```
        Arc arc1 = new Arc(250, 150, 170, 100, 90, 90);
        arc1.setType(ArcType.OPEN);
        arc1.setStroke(Color.RED);
        arc1.setFill(null);

        Arc arc2 = new Arc(250, 150, 170, 100, 20, 50);
        arc2.setType(ArcType.ROUND);
        arc2.setStroke(Color.GREEN);
        arc2.setFill(Color.GREEN);

        Arc arc3 = new Arc(250, 150, 170, 100, 230, 130);
        arc3.setType(ArcType.CHORD);
        arc3.setStroke(Color.BLUE);
        arc3.setFill(null);

        Group root = new Group(backgroundEllipse, arc1, arc2, arc3);
        Scene scene = new Scene(root, 500, 300, Color.LIGHTYELLOW);

        primaryStage.setTitle("Arc Display");
        primaryStage.setScene(scene);
        primaryStage.show();
    }
}
```

DISPLAY

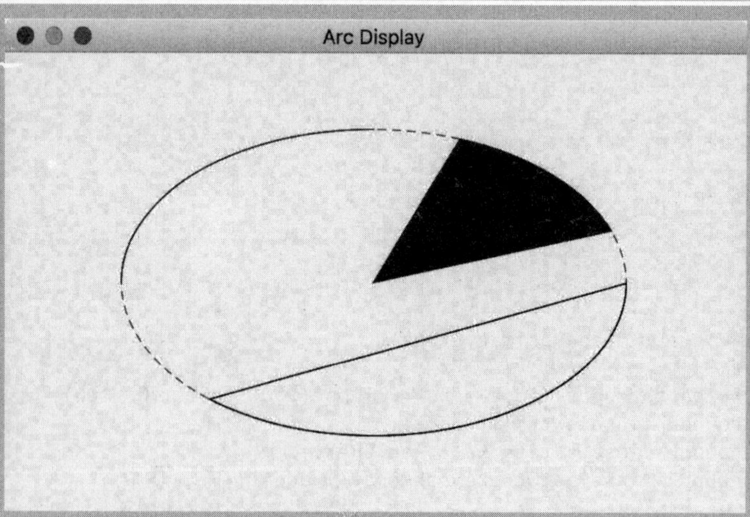

The first arc (red) is an open arc that follows the top left curve of the ellipse, starting at 90 degrees and sweeping for 90 degrees. This arc is unfilled, so it simply follows the ellipse outline. All else being equal, a filled open arc and a filled chord arc are visually the same.

The second (green) arc is a filled round arc, forming a skewed pie shape. It starts at 20 degrees above the horizontal and sweeps for 50 degrees.

The third (blue) arc is an unfilled chord arc, so the outline shows the connection between the two end points of the arc, which starts at 230 degrees and has a length of 130 degrees.

The start angle or the arc length could be specified using negative values. If negative, the angle is measured clockwise instead of counterclockwise. Here's an alternative way to specify the red open arc from the example:

KEY CONCEPT

Positive start angles and lengths are measured counterclockwise. Negative values are measured clockwise.

```
Arc arc1 = new Arc(250, 150, 170, 100, -180, -90);
```

SELF-REVIEW QUESTIONS *(see answers in Appendix L)*

SR 4.26 What is the relationship between an ellipse and an arc?

SR 4.27 Which type of arc is used to display a "pie" shape? A simple curve?

SR 4.28 What start angle and arc length would you specify to include the complete bottom half of the underlying ellipse? What alternative values could you use?

4.7 Images

An `Image` object represents a graphical image and supports loading an image from a file or URL. Supported formats include jpeg, gif, and png.

An `ImageView` is a JavaFX node that is used to display an `Image` object. An `Image` cannot be added directly to a container.

KEY CONCEPT

An image is represented by an `Image` object but is displayed using an `ImageView` object.

The program in Listing 4.6 displays an image (using an image view) centered in a window.

LISTING 4.6

```
import javafx.application.Application;
import javafx.scene.Scene;
import javafx.scene.image.Image;
import javafx.scene.image.ImageView;
import javafx.scene.layout.StackPane;
import javafx.stage.Stage;
```

LISTING 4.6 *continued*

```
//********************************************************************
//  ImageDisplay.java       Author: Lewis/Loftus
//
//  Demonstrates a the use of Image and ImageView objects.
//********************************************************************

public class ImageDisplay extends Application
{
    //-----------------------------------------------------------------
    //  Displays an image centered in a window.
    //-----------------------------------------------------------------
    public void start(Stage primaryStage)
    {
        Image img = new Image("gull.jpg");
        ImageView imgView = new ImageView(img);

        StackPane pane = new StackPane(imgView);
        pane.setStyle("-fx-background-color: cornsilk");

        Scene scene = new Scene(pane, 500, 350);

        primaryStage.setTitle("Image Display");
        primaryStage.setScene(scene);
        primaryStage.show();
    }
}
```

DISPLAY

Unlike previous JavaFX examples, which used a `Group` object as the root node of the scene, this program displays the image in a `StackPane` object. The `StackPane` class is one of several *layout panes* provided with the JavaFX API. A layout pane is a container that governs how controls are arranged and presented visually. A layout pane adjusts the presentation whenever needed, such as when the window is resized.

KEY CONCEPT

A layout pane is a JavaFX container that manages the visual arrangement of the nodes in a particular way.

The nodes in a `StackPane` are stacked on top of each other. For example, you might use a `StackPane` to overlay text on top of a shape. In this example, the `ImageView` object is the only node added to the pane, so it simply serves to keep the image centered in the window. We'll explore other layout panes as needed in upcoming examples and an overview of JavaFX layout panes is presented in Appendix G.

A call to the `setStyle` method of the `StackPane` is used to set the background color of the pane. In previous examples, we've set the background color of the scene itself, but layout panes have their own background color. The `setStyle` method accepts a string that can specify many style properties. JavaFX style properties are modelled after cascading style sheets (CSS), which are used to define the look of HTML elements on a Web page. JavaFX style property names begin with the prefix "-fx-".

The parameter to the `Image` constructor can be a pathname relative to the Java class directory. For example, the following line of code specifies an image in the directory `myPix`:

```
Image logo = new Image("myPix/smallLogo.png");
```

The image can also be obtained from a URL:

```
Image logo = new Image("http://example.com/images/bio.jpg");
```

If a URL is specified, the protocol (such as http://) must be included.

Viewports

A *viewport* is a rectangular area that can be used to restrict the pixels displayed in an `ImageView`. For example:

```
imgView.setViewport(new Rectangle2D(200, 80, 70, 60));
```

If this line was added to the `ImageDisplay` program, the following portion of the image would be visible:

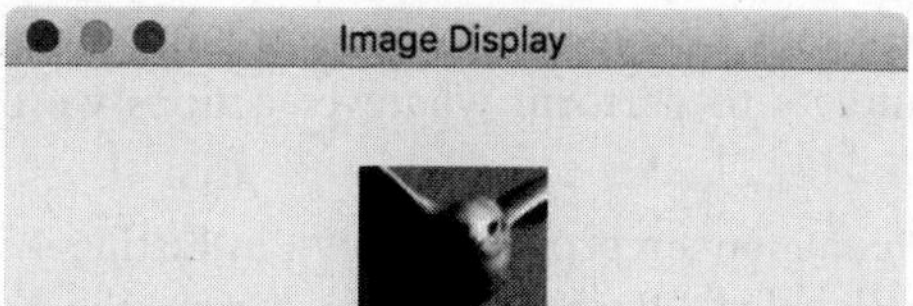

A viewport does not change the underlying image in any way and can be updated programmatically as needed.

SELF-REVIEW QUESTIONS *(see answers in Appendix L)*

SR 4.29 What is the difference between an `Image` and an `ImageView`?

SR 4.30 What is a layout pane?

SR 4.31 How are style properties set for JavaFX nodes?

4.8 Graphical User Interfaces

Unlike a text-based program, or even a graphical program with no interaction, a program that has a graphical user interface (GUI) provides a heightened level of user interaction that often makes a program more effective and interesting.

Three kinds of objects cooperate to create a graphical user interface in JavaFX:

- controls
- events
- event handlers

A GUI *control* is a screen element that displays information and/or allows the user to interact with a program in a certain way. Examples of GUI controls include buttons, text fields, scroll bars, and sliders.

An *event* is an object that represents some occurrence in which we may be interested. Often, event corresponds to user actions, such as processing a mouse button or typing a key on the keyboard. GUI controls generate events to indicate a user action related to that control. For example, a button control will generate an event to indicate that the button has been pushed. A program that is oriented around a GUI, responding to events from the user, is called *event-driven*.

KEY CONCEPT
A GUI is made up of controls, events that represent user actions, and handlers that process those events.

An *event handler* is an object that contains a method that is called when an event occurs. The programmer sets up the relationship between the component that generates an event and the handler that will respond to the event.

For the most part, we will use controls and events that are predefined in the JavaFX API. To set up a GUI program, we present and tailor the necessary controls and provide handlers to perform whatever actions we desire when events occur.

For example, the `PushCounter` program shown in Listing 4.7 presents the user with a single button (labeled "Push Me!"). Each time the button is pushed, a counter is updated and displayed.

LISTING 4.7

```
import javafx.application.Application;
import javafx.event.ActionEvent;
import javafx.geometry.Pos;
import javafx.scene.Scene;
import javafx.scene.control.Button;
import javafx.scene.text.Text;
import javafx.scene.layout.FlowPane;
import javafx.stage.Stage;

//********************************************************************
//  PushCounter.java       Author: Lewis/Loftus
//
//  Demonstrates JavaFX buttons and event handlers.
//********************************************************************

public class PushCounter extends Application
{
   private int count;
   private Text countText;

   //-----------------------------------------------------------------
   //  Presents a GUI containing a button and a label that displays
   //  how many times the button is pushed.
   //-----------------------------------------------------------------
   public void start(Stage primaryStage)
   {
      count = 0;
      countText = new Text("Pushes: 0");

      Button push = new Button("Push Me!");
      push.setOnAction(this::processButtonPress);

      FlowPane pane = new FlowPane(push, countText);
      pane.setAlignment(Pos.CENTER);
      pane.setHgap(20);
      pane.setStyle("-fx-background-color: cyan");

      Scene scene = new Scene(pane, 300, 100);

      primaryStage.setTitle("Push Counter");
      primaryStage.setScene(scene);
      primaryStage.show();
   }
```

LISTING 4.7 *continued*

```
    //-----------------------------------------------------------------
    //  Updates the counter and label when the button is pushed.
    //-----------------------------------------------------------------
    public void processButtonPress(ActionEvent event)
    {
        count++;
        countText.setText("Pushes: " + count);
    }
}
```

DISPLAY

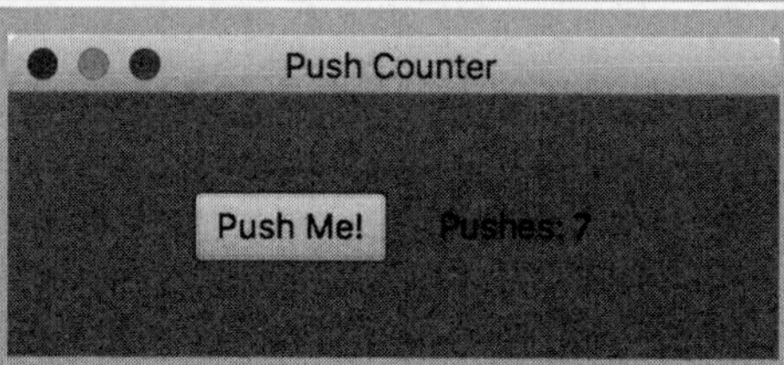

This program displays a `Button` object and a `Text` object. The `Button` class represents a push button that allows the user to initiate an action with a mouse click. The `Button` constructor accepts a `String` parameter that specifies the text shown on the button.

A `Button` object generates an *action event* when it is pushed. The button's `setOnAction` method is used to specify the event handler for the button.

The `::` operator is used to specify a *method reference*, which are new as of Java 8. In this example, the method reference refers to the `processButtonPress` method in this class (the same one as the `start` method). The `this` reference refers to the object that is currently executing the method. So in this example the `PushCounter` class itself serves as the event handler for the button. There are other ways to specify the event handler relationship, which are discussed later in this section.

The `processButtonPress` method increments the counter variable and updates the text displayed. Note that the counter and the `Text` object are declared as instance data (at the class level), so that they can be referenced in both methods in the class.

The `Button` and `Text` controls are added to a `FlowPane`, which is used as the root node of the scene. The `FlowPane` class is a layout pane, similar to the

StackPane used in the previous section. The nodes in a FlowPane are laid out horizontally in rows (which is the default) or vertically in columns. When there is no more room, the next node in the pane flows into the next row or column. In this example, the button and text are arranged horizontally, centered, with a gap of 20 pixels. An overview of JavaFX layout panes is presented in Appendix G.

By the way, the Text object used in this program could be replaced with a Label control to create a similar effect. Labels, however, are most appropriately used when labelling other controls, providing advanced keyboard navigation. Labels have many style properties that Text objects don't have and can also contain images. In this example, a Text object is sufficient.

Alternate Ways to Specify Event Handlers

The PushCounter program used a method reference to define the event handler for the action event generated by the Button object. Let's look at other ways to define an event handler.

An event handler is actually an object that implements the EventHandler interface. An *interface* is a list of methods that the implementing class must define. (Interfaces are discussed in more detail in Chapter 7.) In this case, the EventHandler interface requires an object to define a method called handle to process the event. So an alternative approach to creating an event handler is to define a full class that implements the EventHandler interface, perhaps as a private inner class within the PushCounter class:

```
private class ButtonHandler implements EventHandler<ActionEvent>
{
    public void handle(ActionEvent event)
    {
        count++;
        countText.setText("Pushes: " + count);
    }
}
```

Then the call to setOnAction for the button could specify such an object:

```
push.setOnAction(new ButtonHandler());
```

Instead of defining a separate class, the event handler could also be defined using a *lambda expression*:

```
push.setOnAction((event) -> {
    count++;
    countText.setText("Pushes: " + count);
});
```

A lambda expression is defined by a set of parameters in parentheses, the -> arrow operator, followed by an expression. If one expression is insufficient, a block is used. So the lambda expression in this example accepts the event object, which is passed to a block that contains our handler code.

A lambda expression can be used whenever an object of a *functional interface* is required. A functional interface is one that contains a single abstract method. The `EventHandler` interface is a functional interface.

The method reference approach used in the `PushCounter` program is equivalent to a lambda expression that supplies the parameter to the method. So `this::processButtonPress` is equivalent to `event -> processButtonPress(event)`.

We find the method reference approach to be the cleanest and easiest to follow, so we will usually use that approach in our examples.

SELF-REVIEW QUESTIONS *(see answers in Appendix L)*

SR 4.32 What is the relationship among GUI controls, events, and event handlers?

SR 4.33 What type of event does a `Button` object generate when it is pushed?

SR 4.34 Summarize the three techniques for defining a JavaFX event handler.

SR 4.35 What is a `FlowPane`?

4.9 Text Fields

A *text field* allows the user to enter one line of text that can be used by the program as needed. The `FahrenheitConverter` program shown in Listing 4.8 presents a GUI that includes a text field into which the user can type a Fahrenheit temperature. When the user presses the Return (or Enter) key, the program displays the equivalent Celsius temperature.

LISTING 4.8

```
import javafx.application.Application;
import javafx.scene.Scene;
import javafx.stage.Stage;

//************************************************************************
//  FahrenheitConverter.java       Author: Lewis/Loftus
//
//  Demonstrates the use of a TextField and a GridPane.
//************************************************************************
```

LISTING 4.8 *continued*

```
public class FahrenheitConverter extends Application
{
    //-----------------------------------------------------------------
    //  Launches the temperature converter application.
    //-----------------------------------------------------------------
    public void start(Stage primaryStage)
    {
        Scene scene = new Scene(new FahrenheitPane(), 300, 150);

        primaryStage.setTitle("Fahrenheit Converter");
        primaryStage.setScene(scene);
        primaryStage.show();
    }
}
```

DISPLAY

For this example, the details of the user interface are set up in a separate class, shown in Listing 4.9. The `FahrenheitPane` class extends the `GridPane` class, which is a layout pane from the JavaFX API that displays nodes in a flexible rectangular grid.

The user interface is made up of three `Label` objects and one `TextField` object. The font size of each element is set using a `Font` object and calls to the `setFont` method of each node. Fonts are discussed in more detail in Chapter 5.

At the end of the `FahrenheitPane` constructor, the four elements are added to the pane. (Through inheritance, the `FahrenheitPane` *is* a `GridPane`, and inherits the `add` method.) The parameters to the `add` method specify to which grid cell the node is added. The first value is the row and the second is the column. The rows and columns of a grid pane both start at 0. See Appendix G for more details about grid panes.

LISTING 4.9

```
import javafx.event.ActionEvent;
import javafx.geometry.HPos;
import javafx.geometry.Pos;
import javafx.scene.control.Label;
import javafx.scene.control.TextField;
import javafx.scene.layout.GridPane;
import javafx.scene.text.Font;

//************************************************************************
//  FahrenheitPane.java       Author: Lewis/Loftus
//
//  Demonstrates the use of a TextField and a GridPane.
//************************************************************************

public class FahrenheitPane extends GridPane
{
    private Label result;
    private TextField fahrenheit;

    //-----------------------------------------------------------------------
    //  Sets up a GUI containing a labeled text field for converting
    //  temperatures in Fahrenheit to Celsius.
    //-----------------------------------------------------------------------
    public FahrenheitPane()
    {
        Font font = new Font(18);

        Label inputLabel = new Label("Fahrenheit:");
        inputLabel.setFont(font);
        GridPane.setHalignment(inputLabel, HPos.RIGHT);

        Label outputLabel = new Label("Celsius:");
        outputLabel.setFont(font);
        GridPane.setHalignment(outputLabel, HPos.RIGHT);

        result = new Label("---");
        result.setFont(font);
        GridPane.setHalignment(result, HPos.CENTER);

        fahrenheit = new TextField();
        fahrenheit.setFont(font);
        fahrenheit.setPrefWidth(50);
        fahrenheit.setAlignment(Pos.CENTER);
        fahrenheit.setOnAction(this::processReturn);
```

LISTING 4.9 *continued*

```
        setAlignment(Pos.CENTER);
        setHgap(20);
        setVgap(10);
        setStyle("-fx-background-color: yellow");

        add(inputLabel, 0, 0);
        add(fahrenheit, 1, 0);
        add(outputLabel, 0, 1);
        add(result, 1, 1);
    }

    //--------------------------------------------------------------------
    //  Computes and displays the converted temperature when the user
    //  presses the return key while in the text field.
    //--------------------------------------------------------------------
    public void processReturn(ActionEvent event)
    {
        int fahrenheitTemp = Integer.parseInt(fahrenheit.getText());
        int celsiusTemp = (fahrenheitTemp - 32) * 5 / 9;
        result.setText(celsiusTemp + "");
    }
}
```

The `processReturn` method is used to define the event handler that is triggered when the user presses return while the cursor is in the text field. It is associated with the text field with a call to its `setOnAction` method.

The `processReturn` method obtains the text from the text field using a call to the `getText` method, which returns a character string. The text is converted to an integer using the `parseInt` method of the `Integer` wrapper class. Then the method performs the calculation to determine the equivalent Celsius temperature and sets the text of the appropriate label with the result.

SELF-REVIEW QUESTIONS *(see answers in Appendix L)*

SR 4.36 Describe what happens in the `FahrenheitConverter` program when a user types a number into the text field and presses Return.

SR 4.37 How are rows and columns numbered in a `GridPane` layout? How would you specify the cell that is three over and two down from the upper left corner?

Summary of Key Concepts

- The heart of object-oriented programming is defining classes that represent objects with well-defined state and behavior.
- The scope of a variable, which determines where it can be referenced, depends on where it is declared.
- A UML class diagram helps us visualize the contents of and relationships among the classes of a program.
- An object should be encapsulated, guarding its data from inappropriate access.
- Instance variables should be declared with private visibility to promote encapsulation.
- Most objects contain accessor and mutator methods to allow the client to manage data in a controlled manner.
- The value returned from a method must be consistent with the return type specified in the method header.
- When a method is called, the actual parameters are copied into the formal parameters.
- A variable declared in a method is local to that method and cannot be used outside of it.
- A constructor cannot have any return type, even `void`.
- An arc is defined as a portion of an ellipse.
- Positive start angles and lengths are measured counterclockwise. Negative values are measured clockwise.
- An image is represented by an `Image` object but is displayed using an `ImageView` object.
- A layout pane is a JavaFX container that manages the visual arrangement of the nodes in a particular way.
- A GUI is made up of controls, events that represent user actions, and handlers that process those events.

Exercises

EX 4.1 For each of the following pairs, which represents a class and which represents an object of that class?

a. Ingredient, Stick of Butter

b. Birch, Tree

c. Kentucky, State

d. Ship, Mayflower

e. Toyota, Car

EX 4.2 List some attributes and operations that might be defined for a class called `PictureFrame` that represents a picture frame.

EX 4.3 Consider a class called `HistoricalEvent` that represents an event that occurred in history, such as a war or the declaration of independence. List some attributes and operations that might be defined for this class.

EX 4.4 List some attributes and operations that might be defined for a class called `Course` that represents a college course (not a particular offering of a course, just the course in general).

EX 4.5 Suppose you have a class called `Meal` that includes the instance variables `name` and `price`. Write a method called `printMeal()` that prints the details of a meal.

EX 4.6 Write a method called `cube` that accepts one integer parameter and returns that value raised to the third power.

EX 4.7 Write a method called `random100` that returns a random integer in the range of 1 to 100 (inclusive).

EX 4.8 Write a method called `randomInRange` that accepts two integer parameters representing a range. The method should return a random integer in the specified range (inclusive). Assume that the first parameter is greater than the second.

EX 4.9 Write a method called `randomColor` that creates and returns a `Color` object that represents a random color. Recall that a `Color` object can be defined by three integer values between 0 and 255, representing the contributions of red, green, and blue (its RGB value).

EX 4.10 Suppose you have a class called `City`. Write a constructor for the class that initializes the `name`, `population`, and `geographical area` instance variables based on parameters passed to the constructor.

EX 4.11 Add getter and setter methods for the instance variables of the following class.

```
class Skyscraper {
         String name;
         double height;
         int numberOfFloors;
}
```

EX 4.12 Draw a UML class diagram that shows the relationships among the classes used in the `Transactions` program.

EX 4.13 Write a declaration that creates an `Arc` object that is centered at point (50, 50) and sweeps across the top half of the underlying ellipse. Base it on an ellipse with a horizontal radius of 40 and a vertical radius of 100.

EX 4.14 How do you restrict the pixels displayed of an image?

EX 4.15 What is the purpose of a layout pane?

EX 4.16 How can a method reference be used to define an event handler?

Programming Projects

PP 4.1 Write a class called `Thermometer` that represents a simple thermometer for measuring body temperature. The `Thermometer` class should contain a single double as instance data, representing the current temperature. Write a constructor to initialize the temperature to 37 °C. Write a method called `increase` that increases the temperature by 0.1 °C and another method called `getTemperature` that returns the current temperature. Include a method called `reset` that resets the temperature to 37 °C. Finally, create a driver class called `ThermometerTest` that creates two `Thermometer` objects and tests their methods.

PP 4.2 Write a class called `Bulb` that represents a light bulb that can be turned on and off. Create a driver class called `Lights` whose `main` method instantiates and turns on some `Bulb` objects.

PP 4.3 Write a class called `Cylinder` that contains instance data to represent a cylinder's radius and height. Define the `Cylinder` constructor to accept and initialize the radius and height, and include getter and setter methods. Include methods that calculate and return the volume and surface area of the cylinder. (Volume $= \pi r^2 h$, surface area $= 2\pi rh + 2\pi r^2$.) Include a `toString` method that returns a one-line description of the cylinder. Create a driver class called `MultiCylinder`, whose `main` method instantiates and updates several `Cylinder` objects.

VideoNote
Developing a solution of PP 4.2.

PP 4.4 Write a class called `Dog` that contains instance data that represents the dog's name and age. Define the `Dog` constructor to accept and initialize instance data. Include getter and setter methods for the name and age. Include a method to compute and return the age of the dog in "person years" (seven times the dog's age). Include a `toString` method that returns a one-line description of the dog. Create a driver class called `Kennel`, whose `main` method instantiates and updates several `Dog` objects.

PP 4.5 Write a class called `Car` that contains instance data that represents the make, model, and year of the car. Define the `Car` constructor to initialize these values. Include getter and setter methods for all instance data, and a `toString` method that returns a one-line description of the car. Add a method called `isAntique` that returns a boolean indicating if the car is an antique (if it is more than 45 years old). Create a driver class called `CarTest`, whose `main` method instantiates and updates several `Car` objects.

PP 4.6 Write a class called `Box` that contains instance data that represents the height, width, and depth of the box. Also include a `boolean` variable called `full` as instance data that represents whether the box is full or not. Define the `Box` constructor to accept and initialize the height, width, and depth of the box. Each newly created Box is empty (the constructor should initialize `full` to false). Include getter and setter methods for all instance data. Include a `toString` method that returns a one-line description of the box. Create a driver class called `BoxTest`, whose main method instantiates and updates several `Box` objects.

PP 4.7 Write a class called `Book` that contains instance data for the title, author, publisher, and copyright date. Define the `Book` constructor to accept and initialize this data. Include setter and getter methods for all instance data. Include a `toString` method that returns a nicely formatted, multi-line description of the book. Create a driver class called `Bookshelf`, whose `main` method instantiates and updates several `Book` objects.

PP 4.8 Write a class called `Duration` that represents a duration of time in hours and minutes. It should contain instance data that represents the start hour, end hour, start minute, and end minute. Define the `Duration` constructor to accept and initialize all instance data. Include getter and setter methods for all instance data. Include a `toString` method that returns a String in the format [HH:MM, HH:MM]. Write a method called `length` that returns the length of the duration in minutes. Assume that a 24-hour format is used for all durations of time and no duration will span over multiple days. Create a driver class called `DurationTest`, whose `main` method instantiates and updates several `Duration` objects.

PP 4.9 Using the `Die` class defined in this chapter, write a class called `PairOfDice`, composed of two `Die` objects. Include methods to set and get the individual die values, a method to roll the dice, and a method that returns the current sum of the two die values. Create a driver class called `RollingDice2` to instantiate and use a `PairOfDice` object.

PP 4.10 Write a JavaFX application that displays three images side by side. Use a `FlowPane` with appropriate spacing between images.

PP 4.11 Write a JavaFX application that uses a `GridPane` to display four versions of an image in a 2 × 2 grid. For each version, either use a viewport to display a different part of the image or resize and rotate the image.

PP 4.12 Write a JavaFX application that displays a button and a number. Every time the button is pushed, change the number to a random value between 1 and 100.

PP 4.13 Write a JavaFX application that presents a button and a circle. Every time the button is pushed, the circle should be moved to a new random location within the window.

PP 4.14 Write a JavaFX application that presents two buttons and a number (initially 50) to the user. Label the buttons Increment and Decrement. When the increment button is pushed, increment the displayed value. Likewise, decrement the value when the decrement button is pushed.

PP 4.15 Write a JavaFX application that presents an unlabeled text field in the center of the window surrounded by a circle. When the user enters a radius value in the text field and presses return, redraw the circle accordingly.

PP 4.16 Write a JavaFX application that presents four labeled text fields, allowing the user to enter values for name, age, favorite color, and hobby. Include a button labeled Print. When the button is pushed, the program should print the contents of all fields to the console window (standard output) using `println` statements.

SOFTWARE FAILURE

Denver Airport Baggage Handling System

What Happened?

■ The automated baggage-handling system in Denver resulted in lost luggage and mangled packages.

The designers of the Denver International Airport had big plans to automate the handling of luggage. With as much as a mile to cover between the airport gates and terminals, the hope was to develop a system that whisked your luggage from the check-in counter to the departing plane and from an arriving plane to baggage collection with minimal human intervention. They thought the system would result in fewer flight delays, less waiting at luggage carousels, and reduced labor costs.

The system was designed and created in the late 1980s and early 1990s. Approximately 26 miles of track were constructed to move bags up and down inclines in gray carts under the control of a central computer.

However, the planned March 1994 opening of the airport was delayed continuously due to failures in the baggage system. During tests, bags were misloaded and misrouted. They fell out of carts when making turns. The system loaded bags into carts that already were full and unloaded them onto belts already jammed with luggage. Bags were damaged by being wedged under carts and dropped onto concrete floors.

The airport finally opened for business in February of 1995. At that point, only one airline—United—agreed to use the automated system. This was a stripped-down version of the system, used only for outgoing flights. No other airline used the system at all. They opted for humans driving luggage carts, just as most airports do today. United finally gave up using the system in 2005.

The original cost of the system was $186 million. The delays cost $1 million a day, surpassing the original costs. When United opted to abandon the system in 2005, it did so despite having a lease on the system through 2025 at $60 million per year.

What Caused It?

The fiasco this project represents is considered to be one of the greatest software engineering and overall system-design failures in history. There were many individual issues that contributed to the problems, but in general, the designers simply had too much faith in the technology they were using. They didn't factor in errors and inefficiencies that always occur in a complex system.

The individual problems included the fact that the software misinterpreted data from photoelectric eyes and, therefore, did not detect a pile of existing bags. When the system was restarted after it crashed, it lost information about the status of carts and didn't know which ones were full or not. Sharp corners were not factored in correctly regarding the speed of the conveyors, resulting in spilled carts. A telescoping belt loader called the lizard tongue—designed to reach into a planes cargo hold and pick up bags without human assistance—failed completely.

Lessons Learned

A project of this scope should not be attempted without many localized tests on the technologies in use. The failures were often a result of multiple variables caused by the system as a whole in operation.

When the system was designed in the late 1980s, it relied on a centralized mainframe to control the system. Such an approach seems ridiculous in today's world of distributed processing, but it is a good example of how a large system can be obsolete by the time it is developed. Today, human baggage handlers with handheld scanners result in a far more fast and accurate delivery system than the best goals of the planned automated system.

Source: The International Herald Tribune

5 Conditionals and Loops

CHAPTER OBJECTIVES

- Define the flow of control through a method.
- Explore boolean expressions that can be used to make decisions.
- Perform basic decision-making using `if` statements.
- Discuss issues pertaining to the comparison of certain types of data.
- Execute statements repetitively using `while` loops.
- Discuss the concept of an iterator object and use one to read a text file.
- Introduce the `ArrayList` class.
- Explore more GUI controls and events.

All programming languages have statements that allow you to make decisions to determine what to do next. Some of those statements allow you to repeat a certain activity multiple times. This chapter discusses key Java statements of this type and explores issues related to the comparison of data and objects. It begins with a discussion of boolean expressions, which form the basis of any decision. The Graphics Track sections of this chapter explore some new controls and events.

5.1 Boolean Expressions

The order in which statements are executed in a running program is called the *flow of control*. Unless otherwise specified, the execution of a program proceeds in a linear fashion. That is, a running program starts at the first programming statement and moves down one statement at a time until the program is complete. A Java application begins executing with the first line of the `main` method and proceeds step by step until it gets to the end of the `main` method.

Invoking a method alters the flow of control. When a method is called, control jumps to the code defined for that method. When the method completes, control returns to the place in the calling method where the invocation was made, and processing continues from there.

KEY CONCEPT
Conditionals and loops allow us to control the flow of execution through a method.

Within a given method, we can alter the flow of control through the code by using certain types of programming statements. Statements that control the flow of execution through a method fall into two categories: conditionals and loops.

A *conditional statement* is sometimes called a *selection statement*, because it allows us to choose which statement will be executed next. The conditional statements in Java are the `if` statement, the `if-else` statement, and the `switch` statement. We explore the `if` statement and the `if-else` statement in this chapter and cover the `switch` statement in Chapter 6.

Each decision is based on a *boolean expression* (also called a *condition*), which is an expression that evaluates to either true or false. The result of the expression determines which statement is executed next. The following is an example of an `if` statement:

```
if (count > 20)
    System.out.println("Count exceeded");
```

KEY CONCEPT
An `if` statement allows a program to choose whether to execute a particular statement.

The condition in this statement is `count > 20`. That expression evaluates to a boolean (true or false) result. Either the value stored in `count` is greater than 20 or it's not. If it is, the `println` statement is executed. If it's not, the `println` statement is skipped and processing continues with whatever code follows it.

The need to make decisions like this comes up all the time in programming situations. For example, the cost of life insurance might be dependent on whether the insured person is a smoker. If the person smokes, we calculate the cost using a particular formula; if not, we calculate it using another. The role of a conditional statement is to evaluate a boolean condition (whether the person smokes) and then to execute the proper calculation accordingly.

A *loop*, or *repetition statement*, allows us to execute a programming statement over and over again. Like a conditional, a loop is based on a boolean expression that determines how many times the statement is executed.

KEY CONCEPT
A loop allows a program to execute a statement multiple times.

For example, suppose we wanted to calculate the grade point average of every student in a class. The calculation is the same for each student; it is just performed on different data. We would set up a loop that repeats the calculation for each student until there are no more students to process.

Java has three types of loop statements: the `while` statement, the `do` statement, and the `for` statement. Each type of loop statement has unique characteristics that distinguish it from the others. We cover the `while` statement in this chapter and explore `do` loops and `for` loops in Chapter 6.

The boolean expressions on which conditionals and loops are based use equality operators, relational operators, and logical operators to make decisions. Before we discuss the conditional and loop statements in detail, let's explore these operators.

Equality and Relational Operators

The == and != operators are called *equality operators*. They test whether two values are equal or not equal, respectively. Note that the equality operator consists of two equal signs side by side and should not be mistaken for the assignment operator that uses only one equal sign.

The following `if` statement prints a sentence only if the variables `total` and `sum` contain the same value:

```
if (total == sum)
    System.out.println("total equals sum");
```

Likewise, the following `if` statement prints a sentence only if the variables `total` and `sum` do *not* contain the same value:

```
if (total != sum)
    System.out.println("total does NOT equal sum");
```

Java also has several *relational operators* that let us decide relative ordering between values. Earlier in this section, we used the greater than operator (>) to decide if one value was greater than another. We can ask similar questions using various operators. In Java, relational operators are greater than (>), less than (<), greater than or equal to (>=), and less than or equal to (<=). Figure 5.1 lists the Java equality and relational operators.

Operator	Meaning
==	equal to
!=	not equal to
<	less than
<=	less than or equal to
>	greater than
>=	greater than or equal to

FIGURE 5.1 Java equality and relational operators

The equality and relational operators have precedence lower than the arithmetic operators. Therefore, arithmetic operations are evaluated first, followed by equality and relational operations. As always, parentheses can be used to explicitly specify the order of evaluation.

We'll see more examples of relational operators as we examine conditional and loop statements throughout this chapter.

Logical Operators

In addition to the equality and relational operators, Java has three *logical operators* that produce boolean results. They also take boolean operands. Figure 5.2 lists and describes the logical operators.

The `!` operator is used to perform the *logical NOT* operation, which is also called the *logical complement.* The logical complement of a boolean value yields its opposite value. That is, if a boolean variable called `found` has the value false, then `!found` is true. Likewise, if `found` is true, then `!found` is false. The logical NOT operation does not change the value stored in `found`.

A logical operation can be described by a *truth table* that lists all possible combinations of values for the variables involved in an expression. Because the logical

Operator	Description	Example	Result
!	logical NOT	! a	true if a is false and false if a is true
&&	logical AND	a && b	true if a and b are both true and false otherwise
||	logical OR	a || b	true if a or b or both are true and false otherwise

FIGURE 5.2 Java logical operators

a	!a
false	true
true	false

FIGURE 5.3 Truth table describing the logical NOT operator

NOT operator is unary, there are only two possible values for its one operand: true or false. Figure 5.3 shows a truth table that describes the `!` operator.

The `&&` operator performs a *logical AND* operation. The result is true if both operands are true, but false otherwise. Compare that to the result of the *logical OR* operator (`||`), which is true if one or the other or both operands are true, but false otherwise.

The AND and OR operators are both binary operators since each uses two operands. Therefore, there are four possible combinations to consider: both operands are true, both are false, one is true and the other false, and vice versa. Figure 5.4 depicts a truth table that shows both the `&&` and `||` operators.

The logical NOT has the highest precedence of the three logical operators, followed by logical AND, then logical OR.

Consider the following `if` statement:

```
if (!done && (count > MAX))
   System.out.println("Completed.");
```

Under what conditions would the `println` statement be executed? The value of the boolean variable `done` is either true or false, and the NOT operator reverses that value. The value of `count` is either greater than `MAX` or it isn't. The truth table in Figure 5.5 breaks down all of the possibilities.

KEY CONCEPT
Logical operators are often used to construct sophisticated conditions.

An important characteristic of the `&&` and `||` operators is that they are "short-circuited." That is, if their left operand is sufficient to decide the boolean result of the operation, the right operand is not evaluated. This situation can occur with both operators, but for

a	b	a && b	a || b
false	false	false	false
false	true	false	true
true	false	false	true
true	true	true	true

FIGURE 5.4 Truth table describing the logical AND and OR operators

done	count > MAX	!done	!done && (count > MAX)
false	false	true	false
false	true	true	true
true	false	false	false
true	true	false	false

FIGURE 5.5 A truth table for a specific condition

different reasons. If the left operand of the && operator is false, then the result of the operation will be false no matter what the value of the right operand is. Likewise, if the left operand of the || is true, then the result of the operation is true no matter what the value of the right operand is.

Sometimes you can capitalize on the fact that the operation is short-circuited. For example, the condition in the following if statement will not attempt to divide by zero if the left operand is false. If count has the value zero, the left side of the && operation is false; therefore, the whole expression is false and the right side is not evaluated.

```
if (count != 0 && total/count > MAX)
   System.out.println("Testing.");
```

You should consider carefully whether or not to rely on these kinds of subtle programming language characteristics. Not all programming languages work the same way. As we have stressed before, you should favor readability over clever programming tricks. Always strive to make it clear to any reader of the code how the logic of your program works.

SELF-REVIEW QUESTIONS *(see answers in Appendix L)*

SR 5.1 What is meant by the flow of control through a program?

SR 5.2 What type of conditions are conditionals and loops based on?

SR 5.3 What are the equality operators? The relational operators? The logical operators?

SR 5.4 Given the following declarations, what is the value of each of the listed boolean expressions?

```
int value1 = 5, value2 = 10;
boolean done = true;
```

a. `value1 <= value2`

b. `(value1 + 5) >= value2`

c. `value1 < value2 / 2`

d. `value2 != value1`

e. `!(value1 == value2)`

f. `(value1 < value2) || done`

g. `(value1 > value2) || done`

h. `(value1 < value2) && !done`

i. `done || !done`

j. `((value1 > value2) || done) && (!done || (value2 > value1))`

SR 5.5 What is a truth table?

SR 5.6 Assuming `done` is a `boolean` variable and `value` is an `int` variable, create a truth table for the expression:

```
(value > 0 ) || !done
```

SR 5.7 Assuming `c1` and `c2` are `boolean` variables, create a truth table for the expression:

```
(c1 && !c2) || (!c1 && c2)
```

5.2 The `if` Statement

We've used a basic `if` statement in earlier examples in this chapter. Let's now explore it in detail.

KEY CONCEPT
Proper indentation is important for human readability; it shows the relationship between one statement and another.

An *if statement* consists of the reserved word `if` followed by a boolean expression, followed by a statement. The condition is enclosed in parentheses and must evaluate to true or false. If the condition is true, the statement is executed and processing continues with the next statement. If the condition is false, the statement is skipped and processing continues immediately with the next statement. Figure 5.6 shows this processing.

Consider the following example of an `if` statement:

```
if (total > amount)
    total = total + (amount + 1);
```

In this example, if the value in `total` is greater than the value in `amount`, the assignment statement is executed; otherwise, the assignment statement is skipped.

Note that the assignment statement in this example is indented under the header line of the `if` statement. This communicates that the assignment statement

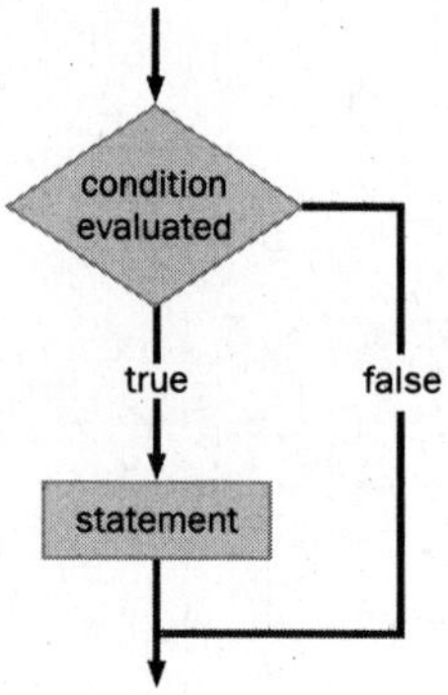

FIGURE 5.6 The logic of an if statement

is part of the if statement; it implies that the if statement governs whether the assignment statement will be executed. Although this indentation is extremely important for the human reader, it is ignored by the compiler.

The example in Listing 5.1 reads the age of the user and then makes a decision as to whether to print a particular sentence based on the age that is entered. The Age program echoes the age value that is entered in all cases. If the age is less than the value of the constant MINOR, the statement about youth is printed. If the age is equal to or greater than the value of MINOR, the println statement is skipped. In either case, the final sentence about age being a state of mind is printed.

LISTING 5.1

```
//********************************************************************
//  Age.java        Author: Lewis/Loftus
//
//  Demonstrates the use of an if statement.
//********************************************************************

import java.util.Scanner;

public class Age
{
   //-----------------------------------------------------------------
   //  Reads the user's age and prints comments accordingly.
   //-----------------------------------------------------------------
   public static void main(String[] args)
   {
      final int MINOR = 21;

      Scanner scan = new Scanner(System.in);
```

LISTING 5.1 *continued*

```
      System.out.print("Enter your age: ");
      int age = scan.nextInt();

      System.out.println("You entered: " + age);

      if (age < MINOR)
         System.out.println("Youth is a wonderful thing. Enjoy.");

      System.out.println("Age is a state of mind.");
   }
}
```

OUTPUT

```
Enter your age: 40
You entered: 40
Age is a state of mind.
```

Let's look at a few more examples of basic `if` statements. The following `if` statement causes the variable `size` to be set to zero if its current value is greater than or equal to the value in the constant `MAX`:

```
if (size >= MAX)
   size = 0;
```

The condition of the following `if` statement first adds three values together, then compares the result to the value stored in `numBooks`:

```
if (numBooks < stackCount + inventoryCount + duplicateCount)
   reorder = true;
```

If `numBooks` is less than the other three values combined, the boolean variable `reorder` is set to `true`. The addition operations are performed before the less than operator, because the arithmetic operators have a higher precedence than the relational operators.

Assuming `generator` refers to an object of the `Random` class, the following `if` statement examines the value returned from a call to `nextInt` to determine a random winner:

```
if (generator.nextInt(CHANCE) == 0)
   System.out.println("You are a randomly selected winner!");
```

The odds of this code picking a winner are based on the value of the `CHANCE` constant. That is, if `CHANCE` contains 20, the odds of winning are 1 in 20. The fact that the condition is looking for a return value of 0 is arbitrary; any value between 0 and `CHANCE-1` would have worked.

The `if-else` Statement

Sometimes we want to do one thing if a condition is true and another thing if that condition is false. We can add an *else clause* to an `if` statement, making it an *if-else statement,* to handle this kind of situation. The following is an example of an `if-else` statement:

```
if (height <= MAX)
   adjustment = 0;
else
   adjustment = MAX - height;
```

KEY CONCEPT

An `if-else` statement allows a program to do one thing if a condition is true and another thing if the condition is false.

If the condition is true, the first assignment statement is executed; if the condition is false, the second assignment statement is executed. Only one or the other will be executed, because a boolean condition evaluates to either true or false. Note that proper indentation is used again to communicate that the statements are part of the governing `if` statement.

If Statement

An `if` statement tests the boolean Expression and, if true, executes the first Statement. The optional `else` clause identifies the Statement that should be executed if the Expression is false.

Examples:

```
if (total < 7)
   System.out.println("Total is less than 7.");
if (firstCh != 'a')
   count++;
else
   count = count / 2;
```

The Wages program shown in Listing 5.2 uses an if-else statement to compute the proper payment amount for an employee.

In the Wages program, if an employee works over 40 hours in a week, the payment amount takes into account the overtime hours. An if-else statement is used to determine whether the number of hours entered by the user is greater than 40. If it is, the extra hours are paid at a rate one and a half times the normal rate. If there are no overtime hours, the total payment is based simply on the number of hours worked and the standard rate.

Let's look at another example of an if-else statement:

```
if (roster.getSize() == FULL)
   roster.expand();
else
   roster.addName(name);
```

LISTING 5.2

```
//********************************************************************
//  Wages.java       Author: Lewis/Loftus
//
//  Demonstrates the use of an if-else statement.
//********************************************************************

import java.text.NumberFormat;
import java.util.Scanner;

public class Wages
{
   //-----------------------------------------------------------------
   //  Reads the number of hours worked and calculates wages.
   //-----------------------------------------------------------------
   public static void main(String[] args)
   {
      final double RATE = 8.25;    // regular pay rate
      final int STANDARD = 40;     // standard hours in a work week

      Scanner scan = new Scanner(System.in);

      double pay = 0.0;

      System.out.print("Enter the number of hours worked: ");
      int hours = scan.nextInt();
```

LISTING 5.2 *continued*

```
      System.out.println();

      // Pay overtime at "time and a half"
      if (hours > STANDARD)
         pay = STANDARD * RATE + (hours-STANDARD) * (RATE * 1.5);
      else
         pay = hours * RATE;

      NumberFormat fmt = NumberFormat.getCurrencyInstance();
      System.out.println("Gross earnings: " + fmt.format(pay));
   }
}
```

OUTPUT

```
Enter the number of hours worked:  46

Gross earnings: $404.25
```

This example makes use of an object called `roster`. Even without knowing what `roster` represents, or from what class it was created, we can see that it has at least three methods: `getSize`, `expand`, and `addName`. The condition of the `if` statement calls `getSize` and compares the result to the constant `FULL`. If the condition is true, the `expand` method is invoked (apparently to expand the size of the roster). If the roster is not yet full, the variable `name` is passed as a parameter to the `addName` method.

The program in Listing 5.3 instantiates a `Coin` object, flips the coin by calling the `flip` method, then uses an `if-else` statement to determine which of two sentences gets printed based on the result.

LISTING 5.3

```
//********************************************************************
//  CoinFlip.java       Author: Lewis/Loftus
//
//  Demonstrates the use of an if-else statement.
//********************************************************************
```

LISTING 5.3 *continued*

```
public class CoinFlip
{
   //-----------------------------------------------------------------
   //  Creates a Coin object, flips it, and prints the results.
   //-----------------------------------------------------------------
   public static void main(String[] args)
   {
      Coin myCoin = new Coin();

      myCoin.flip();

      System.out.println(myCoin);

      if (myCoin.isHeads())
         System.out.println("You win.");
      else
         System.out.println("Better luck next time.");
   }
}
```

OUTPUT

```
Tails
Better luck next time.
```

The `Coin` class is shown in Listing 5.4. It stores two integer constants (`HEADS` and `TAILS`) that represent the two possible states of the coin, and an instance variable called `face` that represents the current state of the coin. The `Coin` constructor initially flips the coin by calling the `flip` method, which determines the new state of the coin by randomly choosing a number (either 0 or 1). The `isHeads` method returns a `boolean` value based on the current face value of the coin. The `toString` method uses an `if-else` statement to determine which character string to return to describe the coin. The `toString` method is automatically called when the `myCoin` object is passed to `println` in the `main` method.

Using Block Statements

We may want to do more than one thing as the result of evaluating a boolean condition. In Java, we can replace any single statement with a *block statement*.

LISTING 5.4

```
//********************************************************************
//  Coin.java       Author: Lewis/Loftus
//
//  Represents a coin with two sides that can be flipped.
//********************************************************************

public class Coin
{
   private final int HEADS = 0;
   private final int TAILS = 1;

   private int face;

   //-----------------------------------------------------------------
   //  Sets up the coin by flipping it initially.
   //-----------------------------------------------------------------
   public Coin()
   {
      flip();
   }

   //-----------------------------------------------------------------
   //  Flips the coin by randomly choosing a face value.
   //-----------------------------------------------------------------
   public void flip()
   {
      face = (int) (Math.random() * 2);
   }

   //-----------------------------------------------------------------
   //  Returns true if the current face of the coin is heads.
   //-----------------------------------------------------------------
   public boolean isHeads()
   {
      return (face == HEADS);
   }

   //-----------------------------------------------------------------
   // Returns the current face of the coin as a string.
   //-----------------------------------------------------------------
   public String toString()
   {
      String faceName;
```

LISTING 5.4 *continued*

```
        if (face == HEADS)
           faceName = "Heads";
        else
           faceName = "Tails";

        return faceName;
    }
}
```

A block statement is a collection of statements enclosed in braces. We've used these braces many times in previous examples to enclose method and class definitions.

The program called `Guessing`, shown in Listing 5.5, uses an `if-else` statement in which the statement of the `else` clause is a block statement.

If the guess entered by the user equals the randomly chosen answer, an appropriate acknowledgment is printed. However, if the answer is incorrect, two statements are printed, one that states that the guess is wrong and one that prints the actual answer. A programming project at the end of this chapter expands the concept of this example into the Hi-Lo game.

Note that if the block braces were not used, the sentence stating that the answer is incorrect would be printed if the answer was wrong, but the sentence revealing the correct answer would be printed in all cases. That is, only the first statement would be considered part of the `else` clause.

Remember that indentation means nothing except to the human reader. Statements that are not blocked properly can lead to the programmer making improper assumptions about how the code will execute. For example, the following code is misleading:

```
if (depth >= UPPER_LIMIT)
    delta = 100;
else
    System.out.println("WARNING: Delta is being reset to ZERO");
    delta = 0;    // not part of the else clause!
```

The indentation (not to mention the logic of the code) implies that the variable `delta` is reset to zero only when `depth` is less than `UPPER_LIMIT`. However, without using a block, the assignment statement that resets `delta` to zero is not governed by the `if-else` statement at all. It is executed in either case, which is clearly not what is intended.

VideoNote
Examples using conditionals.

LISTING 5.5

```
//********************************************************************
//  Guessing.java       Author: Lewis/Loftus
//
//  Demonstrates the use of a block statement in an if-else.
//********************************************************************

import java.util.*;

public class Guessing
{
   //-----------------------------------------------------------------
   //  Plays a simple guessing game with the user.
   //-----------------------------------------------------------------
   public static void main(String[] args)
   {
      final int MAX = 10;
      int answer, guess;

      Scanner scan = new Scanner(System.in);
      Random generator = new Random();

      answer = generator.nextInt(MAX) + 1;

      System.out.print("I'm thinking of a number between 1 and "
                       + MAX + ". Guess what it is: ");

      guess = scan.nextInt();

      if (guess == answer)
         System.out.println("You got it! Good guessing!");
      else
      {
         System.out.println("That is not correct, sorry.");
         System.out.println("The number was " + answer);
      }
   }
}
```

OUTPUT

```
I'm thinking of a number between 1 and 10. Guess what it is:  7
That is not correct, sorry.
The number was 5
```

A block statement can be used anywhere a single statement is called for in Java syntax. For example, the if portion of an if-else statement could be a block, or the else portion could be a block (as we saw in the Guessing program), or both parts could be block statements. For example:

```
if (boxes != warehouse.getCount())
{
    System.out.println("Inventory and warehouse do NOT match.");
    System.out.println("Beginning inventory process again!");
    boxes = 0;
}
else
{
    System.out.println("Inventory and warehouse MATCH.");
    warehouse.ship();
}
```

In this if-else statement, the value of boxes is compared to a value obtained by calling the getCount method of the warehouse object (whatever that is). If they do not match exactly, two println statements and an assignment statement are executed. If they do match, a different message is printed and the ship method of warehouse is invoked.

Nested if Statements

The statement executed as the result of an if statement could be another if statement. This situation is called a *nested if*. It allows us to make another decision after determining the results of a previous decision. The program in Listing 5.6, called MinOfThree, uses nested if statements to determine the smallest of three integer values entered by the user.

Carefully trace the logic of the MinOfThree program, using various input sets with the minimum value in all three positions, to see how it determines the lowest value.

An important situation arises with nested if statements. It may seem that an else clause after a nested if could apply to either if statement. For example:

```
if (code == 'R')
    if (height <= 20)
        System.out.println("Situation Normal");
    else
        System.out.println("Bravo!");
```

LISTING 5.6

```
//********************************************************************
//  MinOfThree.java       Author: Lewis/Loftus
//
//  Demonstrates the use of nested if statements.
//********************************************************************

import java.util.Scanner;

public class MinOfThree
{
   //-----------------------------------------------------------------
   //  Reads three integers from the user and determines the smallest
   //  value.
   //-----------------------------------------------------------------
   public static void main(String[] args)
   {
      int num1, num2, num3, min = 0;

      Scanner scan = new Scanner(System.in);

      System.out.println("Enter three integers: ");
      num1 = scan.nextInt();
      num2 = scan.nextInt();
      num3 = scan.nextInt();

      if (num1 < num2)
         if (num1 < num3)
            min = num1;
         else
            min = num3;
      else
         if (num2 < num3)
            min = num2;
         else
            min = num3;

      System.out.println("Minimum value: " + min);
   }
}
```

OUTPUT

```
Enter three integers:
45  22  69
Minimum value: 22
```

Is the else clause matched to the inner if statement or the outer if statement? The indentation in this example implies that it is part of the inner if statement, and that is correct. An else clause is always matched to the closest unmatched if that preceded it. However, if we're not careful, we can easily mismatch it in our mind and misalign the indentation. This is another reason why accurate, consistent indentation is crucial.

KEY CONCEPT

In a nested if statement, an else clause is matched to the closest unmatched if.

Braces can be used to specify the if statement to which an else clause belongs. For example, if the previous example should have been structured so that the string "Bravo!" is printed if code is not equal to 'R', we could force that relationship (and properly indent) as follows:

```
if (code == 'R')
{
   if (height <= 20)
      System.out.println("Situation Normal");
}
else
   System.out.println("Bravo!");
```

By using the block statement in the first if statement, we establish that the else clause belongs to it.

SELF-REVIEW QUESTIONS *(see answers in Appendix L)*

SR 5.8 What output is produced by the following code fragment given the assumptions below?

```
if (num1 < num2)
   System.out.print(" red ");
if ((num1 + 5) < num2)
   System.out.print(" white ");
else
   System.out.print(" blue ");
System.out.println(" yellow ");
```

a. Assuming the value of num1 is 2 and the value of num2 is 10?
b. Assuming the value of num1 is 10 and the value of num2 is 2?
c. Assuming the value of num1 is 2 and the value of num2 is 2?

SR 5.9 How do block statements help us in the construction of conditionals?

SR 5.10 What is a nested if statement?

SR 5.11 For each assumption, what output is produced by the following code fragment?

```
if (num1 >= num2)
{
   System.out.print(" red ");
   System.out.print(" orange ");
}
if ((num1 + 5) >= num2)
   System.out.print(" white ");

else

   if ((num1 + 10) >= num2)
   {
      System.out.print(" black ");
      System.out.print(" blue ");
   }

   else

      System.out.print(" yellow ");
System.out.println(" green ");
```

a. Assuming the value of `num1` is 5 and the value of `num2` is 4?
b. Assuming the value of `num1` is 5 and the value of `num2` is 12?
c. Assuming the value of `num1` is 5 and the value of `num2` is 27?

SR 5.12 Write an expression that will print a message based on the value of the int variable named `temperature`. If `temperature` is equal to or less than 50, it prints "It is cool." on one line and "Dress warmly." on the next. If `temperature` is greater than 80, it prints "It is warm." on one line and "Dress coolly." on the next. If `temperature` is in between 50 and 80, it prints "It is pleasant." on one line and "Dress pleasantly." on the next.

5.3 Comparing Data

When comparing data using boolean expressions, it's important to understand some nuances that arise depending on the type of data being examined. Let's look at a few key situations.

Comparing Floats

An interesting situation occurs when comparing floating point data. Two floating point values are equal, according to the == operator, only if all the binary digits of their underlying representations match. If the compared values are the results of computation, it may be unlikely that they are exactly equal even if they are close enough for the specific situation. Therefore, you should rarely use the equality operator (==) when comparing floating point values.

A better way to check for floating point equality is to compute the absolute value of the difference between the two values and compare the result to some tolerance level. For example, we may choose a tolerance level of `0.00001`. If the two floating point values are so close that their difference is less than the tolerance, then we are willing to consider them equal. Comparing two floating point values, `f1` and `f2`, could be accomplished as follows:

```
if (Math.abs(f1 - f2) < TOLERANCE)
    System.out.println("Essentially equal.");
```

The value of the constant `TOLERANCE` should be appropriate for the situation.

Comparing Characters

We know what it means when we say that one number is less than another, but what does it mean to say one character is less than another? As we discussed in Chapter 2, characters in Java are based on the Unicode character set, which defines an ordering of all possible characters that can be used. Because the character `'a'` comes before the character `'b'` in the character set, we can say that `'a'` is less than `'b'`.

KEY CONCEPT
The relative order of characters in Java is defined by the Unicode character set.

We can use the equality and relational operators on character data. For example, if two character variables `ch1` and `ch2` hold two characters, we might determine their relative ordering in the Unicode character set with an `if` statement as follows:

```
if (ch1 > ch2)
    System.out.println(ch1 + " is greater than " + ch2);
else
    System.out.println(ch1 + " is NOT greater than " + ch2);
```

The Unicode character set is structured so that all lowercase alphabetic characters (`'a'` through `'z'`) are contiguous and in alphabetical order. The same is true of uppercase alphabetic characters (`'A'` through `'Z'`) and characters that represent digits (`'0'` through `'9'`). The digits precede the uppercase alphabetic characters, which precede the lowercase alphabetic characters. Before, after, and in between these groups are other characters. See the chart in Appendix C for details.

Remember that a character and a character string are two different types of information. A `char` is a primitive value that represents one character. A character string is represented as an object in Java, defined by the `String` class. While comparing strings is based on comparing the characters in the strings, the comparison is governed by the rules for comparing objects.

Comparing Objects

The Unicode relationships among characters make it easy to sort characters and strings of characters. If you have a list of names, for instance, you can put them in alphabetical order based on the inherent relationships among characters in the character set.

However, you should not use the equality or relational operators to compare String objects. The String class contains a method called equals that returns a boolean value that is true if the two strings being compared contain exactly the same characters and is false otherwise. For example:

```
if (name1.equals(name2))
   System.out.println("The names are the same.");
else
   System.out.println("The names are not the same.");
```

KEY CONCEPT

The compareTo method can be used to determine the relative order of strings.

Assuming that name1 and name2 are String objects, this condition determines whether the characters they contain are an exact match. Because both objects were created from the String class, they both respond to the equals message. Therefore, the condition could have been written as name2.equals(name1), and the same result would occur.

It is valid to test the condition (name1 == name2), but that actually tests to see whether both reference variables refer to the same String object. For any object, the == operator tests whether both reference variables are aliases of each other (whether they contain the same address). That's different from testing to see whether two different String objects contain the same characters.

Keep in mind that a string literal (such as "Nathan") is a convenience and is actually a shorthand technique for creating a String object. An interesting issue related to string comparisons is the fact that Java creates a unique object for string literals only when needed. That is, if the string literal "Hi" is used multiple times in a method, only one String object is created to represent it. Therefore, the conditions of both if statements in the following code are true:

```
String str = "software";
if (str == "software")
   System.out.println("References are the same");
if (str.equals("software"))
   System.out.println("Characters are the same");
```

The first time the string literal "software" is used, a String object is created to represent it and the reference variable str is set to its address. Each subsequent time the literal is used, the original object is referenced.

To determine the relative ordering of two strings, use the `compareTo` method of the `String` class. The `compareTo` method is more versatile than the `equals` method. Instead of returning a `boolean` value, the `compareTo` method returns an integer. The return value is negative if the `String` object through which the method is invoked precedes (is less than) the string that is passed in as a parameter. The return value is zero if the two strings contain the same characters. The return value is positive if the `String` object through which the method is invoked follows (is greater than) the string that is passed in as a parameter. For example:

```
int result = name1.compareTo(name2);
if (result < 0)
   System.out.println(name1 + " comes before " + name2);
else
   if (result == 0)
      System.out.println("The names are equal.");
   else
      System.out.println(name1 + " follows " + name2);
```

Keep in mind that comparing characters and strings is based on the Unicode character set (see Appendix C). This is called a *lexicographic ordering*. If all alphabetic characters are in the same case (upper or lower), the lexicographic ordering will be alphabetic ordering as well. However, when comparing two strings, such as `"able"` and `"Baker"`, the `compareTo` method will conclude that `"Baker"` comes first because all of the uppercase letters come before all of the lowercase letters in the Unicode character set. A string that is the prefix of another, longer string is considered to precede the longer string. For example, when comparing the two strings `"horse"` and `"horsefly"`, the `compareTo` method will conclude that `"horse"` comes first.

SELF-REVIEW QUESTIONS *(see answers in Appendix L)*

SR 5.13 Why must we be careful when comparing floating point values for equality?

SR 5.14 How do we compare strings for equality?

SR 5.15 Write an `equals` method for the `Die` class of Section 4.2. The method should return `true` if the `Die` object it is invoked on has the same `faceValue` as the `Die` object passed as a parameter, otherwise it should return `false`.

SR 5.16 Assume the `String` variables `s1` and `s2` have been initialized. Write an expression that prints out the two strings on separate lines in lexicographic order.

5.4 The `while` Statement

As we discussed in the introduction of this chapter, a repetition statement (or loop) allows us to execute another statement multiple times. A *while statement* is a loop that evaluates a boolean condition just as an `if` statement does and executes a statement (called the *body* of the loop) if the condition is true. However, unlike the `if` statement, after the body is executed, the condition is evaluated again. If it is still true, the body is executed again. This repetition continues until the condition becomes false; then processing continues with the statement after the body of the `while` loop. Figure 5.7 shows this processing.

While Statement

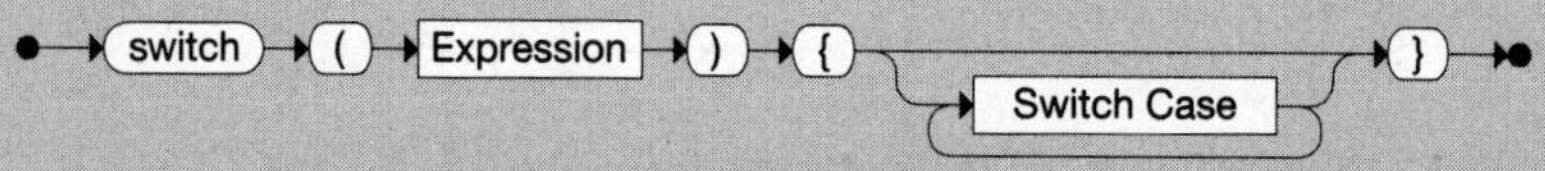

The `while` loop repeatedly executes the specified Statement as long as the boolean Expression is true. The Expression is evaluated first; therefore the Statement might not be executed at all. The Expression is evaluated again after each execution of Statement until the Expression becomes false.

Example:

```
while (total > max)
{
   total = total / 2;
   System.out.println("Current total: " + total);
}
```

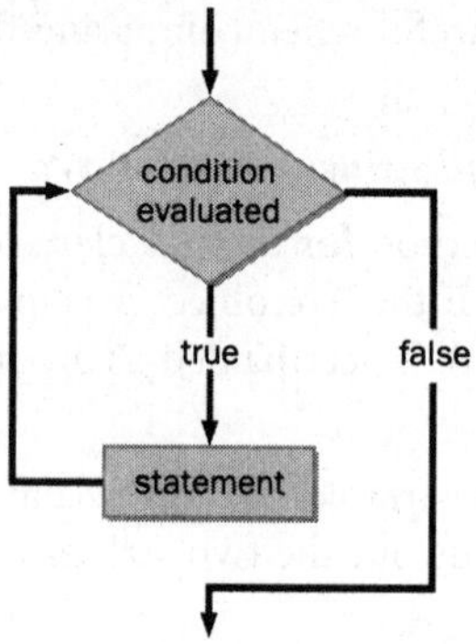

FIGURE 5.7 The logic of a `while` loop

The following loop prints the values from 1 to 5. Each iteration through the loop prints one value, then increments the counter.

```
int count = 1;
while (count <= 5)
{
   System.out.println(count);
   count++;
}
```

KEY CONCEPT

A `while` statement executes the same statement until its condition becomes false.

Note that the body of the `while` loop is a block containing two statements. The entire block is repeated on each iteration of the loop.

Let's look at another program that uses a `while` loop. The `Average` program shown in Listing 5.7 reads a series of integer values from the user, sums them up, and computes their average.

We don't know how many values the user may enter, so we need to have a way to indicate that the user has finished entering numbers. In this program, we designate zero to be a *sentinel value* that indicates the end of the input. The `while` loop continues to process input values until the user enters zero. This assumes that zero

LISTING 5.7

```
//********************************************************************
//  Average.java       Author: Lewis/Loftus
//
//  Demonstrates the use of a while loop, a sentinel value, and a
//  running sum.
//********************************************************************

import java.text.DecimalFormat;
import java.util.Scanner;

public class Average
{
   //-----------------------------------------------------------------
   //  Computes the average of a set of values entered by the user.
   //  The running sum is printed as the numbers are entered.
   //-----------------------------------------------------------------
   public static void main(String[] args)
   {
      int sum = 0, value, count = 0;
      double average;

      Scanner scan = new Scanner(System.in);
```

LISTING 5.7 *continued*

```
      System.out.print("Enter an integer (0 to quit): ");
      value = scan.nextInt();

      while (value != 0)   // sentinel value of 0 to terminate loop
      {
         count++;

         sum += value;
         System.out.println("The sum so far is " + sum);

         System.out.print("Enter an integer (0 to quit): ");
         value = scan.nextInt();
      }

      System.out.println();

      if (count == 0)
         System.out.println("No values were entered.");
      else
      {
         average = (double)sum / count;

         DecimalFormat fmt = new DecimalFormat("0.###");
         System.out.println("The average is " + fmt.format(average));
      }
   }
}
```

OUTPUT

```
Enter an integer (0 to quit):  25
The sum so far is 25
Enter an integer (0 to quit):  164
The sum so far is 189
Enter an integer (0 to quit):  -14
The sum so far is 175
Enter an integer (0 to quit):  84
The sum so far is 259
Enter an integer (0 to quit):  12
The sum so far is 271
Enter an integer (0 to quit):  -35
The sum so far is 236
Enter an integer (0 to quit):  0

The average is 39.333
```

is not one of the valid numbers that should contribute to the average. A sentinel value must always be outside the normal range of values entered.

VideoNote
Examples using while loops.

Note that in the Average program, a variable called sum is used to maintain a *running sum*, which means it is the sum of the values entered thus far. The variable sum is initialized to zero, and each value read is added to and stored back into sum.

We also have to count the number of values that are entered so that after the loop concludes we can divide by the appropriate value to compute the average. Note that the sentinel value is not counted. Consider the unusual situation in which the user immediately enters the sentinel value before entering any valid values. The if statement at the end of the program avoids a divide-by-zero error.

Let's examine yet another program that uses a while loop. The WinPercentage program shown in Listing 5.8 computes the winning percentage of a sports team based on the number of games won.

We use a while loop in the WinPercentage program to *validate the input*, meaning we guarantee that the user enters a value that we consider to be valid. In this example, that means that the number of games won must be greater than or equal to zero and less than or equal to the total number of games played. The while loop continues to execute, repeatedly prompting the user for valid input, until the entered number is indeed valid.

LISTING 5.8

```
//********************************************************************
//  WinPercentage.java        Author: Lewis/Loftus
//
//  Demonstrates the use of a while loop for input validation.
//********************************************************************

import java.text.NumberFormat;
import java.util.Scanner;

public class WinPercentage
{
   //-----------------------------------------------------------------
   //  Computes the percentage of games won by a team.
   //-----------------------------------------------------------------
   public static void main(String[] args)
   {
      final int NUM_GAMES = 12;
      int won;
      double ratio;
```

LISTING 5.8 *continued*

```
      Scanner scan = new Scanner(System.in);

      System.out.print("Enter the number of games won (0 to "
                       + NUM_GAMES + "): ");
      won = scan.nextInt();

      while (won < 0 || won > NUM_GAMES)
      {
         System.out.print("Invalid input. Please reenter: ");
         won = scan.nextInt();
      }

      ratio = (double)won / NUM_GAMES;

      NumberFormat fmt = NumberFormat.getPercentInstance();

      System.out.println();
      System.out.println("Winning percentage: " + fmt.format(ratio));
   }
}
```

OUTPUT

```
Enter the number of games won (0 to 12):  -5
Invalid input. Please reenter:  13
Invalid input. Please reenter:  7

Winning percentage:  58%
```

We generally want our programs to be *robust,* which means that they handle potential problems as elegantly as possible. Validating input data and avoiding errors such as dividing by zero are situations that we should consciously address when designing a program. Loops and conditionals help us recognize and deal with such situations.

Infinite Loops

It is the programmer's responsibility to ensure that the condition of a loop will eventually become false. If it doesn't, the loop body will execute forever, or at least until the program is interrupted. This situation, referred to as an *infinite loop,* is a common mistake.

The following is an example of an infinite loop:

```
int count = 1;
while (count <= 25)    // Warning: this is an infinite loop!
{
    System.out.println(count);
    count = count- 1;
}
```

If you execute this loop, you should be prepared to interrupt it. On most systems, pressing the Control-C keyboard combination (hold down the Control key and press C) terminates a running program.

In this example, the initial value of count is 1, and it is decremented in the loop body. The while loop will continue as long as count is less than or equal to 25. Because count gets smaller with each iteration, the condition will always be true, or at least until the value of count gets so small that an underflow error occurs. The point is that the logic of the code is clearly wrong.

KEY CONCEPT
We must design our programs carefully to avoid infinite loops.

Let's look at some other examples of infinite loops:

```
int count = 1;
while (count != 50)    // infinite loop
    count += 2;
```

In this code fragment, the variable count is initialized to 1 and is moving in a positive direction. However, note that it is being incremented by 2 each time. This loop will never terminate because count will never equal 50. It begins at 1 and then changes to 3, then 5, and so on. Eventually it reaches 49, then changes to 51, then 53, and continues forever.

Now consider the following situation:

```
double num = 1.0;
while (num != 0.0)    // infinite loop
    num = num - 0.1;
```

Once again, the value of the loop control variable seems to be moving in the correct direction. And, in fact, it seems like num will eventually take on the value 0.0. However, this loop is infinite (at least on most systems), because num will never have a value *exactly* equal to 0.0. This situation is similar to one we discussed earlier in this chapter when we explored the idea of comparing floating point values in the condition of an if statement. Because of the way the values are represented in binary, minute computational errors occur internally, making it problematic to compare two floating point values for equality.

Nested Loops

The body of a loop can contain another loop. This situation is called a *nested loop*. Keep in mind that for each iteration of the outer loop, the inner loop executes completely. Consider the following code fragment. How many times does the string "Here again" get printed?

```
int count1, count2;
count1 = 1;
while (count1 <= 10)
{
    count2 = 1;
    while (count2 <= 50)
    {
        System.out.println("Here again");
        count2++;
    }
    count1++;
}
```

The `println` statement is inside the inner loop. The outer loop executes 10 times, as `count1` iterates between 1 and 10. The inner loop executes 50 times, as `count2` iterates between 1 and 50. For each iteration of the outer loop, the inner loop executes completely. Therefore the `println` statement is executed 500 times.

As with any loop situation, we must be careful to scrutinize the conditions of the loops and the initializations of variables. Let's consider some small changes to this code. What if the condition of the outer loop were `(count1 < 10)` instead of `(count1 <= 10)`? How would that change the total number of lines printed? Well, the outer loop would execute 9 times instead of 10, so the `println` statement would be executed 450 times. What if the outer loop were left as it was originally defined, but `count2` were initialized to 11 instead of 1 before the inner loop? The inner loop would then execute 40 times instead of 50, so the total number of lines printed would be 400.

Let's look at another example that uses a nested loop. A *palindrome* is a string of characters that reads the same forward or backward. For example, the following strings are palindromes:

- radar
- drab bard
- ab cde xxxx edc ba
- kayak
- deified
- able was I ere I saw elba

Note that some palindromes have an even number of characters, whereas others have an odd number of characters. The PalindromeTester program shown in Listing 5.9 tests to see whether a string is a palindrome. The user may test as many strings as desired.

The code for PalindromeTester contains two loops, one inside the other. The outer loop controls how many strings are tested, and the inner loop scans through each string, character by character, until it determines whether the string is a palindrome.

LISTING 5.9

```
//********************************************************************
//  PalindromeTester.java       Author: Lewis/Loftus
//
//  Demonstrates the use of nested while loops.
//********************************************************************

import java.util.Scanner;

public class PalindromeTester
{
   //-----------------------------------------------------------------
   //  Tests strings to see if they are palindromes.
   //-----------------------------------------------------------------
   public static void main(String[] args)
   {
      String str, another = "y";
      int left, right;

      Scanner scan = new Scanner(System.in);

      while (another.equalsIgnoreCase("y"))  // allows y or Y
      {
         System.out.println("Enter a potential palindrome:");
         str = scan.nextLine();

         left = 0;
         right = str.length() - 1;

         while (str.charAt(left) == str.charAt(right) && left < right)
         {
            left++;
            right--;
         }

         System.out.println();
```

LISTING 5.9 *continued*

```
         if (left < right)
            System.out.println("That string is NOT a palindrome.");
         else
            System.out.println("That string IS a palindrome.");

          System.out.println();
          System.out.print("Test another palindrome (y/n)? ");
          another = scan.nextLine();
      }
   }
}
```

OUTPUT

```
Enter a potential palindrome:
radar

That string IS a palindrome.

Test another palindrome (y/n)?  y
Enter a potential palindrome:
able was I ere I saw elba

That string IS a palindrome.

Test another palindrome (y/n)?  y
Enter a potential palindrome:
abcddcba

That string IS a palindrome.

Test another palindrome (y/n)?  y
Enter a potential palindrome:
abracadabra

That string is NOT a palindrome.

Test another palindrome (y/n)?  n
```

The variables left and right store the indexes of two characters. They initially indicate the characters on either end of the string. Each iteration of the inner loop compares the two characters indicated by left and right. We fall out of the inner loop when either the characters don't match, meaning the string is not a palindrome, or when the value of left becomes equal to or greater than the value of right, which means the entire string has been tested and it is a palindrome.

Note that the following phrases would not be considered palindromes by the current version of the program:

- A man, a plan, a canal, Panama.
- Dennis and Edna sinned.
- Rise to vote, sir.
- Doom an evil deed, liven a mood.
- Go hang a salami; I'm a lasagna hog.

These strings fail our current criteria for a palindrome because of the spaces, punctuation marks, and changes in uppercase and lowercase. However, if these characteristics were removed or ignored, these strings read the same forward and backward. Consider how the program could be changed to handle these situations. These modifications are included as a programming project at the end of the chapter.

The break and continue Statements

Java includes two statements that affect the processing of conditionals and loops. When a break statement is executed, the flow of execution transfers immediately to the statement after the one governing the current flow. For example, if a break statement is executed within the body of a loop, the execution of the loop is stopped and the statement following the loop is executed. It "breaks" out of the loop.

In Chapter 6, we'll see that using the break statement is usually necessary when writing switch statements. However, it is never necessary to use a break statement in a loop. An equivalent loop can always be written without it. Because the break statement causes program flow to jump from one place to another, using a break in a loop is not good practice. You can and should avoid using the break statement in a loop.

A *continue statement* has a related effect on loop processing. The continue statement is similar to a break, but the loop condition is evaluated again, and the loop body is executed again if it is still true. Like the break statement, the continue statement can always be avoided in a loop, and for the same reasons, it should be.

SELF-REVIEW QUESTIONS *(see answers in Appendix L)*

SR 5.17 What is an infinite loop? Specifically, what causes it?

SR 5.18 What output is produced by the following code fragment?

```
int low = 0, high = 10;
while (low < high)
{
    System.out.println(low);
    low++;
}
```

SR 5.19 What output is produced by the following code fragment?

```
int low = 10, high = 0;
while (low <= high)
{
    System.out.println(low);
    low++;
}
```

SR 5.20 What output is produced by the following code fragment?

```
int low = 0, high = 10;
while (low <= high)
{
    System.out.println(low);
    high = high - low;
}
```

SR 5.21 What output is produced by the following code fragment?

```
int low = 0, high = 10, mid;
while (low <= high)
{
    mid = low;
    while (mid <= high)
    {
        System.out.print(mid + " ");
        mid++;
    }
    System.out.println();
    low++;
}
```

SR 5.22 Assume the `int` variable `value` has been initialized to a positive integer. Write a `while` loop that prints all of the positive divisors of `value`. For example, if `value` is 28, it prints divisors of 28: 1 2 4 7 14 28

SR 5.23 Assume the `int` variable `value` has been initialized to a positive integer. Write a `while` loop that prints all of the positive divisors of each number from one to `value`. For example, if `value` is 4, it prints

divisors of 1: 1
divisors of 2: 1 2
divisors of 3: 1 3
divisors of 4: 1 2 4

5.5 Iterators

An *iterator* is an object that has methods that allow you to process a collection of items one at a time. That is, an iterator lets you step through each item and interact with it as needed. For example, your goal may be to compute the dues for each member of a club or print the distinct parts of a URL. The key is that an iterator provides a consistent and simple mechanism for systematically processing a group of items. Since it is inherently a repetitive process, it is closely related to the idea of loops.

KEY CONCEPT
An iterator is an object that helps you process a group of related items.

Technically an iterator object in Java is defined using the `Iterator` interface, which is discussed in Chapter 7. For now, it is simply helpful to know that such objects exist and that they can make the processing of a collection of items easier.

Every iterator object has a method called `hasNext` that returns a `boolean` value indicating if there is at least one more item to process. Therefore, the `hasNext` method can be used as a condition of a loop to control the processing of each item. An iterator also has a method called `next` to retrieve the next item in the collection to process.

There are several classes in the Java standard class library that define iterator objects. One of these is `Scanner`, a class we've used several times in previous examples to help us read data from the user. The `hasNext` method of the `Scanner` class returns true if there is another input token to process. And, as we've seen previously, it has a `next` method that returns the next input token as a string.

The `Scanner` class also has specific variations of the `hasNext` method, such as the `hasNextInt` and `hasNextDouble` methods, which allow you to determine if the next input token is a particular type. Likewise, as we've seen, there are variations of the `next` method, such as `nextInt` and `nextDouble`, which retrieve values of specific types.

When reading input interactively from the standard input stream, the `hasNext` method of the `Scanner` class will wait until there is input available, then return true. That is, interactive input read from the keyboard is always thought to have more data to process—it just hasn't arrived yet until the user types it in. That's why in previous examples we've used special sentinel values to determine the end of interactive input.

However, the fact that a `Scanner` object is an iterator is particularly helpful when the scanner is being used to process input from a source that has a specific end point, such as processing the lines of a data file or processing the parts of a character string. Let's examine an example of this type of processing.

Reading Text Files

Suppose we have an input file called `urls.inp` that contains a list of URLs that we want to process in some way:

www.google.com

www.linux.org/info/gnu.html

thelyric.com/calendar/

www.cs.vt.edu/undergraduate/about

youtube.com/watch?v=EHCRimwRGLs

The program shown in Listing 5.10 reads the URLs from this file and dissects them to show the various parts of the path. It uses a `Scanner` object to process the input. In fact, it uses multiple `Scanner` objects—one to read the lines of the data file and another to process each URL string.

LISTING 5.10

```
//********************************************************************
//  URLDissector.java       Author: Lewis/Loftus
//
//  Demonstrates the use of Scanner to read file input and parse it
//  using alternative delimiters.
//********************************************************************

import java.util.Scanner;
import java.io.*;

public class URLDissector
{
   //-----------------------------------------------------------------
   //  Reads urls from a file and prints their path components.
   //-----------------------------------------------------------------
   public static void main(String[] args) throws IOException
   {
```

LISTING 5.10 *continued*

```
      String url;
      Scanner fileScan, urlScan;

      fileScan = new Scanner(new File("urls.inp"));

      //  Read and process each line of the file
      while (fileScan.hasNext())
      {
         url = fileScan.nextLine();
         System.out.println("URL: " + url);

         urlScan = new Scanner(url);
         urlScan.useDelimiter("/");

         //  Print each part of the url
         while (urlScan.hasNext())
            System.out.println("   " + urlScan.next());

         System.out.println();
      }
   }
}
```

OUTPUT

```
URL: www.google.com
   www.google.com

URL: www.linux.org/info/gnu.html
   www.linux.org
   info
   gnu.html

URL: thelyric.com/calendar/
   thelyric.com
   calendar

URL: www.cs.vt.edu/undergraduate/about
   www.cs.vt.edu
   undergraduate
   about

URL: youtube.com/watch?v=EHCRimwRGLs
   youtube.com
   watch?v=EHCRimwRGLs
```

There are two `while` loops in this program, one nested within the other. The outer loop processes each line in the file, and the inner loop processes each token in the current line.

The variable `fileScan` is created as a scanner that operates on the input file named `urls.inp`. Instead of passing `System.in` into the `Scanner` constructor, we instantiate a `File` object that represents the input file and pass it into the `Scanner` constructor. At that point, the `fileScan` object is ready to read and process input from the input file.

If for some reason there is a problem finding or opening the input file, the attempt to create a `File` object will throw an `IOException`, which is why we've added the `throws IOException` clause to the `main` method header. (Processing I/O exceptions is discussed further in Chapter 11.)

The body of the outer `while` loop will be executed as long as the `hasNext` method of the input file scanner returns true—that is, as long as there is more input in the data file to process. Each iteration through the loop reads one line (one URL) from the input file and prints it out.

For each URL, a new `Scanner` object is set up to parse the pieces of the URL string, which is passed into the `Scanner` constructor when instantiating the `urlScan` object. The inner `while` loop prints each token of the URL on a separate line.

KEY CONCEPT

The delimiters used to separate tokens in a `Scanner` object can be explicitly set as needed.

Recall that, by default, a `Scanner` object assumes that white space (spaces, tabs, and new lines) is used as the delimiters separating the input tokens. That works in this example for the scanner that is reading each line of the input file. However, if the default delimiters do not suffice, as in the processing of a URL in this example, they can be changed.

In this case, we are interested in each part of the path separated by the slash (/) character. A call to the `useDelimiter` method of the scanner sets the delimiter to a slash prior to processing the URL string.

If you want to use more than one alternate delimiter character, or if you want to parse the input in more complex ways, the `Scanner` class can process patterns called *regular expressions,* which are discussed in Appendix H.

SELF-REVIEW QUESTIONS *(see answers in Appendix L)*

SR 5.24 Devise statements that create each of the following `Scanner` objects.

a. One for interactive input, which reads from `System.in`.
b. One that reads from the file "info.dat".
c. One that reads from the `String` variable `infoString`.

SR 5.25 Assume the `Scanner` object `fileScan` has been initialized to read from a file. Write a `while` loop that calculates the average number of characters per line of the file.

5.6 The ArrayList Class

Now that we have a loop in our arsenal of programming statements, let's introduce a very useful class for managing a set of objects. The `ArrayList` class is part of the `java.util` package of the Java standard class library. An `ArrayList` object stores a list of objects and allows you to refer to each one by an integer *index* value. We will often use loops to scan through the objects in the list and deal with them in one way or another.

Internally, the `ArrayList` class manages the list using a programming construct called an *array* (hence the name). Arrays are discussed in detail in Chapter 8, but we don't have to know the details of arrays to make use of an `ArrayList` object. The `ArrayList` class is part of the Java Collections API, a group of classes that serve to organize and manage other objects. We discuss collection classes further in Chapter 13.

> **KEY CONCEPT**
> An `ArrayList` object stores a list of objects and lets you access them using an integer index.

Figure 5.8 lists several methods of the `ArrayList` class. You can add and remove elements in various ways, determine if the list is empty, and obtain the number of elements currently in the list, among several other operations.

Note that the `ArrayList` class refers to having elements of type `E`. That is a *generic type* (the `E` stands for element), which is determined when an `ArrayList` object is created. So you don't just create an `ArrayList` object, you create an `ArrayList` object that will store a particular type of object. The type parameter for a given object is written in angle brackets after the class name. So we can talk about an `ArrayList<String>` object that manages a list of `String` objects, or an `ArrayList<Book>` that manages a list of `Book` objects.

You can create an `ArrayList` without specifying the type of element, in which case the `ArrayList` stores `Object` references, which means that you can put any type of object in the list. This is usually not a good idea. The point of being able to commit to storing a particular type in a given `ArrayList` object lets the compiler help you check that only the appropriate types of objects are being stored in the object.

> **KEY CONCEPT**
> When an `ArrayList` object is created, you specify the type of element that will be stored in the list.

The index values of an `ArrayList` begin at 0, not 1. So conceptually, for example, an `ArrayList` of `String` objects might be managing the following list:

```
0 "Bashful"
1 "Sleepy"
2 "Happy"
3 "Dopey"
4 "Doc"
```

Also note that an `ArrayList` stores references to objects. You cannot create an `ArrayList` that stores primitive values such as an `int`. But that's where wrapper classes come to the rescue again. For example, you can create an `ArrayList<Integer>` or an `ArrayList<Double>` as appropriate.

ArrayList<E>()
Constructor: creates an initially empty list.

boolean **add(E obj)**
Inserts the specified object to the end of this list.

void **add(int index, E obj)**
Inserts the specified object into this list at the specified index.

void **clear()**
Removes all elements from this list.

E **remove(int index)**
Removes the element at the specified index in this list and returns it.

E **get(int index)**
Returns the object at the specified index in this list without removing it.

int **indexOf(Object obj)**
Returns the index of the first occurrence of the specified object.

boolean **contains(Object obj)**
Returns true if this list contains the specified object.

boolean **isEmpty()**
Returns true if this list contains no elements.

int **size()**
Returns the number of elements in this list.

FIGURE 5.8 Some methods of the ArrayList<E> class.

The program shown in Listing 5.11 instantiates an ArrayList<String> called band. The method add is used to add several String objects to the end of the ArrayList in a specific order. Then one particular string is deleted and another is inserted at a particular index. As with any other object, the toString method of the ArrayList class is automatically called whenever it is sent to the println method, which prints all of the elements surrounded by square brackets. The while loop at the end of the program explicitly prints each element on a separate line.

LISTING 5.11

```
//********************************************************************
//  Beatles.java       Author: Lewis/Loftus
//
//  Demonstrates the use of a ArrayList object.
//********************************************************************
```

LISTING 5.11 *continued*

```java
import java.util.ArrayList;

public class Beatles
{
   //-----------------------------------------------------------------
   //  Stores and modifies a list of band members.
   //-----------------------------------------------------------------
   public static void main(String[] args)
   {
      ArrayList<String> band = new ArrayList<String>();

      band.add("Paul");
      band.add("Pete");
      band.add("John");
      band.add("George");

      System.out.println(band);
      int location = band.indexOf("Pete");
      band.remove(location);

      System.out.println(band);
      System.out.println("At index 1: " + band.get(1));
      band.add(2, "Ringo");

      System.out.println("Size of the band: " + band.size());
      int index = 0;
      while (index < band.size())
      {
         System.out.println(band.get(index));
         index++;
      }
   }
}
```

OUTPUT

```
[Paul, Pete, John, George]
[Paul, John, George]
At index 1: John
Size of the band: 4
Paul
John
Ringo
George
```

SELF-REVIEW QUESTIONS *(see answers in Appendix L)*

SR 5.26 What are the advantages of using an `ArrayList` object?

SR 5.27 What type of elements does an `ArrayList` hold?

SR 5.28 Write a declaration for a variable named `dice` that is an `ArrayList` of `Die` objects.

SR 5.29 What output is produced by the following code fragment?

```
ArrayList<String> names = new ArrayList<String>();
names.add("Andy");
names.add("Betty");
names.add(1, "Chet");
names.add(1, "Don");
names.remove(2);
System.out.println(names);
```

5.7 Determining Event Sources

In Chapter 4, we began to explore programs with a truly interactive graphical user interface (GUI). You'll recall that interactive GUIs require that we set up event handlers to process the user events when they occur. Let's look at an example in which one handler is used to process the events from multiple sources.

Listing 5.12 shows a program that displays two buttons, labeled Red and Blue. When either button is pushed, the background color of the pane is changed accordingly. A `FlowPane` is used to layout the two buttons side by side.

LISTING 5.12

```
import javafx.application.Application;
import javafx.event.ActionEvent;
import javafx.geometry.Pos;
import javafx.scene.Scene;
import javafx.scene.control.Button;
import javafx.scene.layout.FlowPane;
import javafx.stage.Stage;

//************************************************************************
//  RedOrBlue.java       Author: Lewis/Loftus
//
//  Demonstrates the use of one handler for multiple buttons.
//************************************************************************
```

LISTING 5.12 *continued*

```
public class RedOrBlue extends Application
{
    private Button redButton, blueButton;
    private FlowPane pane;

    //-----------------------------------------------------------------
    //  Presents a GUI with two buttons that control the color of the
    //  pane background.
    //-----------------------------------------------------------------
    public void start(Stage primaryStage)
    {
        redButton = new Button("Red!");
        redButton.setOnAction(this::processColorButton);

        blueButton = new Button("Blue!");
        blueButton.setOnAction(this::processColorButton);

        pane = new FlowPane(redButton, blueButton);
        pane.setAlignment(Pos.CENTER);
        pane.setHgap(20);
        pane.setStyle("-fx-background-color: white");

        Scene scene = new Scene(pane, 300, 100);

        primaryStage.setTitle("Red or Blue?");
        primaryStage.setScene(scene);
        primaryStage.show();
    }

    //-----------------------------------------------------------------
    //  Determines which button was pressed and sets the pane color
    //  accordingly.
    //-----------------------------------------------------------------
    public void processColorButton(ActionEvent event)
    {
        if (event.getSource() == redButton)
            pane.setStyle("-fx-background-color: crimson");
        else
            pane.setStyle("-fx-background-color: deepskyblue");

    }
}
```

LISTING 5.12 *continued*

DISPLAY

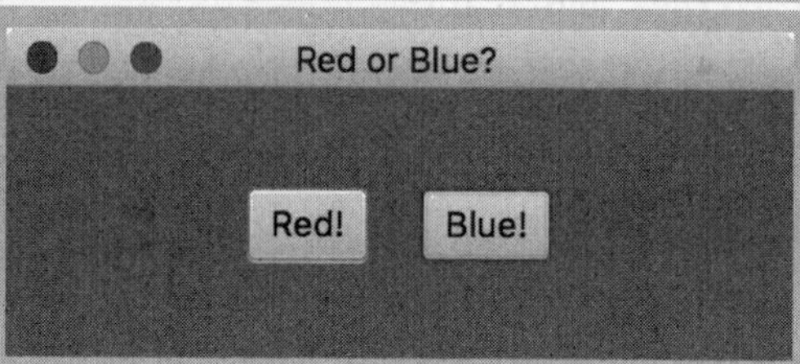

The two buttons use the same method as their event handler. Whenever either button is pressed, the `processColorButton` method is called. It uses an `if` statement to check which button generated the event. If it's the Red button, the background color of the pane is set to red. Otherwise, it must have been the Blue button, so the background color is set to blue.

KEY CONCEPT
A single event handler can be used to process events generated by multiple controls.

As always, the `ActionEvent` object that represents the event is passed into the event handler method. In previous examples we've ignored the event parameter. In this case, we call its `getSource` method which returns the control that generated the event.

Note that the variables representing the two buttons and the pane are declared as instance data at the class level so that they can be accessed in both the `start` method and the event handler method.

We could have created two separate event handler methods, one for the Red button and one for the Blue button. In that case, there would be no need to determine which button generated the event. Whether to have multiple event handlers or determine the event source when it occurs is a design decision that may depend on the situation.

SELF-REVIEW QUESTIONS *(see answers in Appendix L)*

SR 5.30 How do you set up an event handler to process events from multiple sources?

SR 5.31 How can you determine which control generated an event?

5.8 Managing Fonts

A `Font` object is used to affect what text looks like when it is displayed. A font can be applied to a `Text` object or any control that displays text, including `Label` and `Button` objects.

A font is first defined by the *font family* (or *font face*). All characters in a particular font family share the same general design. Examples of font families include Arial, Courier, Helvetica, Garamond, and Times New Roman.

KEY CONCEPT

A character font applied to a `Text`, `Label`, or `Button` object is represented by the `Font` class.

A font is further refined with other characteristics. The *font size* is expressed in units called points. The *font weight* determines how bold the characters are and the *font posture* determines if the characters are shown in italic or not. For example, you might display text in 14 point bold Garamond.

The program in Listing 5.13 displays three `Text` objects with various fonts applied.

LISTING 5.13

```
import javafx.application.Application;
import javafx.scene.Scene;
import javafx.scene.Group;
import javafx.scene.paint.Color;
import javafx.scene.text.Font;
import javafx.scene.text.FontPosture;
import javafx.scene.text.FontWeight;
import javafx.scene.text.Text;
import javafx.stage.Stage;

//************************************************************************
//  FontDemo.java       Author: Lewis/Loftus
//
//  Demonstrates the creation and use of fonts.
//************************************************************************

public class FontDemo extends Application
{
    //--------------------------------------------------------------------
    //  Displays three Text objects using various font styles.
    //--------------------------------------------------------------------
    public void start(Stage primaryStage)
    {
        Font font1 = new Font("Courier", 36);
        Font font2 = Font.font("Times", FontWeight.BOLD,
                FontPosture.ITALIC, 28);
        Font font3 = Font.font("Arial", FontPosture.ITALIC, 14);

        Text text1 = new Text(30, 55, "Dream Big");
        text1.setFont(font1);
```

LISTING 5.13 *continued*

```
        text1.setUnderline(true);

        Text text2 = new Text(150, 110, "Know thyself!");
        text2.setFont(font2);
        text2.setFill(Color.GREEN);

        Text text3 = new Text(50, 150, "In theory, there is no difference " +
            "between theory\nand practice, but in practice there is.");
        text3.setFont(font3);

        Group root = new Group(text1, text2, text3);
        Scene scene = new Scene(root, 400, 200, Color.LIGHTCYAN);

        primaryStage.setTitle("Font Demo");
        primaryStage.setScene(scene);
        primaryStage.show();
    }
}
```

DISPLAY

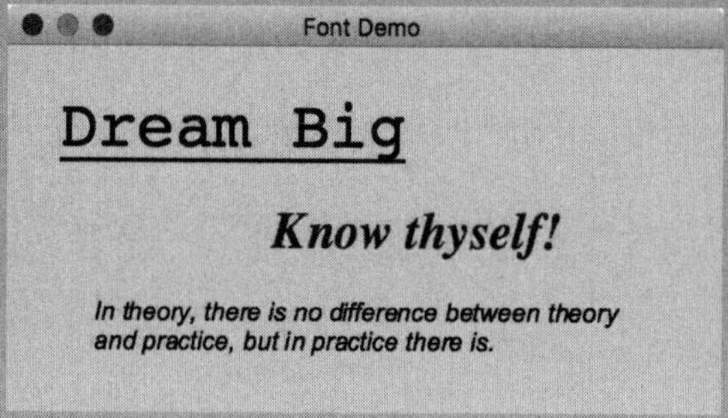

A `Font` object is applied to a particular `Text` object using its `setFont` method. The `Font` itself is created using either the `Font` constructor or by calling the static `font` method.

The `Font` constructor can only take a font size, or a font family and size. In this example, the first font, applied to the text "Dream Big," is set to be 36-point Courier. The font weight and font posture are normal by default.

The other two Font objects created in this program use the font method, which can take many different combinations of the various font characteristics. For example, the second font is created to be both bold and italic, whereas the third font is italic, leaving it at its default font weight.

The font weight is specified using constants defined in the FontWeight enumerated type, which allows you to specify several levels of boldness. Likewise, the font posture is defined by the FontPosture enumerated type, but the only options for posture are Italic or Regular.

Note that underlined text and the color of the text are not governed by the font. These characteristics are determined using calls to setUnderline and setFill on the Text object itself. Characters can also be displayed with a "strike through" effect using a call to the text's setStrikethrough method.

Also note that the third text object uses an embedded \n escape character to display the text on multiple lines.

SELF-REVIEW QUESTIONS *(see answers in Appendix L)*

SR 5.32 What are the two ways to create a Font object?

SR 5.33 What characteristics are represented by a Font object?

SR 5.34 What are some characteristics that affect how text is displayed but are *not* represented as part of a Font object?

5.9 Check Boxes

A *check box* is a button that can be toggled on or off using the mouse, indicating that a particular condition is set or unset. For example, you might use a check box to indicate whether the user has acknowledged and accepted the Terms of Use for your program.

Although you might have a group of check boxes indicating a set of options, each check box operates independently. That is, each can be set to on or off and the status of one does not automatically influence the others. For example, you might use a series of check boxes to indicate which toppings should be included on a pizza. They could be checked or unchecked in any combination.

The program made up of the classes in Listings 5.14 and 5.15 displays two check boxes and a Text object. The check boxes determine whether the text is displayed in bold, italic, both, or neither. Any combination of bold and italic are valid.

The details of the GUI are specified in the StyleOptionsPane class in Listing 5.15. A check box is defined by the CheckBox class from the JavaFX API. When a check box is selected or deselected, it generates an action event. In this example, both check boxes are processed by the same event handler method.

Examine how the processCheckBoxAction method handles a change in the state of either check box. Instead of bothering to determine which check box generated the event, or keep track of whether a box was selected or deselected, the event handler simply examines the current state of both check boxes and resets the font accordingly. Local variables are used to set the font weight and posture,

LISTING 5.14

```
import javafx.application.Application;
import javafx.geometry.Pos;
import javafx.scene.Scene;
import javafx.stage.Stage;

//**************************************************************************
//  StyleOptions.java       Author: Lewis/Loftus
//
//  Demonstrates the use of check boxes.
//**************************************************************************

public class StyleOptions extends Application
{
    //-----------------------------------------------------------------------
    //  Creates and presents the program window.
    //-----------------------------------------------------------------------
    public void start(Stage primaryStage)
    {
        StyleOptionsPane pane = new StyleOptionsPane();
        pane.setAlignment(Pos.CENTER);
        pane.setStyle("-fx-background-color: skyblue");

        Scene scene = new Scene(pane, 400, 150);

        primaryStage.setTitle("Style Options");
        primaryStage.setScene(scene);
        primaryStage.show();
    }
}
```

LISTING 5.14 *continued*

DISPLAY

LISTING 5.15

```
import javafx.event.ActionEvent;
import javafx.geometry.Pos;
import javafx.scene.control.CheckBox;
import javafx.scene.layout.HBox;
import javafx.scene.layout.VBox;
import javafx.scene.text.Text;
import javafx.scene.text.Font;
import javafx.scene.text.FontPosture;
import javafx.scene.text.FontWeight;

//************************************************************************
//  StyleOptionsPane.java       Author: Lewis/Loftus
//
//  Demonstrates the use of check boxes.
//************************************************************************

public class StyleOptionsPane extends VBox
{
    private Text phrase;
    private CheckBox boldCheckBox, italicCheckBox;
```

LISTING 5.15 *continued*

```
   //------------------------------------------------------------------
   //  Sets up this pane with a Text object and check boxes that
   //  determine the style of the text font.
   //------------------------------------------------------------------
   public StyleOptionsPane()
   {
      phrase = new Text("Say it with style!");
      phrase.setFont(new Font("Helvetica", 36));

      boldCheckBox = new CheckBox("Bold");
      boldCheckBox.setOnAction(this::processCheckBoxAction);
      italicCheckBox = new CheckBox("Italic");
      italicCheckBox.setOnAction(this::processCheckBoxAction);

      HBox options = new HBox(boldCheckBox, italicCheckBox);
      options.setAlignment(Pos.CENTER);
      options.setSpacing(20);   // between the check boxes

      setSpacing(20);   // between the text and the check boxes
      getChildren().addAll(phrase, options);
   }

   //------------------------------------------------------------------
   //  Updates the font style of the displayed text.
   //------------------------------------------------------------------
   public void processCheckBoxAction(ActionEvent event)
   {
      FontWeight weight = FontWeight.NORMAL;
      FontPosture posture = FontPosture.REGULAR;

      if (boldCheckBox.isSelected())
         weight = FontWeight.BOLD;

      if (italicCheckBox.isSelected())
         posture = FontPosture.ITALIC;

      phrase.setFont(Font.font("Helvetica", weight, posture, 36));
   }
}
```

which are initially assumed to be unselected. Then the `isSelected` method of each check box is called, which returns `true` if the check box is currently selected. Finally, the font of the text is set appropriately.

There are two new layout panes used in this program. The `HBox` and `VBox` layout panes arrange their nodes, respectively, in a single row (horizontally) or a single column (vertically). Appendix G provides an overview of JavaFX layout panes.

The `StyleOptionsPane` class extends `VBox`, which is used to center the text above the two check boxes. A separate `HBox` is set up to put the check boxes side by side horizontally.

KEY CONCEPT
The `HBox` and `VBox` layout panes arrange their nodes in a single row or column, respectively.

Since the nodes aren't added using the `VBox` constructor, they are added after the fact. But you don't add nodes to a pane directly. Instead, you call the `getChildren` method, which returns all nodes already in the pane (which is none in this case) and then call the `addAll` method to add the new nodes.

SELF-REVIEW QUESTIONS *(see answers in Appendix L)*

SR 5.35 Which of the following could be determined using one or more check boxes? Explain.

a. The condiments that should be put on a hamburger.
b. Whether or not to collate a print job.
c. Your favorite sport.
d. All sports that you play.
e. Your age range (0–12, 13–18, 19–29, 30–50, etc.)

SR 5.36 How do you determine if a particular check box is currently checked?

SR 5.37 How does an `HBox` layout pane arrange its nodes? A `VBox`?

5.10 Radio Buttons

A *radio button* is used with other radio buttons to provide a set of mutually exclusive options. Unlike a check box, a radio button is not particularly useful by itself. It has meaning only when grouped with other radio buttons. Only one option in a group of radio buttons is valid. At any point in time, only one button of a radio button group is selected (on). When a radio button is pushed, the other button in the group that is currently on is automatically toggled off.

KEY CONCEPT
A group of radio buttons provide a set of mutually exclusive options.

The term "radio buttons" comes from the way the pre-set station buttons worked on an old-fashioned car radio. At any point, one button was pushed in to specify the current station. When another was pushed to change the station, the current one automatically popped out.

The program made up of the classes shown in Listings 5.16 and 5.17 displays a group of radio buttons and a `Text` object. The radio buttons determine which phrase is displayed. Because only one phrase is displayed at a time, the use of radio buttons is appropriate.

A radio button control is represented by the JavaFX `RadioButton` class. A `ToggleGroup` object is used to create a set of mutually exclusive radio buttons. To add a button to a group, you pass the group object to the radio button's `setToggleGroup` method.

LISTING 5.16

```
import javafx.application.Application;
import javafx.geometry.Pos;
import javafx.scene.Scene;
import javafx.stage.Stage;

//************************************************************************
//  QuoteOptions.java        Author: Lewis/Loftus
//
//  Demonstrates the use of radio buttons.
//************************************************************************
public class QuoteOptions extends Application
{
   //---------------------------------------------------------------------
   //  Creates and presents the program window.
   //---------------------------------------------------------------------
   public void start(Stage primaryStage)
   {
      QuoteOptionsPane pane = new QuoteOptionsPane();
      pane.setAlignment(Pos.CENTER);
      pane.setStyle("-fx-background-color: lightgreen");

      Scene scene = new Scene(pane, 500, 150);

      primaryStage.setTitle("Quote Options");
      primaryStage.setScene(scene);
      primaryStage.show();
   }
}
```

LISTING 5.16 *continued*

DISPLAY

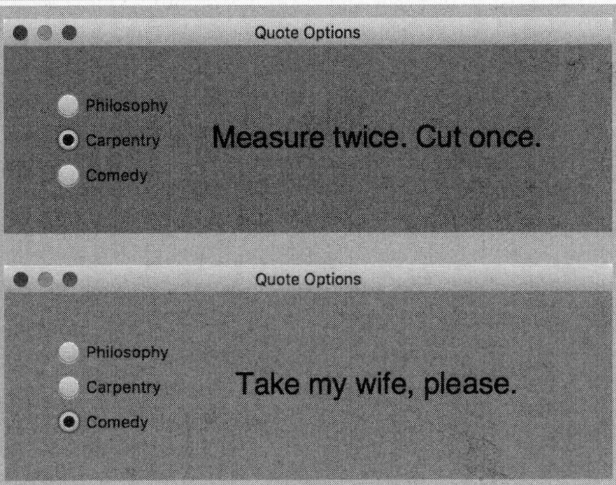

LISTING 5.17

```
import javafx.event.ActionEvent;
import javafx.geometry.Pos;
import javafx.scene.control.RadioButton;
import javafx.scene.control.ToggleGroup;
import javafx.scene.layout.HBox;
import javafx.scene.layout.StackPane;
import javafx.scene.layout.VBox;
import javafx.scene.text.Text;
import javafx.scene.text.Font;

//************************************************************************
//  QuoteOptionsPane.java       Author: Lewis/Loftus
//
//  Demonstrates the use of radio buttons.
//************************************************************************

public class QuoteOptionsPane extends HBox
{
    private Text quote;
```

LISTING 5.17 *continued*

```
private String philosophyQuote, carpentryQuote, comedyQuote;
private RadioButton philosophyButton, carpentryButton, comedyButton;

//-----------------------------------------------------------------
// Sets up this pane with a Text object and radio buttons that
// determine which phrase is displayed.
//-----------------------------------------------------------------
public QuoteOptionsPane()
{
    philosophyQuote = "I think, therefore I am.";
    carpentryQuote = "Measure twice. Cut once.";
    comedyQuote = "Take my wife, please.";

    quote = new Text(philosophyQuote);
    quote.setFont(new Font("Helvetica", 24));

    StackPane quotePane = new StackPane(quote);

    quotePane.setPrefSize(300, 100);

    ToggleGroup group = new ToggleGroup();

    philosophyButton = new RadioButton("Philosophy");
    philosophyButton.setSelected(true);
    philosophyButton.setToggleGroup(group);
    philosophyButton.setOnAction(this::processRadioButtonAction);

    carpentryButton = new RadioButton("Carpentry");
    carpentryButton.setToggleGroup(group);
    carpentryButton.setOnAction(this::processRadioButtonAction);

    comedyButton = new RadioButton("Comedy");
    comedyButton.setToggleGroup(group);
    comedyButton.setOnAction(this::processRadioButtonAction);

    VBox options = new VBox(philosophyButton, carpentryButton,
        comedyButton);
    options.setAlignment(Pos.CENTER_LEFT);
    options.setSpacing(10);

    setSpacing(20);
    getChildren().addAll(options, quotePane);
}

//-----------------------------------------------------------------
// Updates the content of the displayed text.
//-----------------------------------------------------------------
```

LISTING 5.17 *continued*

```
    public void processRadioButtonAction(ActionEvent event)
    {
        if (philosophyButton.isSelected())
            quote.setText(philosophyQuote);
        else if (carpentryButton.isSelected())
            quote.setText(carpentryQuote);
        else
            quote.setText(comedyQuote);
    }
}
```

One event handler is used to process all three radio buttons. A radio button produces an action event when it is selected. The `processRadioButtonAction` method uses a nested `if` statement to determine which button is currently selected and sets the text accordingly.

Like the previous example, this program uses an `HBox` and a `VBox` to organize the GUI elements. This time, however, the `VBox` is used to organize the buttons and is put into an `HBox` to lay it out next to the text.

SELF-REVIEW QUESTIONS *(see answers in Appendix L)*

SR 5.38 Which of the following could be determined using a group of radio buttons? Explain.

a. The condiments that should be put on a hamburger.
b. Whether or not to collate a print job.
c. Your favorite sport.
d. All sports that you play.
e. Your age range (0–12, 13–18, 19–29, 30–50, etc.)

SR 5.39 What is the primary difference between check boxes and radio buttons?

SR 5.40 How do you specify that a particular set of radio buttons work together to provide a set of mutually exclusive options?

Summary of Key Concepts

- Conditionals and loops allow us to control the flow of execution through a method.
- An `if` statement allows a program to choose whether to execute a particular statement.
- A loop allows a program to execute a statement multiple times.
- Logical operators are often used to construct sophisticated conditions.
- Proper indentation is important for human readability; it shows the relationship between one statement and another.
- An `if-else` statement allows a program to do one thing if a condition is true and another thing if the condition is false.
- In a nested `if` statement, an `else` clause is matched to the closest unmatched `if`.
- The relative order of characters in Java is defined by the Unicode character set.
- The `compareTo` method can be used to determine the relative order of strings.
- A `while` statement executes the same statement until its condition becomes false.
- We must design our programs carefully to avoid infinite loops.
- An iterator is an object that helps you process a group of related items.
- The delimiters used to separate tokens in a `Scanner` object can be explicitly set as needed.
- An `ArrayList` object stores a list of objects and lets you access them using an integer index.
- When an `ArrayList` object is created, you specify the type of element that will be stored in the list.
- A single event handler can be used to process events generated by multiple controls.
- A character font applied to a `Text`, `Label`, or `Button` object is represented by the `Font` class.
- The `HBox` and `VBox` layout panes arrange their nodes in a single row or column, respectively.
- A group of radio buttons provide a set of mutually exclusive options.

Exercises

EX 5.1 What happens in the `MinOfThree` program if two or more of the values are equal? If exactly two of the values are equal, does it matter whether the equal values are lower or higher than the third?

EX 5.2 What is wrong with the following code fragment? Rewrite it so that it produces correct output.

```
if (age <= 18)
   System.out.println("Sorry, you are too young");
   System.out.println("Please try again when you are
   older");
else
   System.out.println("Congratulations, welcome to the
   club");
```

EX 5.3 What is wrong with the following code fragment? Will this code compile if it is part of an otherwise valid program? Explain.

```
if (length = MIN_LENGTH)
   System.out.println("The length is minimal.");
```

EX 5.4 What output is produced by the following code fragment?

```
String language = "Java";
int n = 10;
if (n <10)
   System.out.println(language);
   System.out.println("Ada");
   n = n + 2;
System.out.println(language);
```

EX 5.5 What output is produced by the following code fragment?

```
int limit = 100, num1 = 15, num2 = 40;
if (limit <= limit)
{
   if (num1 == num2)
      System.out.println("lemon");
   System.out.println("lime");
}
System.out.println("grape");
```

EX 5.6 Consider the following code:

```
ArrayList<String> scores = new ArrayList<String>();
scores.add("92");
scores.add("120");
```

```
scores.add("73");
scores.add("89");
Collections.sort(scores);
System.out.println(scores);
```

Some values are stored as strings in an `ArrayList`. When this code is executed, the result is as follows:

```
[120, 73, 89, 92]
```

Explain why this is observed.

EX 5.7 What output is produced by the following code fragment?

```
int num = 0, max = 20;
while (num < max)
{
   System.out.println(num);
   num += 4;
}
```

EX 5.8 What output is produced by the following code fragment?

```
int num = 1, max = 20;
while (num < max)
{
   if (num%2 == 0)
      System.out.println(num);
   num++;
}
```

EX 5.9 What is wrong with the following code fragment? How can it be corrected?

```
int i = 50;
while (i ! = 0){
   System.out.println(i);
   i = i -3;
}
```

EX 5.10 Write a `while` loop that verifies that the user enters a positive integer value.

EX 5.11 Write a code fragment that reads and prints integer values entered by a user until a particular sentinel value (stored in `SENTINEL`) is entered. Do not print the sentinel value.

EX 5.12 Write a method called `maxOfTwo` that accepts two integer parameters and returns the larger of the two.

EX 5.13 Write a method called `larger` that accepts two floating point parameters (of type `double`) and returns true if the first parameter is greater than the second, and false otherwise.

EX 5.14 Write a method called `evenlyDivisible` that accepts two integer parameters and returns true if the first parameter is evenly divisible by the second, or vice versa, and false otherwise. Return false if either parameter is zero.

EX 5.15 Write a method called `isAlpha` that accepts a character parameter and returns true if that character is either an uppercase or lowercase alphabetic letter.

EX 5.16 Write a method called `floatEquals` that accepts three floating point values as parameters. The method should return true if the first two parameters are equal within the tolerance of the third parameter.

EX 5.17 Write a method called `isIsosceles` that accepts three integer parameters that represent the lengths of the sides of a triangle. The method returns true if the triangle is isosceles but not equilateral (meaning that exactly two of the sides have an equal length), and false otherwise.

EX 5.18 Would it be better to use check boxes or radio buttons to determine the following? Explain.

a. Your favorite book genre.

b. Whether to make your profile visible or not.

c. Which image format to use (jpg, png, or gif).

d. Which programming languages you know.

Programming Projects

PP 5.1 Write a program that reads an integer value from the user representing a year. The purpose of the program is to determine if the year is a leap year (and therefore has 29 days in February) in the Gregorian calendar. A year is a leap year if it is divisible by 4, unless it is also divisible by 100 but not 400. For example, the year 2003 is not a leap year, but 2004 is. The year 1900 is not a leap year because it is divisible by 100, but the year 2000 is a leap year because even though it is divisible by 100, it is also divisible by 400. Produce an error message for any input value less than 1582 (the year the Gregorian calendar was adopted).

PP 5.2 Modify the solution to the previous project so that the user can evaluate multiple years. Allow the user to terminate the program using an appropriate sentinel value. Validate each input value to ensure it is greater than or equal to 1582.

PP 5.3 Write a program that determines and prints the number of odd, even, and zero digits in an integer value read from the keyboard.

VideoNote
Developing a solution of PP 5.4.

PP 5.4 Write a program that plays the Hi-Lo guessing game with numbers. The program should pick a random number between 1 and 100 (inclusive), then repeatedly prompt the user to guess the number. On each guess, report to the user that he or she is correct or that the guess is high or low. Continue accepting guesses until the user guesses correctly or chooses to quit. Use a sentinel value to determine whether the user wants to quit. Count the number of guesses and report that value when the user guesses correctly. At the end of each game (by quitting or a correct guess), prompt to determine whether the user wants to play again. Continue playing games until the user chooses to stop.

PP 5.5 Write a program that accepts a user's name as an input and calculates the numeric value of the name. The numeric value is calculated by summing each letter of the name, assuming a = 1, b = 2, and so on. The case of the letter does not matter, that is, a = 1 and A = 1.

PP 5.6 Using the `Coin` class defined in this chapter, design and implement a driver class called `FlipRace` whose `main` method creates two `Coin` objects, then continually flips them both to see which coin first comes up heads three flips in a row. Continue flipping the coins until one of the coins wins the race, and consider the possibility that they might tie. Print the results of each turn, and at the end print the winner and total number of flips that were required.

PP 5.7 Write a program that plays the Rock-Paper-Scissors game against the computer. When played between two people, each person picks one of three options (usually shown by a hand gesture) at the same time, and a winner is determined. In the game, Rock beats Scissors, Scissors beats Paper, and Paper beats Rock. The program should randomly choose one of the three options (without revealing it), then prompt for the user's selection. At that point, the program reveals both choices and prints a statement indicating if the user won, the computer won, or if it was a tie. Continue playing until the user chooses to stop, then print the number of user wins, losses, and ties.

PP 5.8 Design and implement an application that simulates a simple slot machine in which three numbers between 0 and 9 are randomly selected and printed side by side. Print an appropriate statement if all three of the numbers are the same, or if any two of the numbers are the same. Continue playing until the user chooses to stop.

PP 5.9 Modify the `Die` class from Chapter 4 so that the `setFaceValue` method does nothing if the parameter is outside of the valid range of values.

PP 5.10 Modify the `Account` class from Chapter 4 so that it performs validity checks on the deposit and withdraw operations. Specifically, don't allow the deposit of a negative number or a withdrawal that exceeds the current balance. Print appropriate error messages if these problems occur.

PP 5.11 Using the `PairOfDice` class from PP 4.9, design and implement a class to play a game called Pig. In this game, the user competes against the computer. On each turn, the current player rolls a pair of dice and accumulates points. The goal is to reach 100 points before your opponent does. If, on any turn, the player rolls a 1, all points accumulated for that round are forfeited and control of the dice moves to the other player. If the player rolls two 1s in one turn, the player loses all points accumulated thus far in the game and loses control of the dice. The player may voluntarily turn over the dice after each roll. Therefore, the player must decide to either roll again (be a pig) and risk losing points, or relinquish control of the dice, possibly allowing the other player to win. Implement the computer player such that it always relinquishes the dice after accumulating 20 or more points in any given round.

PP 5.12 Design and implement a program to process golf scores. The scores of four golfers are stored in a text file. Each line represents one hole, and the file contains 18 lines. Each line contains five values: par for the hole followed by the number of strokes each golfer used on that hole. Store the totals for par and the players in an `ArrayList`. Determine the winner and produce a table showing how well each golfer did (compared to par).

PP 5.13 Design and implement a program that compares two text input files, line by line, for equality. Print any lines that are not equivalent.

PP 5.14 Design and implement a program that counts the number of integer values in a text input file. Produce a table listing the values you identify as integers from the input file.

PP 5.15 Design and implement a program that counts the number of punctuation marks in a text input file. Produce a table that shows how many times each symbol occurred.

PP 5.16 Write a JavaFX application that displays a form similar to the customs form that visitors to a country fill out on arrival. The form should list at least five restricted items and the corresponding fees and give the user the ability to select an item with a check box. Display the total fees and appropriate messages on the form.

PP 5.17 Write a JavaFX application that allows the user to select a color out of five options provided by a set of radio buttons. Change the color of a displayed square accordingly.

PP 5.18 Write a JavaFX application that displays the drawing of a traffic light. Allow the user to select the state of the light (stop, caution, or go) from a set of radio buttons.

PP 5.19 Write a JavaFX application that displays an image and allows the user to select one out of three different sizes to view the image via radio buttons.

SOFTWARE FAILURE

Therac-25

What Happened?

The Therac-25 was a radiation therapy machine used to deliver targeted electron or X-ray beams in order to destroy cancerous tissue. While in use, hundreds of patients were given proper treatments using this device. But in six documented cases from 1985 to 1987, the Therac-25 delivered an overdose of radiation resulting in severe disability and death.

In a typical treatment, the patient lies down and the operator adjusts the machine to target the appropriate area of the body. The operator sets the parameters of the treatment on the machine's computer console and pushes a button to deliver the radiation. Patients are told that a typical side effect is minor skin discomfort similar to that of a mild sunburn.

In the accident cases, some patients reported feeling a "tremendous force of heat" or an "electric tingling shock." In one case, the patient lost the use of her shoulder and arm and had to have her left breast removed because of the radiation damage. Several others died of radiation poisoning.

The amount of radiation delivered is measured in rads (radiation absorbed dose). A standard treatment is around 200 rads. It's estimated that the accidents caused 20,000 rads to be administered.

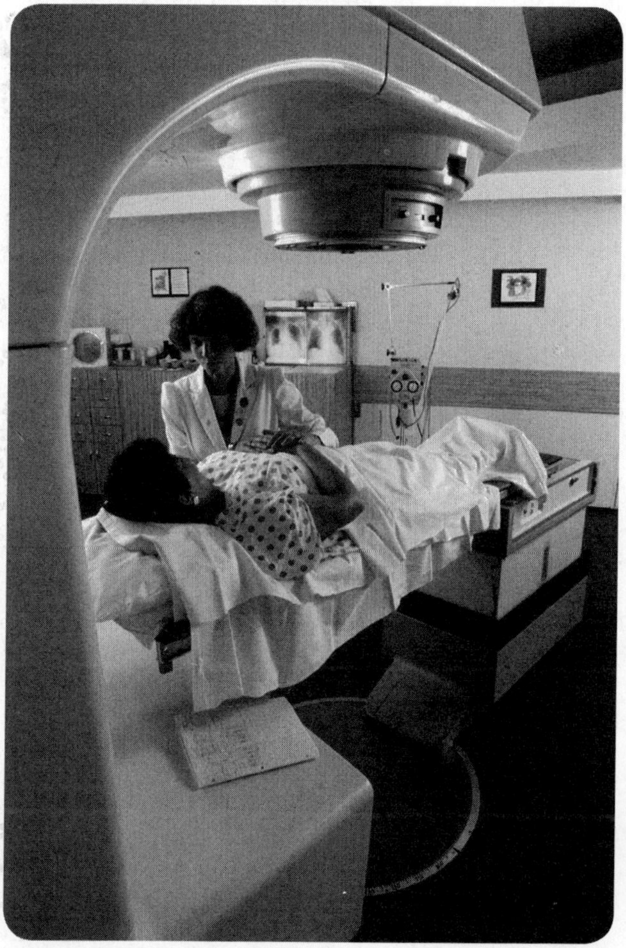

■ Radiation therapy machines deliver precise amounts of targeted radiation.

What Caused It?

The operators were told the Therac-25 had so many safety precautions that it would be "virtually impossible" to overdose a patient. But part of the software used in the Therac-25 was reused from an earlier version of the machine that had included many hardware-based safety precautions. Thus, the hardware features had masked problems with the underlying software. The safety features of the Therac-25 were dominantly software based, and the lurking problems emerged.

It turned out that if the operator mistyped a parameter and then corrected it in a particular way, the software allowed the machine to deliver the maximum radiation dose without diffusing it properly. It was such a strange error that technicians testing the machine failed to reproduce the problem. At one point, one of the machines that had clearly caused an overdose was put back into service after technicians could find nothing wrong with it.

Analysts say that the software problems were only part of the reason the accidents occurred. While there were fundamental programming errors, there was also inadequate attention to safety issues in general. And one reason the machines were used for so long was that the problems were not reported as accurately and thoroughly as they should have been.

Lessons Learned

Software safety is the dominant issue in this case. When human lives are on the line, it's difficult to imagine not doing everything possible to ensure that your software is as robust as possible. It comes down to risk analysis. How much are you willing to risk that a particular piece of software you're developing still contains an error? For many applications, a problem might cause inconvenience to the user and may have business implications, but other applications literally have people's lives at stake.

This case is also an example of the difficulty of isolating the problem. For hundreds of patients, the Therac-25 provided excellent treatment. One of the initial complaints was dismissed without proper investigation or reporting. Later, when a problem had clearly occurred, it could not be replicated. This was an example of a truly exceptional situation—one that does not occur usually or under normal circumstances.

Source: computingcases.org, IEEE Computer

More Conditionals and Loops

6

CHAPTER OBJECTIVES

- Examine conditional processing using `switch` statements.
- Discuss the conditional operator.
- Examine alternative repetition statements: the `do` and `for` loops.
- Draw graphics with the aid of conditionals and loops.
- Apply transformations to graphical objects.

In Chapter 5, we examined the `if` statement for making decisions and the `while` statement for looping. This chapter explores several additional statements in Java for performing similar tasks. In particular, it examines the `switch` conditional statement, as well as the `do` and `for` loops. These alternative statements differ in key details, and any particular situation may lend itself to the use of one over another. The Graphics Track sections of this chapter explore the use of conditionals and loops to control our graphics and examine the role of transformations.

6.1 The switch Statement

Another conditional statement in Java is called the *switch statement,* which causes the executing program to follow one of several paths based on a single value. Similar logic could be constructed with multiple `if` statements, but in the cases where it is warranted, a `switch` statement usually makes code easier to read.

The `switch` statement evaluates an expression to determine a value and then matches that value with one of several possible *cases*. Each case has statements associated with it. After evaluating the expression, control jumps to the statement associated with the first case that matches the value. Consider the following example:

```
switch (idChar)
{
    case 'A':
        aCount = aCount + 1;
        break;
    case 'B':
        bCount = bCount + 1;
        break;
    case 'C':
        cCount = cCount + 1;
        break;
    default:
        System.out.println("Error in Identification Character.");
}
```

First, the expression is evaluated. In this example, the expression is a simple `char` variable called `idChar`. Execution then transfers to the first statement after the case value that matches the result of the expression. Therefore, if `idChar` contains an `'A'`, the variable `aCount` is incremented. If it contains a `'B'`, the case for `'A'` is skipped and processing continues where `bCount` is incremented. Likewise, if `idChar` contains a `'C'`, that case is processed.

KEY CONCEPT
A `switch` statement matches a character or integer value to one of several possible cases.

If no case value matches that of the expression, execution continues with the optional *default case,* indicated by the reserved word `default`. If no default case exists, no statements in the `switch` statement are executed and processing continues with the statement after the `switch` statement. It is often a good idea to include a default case, even if you don't expect it to be executed.

When a `break` statement is encountered, processing jumps to the statement following the `switch` statement. A `break` statement is usually used to break out of each case of a `switch` statement. Without a `break` statement, processing continues into the next case of the `switch`. Therefore, if the `break` statement at the end of the `'A'` case in the previous example was not there, both the `aCount` and `bCount` variables would be incremented when the `idChar` contains an `'A'`. Usually, we want to perform only one case, so a `break` statement is almost always used. Occasionally, though, the "pass through" feature comes in handy.

KEY CONCEPT

A break statement is usually used at the end of each case alternative of a `switch` statement.

You'll remember that the `break` statement was briefly mentioned in Chapter 5, because it could be used in other types of loops and conditionals. We warned then that such processing is usually unnecessary and its use is considered by many developers to be bad practice. The `switch` statement is the exception to this guideline. Using a `break` statement is the only way to make sure the code for only one case is executed.

Switch Statement

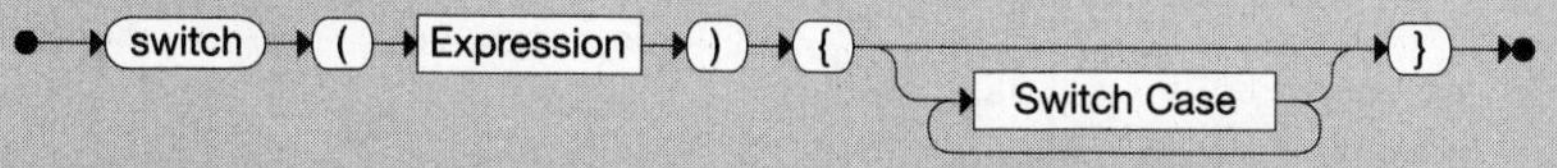

Switch Case

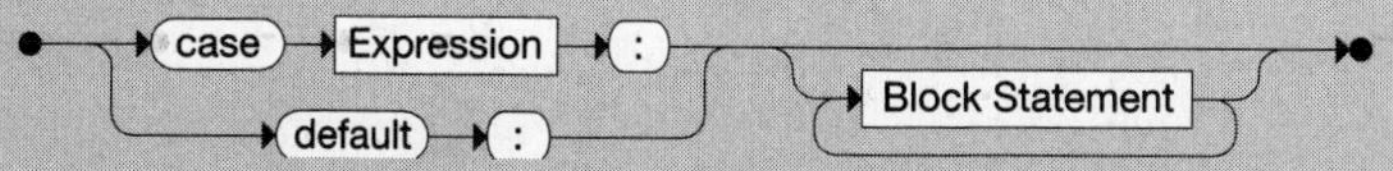

The `switch` statement evaluates the initial Expression and matches its value with one of the cases. Processing continues with the Statement corresponding to that case. The optional `default` case will be executed if no other case matches.

Example:

```
switch (numValues)
{
   case 0:
      System.out.println("No values were entered.");
      break;
   case 1:
      System.out.println("One value was entered.");
      break;
   case 2:
      System.out.println("Two values were entered.");
      break;
   default:
      System.out.println("Too many values were entered.");
}
```

The expression evaluated at the beginning of a `switch` statement must be of type `char`, `byte`, `short`, `int`, or an enumerated type. As of Java 7, a `switch` can also be performed on a `String`. But a switch expression cannot be a boolean or a floating point value. Furthermore, the value of each case must be a constant; it cannot be a variable or other expression. This limits the situations in which a `switch` statement is appropriate. But when it is appropriate, it can make the code easier to read and understand.

Note also that the implicit boolean condition of a `switch` statement is based on equality. The expression at the beginning of the statement is compared to each case value to determine which one it equals. A `switch` statement cannot be used to determine other relational operations (such as less than), unless some preliminary processing is done. For example, the `GradeReport` program in Listing 6.1 prints a comment based on a numeric grade that is entered by the user.

LISTING 6.1

```
//********************************************************************
//  GradeReport.java       Author: Lewis/Loftus
//
//  Demonstrates the use of a switch statement.
//********************************************************************

import java.util.Scanner;

public class GradeReport
{
   //-----------------------------------------------------------------
   //  Reads a grade from the user and prints comments accordingly.
   //-----------------------------------------------------------------
   public static void main(String[] args)
   {
      int grade, category;

      Scanner scan = new Scanner(System.in);

      System.out.print("Enter a numeric grade (0 to 100): ");
      grade = scan.nextInt();

      category = grade / 10;

      System.out.print("That grade is ");

      switch (category)
      {
         case 10:
            System.out.println("a perfect score. Well done.");
            break;
         case 9:
            System.out.println("well above average. Excellent.");
            break;
         case 8:
            System.out.println("above average. Nice job.");
            break;
```

LISTING 6.1 *continued*

```
         case 7:
            System.out.println("average.");
            break;
         case 6:
            System.out.println("below average. You should see the");
            System.out.println("instructor to clarify the material "
                               + "presented in class.");
            break;
         default:
            System.out.println("not passing.");
      }
   }
}
```

OUTPUT

```
Enter a numeric grade (0 to 100): 86
That grade is above average. Nice job.
```

In `GradeReport`, the category of the grade is determined by dividing the grade by 10 using integer division, resulting in an integer value between 0 and 10 (assuming a valid grade is entered). This result is used as the expression of the `switch`, which prints various messages for grades 60 or higher and a default sentence for all other values.

Note that any `switch` statement could be implemented as a set of nested `if` statements. However, nested `if` statements can be difficult for a human reader to understand and are error prone to implement and debug. But because a `switch` can evaluate only equality, sometimes nested `if` statements are necessary. It depends on the situation.

SELF-REVIEW QUESTIONS *(see answers in Appendix L)*

SR 6.1 When a Java program is running, what happens if the expression evaluated for a `switch` statement does not match any of the case values associated with the statement?

SR 6.2 What happens if a case in a `switch` statement does not end with a `break` statement?

SR 6.3 What is the output of the `GradeReport` program if the user enters 72? What if the user enters 46? What if the user enters 123?

SR 6.4 Transform the following nested `if` statement into an equivalent `switch` statement.

```
if (num1 == 5)
   myChar = 'W';
else
   if (num1 == 6)
      myChar = 'X';
   else
      if (num1 == 7)
         myChar = 'Y';
      else
         myChar = 'Z';
```

6.2 The Conditional Operator

The Java *conditional operator* is similar to an `if-else` statement in some ways. It is a *ternary operator* because it requires three operands. The symbol for the conditional operator is usually written `?:`, but it is not like other operators in that the two symbols that make it up are always separated. The following is an example of an expression that contains the conditional operator:

```
(total > MAX) ? total + 1 : total * 2;
```

Preceding the `?` is a boolean condition. Following the `?` are two expressions separated by the `:` symbol. The entire conditional expression returns the value of the first expression if the condition is true, and returns the value of the second expression if the condition is false.

KEY CONCEPT
The conditional operator evaluates to one of two possible values based on a boolean condition.

Keep in mind that this example is an expression that returns a value. The conditional operator is just that, an operator, not a statement that stands on its own. Usually, we want to do something with that value, such as assign it to a variable:

```
total = (total > MAX) ? total + 1 : total * 2;
```

The distinction between the conditional operator and a conditional statement can be subtle. In many ways, the `?:` operator lets us form succinct logic that serves as an abbreviated `if-else` statement. The previous statement is functionally equivalent to, but sometimes more convenient than, the following:

```
if (total > MAX)
   total = total + 1;
else
   total = total * 2;
```

Let's look at a couple more examples. Consider the following declaration:

```
int larger = (num1 > num2) ? num1 : num2;
```

If `num1` is greater than `num2`, the value of `num1` is returned and used to initialize the variable `larger`. If not, the value of `num2` is returned and used to initialize `larger`. Similarly, the following statement prints the smaller of the two values:

```
System.out.println("Smaller: " + ((num1 < num2) ? num1 : num2));
```

The conditional operator is occasionally helpful to evaluate a short condition and return a result. It is not a replacement for an `if-else` statement, however, because the operands to the `?:` operator are expressions, not necessarily full statements. Even when the conditional operator is a viable alternative, you should use it carefully because it may be less readable than an `if-else` statement.

SELF-REVIEW QUESTIONS *(see answers in Appendix L)*

SR 6.5 What is the difference between a conditional operator and a conditional statement?

SR 6.6 Write a declaration that initializes a `char` variable named `id` to `'A'` if the `boolean` variable `first` is true and to `'B'` otherwise.

SR 6.7 Express the following logic in a succinct manner using the conditional operator.

```
if (val <= 10)
    System.out.println("The value is not greater than 10.");
else
    System.out.println("The value is greater than 10.");
```

6.3 The do Statement

Remember from Chapter 5 that the `while` statement first examines its condition, then executes its body if that condition is true. The *do statement* is similar to the `while` statement except that its termination condition is at the end of the loop body. Like the `while` loop, the `do` loop executes the statement in the loop body until the condition becomes false. The condition is written at the end of the loop to indicate that it is not evaluated until the loop body is executed. Note that the body of a `do` loop is always executed at least once. Figure 6.1 shows this processing.

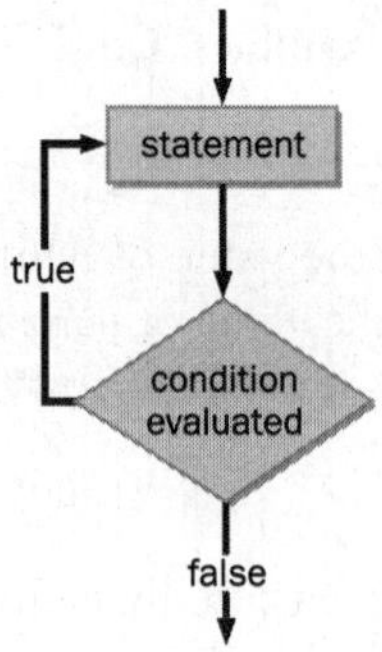

FIGURE 6.1 The logic of a do loop

The following code prints the numbers from 1 to 5 using a do loop. Compare this code with the similar example in Chapter 5 that uses a while loop to accomplish the same task.

```
int count = 0;
do
{
   count++;
   System.out.println(count);
}
while (count < 5);
```

KEY CONCEPT

A do statement executes its loop body at least once.

Note that the do loop begins simply with the reserved word do. The body of the do loop continues until the *while clause* that contains the boolean condition that determines whether the loop body will be executed again. Sometimes it is difficult to determine whether a line of code that begins with the reserved word while is the beginning of a while loop or the end of a do loop.

Let's look at another example of the do loop. The program called ReverseNumber, shown in Listing 6.2, reads an integer from the user and reverses its digits mathematically.

Do Statement

The do loop repeatedly executes the specified Statement as long as the boolean Expression is true. The Statement is executed at least once, then the Expression is evaluated to determine whether the Statement should be executed again.

Example:

```
do
{
   System.out.print("Enter a word:");
   word = scan.next();
   System.out.println(word);
}
while (!word.equals("quit"));
```

LISTING 6.2

```
//********************************************************************
//  ReverseNumber.java       Author: Lewis/Loftus
//
//  Demonstrates the use of a do loop.
//********************************************************************

import java.util.Scanner;

public class ReverseNumber
{
   //-----------------------------------------------------------------
   //  Reverses the digits of an integer mathematically.
   //-----------------------------------------------------------------
   public static void main(String[] args)
   {
      int number, lastDigit, reverse = 0;

      Scanner scan = new Scanner(System.in);

      System.out.print("Enter a positive integer: ");
      number = scan.nextInt();

      do
      {
         lastDigit = number % 10;
         reverse = (reverse * 10) + lastDigit;
         number = number / 10;
      }
      while (number > 0);

      System.out.println("That number reversed is " + reverse);
   }
}
```

LISTING 6.2 *continued*

OUTPUT

```
Enter a positive integer: 2896
That number reversed is 6982
```

The `do` loop in the `ReverseNumber` program uses the remainder operation to determine the digit in the 1's position, then adds it into the reversed number, then truncates that digit from the original number using integer division. The `do` loop terminates when we run out of digits to process, which corresponds to the point when the variable `number` reaches the value zero. Carefully trace the logic of this program with a few examples to see how it works.

If you know you want to perform the body of a loop at least once, then you probably want to use a `do` statement. A `do` loop has many of the same properties as a `while` statement, so it must also be checked for termination conditions to avoid infinite loops.

SELF-REVIEW QUESTIONS *(see answers in Appendix L)*

SR 6.8 Compare and contrast a `while` loop and a `do` loop.

SR 6.9 What output is produced by the following code fragment?

```
int low = 0, high = 10;
do
{
   System.out.println(low);
   low++;
} while (low < high);
```

SR 6.10 What output is produced by the following code fragment?

```
int low = 10, high = 0;
do
{
   System.out.println(low);
   low++;
} while (low <= high);
```

SR 6.11 Write a `do` loop to obtain a sequence of positive integers from the user, using zero as a sentinel value. The program should output the sum of the numbers.

6.4 The for Statement

The while and the do statements are good to use when you don't initially know how many times you want to execute the loop body. The *for statement* is another repetition statement that is particularly well suited for executing the body of a loop a specific number of times that can be determined before the loop is executed.

KEY CONCEPT
A for statement is usually used when a loop will be executed a set number of times.

The following code prints the numbers 1 through 5 using a for loop, just as we did using other loop statements in previous examples:

```
for (int count=1; count <= 5; count++)
   System.out.println(count);
```

The header of a for loop contains three parts separated by semicolons. Before the loop begins, the first part of the header, called the *initialization,* is executed. The second part of the header is the boolean condition, which is evaluated before the loop body (like the while loop). If true, the body of the loop is executed, followed by the execution of the third part of the header, which is called the *increment.* Note that the initialization part is executed only once, but the increment part is executed after each iteration of the loop. Figure 6.2 shows this processing.

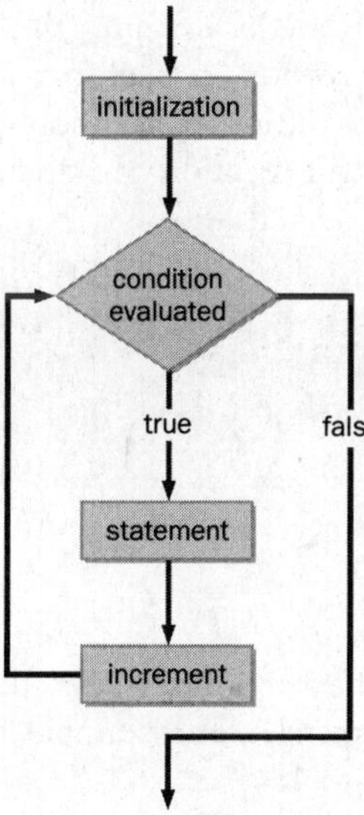

FIGURE 6.2 The logic of a for loop

VideoNote
Examples using `for` loops.

A `for` loop can be a bit tricky to read until you get used to it. The execution of the code doesn't follow a "top to bottom, left to right" reading. The increment code executes after the body of the loop even though it is in the header.

In this example, the initialization portion of the `for` loop header is used to declare the variable `count` as well as to give it an initial value. We are not required to declare a variable there, but it is common practice in situations where the variable is not needed outside of the loop. Because `count` is declared in the `for` loop header, it exists only inside the loop body and cannot be referenced elsewhere. The loop control variable is set up, checked, and modified by the actions in the loop header. It can be referenced inside the loop body, but it should not be modified except by the actions defined in the loop header.

For Statement

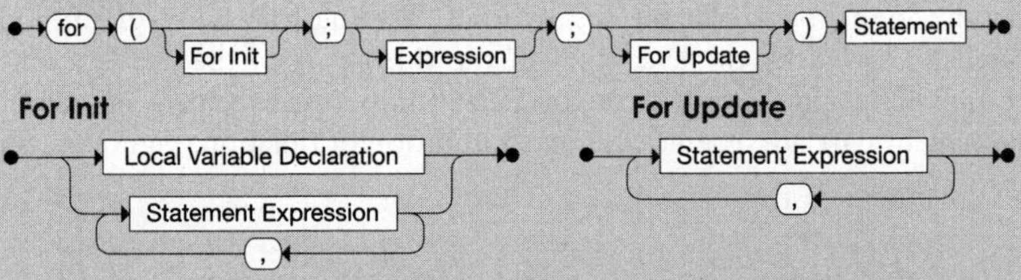

The `for` statement repeatedly executes the specified Statement as long as the boolean Expression is true. The For Init portion of the header is executed only once, before the loop begins. The For Update portion executes after each execution of Statement.

Examples:

```
for (int value=1; value < 25; value++)
   System.out.println(value + " squared is " + value*value);

for (int num=40; num > 0; num-=3)
   sum = sum + num;
```

The increment portion of the `for` loop header, despite its name, could decrement a value rather than increment it. For example, the following loop prints the integer values from 100 down to 1:

```
for (int num = 100; num > 0; num--)
   System.out.println(num);
```

In fact, the increment portion of the `for` loop can perform any calculation, not just a simple increment or decrement. Consider the program shown in Listing 6.3, which prints multiples of a particular value up to a particular limit.

The increment portion of the `for` loop in the `Multiples` program adds the value entered by the user after each iteration. The number of values printed per line is controlled by counting the values printed and then moving to the next line whenever `count` is evenly divisible by the `PER_LINE` constant.

LISTING 6.3

```
//********************************************************************
//  Multiples.java       Author: Lewis/Loftus
//
//  Demonstrates the use of a for loop.
//********************************************************************

import java.util.Scanner;

public class Multiples
{
   //-----------------------------------------------------------------
   //  Prints multiples of a user-specified number up to a user-
   //  specified limit.
   //-----------------------------------------------------------------
   public static void main(String[] args)
   {
      final int PER_LINE = 5;
      int value, limit, mult, count = 0;

      Scanner scan = new Scanner(System.in);

      System.out.print("Enter a positive value: ");
      value = scan.nextInt();

      System.out.print("Enter an upper limit: ");
      limit = scan.nextInt();

      System.out.println();
      System.out.println("The multiples of " + value + " between " +
                         value + " and " + limit + " (inclusive) are:");

      for (mult = value; mult <= limit; mult += value)
      {
         System.out.print(mult + "\t");
```

LISTING 6.3 *continued*

```
            // Print a specific number of values per line of output
            count++;
            if (count % PER_LINE == 0)
               System.out.println();
         }
      }
   }
```

OUTPUT

```
Enter a positive value: 7
Enter an upper limit: 400

The multiples of 7 between 7 and 400 (inclusive) are:
7       14      21      28      35
42      49      56      63      70
77      84      91      98      105
112     119     126     133     140
147     154     161     168     175
182     189     196     203     210
217     224     231     238     245
252     259     266     273     280
287     294     301     308     315
322     329     336     343     350
357     364     371     378     385
392     399
```

The `Stars` program in Listing 6.4 shows the use of nested `for` loops. The output is a triangle shape made of asterisk characters. The outer loop executes exactly 10 times. Each iteration of the outer loop prints one line of the output. The inner loop performs a different number of iterations depending on the line value controlled by the outer loop. Each iteration of the inner loop prints one star on the current line. Writing programs that print variations on this triangle configuration are included in the programming projects at the end of the chapter.

The for-each Loop

A variation of the `for` statement, often called the *for-each loop*, is particularly helpful in situations that involve iterators. In Chapter 5, we discussed that some

LISTING 6.4

```
//********************************************************************
//  Stars.java       Author: Lewis/Loftus
//
//  Demonstrates the use of nested for loops.
//********************************************************************

public class Stars
{
   //-----------------------------------------------------------------
   //  Prints a triangle shape using asterisk (star) characters.
   //-----------------------------------------------------------------
   public static void main(String[] args)
   {
      final int MAX_ROWS = 10;

      for (int row = 1; row <= MAX_ROWS; row++)
      {
         for (int star = 1; star <= row; star++)
            System.out.print("*");

         System.out.println();
      }
   }
}
```

OUTPUT

```
*
**
***
****
*****
******
*******
********
*********
**********
```

objects are considered to be iterators, which have `hasNext` and `next` methods to process each item from a group. If an object has implemented the `Iterable` interface, then we can use a variation of the `for` loop to process items using a simplified syntax.

KEY CONCEPT
The for-each version of a `for` loop simplifies the processing of all elements in an `Iterable` object.

An `ArrayList` object is an `Iterable` object. Therefore, for example, if `library` is an `ArrayList<Book>` object (that is, an `ArrayList` that manages `Book` objects), we can use a `for` loop to process each `Book` object in the collection as follows:

```
for (Book myBook : library)
    System.out.println(myBook);
```

This code can be read as follows: for each `Book` in `library`, print the book object. The variable `myBook` takes the value of each `Book` object in the collection in turn, and the body of the loop can process it appropriately. That succinct for-each loop is essentially equivalent to the following:

```
Book myBook;
while (bookList.hasNext())
{
    myBook = bookList.next();
    System.out.println(myBook);
}
```

This version of the `for` loop can also be used on arrays, which are discussed in Chapter 8. We use the for-each loop as appropriate in various situations throughout the rest of the book.

Comparing Loops

The three basic loop statements (`while`, `do`, and `for`) are functionally equivalent. Any particular loop written using one type of loop can be written using either of the other two loop types. Which type of loop we use depends on the situation.

As we mentioned earlier, the primary difference between a `while` loop and a `do` loop is when the condition is evaluated. The body of a `do` loop is executed at least once, whereas the body of a `while` loop will not be executed at all if the condition is initially false. Therefore, we say that the body of a `while` loop is executed zero or more times, but the body of a `do` loop is executed one or more times.

KEY CONCEPT
The loop statements are functionally equivalent. Which one you use should depend on the situation.

A `for` loop is like a `while` loop in that the condition is evaluated before the loop body is executed. We generally use a `for` loop when the number of times we want to iterate through a loop is fixed or can be easily calculated. In many situations, it is simply more convenient to separate the code that sets up and controls the loop iterations inside the `for` loop header from the body of the loop.

SELF-REVIEW QUESTIONS *(see answers in Appendix L)*

SR 6.12 When would we use a `for` loop instead of a `while` loop?

SR 6.13 What output is produced by the following code fragment?

```
int value = 0;
for (int num = 10; num <= 40; num += 10)
{
   value = value + num;
}
System.out.println(value);
```

SR 6.14 What output is produced by the following code fragment?

```
int value = 0;
for (int num = 10; num < 40; num += 10)
{
   value = value + num;
}
System.out.println(value);
```

SR 6.15 What output is produced by the following code fragment?

```
int value = 6;
for (int num = 1; num <= value; num ++)
{
   for (int i = 1; i <= (value - num); i++)
      System.out.print(" ");
   for (int i = 1; i <= ((2 * num) - 1); i++)
      System.out.print("*");
   System.out.println();
}
```

SR 6.16 Assume `die` is a `Die` object (as defined in Section 4.2). Write a code fragment that will roll `die` 100 times and output the average value rolled.

6.5 Using Loops and Conditionals with Graphics

Conditionals and loops greatly enhance our ability to generate interesting graphics. Let's explore some examples.

The `Bullseye` program shown in Listing 6.5 presents a target with a red bullseye at the center. The drawing is made up of filled circles of decreasing size, alternating black and white, with a common center point. The largest (outer) circle is added first so that the next smaller circle is visible on top of it, and so on, creating the ring effect.

LISTING 6.5

```
import javafx.application.Application;
import javafx.scene.Group;
import javafx.scene.Scene;
import javafx.scene.paint.Color;
import javafx.scene.shape.Circle;
import javafx.stage.Stage;

//************************************************************************
//  Bullseye.java       Author: Lewis/Loftus
//
//  Demonstrates the use of loops and conditionals to draw.
//************************************************************************

public class Bullseye extends Application
{
    //--------------------------------------------------------------------
    //  Displays a target using concentric black and white circles
    //  and a red center.
    //--------------------------------------------------------------------
    public void start(Stage primaryStage)
    {
        Group root = new Group();
        Color ringColor = Color.BLACK;
        Circle ring = null;
        int radius = 150;

        for (int count = 1; count <= 8; count++)
        {
            ring = new Circle(160, 160, radius);
            ring.setFill(ringColor);
            root.getChildren().add(ring);

            if (ringColor.equals(Color.BLACK))
                ringColor = Color.WHITE;
            else
                ringColor = Color.BLACK;

            radius = radius - 20;
        }

        ring.setFill(Color.RED);

        Scene scene = new Scene(root, 320, 320, Color.CYAN);
```

LISTING 6.5 *continued*

```
        primaryStage.setTitle("Bullseye");
        primaryStage.setScene(scene);
        primaryStage.show();
    }
}
```

DISPLAY

A `for` loop is used to draw exactly eight circles. Each time through the loop, one circle is created and added to the group. An `if` statement in the body of the `for` loop is used to set the color for the next circle; if the circle just added was black, the color is changed to white, and vice versa. After falling out of the loop, the fill color of the last ring drawn is changed to red.

Let's look at another example. Listing 6.6 shows a program that draws several rectangles in random locations. The width and height of each rectangle is also randomly selected. The boxes are unfilled unless the width or height is below a certain threshold (10 pixels). Narrow boxes are filled with yellow and short boxes are filled with green.

LISTING 6.6

```
import java.util.Random;
import javafx.application.Application;
import javafx.scene.Group;
import javafx.scene.Scene;
import javafx.scene.paint.Color;
import javafx.scene.shape.Rectangle;
import javafx.stage.Stage;

//************************************************************************
//  Boxes.java       Author: Lewis/Loftus
//
//  Demonstrates the use of loops and conditionals to draw.
//************************************************************************

public class Boxes extends Application
{
    //--------------------------------------------------------------------
    //  Displays multiple rectangles with random width and height in
    //  random locations. Narrow and short boxes are highlighted with
    //  a fill color.
    //--------------------------------------------------------------------
    public void start(Stage primaryStage)
    {
        Group root = new Group();
        Random gen = new Random();

        for (int count = 1; count <= 50; count++)
        {
            int x = gen.nextInt(350) + 1;
            int y = gen.nextInt(350) + 1;

            int width = gen.nextInt(50) + 1;
            int height = gen.nextInt(50) + 1;

            Color fill = null;
            if (width < 10)
                fill = Color.YELLOW;
            else if (height < 10)
                fill = Color.GREEN;

            Rectangle box = new Rectangle(x, y, width, height);
            box.setStroke(Color.WHITE);
            box.setFill(fill);

            root.getChildren().add(box);
        }
```

LISTING 6.6 *continued*

```
        Scene scene = new Scene(root, 400, 400, Color.BLACK);

        primaryStage.setTitle("Boxes");
        primaryStage.setScene(scene);
        primaryStage.show();
    }
}
```

DISPLAY

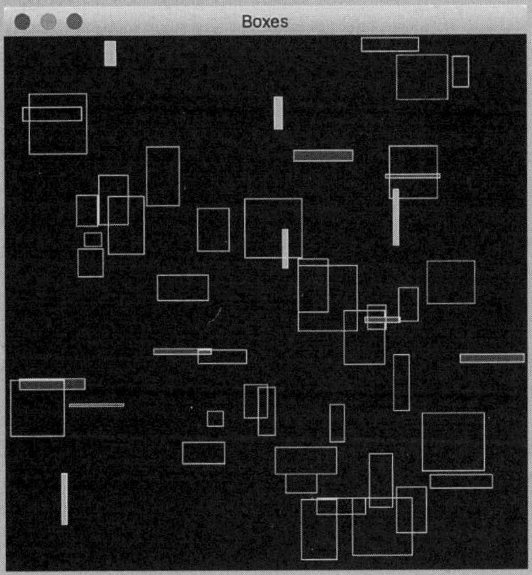

A `for` loop is used to create 50 boxes. The body of the `for` loop creates and adds one box. A nested `if` statement is used to check the randomly generated width and height of the current box, setting the color appropriately. For each box, the fill color is initially set to `null` and only changed if either dimension is too small.

SELF-REVIEW QUESTIONS *(see answers in Appendix L)*

SR 6.17 What changes would have to be made to the `Bullseye` program to have a 10-ring target?

SR 6.18 How would you modify the `Boxes` program so that boxes that are neither narrow or short are filled with white instead of just being outlined in white.

6.6 Graphic Transformations

A JavaFX *transformation* is an effect applied to a node that changes the way it is presented visually. The four basic transformation types are:

- *Translation*—changes the position of the node along the x or y axis.
- *Scaling*—causes the node to appear larger or smaller.
- *Rotation*—rotates the node around its center point.
- *Shearing*—rotates one axis so that the x and y axes are no longer perpendicular.

KEY CONCEPT
A transformation changes the visual presentation of a node.

Applying a transformation to an object sets its transformation properties but does not change its underlying characteristics. For example, translating a shape along an axis does not change the node's original position value.

Translation

A translation is accomplished using a call to the `setTranslateX` and `setTranslateY` methods. The following code creates two rectangles in the same position, but then translates the position of the second one.

```
Rectangle rec1 = new Rectangle(100, 100, 200, 50);
rec1.setFill(Color.STEELBLUE);

Rectangle rec2 = new Rectangle(100, 100, 200, 50);
rec2.setFill(Color.ORANGE);
rec2.setTranslateX(70);
rec2.setTranslateY(10);
```

Here's the result:

If the orange rectangle was not translated, it would completely block the blue one. But its position is shifted by 70 along the x axis and by 10 along the y axis. The translation values are added to the original, so that the translated position of the upper left corner of the orange rectangle is (170, 110).

Scaling

Scaling a node is accomplished with calls to the `setScaleX` and `setScaleY` methods, which take a `double` value representing the scaling factor. For example, a scaling factor of 0.5 will display a node at half its original size on that axis. A scaling factor of 1.3 will display it 30% larger than the original.

The following code creates two `ImageView` objects from the same image, and scales the second one:

```
Image img = new Image("water lily.jpg");
ImageView imgView1 = new ImageView(img);

ImageView imgView2 = new ImageView(img);
imgView2.setX(300);
imgView2.setScaleX(0.7);
imgView2.setScaleY(0.7);
```

Note that it is the `ImageView` that is scaled, not the image itself. The second image view is displayed at 70% of its original size (30% smaller) on both the x and y axes. The x position of the second `ImageView` is set just to move it to a different position than the first. Here's the result:

This example keeps the image in proportion to the original by using the same scaling factor on both the x and y axes. If only one axis is scaled, or they are scaled a different amount, the result will be distorted.

KEY CONCEPT
Use the same scaling factor on both axes to keep a node in proportion to the original.

Rotation

A call to `setRotate` causes a node to be rotated around its center point. Its parameter specifies the number of degrees the node is rotated. Consider the following lines of code:

```
Rectangle rec = new Rectangle(50, 100, 200, 50);
rec.setFill(Color.STEELBLUE);
rec.setRotate(40);

Text text = new Text(270, 125, "Tilted Text!");
text.setFont(new Font("Courier", 24));
text.setRotate(-15);
```

If the value passed to `setRotate` is positive, the node is rotated clockwise. If the value is negative, the node is rotated counterclockwise. So the first three lines of this code create a blue rectangle and rotate it 40 degrees clockwise. The next three lines create a `Text` object and rotate it 15 degrees counterclockwise. Here's the result:

To rotate a node around a point other than its center point, you can create a `Rotate` object and add it to the list of transformations that are applied to the node. For example, to rotate a node 45 degrees around the point (70, 150):

```
node.getTransforms().add(new Rotate(45, 70, 150));
```

Each transformation has a corresponding class that represents it, so all transformations can be applied in this way.

Shearing

A shearing transformation can only be applied by creating a `Shear` object and adding it to the list of transformations for the node. The following code creates an `ImageView` and applies a shear of 40% on the x axis and 20% on the y axis:

```
Image img = new Image("duck.jpg");
ImageView imgView = new ImageView(img);
imgView.getTransforms().add(new Shear(0.4, 0.2));
```

Here is the result:

Applying Transformations on Groups

Transformations can be applied to any JavaFX nodes, which means they can be applied not only to individual shapes, images, and controls, but also to groups and panes as well. When a transformation is applied to a group or pane, it is applied to each node in the container.

KEY CONCEPT
A transformation applied to a group or pane is applied automatically to all nodes in the container.

The class shown in Listing 6.7 is derived from the Group class. Its constructor creates the elements needed to display a robot face and adds them to the group.

LISTING 6.7

```
import javafx.scene.Group;
import javafx.scene.paint.Color;
import javafx.scene.shape.Rectangle;

//************************************************************************
//  RobotFace.java        Author: Lewis/Loftus
//
//  Presents the face of a robot.
//************************************************************************

public class RobotFace extends Group
{
    //--------------------------------------------------------------------
    //  Sets up the elements that make up the robots face, positioned
    //  in the upper left corner of the coordinate system.
    //--------------------------------------------------------------------
    public RobotFace()
    {
        Rectangle head = new Rectangle(5, 0, 100, 70);
        head.setFill(Color.SILVER);
        head.setArcHeight(10);
        head.setArcWidth(10);

        Rectangle ears = new Rectangle(0, 20, 110, 30);
        ears.setFill(Color.DARKBLUE);
        ears.setArcHeight(10);
        ears.setArcWidth(10);

        Rectangle eye1 = new Rectangle(25, 15, 20, 10);
        eye1.setFill(Color.GOLD);

        Rectangle eye2 = new Rectangle(65, 15, 20, 10);
        eye2.setFill(Color.GOLD);
```

LISTING 6.7 *continued*

```
        Rectangle nose = new Rectangle(52, 25, 6, 15);
        nose.setFill(Color.BLACK);

        Rectangle mouth = new Rectangle(35, 45, 40, 10);
        mouth.setFill(Color.RED);

        getChildren().addAll(ears, head, eye1, eye2, nose, mouth);
    }
}
```

If a `RobotFace` object were added to a container as originally defined, it would be displayed in the upper left corner:

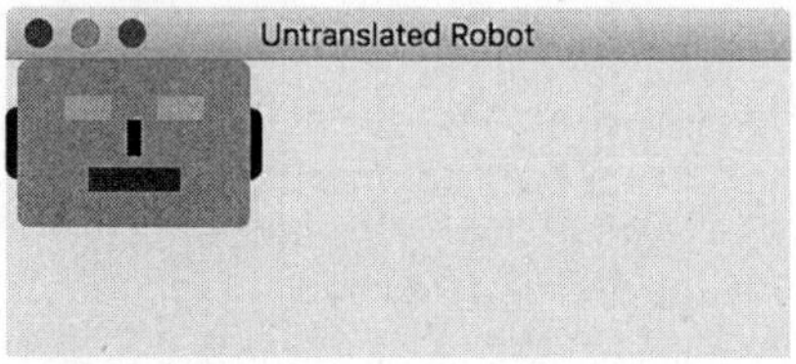

Listing 6.8 shows a program that creates and displays three robot faces with various transformations applied.

LISTING 6.8

```
import javafx.application.Application;
import javafx.scene.Group;
import javafx.scene.Scene;
import javafx.scene.paint.Color;
import javafx.stage.Stage;

//************************************************************************
//  Robots.java       Author: Lewis/Loftus
//
//  Demonstrates graphical transformations.
//************************************************************************

public class Robots extends Application
{
```

LISTING 6.8 *continued*

```
    //-----------------------------------------------------------------
    //  Displays three robot faces, applying various transformations.
    //-----------------------------------------------------------------
    public void start(Stage primaryStage)
    {
        RobotFace robot1 = new RobotFace();
        robot1.setTranslateX(70);
        robot1.setTranslateY(40);

        RobotFace robot2 = new RobotFace();
        robot2.setTranslateX(300);
        robot2.setTranslateY(40);
        robot2.setRotate(20);

        RobotFace robot3 = new RobotFace();
        robot3.setTranslateX(200);
        robot3.setTranslateY(200);
        robot3.setScaleX(2.5);
        robot3.setScaleY(2.5);

        Group root = new Group(robot1, robot2, robot3);

        Scene scene = new Scene(root, 500, 380, Color.WHITE);

        primaryStage.setTitle("Robots");
        primaryStage.setScene(scene);
        primaryStage.show();
    }
}
```

DISPLAY

The first robot is displayed in the upper left portion of the window. The only transformation that has been applied to it is that its position is translated 70 pixels along the x axis and 40 pixels along the y axis, shifting it out of the corner of the window.

The second robot (upper right) has been translated to its new position and has been rotated 20 degrees clockwise.

The third robot's position is also translated, and it is scaled to display at two and a half times its normal size.

Note that all of these transformations were applied to `RobotFace` objects, which are `Group` objects by inheritance. Then all three of those groups were added to the root node (also a group) of the scene.

SELF-REVIEW QUESTIONS *(see answers in Appendix L)*

SR 6.19 How would you shift the position of a `Circle` named `ring` 100 pixels lower than its original position?

SR 6.20 How would you display an `ImageView` named `view` at twice its original size?

SR 6.21 What happens if you scale a node by a different factor along the x and y axes?

SR 6.22 How would you rotate an `Ellipse` named `oval` 40 degrees clockwise? What if you wanted to rotate it 10 degrees counterclockwise?

Summary of Key Concepts

- A `switch` statement matches a character or integer value to one of several possible cases.
- A `break` statement is usually used at the end of each case alternative of a `switch` statement.
- The conditional operator evaluates to one of two possible values based on a boolean condition.
- A `do` statement executes its loop body at least once.
- A `for` statement is usually used when a loop will be executed a set number of times.
- The for-each version of a `for` loop simplifies the processing of all elements in an `Iterable` object.
- The loop statements are functionally equivalent. Which one you use should depend on the situation.
- A transformation changes the visual presentation of a node.
- Use the same scaling factor on both axes to keep a node in proportion to the original.
- A transformation applied to a group or pane is applied automatically to all nodes in the container.

Exercises

EX 6.1 How many iterations will the following for loops execute?

a. `for (int i = 0; i < 20; i++) { }`

b. `for (int i = 1; i <= 20; i++) { }`

c. `for (int i = 5; i < 20; i++) { }`

d. `for (int i = 20; i > 0; i--) { }`

e. `for (int i = 1; i < 20; i = i + 2) { }`

f. `for (int i = 1; i < 20; i *= 2) { }`

EX 6.2 What output is produced by the following code fragment?

```
for (int num = 100; num >= 1; num /= 2)
   System.out.println(num);
```

EX 6.3 What output is produced by the following code fragment?

```
for (int val = 200; val >= 0; val -= 1)
if (val % 4 != 0)
    System.out.println(val);
```

EX 6.4 Transform the following `while` loop into an equivalent `do` loop (make sure it produces the same output).

```
int num = 1;
while (num < 20)
{
   num++;
   System.out.println(num);
}
```

EX 6.5 Transform the `while` loop from the previous exercise into an equivalent `for` loop (make sure it produces the same output).

EX 6.6 Write a `do` loop that verifies that the user enters an even integer value.

EX 6.7 Write a `for` loop to print all numbers from 15 to 25 (inclusive).

EX 6.8 Write a `for` loop to print all multiples of 3 that are less than 100.

EX 6.9 Write a code fragment that reads 10 integer values from the user and prints the highest value entered.

EX 6.10 Write a code fragment that determines and prints the total number of uppercase characters in a `String` object named `title`.

EX 6.11 Write a code fragment that prints the characters stored in a `String` object called `str` backward.

EX 6.12 Write a code fragment that prints every other character in a `String` object called `word` starting with the first character.

EX 6.13 Write a method called `powersOfTwo` that prints the first 10 powers of 2 (starting with 2). The method takes no parameters and doesn't return anything.

EX 6.14 Write a method called `pad` that accepts a string called `str` and an integer called `length`. Return a string with `length` number of characters by adding an appropriate number of `'0'` characters to the end of the string. If the string is longer than `length`, then return the original string unchanged. For example, `pad("aaa", 6)` will return `"aaa000"`.

EX 6.15 Write a method called `sum100` that returns the sum of the integers from 1 to 100, inclusive.

EX 6.16 Write a method called `sumRange` that accepts two integer parameters that represent a range. Issue an error message and return zero if the second parameter is less than the first. Otherwise, the method should return the sum of the integers in that range (inclusive).

EX 6.17 Write a method called `countA` that accepts a `String` parameter and returns the number of times the character `'A'` is found in the string.

EX 6.18 Write a method called `pigly` that accepts a `String` containing a single word and converts that word into Pig Latin. The rule for Pig Latin is that, if a word starts with a consonant, you need to remove the consonant from the beginning of the word and add it to the end of the word and suffix “ay”. If a word starts with a vowel, you need to suffix “way”.

EX 6.19 In the `Bullseye` program, what is the fill color of the innermost circle before it is changed to red? Explain.

EX 6.20 Given the way the `Boxes` program is written, what color will a rectangle be if it is both narrow and short? Explain.

EX 6.21 Rewrite the `if` statement used in the `Boxes` program so that if a box is both narrow and short, its fill color will be orange. Otherwise, keep narrow boxes yellow and short boxes green.

EX 6.22 Write code that will shift a `Rectangle` named `rec` 50 pixels right and 10 pixels down, rotate it 45 degrees clockwise, and display it at half its original size.

EX 6.23 Write code that will rotate a shape named `square` by 60 degrees around its center and will double its size using a scale.

EX 6.24 What happens when you apply a transformation to a group?

Programming Projects

PP 6.1 Write a program that reads an integer value and prints the sum of all even integers between 2 and the input value, inclusive. Print an error message if the input value is less than 2. Prompt accordingly.

PP 6.2 Write a program that reads a string from the user and prints it one character per line.

VideoNote
Developing a solution of PP 6.2.

PP 6.3 Write a program that produces a multiplication table, showing the results of multiplying the integers 1 through 12 by themselves.

PP 6.4 Write a program that prints the first few verses of the traveling song "One Hundred Bottles of Beer." Use a loop such that each iteration prints one verse. Read the number of verses to print from the user. Validate the input. The following are the first two verses of the song:

100 bottles of beer on the wall
100 bottles of beer
If one of those bottles should happen to fall
99 bottles of beer on the wall

99 bottles of beer on the wall
99 bottles of beer
If one of those bottles should happen to fall
98 bottles of beer on the wall

PP 6.5 Using the `PairOfDice` class from PP 4.9, write a program that rolls a pair of dice 1000 times, counting the number of box cars (two sixes) that occur.

PP 6.6 Using the `Coin` class defined in Chapter 5, write a program called `FourHeads` whose `main` method flips a coin until it gets four heads in a row. Print the total number of flips needed to get four heads in a row.

PP 6.7 Create modified versions of the `Stars` program to print the following patterns. Create a separate program to produce each pattern. *Hint:* Parts b, c, and d require several loops, some of which print a specific number of spaces.

```
a. **********  b.          *  c. **********  d.     *
   *********              **      *********        ***
   ********              ***       ********       *****
   *******              ****        *******      *******
   ******              *****         ******     *********
   *****              ******          *****     *********
   ****              *******           ****      *******
   ***              ********            ***       *****
   **              *********             **        ***
   *              **********              *         *
```

PP 6.8 Write a program that prints a table showing a subset of the Unicode characters and their numeric values. Print five number/character pairs per line, separated by tab characters. Print the table for numeric values from 32 (the space character) to 126 (the ~ character), which corresponds to the printable ASCII subset of the Unicode character set. Compare your output to the table in Appendix C. Unlike the table in Appendix C, the values in your table can increase as they go across a row.

PP 6.9 Write a program that reads a string from the user, then determines and prints how many of each lowercase vowel (a, e, i, o, and u) appear in the entire string. Have a separate counter for each vowel. Also count and print the number of nonvowel characters.

PP 6.10 Write a program that prints the verses of the song "The Twelve Days of Christmas," in which each verse adds one line. The first two verses of the song are:

On the 1st day of Christmas my true love gave to me
A partridge in a pear tree.
On the 2nd day of Christmas my true love gave to me
Two turtle doves, and
A partridge in a pear tree.

Use a `switch` statement in a loop to control which lines get printed. *Hint:* Order the cases carefully and avoid the `break` statement. Use a separate `switch` statement to put the appropriate suffix on the day number (1st, 2nd, 3rd, etc.). The final verse of the song involves all 12 days, as follows:

On the 12th day of Christmas, my true love gave to me
Twelve drummers drumming,
Eleven pipers piping,
Ten lords a-leaping,
Nine ladies dancing,
Eight maids a-milking,
Seven swans a-swimming,
Six geese a-laying,
Five golden rings,
Four calling birds,
Three French hens,
Two turtle doves, and
A partridge in a pear tree.

PP 6.11 Write a JavaFX application that draws 20 horizontal, evenly spaced parallel lines of random length.

PP 6.12 Write a JavaFX application that displays a starfield with stars of random sizes distributed randomly across the night sky. There should be 1000 stars in the starfield.

PP 6.13 Write a JavaFX application that draws 10 concentric circles of random radius.

PP 6.14 Write a JavaFX application that draws 100 circles of random color and random size in random locations. Ensure that the entire circle appears in the visible area of the scene.

PP 6.15 Write a JavaFX application that displays 10,000 very small circles (radius of 1 pixel) in random locations within the visible area. Fill the dots on the left half of the scene red and the dots on the right half of the scene green. Use the `getWidth` method of the scene to help determine the halfway point.

PP 6.16 Write a JavaFX application that displays a brick wall pattern in which each row of bricks is offset from the row above and below it.

PP 6.17 Write a JavaFX application called `Quilt` that displays a quilt made up of two alternating square patterns. Define a class called `QuiltSquare` that represents a pattern of your choice. Allow the constructor of the `QuiltSquare` class to vary some characteristics of the pattern, such as its color scheme. Instantiate two `QuiltSquare` objects and incorporate them in a checkerboard layout in the quilt.

PP 6.18 Write a JavaFX application that draws 10 circles of random radius in random locations. Leave all circles unfilled except for the largest circle, which should be filled with a translucent red (30% opaque). If multiple circles have the same largest size, fill any one of them. Hint: keep track of the largest circle as you generate them; then change its fill color at the end.

PP 6.19 Write a JavaFX application that displays the same square image four times, once right side up, then on its right side, then upside down, and finally, on its left side.

PP 6.20 Write a JavaFX application that displays a rug pattern consisting of rows of stars. Each star should be constructed by placing two squares on top of each other, with one square rotated by 45 degrees. There should be at least five rows and each row should have five stars.

PP 6.21 Write a JavaFX application that displays a group of four alien spaceships in space. Define the spaceship once in a separate class, made up of whatever shapes you'd like. Then create four of them to be displayed, adjusting the position and size of each ship to make it appear that some are closer than others. Include a field of randomly generated stars (small white dots) behind the ships.

7

Object-Oriented Design

CHAPTER OBJECTIVES

- Establish key issues related to the design of object-oriented software.
- Explore techniques for identifying the classes and objects needed in a program.
- Discuss the relationships among classes.
- Describe the effect of the `static` modifier on methods and data.
- Discuss the creation of a formal object interface.
- Further explore the definition of enumerated type classes.
- Discuss issues related to the design of methods, including method overloading.
- Explore issues related to the design of graphical user interfaces.
- Discuss events generated by the mouse and the keyboard.

This chapter extends our discussion of the design of object-oriented software. We first focus on the stages of software development and the process of identifying classes and objects in the problem domain. We then discuss various issues that affect the design of a class, including static members, class relationships, interfaces, and enumerated types. We also explore design issues at the method level and introduce the concept of method overloading. A discussion of testing strategies rounds out these issues. In the Graphics Track sections of this chapter, we discuss the characteristics of a well-designed graphical user interface (GUI) and explore mouse and keyboard events.

7.1 Software Development Activities

Creating software involves much more than just writing code. As the problems you tackle get bigger, and the solutions include more classes, it becomes crucial to carefully think through the design of the software. Any proper software development effort consists of four basic *development activities*:

- establishing the requirements
- creating a design
- implementing the design
- testing

It would be nice if these activities, in this order, defined a step-by-step approach for developing software. However, although they may seem to be sequential, they are almost never completely linear in reality. They overlap and interact. Let's discuss each development activity briefly.

Software requirements specify *what* a program must accomplish. They indicate the tasks that a program should perform, not how it performs them. Often, requirements are expressed in a document called a *functional specification.*

We discussed in Chapter 1 the basic premise that programming is really about problem solving; we create a program to solve a particular problem. Requirements are the clear expression of that problem. Until we truly know what problem we are trying to solve, we can't actually solve it.

The person or group who wants a software product developed (the *client*) will often provide an initial set of requirements. However, these initial requirements are often incomplete, ambiguous, and perhaps even contradictory. The software developer must work with the client to refine the requirements until all key decisions about what the system will do have been addressed.

Requirements often address user interface issues such as output format, screen layouts, and graphical interface components. Essentially, the requirements establish the characteristics that make the program useful for the end user. They may also apply constraints to your program, such as how fast a task must be performed.

A *software design* indicates *how* a program will accomplish its requirements. The design specifies the classes and objects needed in a program and defines how they interact. It also specifies the relationships among the classes. Low-level design issues deal with how individual methods accomplish their tasks.

A civil engineer would never consider building a bridge without designing it first. The design of software is no less essential. Many problems that occur in software are directly attributable to a lack of good design effort. It has been shown time and again that the effort spent on the design of a program is well worth it, saving both time and money in the long run.

During software design, alternatives need to be considered and explored. Often, the first attempt at a design is not the best solution. Fortunately, changes are relatively easy to make during the design stage.

KEY CONCEPT
The effort put into design is both crucial and cost effective.

Implementation is the process of writing the source code that will solve the problem. More precisely, implementation is the act of translating the design into a particular programming language. Too many programmers focus on implementation exclusively when actually it should be the least creative of all development activities. The important decisions should be made when establishing the requirements and creating the design.

Testing is the act of ensuring that a program will solve the intended problem given all of the constraints under which it must perform. Testing includes running a program multiple times with various inputs and carefully scrutinizing the results. But it means far more than that. We revisit the issues related to testing in Section 7.9.

SELF-REVIEW QUESTIONS *(see answers in Appendix L)*

SR 7.1 Name the four basic activities that are involved in a software development process.

SR 7.2 Who creates/specifies software requirements, the client or the developer? Discuss.

SR 7.3 Compare and contrast the four basic development activities presented in this section with the five general problem-solving steps presented in Chapter 1 (Section 1.6).

7.2 Identifying Classes and Objects

A fundamental part of object-oriented software design is determining the classes that will contribute to the program. We have to carefully consider how we want to represent the various elements that make up the overall solution. These classes determine the objects that we will manage in the system.

One way to identify potential classes is to identify the objects discussed in the program requirements. Objects are generally nouns. You literally may want to scrutinize a problem description, or a functional specification if available, to identify the nouns found in it. For example, Figure 7.1 shows part of a problem description with the nouns circled.

Of course, not every noun in the problem specification will correspond to a class in your program. This activity is just a starting point that allows you to think about the types of objects a program will manage.

KEY CONCEPT
The nouns in a problem description may indicate some of the classes and objects needed in a program.

```
The user must be allowed to specify each product by
its primary characteristics, including its name and
product number. If the bar code does not match the
product, then an error should be generated to the
message window and entered into the error log. The
summary report of all transactions must be structured
as specified in section 7.A.
```

FIGURE 7.1 A partial problem description with the nouns circled

Remember that a class represents a group of objects with similar behavior. A plural noun in the specification, such as products, may indicate the need for a class that represents one of those items, such as `Product`. Even if there is only one of a particular kind of object needed in your system, it may best be represented as a class.

Classes that represent objects should generally be given names that are singular nouns, such as `Coin`, `Student`, and `Message`. A class represents a single item from which we are free to create as many instances as we choose.

Another key decision is whether to represent something as an object or as a primitive attribute of another object. For example, we may initially think that an employee's salary should be represented as an integer, and that may work for much of the system's processing. But upon further reflection we might realize that the salary is based on the person's rank, which has upper and lower salary bounds that must be managed with care. Therefore the final conclusion may be that we'd be better off representing all of that data and the associated behavior as a separate class.

Given the needs of a particular program, we want to strike a good balance between classes that are too general and those that are too specific. For example, it may complicate our design unnecessarily to create a separate class for each type of appliance that exists in a house. It may be sufficient to have a single `Appliance` class, with perhaps a piece of instance data that indicates what type of appliance it is. Then again, it may not. It all depends on what the software is intended to accomplish.

In addition to classes that represent objects from the problem domain, we likely will need classes that support the work necessary to get the job done. For example, in addition to `Member` objects, we may want a separate class to help us manage all of the members of a club.

Keep in mind that when producing a real system, some of the classes we identify during design may already exist. Even if nothing matches exactly, there may be an old class that's similar enough to serve as the basis for our new class. The existing class may be part of the Java standard class library, part of a solution to a problem we've solved previously, or part of a library that can be bought from a third party. These are all examples of software reuse.

Assigning Responsibilities

Part of the process of identifying the classes needed in a program is the process of assigning responsibilities to each class. Each class represents an object with certain behaviors that are defined by the methods of the class. Any activity that the program must accomplish must be represented somewhere in the behaviors of the classes. That is, each class is responsible for carrying out certain activities, and those responsibilities must be assigned as part of designing a program.

The behaviors of a class perform actions that make up the functionality of a program. Thus we generally use verbs for the names of behaviors and the methods that accomplish them.

Sometimes it is challenging to determine which is the best class to carry out a particular responsibility. Consider multiple possibilities. Sometimes such analysis makes you realize that you could benefit from defining another class to shoulder the responsibility.

It's not necessary in the early stages of a design to identify all the methods that a class will contain. It is often sufficient to assign primary responsibilities and consider how those responsibilities translate to particular methods.

SELF-REVIEW QUESTIONS *(see answers in Appendix L)*

SR 7.4 How can identifying the nouns in a problem specification help you design an object-oriented solution to the problem?

SR 7.5 Is it important to identify and define all of the methods that a class will contain during the early stages of problem solution design? Discuss.

7.3 Static Class Members

We've used static methods in various situations in previous examples in the book. For example, all the methods of the `Math` class are static. Recall that a static method is one that is invoked through its class name, instead of through an object of that class.

VideoNote
Exploring the `static` modifier.

Not only can methods be static, but variables can be static as well. We declare static class members using the `static` modifier.

Deciding whether to declare a method or variable as static is a key step in class design. Let's examine the implications of static variables and methods more closely.

Static Variables

So far, we've seen two categories of variables: local variables that are declared inside a method, and instance variables that are declared in a class but not inside a method. The term *instance variable* is used, because each instance of the class has its own version of the variable. That is, each object has distinct memory space for each variable so that each object can have a distinct value for that variable.

KEY CONCEPT
A static variable is shared among all instances of a class.

A *static variable,* which is sometimes called a *class variable*, is shared among all instances of a class. There is only one copy of a static variable for all objects of the class. Therefore, changing the value of a static variable in one object changes it for all of the others. The reserved word `static` is used as a modifier to declare a static variable as follows:

```
private static int count = 0;
```

Memory space for a static variable is established when the class that contains it is referenced for the first time in a program. A local variable declared within a method cannot be static.

Constants, which are declared using the `final` modifier, are often declared using the `static` modifier. Because the value of constants cannot be changed, there might as well be only one copy of the value across all objects of the class.

Static Methods

In Chapter 3, we briefly introduced the concept of a *static method* (also called a *class method*). Static methods can be invoked through the class name. We don't have to instantiate an object of the class in order to invoke the method. In Chapter 3, we noted that all the methods of the `Math` class are static methods. For example, in the following line of code the `sqrt` method is invoked through the `Math` class name:

```
System.out.println("Square root of 27: " + Math.sqrt(27));
```

The methods in the `Math` class perform basic computations based on values passed as parameters. There is no object state to maintain in these situations; therefore, there is no good reason to create an object in order to request these services.

A method is made static by using the `static` modifier in the method declaration. As we've seen many times, the `main` method of a Java program must be declared with the `static` modifier; this is done so that `main` can be executed by the interpreter without instantiating an object from the class that contains `main`.

Because static methods do not operate in the context of a particular object, they cannot reference instance variables, which exist only in an instance of a class. The compiler will issue an error if a static method attempts to use a nonstatic variable. A static method can, however, reference static variables, because static variables exist independent of specific objects. Therefore, the `main` method can access only static or local variables.

The program in Listing 7.1 instantiates several objects of the `Slogan` class, printing each one out in turn. At the end of the program, it invokes a method called `getCount` through the class name, which returns the number of `Slogan` objects that were instantiated in the program.

LISTING 7.1

```
//********************************************************************
//  SloganCounter.java       Author: Lewis/Loftus
//
//  Demonstrates the use of the static modifier.
//********************************************************************

public class SloganCounter
{
   //-----------------------------------------------------------------
   //  Creates several Slogan objects and prints the number of
   //  objects that were created.
   //-----------------------------------------------------------------
   public static void main(String[] args)
   {
      Slogan obj;

      obj = new Slogan("Remember the Alamo.");
      System.out.println(obj);

      obj = new Slogan("Don't Worry. Be Happy.");
      System.out.println(obj);

      obj = new Slogan("Live Free or Die.");
      System.out.println(obj);

      obj = new Slogan("Talk is Cheap.");
      System.out.println(obj);

      obj = new Slogan("Write Once, Run Anywhere.");
      System.out.println(obj);
```

LISTING 7.1 *continued*

```
      System.out.println();
      System.out.println("Slogans created: " + Slogan.getCount());
   }
}
```

OUTPUT

```
Remember the Alamo.
Don't Worry. Be Happy.
Live Free or Die.
Talk is Cheap.
Write Once, Run Anywhere.

Slogans created: 5
```

Listing 7.2 shows the `Slogan` class. The constructor of `Slogan` increments a static variable called `count`, which is initialized to zero when it is declared. Therefore, `count` serves to keep track of the number of instances of `Slogan` that are created.

The `getCount` method of `Slogan` is also declared as `static`, which allows it to be invoked through the class name in the `main` method. Note that the only data referenced in the `getCount` method is the integer variable `count`, which is static. As a static method, `getCount` cannot reference any nonstatic data.

The `getCount` method could have been declared without the `static` modifier, but then its invocation in the `main` method would have to have been done through an instance of the `Slogan` class instead of the class itself.

LISTING 7.2

```
//********************************************************************
//  Slogan.java       Author: Lewis/Loftus
//
//  Represents a single slogan string.
//********************************************************************

public class Slogan
{
   private String phrase;
   private static int count = 0;
```

LISTING 7.2 *continued*

```
   //-----------------------------------------------------------------
   //  Constructor: Sets up the slogan and counts the number of
   //  instances created.
   //-----------------------------------------------------------------
   public Slogan(String str)
   {
      phrase = str;
      count++;
   }

   //-----------------------------------------------------------------
   //  Returns this slogan as a string.
   //-----------------------------------------------------------------
   public String toString()
   {
      return phrase;
   }

   //-----------------------------------------------------------------
   //  Returns the number of instances of this class that have been
   //  created.
   //-----------------------------------------------------------------
   public static int getCount()
   {
      return count;
   }
}
```

SELF-REVIEW QUESTIONS *(see answers in Appendix L)*

SR 7.6 What is the difference between a static variable and an instance variable?

SR 7.7 Assume you are defining a `BankAccount` class whose objects each represent a separate bank account. Write a declaration for a variable of the class that will hold the combined total balance of all the bank accounts represented by the class.

SR 7.8 Assume you are defining a `BankAccount` class whose objects each represent a separate bank account. Write a declaration for a variable of the class that will hold the minimum balance that each account must maintain.

SR 7.9 What kinds of variables can the `main` method of any program reference? Why?

7.4 Class Relationships

The classes in a software system have various types of relationships to each other. Three of the more common relationships are dependency, aggregation, and inheritance.

We've seen dependency relationships in many examples in which one class "uses" another. This section revisits the dependency relationship and explores the situation where a class depends on itself. We then explore aggregation, in which the objects of one class contain objects of another, creating a "has-a" relationship. Inheritance, which we introduced in Chapter 1, creates an "is-a" relationship between classes. We defer our detailed examination of inheritance until Chapter 9.

Dependency

In many previous examples, we've seen the idea of one class being dependent on another. This means that one class relies on another in some sense. Often the methods of one class will invoke the methods of the other class. This establishes a "uses" relationship.

Generally, if class `A` uses class `B`, then one or more methods of class `A` invoke one or more methods of class `B`. If an invoked method is static, then `A` merely references `B` by name. If the invoked method is not static, then `A` must have access to a specific instance of class `B` in order to invoke the method. That is, `A` must have a reference to an object of class `B`.

The way in which one object gains access to an object of another class is an important design decision. It occurs when one class instantiates the objects of another, but that's often the basis of an aggregation relationship. The access can also be accomplished by passing one object to another as a method parameter.

In general, we want to minimize the number of dependencies among classes. The less dependent our classes are on each other, the less impact changes and errors will have on the system.

Dependencies Among Objects of the Same Class

In some cases, a class depends on itself. That is, an object of one class interacts with another object of the same class. To accomplish this, a method of the class may accept as a parameter an object of the same class. Designing such a class drives home the idea that a class represents a particular object.

The concat method of the String class is an example of this situation. The method is executed through one String object and is passed another String object as a parameter. For example:

```
str3 = str1.concat(str2);
```

The String object executing the method (str1) appends its characters to those of the String passed as a parameter (str2). A new String object is returned as a result and stored as str3.

The RationalTester program shown in Listing 7.3 demonstrates a similar situation. A rational number is a value that can be represented as a ratio of two integers (a fraction). The RationalTester program creates two objects representing rational numbers and then performs various operations on them to produce new rational numbers.

LISTING 7.3

```
//********************************************************************
//  RationalTester.java       Author: Lewis/Loftus
//
//  Driver to exercise the use of multiple Rational objects.
//********************************************************************

public class RationalTester
{
   //-----------------------------------------------------------------
   //  Creates some rational number objects and performs various
   //  operations on them.
   //-----------------------------------------------------------------
   public static void main(String[] args)
   {
      RationalNumber r1 = new RationalNumber(6, 8);
      RationalNumber r2 = new RationalNumber(1, 3);
      RationalNumber r3, r4, r5, r6, r7;

      System.out.println("First rational number: " + r1);
      System.out.println("Second rational number: " + r2);

      if (r1.isLike(r2))
         System.out.println("r1 and r2 are equal.");
      else
         System.out.println("r1 and r2 are NOT equal.");

      r3 = r1.reciprocal();
      System.out.println("The reciprocal of r1 is: " + r3);
```

LISTING 7.3 *continued*

```
      r4 = r1.add(r2);
      r5 = r1.subtract(r2);
      r6 = r1.multiply(r2);
      r7 = r1.divide(r2);

      System.out.println("r1 + r2: " + r4);
      System.out.println("r1 - r2: " + r5);
      System.out.println("r1 * r2: " + r6);
      System.out.println("r1 / r2: " + r7);
   }
}
```

OUTPUT

```
First rational number: 3/4
Second rational number: 1/3
r1 and r2 are NOT equal.
The reciprocal of r1 is: 4/3
r1 + r2: 13/12
r1 - r2: 5/12
r1 * r2: 1/4
r1 / r2: 9/4
```

The RationalNumber class is shown in Listing 7.4. Keep in mind as you examine this class that each object created from the RationalNumber class represents a single rational number. The RationalNumber class contains various operations on rational numbers, such as addition and subtraction.

LISTING 7.4

```
//********************************************************************
//  RationalNumber.java       Author: Lewis/Loftus
//
//  Represents one rational number with a numerator and denominator.
//********************************************************************

public class RationalNumber
{
   private int numerator, denominator;
```

LISTING 7.4 *continued*

```
   //-----------------------------------------------------------------
   //  Constructor: Sets up the rational number by ensuring a nonzero
   //  denominator and making only the numerator signed.
   //-----------------------------------------------------------------
   public RationalNumber(int numer, int denom)
   {
      if (denom == 0)
         denom = 1;

      //  Make the numerator "store" the sign
      if (denom < 0)
      {
         numer = numer * -1;
         denom = denom * -1;
      }

      numerator = numer;
      denominator = denom;

      reduce();
   }

   //-----------------------------------------------------------------
   //  Returns the numerator of this rational number.
   //-----------------------------------------------------------------
   public int getNumerator()
   {
      return numerator;
   }

   //-----------------------------------------------------------------
   //  Returns the denominator of this rational number.
   //-----------------------------------------------------------------
   public int getDenominator()
   {
      return denominator;
   }

   //-----------------------------------------------------------------
   //  Returns the reciprocal of this rational number.
   //-----------------------------------------------------------------
   public RationalNumber reciprocal()
   {
      return new RationalNumber(denominator, numerator);
   }
```

LISTING 7.4 *continued*

```
   //-----------------------------------------------------------------
   //  Adds this rational number to the one passed as a parameter.
   //  A common denominator is found by multiplying the individual
   //  denominators.
   //-----------------------------------------------------------------
   public RationalNumber add(RationalNumber op2)
   {
      int commonDenominator = denominator * op2.getDenominator();
      int numerator1 = numerator * op2.getDenominator();
      int numerator2 = op2.getNumerator() * denominator;
      int sum = numerator1 + numerator2;

      return new RationalNumber(sum, commonDenominator);
   }

   //-----------------------------------------------------------------
   //  Subtracts the rational number passed as a parameter from this
   //  rational number.
   //-----------------------------------------------------------------
   public RationalNumber subtract(RationalNumber op2)
   {
      int commonDenominator = denominator * op2.getDenominator();
      int numerator1 = numerator * op2.getDenominator();
      int numerator2 = op2.getNumerator() * denominator;
      int difference = numerator1 - numerator2;

      return new RationalNumber(difference, commonDenominator);
   }

   //-----------------------------------------------------------------
   //  Multiplies this rational number by the one passed as a
   //  parameter.
   //-----------------------------------------------------------------
   public RationalNumber multiply(RationalNumber op2)
   {
      int numer = numerator * op2.getNumerator();
      int denom = denominator * op2.getDenominator();

      return new RationalNumber(numer, denom);
   }

   //-----------------------------------------------------------------
   //  Divides this rational number by the one passed as a parameter
   //  by multiplying by the reciprocal of the second rational.
   //-----------------------------------------------------------------
```

LISTING 7.4 *continued*

```
   public RationalNumber divide(RationalNumber op2)
   {
      return multiply(op2.reciprocal());
   }

   //-----------------------------------------------------------------
   //  Determines if this rational number is equal to the one passed
   //  as a parameter. Assumes they are both reduced.
   //-----------------------------------------------------------------
   public boolean isLike(RationalNumber op2)
   {
      return (numerator == op2.getNumerator() &&
              denominator == op2.getDenominator() );
   }

   //-----------------------------------------------------------------
   //  Returns this rational number as a string.
   //-----------------------------------------------------------------
   public String toString()
   {
      String result;
      if (numerator == 0)
         result = "0";
      else
         if (denominator == 1)
            result = numerator + "";
         else
         result = numerator + "/" + denominator;
      return result;
   }

   //-----------------------------------------------------------------
   //  Reduces this rational number by dividing both the numerator
   //  and the denominator by their greatest common divisor.
   //-----------------------------------------------------------------
   private void reduce()
   {
      if (numerator != 0)
      {
         int common = gcd(Math.abs(numerator), denominator);

         numerator = numerator / common;
         denominator = denominator / common;
      }
```

LISTING 7.4 *continued*

```
   }

   //-----------------------------------------------------------------
   //  Computes and returns the greatest common divisor of the two
   //  positive parameters. Uses Euclid's algorithm.
   //-----------------------------------------------------------------
   private int gcd(int num1, int num2)
   {
      while (num1 != num2)
         if (num1 > num2)
            num1 = num1 - num2;
         else
           num2 = num2 - num1;

      return num1;
   }
}
```

The methods of the `RationalNumber` class, such as `add`, `subtract`, `multiply`, and `divide`, use the `RationalNumber` object that is executing the method as the first (left) operand and the `RationalNumber` object passed as a parameter as the second (right) operand.

The `isLike` method of the `RationalNumber` class is used to determine if two rational numbers are essentially equal. It's tempting, therefore, to call that method `equals`, similar to the method used to compare `String` objects (discussed in Chapter 5). In Chapter 9, however, we will discuss how the `equals` method is somewhat special due to inheritance, and that it should be implemented in a particular way. So to avoid confusion we call this method `isLike` for now.

Note that some of the methods in the `RationalNumber` class, including `reduce` and `gcd`, are declared with private visibility. These methods are `private` because we don't want them executed directly from outside a `RationalNumber` object. They exist only to support the other services of the object.

Aggregation

Some objects are made up of other objects. A car, for instance, is made up of its engine, its chassis, its wheels, and several other parts. Each of these other parts could be considered a separate object. Therefore, we can say that a car is an *aggregation*—it is composed, at least in part, of other objects. Aggregation is sometimes described as a *has-a relationship*. For instance, a car has a chassis.

KEY CONCEPT

An aggregate object is composed of other objects, forming a has-a relationship.

In the software world, we define an *aggregate object* as any object that contains references to other objects as instance data. For example, an Account object contains, among other things, a String object that represents the name of the account owner. We sometimes forget that strings are objects, but technically that makes each Account object an aggregate object.

Aggregation is a special type of dependency. That is, a class that is defined in part by another class is dependent on that class. The methods of the aggregate object generally invoke the methods of the objects from which it is composed.

Let's consider another example. The program StudentBody shown in Listing 7.5 creates two Student objects. Each Student object is composed, in part, of two Address objects, one for the student's address at school and another for the student's home address. The main method does nothing more than create the Student objects and print them out. Once again we are passing objects to the println method, relying on the automatic call to the toString method to create a valid representation of the object that is suitable for printing.

The Student class shown in Listing 7.6 represents a single student. This class would have to be greatly expanded if it were to represent all aspects of a student. We deliberately keep it simple for now so that the object aggregation is clearly shown. The instance data of the Student class includes two references to Address objects. We refer to those objects in the toString method as we create a string representation of the student. By concatenating an Address object to another string, the toString method in Address is automatically invoked.

LISTING 7.5

```
//********************************************************************
//  StudentBody.java       Author: Lewis/Loftus
//
//  Demonstrates the use of an aggregate class.
//********************************************************************

public class StudentBody
{
   //-----------------------------------------------------------------
   //  Creates some Address and Student objects and prints them.
   //-----------------------------------------------------------------
   public static void main(String[] args)
   {
      Address school = new Address("800 Lancaster Ave.", "Villanova",
                                   "PA", 19085);
      Address jHome = new Address("21 Jump Street", "Blacksburg",
                                  "VA", 24551);
```

LISTING 7.5 *continued*

```
      Student john = new Student("John", "Smith", jHome, school);


      Address mHome = new Address("123 Main Street", "Euclid", "OH",
                                  44132);
      Student marsha = new Student("Marsha", "Jones", mHome, school);

      System.out.println(john);
      System.out.println();
      System.out.println(marsha);
   }
}
```

OUTPUT

```
John Smith
Home Address:
21 Jump Street
Blacksburg, VA 24551
School Address:
800 Lancaster Ave.
Villanova, PA 19085

Marsha Jones
Home Address:
123 Main Street
Euclid, OH 44132
School Address:
800 Lancaster Ave.
Villanova, PA 19085
```

LISTING 7.6

```
//********************************************************************
//  Student.java       Author: Lewis/Loftus
//
//  Represents a college student.
//********************************************************************

public class Student
{
   private String firstName, lastName;
   private Address homeAddress, schoolAddress;
```

LISTING 7.6 *continued*

```
   //-----------------------------------------------------------------
   //  Constructor: Sets up this student with the specified values.
   //-----------------------------------------------------------------
   public Student(String first, String last, Address home,
                  Address school)
   {
      firstName = first;
      lastName = last;
      homeAddress = home;
      schoolAddress = school;
   }

   //-----------------------------------------------------------------
   //  Returns a string description of this Student object.
   //-----------------------------------------------------------------
   public String toString()
   {
      String result;

      result = firstName + " " + lastName + "\n";
      result += "Home Address:\n" + homeAddress + "\n";
      result += "School Address:\n" + schoolAddress;

      return result;
   }
}
```

The Address class is shown in Listing 7.7. It represents a street address. Note that nothing about the Address class indicates that it is part of a Student object. The Address class is kept generic by design and therefore could be used in any situation in which a street address is needed.

LISTING 7.7

```
//********************************************************************
//  Address.java       Author: Lewis/Loftus
//
//  Represents a street address.
//********************************************************************

public class Address
{
```

LISTING 7.7 *continued*

```
   private String streetAddress, city, state;
   private long zipCode;

   //-----------------------------------------------------------------
   //  Constructor: Sets up this address with the specified data.
   //-----------------------------------------------------------------
   public Address(String street, String town, String st, long zip)
   {
      streetAddress = street;
      city = town;
      state = st;
      zipCode = zip;
   }

   //-----------------------------------------------------------------
   // Returns a description of this Address object.
   //-----------------------------------------------------------------
   public String toString()
   {
      String result;

      result = streetAddress + "\n";
      result += city + ", " + state + " " + zipCode;

      return result;
   }
}
```

The more complex an object, the more likely it will need to be represented as an aggregate object. In UML, aggregation is represented by a connection between two classes, with an open diamond at the end near the class that is the aggregate. Figure 7.2 shows a UML class diagram for the `StudentBody` program.

Note that in previous UML diagram examples and in Figure 7.2, strings are not represented as separate classes with aggregation relationships, though technically they could be. Strings are so fundamental to programming that often they are represented as though they were a primitive type in a UML diagram.

The `this` Reference

Before we leave the topic of relationships among classes, we should examine another special reference used in Java programs called the `this` reference. The word `this` is a reserved word in Java. It allows an object to refer to itself. As we

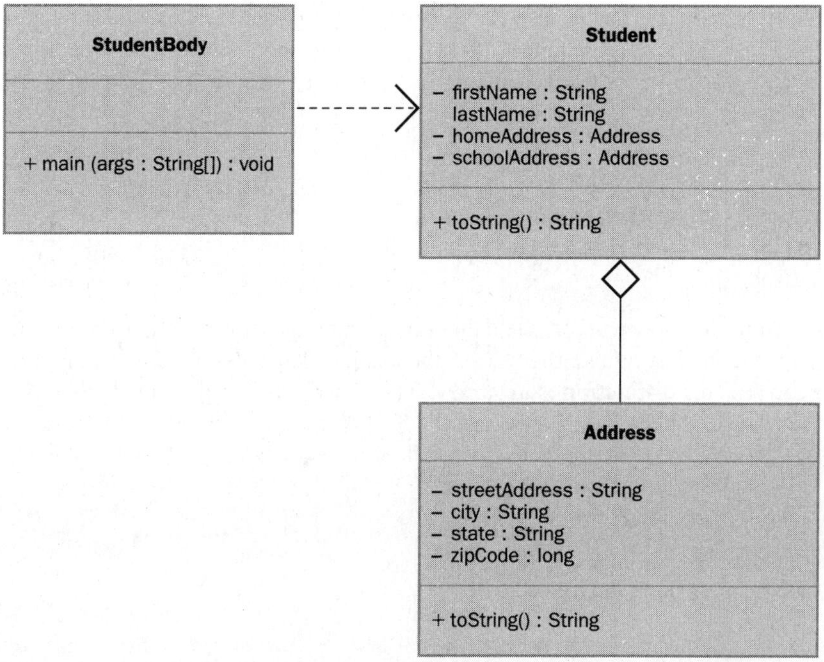

FIGURE 7.2 A UML class diagram showing aggregation

have discussed, a nonstatic method is invoked through (or by) a particular object or class. Inside that method, the `this` reference can be used to refer to the currently executing object.

For example, in a class called `ChessPiece` there could be a method called `move`, which could contain the following line:

```
if (this.position == piece2.position)
    result =  false;
```

In this situation, the `this` reference is being used to clarify which position is being referenced. The `this` reference refers to the object through which the method was invoked. So when the following line is used to invoke the method, the `this` reference refers to `bishop1`:

```
bishop1.move();
```

However, when a different object is used to invoke the method, the `this` reference refers to that object. Therefore, when the following invocation is used, the `this` reference in the `move` method refers to `bishop2`:

```
bishop2.move();
```

Often, the `this` reference is used to distinguish the parameters of a constructor from their corresponding instance variables with the same names. For example, the constructor of the `Account` class was presented in Chapter 4 as follows:

```
public Account(String owner, long account, double initial)
{
    name = owner;
    acctNumber = account;
    balance = initial;
}
```

When writing that constructor, we deliberately came up with different names for the parameters to distinguish them from the instance variables `name`, `acctNumber`, and `balance`. This distinction is arbitrary. The constructor could have been written as follows using the `this` reference:

```
public Account(String name, long acctNumber, double balance)
{
    this.name = name;
    this.acctNumber = acctNumber;
    this.balance = balance;
}
```

In this version of the constructor, the `this` reference specifically refers to the instance variables of the object. The variables on the right-hand side of the assignment statements refer to the formal parameters. This approach eliminates the need to come up with different yet equivalent names. This situation sometimes occurs in other methods but comes up often in constructors.

SELF-REVIEW QUESTIONS *(see answers in Appendix L)*

SR 7.10 Describe a dependency relationship between two classes.

SR 7.11 Explain how a class can have an association with itself.

SR 7.12 What is an aggregate object?

SR 7.13 What does the `this` reference refer to?

7.5 Interfaces

We've used the term interface to refer to the set of public methods through which we can interact with an object. That definition is consistent with our use of it in this section, but now we are going to formalize this concept using a particular language construct in Java.

LISTING 7.8

```
//********************************************************************
//  Complexity.java        Author: Lewis/Loftus
//
//  Represents the interface for an object that can be assigned an
//  explicit complexity.
//********************************************************************

public interface Complexity
{
   public void setComplexity(int complexity);
   public int getComplexity();
}
```

A Java *interface* is a collection of constants and abstract methods. An *abstract method* is a method that does not have an implementation. That is, there is no body of code defined for an abstract method. The header of the method, including its parameter list, is simply followed by a semicolon. An interface cannot be instantiated.

KEY CONCEPT
An interface is a collection of abstract methods and therefore cannot be instantiated.

Listing 7.8 shows an interface called `Complexity`. It contains two abstract methods: `setComplexity` and `getComplexity`.

An abstract method can be preceded by the reserved word `abstract`, though in interfaces it usually is not. Methods in interfaces have public visibility by default.

A class *implements* an interface by providing method implementations for each of the abstract methods defined in the interface. A class that implements an interface uses the reserved word `implements` followed by the interface name in the class header. If a class asserts that it implements a particular interface, it must provide a definition for all methods in the interface. The compiler will produce errors if any of the methods in the interface are not given a definition in the class.

The `Question` class, shown in Listing 7.9, implements the `Complexity` interface. Both the `setComplexity` and `getComplexity` methods are implemented. They must be declared with the same signatures as their abstract counterparts in the interface. In the `Question` class, the methods are defined simply to set or return a numeric value representing the complexity level of the question that the object represents.

Note that the `Question` class also implements additional methods that are not part of the `Complexity` interface. Specifically, it defines methods called `getQuestion`, `getAnswer`, `answerCorrect`, and `toString`, which have nothing to do with the interface. The interface guarantees that the class implements certain methods,

LISTING 7.9

```
//********************************************************************
//  Question.java       Author: Lewis/Loftus
//
//  Represents a question (and its answer).
//********************************************************************

public class Question implements Complexity
{
   private String question, answer;
   private int complexityLevel;

   //-----------------------------------------------------------------
   //  Constructor: Sets up the question with a default complexity.
   //-----------------------------------------------------------------
   public Question(String query, String result)
   {
      question = query;
      answer = result;
      complexityLevel = 1;
   }

   //-----------------------------------------------------------------
   //  Sets the complexity level for this question.
   //-----------------------------------------------------------------
   public void setComplexity(int level)
   {
      complexityLevel = level;
   }

   //-----------------------------------------------------------------
   //  Returns the complexity level for this question.
   //-----------------------------------------------------------------
   public int getComplexity()
   {
      return complexityLevel;
   }

   //-----------------------------------------------------------------
   //  Returns the question.
   //-----------------------------------------------------------------
   public String getQuestion()
   {
      return question;
   }
```

LISTING 7.9 *continued*

```
   //-----------------------------------------------------------------
   //  Returns the answer to this question.
   //-----------------------------------------------------------------
   public String getAnswer()
   {
      return answer;
   }

   //-----------------------------------------------------------------
   //  Returns true if the candidate answer matches the answer.
   //-----------------------------------------------------------------
   public boolean answerCorrect(String candidateAnswer)
   {
      return answer.equals(candidateAnswer);
   }

   //-----------------------------------------------------------------
   //  Returns this question (and its answer) as a string.
   //-----------------------------------------------------------------
   public String toString()
   {
      return question + "\n" + answer;
   }
}
```

but it does not restrict it from having additional ones. It is common for a class that implements an interface to have other methods.

Listing 7.10 shows a program called `MiniQuiz`, which uses some `Question` objects.

An interface and its relationship to a class that implements it can be shown in a UML class diagram. An interface is represented similarly to a class node except that the designation `<<interface>>` is inserted above the interface name. A dotted arrow with a closed arrowhead is drawn from the class to the interface that it implements. Figure 7.3 shows a UML class diagram for the `MiniQuiz` program.

Multiple classes can implement the same interface, providing alternative definitions for the methods. For example, we could implement a class called `Task` that also implements the `Complexity` interface. In it we could choose to manage the complexity of a task in a different way (though it would still have to implement all the methods of the interface).

A class can implement more than one interface. In these cases, the class must provide an implementation for all methods in all interfaces listed. To show that

LISTING 7.10

```
//********************************************************************
//  MiniQuiz.java        Author: Lewis/Loftus
//
//  Demonstrates the use of a class that implements an interface.
//********************************************************************

import java.util.Scanner;

public class MiniQuiz
{
   //-----------------------------------------------------------------
   //  Presents a short quiz.
   //-----------------------------------------------------------------
   public static void main(String[] args)
   {
      Question q1, q2;
      String possible;

      Scanner scan = new Scanner(System.in);

      q1 = new Question("What is the capital of Jamaica?",
                        "Kingston");
      q1.setComplexity(4);

      q2 = new Question("Which is worse, ignorance or apathy?",
                        "I don't know and I don't care");
      q2.setComplexity(10);

      System.out.print(q1.getQuestion());
      System.out.println(" (Level: " + q1.getComplexity() + ")");
      possible = scan.nextLine();
      if (q1.answerCorrect(possible))
         System.out.println("Correct");
      else
         System.out.println("No, the answer is " + q1.getAnswer());

      System.out.println();
      System.out.print(q2.getQuestion());
      System.out.println(" (Level: " + q2.getComplexity() + ")");
      possible = scan.nextLine();
      if (q2.answerCorrect(possible))
         System.out.println("Correct");
      else
```

LISTING 7.10 *continued*

```
            System.out.println("No, the answer is " + q2.getAnswer());
    }
}
```

OUTPUT

```
What is the capital of Jamaica? (Level: 4)
Kingston
Correct

Which is worse, ignorance or apathy? (Level: 10)
apathy
No, the answer is I don't know and I don't care
```

a class implements multiple interfaces, they are listed in the `implements` clause, separated by commas. For example:

```
class ManyThings implements Interface1, Interface2, Interface3
{
    // contains all methods of all interfaces
}
```

In addition to, or instead of, abstract methods, an interface can also contain constants, defined using the `final` modifier. When a class implements an interface, it gains access to all the constants defined in it.

The interface construct formally defines the ways in which we can interact with a class. It also serves as a basis for a powerful programming technique called polymorphism, which we discuss in Chapter 10.

The `Comparable` Interface

The Java standard class library contains interfaces as well as classes. The `Comparable` interface, for example, is defined in the `java.lang` package. The `Comparable` interface contains only one method, `compareTo`, which takes an object as a parameter and returns an integer.

The intention of this interface is to provide a common mechanism for comparing one object to another. One object calls the method and passes another as a parameter as follows:

```
if (obj1.compareTo(obj2) < 0)
    System.out.println("obj1 is less than obj2");
```

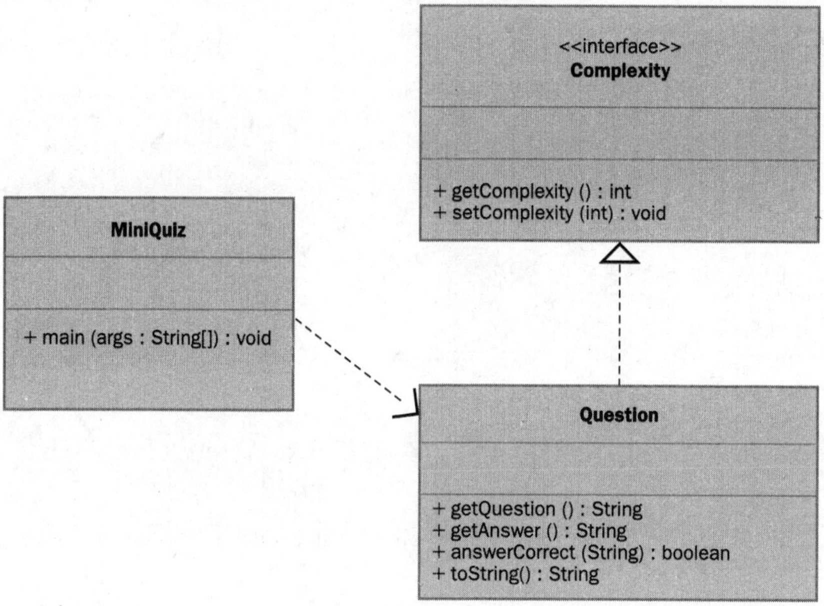

FIGURE 7.3 A UML class diagram for the `MiniQuiz` program

As specified by the documentation for the interface, the integer that is returned from the `compareTo` method should be negative if `obj1` is less than `obj2`, 0 if they are equal, and positive if `obj1` is greater than `obj2`. It is up to the designer of each class to decide what it means for one object of that class to be less than, equal to, or greater than another.

In Chapter 5, we mentioned that the `String` class contains a `compareTo` method that operates in this manner. Now we can clarify that the `String` class has this method because it implements the `Comparable` interface. The `String` class implementation of this method bases the comparison on the lexicographic ordering defined by the Unicode character set.

The `Iterator` Interface

The `Iterator` interface is another interface defined as part of the Java standard class library. It is used by a class that represents a collection of objects, providing a means to move through the collection one object at a time.

In Chapter 5, we defined the concept of an iterator, using a loop to process all elements in the collection. Most iterators, including objects of the `Scanner` class, are defined using the `Iterator` interface.

The two primary methods in the `Iterator` interface are `hasNext`, which returns a boolean result, and `next`, which returns an object. Neither of these methods takes any parameters. The `hasNext` method returns true if there are items left to process, and `next` returns the next object. It is up to the designer of the class that implements the `Iterator` interface to decide the order in which objects will be delivered by the `next` method.

We should note that, according to the spirit of the interface, the `next` method does not remove the object from the underlying collection; it simply returns a reference to it. The `Iterator` interface also has a method called `remove`, which takes no parameters and has a `void` return type. A call to the `remove` method removes the object that was most recently returned by the `next` method from the underlying collection.

SELF-REVIEW QUESTIONS *(see answers in Appendix L)*

SR 7.14 What is the difference between a class and an interface?

SR 7.15 Define a Java interface called `Nameable`. Classes that implement this interface must provide a `setName` method that requires a single `String` parameter and returns nothing, and a `getName` method that has no parameters and returns a `String`.

SR 7.16 True or False? Explain.

a. A Java interface can include only abstract methods, nothing else.
b. An abstract method is a method that does not have an implementation.
c. All of the methods included in a Java interface definition must be abstract.
d. A class that implements an interface can define only those methods that are included in the interface.
e. Multiple classes can implement the same interface.
f. A class can implement more than one interface.
g. All classes that implement an interface must provide the exact same definitions of the methods that are included in the interface.

7.6 Enumerated Types Revisited

In Chapter 3, we introduced the concept of an enumerated type, which defines a new data type and lists all possible values of that type. We gave an example that defined an enumerated type called `Season`, which was declared as follows:

```
enum Season {winter, spring, summer, fall}
```

We mentioned that an enumerated type is a special kind of class, and that the values of the enumerated type are objects. The values are, in fact, instances of its own enumerated type. For example, `winter` is an object of the `Season` class. Let's explore this concept a bit further.

Suppose we declare a variable of the `Season` type as follows:

```
Season time;
```

KEY CONCEPT
The values of an enumerated type are static variables of that type.

Because an enumerated type is a special kind of class, the variable `time` is an object reference variable. Furthermore, as an enumerated type, it can be assigned only the values listed in the `Season` definition. These values (`winter`, `spring`, `summer`, and `fall`) are actually references to `Season` objects that are stored as `public static` variables within the `Season` class. Thus we can make an assignment such as the following:

```
time = Season.spring;
```

Now let's take this idea a step further. In Listing 7.11, we redefine the `Season` type, giving it a more substantial definition. Note that we still use the `enum` reserved word to declare the enumerated type, and we still list all possible values of the type. In addition, in this definition we add a private `String` called `span`, a constructor for the `Season` class, and a method named `getSpan`. Each value in the list of values for the enumerated type invokes the constructor, passing it a character string that is then stored in the `span` variable of each value.

LISTING 7.11

```
//********************************************************************
//  Season.java          Author: Lewis/Loftus
//
//  Enumerates the values for Season.
//********************************************************************

public enum Season
{
   winter ("December through February"),
   spring ("March through May"),
   summer ("June through August"),
   fall ("September through November");

   private String span;
```

LISTING 7.11 *continued*

```
   //-----------------------------------------------------------------
   //  Constructor: Sets up each value with an associated string.
   //-----------------------------------------------------------------
   Season(String months)
   {
      span = months;
   }

   //-----------------------------------------------------------------
   //  Returns the span message for this value.
   //-----------------------------------------------------------------
   public String getSpan()
   {
      return span;
   }
}
```

The main method of the SeasonTester class, shown in Listing 7.12, prints each value of the Season enumerated type, as well as the span statement for each. Every enumerated type contains a static method called values that returns a list of all possible values for that type. This list is an iterator, so we can use the enhanced version of a for loop to process each value.

LISTING 7.12

```
//********************************************************************
//  SeasonTester.java       Author: Lewis/Loftus
//
//  Demonstrates the use of a full enumerated type.
//********************************************************************

public class SeasonTester
{
   //-----------------------------------------------------------------
   //  Iterates through the values of the Season enumerated type.
   //-----------------------------------------------------------------
   public static void main(String[] args)
   {
```

LISTING 7.12 *continued*

```
      for (Season time : Season.values())
         System.out.println(time + "\t" + time.getSpan());
   }
}
```

OUTPUT

```
winter   December through February
spring   March through May
summer   June through August
fall     September through November
```

KEY CONCEPT
We can add attributes and methods to the definition of an enumerated type.

In addition to the list of possible values defined in every enumerated type, we can include any number of attributes or methods of our own choosing. This provides various opportunities for creative class design.

SELF-REVIEW QUESTION *(see answer in Appendix L)*

SR 7.17 Using the enumerated type `Season` as defined in this section, what is the output from the following code sequence?

```
Season time1, time2;
time1 = Season.winter;
time2 = Season.summer;
System.out.println(time1);
System.out.println(time2.name());
System.out.println(time1.ordinal());
System.out.println(time2.getSpan());
```

7.7 Method Design

Once you have identified classes and assigned basic responsibilities, the design of each method will determine how exactly the class will define its behaviors. Some methods are straightforward and require little thought. Others are more interesting and require careful planning.

An *algorithm* is a step-by-step process for solving a problem. A recipe is an example of an algorithm. Travel directions are another example of an algorithm. Every method implements an algorithm that determines how that method accomplishes its goals.

An algorithm is often described using *pseudocode,* which is a mixture of code statements and English phrases. Pseudocode provides enough structure to show how the code will operate, without getting bogged down in the syntactic details of a particular programming language or becoming prematurely constrained by the characteristics of particular programming constructs.

This section discusses two important aspects of program design at the method level: method decomposition and the implications of passing objects as parameters.

Method Decomposition

Occasionally, a service that an object provides is so complicated that it cannot reasonably be implemented using one method. Therefore, we sometimes need to decompose a method into multiple methods to create a more understandable design. As an example, let's examine a program that translates English sentences into Pig Latin.

KEY CONCEPT
A complex service provided by an object can be decomposed to make use of private support methods.

Pig Latin is a made-up language in which each word of a sentence is modified, in general, by moving the initial sound of the word to the end and adding an "ay" sound. For example, the word *happy* would be written and pronounced *appyhay* and the word *birthday* would become *irthdaybay*. Words that begin with vowels simply have a "yay" sound added on the end, turning the word *enough* into *enoughyay*. Consonant blends such as "ch" and "st" at the beginning of a word are moved to the end together before adding the "ay" sound. Therefore, the word *grapefruit* becomes *apefruitgray*.

The `PigLatin` program shown in Listing 7.13 reads one or more sentences, translating each into Pig Latin.

The workhorse behind the `PigLatin` program is the `PigLatinTranslator` class, shown in Listing 7.14. The `PigLatinTranslator` class provides one fundamental service, a static method called `translate`, which accepts a string and translates it into Pig Latin. Note that the `PigLatinTranslator` class does not contain a constructor because none is needed.

LISTING 7.13

```
//********************************************************************
//  PigLatin.java       Author: Lewis/Loftus
//
//  Demonstrates the concept of method decomposition.
//********************************************************************

import java.util.Scanner;
```

LISTING 7.13 *continued*

```
public class PigLatin
{
   //-----------------------------------------------------------------
   //  Reads sentences and translates them into Pig Latin.
   //-----------------------------------------------------------------
   public static void main(String[] args)
   {
      String sentence, result, another;

      Scanner scan = new Scanner(System.in);

      do
      {
         System.out.println();
         System.out.println("Enter a sentence (no punctuation):");
         sentence = scan.nextLine();

         System.out.println();
         result = PigLatinTranslator.translate(sentence);
         System.out.println("That sentence in Pig Latin is:");
         System.out.println(result);

         System.out.println();
         System.out.print("Translate another sentence (y/n)? ");
         another = scan.nextLine();
      }
      while (another.equalsIgnoreCase("y"));
   }
}
```

OUTPUT

```
Enter a sentence (no punctuation):
Do you speak Pig Latin
That sentence in Pig Latin is:
oday ouyay eakspay igpay atinlay

Translate another sentence (y/n)?  y

Enter a sentence (no punctuation):
Play it again Sam

That sentence in Pig Latin is:
ayplay ityay againyay amsay

Translate another sentence (y/n)?  n
```

LISTING 7.14

```
//********************************************************************
//  PigLatinTranslator.java       Author: Lewis/Loftus
//
//  Represents a translator from English to Pig Latin. Demonstrates
//  method decomposition.
//********************************************************************

import java.util.Scanner;

public class PigLatinTranslator
{
   //-----------------------------------------------------------------
   //  Translates a sentence of words into Pig Latin.
   //-----------------------------------------------------------------
   public static String translate(String sentence)
   {
      String result = "";

      sentence = sentence.toLowerCase();

      Scanner scan = new Scanner(sentence);

      while (scan.hasNext())
      {
         result += translateWord(scan.next());
         result += " ";
      }

      return result;
   }

   //-----------------------------------------------------------------
   //  Translates one word into Pig Latin. If the word begins with a
   //  vowel, the suffix "yay" is appended to the word. Otherwise,
   //  the first letter or two are moved to the end of the word,
   //  and "ay" is appended.
   //-----------------------------------------------------------------
   private static String translateWord(String word)
   {
      String result = "";

      if (beginsWithVowel(word))
         result = word + "yay";
      else
         if (beginsWithBlend(word))
```

LISTING 7.14 *continued*

```
         result = word.substring(2) + word.substring(0,2) + "ay";
      else
         result = word.substring(1) + word.charAt(0) + "ay";

      return result;
   }

   //-----------------------------------------------------------------
   //  Determines if the specified word begins with a vowel.
   //-----------------------------------------------------------------
   private static boolean beginsWithVowel(String word)
   {
      String vowels = "aeiou";

      char letter = word.charAt(0);

      return (vowels.indexOf(letter) != -1);
   }

   //-----------------------------------------------------------------
   //  Determines if the specified word begins with a particular
   //  two-character consonant blend.
   //-----------------------------------------------------------------
   private static boolean beginsWithBlend(String word)
   {
      return ( word.startsWith("bl") || word.startsWith("sc") ||
               word.startsWith("br") || word.startsWith("sh") ||
               word.startsWith("ch") || word.startsWith("sk") ||
               word.startsWith("cl") || word.startsWith("sl") ||
               word.startsWith("cr") || word.startsWith("sn") ||
               word.startsWith("dr") || word.startsWith("sm") ||
               word.startsWith("dw") || word.startsWith("sp") ||
               word.startsWith("fl") || word.startsWith("sq") ||
               word.startsWith("fr") || word.startsWith("st") ||
               word.startsWith("gl") || word.startsWith("sw") ||
               word.startsWith("gr") || word.startsWith("th") ||
               word.startsWith("kl") || word.startsWith("tr") ||
               word.startsWith("ph") || word.startsWith("tw") ||
               word.startsWith("pl") || word.startsWith("wh") ||
               word.startsWith("pr") || word.startsWith("wr") );
   }
}
```

The act of translating an entire sentence into Pig Latin is not trivial. If written in one big method, it would be very long and difficult to follow. A better solution, as implemented in the `PigLatinTranslator` class, is to decompose the `translate` method and use several other support methods to help with the task.

The `translate` method uses a `Scanner` object to separate the string into words. Recall that one role of the `Scanner` class (discussed in Chapter 3) is to separate a string into smaller elements called tokens. In this case, the tokens are separated by space characters so we can use the default white space delimiters. The `PigLatin` program assumes that no punctuation is included in the input.

The `translate` method passes each word to the private support method `translateWord`. Even the job of translating one word is somewhat involved, so the `translateWord` method makes use of two other private methods, `beginsWith-Vowel` and `beginsWithBlend`.

The `beginsWithVowel` method returns a `boolean` value that indicates whether the word passed as a parameter begins with a vowel. Note that instead of checking each vowel separately, the code for this method declares a string that contains all the vowels, and then invokes the `String` method `indexOf` to determine whether the first character of the word is in the vowel string. If the specified character cannot be found, the `indexOf` method returns a value of `–1`.

The `beginsWithBlend` method also returns a `boolean` value. The body of the method contains only a `return` statement with one large expression that makes several calls to the `startsWith` method of the `String` class. If any of these calls returns true, then the `beginsWithBlend` method returns true as well.

Note that the `translateWord`, `beginsWithVowel`, and `beginsWithBlend` methods are all declared with private visibility. They are not intended to provide services directly to clients outside the class. Instead, they exist to help the `translate` method, which is the only true service method in this class, to do its job. By declaring them with private visibility, they cannot be invoked from outside this class. If the `main` method of the `PigLatin` class attempted to invoke the `translateWord` method, for instance, the compiler would issue an error message.

Figure 7.4 shows a UML class diagram for the `PigLatin` program. Note the notation showing the visibility of various methods.

Whenever a method becomes large or complex, we should consider decomposing it into multiple methods to create a more understandable class design. First, however, we must consider how other classes and objects can be defined to create better overall system design. In an object-oriented design, method decomposition must be subordinate to object decomposition.

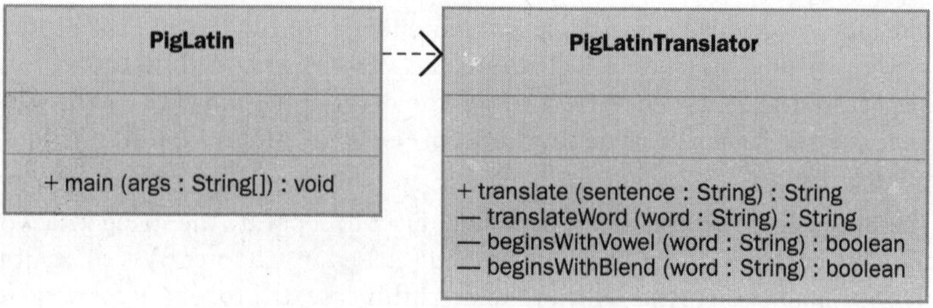

FIGURE 7.4 A UML class diagram for the `PigLatin` program

Method Parameters Revisited

Another important issue related to method design involves the way parameters are passed into a method. In Java, all parameters are passed *by value.* That is, the current value of the actual parameter (in the invocation) is copied into the formal parameter in the method header. We mentioned this issue in Chapter 4; let's examine it now in more detail.

Essentially, parameter passing is like an assignment statement, assigning to the formal parameter a copy of the value stored in the actual parameter. This issue must be considered when making changes to a formal parameter inside a method. The formal parameter is a separate copy of the value that is passed in, so any changes made to it have no effect on the actual parameter. After control returns to the calling method, the actual parameter will have the same value as it did before the method was called.

However, when we pass an object to a method, we are actually passing a reference to that object. The value that gets copied is the address of the object. Therefore, the formal parameter and the actual parameter become aliases of each other. If we change the state of the object through the formal parameter reference inside the method, we are changing the object referenced by the actual parameter, because they refer to the same object. On the other hand, if we change the formal parameter reference itself (to make it point to a new object, for instance), we have not changed the fact that the actual parameter still refers to the original object.

KEY CONCEPT

When an object is passed to a method, the actual and formal parameters become aliases.

The program in Listing 7.15 illustrates the nuances of parameter passing. Carefully trace the processing of this program and note the values that are output. The `ParameterTester` class contains a `main` method that calls the `changeValues` method in a `ParameterModifier` object. Two of the parameters to `changeValues` are `Num` objects, each of which simply stores an integer value. The other parameter is a primitive integer value.

LISTING 7.15

```
//********************************************************************
//  ParameterTester.java       Author: Lewis/Loftus
//
//  Demonstrates the effects of passing various types of parameters.
//********************************************************************

public class ParameterTester
{
   //-----------------------------------------------------------------
   //  Sets up three variables (one primitive and two objects) to
   //  serve as actual parameters to the changeValues method. Prints
   //  their values before and after calling the method.
   //-----------------------------------------------------------------
   public static void main(String[] args)
   {
      ParameterModifier modifier = new ParameterModifier();

      int a1 = 111;
      Num a2 = new Num(222);
      Num a3 = new Num(333);

      System.out.println("Before calling changeValues:");
      System.out.println("a1\ta2\ta3");
      System.out.println(a1 + "\t" + a2 + "\t" + a3 + "\n");

      modifier.changeValues(a1, a2, a3);

      System.out.println("After calling changeValues:");
      System.out.println("a1\ta2\ta3");
      System.out.println(a1 + "\t" + a2 + "\t" + a3 + "\n");
   }
}
```

OUTPUT

```
Before calling changeValues
a1      a2      a3
111     222     333

Before changing the values:
f1      f2      f3
111     222     333
```

LISTING 7.15 *continued*

```
After changing the values:
f1      f2      f3
999     888     777

After calling changeValues:
a1      a2      a3
111     888     333
```

Listing 7.16 shows the ParameterModifier class and Listing 7.17 shows the Num class. Inside the changeValues method, a modification is made to each of the three formal parameters: the integer parameter is set to a different value, the value stored in the first Num parameter is changed using its setValue method,

LISTING 7.16

```
//********************************************************************
//  ParameterModifier.java       Author: Lewis/Loftus
//
//  Demonstrates the effects of changing parameter values.
//********************************************************************

public class ParameterModifier
{
   //-----------------------------------------------------------------
   //  Modifies the parameters, printing their values before and
   //  after making the changes.
   //-----------------------------------------------------------------
   public void changeValues(int f1, Num f2, Num f3)
   {
      System.out.println("Before changing the values:");
      System.out.println("f1\tf2\tf3");
      System.out.println(f1 + "\t" + f2 + "\t" + f3 + "\n");

      f1 = 999;
      f2.setValue(888);
      f3 = new Num(777);

      System.out.println("After changing the values:");
      System.out.println("f1\tf2\tf3");
      System.out.println(f1 + "\t" + f2 + "\t" + f3 + "\n");
   }
}
```

LISTING 7.17

```
//********************************************************************
//  Num.java       Author: Lewis/Loftus
//
//  Represents a single integer as an object.
//********************************************************************

public class Num
{
   private int value;

   //-----------------------------------------------------------------
   //  Sets up the new Num object, storing an initial value.
   //-----------------------------------------------------------------
   public Num(int update)
   {
      value = update;
   }

   //-----------------------------------------------------------------
   //  Sets the stored value to the newly specified value.
   //-----------------------------------------------------------------
   public void setValue(int update)
   {
      value = update;
   }

   //-----------------------------------------------------------------
   //  Returns the stored integer value as a string.
   //-----------------------------------------------------------------
   public String toString()
   {
      return value + "";
   }
}
```

and a new `Num` object is created and assigned to the second `Num` parameter. These changes are reflected in the output printed at the end of the `changeValues` method.

However, note the final values that are printed after returning from the method. The primitive integer was not changed from its original value, because the change was made to a copy inside the method. Likewise, the last parameter still refers to its original object with its original value. This is because the new `Num` object created in the method was referred to only by the formal parameter. When the method returned, that formal parameter was destroyed and the `Num` object it referred to was marked for garbage collection. The only change that is "permanent" is the change made to the state of the second parameter. Figure 7.5 shows the step-by-step processing of this program.

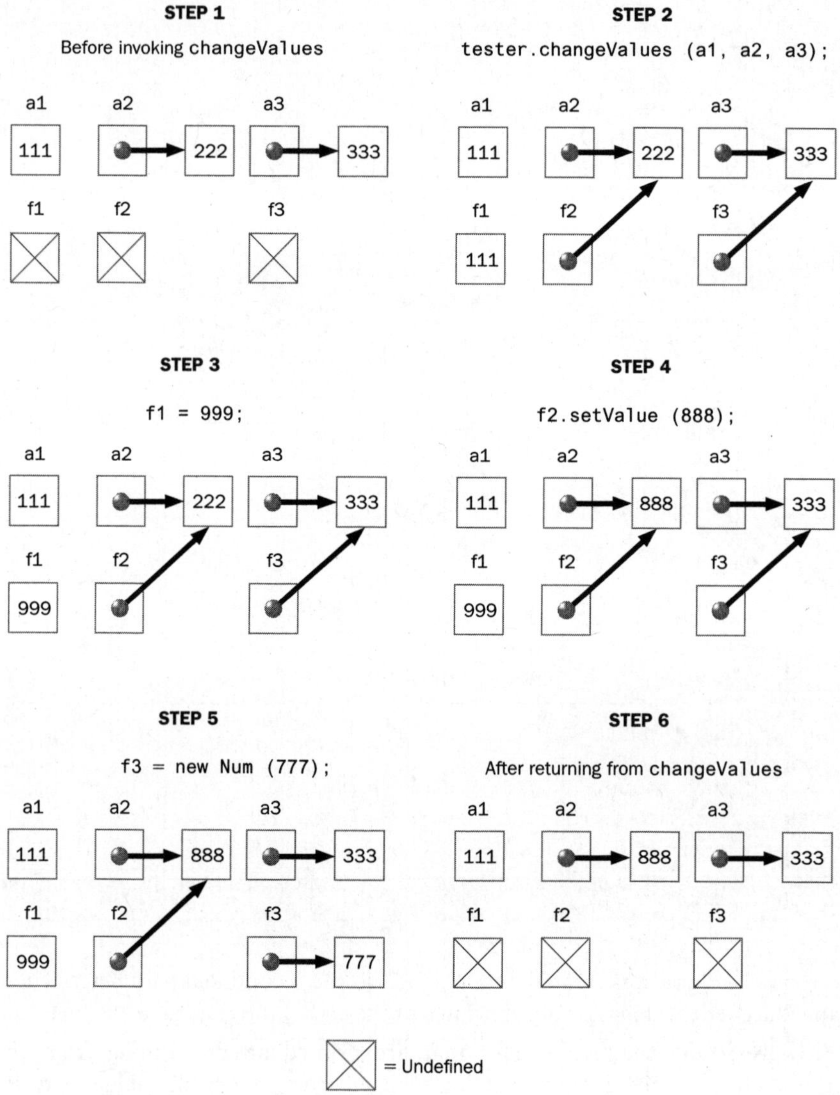

FIGURE 7.5 Tracing the parameters in the `ParameterTesting` program

SELF-REVIEW QUESTIONS *(see answers in Appendix L)*

SR 7.18 What is method decomposition?

SR 7.19 Answer the following questions about the `PigLatinTranslator` class.

a. No constructor is defined. Why not?
b. Some of the defined methods are private. Why?
c. A `Scanner` object is declared in the `translate` method. What is it used to scan?

SR 7.20 Identify the resultant sequence of calls/returns of `PigLatinTranslator` support methods when `translate` is invoked with the following actual parameters.

a. `"animal"`
b. `"hello"`
c. `"We are the champions"`

SR 7.21 How are objects passed as parameters?

7.8 Method Overloading

As we've discussed, when a method is invoked, the flow of control transfers to the code that defines the method. After the method has been executed, control returns to the location of the call and processing continues.

Often the method name is sufficient to indicate which method is being called by a specific invocation. But in Java, as in other object-oriented languages, you can use the same method name with different parameter lists for multiple methods. This technique is called *method overloading*. It is useful when you need to perform similar methods on different types of data.

The compiler must still be able to associate each invocation to a specific method declaration. If the method name for two or more methods is the same, additional information is used to uniquely identify the version that is being invoked. In Java, a method name can be used for multiple methods as long as the number of parameters, the types of those parameters, and/or the order of the types of parameters is distinct.

KEY CONCEPT

The versions of an overloaded method are distinguished by the number, type, and order of their parameters.

For example, we could declare a method called `sum` as follows:

```
public int sum(int num1, int num2)
{
   return num1 + num2;
}
```

Then we could declare another method called sum, within the same class, as follows:

```
public int sum(int num1, int num2, int num3)
{
   return num1 + num2 + num3;
}
```

Now, when an invocation is made, the compiler looks at the number of parameters to determine which version of the sum method to call. For instance, the following invocation will call the second version of the sum method:

```
sum(25, 69, 13);
```

A method's name, along with the number, type, and order of its parameters, is called the method's *signature*. The compiler uses the complete method signature to *bind* a method invocation to the appropriate definition.

The compiler must be able to examine a method invocation to determine which specific method is being invoked. If you attempt to specify two method names with the same signature, the compiler will issue an appropriate error message and will not create an executable program. There can be no ambiguity.

Note that the return type of a method is not part of the method signature. That is, two overloaded methods cannot differ only by their return type. This is because the value returned by a method can be ignored by the invocation. The compiler would not be able to distinguish which version of an overloaded method is being referenced in such situations.

VideoNote
Examples of method overloading.

The println method is an example of a method that is overloaded several times, each accepting a single type. The following is a partial list of its various signatures:

- println(String s)
- println(int i)
- println(double d)
- println(char c)
- println(boolean b)

The following two lines of code actually invoke different methods that have the same name:

```
System.out.println("Number of students: ");
System.out.println(count);
```

The first line invokes the version of println that accepts a string. The second line, assuming count is an integer variable, invokes the version of println that accepts an integer.

We often use a `println` statement that prints several distinct types, such as

```
System.out.println("Number of students: " + count);
```

Remember, in this case the plus sign is the string concatenation operator. First, the value in the variable `count` is converted to a string representation, then the two strings are concatenated into one longer string, and finally the definition of `println` that accepts a single string is invoked.

Constructors can be overloaded, and often are. By providing multiple versions of a constructor, we provide multiple ways to set up an object.

SELF-REVIEW QUESTIONS *(see answers in Appendix L)*

SR 7.22 How are overloaded methods distinguished from each other?

SR 7.23 For each of the following pairs of method headers, state whether or not the signatures are distinct. If not, explain why not.

a.
```
String describe(String name, int count)
String describe(int count, String name)
```
b.
```
void count( )
int count( )
```
c.
```
int howMany(int compareValue)
int howMany(int ceiling)
```
d.
```
boolean greater(int value1)
boolean greater(int value1, int value2)
```

SR 7.24 The `Num` class is defined in Section 7.7. Overload the constructor of that class by defining a second constructor which takes no parameters and sets the `value` attribute to zero.

7.9 Testing

The term *testing* can be applied in many ways to software development. Testing certainly includes its traditional definition: the act of running a completed program with various inputs to discover problems. But it also includes any evaluation that is performed by human or machine to assess the quality of the evolving system. These evaluations should occur long before a single line of code is written.

The goal of testing is to find errors. By finding errors and fixing them, we improve the quality of our program. It's likely that later on someone else will find any errors that remain hidden during development. The earlier the errors are found, the easier and cheaper they are to fix. Taking the time to uncover problems as early as possible is almost always worth the effort.

KEY CONCEPT
Testing a program can never guarantee the absence of errors.

Running a program with specific input and producing the correct results establishes only that the program works for that particular input. As more and more test cases execute without revealing errors, our confidence in the program rises, but we can never really be sure that all errors have been eliminated. There could always be another error still undiscovered. Because of that, it is important to thoroughly test a program in as many ways as possible and with well-designed test cases.

It is possible to prove that a program is correct, but that technique is enormously complex for large systems, and errors can be made in the proof itself. Therefore, we generally rely on testing to determine the quality of a program.

After determining that an error exists, we determine the cause of the error and fix it. After a problem is fixed, we should run previous tests again to make sure that while fixing the problem we didn't create another. This technique is called *regression testing*.

Reviews

One technique used to evaluate design or code is called a *review*, which is a meeting in which several people carefully examine a design document or section of code. Presenting our design or code to others causes us to think more carefully about it and permits others to share their suggestions with us. The participants discuss its merits and problems, and create a list of issues that must be addressed. The goal of a review is to identify problems, not to solve them, which usually takes much more time.

A design review should determine whether the requirements have been addressed. It should also assess the way the system is decomposed into classes and objects. A code review should determine how faithfully the design satisfies the requirements and how faithfully the implementation represents the design. It should identify any specific problems that would cause the design or the implementation to fail in its responsibilities.

Sometimes a review is called a *walkthrough,* because its goal is to step carefully through a document and evaluate each section.

Defect Testing

Since the goal of testing is to find errors, it is often referred to as *defect testing*. With that goal in mind, a good test is one that uncovers any deficiencies in a program. This might seem strange, because we ultimately don't want to have problems in our system. But keep in mind that errors almost certainly exist. Our testing efforts should make every attempt to find them. We want to increase the reliability of our program by finding and fixing the errors that exist, rather than letting users discover them.

> **KEY CONCEPT**
> A good test is one that uncovers an error.

A *test case* consists of a set of inputs, user actions, or other initial conditions, along with the expected output. A test case should be appropriately documented so that it can be repeated later as needed. Developers often create a complete *test suite,* which is a set of test cases that covers various aspects of the system.

> **KEY CONCEPT**
> It is not feasible to exhaustively test a program for all possible input and user actions.

Because programs operate on a large number of possible inputs, it is not feasible to create test cases for all possible input or user actions. Nor is it usually necessary to test every single situation. Two specific test cases may be so similar that they actually do not test unique aspects of the program. To do both would be a wasted effort. We'd rather execute a test case that stresses the program in some new way. Therefore, we want to choose our test cases carefully. To that end, let's examine two approaches to defect testing: black-box testing and white-box testing.

As the name implies, *black-box testing* treats the thing being tested as a black box. In black-box testing, test cases are developed without regard to the internal workings. Black-box tests are based on inputs and outputs. An entire program can be tested using a black-box technique, in which case the inputs are the user-provided information and user actions such as button pushes. A test case is successful only if the input produces the expected output. A single class can also be tested using a black-box technique, which focuses on the system interface (its public methods) of the class. Certain parameters are passed in, producing certain results. Black-box test cases are often derived directly from the requirements of the system or from the stated purpose of a method.

The input data for a black-box test case are often selected by defining equivalence categories. An *equivalence category* is a collection of inputs that are expected to produce similar outputs. Generally, if a method will work for one value in the equivalence category, we have every reason to believe it will work for the others. For example, the input to a method that computes the square root of an integer can be divided into two equivalence categories: nonnegative integers and negative integers. If it works appropriately for one nonnegative value, it will likely work for all nonnegative values. Likewise, if it works appropriately for one negative value, it will likely work for all negative values.

Equivalence categories have defined boundaries. Because all values of an equivalence category essentially test the same features of a program, only one test case inside the equivalence boundary is needed. However, because programming often produces "off by one" errors, the values on and around the boundary should be tested exhaustively. For an integer boundary, a good test suite would include at least the exact value of the boundary, the boundary minus 1, and the boundary plus 1. Test cases that use these cases, plus at least one from within the general field of the category, should be defined.

Let's look at an example. Consider a method whose purpose is to validate that a particular integer value is in the range 0 to 99, inclusive. There are three equivalence categories in this case: values below 0, values in the range of 0 to 99, and values above 99. Black-box testing dictates that we use test values that surround and fall on the boundaries, as well as some general values from the equivalence categories. Therefore, a set of black-box test cases for this situation might be: −500, −1, 0, 1, 50, 98, 99, 100, and 500.

White-box testing, also known as *glass-box testing*, exercises the internal structure and implementation of a method. A white-box test case is based on the logic of the code. The goal is to ensure that every path through a program is executed at least once. A white-box test maps the possible paths through the code and ensures that the test cases cause every path to be executed. This type of testing is often called *statement coverage*.

Paths through code are controlled by various control flow statements that use conditional expressions, such as `if` statements. In order to have every path through the program executed at least once, the input data values for the test cases need to control the values for the conditional expressions. The input data of one or more test cases should cause the condition of an `if` statement to evaluate to `true` in at least one case and to `false` in at least one case. Covering both true and false values in an `if` statement guarantees that both the paths through the `if` statement will be executed. Similar situations can be created for loops and other constructs.

In both black-box and white-box testing, the expected output for each test should be established prior to running the test. It's too easy to be persuaded that the results of a test are appropriate if you haven't first carefully determined what the results should be.

SELF-REVIEW QUESTION *(see answer in Appendix L)*

SR 7.25 Select the term from the following list that best matches each of the following phrases:

black-box, defects, regression, review, test case, test suite, walk-through, white-box

a. Running previous test cases after a change is made to a program to help ensure that the change did not introduce an error.
b. A meeting in which several people collectively evaluate an artifact.
c. A review that steps carefully through a document, evaluating each section.
d. The goal of testing is to discover these.

e. A description of the input and corresponding expected output of a code unit being tested.
f. A set of test cases that covers various aspects of a system.
g. With this testing approach, test cases are based solely on requirement specifications.
h. With this testing approach, test cases are based on the internal workings of the program.

7.10 GUI Design

As we focus on the details that allow us to create GUIs, we may sometimes lose sight of the big picture. As we continue to explore GUI construction, we should keep in mind that our goal is to solve a problem. Specifically, we want to create software that is useful. Knowing the details of controls, events, and other language elements gives us the tools to put GUIs together, but we must guide that knowledge with the following fundamental ideas of good GUI design:

- Know the user.
- Prevent user errors.
- Optimize user abilities.
- Be consistent.

KEY CONCEPT
The design of any GUI should adhere to basic guidelines regarding consistency and usability.

The software designer must understand the user's needs and potential activities in order to develop an interface that will serve that user well. Keep in mind that, to the user, the interface *is* the software. It is the only way the user interacts with the system. As such, the interface must satisfy the user's needs.

Whenever possible, we should design interfaces so that the user can make as few mistakes as possible. In many situations, we have the flexibility to choose one of several controls to accomplish a specific task. We should always try to choose controls that will prevent inappropriate actions and avoid invalid input. For example, if an input value must be one of a set of particular values, we should use controls that allow the user to make only a valid choice. That is, constraining the user to a few valid choices with, for instance, a set of radio buttons is better than allowing the user to type arbitrary and possibly invalid data into a text field.

Not all users are alike. Some are more adept than others at using a particular GUI or GUI controls in general. We shouldn't design with only the lowest common denominator in mind. For example, we should provide shortcuts whenever reasonable. That is, in addition to a normal series of actions that will allow a user to accomplish a task, we should also provide redundant ways to accomplish the same task. Using keyboard shortcuts (mnemonics) is a good example. Sometimes these additional mechanisms are less intuitive, but they may be faster for the experienced user.

Finally, consistency is important when dealing with large systems or multiple systems in a common environment. Users become familiar with a particular organization or color scheme; these should not be changed arbitrarily.

SELF-REVIEW QUESTIONS *(see answers in Appendix L)*

SR 7.26 What general guidelines for GUI design are presented in this section?

SR 7.27 Why is a good user interface design so important?

7.11 Mouse Events

Let's examine the events that are generated when using a mouse, described in Figure 7.6. The coordinates of the mouse are captured in the event object when any of these events occur.

When you click the mouse button while the mouse pointer is over a JavaFX node, three events occur: one when the mouse button is pushed down (*mouse pressed*) and two when it is let up (*mouse released* and *mouse clicked*).

KEY CONCEPT
Moving the mouse and clicking the mouse button generate events to which a program can respond.

A node will generate a *mouse entered* event when the mouse pointer passes into its graphical space. Likewise, it generates a *mouse exited* event when the mouse pointer is moved off of the node.

A stream of *mouse moved* events occur while the mouse is in motion. If the mouse button is pressed down while the mouse is being moved, *mouse dragged* events are generated. These events are generated very quickly while the mouse is in motion, allowing a program to track and respond to the ongoing movement of the mouse.

Mouse Event	Description
mouse pressed	The mouse button is pressed down.
mouse released	The mouse button is released.
mouse clicked	The mouse button is pressed down and released on the same node.
mouse entered	The mouse pointer is moved onto (over) a node.
mouse exited	The mouse pointer is moved off of a node.
mouse moved	The mouse is moved.
mouse dragged	The mouse is moved while the mouse button is pressed down.

FIGURE 7.6 JavaFX mouse events

There is a corresponding convenience method for setting the handler for each of the mouse events, such as setOnMousePressed, setOnMouseReleased, etc.

The program shown in Listing 7.18 responds to one mouse event. When the mouse button is clicked anywhere on the scene, a line is displayed from the origin point (0, 0) in the upper left corner to the location of the mouse pointer. Also, the distance between those two points is calculated and displayed.

LISTING 7.18

```
import javafx.application.Application;
import javafx.scene.Group;
import javafx.scene.Scene;
import javafx.scene.input.MouseEvent;
import javafx.scene.paint.Color;
import javafx.scene.shape.Line;
import javafx.scene.text.Text;
import javafx.stage.Stage;

//************************************************************************
//  ClickDistance.java       Author: Lewis/Loftus
//
//  Demonstrates the handling of a mouse click event.
//************************************************************************

public class ClickDistance extends Application
{
   private Line line;
   private Text distanceText;

   //--------------------------------------------------------------------
   //  Shows the distance between the origin (0, 0) and the point where
   //  the mouse is clicked.
   //--------------------------------------------------------------------
   public void start(Stage primaryStage)
   {
      line =  new Line(0, 0, 0, 0);
      distanceText = new Text(150, 30, "Distance:  --");

      Group root = new Group(distanceText, line);

      Scene scene = new Scene(root, 400, 300, Color.LIGHTYELLOW);

      scene.setOnMouseClicked(this::processMouseClick);

      primaryStage.setTitle("Click Distance");
```

LISTING 7.18 *continued*

```
      primaryStage.setScene(scene);
      primaryStage.show();
   }

   //-----------------------------------------------------------------
   //  Resets the end point of the line to the location of the mouse
   //  click event and updates the distance displayed.
   //-----------------------------------------------------------------
   public void processMouseClick(MouseEvent event)
   {
      double clickX = event.getX();
      double clickY = event.getY();

      line.setEndX(clickX);
      line.setEndY(clickY);

      double distance = Math.sqrt(clickX * clickX + clickY * clickY);

      String distanceStr = String.format("%.2f", distance);
      distanceText.setText("Distance:  " + distanceStr);
   }
}
```

DISPLAY

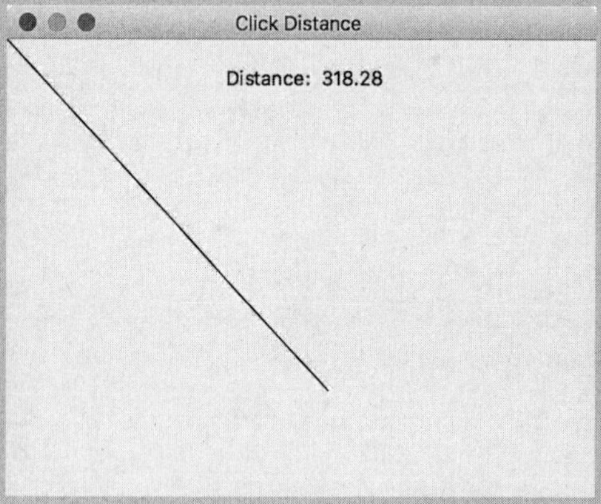

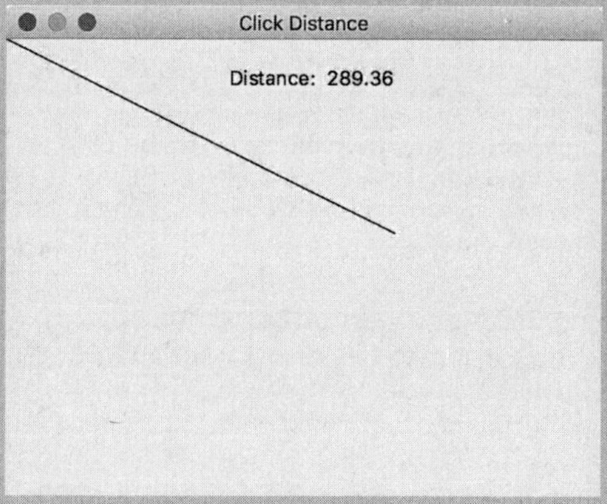

The `processMouseClick` method is set as the event handler, which is passed the `MouseEvent` object that represents the event. Calling the `getX` and `getY` methods of the event return coordinates that indicate where the mouse was clicked. Using those values, the end point of the line is reset and the distance to the origin point is calculated and displayed.

Now let's look at an example that responds to two mouse-oriented events. The `RubberLines` program shown in Listing 7.19 allows the user to draw a line between two points by clicking the mouse button to establish one end point and dragging the mouse to the other end point. The line is constantly redrawn as the mouse is being dragged, giving the illusion that the user is stretching the line into existence. This effect is called *rubberbanding*.

KEY CONCEPT
Rubberbanding is the graphical effect caused when a shape seems to resize as the mouse is dragged.

LISTING 7.19

```
import javafx.application.Application;
import javafx.scene.Group;
import javafx.scene.Scene;
import javafx.scene.input.MouseEvent;
import javafx.scene.paint.Color;
import javafx.scene.shape.Line;
import javafx.stage.Stage;

//************************************************************************
//  RubberLines.java       Author: Lewis/Loftus
//
//  Demonstrates the handling of mouse press and mouse drag events.
//************************************************************************

public class RubberLines extends Application
{
   private Line currentLine;
   private Group root;

   //--------------------------------------------------------------------
   //  Displays an initially empty scene, waiting for the user to
   //  draw lines with the mouse.
   //--------------------------------------------------------------------
   public void start(Stage primaryStage)
   {
      root = new Group();

      Scene scene = new Scene(root, 500, 300, Color.BLACK);

      scene.setOnMousePressed(this::processMousePress);
      scene.setOnMouseDragged(this::processMouseDrag);
```

LISTING 7.19 *continued*

```
      primaryStage.setTitle("Rubber Lines");
      primaryStage.setScene(scene);
      primaryStage.show();
   }

   //--------------------------------------------------------------------
   //  Adds a new line to the scene when the mouse button is pressed.
   //--------------------------------------------------------------------
   public void processMousePress(MouseEvent event)
   {
      currentLine = new Line(event.getX(), event.getY(), event.getX(),
          event.getY());
      currentLine.setStroke(Color.CYAN);
      currentLine.setStrokeWidth(3);
      root.getChildren().add(currentLine);
   }

   //--------------------------------------------------------------------
   //  Updates the end point of the current line as the mouse is
   //  dragged, creating the rubber band effect.
   //--------------------------------------------------------------------
   public void processMouseDrag(MouseEvent event)
   {
      currentLine.setEndX(event.getX());
      currentLine.setEndY(event.getY());
   }
}
```

DISPLAY

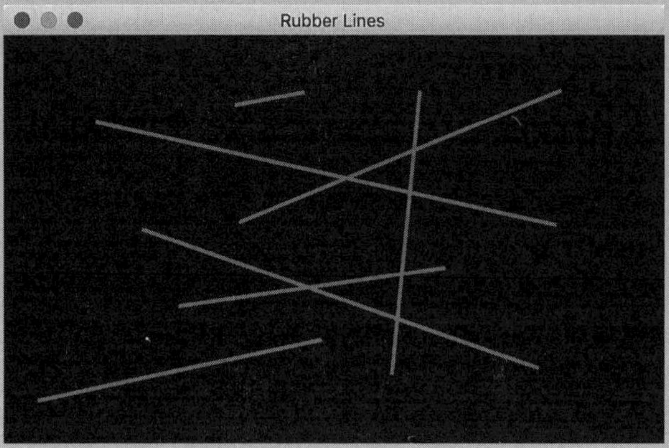

Two event handlers are established in this program: one to handle the mouse being pressed and the other to handle the mouse being dragged. When the mouse button is pressed, a new `Line` object is created and added to the root node of the scene. The line is initially only one pixel long, corresponding to the location of the mouse.

As the mouse is being dragged, multiple mouse drag events are generated. Each time, the end point of the line is updated to the current position of the mouse pointer. These changes happen so quickly that it appears as if one line is being stretched. When the user releases the mouse button, the drag effects stop and the line's position is now fixed. The user can then draw another line if desired.

SELF-REVIEW QUESTIONS *(see answers in Appendix L)*

SR 7.28 What events are generated when the mouse button is clicked?

SR 7.29 What events are generated when the mouse pointer is moved from one location in a window to another?

SR 7.30 How do you obtain the location of the mouse when a mouse event occurs?

7.12 Key Events

A key event is generated when a keyboard key is pressed. Key events allow a program to respond immediately to the user when he or she is typing or pressing other keys such as the arrow keys. If key events are being handled, there is no need to wait for the user to press the Enter key as there is in other keyboard input situations.

KEY CONCEPT
Key events allow a program to respond immediately to the user pressing keyboard keys.

There are three types of key events, as listed in Figure 7.7. The methods `setOnKeyPressed`, `setOnKeyReleased`, and `setOnKeyTyped` can be used to set the event handlers for these methods.

Mouse Event	Description
key pressed	A keyboard key is pressed down.
key released	A keyboard key is released.
key typed	A keyboard key that generates a character is typed (pressed and released).

FIGURE 7.7 JavaFX key events

A key typed event is slightly different than the other two. A key typed event is not a function of the underlying platform, while the other two are. A key typed event is only generated when a key representing a Unicode character is entered.

The program shown in Listing 7.20 responds to key pressed events. It displays an image of an alien that can be moved around the screen using the arrow keys on the keyboard. When the up arrow key is pressed, for instance, the alien immediately moves upward on the screen.

LISTING 7.20

```
import javafx.application.Application;
import javafx.scene.Group;
import javafx.scene.Scene;
import javafx.scene.image.Image;
import javafx.scene.image.ImageView;
import javafx.scene.input.KeyEvent;
import javafx.scene.paint.Color;
import javafx.stage.Stage;

//************************************************************************
//  AlienDirection.java       Author: Lewis/Loftus
//
//  Demonstrates the handling of keyboard events.
//************************************************************************

public class AlienDirection extends Application
{
   public final static int JUMP = 10;

   private ImageView imageView;

   //---------------------------------------------------------------------
   //  Displays an image that can be moved using the arrow keys.
   //---------------------------------------------------------------------
   public void start(Stage primaryStage)
   {
      Image alien = new Image("alien.png");

      imageView = new ImageView(alien);
      imageView.setX(20);
      imageView.setY(20);

      Group root = new Group(imageView);

      Scene scene = new Scene(root, 400, 200, Color.BLACK);
      scene.setOnKeyPressed(this::processKeyPress);
```

LISTING 7.20 *continued*

```
        primaryStage.setTitle("Alien Direction");
        primaryStage.setScene(scene);
        primaryStage.show();
    }

    //-----------------------------------------------------------------
    //  Modifies the position of the image view when an arrow key is
    //  pressed.
    //-----------------------------------------------------------------
    public void processKeyPress(KeyEvent event)
    {
        switch (event.getCode())
        {
            case UP:
                imageView.setY(imageView.getY() - JUMP);
                break;
            case DOWN:
                imageView.setY(imageView.getY() + JUMP);
                break;
            case RIGHT:
                imageView.setX(imageView.getX() + JUMP);
                break;
            case LEFT:
                imageView.setX(imageView.getX() - JUMP);
                break;
            default:
                break;  // do nothing if it's not an arrow key
        }
    }
}
```

DISPLAY

The `start` method of this example loads the alien image and sets up an `ImageView` object to display it. The initial position of the image view is explicitly set.

Key events are processed by the node that has the *keyboard focus*. In this example, the events are processed by the scene itself. So the `setOnKeyPressed` method of the scene is called to set the handler for keys that are pressed.

When a keyboard key is pressed, the event handler method is called and passed a `KeyEvent` object. The `getCode` method of the event object returns a code that represents the key that was pressed. More specifically, it returns a `KeyCode` object, which is an enumerated type representing the various keys.

A `switch` statement is used to handle each of the four arrow keys to which we want the program to respond. For instance, when the right arrow key is pressed, a specific number of pixels (represented by the constant `jump`) is added to the x position of the image view. If the user presses any key than the arrow keys, it is ignored.

It should be noted that if a key typed event is generated, its `getCode` method will always return `KeyCode.UNDEFINED`. In that case, the `getCharacter` method of the event can be used to get the character.

SELF-REVIEW QUESTIONS *(see answers in Appendix L)*

SR 7.31 What events are generated when a keyboard key is typed?

SR 7.32 In a program, how do you determine which key has been pressed?

SR 7.33 What does the `AlienDirection` program do when an arrow key is pressed?

Summary of Key Concepts

- The effort put into design is both crucial and cost effective.
- The nouns in a problem description may indicate some of the classes and objects needed in a program.
- A static variable is shared among all instances of a class.
- An aggregate object is composed of other objects, forming a has-a relationship.
- An interface is a collection of abstract methods and therefore cannot be instantiated.
- The values of an enumerated type are static variables of that type.
- We can add attributes and methods to the definition of an enumerated type.
- A complex service provided by an object can be decomposed to make use of private support methods.
- When an object is passed to a method, the actual and formal parameters become aliases.
- The versions of an overloaded method are distinguished by the number, type, and order of their parameters.
- Testing a program can never guarantee the absence of errors.
- A good test is one that uncovers an error.
- It is not feasible to exhaustively test a program for all possible input and user actions.
- The design of any GUI should adhere to basic guidelines regarding consistency and usability.
- Moving the mouse and clicking the mouse button generate events to which a program can respond.
- Rubberbanding is the graphical effect caused when a shape seems to resize as the mouse is dragged.
- Key events allow a program to respond immediately to the user pressing keyboard keys.

Exercises

EX 7.1 Write a method called `average` that accepts two integer parameters and returns their average as a floating point value.

EX 7.2 Overload the `average` method of Exercise 7.1 such that if three integers are provided as parameters, the method returns the average of all three.

EX 7.3 Overload the `average` method of Exercise 7.1 to accept four integer parameters and return their average.

EX 7.4 Write a method called `splice` that takes a `String` and two integers named `startingIndex` and `deleteLength`. Remove `deleteLength` characters from the `String`, starting with index `startingIndex`. Return the resulting string. If `startingIndex` is less than 0, then start removing characters from index 0. If `deleteLength` is 0, then return the original string.

EX 7.5 Overload the `splice` method from Exercise 7.4 such that it accepts an additional `String` named `replace`. Insert `replace` at the beginning of `startingIndex`. If the length of `replace` is different from that of `deleteLength`, then the resulting string will be of a different length.

EX 7.6 Write a method called `makeCircle` that returns a new `Circle` object based on the method's parameters: two integer values representing the (x, y) coordinates of the center of the circle, an integer representing the circles radius, and a `Color` object that defines the circle's fill color.

EX 7.7 Write a method named `shiftLeft` that accepts a `String` and removes the first character from the `String` and adds it to the end of the `String`.

EX 7.8 Overload the `shiftLeft` method of Exercise 7.7 to accept the integer `n` representing the number of characters to be moved. That is, remove `n` characters from the beginning of the `String` and add them to the end of the `String`. If `n` is 0, return the original `String`.

EX 7.9 Overload the `shiftLeft` method of Exercise 7.8 such that it also accepts an additional `char` value named `c`. Remove `n` characters from the beginning of the `String` and add `c` to the end of the `String` `n` times.

EX 7.10 Discuss the manner in which Java passes parameters to a method. Is this technique consistent between primitive types and objects? Explain.

EX 7.11 Explain why a static method cannot refer to an instance variable.

EX 7.12 Can a class implement two interfaces that each contains the same method signature? Explain.

EX 7.13 Create an interface called `Visible` that includes two methods: `makeVisible` and `makeInvisible`. Both methods should take no parameters and should return a `boolean` result. Describe how a class might implement this interface.

EX 7.14 Draw a UML class diagram that shows the relationships among the elements of Exercise 7.13.

EX 7.15 Imagine a game in which some game elements can be broken by the player and others can't. Create an interface called `Breakable` that has a method called `break` that takes no parameters and another called `broken` that returns a `boolean` result indicating whether that object is currently broken.

EX 7.16 Create an interface called `VCR` that has methods that represent the standard operations on a video cassette recorder (play, stop, etc.). Define the method signatures any way you desire. Describe how a class might implement this interface.

EX 7.17 Draw a UML class diagram that shows the relationships among the elements of Exercise 7.16.

EX 7.18 Compare and contrast a mouse clicked event and a key typed event.

EX 7.19 What is rubberbanding? How can it be accomplished?

Programming Projects

PP 7.1 Modify the `Account` class from Chapter 4 so that it also permits an account to be opened with just a name and an account number, assuming an initial balance of zero. Modify the `main` method of the `Transactions` class to demonstrate this new capability.

VideoNote
Developing a solution of PP 7.1.

PP 7.2 Create a class called `SalesPerson` that represents a salesperson in an organization. The `SalesPerson` class should have the name, the phone number, and the assigned district of a salesperson. Each salesperson acquires a certain sale amount every day. Provide a constructor that sets all instance values based on parameter values. Overload the constructor such that each daily sale amount for a week is set to zero. Provide a method called `setDailyAmount` that accepts a day of a week as a number (0 for Sunday, 1 for Monday, and so on) and an amount and sets that amount as the daily sale amount. Provide another method called `getDailyAmount` that accepts a day of a week and returns the amount for that day. Provide a method called `total` that calculates the total sale amount for the week and a method called `average` that calculates the average daily sale amount for the week. Write a `toString` method that prints all the details of the salesperson. Write a driver class to exercise the `SalesPerson` class.

PP 7.3 Write a class called `SalesTeam` that represents a team of salespeople. Each salesperson on the team is represented by the

SalesPerson class of PP 7.2. Each team has a name, and the constructor needs only to accept the name of the team. Use an ArrayList to store the team members. Provide a method called addSalesPerson that accepts a SalesPerson object. Provide a method called weeklyReport that prints the name and the total sale amount of each team member and the total amount for the entire team. Write a driver class that fully exercises the SalesTeam class.

PP 7.4 Modify the RationalNumber class so that it implements the Comparable interface. To perform the comparison, compute an equivalent floating point value from the numerator and denominator for both RationalNumber objects, then compare them using a tolerance value of 0.0001. Write a main driver to test your modifications.

PP 7.5 Write a Java interface called Priority that includes two methods: setPriority and getPriority. The interface should define a way to establish numeric priority among a set of objects. Design and implement a class called Task that represents a task (such as on a to-do list) that implements the Priority interface. Create a driver class to exercise some Task objects.

PP 7.6 Modify the Task class from PP 7.5 so that it also implements the Complexity interface defined in this chapter. Modify the driver class to show these new features of Task objects.

PP 7.7 Modify the Task class from PPs 7.5 and 7.6 so that it also implements the Comparable interface from the Java standard class library. Implement the interface such that the tasks are ranked by priority. Create a driver class whose main method shows these new features of Task objects.

PP 7.8 Write a Java interface called Lockable that includes the following methods: setKey, lock, unlock, and locked. The setKey, lock, and unlock methods take an integer parameter that represents the key. The setKey method establishes the key. The lock and unlock methods lock and unlock the object, but only if the key passed in is correct. The locked method returns a boolean that indicates whether or not the object is locked. A Lockable object represents an object whose regular methods are protected: if the object is locked, the methods cannot be invoked; if it is unlocked, they can be invoked. Write a version of the Coin class from Chapter 5 so that it is Lockable.

PP 7.9 Write a version of the `Account` class from Chapter 4 so that it is `Lockable` as defined by PP 7.8.

PP 7.10 Write a JavaFX application that counts the number of times the mouse button has been clicked on the scene. Display that number at the top of the window.

PP 7.11 Write a JavaFX application that changes its background color depending on where the mouse pointer is located. If the mouse pointer is on the left half of the program window, display red; if it is on the right half, display green.

PP 7.12 Write a JavaFX application that draws multiple circles using a rubberbanding technique. The circle size is determined by a mouse drag. Use the initial mouse press location as the fixed center point of the circle. Compute the distance between the current location of the mouse pointer and the center point to determine the current radius of the circle.

PP 7.13 Write a JavaFX application that serves as a mouse odometer, continually displaying how far, in pixels, the mouse has moved while it is over the program window. Display the current odometer value at the top of the window. Hint: As the mouse moves, use the distance formula to calculate how far the mouse has traveled since the last event, and add that to a running total.

PP 7.14 Write a JavaFX application that displays the top view of a battle tank that follows the movement of the mouse. When the mouse button is pressed down, have a laser beam shoot out of the gun mounted on the tank (one continuous beam, not a moving projectile) until the mouse button is released. Define the tank using a separate class.

PP 7.15 Modify the `AlienDirection` program from this chapter so that the image is not allowed to move out of the visible area of the window. Ignore any key event that would cause that to happen.

SOFTWARE FAILURE

2003 Northeast Blackout

What Happened?

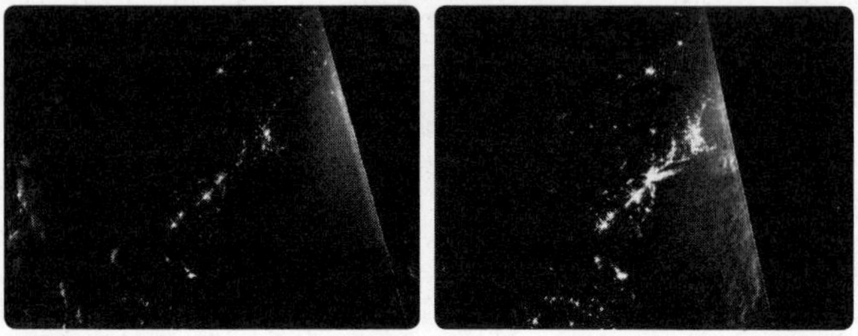

■ The northeastern United States before and after the blackout.

On August 14, 2003, the largest electrical blackout in American history hit the northeastern United States and parts of Canada. Several metropolitan areas were affected, including New York, Cleveland, Detroit, Toronto, and Ottawa. Within a span of three minutes, 21 power plants had shut down, affecting approximately 50 million people.

The typical problems resulted in the blackout areas. Lack of traffic lights caused traffic problems. Trains and elevators were stuck. Airports delayed flights. Water pressure that relied on electric pumps failed. Cell phone usage was disrupted. (Wired telephone usage was still available, but it was overtaxed during the emergency.) Internet traffic slowed due to downed servers and the attempt to reroute messages. Some incidents of looting were reported.

Estimates place the total financial cost of the blackout anywhere between $4 and $8 billion. Nine people died from various causes related to the blackout.

What Caused It?

Many sources of the problem were blamed during the early hours and days after the blackout. Because of the heightened consciousness after the September 11, 2001 attacks, authorities were quick to rule out terrorism. Downed trees and lightning strikes throughout the affected region were blamed. Officials even considered—but quickly ruled out—the "Blaster" computer worm that was spreading at the time.

Over the course of the next few months, a task force sorted out the issues. The initial cause was determined to be in Akron, Ohio, where the FirstEnergy Corp. had failed to keep trees near the power lines trimmed appropriately. On August 14, 2003, tree limbs caused three power lines to fail simultaneously. When such failures occur, the operators at the power control center are responsible for keeping the load balanced. In this case, they failed to do so, because the computer-based alarm system that would have informed them of the problem failed to operate correctly. The load imbalance quickly spread to neighboring power plants, resulting in the cascading blackout.

So although there were various contributing factors, a big part of the problem was the failure of the alarm system. This issue eventually was traced to a race condition bug in the computer General Electric Energys used to monitor alarms. A race condition in a computer program occurs when two or more processes running concurrently access some shared data. One modifies the data after another has read it, and they both continue processing under the wrong assumptions. In this case, three power lines failing simultaneously caused the race condition that caused the alarm system to fail, which went unnoticed by the operators. Resulting problems caused the entire system to crash shortly thereafter. The backup system crashed for the same reasons. After the bug was discovered, GE issued a patch to correct it.

Lessons Learned

The problems of this event stemmed not from a lack of power but on the inability to get the power where it was needed. This blackout highlighted the poor infrastructure of power lines that exist and the danger of relying on voluntary rules for maintaining the reliability of the power grid.

Regarding the software culpability, race conditions are a known source of failure in concurrent systems and must be tested for thoroughly. Formal analysis is warranted in situations like this one where so much is at stake.

Sources: CNN.com, WashingtonPost.com

Arrays

8

CHAPTER OBJECTIVES

- Define and use arrays for basic data organization.
- Discuss bounds checking and techniques for managing capacity.
- Discuss the issues related to arrays as objects and arrays of objects.
- Explore the use of command-line arguments.
- Describe the syntax and use of variable-length parameter lists.
- Discuss the creation and use of multidimensional arrays.
- Explore polygon and polyline shapes

In our programming efforts, we often want to organize objects or primitive data in a form that is easy to access and modify. The `ArrayList` class, explored in Chapter 5, was used for exactly that purpose. As the class name implies, an `ArrayList` is implemented using arrays, which are programming constructs that group data into lists. In this chapter, we'll explore the details of arrays, which are a fundamental component of most high-level languages. In the Graphics Track sections of this chapter, we explore methods that let us draw complex multisided figures, introduce the choice box control, and see how audio clips can be played in a JavaFX program.

8.1 Array Elements

An *array* is a simple but powerful programming language construct used to group and organize data. When writing a program that manages a large amount of information, such as a list of 100 names, it is not practical to declare separate variables for each piece of data. Arrays solve this problem by letting us declare one variable that can hold multiple, individually accessible values.

An array is a list of values. Each value is stored at a specific, numbered position in the array. The number corresponding to each position is called an *index* or a *subscript*. Figure 8.1 shows an array of integers and the indexes that correspond to each position. The array is called `height`; it contains integers that represent several peoples' heights in inches.

In Java, array indexes always begin at zero. Therefore, the value stored at index 5 is actually the sixth value in the array. The array shown in Figure 8.1 has 11 values, indexed from 0 to 10.

KEY CONCEPT
An array of size N is indexed from 0 to N–1.

To access a value in an array, we use the name of the array followed by the index in square brackets. For example, the following expression refers to the ninth value in the array `height`:

```
height[8]
```

According to Figure 8.1, `height[8]` (pronounced height-sub-eight) contains the value 79. Don't confuse the value of the index, in this case 8, with the value stored in the array at that index, in this case 79.

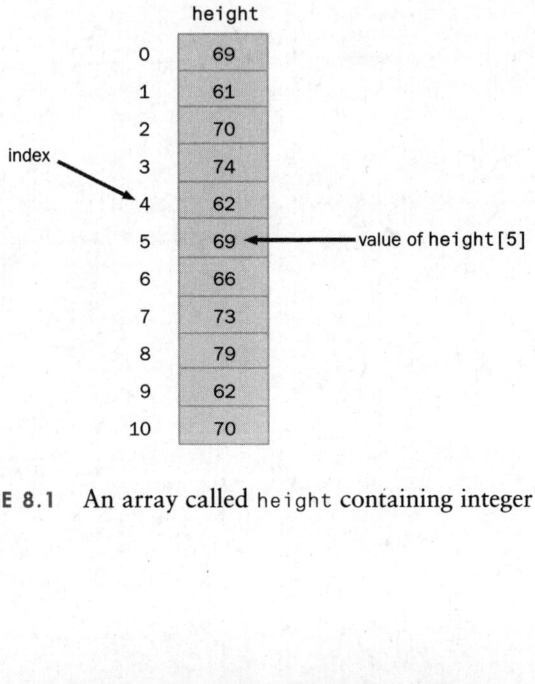

FIGURE 8.1 An array called `height` containing integer values

The expression `height[8]` refers to a single integer stored at a particular memory location. It can be used wherever an integer variable can be used. Therefore, you can assign a value to it, use it in calculations, print its value, and so on. Furthermore, because array indexes are integers, you can use integer expressions to specify the index used to access an array. These concepts are demonstrated in the following lines of code:

```
height[2] = 72;
height[count] = feet * 12;
average = (height[0] + height[1] + height[2]) / 3;
System.out.println("The middle value is " + height[MAX/2]);
pick = height[rand.nextInt(11)];
```

Arrays are stored contiguously in memory, meaning that the elements are stored one right after the other in memory just as we picture them conceptually. This makes an array extremely efficient in terms of accessing any particular element by its index. Internally, to determine the address of any particular element, the index is multiplied by the size of each element, and added to the memory address of the starting point of the array. That's why array indexes begin at zero instead of one—to make that computation as easy as possible. So from an efficiency point of view, it's as easy to access the 500th element in the array as it is to access the first element.

SELF-REVIEW QUESTIONS *(see answers in Appendix L)*

SR 8.1 What is an array?

SR 8.2 How is each element of an array referenced?

SR 8.3 Based on the array shown in Figure 8.1, what are each of the following?

a. `height[1]`
b. `height[2] + height[5]`
c. `height[2 + 5]`
d. the value stored at index 8
e. the fourth value
f. `height.length`

8.2 Declaring and Using Arrays

In Java, arrays are objects. To create an array, the reference to the array must be declared. The array can then be instantiated using the `new` operator, which allocates memory space to store values. The following code represents the declaration for the array shown in Figure 8.1:

```
int[] height = new int[11];
```

KEY CONCEPT
In Java, an array is an object that must be instantiated.

The variable `height` is declared to be an array of integers whose type is written as `int[]`. All values stored in an array have the same type (or are at least compatible). For example, we can create an array that can hold integers or an array that can hold strings, but not an array that can hold both integers and strings. An array can be set up to hold any primitive type or any object (class) type. A value stored in an array is sometimes called an *array element*, and the type of values that an array holds is called the *element type* of the array.

LISTING 8.1

```
//********************************************************************
//  BasicArray.java       Author: Lewis/Loftus
//
//  Demonstrates basic array declaration and use.
//********************************************************************

public class BasicArray
{
   //-----------------------------------------------------------------
   //  Creates an array, fills it with various integer values,
   //  modifies one value, then prints them out.
   //-----------------------------------------------------------------
   public static void main(String[] args)
   {
      final int LIMIT = 15, MULTIPLE = 10;

      int[] list = new int[LIMIT];

      // Initialize the array values
      for (int index = 0; index < LIMIT; index++)
         list[index] = index * MULTIPLE;

      list[5] = 999; // change one array value

      // Print the array values
      for (int value : list)
         System.out.print(value + " ");
   }
}
```

OUTPUT

```
0 10 20 30 40 999 60 70 80 90 100 110 120 130 140
```

Note that the type of the array variable (`int[]`) does not include the size of the array. The instantiation of `height`, using the `new` operator, reserves the memory space to store 11 integers indexed from 0 to 10. Once an array is declared to be a certain size, the number of values it can hold cannot be changed.

VideoNote
Overview of arrays.

The example shown in Listing 8.1 creates an array called `list` that can hold 15 integers, which it loads with successive increments of 10. It then changes the value of the sixth element in the array (at index 5). Finally, it prints all values stored in the array.

Figure 8.2 shows the array as it changes during the execution of the `BasicArray` program. It is often convenient to use `for` loops when handling arrays, because the number of positions in the array is constant. Note that a constant called `LIMIT` is used in several places in the `BasicArray` program. This constant is used to declare the size of the array and to control the `for` loop that initializes the array values.

The iterator version of the `for` loop is used to print the values in the array. Recall from Chapter 5 that this version of the `for` loop extracts each value in the

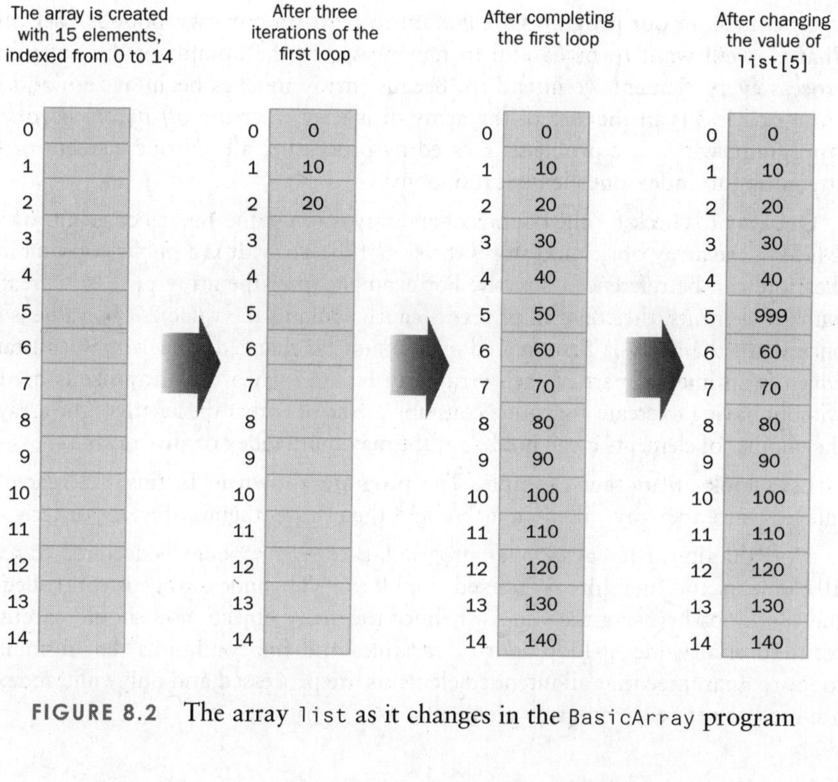

FIGURE 8.2 The array `list` as it changes in the `BasicArray` program

specified iterator. Every Java array is an iterator, so this type of loop can be used whenever we want to process every element stored in an array.

The square brackets used to indicate the index of an array are treated as an operator in Java. Therefore, just like the + operator or the <= operator, the index operator (`[]`) has a precedence relative to the other Java operators that determines when it is executed. It has the highest precedence of all Java operators.

Bounds Checking

Java performs *automatic bounds checking*, which ensures that the index is in range for the array being referenced. Whenever a reference to an array element is made, the index must be greater than or equal to zero and less than the size of the array. For example, suppose an array called `prices` is created with 25 elements. The valid indexes for the array are from 0 to 24. Whenever a reference is made to a particular element in the array (such as `prices[count]`), the value of the index is checked. If it is in the valid range of indexes for the array (0 to 24), the reference is carried out. If the index is not valid, an exception called `ArrayIndexOutOfBoundsException` is thrown.

KEY CONCEPT
Bounds checking ensures that an index used to refer to an array element is in range.

Of course, in our programs we'll want to perform our own bounds checking. That is, we'll want to be careful to remain within the bounds of the array and process every element we intend to. Because array indexes begin at zero and go up to one less than the size of the array, it is easy to create *off-by-one errors* in a program, which are problems created by processing all but one element or by attempting to index one element too many.

One way to check for the bounds of an array is to use the `length` constant, which is held in the array object and stores the size of the array. It is a public constant and therefore can be referenced directly. For example, after the array `prices` is created with 25 elements, the constant `prices.length` contains the value 25. Its value is set once when the array is first created and cannot be changed. The `length` constant, which is an integral part of each array, can be used when the array size is needed without having to create a separate constant. Remember that the length of the array is the number of elements it can hold, thus the maximum index of an array is `length-1`.

Let's look at another example. The program shown in Listing 8.2 reads 10 integers into an array called `numbers`, and then prints them in reverse order.

Note that in the `ReverseOrder` program, the array `numbers` is declared to have 10 elements and therefore is indexed from 0 to 9. The index range is controlled in the `for` loops by using the `length` field of the array object. You should carefully set the initial value of loop control variables and the conditions that terminate loops to guarantee that all intended elements are processed and only valid indexes are used to reference an array element.

LISTING 8.2

```
//********************************************************************
//  ReverseOrder.java        Author: Lewis/Loftus
//
//  Demonstrates array index processing.
//********************************************************************

import java.util.Scanner;

public class ReverseOrder
{
   //-----------------------------------------------------------------
   //  Reads a list of numbers from the user, storing them in an
   //  array, then prints them in the opposite order.
   //-----------------------------------------------------------------
   public static void main(String[] args)
   {
      Scanner scan = new Scanner(System.in);

      double[] numbers = new double[10];

      System.out.println("The size of the array: " + numbers.length);

      for (int index = 0; index < numbers.length; index++)
      {
         System.out.print("Enter number " + (index+1) + ": ");
         numbers[index] = scan.nextDouble();
      }

      System.out.println("The numbers in reverse order:");

      for (int index = numbers.length-1; index >= 0; index--)
         System.out.print(numbers[index] + " ");
   }
}
```

OUTPUT

```
The size of the array: 10
Enter number 1: 18.36
Enter number 2: 48.9
Enter number 3: 53.5
Enter number 4: 29.06
```

LISTING 8.2 *continued*

```
Enter number 5: 72.404
Enter number 6: 34.8
Enter number 7: 63.41
Enter number 8: 45.55
Enter number 9: 69.0
Enter number 10: 99.18
The numbers in reverse order:
99.18  69.0  45.55  63.41  34.8  72.404  29.06  53.5  48.9  18.36
```

The `LetterCount` example, shown in Listing 8.3, uses two arrays and a `String` object. The array called `upper` is used to store the number of times each uppercase alphabetic letter is found in the string. The array called `lower` serves the same purpose for lowercase letters.

Because there are 26 letters in the English alphabet, both the `upper` and `lower` arrays are declared with 26 elements. Each element contains an integer that is initially zero by default. The for loop scans through the string one character at a time. The appropriate counter in the appropriate array is incremented for each character found in the string.

LISTING 8.3

```
//********************************************************************
//  LetterCount.java      Author: Lewis/Loftus
//
//  Demonstrates the relationship between arrays an strings.
//********************************************************************

import java.util.Scanner;

public class LetterCount
{
   //-----------------------------------------------------------------
   //  Reads a sentence from the user and counts the number of
   //  uppercase and lowercase letters contained in it.
   //-----------------------------------------------------------------
   public static void main(String[] args)
   {
      final int NUMCHARS = 26;
```

LISTING 8.3 *continued*

```
      Scanner scan = new Scanner(System.in);

      int[] upper = new int[NUMCHARS];
      int[] lower = new int[NUMCHARS];

      char current;    // the current character being processed
      int other = 0;   // counter for non-alphabetics

      System.out.println("Enter a sentence:");
      String line = scan.nextLine();

      //Count the number of each letter occurrence
      for (int ch = 0; ch < line.length(); ch++)
      {
         current = line.charAt(ch);
         if (current >= 'A' && current <= 'Z')
           upper[current-'A']++;
         else
            if (current >= 'a' && current <= 'z')
               lower[current-'a']++;
            else
               other++;
      }

      //Print the results
      System.out.println();
      for (int letter=0; letter < upper.length; letter++)
      {
         System.out.print((char)(letter + 'A'));
         System.out.print(": " + upper[letter]);
         System.out.print("\t\t" + (char)(letter + 'a'));
         System.out.println(": " + lower[letter]);
      }

      System.out.println();
      System.out.println("Non-alphabetic characters: " + other);
   }
}
```

LISTING 8.3 *continued*

OUTPUT

```
Enter a sentence:
In Casablanca, Humphrey Bogart never says "Play it again, Sam."

A: 0          a: 10
B: 1          b: 1
C: 1          c: 1
D: 0          d: 0
E: 0          e: 3
F: 0          f: 0
G: 0          g: 2
H: 1          h: 1
I: 1          i: 2
J: 0          j: 0
K: 0          k: 0
L: 0          l: 2
M: 0          m: 2
N: 0          n: 4
O: 0          o: 1
P: 1          p: 1
Q: 0          q: 0
R: 0          r: 3
S: 1          s: 3
T: 0          t: 2
U: 0          u: 1
V: 0          v: 1
W: 0          w: 0
X: 0          x: 0
Y: 0          y: 3
Z: 0          z: 0

Non-alphabetic characters: 14
```

VideoNote
Discussion of the `LetterCount` example.

Both the counter arrays are indexed from 0 to 25. We have to map each character to a counter. A logical way to do this is to use `upper[0]` to count the number of `'A'` characters found, `upper[1]` to count the number of `'B'` characters found, and so on. Likewise, `lower[0]` is used to count `'a'` characters, `lower[1]` is used to count `'b'` characters, and so on. A separate variable called `other` is used to count any nonalphabetic characters that are encountered.

Note that to determine if a character is an uppercase letter we used the boolean expression `(current >= 'A' && current <= 'Z')`. A similar expression is used for determining the lowercase letters. We could have used the static methods `isUpperCase` and `isLowerCase` in the `Character` class to make these determinations but didn't in this example to drive home the point that because characters are based on the Unicode character set, they have a specific numeric value and order that we can use in our programming.

We use the current character to calculate which index in the array to reference. We have to be careful when calculating an index to ensure that it remains within the bounds of the array and matches to the correct element. Remember that in the Unicode character set, the uppercase and lowercase alphabetic letters are continuous and in order (see Appendix C). Therefore, taking the numeric value of an uppercase letter such as `'E'` (which is 69) and subtracting the numeric value of the character `'A'` (which is 65) yields 4, which is the correct index for the counter of the character `'E'`. Note that nowhere in the program do we actually need to know the specific numeric values for each letter.

Alternate Array Syntax

Syntactically, there are two ways to declare an array reference in Java. The first technique, which is used in the previous examples and throughout this text, is to associate the brackets with the type of values stored in the array. The second technique is to associate the brackets with the name of the array. Therefore, the following two declarations are equivalent:

```
int[] grades;
int grades[];
```

Although there is no difference between these declaration techniques as far as the compiler is concerned, the first is consistent with other types of declarations. The declared type is explicit if the array brackets are associated with the element type, especially if there are multiple variables declared on the same line. Therefore, we associate the brackets with the element type throughout this text.

Initializer Lists

You can use an *initializer list* to instantiate an array and provide the initial values for the elements of the array. It is essentially the same idea as initializing a

KEY CONCEPT
An initializer list can be used to instantiate an array object instead of using the new operator.

variable of a primitive data type in its declaration except that an array requires several values.

The items in an initializer list are separated by commas and delimited by braces ({}). When an initializer list is used, the new operator is not used. The size of the array is determined by the number of items in the initializer list. For example, the following declaration instantiates the array scores as an array of eight integers, indexed from 0 to 7 with the specified initial values:

```
int[] scores = {87, 98, 69, 87, 65, 76, 99, 83};
```

An initializer list can be used only when an array is first declared.

The type of each value in an initializer list must match the type of the array elements. Let's look at another example:

```
char[] vowels = {'A', 'E', 'I', 'O', 'U'};
```

In this case, the variable vowels is declared to be an array of five characters, and the initializer list contains character literals.

The program shown in Listing 8.4 demonstrates the use of an initializer list to instantiate an array.

Arrays as Parameters

KEY CONCEPT
An entire array can be passed as a parameter, making the formal parameter an alias of the original.

An entire array can be passed as a parameter to a method. Because an array is an object, when an entire array is passed as a parameter, a copy of the reference to the original array is passed. We discussed this issue as it applies to all objects in Chapter 7.

A method that receives an array as a parameter can permanently change an element of the array, because it is referring to the original element value. The method cannot permanently change the reference to the array itself, because a copy of the original reference is sent to the method. These rules are consistent with the rules that govern any object type.

An element of an array can be passed to a method as well. If the element type is a primitive type, a copy of the value is passed. If that element is a reference to an object, a copy of the object reference is passed. As always, the impact of changes made to a parameter inside the method depends on the type of the parameter. We discuss arrays of objects further in the next section.

LISTING 8.4

```
//********************************************************************
//  Primes.java       Author: Lewis/Loftus
//
//  Demonstrates the use of an initializer list for an array.
//********************************************************************

public class Primes
{
   //-----------------------------------------------------------------
   //  Stores some prime numbers in an array and prints them.
   //-----------------------------------------------------------------
   public static void main(String[] args)
   {
      int[] primeNums = {2, 3, 5, 7, 11, 13, 17, 19};

      System.out.println("Array length: " + primeNums.length);

      System.out.println("The first few prime numbers are:");

      for (int prime : primeNums)
         System.out.print(prime + " ");
   }
}
```

OUTPUT

```
Array length: 8
The first few prime numbers are:
2  3  5  7  11  13  17  19
```

SELF-REVIEW QUESTIONS *(see answers in Appendix L)*

SR 8.4 What is an array's element type?

SR 8.5 Describe the process of creating an array. When is memory allocated for the array?

SR 8.6 Write an array declaration to represent the ages of all 100 children attending a summer camp.

SR 8.7 Write an array declaration to represent the counts of how many times each face appeared when a standard six-sided die is rolled.

SR 8.8 Explain the concept of array bounds checking. What happens when a Java array is indexed with an invalid value?

SR 8.9 What is an off-by-one error? How does it relate to arrays?

SR 8.10 Write code that increments (by one) each element of an array of integers named `values`.

SR 8.11 Write code that computes and prints the sum of the elements of an array of integers named `values`.

SR 8.12 What does an array initializer list accomplish?

SR 8.13 Can an entire array be passed as a parameter? How is this accomplished?

8.3 Arrays of Objects

In the previous examples in this chapter, we used arrays to store primitive types such as integers and characters. Arrays can also store references to objects as elements. Fairly complex information management structures can be created using only arrays and other objects. For example, an array could contain objects, and each of those objects could consist of several variables and the methods that use them. Those variables could themselves be arrays, and so on. The design of a program should capitalize on the ability to combine these constructs to create the most appropriate representation for the information.

Keep in mind that the array itself is an object. So it would be appropriate to picture an array of `int` values called `weight` as follows:

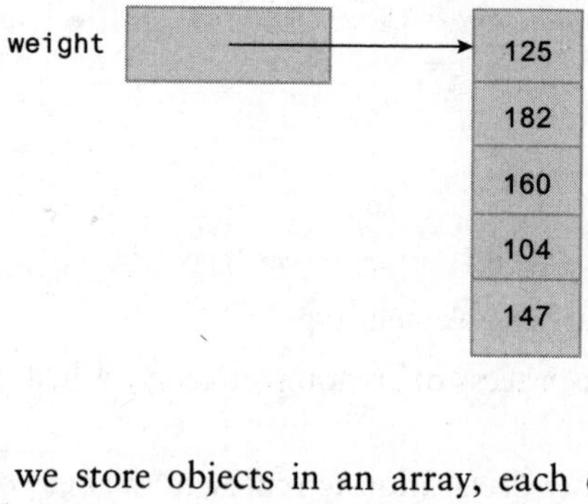

KEY CONCEPT
Instantiating an array of objects reserves room to store references only. The objects that are stored in each element must be instantiated separately.

When we store objects in an array, each element is a separate object. That is, an array of objects is really an array of object references. Consider the following declaration:

```
String[] words = new String[5];
```

The variable `words` is an array of references to `String` objects. The `new` operator in the declaration instantiates the array and reserves space for five `String` references. This declaration does not create any `String` objects; it merely creates an array that holds references to `String` objects. Initially, the array looks like this:

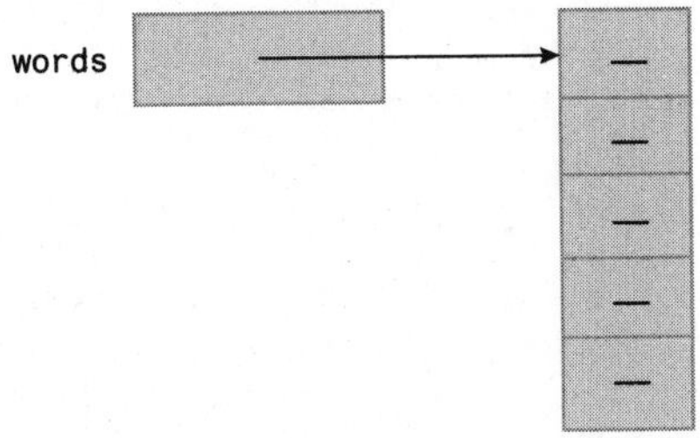

After a few `String` objects are created and put in the array, it might look like this:

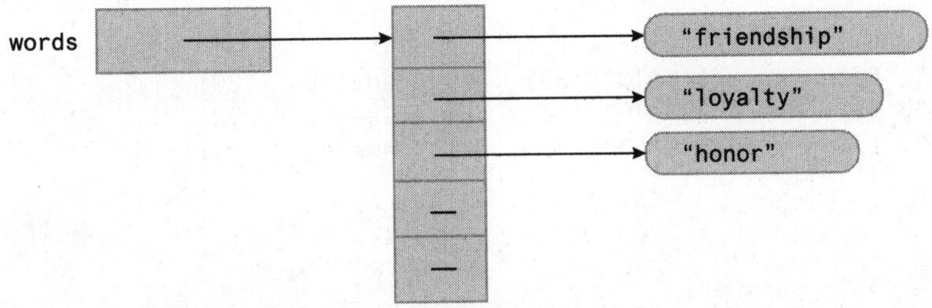

The `words` array is an object, and each character string it holds is its own object. Each object contained in an array has to be instantiated separately.

Keep in mind that `String` objects can be represented as string literals. So the following declaration creates an array called `verbs` and uses an initializer list to populate it with several `String` objects, each instantiated using a string literal:

```
String[] verbs = {"play", "work", "eat", "sleep"};
```

The program called `GradeRange` shown in Listing 8.5 creates an array of `Grade` objects, then prints them. The `Grade` objects are created using several `new` operators in the initialization list of the array.

The `Grade` class is shown in Listing 8.6. Each `Grade` object represents a letter grade for a school course and includes a numerical lower bound. The values for the grade name and lower bound can be set using the `Grade` constructor, or using appropriate mutator methods. Accessor methods are also defined, as is a `toString` method to return a string representation of the grade. The `toString` method is automatically invoked when the grades are printed in the `main` method.

Let's look at another example. Listing 8.7 shows the `Movies` class, which contains a `main` method that creates, modifies, and examines a DVD collection.

LISTING 8.5

```
//********************************************************************
//  GradeRange.java        Author: Lewis/Loftus
//
// Demonstrates the use of an array of objects.
//********************************************************************

public class GradeRange
{
   //-----------------------------------------------------------------
   //  Creates an array of Grade objects and prints them.
   //-----------------------------------------------------------------
   public static void main(String[] args)
   {
      Grade[] grades =
      {
         new Grade("A", 95), new Grade("A-", 90),
         new Grade("B+", 87), new Grade("B", 85), new Grade("B-", 80),
         new Grade("C+", 77), new Grade("C", 75), new Grade("C-", 70),
         new Grade("D+", 67), new Grade("D", 65), new Grade("D-", 60),
         new Grade("F", 0)
      };

      for (Grade letterGrade : grades)
         System.out.println(letterGrade);
   }
}
```

OUTPUT

```
A       95
A-      90
B+      87
B       85
B-      80
C+      77
C       75
C-      70
D+      67
D       65
D-      60
F       0
```

LISTING 8.6

```
//********************************************************************
//  Grade.java       Author: Lewis/Loftus
//
//  Represents a school grade.
//********************************************************************

public class Grade
{
   private String name;
   private int lowerBound;

   //-----------------------------------------------------------------
   // Constructor: Sets up this Grade object with the specified
   // grade name and numeric lower bound.
   //-----------------------------------------------------------------
   public Grade(String grade, int cutoff)
   {
      name = grade;
      lowerBound = cutoff;
   }

   //-----------------------------------------------------------------
   // Returns a string representation of this grade.
   //-----------------------------------------------------------------
   public String toString()
   {
      return name + "\t" + lowerBound;
   }

   //-----------------------------------------------------------------
   // Name mutator.
   //-----------------------------------------------------------------
   public void setName(String grade)
   {
      name = grade;
   }

   //-----------------------------------------------------------------
   // Lower bound mutator.
   //-----------------------------------------------------------------
   public void setLowerBound(int cutoff)
   {
      lowerBound = cutoff;
   }
```

LISTING 8.6 *continued*

```
   //-----------------------------------------------------------------
   // Name accessor.
   //-----------------------------------------------------------------
   public String getName()
   {
      return name;
   }

   //-----------------------------------------------------------------
   // Lower bound accessor.
   //-----------------------------------------------------------------
   public int getLowerBound()
   {
      return lowerBound;
   }
}
```

LISTING 8.7

```
//********************************************************************
//  Movies.java       Author: Lewis/Loftus
//
//  Demonstrates the use of an array of objects.
//********************************************************************

public class Movies
{
   //-----------------------------------------------------------------
   // Creates a DVDCollection object and adds some DVDs to it. Prints
   // reports on the status of the collection.
   //-----------------------------------------------------------------
   public static void main(String[] args)
   {
      DVDCollection movies = new DVDCollection();

      movies.addDVD("The Godfather", "Francis Ford Coppola", 1972, 24.95, true);
      movies.addDVD("District 9", "Neill Blomkamp", 2009, 19.95, false);
      movies.addDVD("Iron Man", "Jon Favreau", 2008, 15.95, false);
      movies.addDVD("All About Eve", "Joseph Mankiewicz", 1950, 17.50, false);
      movies.addDVD("The Matrix", "Andy & Lana Wachowski", 1999, 19.95, true);
```

LISTING 8.7 *continued*

```
      System.out.println(movies);

      movies.addDVD("Iron Man 2", "Jon Favreau", 2010, 22.99, false);
      movies.addDVD("Casablanca", "Michael Curtiz", 1942, 19.95, false);

      System.out.println(movies);
   }
}
```

OUTPUT

```
~~~~~~~~~~~~~~~~~~~~~~~~~~~~~~~~~~~~~~~~~~~~~~
My DVD Collection

Number of DVDs: 5
Total cost: $98.30
Average cost: $19.66


DVD List:

$24.95   1972       The Godfather     Francis Ford Coppola      Blu-ray
$19.95   2009       District 9        Neill Blomkamp
$15.95   2008       Iron Man          Jon Favreau
$17.50   1950       All About Eve     Joseph Mankiewicz
$19.95   1999       The Matrix        Andy & Lana Wachowski     Blu-ray

~~~~~~~~~~~~~~~~~~~~~~~~~~~~~~~~~~~~~~~~~~~~~~
My DVD Collection

Number of DVDs: 7
Total cost: $141.24
Average cost: $20.18

DVD List:

$24.95   1972       The Godfather     Francis Ford Coppola      Blu-ray
$19.95   2009       District 9        Neill Blomkamp
$15.95   2008       Iron Man          Jon Favreau
$17.50   1950       All About Eve     Joseph Mankiewicz
$19.95   1999       The Matrix        Andy & Lana Wachowski     Blu-ray
$22.99   2010       Iron Man 2        Jon Favreau
$19.95   1942       Casablanca        Michael Curtiz
```

Each DVD added to the collection is specified by its title, director, year of release, purchase price, and whether or not it is in Blu-ray format.

Listing 8.8 shows the `DVDCollection` class. It contains an array of `DVD` objects representing the collection. It maintains a count of the DVDs in the collection and their combined value. It also keeps track of the current size of the collection array so that a larger array can be created if too many DVDs are added to the collection.

LISTING 8.8

```
//********************************************************************
//  DVDCollection.java       Author: Lewis/Loftus
//
//  Represents a collection of DVD movies.
//********************************************************************

import java.text.NumberFormat;

public class DVDCollection
{
   private DVD[] collection;
   private int count;
   private double totalCost;

   //-----------------------------------------------------------------
   // Constructor: Creates an initially empty collection.
   //-----------------------------------------------------------------
   public DVDCollection()
   {
      collection = new DVD[100];
      count = 0;
      totalCost = 0.0;
   }

   //-----------------------------------------------------------------
   // Adds a DVD to the collection, increasing the size of the
   // collection array if necessary.
   //-----------------------------------------------------------------
   public void addDVD(String title, String director, int year,
                      double cost, boolean bluray)
   {
      if (count == collection.length)
         increaseSize();

      collection[count] = new DVD(title, director, year, cost, bluray);
```

LISTING 8.8 *continued*

```
      totalCost += cost;
      count++;
   }

   //-----------------------------------------------------------------
   // Returns a report describing the DVD collection.
   //-----------------------------------------------------------------
   public String toString()
   {
      NumberFormat fmt = NumberFormat.getCurrencyInstance();

      String report = "~~~~~~~~~~~~~~~~~~~~~~~~~~~~~~~~~~~~~~~~~~~~~~\n";
      report += "My DVD Collection\n\n";

      report += "Number of DVDs: " + count + "\n";
      report += "Total cost: " + fmt.format(totalCost) + "\n";
      report += "Average cost: " + fmt.format(totalCost/count);

      report += "\n\nDVD List:\n\n";

      for (int dvd = 0; dvd < count; dvd++)
         report += collection[dvd].toString() + "\n";

      return report;
   }

   //-----------------------------------------------------------------
   // Increases the capacity of the collection by creating a
   // larger array and copying the existing collection into it.
   //-----------------------------------------------------------------
   private void increaseSize()
   {
      DVD[] temp = new DVD[collection.length * 2];

      for (int dvd = 0; dvd < collection.length; dvd++)
         temp[dvd] = collection[dvd];

      collection = temp;
   }
}
```

The `collection` array is instantiated in the `DVDCollection` constructor. Every time a DVD is added to the collection (using the `addDVD` method), a new `DVD` object is created and a reference to it is stored in the `collection` array.

Each time a DVD is added to the collection, we check to see whether we have reached the current capacity of the `collection` array. If we didn't perform this check, an exception would eventually be thrown when we try to store a new `DVD` object at an invalid index. If the current capacity has been reached, the private `increaseSize` method is invoked, which first creates an array that is twice as big as the current `collection` array. Each DVD in the existing collection is then copied into the new array. Finally, the `collection` reference is set to the larger array. Using this technique, we theoretically never run out of room in our DVD collection. The user of the `DVDCollection` object (the `main` method in this case) never has to worry about running out of space, because it's all handled internally.

Figure 8.3 shows a UML class diagram of the `Movies` program. Recall that the open diamond indicates aggregation. The cardinality of the relationship is also noted: a `DVDCollection` object contains zero or more `DVD` objects.

The `toString` method of the `DVDCollection` class returns an entire report summarizing the collection. The report is created, in part, using calls to the `toString` method of each `DVD` object stored in the collection. Listing 8.9 shows the `DVD` class.

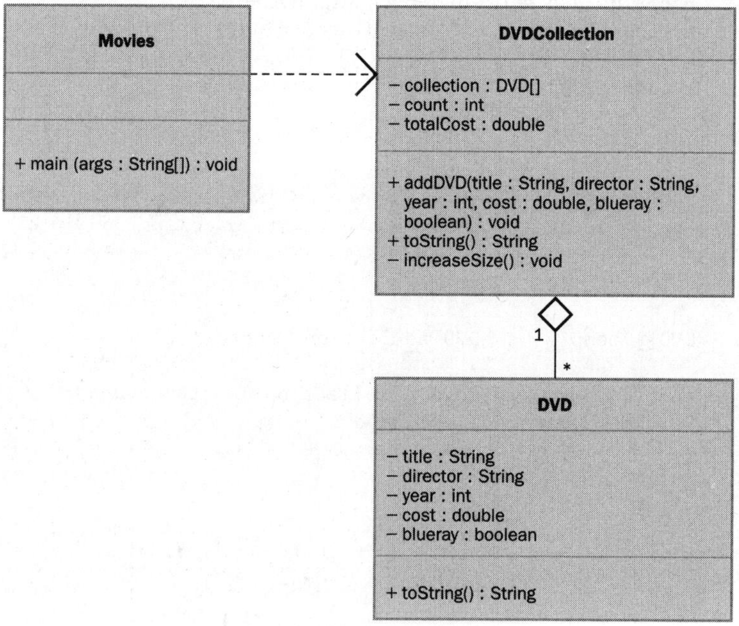

FIGURE 8.3 A UML class diagram of the `Movies` program

LISTING 8.9

```
//********************************************************************
//  DVD.java       Author: Lewis/Loftus
//
//  Represents a DVD video disc.
//********************************************************************

import java.text.NumberFormat;

public class DVD
{
   private String title, director;
   private int year;
   private double cost;
   private boolean bluray;

   //-----------------------------------------------------------------
   //  Creates a new DVD with the specified information.
   //-----------------------------------------------------------------
   public DVD(String title, String director, int year, double cost,
         boolean bluray)
   {
      this.title = title;
      this.director = director;
      this.year = year;
      this.cost = cost;
      this.bluray = bluray;
   }

   //-----------------------------------------------------------------
   // Returns a string description of this DVD.
   //-----------------------------------------------------------------
   public String toString()
   {
      NumberFormat fmt = NumberFormat.getCurrencyInstance();

      String description;

      description = fmt.format(cost) + "\t" + year + "\t";
      description += title + "\t" + director;
      if (bluray)
         description += "\t" + "Blu-ray";

      return description;
   }
}
```

SELF-REVIEW QUESTIONS *(see answers in Appendix L)*

SR 8.14 How is an array of objects created?

SR 8.15 Suppose `team` is an array of strings meant to hold the names of the six players on a volleyball team: Amanda, Clare, Emily, Julie, Katie, and Maria.

a. Write an array declaration for `team`.
b. Show how to both declare and populate `team` using an initializer list.

SR 8.16 Assume `Book` is a class whose objects represent books. Assume a constructor of the `Book` class accepts two parameters—the name of the book and the number of pages.

a. Write a declaration for a variable named `library` that is an array of ten books.
b. Write a `new` statement that sets the first book in the `library` array to `"Starship Troopers"`, which is 208 pages long.

8.4 Command-Line Arguments

The parameter to the `main` method of a Java application is always an array of `String` objects. We've ignored that parameter in previous examples, but now we can discuss how it might occasionally be useful.

KEY CONCEPT
Command-line arguments are stored in an array of `String` objects and are passed to the `main` method.

The Java run-time environment invokes the `main` method when an application is submitted to the interpreter. The `String[]` parameter, which we typically call `args`, represents *command-line arguments* that are provided when the interpreter is invoked. Any extra information on the command line when the interpreter is invoked is stored in the `args` array for use by the program. This technique is another way to provide input to a program.

The program shown in Listing 8.10 uses command-line arguments to print a nametag. It assumes the first argument represents some type of greeting and the second argument represents a person's name.

If two strings are not provided on the command line for the `NameTag` program, the `args` array will not contain enough (if any) elements, and the references in the program will cause an `ArrayIndexOutOfBoundsException` to be thrown. If extra information is included on the command line, it will be stored in the `args` array but ignored by the program.

LISTING 8.10

```
//********************************************************************
//  NameTag.java       Author: Lewis/Loftus
//
//  Demonstrates the use of command line arguments.
//********************************************************************

public class NameTag
{
   //-----------------------------------------------------------------
   // Prints a simple name tag using a greeting and a name that is
   // specified by the user.
   //-----------------------------------------------------------------
   public static void main(String[] args)
   {
      System.out.println();
      System.out.println("     " + args[0]);
      System.out.println("My name is " + args[1]);
   }
}
```

OUTPUT

```
> java NameTag Howdy John

     Howdy
My name is John

> java NameTag Hello Bill

     Hello
My name is Bill
```

Remember that the parameter to the `main` method is always an array of `String` objects. If you want numeric information to be input as a command-line argument, the program has to convert it from its string representation.

You also should be aware that in some program development environments, a command line is not used to submit a program to the interpreter. In such situations, the command-line information can be specified in some other way. Consult the documentation for these specifics if necessary.

SELF-REVIEW QUESTIONS *(see answers in Appendix L)*

SR 8.17 What is a command-line argument?

SR 8.18 Write a `main` method for a program that outputs the sum of the string lengths of its first two command-line arguments.

SR 8.19 Write a `main` method for a program that outputs the sum of the values of its first two command-line arguments, which are integers.

8.5 Variable Length Parameter Lists

Suppose we wanted to design a method that processed a different amount of data from one invocation to the next. For example, let's design a method called `average` that accepts a few integer values and returns their average. In one invocation of the method, we might pass in three integers to average:

```
mean1 = average(42, 69, 37);
```

In another invocation of the same method, we might pass in seven integers to average:

```
mean2 = average(35, 43, 93, 23, 40, 21, 75);
```

KEY CONCEPT

A Java method can be defined to accept a varying number of parameters.

To accomplish this, we could define overloaded versions of the `average` method, but that would require that we know the maximum number of parameters there might be and create a separate version of the method for each possibility. Alternatively, we could define the method to accept an array of integers, which could be of different sizes for each call. But that would require packaging the integers into an array in the calling method and passing in one parameter.

Java provides a way to define methods that accept variable-length parameter lists. By using some special syntax in the formal parameter list of the method, we can define the method to accept any number of parameters. The parameters are automatically put into an array for easy processing in the method. For example, the `average` method could be written as follows:

```
public double average(int ... list)
{
   double result = 0.0;

   if (list.length != 0)
```

```
    {
        int sum = 0;
        for (int num : list)
          sum += num;
        result = (double)sum / list.length;
    }

    return result;
}
```

Note the way the formal parameters are defined. The ellipsis (three periods in a row) indicates that the method accepts a variable number of parameters. In this case, the method accepts any number of `int` parameters, which it automatically puts into an array called `list`. In the method, we process the array normally.

We can now pass any number of `int` parameters to the `average` method, including none at all. That's why we check to see if the length of the array is zero before we compute the average.

The type of the multiple parameters can be any primitive or object type. For example, the following method accepts and prints multiple `Grade` objects (we defined the `Grade` class earlier in this chapter):

```
public void printGrades(Grade ... grades)
{
    for (Grade letterGrade : grades)
        System.out.println(letterGrade);
}
```

A method that accepts a variable number of parameters can also accept other parameters. For example, the following method accepts an `int`, a `String` object, and then a variable number of `double` values that will be stored in an array called `nums`:

```
public void test(int count, String name, double ... nums)
{
    // whatever
}
```

The varying parameters must come last in the formal arguments. A single method cannot accept two sets of varying parameters.

Constructors can also be set up to accept a varying number of parameters. The program shown in Listing 8.11 creates two `Family` objects, passing a varying number of strings (representing the family member names) into the `Family` constructor.

LISTING 8.11

```
//********************************************************************
//  VariableParameters.java       Author: Lewis/Loftus
//
//  Demonstrates the use of a variable length parameter list.
//********************************************************************

public class VariableParameters
{
   //-----------------------------------------------------------------
   //  Creates two Family objects using a constructor that accepts
   //  a variable number of String objects as parameters.
   //-----------------------------------------------------------------
   public static void main(String[] args)
   {
      Family lewis = new Family("John", "Sharon", "Justin", "Kayla",
         "Nathan", "Samantha");

      Family camden = new Family("Stephen", "Annie", "Matt", "Mary",
         "Simon", "Lucy", "Ruthie", "Sam", "David");

      System.out.println(lewis);
      System.out.println();
      System.out.println(camden);
   }
}
```

OUTPUT

```
John
Sharon
Justin
Kayla
Nathan
Samantha

Stephen
Annie
Matt
Mary
Simon
Lucy
Ruthie
Sam
David
```

LISTING 8.12

```
//********************************************************************
//  Family.java       Author: Lewis/Loftus
//
//  Demonstrates the use of variable length parameter lists.
//********************************************************************

public class Family
{
   private String[] members;

   //-----------------------------------------------------------------
   // Constructor: Sets up this family by storing the (possibly
   // multiple) names that are passed in as parameters.
   //-----------------------------------------------------------------
   public Family(String ... names)
   {
      members = names;
   }

   //-----------------------------------------------------------------
   //  Returns a string representation of this family.
   //-----------------------------------------------------------------
   public String toString()
   {
      String result = "";

      for (String name : members)
         result += name + "\n";

      return result;
   }
}
```

The `Family` class is shown in Listing 8.12. The constructor simply stores a reference to the array parameter until it is needed. By using a variable-length parameter list for the constructor, we make it easy to create a family of any size.

SELF-REVIEW QUESTIONS *(see answers in Appendix L)*

SR 8.20 How can Java methods have variable-length parameter lists?

SR 8.21 Write a method called `distance` that accepts a multiple number of integer parameters (each of which represents the distance of one leg of a journey) and returns the total distance of the trip.

SR 8.22 Write a method called `travelTime` that accepts an integer parameter indicating average speed followed by a multiple number of integer parameters (each of which represents the distance of one leg of a journey) and returns the total time of the trip.

8.6 Two-Dimensional Arrays

The arrays we've examined so far have all been *one-dimensional arrays* in the sense that they represent a simple list of values. As the name implies, a *two-dimensional array* has values in two dimensions, which are often thought of as the rows and columns of a table. Figure 8.4 graphically compares a one-dimensional array with a two-dimensional array. We must use two indexes to refer to a value in a two-dimensional array, one specifying the row and another the column.

Brackets are used to represent each dimension in the array. Therefore, the type of a two-dimensional array that stores integers is `int[][]`. Technically, Java represents two-dimensional arrays as an array of arrays. A two-dimensional integer array is really a one-dimensional array of references to one-dimensional integer arrays.

The `TwoDArray` program shown in Listing 8.13 instantiates a two-dimensional array of integers. As with one-dimensional arrays, the size of the dimensions is specified when the array is created. The size of the dimensions can be different.

Nested `for` loops are used in the `TwoDArray` program to load the array with values and also to print those values in a table format. Carefully trace the processing to see how the nested loops eventually visit each element in the two-dimensional array. Note that the outer loops are governed by `table.length`, which represents the number of rows, and the inner loops are governed by `table[row].length`, which represents the number of columns in that row.

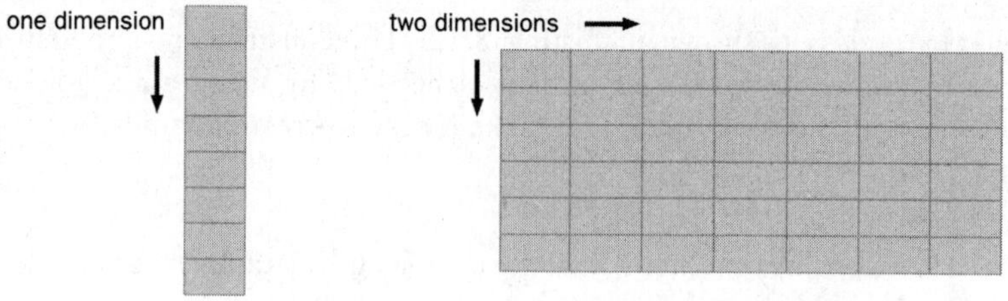

FIGURE 8.4 A one-dimensional array and a two-dimensional array

LISTING 8.13

```
//********************************************************************
//  TwoDArray.java       Author: Lewis/Loftus
//
//  Demonstrates the use of a two-dimensional array.
//********************************************************************

public class TwoDArray
{
   //-----------------------------------------------------------------
   //  Creates a 2D array of integers, fills it with increasing
   //  integer values, then prints them out.
   //-----------------------------------------------------------------
   public static void main(String[] args)
   {
      int[][] table = new int[5][10];

      // Load the table with values
      for (int row = 0; row < table.length; row++)
         for (int col = 0; col < table[row].length; col++)
            table[row][col] = row * 10 + col;

      // Print the table
      for (int row = 0; row < table.length; row++)
      {
         for (int col = 0; col < table[row].length; col++)
            System.out.print(table[row][col] + "\t");
         System.out.println();
      }
   }
}
```

OUTPUT

```
0	1	2	3	4	5	6	7	8	9
10	11	12	13	14	15	16	17	18	19
20	21	22	23	24	25	26	27	28	29
30	31	32	33	34	35	36	37	38	39
40	41	42	43	44	45	46	47	48	49
```

As with one-dimensional arrays, an initializer list can be used to instantiate a two-dimensional array, where each element is itself an array initializer list. This technique is used in the SodaSurvey program, which is shown in Listing 8.14.

LISTING 8.14

```
//********************************************************************
//  SodaSurvey.java       Author: Lewis/Loftus
//
//  Demonstrates the use of a two-dimensional array.
//********************************************************************

import java.text.DecimalFormat;

public class SodaSurvey
{
   //-----------------------------------------------------------------
   //  Determines and prints the average of each row (soda) and each
   //  column (respondent) of the survey scores.
   //-----------------------------------------------------------------
   public static void main(String[] args)
   {
      int[][] scores = { {3, 4, 5, 2, 1, 4, 3, 2, 4, 4},
                         {2, 4, 3, 4, 3, 3, 2, 1, 2, 2},
                         {3, 5, 4, 5, 5, 3, 2, 5, 5, 5},
                         {1, 1, 1, 3, 1, 2, 1, 3, 2, 4} };

      final int SODAS = scores.length;
      final int PEOPLE = scores[0].length;

      int[] sodaSum = new int[SODAS];
      int[] personSum = new int[PEOPLE];

      for (int soda = 0; soda < SODAS; soda++)
         for (int person = 0; person < PEOPLE; person++)
         {
            sodaSum[soda] += scores[soda][person];
            personSum[person] += scores[soda][person];
         }

      DecimalFormat fmt = new DecimalFormat("0.#");
      System.out.println("Averages:\n");
```

LISTING 8.14 *continued*

```
      for (int soda = 0; soda < SODAS; soda++)
         System.out.println("Soda #" + (soda+1) + ": " +
                    fmt.format((float)sodaSum[soda]/PEOPLE));

      System.out.println();
      for (int person = 0; person < PEOPLE; person++)
         System.out.println("Person #" + (person+1) + ": " +
                    fmt.format((float)personSum[person]/SODAS));
   }
}
```

OUTPUT

```
Averages:

Soda #1: 3.2
Soda #2: 2.6
Soda #3: 4.2
Soda #4: 1.9

Person #1: 2.2
Person #2: 3.5
Person #3: 3.2
Person #4: 3.5
Person #5: 2.5
Person #6: 3
Person #7: 2
Person #8: 2.8
Person #9: 3.2
Person #10: 3.8
```

Suppose a soda manufacturer held a taste test for four new flavors to see how people liked them. The manufacturer got 10 people to try each new flavor and give it a score from 1 to 5, where 1 equals poor and 5 equals excellent. The two-dimensional array called `scores` in the `SodaSurvey` program stores the results of that survey. Each row corresponds to a soda and each column in that row corresponds to the person who tasted it. More generally, each row holds the responses that all testers gave for one particular soda flavor, and each column holds the responses of one person for all sodas.

The SodaSurvey program computes and prints the average responses for each soda and for each respondent. The sums of each soda and person are first stored in one-dimensional arrays of integers. Then the averages are computed and printed.

Multidimensional Arrays

An array can have one, two, three, or even more dimensions. Any array with more than one dimension is called a *multidimensional array*.

It's fairly easy to picture a two-dimensional array as a table. A three-dimensional array could be drawn as a cube. However, once you are past three dimensions, multidimensional arrays might seem hard to visualize. Yet, consider that each subsequent dimension is simply a subdivision of the previous one. It is often best to think of larger multidimensional arrays in this way.

For example, suppose we wanted to store the number of students attending universities across the United States, broken down in a meaningful way. We might represent it as a four-dimensional array of integers. The first dimension represents the state. The second dimension represents the universities in each state. The third dimension represents the colleges in each university. Finally, the fourth dimension represents departments in each college. The value stored at each location is the number of students in one particular department. Figure 8.5 shows these subdivisions.

KEY CONCEPT

Using an array with more than two dimensions is rare in an object-oriented system.

Two-dimensional arrays are fairly common. However, care should be taken when deciding to create multidimensional arrays in a program. When dealing with large amounts of data that are managed at multiple levels, additional information and the methods needed to manage that information will probably be required. It is far more likely, for instance, that in the previous example, each state would be represented by an object, which may contain, among other things, an array to store information about each university, and so on.

There is one other important characteristic of Java arrays to consider. As we established previously, Java does not directly support multidimensional arrays.

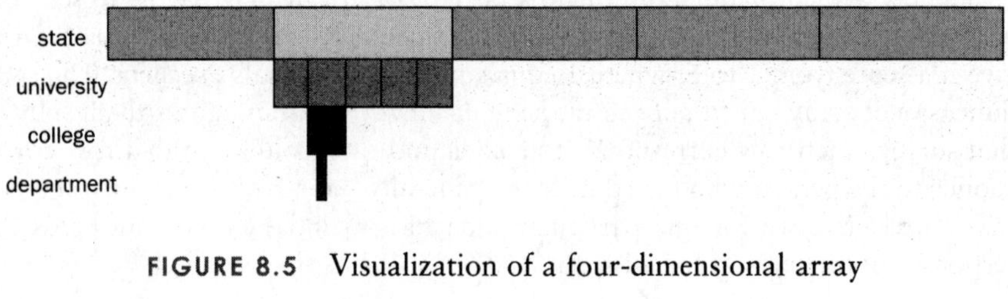

FIGURE 8.5 Visualization of a four-dimensional array

Instead, they are represented as arrays of references to array objects. Those arrays could themselves contain references to other arrays. This layering continues for as many dimensions as required. Because of this technique for representing each dimension, the arrays in any one dimension could be of different lengths. These are sometimes called *ragged arrays*. For example, the number of elements in each row of a two-dimensional array may not be the same. In such situations, care must be taken to make sure the arrays are managed appropriately.

SELF-REVIEW QUESTIONS *(see answers in Appendix L)*

SR 8.23 How are multidimensional arrays implemented in Java?

SR 8.24 A two-dimensional array named `scores` holds the test scores for a class of students for a semester. Write code that prints out a single value that represents the range of scores held in the array. It prints out the value of the highest score minus the value of the lowest score. Each test score is represented as an integer.

8.7 Polygons and Polylines

A *polygon* is a multisided figure that is represented in the JavaFX API by the `Polygon` class. A polygon is defined using a series of (x, y) points that specify the vertices of the polygon. Arrays are often used to store the list of coordinates used to define a polygon.

A polygon is always a closed shape. A line segment is always drawn from the last point in the polygon's list of vertices to the first point.

A *polyline*, on the other hand, is an open shape. A polyline is simply a series of points connected by line segments. The first and last vertices of a polyline are not automatically connected.

KEY CONCEPT
A polyline is similar to a polygon except that a polyline is not a closed shape.

The program in Listing 8.15 uses two `Polygon` objects and a `Polyline` object to display a rocket blasting off. One polygon forms

LISTING 8.15

```
import javafx.application.Application;
import javafx.scene.Group;
import javafx.scene.Scene;
import javafx.scene.paint.Color;
import javafx.scene.shape.Polygon;
import javafx.scene.shape.Polyline;
import javafx.stage.Stage;
```

LISTING 8.15 *continued*

```
//********************************************************************
//  Rocket.java       Author: Lewis/Loftus
//
//  Demonstrates the use of polygons and polylines.
//********************************************************************

public class Rocket extends Application
{
   //-----------------------------------------------------------------
   //  Displays a rocket lifting off. The rocket and hatch are polygons
   //  and the flame is a polyline.
   //-----------------------------------------------------------------
   public void start(Stage primaryStage)
   {
      double[] hullPoints = {200, 25, 240, 60, 240, 230, 270, 260,
         270, 300, 140, 300, 140, 260, 160, 230, 160, 60};

      Polygon rocket = new Polygon(hullPoints);
      rocket.setFill(Color.BEIGE);

      double[] hatchPoints = {185, 70, 215, 70, 220, 120, 180, 120};
      Polygon hatch = new Polygon(hatchPoints);
      hatch.setFill(Color.MAROON);

      double[] flamePoints = {142, 310, 142, 330, 150, 325, 155, 380,
         165, 340, 175, 360, 190, 350, 200, 375, 215, 330, 220, 360,
         225, 355, 230, 370, 240, 340, 255, 370, 260, 335, 268, 340,
         268, 310};

      Polyline flame = new Polyline(flamePoints);
      flame.setStroke(Color.RED);
      flame.setStrokeWidth(3);

      Group root = new Group(rocket, hatch, flame);

      Scene scene = new Scene(root, 400, 400, Color.BLACK);

      primaryStage.setTitle("Rocket");
      primaryStage.setScene(scene);
      primaryStage.show();
   }
}
```

LISTING 8.15 *continued*

DISPLAY

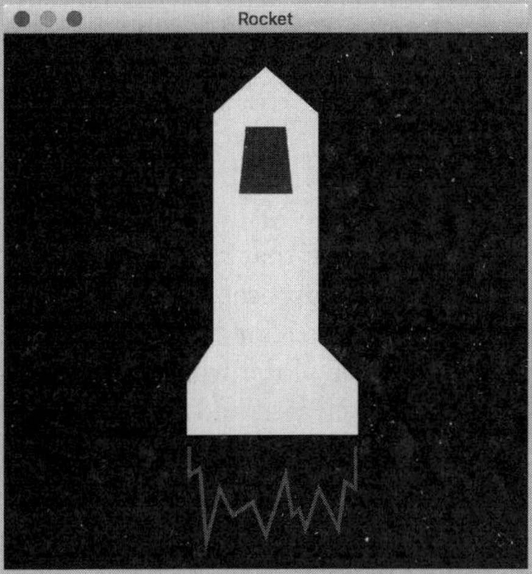

the hull of the rocket itself, and the other forms the hatch in the side of the rocket. The polyline is used to represent the flames coming out of the bottom of the rocket.

For each shape, the coordinate values that make up the vertices are stored in an array of `double` values, and the array is passed to the `Polygon` or `Polyline` constructor when the shape object is created. Each array is created using an initialization list.

Each pair of coordinates in the array represents a point. For example, the first point in the polygon that makes up the hull is (200, 25), which is the nose of the rocket. The next point is (240, 60). The third is (240, 230), and so on moving clockwise around the hull.

If you don't know all the coordinates initially, you can add vertices after the shapes are created by retrieving the current list of vertices and adding additional ones. The following line of code adds two more vertices, one at (50, 75) and another at (100, 30), to the specified polygon:

```
myPolygon.getPoints().addAll(50, 75, 100, 30);
```

Note that the arrays can hold floating-point values (`double`), but we store integers in them. All coordinates in JavaFX are stored as doubles so that they can be determined by computations that may involve floating-point calculations.

Like other shapes, the fill color, stroke color, and stroke width of polygons and polylines can be set using calls to the appropriate methods.

SELF-REVIEW QUESTIONS *(see answers in Appendix L)*

SR 8.25 What is a polyline? How do we specify its shape?

SR 8.26 What is the difference between a polygon and a polyline?

SR 8.27 Why are coordinates in JavaFX stored as `double` values?

8.8 An Array of Color Objects

Let's look at an example that makes use of an array of `Color` objects. The program in Listing 8.16 allows the user to click the mouse pointer anywhere in the window to make a colored dot appear. A count of the number of dots is displayed in the upper left corner of the window. If the user double clicks anywhere in the window, the dots are cleared and the count is reset.

LISTING 8.16

```
import javafx.application.Application;
import javafx.scene.Group;
import javafx.scene.Scene;
import javafx.scene.input.MouseEvent;
import javafx.scene.paint.Color;
import javafx.scene.shape.Circle;
import javafx.scene.text.Font;
import javafx.scene.text.Text;
import javafx.stage.Stage;

//************************************************************************
//  Dots.java       Author: Lewis/Loftus
//
//  Demonstrates the use of an array of Color objects and the capture of
//  a double mouse click.
//************************************************************************

public class Dots extends Application
{
   private Color[] colorList = {Color.RED, Color.CYAN, Color.MAGENTA,
           Color.YELLOW, Color.LIME, Color.WHITE};

   private int colorIndex = 0;
   private int count = 0;
```

LISTING 8.16 *continued*

```
   private Text countText;
   private Group root;

   //-----------------------------------------------------------------
   //  Displays a scene on which the user can add colored dots with
   //  mouse clicks.
   //-----------------------------------------------------------------
   public void start(Stage primaryStage)
   {
      countText = new Text(20, 30, "Count: 0");
      countText.setFont(new Font(18));
      countText.setFill(Color.WHITE);

      root = new Group(countText);

      Scene scene = new Scene(root, 400, 300, Color.BLACK);
      scene.setOnMouseClicked(this::processMouseClick);

      primaryStage.setTitle("Dots");
      primaryStage.setScene(scene);
      primaryStage.show();
   }

   //-----------------------------------------------------------------
   //  Process a mouse click by adding a circle to that location. Circle
   //  colors rotate through a set list of colors. A double click clears
   //  the dots and resets the counter.
   //-----------------------------------------------------------------
   public void processMouseClick(MouseEvent event)
   {
      if (event.getClickCount() == 2)   // double click
      {
         count = 0;
         colorIndex = 0;
         root.getChildren().clear();
         countText.setText("Count: 0");
         root.getChildren().add(countText);
      }
      else
      {
         Circle circle = new Circle(event.getX(), event.getY(), 10);
         circle.setFill(colorList[colorIndex]);
         root.getChildren().add(circle);
```

LISTING 8.16 *continued*

```
            colorIndex = (colorIndex + 1) % colorList.length;

            count++;
            countText.setText("Count: " + count);
        }
    }
}
```

DISPLAY

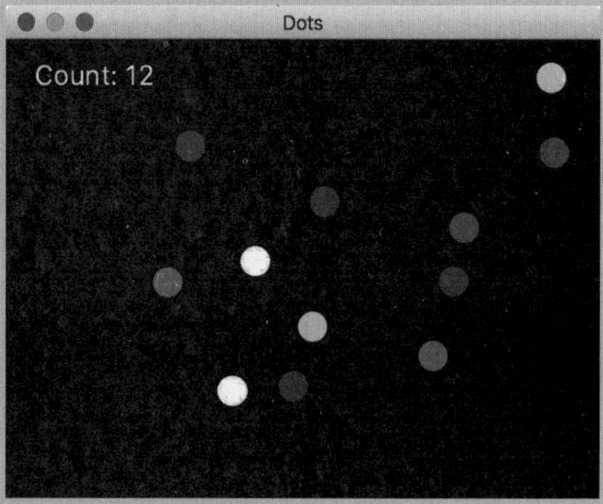

The `Dots` example is set up to handle mouse click events. Whenever a mouse click event occurs, the event handler method is called. The event handler method, which we happened to call `processMouseClick`, is specified in the `start` method using a call to the `setOnMouseClick` method.

The first thing the event handling method does is check for a *double click* (two clicks that occur very quickly in the same location) by calling the `getClickCount` method of the event object. If a double click is detected, all nodes in the scene are cleared, and then the count text (with a count of 0) is added again to the scene.

If it is not a double click, the `else` portion of the `if` statement is executed, which creates and adds a colored dot to the scene at the location where the mouse click occurred. The `getX` and `getY` methods of the event object are used to get the coordinates of the mouse click.

The colors of the dots added to the scene rotate among a set of six colors stored in an array called `colorList`, created at the class level using an initialization list. The first dot added is colored red. The second is cyan, following the order of the colors in the array. The third is magenta, and so on. After a white dot is added, the cycle begins again with red.

The rotating colors are controlled by an integer variable called `colorIndex`. It represents the array index of the color of the next dot to be added. After a colored dot is added, the `colorIndex` value is incremented so that the next dot will be the next color. The increment is done with the following line of code:

```
colorIndex = (colorIndex + 1) % colorList.length;
```

That line of code not only increments the value in `colorIndex`, it uses the remainder operator (`%`) to wrap the index back to the beginning of the array when it reaches the end. Not that it is dividing the updated index by the length of the `colorList` array (which is 6). If the index is incremented from 2 to 3, for instance, the remainder operator returns 3. If the index is incremented from 5 to 6, however, the remainder operator returns 0 and the cycle begins again.

KEY CONCEPT

The remainder operator can be used to wrap a sequence of values back to zero.

SELF-REVIEW QUESTIONS *(see answers in Appendix L)*

SR 8.28 How can you determine if the user has double clicked the mouse button?

SR 8.29 The display for Listing 8.16 shows 12 dots. What would the color of the next dot be?

SR 8.30 What modifications would be necessary to the `Dots` program to add more colors to the rotating set of dot colors?

8.9 Choice Boxes

A *choice box* is a JavaFX GUI control that allows the user to select one of several options from a drop down menu. When the user clicks on the choice box, a list of options is displayed from which the user can choose. The current selection is displayed in the choice box.

KEY CONCEPT

A choice box provides a drop down menu of options to the user.

The `JukeBox` program shown in Listing 8.17 allows the user to choose a song to play using a choice box. The Play button begins playing the current selection from the beginning, and the Stop button stops the current song. Selecting a new song while one is playing also stops the current song.

LISTING 8.17

```
import java.io.File;
import javafx.application.Application;
import javafx.event.ActionEvent;
import javafx.geometry.Insets;
import javafx.geometry.Pos;
import javafx.scene.Scene;
import javafx.scene.control.Button;
import javafx.scene.control.ChoiceBox;
import javafx.scene.control.Label;
import javafx.scene.layout.HBox;
import javafx.scene.layout.VBox;
import javafx.scene.media.AudioClip;
import javafx.stage.Stage;

//********************************************************************
//  JukeBox.java       Author: Lewis/Loftus
//
//  Demonstrates the use of a combo box and audio clips.
//********************************************************************

public class JukeBox extends Application
{
   private ChoiceBox<String> choice;
   private AudioClip[] tunes;
   private AudioClip current;
   private Button playButton, stopButton;

   //-----------------------------------------------------------------
   //  Presents an interface that allows the user to select and play
   //  a tune from a drop down box.
   //-----------------------------------------------------------------
   public void start(Stage primaryStage)
   {
      String[] names = {"Western Beat", "Classical Melody",
         "Jeopardy Theme", "Eighties Jam", "New Age Rythm",
         "Lullaby", "Alfred Hitchcock's Theme"};

      File[] audioFiles = {new File("westernBeat.wav"),
         new File("classical.wav"), new File("jeopardy.mp3"),
         new File("eightiesJam.wav"), new File("newAgeRythm.wav"),
         new File("lullaby.mp3"), new File("hitchcock.wav")};

      tunes = new AudioClip[audioFiles.length];
      for (int i = 0; i < audioFiles.length; i++)
          tunes[i] = new AudioClip(audioFiles[i].toURI().toString());
```

LISTING 8.17 *continued*

```
        current = tunes[0];

        Label label = new Label("Select a tune:");

        choice = new ChoiceBox<String>();
        choice.getItems().addAll(names);
        choice.getSelectionModel().selectFirst();
        choice.setOnAction(this::processChoice);

        playButton = new Button("Play");
        stopButton = new Button("Stop");
        HBox buttons = new HBox(playButton, stopButton);
        buttons.setSpacing(10);
        buttons.setPadding(new Insets(15, 0, 0, 0));
        buttons.setAlignment(Pos.CENTER);

        playButton.setOnAction(this::processButtonPush);
        stopButton.setOnAction(this::processButtonPush);

        VBox root = new VBox(label, choice, buttons);
        root.setPadding(new Insets(15, 15, 15, 25));
        root.setSpacing(10);
        root.setStyle("-fx-background-color: skyblue");

        Scene scene = new Scene(root, 300, 150);

        primaryStage.setTitle("Java Juke Box");
        primaryStage.setScene(scene);
        primaryStage.show();
    }

    //--------------------------------------------------------------------
    //  When a choice box selection is made, stops the current clip (if
    //  one was playing) and sets the current tune.
    //--------------------------------------------------------------------
    public void processChoice(ActionEvent event)
    {
        current.stop();
        current = tunes[choice.getSelectionModel().getSelectedIndex()];
    }

    //--------------------------------------------------------------------
    //  Handles the play and stop buttons. Stops the current clip in
    //  either case. If the play button was pressed, (re)starts the
```

LISTING 8.17 *continued*

```
   //  current clip.
   //----------------------------------------------------------------
   public void processButtonPush(ActionEvent event)
   {
      current.stop();

      if (event.getSource() == playButton)
         current.play();
   }
}
```

DISPLAY

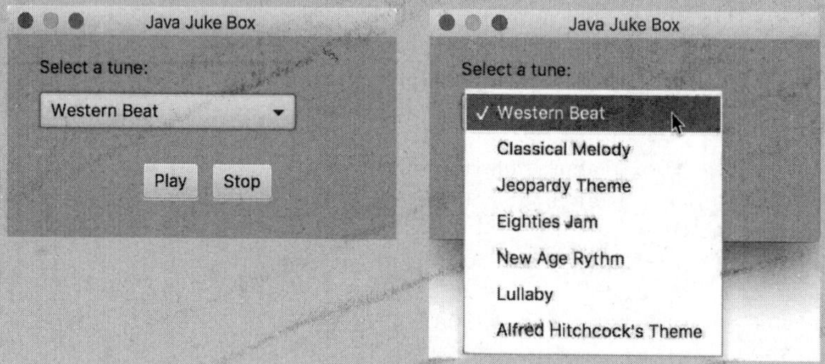

There are several arrays used in the JukeBox program. First, an array of strings called names is used to store the names of the song options displayed in the choice box. After the ChoiceBox object is created, the array of names is added to the list of items displayed.

An array of File objects is used to represent the audio files of individual songs. They are then used to create an array of AudioClip objects. The AudioClip class is part of the javafx.scene.media package and provides basic playback control of an uncompressed audio file. For more complex control, longer audio clips, or compressed file formats, use Media objects.

There are two event handler methods in the JukeBox program. One responds to the action event that occurs when an option is selected in the choice box. The other responds to the action even that is generated by either button.

When the user selects a new option in the choice box, the current song is stopped if one is playing; if the current song is not playing the call to the stop method does nothing. Then the variable that represents the currently selected song is set to the appropriate `AudioClip` object from the `tunes` array. The index is obtained by calling the `getSelectedIndex` method of the underlying *selection model* used by the choice box.

When either the Play or Stop button is pushed, the current song playing is stopped (if there is one). Then, if it is the Play button that was pushed, the current song is started from the beginning.

It should be noted that a choice box can be either editable or uneditable. By default, a choice box is uneditable. Changing the option in an uneditable choice box can only be accomplished by selecting an item from the list. If the choice box is editable, the user can either select an item from the list or type a particular value into the choice box (as you would a text field). For the `JukeBox` program, an uneditable choice box was appropriate.

A *combo box* is another control that is very similar in behavior to a choice box. The differences are subtle and have to do with the way the options are displayed. Internally, a `ChoiceBox` uses menus, whereas a `ComboBox` uses a `ListView`. An implication of that is that you can only select one option in a choice box but you can set up the selection model of a combo box to allow multiple selections. Choice boxes are well-suited to a small number of choices. If the number of options you're presenting is very large, consider using a combo box.

SELF-REVIEW QUESTIONS *(see answers in Appendix L)*

SR 8.31 What is a choice box?

SR 8.32 How many action event handlers are defined in the `JukeBox` program, and what do they respond to?

SR 8.33 Describe how the `JukeBox` program associates the choice box selection made by the user with a specific audio clip.

Summary of Key Concepts

- An array of size N is indexed from 0 to N–1.
- In Java, an array is an object that must be instantiated.
- Bounds checking ensures that an index used to refer to an array element is in range.
- An initializer list can be used to instantiate an array object instead of using the `new` operator.
- An entire array can be passed as a parameter, making the formal parameter an alias of the original.
- Instantiating an array of objects reserves room to store references only. The objects that are stored in each element must be instantiated separately.
- Command-line arguments are stored in an array of `String` objects and are passed to the `main` method.
- A Java method can be defined to accept a varying number of parameters.
- Using an array with more than two dimensions is rare in an object-oriented system.
- A polyline is similar to a polygon except that a polyline is not a closed shape.
- The remainder operator can be used to wrap a sequence of values back to zero.
- A choice box provides a drop down menu of options to the user.

Exercises

EX 8.1 Which of the following are valid declarations? Which instantiate an array object? Explain your answers. If a declaration creates an array object, describe the array.

```
boolean completed[] = {true, true, false, false};
int powersOfTwo = {1, 2, 4, 8, 16, 32, 62, 128};
char[] vowels = new char[5];
float[] length = float[100];
String[] names = new {"Sam", "Frodo", "Merry", "Pippin"};
char vowels[] = {'a', 'e', 'i', 'o', 'u'};
double[] standardDeviation = new double[];
```

EX 8.2 Describe five programs that would be difficult to implement without using arrays.

EX 8.3 Describe how an element in an array is accessed in memory. For example, where is `myArray[25]` stored in memory?

EX 8.4 Describe what problem occurs in the following code. What modifications should be made to it to eliminate the problem?

```
double[] masses = {123,6, 34.2, 765.87, 987.43, 90, 321,5};
double totalMass = 0;
for (int index = 1; index < masses.length + 1; index++){
     totalMass += masses[index];
}
```

EX 8.5 Write an array declaration and any necessary supporting classes for each of the following statements:

a. names of the planets of the solar system

b. for each flight leaving an airport on a particular day: the flight number, departure time, and duration

c. for each product on an online store: the product name, description, cost, number in stock, and rating

d. the average temperature of a year

e. for each track played on a music player: the title, length, genre, and artist

EX 8.6 Write code that sets each element of an array called `nums` to the value of the constant `INITIAL`.

EX 8.7 Write code that prints the values stored in an array called `names` backwards.

EX 8.8 Write code that sets each element of a `boolean` array called `flags` to alternating values (`true` at index 0, `false` at index 1, etc.).

EX 8.9 Write a method called `sumArray` that accepts an array of floating point values and returns the sum of the values stored in the array.

EX 8.10 Write a method called `switchThem` that accepts two integer arrays as parameters and switches the contents of the arrays. Take into account that the arrays may be of different sizes.

EX 8.11 Describe a program for which you would use the `ArrayList` class instead of arrays. Describe a program for which you would use arrays instead of the `ArrayList` class. Explain your choices.

EX 8.12 The `Dots` program handles mouse click events to draw the dots. How would the program behave differently if it handled mouse pressed events instead? Mouse released events?

EX 8.13 Modify the `JukeBox` program so that it will play the selected song when the user presses the P key on the keyboard (without having to press the Play button).

EX 8.14 How can the JukeBox program be modified to use a single array of songs rather than three separate arrays for names, audio files, and tunes?

Programming Projects

PP 8.1 Write a program that reads an arbitrary number of integers that are in the range 0 to 50 inclusive and counts how many occurrences of each are entered. Indicate the end of the input by a value outside of the range. After all input has been processed, print all of the values (with the number of occurrences) that were entered one or more times.

PP 8.2 Modify the program from PP 8.1 so that it works for numbers in the range between −25 and 25.

```
1  -  10  | *****
11 -  20  | **
21 -  30  | *******************
31 -  40  |
41 -  50  | ***
51 -  60  | ********
61 -  70  | **
71 -  80  | *****
81 -  90  | *******
91 - 100  | *********
```

PP 8.3 Write a program that creates a histogram that allows you to visually inspect the frequency distribution of a set of values. The program should read in an arbitrary number of integers from a text input file that are in the range 1 to 100 inclusive; then produce a chart similar to the one below that indicates how many input values fell in the range 1 to 10, 11 to 20, and so on. Print one asterisk for each value entered.

PP 8.4 The lines in the histogram in PP 8.3 will be too long if a large number of values is entered. Modify the program so that it prints an asterisk for every five values in each category. Ignore leftovers. For example, if a category had 17 values, print three asterisks in that row. If a category had 4 values, do not print any asterisks in that row.

PP 8.5 Write a program that computes and prints the mean and standard deviation of a list of integers x_1 through x_n. Assume that there will be no more than 50 input values. Compute both the mean and standard deviation as floating point values, using the following formulas.

$$\text{mean} = \frac{\sum_{i=1}^{n} X_i}{n}$$

$$\text{sd} = \sqrt{\sum_{i=1}^{n} (X_i - \text{mean})^2}$$

PP 8.6 The L&L Bank can handle up to 30 customers who have savings accounts. Design and implement a program that manages the accounts. Keep track of key information and allow each customer to make deposits and withdrawals. Produce appropriate error messages for invalid transactions. *Hint*: You may want to base your accounts on the `Account` class from Chapter 4. Also provide a method to add 3 percent interest to all accounts whenever the method is invoked.

VideoNote
Developing a solution of PP 8.5.

PP 8.7 Create a class called `ScrabbleTile` that represents a Scrabble tile with a letter and a point value. Then create a class called `TileBag` that contains 100 Scrabble tiles. The `TileBag` class should contain methods to shuffle the tiles and pick a tile, removing it from the bag. Write a `main` class to create an instance of `TileBag`, select seven tiles from the bag, and print the chosen tiles. Report the number of tiles left in the bag.

PP 8.8 Write a program that reads a sequence of up to 25 pairs of names and postal (ZIP) codes for individuals. Store the data in an object designed to store a first name (string), last name (string), and postal code (integer). Assume each line of input will contain two strings followed by an integer value, each separated by a tab character. Then, after the input has been read in, print the list in an appropriate format to the screen.

PP 8.9 Modify the program you created in PP 8.8 to accomplish the following:

- Support the storing of additional user information: street address (string), city (string), state (string), and 10-digit phone number (long integer, contains area code and does not include special characters such as `'('`, `')'`, or `'-'`)
- Store the data in an `ArrayList` object.

PP 8.10 Use the `Question` class from Chapter 7 to define a `Quiz` class. A quiz can be composed of up to 25 questions. Define the `add` method of the `Quiz` class to add a question to a quiz. Define the `giveQuiz` method of the `Quiz` class to present each question in turn to the user, accept an answer for each one, and keep track of the results. Define a class called `QuizTime` with a `main` method that populates a quiz, presents it, and prints the final results.

PP 8.11 Modify your answer to PP 8.10 so that the complexity level of the questions given in the quiz is taken into account. Overload the `giveQuiz` method so that it accepts two integer parameters that specify the minimum and maximum complexity levels for the quiz questions and presents only questions in that complexity range. Modify the `main` method to demonstrate this feature.

PP 8.12 Define a class called `Star` that extends `Polygon` and is shaped like a five-pointed star. Use parameters to the `Star` constructor to specify the color, position, and scale of the star. Write a JavaFX application that presents 5 stars of different colors, scaled to various sizes.

PP 8.13 Define a class called `PieChart` that extends `Group` and presents a pie chart for a given array of values. Each slice of the chart should have a different color and correspond to the value provided. Use the shapes found in the `javafx.scene.shape` package to construct the chart. Write a JavaFX application to display the pie chart.

PP 8.14 Modify the `QuoteOptions` program from Chapter 5 so that it provides three additional quote options. Use arrays to store the category options and quotes, and a choice box to present the options (instead of radio buttons).

PP 8.15 Write a JavaFX application that displays an image and plays a sound effect with each mouse click. Rotate through four images and five sound effects, so the image/sound effect pairing is different each time.

PP 8.16 Write a JavaFX application that presents 20 circles, each with a random radius and location. If a circle does not overlap any other circle, fill the circle with black. Fill overlapping circles with a translucent blue (alpha value of 0.3). Hint: Use an array to store the `Circle` objects, and check each new circle to see if it overlaps any previously created circle. Two circles overlap if the distance between their center points is less than the sum of their radii.

PP 8.17 Write a JavaFX application that creates polyline shapes dynamically using mouse clicks. Each mouse click adds a new line segment to the current polyline from the previous point to the current mouse position. Allow the user to end the current polyline with a double click. And provide a button that clears the window and allows the user to begin again.

SOFTWARE FAILURE

LA Air Traffic Control

What Happened?

At about 5 pm on Tuesday, September 14, 2004, the Los Angeles air traffic-control center suddenly lost voice contact with 400 planes they were tracking in the southwestern United States. The Voice Switching and Control System (VSCS), designed by the Harris Corp. of Melbourne, Florida, had unexpectedly shut down. Then the backup system designed to take over when such a failure occurred crashed within a minute after it was activated. Without the controller's guidance, planes began coming dangerously close to each other, resulting in several near misses.

■ Air traffic controllers in action, using voice and imaging systems.

Collisions were avoided due in part to the quick thinking of some controllers, who used their cell phones to alert other traffic-control centers and the airlines. But the main reason the incident wasn't a disaster was the on-board collision avoidance systems now found in commercial jets. These systems track the transponders of nearby aircraft and give emergency instructions to the pilots to climb or descend at the last minute. It's likely that several midair collisions would have resulted if the problem had occurred 10 to 15 years earlier, before planes had such avoidance systems.

What Caused It?

Officially, the incident was blamed on human error. The FAA reported that the problem was "not the result of system reliability" and would have been avoided if FAA procedures had been followed. The key procedure in this case requires that the voice switching system be rebooted every 30 days.

The root cause, however, was traced to a software problem. The VSCS relies on a subsystem that periodically runs built-in tests. A countdown timer in the subsystem is used to determine when the tests will run. The timer counts down in milliseconds, starting at the highest numeric value that the system could handle: 232. That's just over four billion milliseconds. It takes just under 50 days for the timer to go from 232 down to zero. Unfortunately, when the timer reaches zero, the tests cannot be run, and the system shuts down. By rebooting the system every 30 days, the timer is reset almost three weeks before it expires.

The FAA first discovered the problem when it ran tests on the system in the field. It ran for 49.7 days, and then crashed. After rebooting, everything seemed fine. When a similar crash happened with another system, the FAA instituted the 30 day reboot procedure.

After the incident in Los Angeles, the issue was tracked down, and a software patch was created to fix the problem. Now the system periodically resets the counter without the need for human intervention.

Lessons Learned

In this situation, the problem (if not its implications) was known beforehand. Harris (the manufacturer) knew about the potential for the timer to expire but hadn't determined the impact it might have on the system. The FAA discovered the problem during tests—although not the root cause. Instead of delving further, they instituted a human-based, manual solution—the ultimate "when in doubt, reboot" scenario.

It's true that the problem would have been avoided if the FAA procedures had been followed, but that's of little comfort when the software can make such procedures unnecessary. It's also true that the incident would have been negligible if the backup system had not failed. Having redundant backup systems would lessen the chance of complete failure.

In this case, though, the bottom line is that thorough testing and investigation would have brought the problem to light. In safety-critical systems, nothing less should be acceptable.

Source: IEEE Spectrum, November 2004

9 Inheritance

CHAPTER OBJECTIVES

- Explore the derivation of new classes from existing ones.
- Define the concept and purpose of method overriding.
- Discuss the design of class hierarchies.
- Discuss the issue of visibility as it relates to inheritance.
- Explore the ability to derive one interface from another.
- Discuss object-oriented design in the context of inheritance.
- Describe the inheritance structure for JavaFX controls and shapes.
- Explore color and date pickers and dialog boxes.

This chapter explains inheritance, a fundamental technique for organizing and creating classes. It is a powerful idea that influences the way we design object-oriented software and enhances our ability to reuse classes in other situations and programs. In this chapter, we explore the technique for creating subclasses and class hierarchies, and we discuss a technique for overriding the definition of an inherited method. We examine the `protected` modifier and discuss the effect all visibility modifiers have on inherited attributes and methods. Finally, we discuss how inheritance plays a role in JavaFX graphical user interfaces, as well as more controls and dialog boxes.

9.1 Creating Subclasses

In our introduction to object-oriented concepts in Chapter 1, we presented the analogy that a class is to an object what a blueprint is to a house. In subsequent chapters we've reinforced that idea, writing classes that define a set of similar objects. A class establishes the characteristics and behaviors of an object but reserves no memory space for variables (unless those variables are declared as `static`). Classes are the plan, and objects are the embodiment of that plan.

Many houses can be created from the same blueprint. They are essentially the same house in different locations with different people living in them. Now suppose you want a house that is similar to another but with some different or additional features. You want to start with the same basic blueprint but modify it to suit new, slightly different, needs. Many housing developments are created this way. The houses in the development have the same core layout, but they have unique features. For instance, they might all be split-level homes with the same basic room configuration, but some have a fireplace or full basement while others do not, or an upgraded gourmet kitchen instead of the standard version.

It's likely that the housing developer commissioned a master architect to create a single blueprint to establish the basic design of all houses in the development, then a series of new blueprints that include variations designed to appeal to different buyers. The act of creating the series of blueprints was simplified since they all begin with the same underlying structure, while the variations give them unique characteristics that may be important to the prospective owners.

KEY CONCEPT
Inheritance is the process of deriving a new class from an existing one.

Creating a new blueprint that is based on an existing blueprint is analogous to the object-oriented concept of *inheritance*, which is the process in which a new class is derived from an existing one. Inheritance is a powerful software development technique and a defining characteristic of object-oriented programming. We've used inheritance in basic ways in earlier examples; in this chapter we explore it in detail.

Via inheritance, the new class automatically contains the variables and methods in the original class. Then, to tailor the class as needed, the programmer can add new variables and methods to the derived class or modify the inherited ones.

KEY CONCEPT
One purpose of inheritance is to reuse existing software.

In general, new classes can be created via inheritance faster, easier, and cheaper than by writing them from scratch. Inheritance is one way to support the idea of *software reuse*. By using existing software components to create new ones, we capitalize on the effort that went into the design, implementation, and testing of the existing software.

Keep in mind that the word *class* comes from the idea of classifying groups of objects with similar characteristics. Classification schemes often use levels of classes that relate to each other. For example, all mammals share certain characteristics: They are warmblooded, have hair, and produce milk to feed their young. Now consider a subset of mammals, such as horses. All horses are mammals and have all of the characteristics of mammals, but they also have unique features that make them different from other mammals such as dogs.

If we translate this idea into software terms, an existing class called `Mammal` would have certain variables and methods that describe the state and behavior of mammals. A `Horse` class could be derived from the existing `Mammal` class, automatically inheriting the variables and methods contained in `Mammal`. The `Horse` class can refer to the inherited variables and methods as if they had been declared locally in that class. New variables and methods can then be added to the derived class to distinguish a horse from other mammals.

The original class that is used to derive a new one is called the *parent class*, *superclass*, or *base class*. The derived class is called a *child class*, or *subclass*. Java uses the reserved word `extends` to indicate that a new class is being derived from an existing class.

KEY CONCEPT

Inheritance creates an is-a relationship between the parent and child classes.

The process of inheritance should establish an *is-a relationship* between two classes. That is, the child class should be a more specific version of the parent. For example, a horse is a mammal. Not all mammals are horses, but all horses are mammals. For any class X that is derived from class Y, you should be able to say that "X is a Y." If such a statement doesn't make sense, then that relationship is probably not an appropriate use of inheritance.

Let's look at an example. The program shown in Listing 9.1 instantiates an object of class `Dictionary`, which is derived from a class called `Book`. In the `main` method, three methods are invoked through the `Dictionary` object: two that were declared locally in the `Dictionary` class and one that was inherited from the `Book` class.

The `Book` class (see Listing 9.2) is used to derive the `Dictionary` class (see Listing 9.3) using the reserved word `extends` in the header of `Dictionary`. The `Dictionary` class automatically inherits the definition of the `setPages` and `getPages` methods, as well as the `pages` variable. It is as if those methods and the `pages` variable were declared inside the `Dictionary` class. Note that, in the `Dictionary` class, the `computeRatio` method explicitly references the `pages` variable, even though the variable is declared in the `Book` class.

Also note that although the `Book` class is needed to create the definition of `Dictionary`, no `Book` object is ever instantiated in the program. An instance of a child class does not rely on an instance of the parent class.

Inheritance is a one-way street. The `Book` class cannot use variables or methods that are declared explicitly in the `Dictionary` class. For instance, if we created an object from the `Book` class, it could not be used to invoke the `setDefinitions` method. This restriction makes sense, because a child class is a more specific

LISTING 9.1

```
//********************************************************************
//  Words.java       Author: Lewis/Loftus
//
//  Demonstrates the use of an inherited method.
//********************************************************************

public class Words
{
   //-----------------------------------------------------------------
   //  Instantiates a derived class and invokes its inherited and
   //  local methods.
   //-----------------------------------------------------------------
   public static void main(String[] args)
   {
      Dictionary webster = new Dictionary();

      System.out.println("Number of pages: " + webster.getPages());

      System.out.println("Number of definitions: " +
                         webster.getDefinitions());

      System.out.println("Definitions per page: " +
                         webster.computeRatio());
   }
}
```

OUTPUT

```
Number of pages: 1500
Number of definitions: 52500
Definitions per page: 35.0
```

version of the parent class. A dictionary has pages, because all books have pages; but although a dictionary has definitions, not all books do.

Inheritance relationships are often represented in UML class diagrams. Figure 9.1 shows the inheritance relationship between the `Book` and `Dictionary` classes. An arrow with an open arrowhead is used to show inheritance in a UML diagram, with the arrow pointing from the child class to the parent class.

LISTING 9.2

```
//********************************************************************
//  Book.java       Author: Lewis/Loftus
//
//  Represents a book. Used as the parent of a derived class to
//  demonstrate inheritance.
//********************************************************************

public class Book
{
   protected int pages = 1500;

   //----------------------------------------------------------------
   //  Pages mutator.
   //----------------------------------------------------------------
   public void setPages(int numPages)
   {
      pages = numPages;
   }

   //----------------------------------------------------------------
   //  Pages accessor.
   //----------------------------------------------------------------
   public int getPages()
   {
      return pages;
   }
}
```

The `protected` Modifier

As we've seen, visibility modifiers are used to control access to the members of a class. This effect extends into the process of inheritance as well. Any public method or variable in a parent class can be explicitly referenced by name in the child class and through objects of that child class. On the other hand, private methods and variables of the parent class cannot be referenced in the child class or through an object of the child class.

However, if we declare a variable with public visibility so that a derived class can reference it, we violate the principle of encapsulation. Therefore, Java provides a third visibility modifier: `protected`. Note that the variable `pages` is declared with protected visibility in the `Book` class. When a variable or method is

LISTING 9.3

```
//********************************************************************
//  Dictionary.java       Author: Lewis/Loftus
//
//  Represents a dictionary, which is a book. Used to demonstrate
//  inheritance.
//********************************************************************

public class Dictionary extends Book
{
   private int definitions = 52500;

   //-----------------------------------------------------------------
   //  Prints a message using both local and inherited values.
   //-----------------------------------------------------------------
   public double computeRatio()
   {
      return  (double) definitions / pages;
   }

   //-----------------------------------------------------------------
   //  Definitions mutator.
   //-----------------------------------------------------------------
   public void setDefinitions(int numDefinitions)
   {
      definitions = numDefinitions;
   }

   //-----------------------------------------------------------------
   //  Definitions accessor.
   //-----------------------------------------------------------------
   public int getDefinitions()
   {
      return definitions;
   }
}
```

declared with protected visibility, a derived class can reference it. And protected visibility allows the class to retain some encapsulation properties. The encapsulation with protected visibility is not as tight as it would be if the variable or method were declared private, but it is better than if it were declared public. Specifically, a

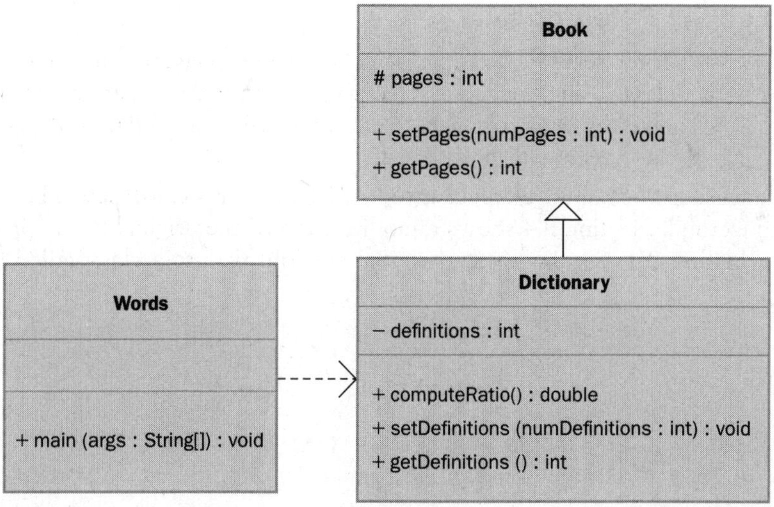

FIGURE 9.1 A UML class diagram showing an inheritance relationship

variable or method declared with protected visibility may be accessed by any class in the same package, in addition to being accessible by any derived classes. The relationships among all Java modifiers are explained completely in Appendix E.

KEY CONCEPT
Protected visibility provides the best possible encapsulation that permits inheritance.

In a UML diagram, protected visibility can be indicated by preceding the protected member with a hash mark (#). The `pages` variable of the `Book` class has this annotation in Figure 9.1.

Each variable or method retains the effect of its original visibility modifier. For example, the `setPages` method is still considered to be public in its inherited form in the `Dictionary` class.

VideoNote
Overview of inheritance.

Let's be clear about our terms. All methods and variables, even those declared with private visibility, are inherited by the child class. That is, their definitions exist and memory space is reserved for the variables. It's just that they can't be referenced by name. This issue is explored in more detail in Section 9.4.

Constructors, however, are not inherited. Constructors are special methods that are used to set up a particular type of object, so it doesn't make sense for a class called `Dictionary` to have a constructor called `Book`. But you can imagine that a child class may want to refer to the constructor of the parent class, which is one of the reasons for the `super` reference, described next.

The super Reference

KEY CONCEPT
A parent's constructor can be invoked using the super reference.

The reserved word super can be used in a class to refer to its parent class. Using the super reference, we can access a parent's members. Like the this reference, what the word super refers to depends on the class in which it is used.

One use of the super reference is to invoke a parent's constructor. Let's look at an example. Listing 9.4 shows a modification of the original Words program from Listing 9.1. Similar to the original version, we use a class called Book2

LISTING 9.4

```
//********************************************************************
//  Words2.java       Author: Lewis/Loftus
//
//  Demonstrates the use of the super reference.
//********************************************************************

public class Words2
{
   //-----------------------------------------------------------------
   //  Instantiates a derived class and invokes its inherited and
   //  local methods.
   //-----------------------------------------------------------------
   public static void main(String[] args)
   {
      Dictionary2 webster = new Dictionary2(1500, 52500);

      System.out.println("Number of pages: " + webster.getPages());

      System.out.println("Number of definitions: " +
                         webster.getDefinitions());

      System.out.println("Definitions per page: " +
                         webster.computeRatio());
   }
}
```

OUTPUT

```
Number of pages: 1500
Number of definitions: 52500
Definitions per page: 35.0
```

LISTING 9.5

```
//********************************************************************
//  Book2.java       Author: Lewis/Loftus
//
//  Represents a book. Used as the parent of a derived class to
//  demonstrate inheritance and the use of the super reference.
//********************************************************************

public class Book2
{
   protected int pages;

   //-----------------------------------------------------------------
   //  Constructor: Sets up the book with the specified number of
   //  pages.
   //-----------------------------------------------------------------
   public Book2(int numPages)
   {
      pages = numPages;
   }

   //-----------------------------------------------------------------
   //  Pages mutator.
   //-----------------------------------------------------------------
   public void setPages(int numPages)
   {
      pages = numPages;
   }

   //-----------------------------------------------------------------
   //  Pages accessor.
   //-----------------------------------------------------------------
   public int getPages()
   {
      return pages;
   }
}
```

(see Listing 9.5) as the parent of the derived class `Dictionary2` (see Listing 9.6). However, unlike earlier versions of these classes, `Book2` and `Dictionary2` have explicit constructors used to initialize their instance variables. The output of the `Words2` program is the same as it is for the original `Words` program.

LISTING 9.6

```
//********************************************************************
//  Dictionary2.java       Author: Lewis/Loftus
//
//  Represents a dictionary, which is a book. Used to demonstrate
//  the use of the super reference.
//********************************************************************

public class Dictionary2 extends Book2
{
   private int definitions;

   //-----------------------------------------------------------------
   //  Constructor: Sets up the dictionary with the specified number
   //  of pages and definitions.
   //-----------------------------------------------------------------
   public Dictionary2(int numPages, int numDefinitions)
   {
      super(numPages);

      definitions = numDefinitions;
   }

   //-----------------------------------------------------------------
   //  Prints a message using both local and inherited values.
   //-----------------------------------------------------------------
   public double computeRatio()
   {
      return (double) definitions / pages;
   }

   //-----------------------------------------------------------------
   //  Definitions mutator.
   //-----------------------------------------------------------------
   public void setDefinitions(int numDefinitions)
   {
      definitions = numDefinitions;
   }

   //-----------------------------------------------------------------
   //  Definitions accessor.
   //-----------------------------------------------------------------
```

LISTING 9.6 *continued*

```
    public int getDefinitions()
    {
       return definitions;
    }
}
```

The Dictionary2 constructor takes two integer values as parameters, representing the number of pages and definitions in the book. Because the Book2 class already has a constructor that performs the work to set up the parts of the dictionary that were inherited, we rely on that constructor to do that work. However, since the constructor is not inherited, we cannot invoke it directly, and so we use the super reference to get to it in the parent class. The Dictionary2 constructor then proceeds to initialize its definitions variable.

In this case, it would have been just as easy to set the pages variable explicitly in the Dictionary2 constructor instead of using super to call the Book2 constructor. However, it is good practice to let each class "take care of itself." If we choose to change the way that the Book2 constructor sets up its pages variable, we would also have to remember to make that change in Dictionary2. By using the super reference, a change made in Book2 is automatically reflected in Dictionary2.

A child's constructor is responsible for calling its parent's constructor. Generally, the first line of a constructor should use the super reference call to a constructor of the parent class. If no such call exists, Java will automatically make a call to super() at the beginning of the constructor. This rule ensures that a parent class initializes its variables before the child class constructor begins to execute. Using the super reference to invoke a parent's constructor can be done only in the child's constructor, and if included it must be the first line of the constructor.

The super reference can also be used to reference other variables and methods defined in the parent's class. We use this technique in later sections of this chapter.

Multiple Inheritance

Java's approach to inheritance is called *single inheritance.* This term means that a derived class can have only one parent. Some object-oriented languages allow a

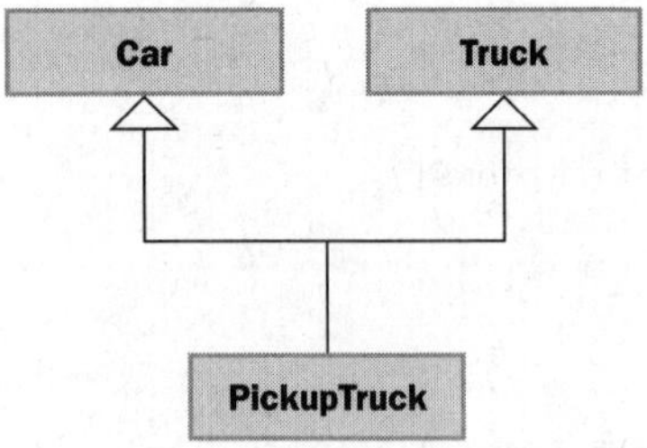

FIGURE 9.2 A UML class diagram showing multiple inheritance

child class to have multiple parents. This approach is called *multiple inheritance* and is occasionally useful for describing objects that are in between two categories or classes. For example, suppose we had a class `Car` and a class `Truck` and we wanted to create a new class called `PickupTruck`. A pickup truck is somewhat like a car and somewhat like a truck. With single inheritance, we must decide whether it is better to derive the new class from `Car` or `Truck`. With multiple inheritance, it can be derived from both, as shown in Figure 9.2.

Multiple inheritance works well in some situations, but it comes with a price. What if both `Truck` and `Car` have methods with the same name? Which method would `PickupTruck` inherit? The answer to this question is complex, and it depends on the rules of the language that supports multiple inheritance.

The designers of the Java language explicitly decided not to support multiple inheritance. Instead, we can rely on interfaces to provide the best features of multiple inheritance without the added complexity. Although a Java class can be derived from only one parent class, it can implement multiple interfaces. Therefore, we can interact with a particular class in specific ways while inheriting the core information from one parent class.

SELF-REVIEW QUESTIONS *(see answers in Appendix L)*

SR 9.1 Describe the relationship between a parent class and a child class.

SR 9.2 How does inheritance support software reuse?

SR 9.3 What relationship should every class derivation represent?

SR 9.4 What does the `protected` modifier accomplish?

SR 9.5 Why is the `super` reference important to a child class?

SR 9.6 Define a class `SchoolBook2` that extends `Book2` to include an attribute indicating the age (4 through 16) that a book targets. The constructor accepts the age as a parameter. The class also provides a `level` method that returns a string as follows: "Pre-school" if the target age is 4 through 6, "Early" if the target age is 7 through 9, "Middle" if the target age is 10 through 12, and "Upper" if the target age is 13 through 16.

SR 9.7 What is the difference between single inheritance and multiple inheritance?

9.2 Overriding Methods

When a child class defines a method with the same name and signature as a method in the parent class, we say that the child's version *overrides* the parent's version in favor of its own. The need for overriding occurs often in inheritance situations.

KEY CONCEPT

A child class can override (redefine) the parent's definition of an inherited method.

The program in Listing 9.7 provides a simple demonstration of method overriding in Java. The `Messages` class contains a `main` method that instantiates two objects: one from class `Thought` and one from class `Advice`. The `Thought` class is the parent of the `Advice` class.

LISTING 9.7

```
//********************************************************************
//  Messages.java       Author: Lewis/Loftus
//
//  Demonstrates the use of an overridden method.
//********************************************************************
public class Messages
{
   //-----------------------------------------------------------------
   //  Creates two objects and invokes the message method in each.
   //-----------------------------------------------------------------
   public static void main(String[] args)
   {
      Thought parked = new Thought();
      Advice dates = new Advice();

      parked.message();

      dates.message();   // overridden
   }
}
```

LISTING 9.7 *continued*

OUTPUT

```
I feel like I'm diagonally parked in a parallel universe.

Warning: Dates in calendar are closer than they appear.

I feel like I'm diagonally parked in a parallel universe.
```

Both the `Thought` class (see Listing 9.8) and the `Advice` class (see Listing 9.9) contain a definition for a method called `message`. The version of `message` defined in the `Thought` class is inherited by `Advice`, but `Advice` overrides it with an alternative version. The new version of the method prints out an entirely different message and then invokes the parent's version of the `message` method using the `super` reference.

The object that is used to invoke a method determines which version of the method is actually executed. When `message` is invoked using the `parked` object in

LISTING 9.8

```
//********************************************************************
//  Thought.java       Author: Lewis/Loftus
//
//  Represents a stray thought. Used as the parent of a derived
//  class to demonstrate the use of an overridden method.
//********************************************************************

public class Thought
{
   //-----------------------------------------------------------------
   //  Prints a message.
   //-----------------------------------------------------------------
   public void message()
   {
      System.out.println("I feel like I'm diagonally parked in a " +
                         "parallel universe.");

      System.out.println();
   }
}
```

LISTING 9.9

```
//********************************************************************
//  Advice.java       Author: Lewis/Loftus
//
//  Represents some thoughtful advice. Used to demonstrate the use
//  of an overridden method.
//********************************************************************

public class Advice extends Thought
{
   //-----------------------------------------------------------------
   //  Prints a message. This method overrides the parent's version.
   //-----------------------------------------------------------------
   public void message()
   {
      System.out.println("Warning: Dates in calendar are closer " +
                         "than they appear.");

      System.out.println();

      super.message();   // explicitly invokes the parent's version
   }
}
```

the `main` method, the `Thought` version of `message` is executed. When `message` is invoked using the `dates` object, the `Advice` version of `message` is executed.

A method can be defined with the `final` modifier. A child class cannot override a final method. This technique is used to ensure that a derived class uses a particular definition of a method.

Method overriding is a key element in object-oriented design. It allows two objects that are related by inheritance to use the same naming conventions for methods that accomplish the same general task in different ways. Overriding becomes even more important when it comes to polymorphism, which is discussed in Chapter 10.

Shadowing Variables

It is possible, although not recommended, for a child class to declare a variable with the same name as one that is inherited from the parent. Note the distinction between redeclaring a variable and simply giving an inherited variable a particular value. If a variable of the same name is declared in a child class, it is called a *shadow variable*. It is similar in concept to the process of overriding methods but creates confusing subtleties.

Because an inherited variable is already available to the child class, there is usually no good reason to redeclare it. Someone reading code with a shadowed variable will find two different declarations that seem to apply to a variable used in the child class. This confusion causes problems and serves no useful purpose. A redeclaration of a particular variable name could change its type, but that is usually unnecessary. In general, shadowing variables should be avoided.

SELF-REVIEW QUESTIONS *(see answers in Appendix L)*

SR 9.8 Why would a child class override one or more of the methods of its parent class?

SR 9.9 True or False? Explain.

a. A child class may define a method with the same name as a method in the parent class.
b. A child class can override the constructor of the parent class.
c. A child class can override a `final` method of the parent class.
d. It is considered poor design when a child class overrides a method from the parent class.
e. A child class may define a variable with the same name as a variable in the parent class.

9.3 Class Hierarchies

KEY CONCEPT
The child of one class can be the parent of one or more other classes, creating a class hierarchy.

A child class derived from one parent can be the parent of its own child class. Furthermore, multiple classes can be derived from a single parent. Therefore, inheritance relationships often develop

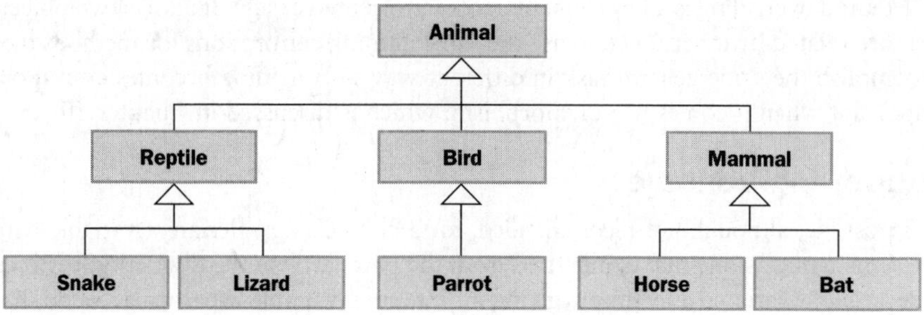

FIGURE 9.3 A UML class diagram showing a class hierarchy

into *class hierarchies*. Figure 9.3 shows a class hierarchy that includes the inheritance relationship between the `Mammal` and `Horse` classes.

There is no limit to the number of children a class can have or to the number of levels to which a class hierarchy can extend. Two children of the same parent are called *siblings*. Although siblings share the characteristics passed on by their common parent, they are not related by inheritance, because one is not used to derive the other.

In class hierarchies, common features should be kept as high in the hierarchy as reasonably possible. That way, the only characteristics explicitly established in a child class are those that make the class distinct from its parent and from its siblings. This approach maximizes the potential to reuse classes. It also facilitates maintenance activities, because when changes are made to the parent, they are automatically reflected in the descendants. Always remember to maintain the is-a relationship when building class hierarchies.

The inheritance mechanism is transitive. That is, a parent passes along a trait to a child class, and that child class passes it along to its children, and so on. An inherited feature might have originated in the immediate parent or possibly several levels higher in a more distant ancestor class.

KEY CONCEPT
Common features should be located as high in a class hierarchy as is reasonably possible.

There is no single best hierarchy organization for all situations. The decisions you make when you are designing a class hierarchy restrict and guide more detailed design decisions and implementation options, so you must make them carefully.

Earlier in this chapter we discussed a class hierarchy that organized animals by their major biological classifications, such as `Mammal`, `Bird`, and `Reptile`. However, in a different situation, the same animals might logically be organized in a different way. For example, as shown in Figure 9.4, the class hierarchy might be organized around a function of the animals, such as their ability to fly. In this case, a `Parrot` class and a `Bat` class would be siblings derived from a general `FlyingAnimal` class. This class hierarchy is as valid and reasonable as the original one. The needs of the programs that use the classes will determine which is best for the particular situation.

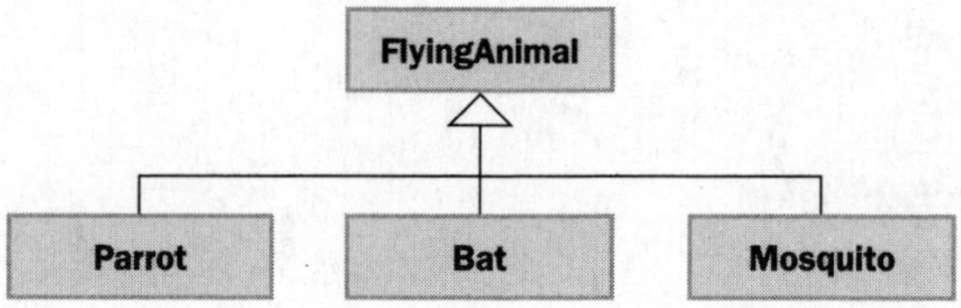

FIGURE 9.4 An alternative hierarchy for organizing animals

The `Object` Class

In Java, all classes are derived ultimately from the `Object` class. If a class definition doesn't use the `extends` clause to derive itself explicitly from another class, then that class is automatically derived from the `Object` class by default. Therefore, the following two class definitions are equivalent:

```
class Thing
{
   //  whatever
}
```

and

```
class Thing extends Object
{
   //  whatever
}
```

KEY CONCEPT
All Java classes are derived, directly or indirectly, from the `Object` class.

Because all classes are derived from `Object`, all public methods of `Object` are inherited by every Java class. They can be invoked through any object created in any Java program. The `Object` class is defined in the `java.lang` package of the Java standard class library. Figure 9.5 lists some of the methods of the `Object` class.

As it turns out, we've been using `Object` methods quite often in our examples. The `toString` method, for instance, is defined in the `Object` class, so the `toString` method can be called on any object. As we've seen several times, when a `println` method is called with an object parameter, `toString` is called to determine what to print.

KEY CONCEPT
The `toString` and `equals` methods are inherited by every class in every Java program.

Therefore, when we define a `toString` method in a class, we are actually overriding an inherited definition. The definition for `toString` that is provided by the `Object` class returns a string containing the

```
boolean equals(Object obj)
    Returns true if this object is an alias of the specified object.

String toString()
    Returns a string representation of this object.

Object clone()
    Creates and returns a copy of this object.
```

FIGURE 9.5 Some methods of the `Object` class

object's class name followed by a numeric value that is unique for that object. Usually, we override the `Object` version of `toString` to fit our own needs. The `String` class has overridden the `toString` method so that it returns its stored string value.

We are also overriding an inherited method when we define an `equals` method for a class. As we've discussed previously, the purpose of the `equals` method is to determine whether two objects are equal. The definition of the `equals` method provided by the `Object` class returns true if the two object references actually refer to the same object (that is, if they are aliases). Classes often override the inherited definition of the `equals` method in favor of a more appropriate definition. For instance, the `String` class overrides `equals` so that it returns true only if both strings contain the same characters in the same order.

Abstract Classes

An *abstract class* represents a generic concept in a class hierarchy. An abstract class cannot be instantiated and usually contains one or more *abstract methods*, which have no definition. We've discussed abstract methods in Chapter 7 when they are used to define a Java interface. An abstract class is similar to an interface in some ways. However, unlike interfaces, an abstract class can contain methods that are not abstract. It can also contain data declarations other than constants.

A class is declared as abstract by including the `abstract` modifier in the class header. Any class that contains one or more abstract methods must be declared as abstract. In abstract classes (unlike interfaces), the `abstract` modifier must be applied to each abstract method. A class declared as abstract does not have to contain abstract methods.

KEY CONCEPT

An abstract class cannot be instantiated. It represents a concept on which other classes can build their definitions.

Abstract classes serve as placeholders in a class hierarchy. As the name implies, an abstract class represents an abstract entity that is usually insufficiently defined to be useful by itself. Instead, an abstract class may contain a partial description that is inherited by all of its descendants in the class hierarchy. Its children, which are more specific, fill in the gaps.

Consider the class hierarchy shown in Figure 9.6. The `Vehicle` class at the top of the hierarchy may be too generic for a particular application. Therefore we may choose to implement it as an abstract class. In UML diagrams, abstract class names are shown in italic.

Concepts that apply to all vehicles can be represented in the `Vehicle` class and are inherited by its descendants. That way, each of its descendants doesn't have to define the same concept redundantly (and perhaps inconsistently). For example, we may say that all vehicles have a particular speed. Therefore we declare a `speed` variable in the `Vehicle` class, and all specific vehicles below it in the hierarchy

VideoNote

Example using a class hierarchy.

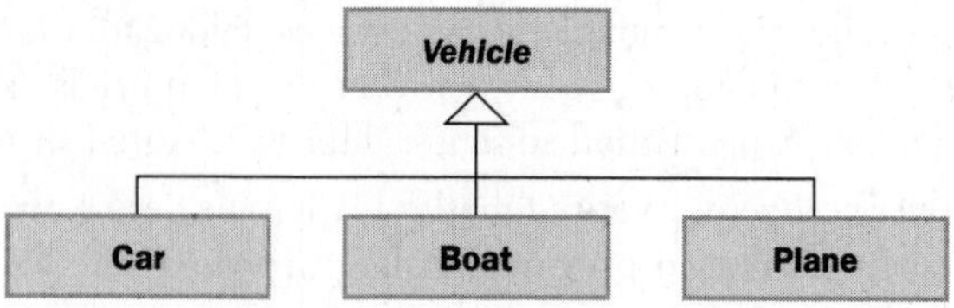

FIGURE 9.6 A vehicle class hierarchy

automatically have that variable because of inheritance. Any change we make to the representation of the speed of a vehicle is automatically reflected in all descendant classes. Similarly, we may declare an abstract method called `fuelConsumption`, whose purpose is to calculate how quickly fuel is being consumed by a particular vehicle. The details of the `fuelConsumption` method must be defined by each type of vehicle, but the `Vehicle` class establishes that all vehicles consume fuel and provides a consistent way to compute that value.

Some concepts don't apply to all vehicles, so we wouldn't represent those concepts at the `Vehicle` level. For instance, we wouldn't include a variable called `numberOfWheels` in the `Vehicle` class, because not all vehicles have wheels. The child classes for which wheels are appropriate can add that concept at the appropriate level in the hierarchy.

There are no restrictions as to where in a class hierarchy an abstract class can be defined. Usually, they are located at the upper levels of a class hierarchy. However, it is possible to derive an abstract class from a nonabstract parent.

Usually, a child of an abstract class will provide a specific definition for an abstract method inherited from its parent. Note that this is just a specific case of overriding a method, giving a different definition than the one the parent provides. If a child of an abstract class does not give a definition for every abstract method that it inherits from its parent, then the child class is also considered abstract.

KEY CONCEPT

A class derived from an abstract parent must override all of its parent's abstract methods, or the derived class will also be considered abstract.

Note that it would be a contradiction for an abstract method to be modified as `final` or `static`. Because a final method cannot be overridden in subclasses, an abstract final method would have no way of being given a definition in subclasses. A static method can be invoked using the class name without declaring an object of the class. Because abstract methods have no implementation, an abstract static method would make no sense.

Choosing which classes and methods to make abstract is an important part of the design process. You should make such choices only after careful consideration. By using abstract classes wisely, you can create flexible, extensible software designs.

Interface Hierarchies

The concept of inheritance can be applied to interfaces as well as classes. That is, one interface can be derived from another interface. These relationships can form an *interface hierarchy*, which is similar to a class hierarchy. Inheritance relationships between interfaces are shown in UML diagrams using the same connection (an arrow with an open arrowhead) as they are with classes.

> **KEY CONCEPT**
> Inheritance can be applied to interfaces so that one interface can be derived from another.

When a parent interface is used to derive a child interface, the child inherits all abstract methods and constants of the parent. Any class that implements the child interface must implement all of the methods. There are no visibility issues when dealing with inheritance between interfaces (as there are with protected and private members of a class), because all members of an interface are public.

Class hierarchies and interface hierarchies do not overlap. That is, an interface cannot be used to derive a class, and a class cannot be used to derive an interface. A class and an interface interact only when a class is designed to implement a particular interface.

SELF-REVIEW QUESTIONS *(see answers in Appendix L)*

SR 9.10 Draw a UML class diagram showing an inheritance hierarchy containing classes that represent different types of food. Show some appropriate variables and method names for at least two of these classes.

SR 9.11 What is the significance of the `Object` class?

SR 9.12 Which is the only Java class that does not have a parent class? Explain.

SR 9.13 What is the role of an abstract class?

SR 9.14 Why is it a contradiction to define a `final`, `abstract` class?

SR 9.15 What is an interface hierarchy?

9.4 Visibility

As we discussed earlier in this chapter, all variables and methods, even private members, that are defined in a parent class are inherited by a child class. They exist for an object of a derived class, even though they can't be referenced directly. They can, however, be referenced indirectly.

> **KEY CONCEPT**
> Private members are inherited by the child class, but cannot be referenced directly by name. They may be used indirectly, however.

Let's look at an example that demonstrates this situation. The program shown in Listing 9.10 contains a `main` method that instantiates a `Pizza`

LISTING 9.10

```
//********************************************************************
//  FoodAnalyzer.java       Author: Lewis/Loftus
//
//  Demonstrates indirect access to inherited private members.
//********************************************************************

public class FoodAnalyzer
{
   //-----------------------------------------------------------------
   //  Instantiates a Pizza object and prints its calories per
   //  serving.
   //-----------------------------------------------------------------
   public static void main(String[] args)
   {
      Pizza special = new Pizza(275);

      System.out.println("Calories per serving: " +
                         special.caloriesPerServing());
   }
}
```

OUTPUT

```
Calories per serving: 309
```

object and invokes a method to determine how many calories the pizza has per serving due to its fat content.

The FoodItem class shown in Listing 9.11 represents a generic type of food. The constructor of FoodItem accepts the number of grams of fat and the number of servings of that food. The calories method returns the number of calories due to fat, which the caloriesPerServing method invokes to help compute the number of fat calories per serving.

The Pizza class, shown in Listing 9.12, is derived from the FoodItem class, but it adds no special functionality or data. Its constructor calls the constructor of FoodItem using the super reference, asserting that there are eight servings per pizza.

The Pizza object called special in the main method is used to invoke the method caloriesPerServing, which is defined as a public method of FoodItem. Note that caloriesPerServing calls calories, which is declared with private visibility. Furthermore, calories references the variable fatGrams and the constant CALORIES_PER_GRAM, which are also declared with private visibility.

LISTING 9.11

```java
//********************************************************************
//  FoodItem.java       Author: Lewis/Loftus
//
//  Represents an item of food. Used as the parent of a derived class
//  to demonstrate indirect referencing.
//********************************************************************

public class FoodItem
{
   final private int CALORIES_PER_GRAM = 9;
   private int fatGrams;
   protected int servings;

   //-----------------------------------------------------------------
   //  Sets up this food item with the specified number of fat grams
   //  and number of servings.
   //-----------------------------------------------------------------
   public FoodItem(int numFatGrams, int numServings)
   {
      fatGrams = numFatGrams;
      servings = numServings;
   }

   //-----------------------------------------------------------------
   //  Computes and returns the number of calories in this food item
   //  due to fat.
   //-----------------------------------------------------------------
   private int calories()
   {
      return fatGrams * CALORIES_PER_GRAM;
   }

   //-----------------------------------------------------------------
   //  Computes and returns the number of fat calories per serving.
   //-----------------------------------------------------------------
   public int caloriesPerServing()
   {
      return  (calories() / servings);
   }
}
```

LISTING 9.12

```
//********************************************************************
//  Pizza.java       Author: Lewis/Loftus
//
//  Represents a pizza, which is a food item. Used to demonstrate
//  indirect referencing through inheritance.
//********************************************************************

public class Pizza extends FoodItem
{
   //-----------------------------------------------------------------
   //  Sets up a pizza with the specified amount of fat (assumes
   //  eight servings).
   //-----------------------------------------------------------------
   public Pizza(int fatGrams)
   {
      super(fatGrams, 8);
   }
}
```

Even though the `Pizza` class cannot explicitly reference `calories`, `fatGrams`, or `CALORIES_PER_GRAM`, they are available for use indirectly when the `Pizza` object needs them. A `Pizza` object cannot be used to invoke the `calories` method, but it can call a method that can. Note that a `FoodItem` object was never created or needed.

SELF-REVIEW QUESTIONS *(see answers in Appendix L)*

SR 9.16 Are all members of a parent class inherited by the child? Explain.

SR 9.17 Could the `Pizza` class refer to the variable servings explicitly? What about the `calories` method? Explain.

9.5 Designing for Inheritance

KEY CONCEPT
Software design must carefully and specifically address inheritance.

As a major characteristic of object-oriented software, inheritance must be carefully and specifically addressed during software design. A little thought about inheritance relationships can lead to a far more elegant design, which pays huge dividends in the long term.

Throughout this chapter, several design issues have been addressed in the discussion of the nuts and bolts of inheritance in Java. The following list summarizes some of the inheritance issues that you should keep in mind during the program design stage:

- Every derivation should be an is-a relationship. The child should be a more specific version of the parent.
- Design a class hierarchy to capitalize on reuse and potential reuse in the future.
- As classes and objects are identified in the problem domain, find their commonality. Push common features as high in the class hierarchy as appropriate for consistency and ease of maintenance.
- Override methods as appropriate to tailor or change the functionality of a child.
- Add new variables to the child class as needed, but don't shadow (redefine) any inherited variables.
- Allow each class to manage its own data. Therefore, use the `super` reference to invoke a parent's constructor and to call overridden versions of methods if appropriate.
- Use interfaces to create a class that serves multiple roles (simulating multiple inheritance).
- Design a class hierarchy to fit the needs of the application, with attention to how it may be useful in the future.
- Even if there are no current uses for them, override general methods such as `toString` and `equals` appropriately in child classes so that the inherited versions don't cause unintentional problems later.
- Use abstract classes to specify a common class interface for the concrete classes lower in the hierarchy.
- Use visibility modifiers carefully to provide the needed access in derived classes without violating encapsulation.

Restricting Inheritance

We've seen the `final` modifier used in declarations to create constants many times. The other uses of the `final` modifier involve inheritance and can have a significant influence on software design. Specifically, the `final` modifier can be used to curtail the abilities related to inheritance.

Earlier in this chapter, we mentioned that a method can be declared as `final`, which means it cannot be overridden in any classes that extend the one it is in. A final method is often used to insist that particular functionality be used in all child classes.

> **KEY CONCEPT**
> The `final` modifier can be used to restrict inheritance.

The `final` modifier can also be applied to an entire class. A final class cannot be extended at all. Consider the following declaration:

```
public final class Standards
{
   // whatever
}
```

Given this declaration, the `Standards` class cannot be used in the `extends` clause of another class. The compiler will generate an error message in such a case. The `Standards` class can be used normally, but it cannot be the parent of another class.

Using the `final` modifier to restrict inheritance abilities is a key design decision. It should be done in situations in which a child class could possibly be used to change functionality that you, as the designer, specifically want to be handled a certain way. This issue comes up again in the discussion of polymorphism in Chapter 10.

SELF-REVIEW QUESTIONS *(see answers in Appendix L)*

SR 9.18 What does it mean for an inheritance derivation to represent an is-a relationship?

SR 9.19 Where should common features of classes appear in a class hierarchy? Why?

SR 9.20 How can you define a class with multiple roles?

SR 9.21 Why should you override the `toString` method of a parent in its child class, even when the method is not invoked through the child by your current applications?

SR 9.22 How can the `final` modifier be used to restrict inheritance? Why would you do this?

9.6 Inheritance in JavaFX

In Chapter 3, when we first began discussing JavaFX applications, we established the analogy of a scene being set on a stage, and that a `Scene` object had a root node, to which other nodes in the scene are added, forming a scene graph. Depending on what they are, those nodes, in turn, may hold other nodes.

KEY CONCEPT
The classes that define the nodes of a JavaFX scene are organized into a class hierarchy.

This approach is made possible by the inheritance relationships among many of the classes in the JavaFX API. Part of that hierarchy, with the `Node` class at the top, is shown in Figure 9.7. The `Node` class is derived directly from the `java.lang.Object` class. Not all derived classes are shown in this hierarchy, but it presents a representative sample.

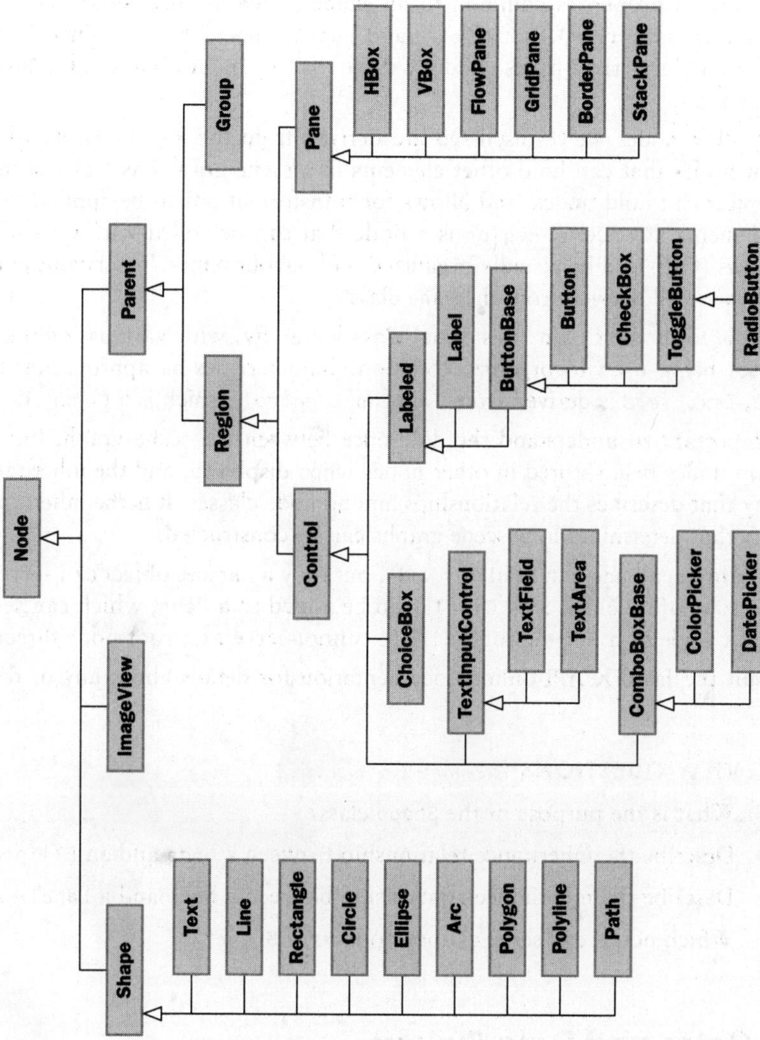

FIGURE 9.7 Part of the Node class hierarchy in the JavaFX API

Remember that inheritance establishes an is-a relationship, and that relationship applies to all derived classes. For example, a `Polygon` is a `Shape`, which is derived from `Node`. So a `Polygon` is also a `Node`. In fact, all classes in Figure 9.7 are nodes.

All of the classes that define geometric shapes are derived from the `Shape` class, which manages properties common to all shapes, such as their stroke and fill. Methods such as `setFill`, `setStroke`, and `setStrokeWidth` are defined in the `Shape` class and inherited by its children. Note that an `ImageView` is not a `Shape`, but it is a `Node`.

Most other nodes we've discussed are derived from the `Parent` class, which represent nodes that can hold other elements in a scene graph. As we've seen, a `Group` object can hold nodes, and allows for transformations to be applied to all group elements at once. A `Region` is a node that can be styled with Cascading Style Sheets (CSS) and be visually organized with layout panes. The layout panes themselves are all derived from the `Pane` class.

Controls form their own substantial class hierarchy, with various intermediate classes being used to organize common characteristics as appropriate. For example, `TextField` is derived from `TextInputControl`, which is a `Control`.

It's important to understand the difference between the scene graph, formed by certain nodes being stored in other nodes when displayed, and the inheritance hierarchy that describes the relationships among node classes. It is the inheritance hierarchy that determines how scene graphs can be constructed.

For example, a `Pane` can hold any `Node`, but only a `Parent` object can serve as the root node of a `Scene`. So a `Circle` can be added to a `Pane`, which can serve as the root node of a `Scene`, but a `Circle` cannot serve as a root node directly.

Consult the JavaFX API online documentation for details about any of these classes.

SELF-REVIEW QUESTIONS *(see answers in Appendix L)*

SR 9.23 What is the purpose of the `Shape` class?

SR 9.24 Describe the inheritance relationship between a `Node` and an `Ellipse`.

SR 9.25 Describe the inheritance relationship between a `Node` and a `Label`.

SR 9.26 Which nodes can serve as root nodes of a `Scene`?

9.7 Color and Date Pickers

The JavaFX API includes the `ColorPicker` class which represents a control that lets the user select a color. The control appears as a single field displaying the current color and its corresponding RGB value in hexadecimal.

When clicked, a color picker displays a drop-down palette of colors from which to choose. If none of the palette colors will do, you can also pick a custom color from a more complicated selection pane, or specify the color using RGB values or another color representation model.

Similarly, a `DatePicker` object allows the user to select a calendar date. Like the color picker, a date picker appears as a single field. It displays the currently selected date in m/d/y format by default. When clicked, the date picker displays a drop-down calendar that allows the user to change months and years, and ultimately click on a specific date.

KEY CONCEPT

Color and date pickers are controls that allow the user to specify a color or calendar date, respectively.

The program in Listing 9.13 demonstrates a date picker and a color picker. When a date is selected, a message below the picker fields displays the corresponding day of the week. When a color is selected, the message fill color changes accordingly.

LISTING 9.13

```
import java.time.LocalDate;
import javafx.application.Application;
import javafx.event.ActionEvent;
import javafx.geometry.Pos;
import javafx.scene.Scene;
import javafx.scene.control.ColorPicker;
import javafx.scene.control.DatePicker;
import javafx.scene.layout.HBox;
import javafx.scene.layout.VBox;
import javafx.scene.paint.Color;
import javafx.scene.text.Font;
import javafx.scene.text.FontPosture;
import javafx.scene.text.FontWeight;
import javafx.scene.text.Text;
import javafx.stage.Stage;

//************************************************************************
//  PickerDemo.java       Author: Lewis/Loftus
//
//  Demonstrates the use of color picker and date picker controls.
//************************************************************************

public class PickerDemo extends Application
{
    private Text message;
    private DatePicker datePicker;
    private ColorPicker colorPicker;
```

LISTING 9.13 *continued*

```
//--------------------------------------------------------------------
//  Allows the user to select a date and a color. A Text object
//  displays the day of the week in the color specified.
//--------------------------------------------------------------------
public void start(Stage primaryStage)
{
   datePicker = new DatePicker(LocalDate.now());
   datePicker.setOnAction(this::processDateChoice);

   colorPicker = new ColorPicker(Color.BLACK);
   colorPicker.setOnAction(this::processColorChoice);

   message = new Text("HAPPY " + LocalDate.now().getDayOfWeek());
   message.setFont(Font.font("Helvetica", FontWeight.BOLD,
      FontPosture.REGULAR, 24));

   HBox pickers = new HBox(datePicker, colorPicker);
   pickers.setSpacing(15);
   pickers.setAlignment(Pos.CENTER);

   VBox root = new VBox();
   root.setStyle("-fx-background-color: white");
   root.setSpacing(20);
   root.setAlignment(Pos.CENTER);
   root.getChildren().addAll(pickers, message);

   Scene scene = new Scene(root, 400, 150);

   primaryStage.setTitle("Picker Demo");
   primaryStage.setScene(scene);
   primaryStage.show();
}

//--------------------------------------------------------------------
//  Gets the value of the date from the date picker and updates the
//  message with the corresponding day of the week.
//--------------------------------------------------------------------
public void processDateChoice(ActionEvent event)
{
   LocalDate date = datePicker.getValue();
   message.setText("HAPPY " + date.getDayOfWeek());
}
```

LISTING 9.13 *continued*

```
   //-----------------------------------------------------------------
   //  Gets the color specified in the color picker and sets the
   //  color of the displayed message.
   //-----------------------------------------------------------------
   public void processColorChoice(ActionEvent event)
   {
      message.setFill(colorPicker.getValue());
   }
}
```

DISPLAY

This program makes use of the `java.time.LocalDate` class, which represents a calendar date. Among other, the `LocalDate` class has a static method called `now` that returns the current date, and an object method called `getDayOfWeek` that returns the day of the week corresponding to the date.

If no date is specified when a `DatePicker` object is instantiated, the field will initially be blank. In this program, however, the current date is passed to the `DatePicker` constructor to set the initial date. If no color is specified when a `ColorPicker` is created, the default color is white. This example passes the color black to the `ColorPicker` constructor to match the initial color of the message.

In this program, two separate action event handler methods are used to process a selection made using the date picker and color picker. Both use the `getValue` method of the appropriate picker to get the current value selected by the user. The `getValue` method of a color picker returns a `Color` object, while the `getValue` method of a date picker returns a `LocalDate` object.

SELF-REVIEW QUESTIONS *(see answers in Appendix L)*

SR 9.27 What are some ways a color picker allows the user to specify a color?

SR 9.28 What does the `getValue` method of a `DatePicker` object return? What does the `getValue` method of a `ColorPicker` object return?

9.8 Dialog Boxes

KEY CONCEPT
A dialog box is a pop-up window that allows brief, specific user interaction.

A *dialog box* is a window that pops up on top of any currently active window so that the user can interact with it. A dialog box can serve a variety of purposes, such as conveying some information, confirming an action, or allowing the user to enter some information. Usually, a dialog box has a solitary purpose, and the user's interaction with it is brief.

Support for dialog boxes in GUIs comes from a few classes in the JavaFX API. The `Alert` class provides support for several basic dialog boxes that can be easily created and displayed. There are several types of alerts, specified by the `Alert.AlertType` enumerated type:

- `AlertType.INFORMATION`—conveys information
- `AlertType.CONFIRMATION`—allows the user to confirm an action
- `AlertType.WARNING`—conveys a warning
- `AlertType.ERROR`—indicates something has gone wrong

The differences in the alert types include the title, header, buttons, and graphic used. All of these elements can be tailored if desired.

Two other classes that define dialog boxes in JavaFX are the `TextInputDialog` class and the `ChoiceDialog` class. They allow the user to enter input using a text field and a drop-down choice box, respectively.

The program in Listing 9.14 uses dialog boxes exclusively to interact with the user. It first presents the user with a `TextInputDialog` that prompts the user to enter an integer. After the user presses the OK button, a second dialog box appears, informing the user whether the numbered entered was even or odd. After the user dismisses that box, a third dialog box appears to determine whether the user would like to test another number.

LISTING 9.14

```
import java.util.Optional;
import javafx.application.Application;
import javafx.scene.control.Alert;
```

LISTING 9.14 *continued*

```
import javafx.scene.control.Alert.AlertType;
import javafx.scene.control.ButtonType;
import javafx.scene.control.TextInputDialog;
import javafx.stage.Stage;

//************************************************************************
//  EvenOdd.java       Author: Lewis/Loftus
//
//  Demonstrates the use of information and confirmation alerts, as well
//  as text input dialog boxes.
//************************************************************************

public class EvenOdd extends Application
{
   //---------------------------------------------------------------------
   //  Prompts the user for an integer, informs the user if that value
   //  is even or odd, then asks if the user would like to process
   //  another value. All interaction is performed using dialog boxes.
   //---------------------------------------------------------------------
   public void start(Stage primaryStage) throws Exception
   {
      boolean doAnother = true;

      while (doAnother)
      {
         TextInputDialog inputDialog = new TextInputDialog();
         inputDialog.setHeaderText(null);
         inputDialog.setTitle(null);
         inputDialog.setContentText("Enter an integer:");
         Optional<String> numString = inputDialog.showAndWait();

         if (numString.isPresent())
         {
            int num = Integer.parseInt(numString.get());

            String result = "That number is " +
               ((num % 2 == 0) ? "even." : "odd.");

            Alert answerDialog = new Alert(AlertType.INFORMATION);
            answerDialog.setHeaderText(null);
            answerDialog.setContentText(result);
            answerDialog.showAndWait();

            Alert confirmDialog = new Alert(AlertType.CONFIRMATION);
            confirmDialog.setHeaderText(null);
```

LISTING 9.14 *continued*

```
              confirmDialog.setContentText("Do another?");
              Optional<ButtonType> another = confirmDialog.showAndWait();

              if (another.get() != ButtonType.OK)
                  doAnother = false;
          }
          else
             doAnother = false;
      }
   }
}
```

DISPLAY

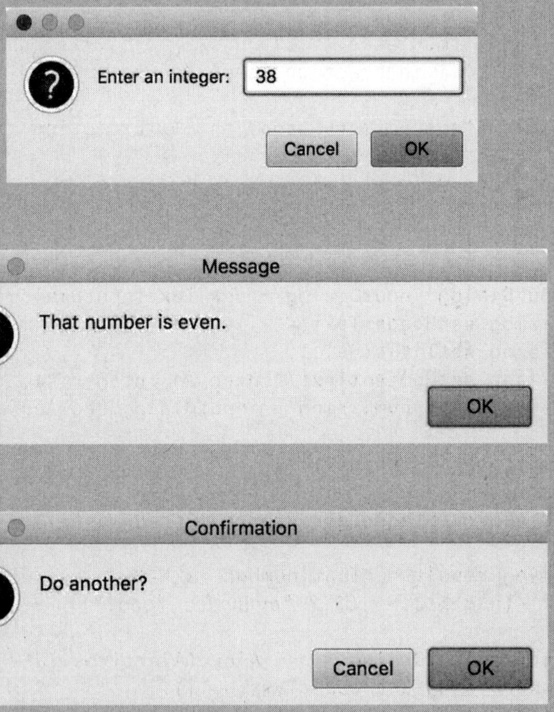

The headers for all of the dialog boxes shown in Listing 9.14 are set to `null` to keep them small and simple. The title (the text in the title bar) on the first one is also set to `null`, but on the others the default value is used.

After the first dialog box is set up, its `showAndWait` method is called, which causes the program to block at that point, waiting for the user to enter a value and press a button. When the user presses a button, this method returns an `Optional<String>` object that represents the text entered in the text field.

If the user entered something into the text field, it is converted to an integer, then the program determines if it is even or odd using a conditional statement. The appropriate text is used to set up an information `Alert`, then it is displayed using its `showAndWait` method. This time, its return value is ignored.

The third dialog box is set up and displayed, again using the `showAndWait` method. If the user presses the OK button, loop executes another time to process another number. If the user presses the Cancel button, or simply closes the dialog window, the `doAnother` `boolean` variable is set to false, and the loop terminates.

The `Optional` class is simply a container for a particular type of value. The value returned by the `showAndWait` method of a `TextInputDialog` is an `Optional<String>`. For a confirmation `Alert`, the value returned by `showAndWait` is an `Optional<ButtonType>`. By setting it up this way, the `showAndWait` method of any dialog box returns the same type of object (an `Optional` object), but it contains whatever type of value is appropriate for that interaction.

File Choosers

A specialized dialog box called a *file chooser* allows the user to select a file from a hard drive or other storage medium. You have probably run many programs that allow you to specify a file using a similar dialog box.

The program in Listing 9.15 displays a file chooser dialog box to the user. When a file is selected, the contents of the file are read and displayed in a window containing a text area.

LISTING 9.15

```
import java.io.File;
import java.io.IOException;
import java.util.Scanner;
import javafx.application.Application;
import javafx.scene.Scene;
import javafx.scene.control.TextArea;
```

LISTING 9.15 *continued*

```
import javafx.scene.text.Font;
import javafx.stage.FileChooser;
import javafx.stage.Stage;

//********************************************************************
//  DisplayFile.java       Author: Lewis/Loftus
//
//  Demonstrates the use of a file chooser dialog box and a text area.
//********************************************************************

public class DisplayFile extends Application
{
   //-----------------------------------------------------------------
   //  Presents a file chooser dialog, reads the selected file and
   //  loads it into a text area.
   //-----------------------------------------------------------------
   public void start(Stage primaryStage) throws IOException
   {
      FileChooser chooser = new FileChooser();
      File selectedFile = chooser.showOpenDialog(primaryStage);

      TextArea content = new TextArea();
      content.setFont(new Font("Courier", 12));
      content.setEditable(false);

      if (selectedFile == null)
         content.setText("No file chosen.");
      else
      {
         Scanner scan = new Scanner(selectedFile);

         String info = "";
         while (scan.hasNext())
            info += scan.nextLine() + "\n";

         content.setText(info);
      }

      Scene scene = new Scene(content, 500, 500);

      primaryStage.setTitle("Display File");
      primaryStage.setScene(scene);
      primaryStage.show();
   }
}
```

LISTING 9.15 *continued*

DISPLAY

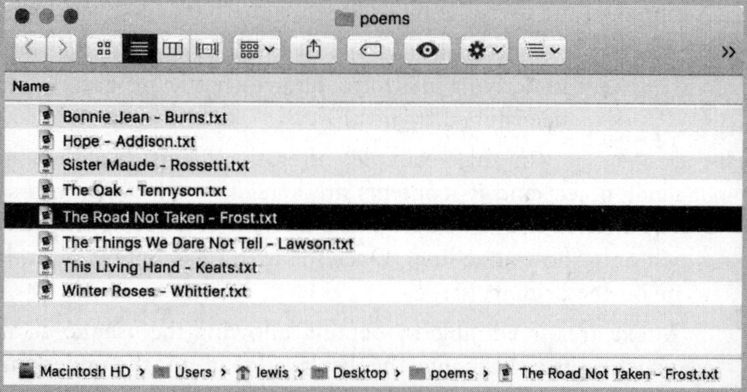

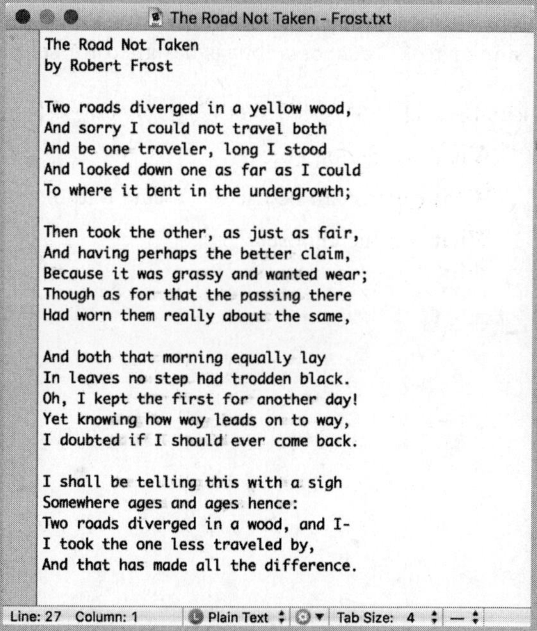

The `showOpenDialog` method of a `FileChooser` object presents a dialog box that allows the user to specify a file to be opened. Similarly, the `showOpenMultipleDialog` method presents a dialog box that lets the user specify multiple files at once, and the `showSaveDialog` method presents a dialog box that allows the user to specify a file in which to save information.

All of these methods accept a parameter that represents the "owner" window. All input to the owner is blocked while the file dialog is being shown.

KEY CONCEPT
The look and feel of a file chooser is based on the underlying platform.

The look and feel of a file chooser dialog box is based on the underlying platform on which the program is running—it is not determined by JavaFX.

In this example, after the file is specified, it is read using a `Scanner` object and its contents are loaded, line by line, into a `TextArea` object. A *text area* is a control that presents multiple lines of text (unlike a `TextField`, which only shows one line). Once the text area content is set, it is displayed in a scene on the primary stage.

A text area is editable by default, allowing the user to change the text. Note that such edits only change the displayed text, not the underlying file. To save the changes, the text must be written back to the file, or saved in another file. A save dialog of the `FileChooser` class may be helpful in this case.

It should be noted that there is another JavaFX class called `DirectoryChooser` that is similar to `FileChooser` but is designed for selecting directories (folders).

SELF-REVIEW QUESTIONS *(see answers in Appendix L)*

SR 9.29 What is a dialog box?

SR 9.30 What classes can be used to create and display dialog boxes?

SR 9.31 What is a file chooser?

Summary of Key Concepts

- Inheritance is the process of deriving a new class from an existing one.
- One purpose of inheritance is to reuse existing software.
- Inheritance creates an is-a relationship between the parent and child classes.
- Protected visibility provides the best possible encapsulation that permits inheritance.
- A parent's constructor can be invoked using the `super` reference.
- A child class can override (redefine) the parent's definition of an inherited method.
- The child of one class can be the parent of one or more other classes, creating a class hierarchy.
- Common features should be located as high in a class hierarchy as is reasonably possible.
- All Java classes are derived, directly or indirectly, from the `Object` class.
- The `toString` and `equals` methods are inherited by every class in every Java program.
- An abstract class cannot be instantiated. It represents a concept on which other classes can build their definitions.
- A class derived from an abstract parent must override all of its parent's abstract methods, or the derived class will also be considered abstract.
- Inheritance can be applied to interfaces so that one interface can be derived from another.
- Private members are inherited by the child class, but cannot be referenced directly by name. They may be used indirectly, however.
- Software design must carefully and specifically address inheritance.
- The `final` modifier can be used to restrict inheritance.
- The classes that define the nodes of a JavaFX scene are organized into a class hierarchy.
- Color and date pickers are controls that allow the user to specify a color or calendar date, respectively.
- A dialog box is a pop-up window that allows brief, specific user interaction.
- The look and feel of a file chooser is based on the underlying platform.

Exercises

EX 9.1 Draw a UML class diagram showing an inheritance hierarchy containing classes that represent different types of clocks. Show the variables and method names for two of these classes.

EX 9.2 Show an alternative diagram for the hierarchy in Exercise 9.1. Explain why it may be a better or worse approach than the original.

EX 9.3 Draw a UML class diagram showing an inheritance hierarchy containing classes that represent different types of cars, organized first by manufacturer. Show some appropriate variables and method names for at least two of these classes.

EX 9.4 Show an alternative diagram for the hierarchy in Exercise 9.3 in which the cars are organized first by type (sports car, sedan, SUV, etc.). Show some appropriate variables and method names for at least two of these classes. Compare and contrast the two approaches.

EX 9.5 Draw a UML class diagram showing an inheritance hierarchy containing classes that represent different types of airplanes. Show some appropriate variables and method names for at least two of these classes.

EX 9.6 Draw a UML class diagram showing an inheritance hierarchy containing classes that represent different types of trees (oak, elm, etc.). Show some appropriate variables and method names for at least two of these classes.

EX 9.7 Use the online Java API documentation to look up JavaFX scene Node, Shape, and at least four subclasses of Shape. Draw a UML class diagram showing an inheritance hierarchy containing these classes. Show some appropriate variables and method names for at least two of these classes.

EX 9.8 Experiment with a simple derivation relationship between two classes. Put `println` statements in constructors of both the parent and child classes. Do not explicitly call the constructor of the parent in the child. What happens? Why? Change the child's constructor to explicitly call the constructor of the parent. Now what happens?

EX 9.9 Which of the following classes are allowed to contain children in a scene graph? What is the determining factor?

a. `Line`

b. `Canvas`

c. `Region`

d. `WebView`

e. `CubicCurve`

EX 9.10 Describe the role of the `Alert` class.

Programming Projects

PP 9.1 Write a class called `MonetaryCoin` that is derived from the `Coin` class presented in Chapter 5. Store an integer in the `MonetaryCoin` that represents its value and add a method that returns its value. Create a `main` driver class to instantiate and compute the sum of several `MonetaryCoin` objects. Demonstrate that a monetary coin inherits its parent's ability to be flipped.

PP 9.2 Design and implement a set of classes that define the employees of a hospital: doctor, nurse, administrator, surgeon, receptionist, janitor, and so on. Include methods in each class that are named according to the services provided by that person and that print an appropriate message. Create a `main` driver class to instantiate and exercise several of the classes.

PP 9.3 Design and implement a set of classes that define various types of reading material: books, novels, magazines, technical journals, textbooks, and so on. Include data values that describe various attributes of the material, such as the number of pages and the names of the primary characters. Include methods that are named appropriately for each class and that print an appropriate message. Create a `main` driver class to instantiate and exercise several of the classes.

PP 9.4 Design and implement a set of classes that keeps track of various apps in an app store. Have each low-level class represent a specific type of app, such as games or utility. Tailor the services of the classes to the type of app in question, and move common attributes to the higher-level classes as appropriate. Create a `main` driver class to instantiate and exercise several of the classes.

PP 9.5 Design and implement a set of classes that keeps track of demographic information about a set of people, such as age, nationality, occupation, income, and so on. Design each class to focus on a particular aspect of data collection. Create a `main` driver class to instantiate and exercise several of the classes.

PP 9.6 Design and implement a set of classes that define a series of three-dimensional geometric shapes (these are not like JavaFX classes and have no graphic representation). For each, store fundamental data about their size and provide methods to access and modify this data. In addition, provide appropriate methods to compute each shape's circumference, area, and volume. In your design, consider how shapes are related and thus where inheritance can be implemented. Create a `main` driver class to instantiate several shapes of differing types and exercise the behavior you provided.

PP 9.7 Design and implement a set of classes that define various types of electronics equipment (computers, cell phones, pagers, digital cameras, etc.). Include data values that describe various attributes of the electronics, such as the weight, cost, power usage, and the names of the manufacturers. Include methods that are named appropriately for each class and that print an appropriate message. Create a `main` driver class to instantiate and exercise several of the classes.

PP 9.8 Design and implement a set of classes that define various courses in your curriculum. Include information about each course such as the title, number, description, and department that teaches the course. Consider the categories of classes that constitutes your curriculum when designing your inheritance structure. Create a `main` driver class to instantiate and exercise several of the classes.

PP 9.9 Write a JavaFX application that displays a text field, a color picker, and a button. When the user presses the button, or presses return while in the text field, display the text obtained from the text field in the color selected by the color picker.

PP 9.10 Modify the `RubberLines` program from Chapter 7 so that a color picker is displayed in the upper left corner of the window. Let the value of the color picker determine the color of the next line drawn.

PP 9.11 Write a JavaFX application that allows the user to draw (scribble) on the scene by dragging the mouse. In the upper-left corner, provide a button to clear the scene and a color picker to choose the current drawing color. Hint: Add a new polyline to the scene each time the mouse button is pressed. As the mouse is dragged, add points to current polyline.

SOFTWARE FAILURE

Ariane 5 Flight 501

What Happened?

Ariane 5 is an expendable launch system designed by the European Space Agency (ESA) to deliver payloads into earth orbit. On June 4, 1996, the first flight of the rocket (Flight 501) exploded 37 seconds after liftoff.

The control system had malfunctioned, causing the rocket to veer off course. Strong aerodynamic forces caused the main portion of the rocket to break apart. An on-board monitor detected the break up and initiated an automatic destruct system to destroy the vehicle in the air.

Flight 501 was carrying four unmanned spacecraft designed to study the magnetic field of the Earth. The rocket's destruction resulted in a complete loss of the payload at an estimated cost of $370 million.

■ The first flight of the Ariane 5 rocket exploded shortly after liftoff.

What Caused It?

The Ariane 5 rocket reused some of the software that was used to control its predecessor, the Ariane 4. That software contained a segment for converting a floating-point number to a signed 16-bit integer. On Flight 501, this value was outside of the range that a 16-bit integer could represent, causing an overflow error. In the Ariane 4, the converted value had always been small enough to avoid this problem.

The overflow error would have been caught by an exception handler, but that part of the system had been disabled for efficiency reasons. The error occurred almost simultaneously in both the main and backup computers, causing them to shut down. This led to the rocket veering off course and its destruction.

Lessons Learned

The success of the Ariane 4 gave the designers of the Ariane 5 confidence in the software. Therefore, minimal testing was done for some parts of the system. The potential problem had always existed in the previous system, but the data (which represented a measurement) was always small. The varying parameters of the new system were not taken into account. So while the root cause was a software bug, the failure resulted from changes in the dynamics of the system and its environment. It is a failure of design and testing—more so than a software bug.

Better reactions to such a problem would have been helpful as well. The exception handling system, if left in place, could have handled the problem more gracefully, rather than simply shutting down the control computer. Ironically, in this case, the measurement in question wasn't even needed after liftoff.

Sources: IEEE Software, cnn.com

Polymorphism 10

CHAPTER OBJECTIVES

- Define polymorphism and explore its benefits.
- Discuss the concept of dynamic binding.
- Use inheritance relationships to create polymorphic references.
- Use interfaces to create polymorphic references.
- Explore sorting and searching using polymorphic implementations.
- Discuss object-oriented design in the context of polymorphism.
- Explore the concept of property binding.
- Examine slider and spinner controls.

This chapter discusses polymorphism, another fundamental principle of object-oriented software. We first explore the concept of binding and discuss how it relates to polymorphism. Then we examine how polymorphic references can be accomplished using either inheritance or interfaces. Design issues related to polymorphism are examined. The Graphics Track of this chapter introduces JavaFX properties and explores how they can be bound together to keep data in sync. We also explore more GUI controls.

10.1 Late Binding

Often, the type of a reference variable matches the class of the object to which it refers exactly. For example, consider the following reference:

```
ChessPiece bishop;
```

The `bishop` variable may be used to point to an object that is created by instantiating the `ChessPiece` class. However, it doesn't have to. The variable type and the object it refers to must be compatible, but their types need not be exactly the same. The relationship between a reference variable and the object it refers to is more flexible than that.

KEY CONCEPT

A polymorphic reference can refer to different types of objects over time.

The term *polymorphism* can be defined as "having many forms." A *polymorphic reference* is a reference variable that can refer to different types of objects at different points in time. The specific method invoked through a polymorphic reference can change from one invocation to the next.

Consider the following line of code:

```
obj.doIt();
```

If the reference `obj` is polymorphic, it can refer to different types of objects at different times. So if that line of code is in a loop, or if it's in a method that is called more than once, that line of code could call a different version of the `doIt` method each time it is invoked.

At some point, the commitment is made to execute certain code to carry out a method invocation. This commitment is referred to as *binding* a method invocation to a method definition. In many situations, the binding of a method invocation to a method definition can occur at compile time. For polymorphic references, however, the decision cannot be made until run time. The method definition that is used is based on the object that is being referred to by the reference variable at that moment. This deferred commitment is called *late binding* or *dynamic binding*. It is less efficient than binding at compile time, because the decision must be made during the execution of the program. This overhead is generally acceptable in light of the flexibility that a polymorphic reference provides.

KEY CONCEPT

The binding of a method invocation to its definition is performed at run time for a polymorphic reference.

We can create a polymorphic reference in Java in two ways: using inheritance and using interfaces. Let's look at each in turn.

SELF-REVIEW QUESTIONS *(see answers in Appendix L)*

SR 10.1 What is polymorphism?

SR 10.2 Why is compile time binding considered more efficient than dynamic binding?

10.2 Polymorphism via Inheritance

When we declare a reference variable using a particular class name, it can be used to refer to any object of that class. In addition, it can also refer to any object of any class that is related to its declared type by inheritance. For example, if the class `Mammal` is the parent of the class `Horse`, then a `Mammal` reference can be used to refer to any object of class `Horse`. This ability is shown in the following code segment:

KEY CONCEPT
A reference variable can refer to any object created from any class related to it by inheritance.

```
Mammal pet;
Horse secretariat = new Horse();
pet = secretariat;  // a valid assignment
```

The reverse operation, assigning the `Mammal` object to a `Horse` reference, can also be done but it requires an explicit cast. Assigning a reference in this direction is generally less useful and more likely to cause problems, because although a horse has all the functionality of a mammal (because a horse *is-a* mammal), the reverse is not necessarily true.

This relationship works throughout a class hierarchy. If the `Mammal` class were derived from a class called `Animal`, the following assignment would also be valid:

```
Animal creature = new Horse();
```

Carrying this to the limit, an `Object` reference can be used to refer to any object, because ultimately all classes are descendants of the `Object` class. An `ArrayList`, for example, uses polymorphism in that it is designed to hold `Object` references. That's why an `ArrayList` that doesn't specify an element type can be used to store any kind of object. In fact, a particular `ArrayList` can be used to hold several different types of objects at one time, because, by inheritance, they are all `Object` objects.

The reference variable `creature` can be polymorphic, because at any point in time it can refer to an `Animal` object, a `Mammal` object, or a `Horse` object. Suppose that all three of these classes have a method called `move` that is implemented in different ways (because

KEY CONCEPT
The type of the object, not the type of the reference, is used to determine which version of a method to invoke.

the child class overrode the definition it inherited). The following invocation calls the `move` method, but the particular version of the method it calls is determined at run time:

```
creature.move();
```

When this line is executed, if `creature` currently refers to an `Animal` object, the `move` method of the `Animal` class is invoked. Likewise, if `creature` currently refers to a `Mammal` object, the `Mammal` version of `move` is invoked. Likewise if it currently refers to a `Horse` object.

Of course, since `Animal` and `Mammal` represent general concepts, they may be defined as abstract classes. This situation does not eliminate the ability to have polymorphic references. Suppose the `move` method in the `Mammal` class is abstract and is given unique definitions in the `Horse`, `Dog`, and `Whale` classes (all derived from `Mammal`). A `Mammal` reference variable can be used to refer to any objects created from any of the `Horse`, `Dog`, and `Whale` classes, and can be used to execute the `move` method on any of them.

Let's look at another situation. Consider the class hierarchy shown in Figure 10.1. The classes in it represent various types of employees that might be employed at a particular company. Let's explore an example that uses this hierarchy to pay a set of employees of various types.

The `Firm` class shown in Listing 10.1 contains a `main` driver that creates a `Staff` of employees and invokes the `payday` method to pay them all. The program output includes information about each employee and how much each is paid (if anything).

The `Staff` class shown in Listing 10.2 maintains an array of objects that represent individual employees of various kinds. Note that the array is declared to hold `StaffMember` references, but it is actually filled with objects created from several other classes, such as `Executive` and `Employee`. These classes are all descendants of the `StaffMember` class, so the assignments are valid. The `staffList` array is filled with polymorphic references.

VideoNote
Exploring the Firm program.

The `payday` method of the `Staff` class scans through the list of employees, printing their information and invoking their `pay` methods to determine how much each employee should be paid. The invocation of the `pay` method is polymorphic, because each class has its own version of the `pay` method.

The `StaffMember` class shown in Listing 10.3 is abstract. It does not represent a particular type of employee and is not intended to be instantiated. Rather, it serves as the ancestor of all employee classes and contains information that applies to all employees. Each employee has a name, address, and phone number, so variables to store these values are declared in the `StaffMember` class and are inherited by all descendants.

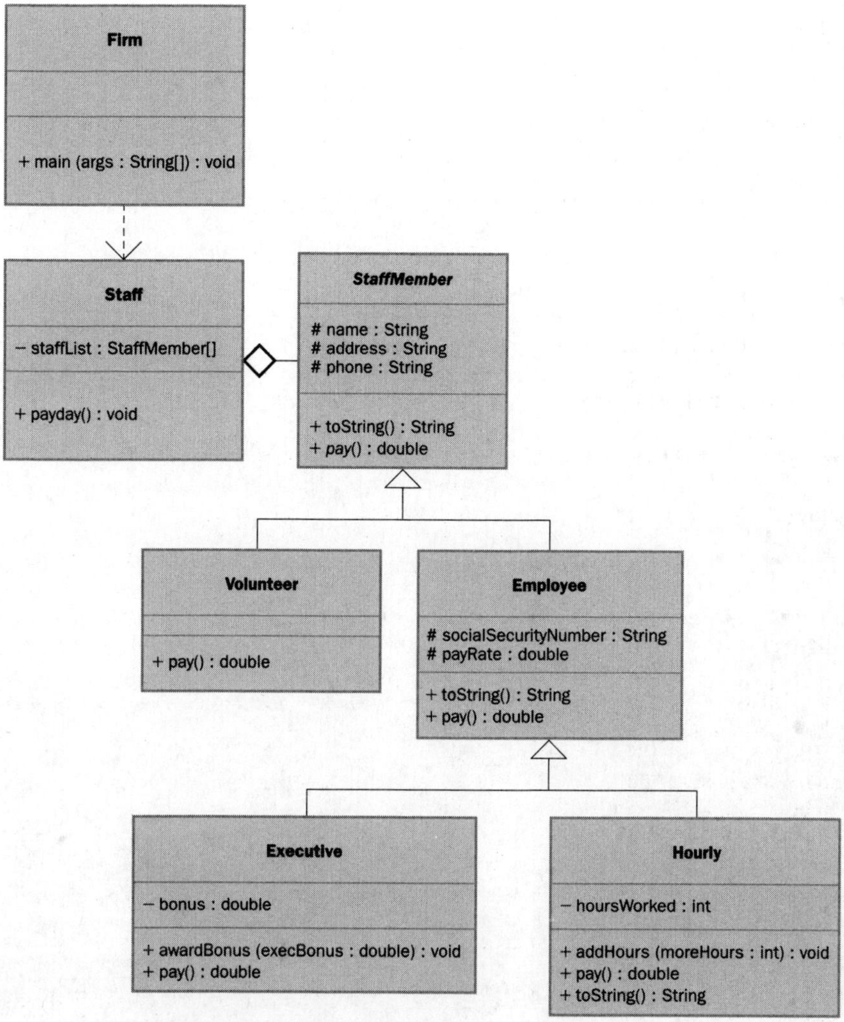

FIGURE 10.1 A class hierarchy of employees

The `StaffMember` class contains a `toString` method to return the information managed by the `StaffMember` class. It also contains an abstract method called `pay`, which takes no parameters and returns a value of type `double`. At the generic `StaffMember` level, it would be inappropriate to give a definition for this method.

LISTING 10.1

```
//********************************************************************
//  Firm.java       Author: Lewis/Loftus
//
//  Demonstrates polymorphism via inheritance.
//********************************************************************

public class Firm
{
   //-----------------------------------------------------------------
   //  Creates a staff of employees for a firm and pays them.
   //-----------------------------------------------------------------
   public static void main(String[] args)
   {
      Staff personnel = new Staff();

      personnel.payday();
   }
}
```

OUTPUT

```
Name: Sam
Address: 123 Main Line
Phone: 555-0469
Social Security Number: 123-45-6789
Paid: 2923.07
-----------------------------------
Name: Carla
Address: 456 Off Line
Phone: 555-0101
Social Security Number: 987-65-4321
Paid: 1246.15
-----------------------------------
Name: Woody
Address: 789 Off Rocker
Phone: 555-0000
Social Security Number: 010-20-3040
Paid: 1169.23
-----------------------------------
Name: Diane
Address: 678 Fifth Ave.
Phone: 555-0690
```

LISTING 10.1 *continued*

```
Social Security Number: 958-47-3625
Current hours: 40
Paid: 422.0
-----------------------------------
Name: Norm
Address: 987 Suds Blvd.
Phone: 555-8374
Thanks!
-----------------------------------
Name: Cliff
Address: 321 Duds Lane
Phone: 555-7282
Thanks!
-----------------------------------
```

LISTING 10.2

```java
//********************************************************************
//  Staff.java       Author: Lewis/Loftus
//
//  Represents the personnel staff of a particular business.
//********************************************************************

public class Staff
{
   private StaffMember[] staffList;

   //-----------------------------------------------------------------
   //  Constructor: Sets up the list of staff members.
   //-----------------------------------------------------------------
   public Staff()
   {
      staffList = new StaffMember[6];

      staffList[0] = new Executive("Sam", "123 Main Line",
         "555-0469", "123-45-6789", 2423.07);
```

LISTING 10.2 *continued*

```
      staffList[1] = new Employee("Carla", "456 Off Line",
         "555-0101", "987-65-4321", 1246.15);
      staffList[2] = new Employee("Woody", "789 Off Rocker",
         "555-0000", "010-20-3040", 1169.23);

      staffList[3] = new Hourly("Diane", "678 Fifth Ave.",
         "555-0690", "958-47-3625", 10.55);

      staffList[4] = new Volunteer("Norm", "987 Suds Blvd.",
         "555-8374");
      staffList[5] = new Volunteer("Cliff", "321 Duds Lane",
         "555-7282");

      ((Executive)staffList[0]).awardBonus(500.00);

      ((Hourly)staffList[3]).addHours(40);
   }

   //-----------------------------------------------------------------
   //  Pays all staff members.
   //-----------------------------------------------------------------
   public void payday()
   {
      double amount;

      for (int count=0; count < staffList.length; count++)
      {
         System.out.println(staffList[count]);

         amount = staffList[count].pay();   // polymorphic

         if (amount == 0.0)
            System.out.println("Thanks!");
         else
            System.out.println("Paid: " + amount);

         System.out.println("-----------------------------------");
      }
   }
}
```

LISTING 10.3

```
//********************************************************************
//  StaffMember.java       Author: Lewis/Loftus
//
//  Represents a generic staff member.
//********************************************************************

abstract public class StaffMember
{
   protected String name;
   protected String address;
   protected String phone;

   //-----------------------------------------------------------------
   //  Constructor: Sets up this staff member using the specified
   //  information.
   //-----------------------------------------------------------------
   public StaffMember(String eName, String eAddress, String ePhone)
   {
      name = eName;
      address = eAddress;
      phone = ePhone;
   }

   //-----------------------------------------------------------------
   //  Returns a string including the basic employee information.
   //-----------------------------------------------------------------
   public String toString()
   {
      String result = "Name: " + name + "\n";

      result += "Address: " + address + "\n";
      result += "Phone: " + phone;

      return result;
   }

   //-----------------------------------------------------------------
   //  Derived classes must define the pay method for each type of
   //  employee.
   //-----------------------------------------------------------------
   public abstract double pay();
}
```

However, the descendants of StaffMember each provide their own specific definition for pay. By defining pay abstractly in StaffMember, the payday method of Staff can polymorphically pay each employee.

This is the essence of polymorphism. Each class knows best how it should handle a specific behavior; in this case, paying an employee. Yet in one sense it's all the same behavior—the employee is getting paid. Polymorphism lets us treat similar objects in consistent but unique ways.

The Volunteer class shown in Listing 10.4 represents a person that is not compensated monetarily for his or her work. We keep track only of a volunteer's basic information, which is passed into the constructor of Volunteer, which in turn passes it to the StaffMember constructor using the super reference. The pay method of Volunteer simply returns a zero pay value. If pay had not been

LISTING 10.4

```
//********************************************************************
//  Volunteer.java       Author: Lewis/Loftus
//
//  Represents a staff member that works as a volunteer.
//********************************************************************

public class Volunteer extends StaffMember
{
   //-----------------------------------------------------------------
   //  Constructor: Sets up this volunteer using the specified
   //  information.
   //-----------------------------------------------------------------
   public Volunteer(String eName, String eAddress, String ePhone)
   {
      super(eName, eAddress, ePhone);
   }

   //-----------------------------------------------------------------
   //  Returns a zero pay value for this volunteer.
   //-----------------------------------------------------------------
   public double pay()
   {
      return 0.0;
   }
}
```

overridden, the Volunteer class would have been considered abstract and could not have been instantiated.

Note that when a volunteer gets "paid" in the payday method of Staff, a simple expression of thanks is printed. In all other situations, where the pay value is greater than zero, the payment itself is printed.

The Employee class shown in Listing 10.5 represents an employee that gets paid at a particular rate each pay period. The pay rate, as well as the employee's Social Security number, is passed along with the other basic information to the Employee constructor. The basic information is passed to the constructor of StaffMember using the super reference.

The toString method of Employee is overridden to concatenate the additional information that Employee manages to the information returned by the parent's version of toString, which is called using the super reference. The pay method of an Employee simply returns the pay rate for that employee.

The Executive class shown in Listing 10.6 represents an employee that may earn a bonus in addition to his or her normal pay rate. The Executive class is derived from Employee and therefore inherits from both StaffMember and Employee. The constructor of Executive passes along its information to the Employee constructor and sets the executive bonus to zero.

A bonus is awarded to an executive using the awardBonus method. This method is called in the Staff constructor for the only executive that is part of the staffList array. Note that the generic StaffMember reference must be cast into an Executive reference to invoke the awardBonus method (which doesn't exist for a StaffMember).

The Executive class overrides the pay method so that it first determines the payment as it would for any employee, then adds the bonus. The pay method of the Employee class is invoked using super to obtain the normal payment amount. This technique is better than using just the payRate variable, because if we choose to change how Employee objects get paid, the change will automatically be reflected in Executive. After the bonus is awarded, it is reset to zero.

The Hourly class shown in Listing 10.7 represents an employee whose pay rate is applied on an hourly basis. It keeps track of the number of hours worked in the current pay period, which can be modified by calls to the addHours method. This method is called from the payday method of Staff. The pay method of Hourly determines the payment based on the number of hours worked and then resets the hours to zero.

LISTING 10.5

```
//********************************************************************
//  Employee.java       Author: Lewis/Loftus
//
//  Represents a general paid employee.
//********************************************************************

public class Employee extends StaffMember
{
   protected String socialSecurityNumber;
   protected double payRate;

   //-----------------------------------------------------------------
   //  Constructor: Sets up this employee with the specified
   //  information.
   //-----------------------------------------------------------------
   public Employee(String eName, String eAddress, String ePhone,
                   String socSecNumber, double rate)
   {
      super(eName, eAddress, ePhone);

      socialSecurityNumber = socSecNumber;
      payRate = rate;
   }

   //-----------------------------------------------------------------
   //  Returns information about an employee as a string.
   //-----------------------------------------------------------------
   public String toString()
   {
      String result = super.toString();

      result += "\nSocial Security Number: " + socialSecurityNumber;

      return result;
   }

   //-----------------------------------------------------------------
   //  Returns the pay rate for this employee.
   //-----------------------------------------------------------------
   public double pay()
   {
      return payRate;
   }
}
```

LISTING 10.6

```
//********************************************************************
//  Executive.java       Author: Lewis/Loftus
//
//  Represents an executive staff member, who can earn a bonus.
//********************************************************************

public class Executive extends Employee
{
   private double bonus;

   //-----------------------------------------------------------------
   //  Constructor: Sets up this executive with the specified
   //  information.
   //-----------------------------------------------------------------
   public Executive(String eName, String eAddress, String ePhone,
                    String socSecNumber, double rate)
   {
      super(eName, eAddress, ePhone, socSecNumber, rate);

      bonus = 0;   // bonus has yet to be awarded
   }

   //-----------------------------------------------------------------
   //  Awards the specified bonus to this executive.
   //-----------------------------------------------------------------
   public void awardBonus(double execBonus)
   {
      bonus = execBonus;
   }

   //-----------------------------------------------------------------
   //  Computes and returns the pay for an executive, which is the
   //  regular employee payment plus a one-time bonus.
   //-----------------------------------------------------------------
   public double pay()
   {
      double payment = super.pay() + bonus;

      bonus = 0;

      return payment;
   }
}
```

LISTING 10.7

```java
//********************************************************************
//  Hourly.java       Author: Lewis/Loftus
//
//  Represents an employee that gets paid by the hour.
//********************************************************************

public class Hourly extends Employee
{
   private int hoursWorked;

   //-----------------------------------------------------------------
   //  Constructor: Sets up this hourly employee using the specified
   //  information.
   //-----------------------------------------------------------------
   public Hourly(String eName, String eAddress, String ePhone,
                 String socSecNumber, double rate)
   {
      super(eName, eAddress, ePhone, socSecNumber, rate);

      hoursWorked = 0;
   }

   //-----------------------------------------------------------------
   //  Adds the specified number of hours to this employee's
   //  accumulated hours.
   //-----------------------------------------------------------------
   public void addHours(int moreHours)
   {
      hoursWorked += moreHours;
   }

   //-----------------------------------------------------------------
   //  Computes and returns the pay for this hourly employee.
   //-----------------------------------------------------------------
   public double pay()
   {
      double payment = payRate * hoursWorked;

      hoursWorked = 0;

      return payment;
   }
```

LISTING 10.7 *continued*

```
   //-----------------------------------------------------------------
   //  Returns information about this hourly employee as a string.
   //-----------------------------------------------------------------
   public String toString()
   {
      String result = super.toString();

      result += "\nCurrent hours: " + hoursWorked;

      return result;
   }
}
```

SELF-REVIEW QUESTIONS *(see answers in Appendix L)*

SR 10.3 How does inheritance support polymorphism?

SR 10.4 Suppose the class `MusicPlayer` is the parent of the class `CDPlayer`. Is the following sequence of statements allowed in Java? Explain.

```
MusicPlayer mplayer = new MusicPlayer();
CDPlayer cdplayer = new CDPlayer();
mplayer = cdplayer;
```

SR 10.5 Suppose the class `MusicPlayer` is the parent of the class `CDPlayer`. Is the following sequence of statements allowed in Java? Explain.

```
MusicPlayer mplayer = new MusicPlayer();
CDPlayer cdplayer = new CDPlayer();
cdplayer = mplayer;
```

SR 10.6 How is overriding related to polymorphism?

SR 10.7 Why is the `StaffMember` class in the `Firm` example declared as abstract?

SR 10.8 Why is the `pay` method declared in the `StaffMember` class, given that it is abstract and has no body at that level?

SR 10.9 Which `pay` method is invoked by the following line from the `payday` method of the `Staff` class?

```
amount = staffList[count].pay();
```

10.3 Polymorphism via Interfaces

KEY CONCEPT
An interface name can be used to declare an object reference variable.

Now let's examine how we can create polymorphic references using interfaces. As we've seen many times, a class name can be used to declare the type of an object reference variable. Similarly, an interface name can be used as the type of a reference variable as well. An interface reference variable can be used to refer to any object of any class that implements that interface.

Suppose we declare an interface called `Speaker` as follows:

```
public interface Speaker
{
   public void speak();
   public void announce(String str);
}
```

The interface name, `Speaker`, can now be used to declare an object reference variable:

```
Speaker current;
```

KEY CONCEPT
An interface reference can refer to any object of any class that implements that interface.

The reference variable `current` can be used to refer to any object of any class that implements the `Speaker` interface. For example, if we define a class called `Philosopher` such that it implements the `Speaker` interface, we can then assign a `Philosopher` object to a `Speaker` reference as follows:

```
current = new Philosopher();
```

This assignment is valid, because a `Philosopher` is a `Speaker`. In this sense the relationship between a class and its interface is the same as the relationship between a child class and its parent. It is an is-a relationship. And that relationship forms the basis of the polymorphism.

The flexibility of an interface reference allows us to create polymorphic references. As we saw earlier in this chapter, using inheritance, we can create a polymorphic reference that can refer to any one of a set of objects as long as they are related by inheritance. Using interfaces, we can create similar polymorphic references among objects that implement the same interface.

For example, if we create a class called `Dog` that also implements the `Speaker` interface, it can be assigned to a `Speaker` reference variable as well. The same reference variable, in fact, can at one point refer to a `Philosopher` object and then later refer to a `Dog` object. The following lines of code illustrate this:

```
Speaker guest;
guest = new Philosopher();
guest.speak();
guest = new Dog();
guest.speak();
```

In this code, the first time the `speak` method is called, it invokes the `speak` method defined in the `Philosopher` class. The second time it is called, it invokes the `speak` method of the `Dog` class. As with polymorphic references via inheritance, it is not the type of the reference that determines which method gets invoked; it is based on the type of the object that the reference points to at the moment of invocation.

Note that when we are using an interface reference variable, we can invoke only the methods defined in the interface, even if the object it refers to has other methods to which it can respond. For example, suppose the `Philosopher` class also defined a public method called `pontificate`. The second line of the following code would generate a compiler error, even though the object can in fact respond to the `pontificate` method:

```
Speaker special = new Philosopher();
special.pontificate();    // generates a compiler error
```

The problem is that the compiler can determine only that the object is a `Speaker`, and therefore can guarantee only that the object can respond to the `speak` and `announce` methods. Because the reference variable `special` could refer to a `Dog` object (which cannot pontificate), it does not allow the invocation. If we know in a particular situation that such an invocation is valid, we can cast the object into the appropriate reference so that the compiler will accept it, as follows:

```
((Philosopher)special).pontificate();
```

As we can with polymorphic references based in inheritance, an interface name can be used as the type of a method parameter. In such situations, any object of any class that implements the interface can be passed into the method. For example, the following method takes a `Speaker` object as a parameter. Therefore, both a `Dog` object and a `Philosopher` object can be passed into it in separate invocations:

KEY CONCEPT
A parameter to a method can be polymorphic, giving the method flexible control of its arguments.

```
public void sayIt(Speaker current)
{
   current.speak();
}
```

Using a polymorphic reference as the formal parameter to a method is a powerful technique. It allows the method to control the types of parameters passed into it, yet gives it the flexibility to accept arguments of various types.

SELF-REVIEW QUESTIONS *(see answers in Appendix L)*

SR 10.10 How can polymorphism be accomplished using interfaces?

SR 10.11 Suppose that the `Speaker` interface and the `Philosopher` and `Dog` classes are as described in this section. Are the following sequences of statements allowed in Java? Explain.

a.
```
Speaker current = new Speaker();
```

b.
```
Speaker current = new Dog();
```

c.
```
Speaker first, second;
first = new Dog();
second = new Philosopher();
first.speak();
first = second;
```

d.
```
Speaker first = new Dog();
Philospher second = new Philosopher();
second.pontificate();
first = second;
```

e.
```
Speaker first = new Dog();
Philospher second = new Philosopher();
first = second;
second.pontificate();
first.pontificate();
```

10.4 Sorting

Let's examine a problem that lends itself to a polymorphic solution. *Sorting* is the process of arranging a list of items in a well-defined order. For example, you may want to alphabetize a list of names or put a list of survey results into descending numeric order. Many sorting algorithms have been developed and critiqued over the years. In fact, sorting is considered to be a classic area of study in computer science.

This section examines two sorting algorithms: selection sort and insertion sort. Complete coverage of various sorting techniques is beyond the scope of this text. Instead, we introduce the topic and establish some of the fundamental ideas involved. We do not delve into a detailed analysis of the algorithms but instead focus on the strategies involved and general characteristics.

Selection Sort

The *selection sort* algorithm sorts a list of values by successively putting particular values in their final, sorted positions. In other words, for each position in the list, the algorithm selects the value that should go in that position and puts it there.

The general strategy of selection sort is: Scan the entire list to find the smallest value. Exchange that value with the value in the first position of the list. Scan the rest of the list (all but the first value) to find the smallest value, then exchange it with the value in the second position of the list. Scan the rest of the list (all but the first two values) to find the smallest value, then exchange it with the value in the third position of the list. Continue this process for all but the last position in the list (which will end up containing the largest value). When the process is complete, the list is sorted. Figure 10.2 demonstrates the use of the selection sort algorithm.

The program shown in Listing 10.8 uses a selection sort to arrange a list of `Contact` objects into ascending order.

Listing 10.9 shows the `Sorting` class, which contains two sorting algorithms. The `PhoneList` program uses only the `selectionSort` method. The other method is discussed later in this section.

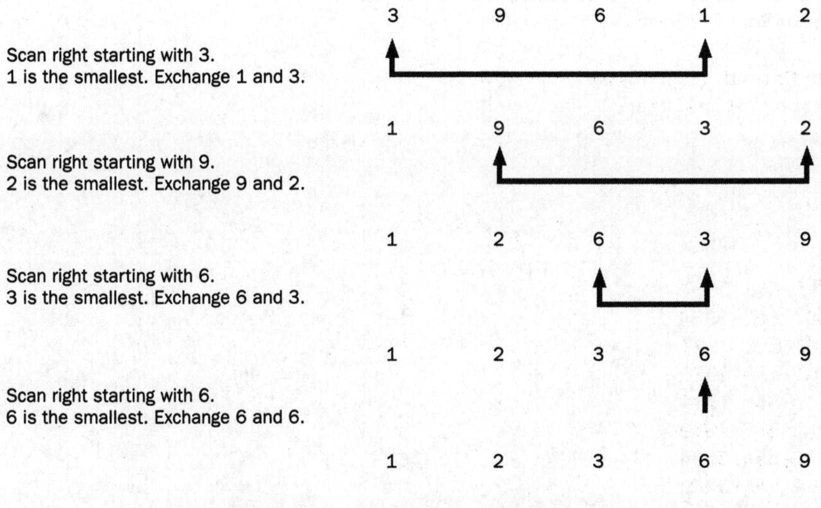

FIGURE 10.2 Selection sort processing

LISTING 10.8

```
//********************************************************************
//  PhoneList.java       Author: Lewis/Loftus
//
//  Driver for testing a sorting algorithm.
//********************************************************************

public class PhoneList
{
   //-----------------------------------------------------------------
   //  Creates an array of Contact objects, sorts them, then prints
   //  them.
   //-----------------------------------------------------------------
   public static void main(String[] args)
   {
      Contact[] friends = new Contact[8];

      friends[0] = new Contact("John", "Smith", "610-555-7384");
      friends[1] = new Contact("Sarah", "Barnes", "215-555-3827");
      friends[2] = new Contact("Mark", "Riley", "733-555-2969");
      friends[3] = new Contact("Laura", "Getz", "663-555-3984");
      friends[4] = new Contact("Larry", "Smith", "464-555-3489");
      friends[5] = new Contact("Frank", "Phelps", "322-555-2284");
      friends[6] = new Contact("Mario", "Guzman", "804-555-9066");
      friends[7] = new Contact("Marsha", "Grant", "243-555-2837");

      Sorting<Contact> sorts = new Sorting<Contact>();
      sorts.selectionSort(friends);

      for (Contact friend : friends)
         System.out.println(friend);
   }
}
```

OUTPUT

```
Barnes, Sarah   215-555-3827
Getz, Laura     663-555-3984
Grant, Marsha   243-555-2837
Guzman, Mario   804-555-9066
Phelps, Frank   322-555-2284
Riley, Mark     733-555-2969
Smith, John     610-555-7384
Smith, Larry    464-555-3489
```

LISTING 10.9

```
//********************************************************************
//  Sorting.java       Author: Lewis/Loftus
//
//  Demonstrates the selection sort and insertion sort algorithms.
//********************************************************************

public class Sorting<T>
{
   //-----------------------------------------------------------------
   //  Sorts the specified array of objects using the selection
   //  sort algorithm.
   //-----------------------------------------------------------------
   public void selectionSort(Comparable<T>[] list)
   {
      int min;
      Comparable<T> temp;

      for (int index = 0; index < list.length-1; index++)
      {
         min = index;
         for (int scan = index+1; scan < list.length; scan++)
            if (list[scan].compareTo((T)list[min]) < 0)
               min = scan;

         // Swap the values
         temp = list[min];
         list[min] = list[index];
         list[index] = temp;
      }
   }

   //-----------------------------------------------------------------
   //  Sorts the specified array of objects using the insertion
   //  sort algorithm.
   //-----------------------------------------------------------------
   public void insertionSort(Comparable<T>[] list)
   {
      for (int index = 1; index < list.length; index++)
      {
         Comparable<T> key = list[index];
         int position = index;
```

LISTING 10.9 *continued*

```
         // Shift larger values to the right
         while (position > 0 && key.compareTo((T)list[position-1]) < 0)
         {
            list[position] = list[position-1];
            position--;
         }

         list[position] = key;
      }
   }
}
```

The selectionSort method accepts an array of Comparable objects to sort. Recall that Comparable is an interface that includes only one method, compareTo, which is designed to return an integer that is less than zero, equal to zero, or greater than zero if the executing object is less than, equal to, or greater than the object to which it is being compared, respectively.

Comparable is a generic interface, operating on a generic type T, which specifies what type of object the comparable object can be compared to.

Any class that implements the Comparable interface must specify what an object of that class can be compared to (what T is) and must define the compareTo method accordingly. For example, if a Book class implements Comparable<Book>, any Book object can then be compared to any other Book object to determine their relative order.

The selectionSort method is polymorphic. Note that it doesn't refer to Contact objects at all and yet is used to sort an array of Contact objects. The selectionSort method is set up to sort any array of objects, as long as those objects can be compared to determine their order. You can call selectionSort multiple times, passing in arrays of different types of objects, as long as they are Comparable.

KEY CONCEPT

Implementing a sort algorithm polymorphically allows it to sort any comparable set of objects.

Each Contact object represents a person with a last name, a first name, and a phone number. Listing 10.10 shows the Contact class.

The Contact class implements the Comparable interface and therefore provides a definition of the compareTo method. In this case, the contacts are sorted by last name; if two contacts have the same last name, their first names are used.

LISTING 10.10

```
//********************************************************************
//  Contact.java       Author: Lewis/Loftus
//
//  Represents a phone contact.
//********************************************************************

public class Contact implements Comparable<Contact>
{
   private String firstName, lastName, phone;

   //-----------------------------------------------------------------
   //  Constructor: Sets up this contact with the specified data.
   //-----------------------------------------------------------------
   public Contact(String first, String last, String telephone)
   {
      firstName = first;
      lastName = last;
      phone = telephone;
   }

   //-----------------------------------------------------------------
   //  Returns a description of this contact as a string.
   //-----------------------------------------------------------------
   public String toString()
   {
      return lastName + ", " + firstName + "\t" + phone;
   }

   //-----------------------------------------------------------------
   //  Returns true if the first and last names of this contact match
   //  those of the parameter.
   //-----------------------------------------------------------------
   public boolean equals(Object other)
   {
      return (lastName.equals(((Contact)other).getLastName()) &&
              firstName.equals(((Contact)other).getFirstName()));
   }

   //-----------------------------------------------------------------
   //  Uses both last and first names to determine ordering.
   //-----------------------------------------------------------------
   public int compareTo(Contact other)
   {
      int result;
```

LISTING 10.10 *continued*

```
      if (lastName.equals(other.getLastName()))
         result = firstName.compareTo(other.getFirstName());
      else
         result = lastName.compareTo(other.getLastName());

      return result;
   }

   //-----------------------------------------------------------------
   //  First name accessor.
   //-----------------------------------------------------------------
   public String getFirstName()
   {
      return firstName;
   }

   //-----------------------------------------------------------------
   //  Last name accessor.
   //-----------------------------------------------------------------
   public String getLastName()
   {
      return lastName;
   }
}
```

The implementation of the `selectionSort` method uses two `for` loops to sort the array. The outer loop controls the position in the array where the next smallest value will be stored. The inner loop finds the smallest value in the rest of the list by scanning all positions greater than or equal to the index specified by the outer loop. When the smallest value is determined, it is exchanged with the value stored at the index. This exchange is done in three assignment statements by using an extra variable called `temp`. This type of exchange is often called *swapping*.

VideoNote
Sorting `Comparable` objects.

Note that because this algorithm finds the smallest value during each iteration, the result is an array sorted in ascending order (that is, smallest to largest). The algorithm can easily be changed to put values in descending order by finding the largest value each time.

Also note that we've set up the sorting methods to sort arrays of objects. Therefore, if your goal is to sort an array of a primitive type, such as an array of integer values, they would have to be put into an array of `Integer` objects to be processed. All of the wrapper classes implement the `Comparable` interface.

Insertion Sort

The `Sorting` class also contains a method that performs an insertion sort on an array of `Comparable` objects. If used to sort the array of `Contact` objects in the `PhoneList` program, it would produce the same results as the selection sort did. However, the logic used to put the objects in order is different.

The *insertion sort* algorithm sorts a list of values by repetitively inserting a particular value into a subset of the list that has already been sorted. One at a time, each unsorted element is inserted at the appropriate position in that sorted subset until the entire list is in order.

The general strategy of insertion sort is: Begin with a "sorted" list containing only one value. Sort the first two values in the list relative to each other by exchanging them if necessary. Insert the list's third value into the appropriate position relative to the first two (sorted) values. Then insert the fourth value into its proper position relative to the first three values in the list. Each time an insertion is made, the number of values in the sorted subset increases by one. Continue this process until all values are inserted in their proper places, at which point the list is completely sorted.

The insertion process requires that the other values in the array shift to make room for the inserted element. Figure 10.3 demonstrates the behavior of the insertion sort algorithm with integers.

Similar to the selection sort implementation, the `insertionSort` method uses two `for` loops to sort the array. In the insertion sort, however, the outer loop

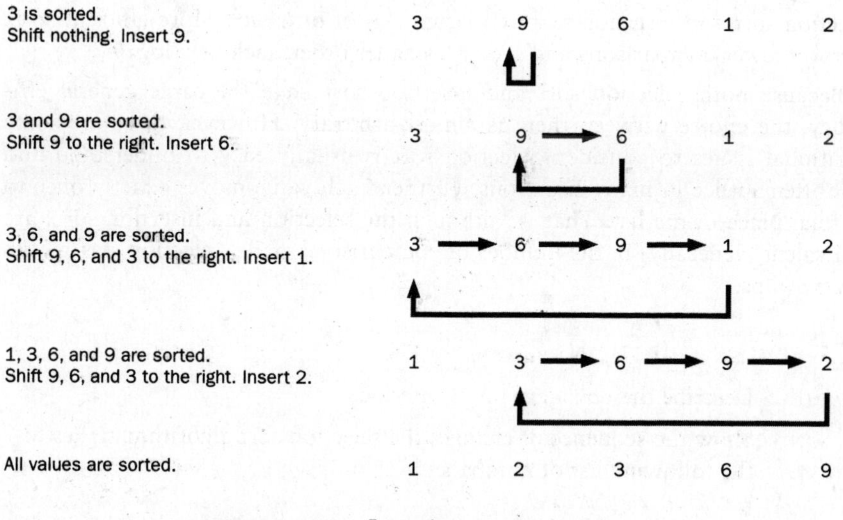

FIGURE 10.3 Insertion sort processing

controls the index in the array of the next value to be inserted. The inner loop compares the current insert value with values stored at lower indexes (which make up a sorted subset of the entire list). If the current insert value is less than the value at `position`, that value is shifted to the right. Shifting continues until the proper position is opened to accept the insert value. Each iteration of the outer loop adds one more value to the sorted subset of the list, until the entire list is sorted.

Comparing Sorts

There are various reasons for choosing one sorting algorithm over another, including the algorithm's simplicity, its level of efficiency, and the amount of memory it uses. An algorithm that is easier to understand is also easier to implement and debug. However, often the simplest sorts are the most inefficient ones. Efficiency is usually considered to be the primary criterion when comparing sorting algorithms. In general, one sorting algorithm is less efficient than another if it performs more comparisons than the other. There are several algorithms that are more efficient than the two we examined, but they are also more complex.

Both selection sort and insertion sort have essentially the same level of efficiency. Both have an outer loop and an inner loop with similar properties, if not purposes. The outer loop is executed once for each value in the list, and the inner loop compares the value in the outer loop with most, if not all, of the values in the rest of the list. Therefore, both algorithms perform approximately n^2 number of comparisons, where n is the number of values in the list. We say that both selection sort and insertion sort are algorithms of *order* n^2. More efficient sorts perform fewer comparisons and are of a smaller order, such as $n \log_2 n$.

Because both selection sort and insertion sort have the same general efficiency, the choice between them is almost arbitrary. However, there are some additional issues to consider. Selection sort is usually easy to understand and will often suffice in many situations. Further, each value moves exactly once to its final place in the list. That is, although the selection and insertion sorts are equivalent (generally) in the number of comparisons made, selection sort makes fewer swaps.

SELF-REVIEW QUESTIONS *(see answers in Appendix L)*

SR 10.12 Describe the `Comparable<T>` interface.

SR 10.13 Show the sequence of changes the selection sort algorithm makes to the following list of numbers:

```
5 7 1 8 2 4 3
```

SR 10.14 Show the sequence of changes the insertion sort algorithm makes to the following list of numbers:

`5 7 1 8 2 4 3`

SR 10.15 In what way are the sort methods defined in this chapter polymorphic?

SR 10.16 Which is better: selection sort or insertion sort? Explain.

10.5 Searching

Like sorting, searching for an item is another classic computing problem, and also lends itself to a polymorphic solution. *Searching* is the process of finding a designated *target element* within a group of items. For example, we may need to search for a person named Vito Andolini in a club roster.

The group of items to be searched is sometimes called the *search pool*. The search pool is usually organized into a collection of objects of some kind, such as an array.

Whenever we perform a search, we must consider the possibility that the target is not present in the group. Furthermore, we would like to perform a search efficiently. We don't want to make any more comparisons than we have to.

In this section we examine two search algorithms, linear search and binary search. We explore versatile, polymorphic implementations of these algorithms and compare their efficiency.

Linear Search

If the search pool can be examined one element at a time in any order, one straightforward way to perform the search is to start at the beginning of the list and compare each value in turn to the target element. Eventually, either the target element will be found or we will come to the end of the list and conclude that the target doesn't exist in the group.

This approach is called a *linear search*, because it begins at one end and scans the search pool in a linear manner. This process is depicted in Figure 10.4. When items are stored in an array, a linear search is relatively simple.

The program shown in Listing 10.11 is similar to the `PhoneList` program from the previous section. It begins with the same, unsorted array of `Contact` objects. It then performs a linear search for a contact and prints the result. Then it calls the `selectionSort` method, which was discussed in the previous section, to sort the contacts. It then searches for another contact using a binary search, which is discussed later in this section.

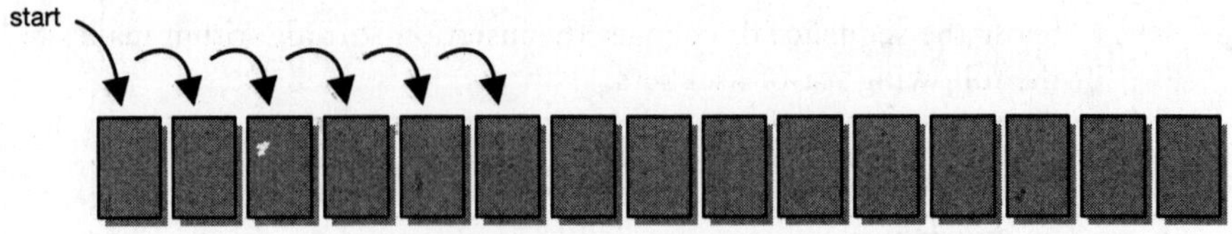

FIGURE 10.4 A linear search

LISTING 10.11

```
//********************************************************************
//  PhoneList2.java       Author: Lewis/Loftus
//
//  Driver for testing searching algorithms.
//********************************************************************

public class PhoneList2
{
   //-----------------------------------------------------------------
   //  Creates an array of Contact objects, sorts them, then prints
   //  them.
   //-----------------------------------------------------------------
   public static void main(String[] args)
   {
      Contact test, found;
      Contact[] friends = new Contact[8];

      friends[0] = new Contact("John", "Smith", "610-555-7384");
      friends[1] = new Contact("Sarah", "Barnes", "215-555-3827");
      friends[2] = new Contact("Mark", "Riley", "733-555-2969");
      friends[3] = new Contact("Laura", "Getz", "663-555-3984");
      friends[4] = new Contact("Larry", "Smith", "464-555-3489");
      friends[5] = new Contact("Frank", "Phelps", "322-555-2284");
      friends[6] = new Contact("Mario", "Guzman", "804-555-9066");
      friends[7] = new Contact("Marsha", "Grant", "243-555-2837");

      Searching<Contact> searches = new Searching<Contact>();

      test = new Contact("Frank", "Phelps", "");
      found = searches.linearSearch(friends, test);
      if (found != null)
         System.out.println("Found: " + found);
      else
```

LISTING 10.11 *continued*

```
            System.out.println("The contact was not found.");
         System.out.println();

         Sorting<Contact> sorts = new Sorting<Contact>();
         sorts.selectionSort(friends);

         test = new Contact("Mario", "Guzman", "");
         found = (Contact) searches.binarySearch(friends, test);
         if (found != null)
            System.out.println("Found: " + found);
         else
            System.out.println("The contact was not found.");
      }
   }
```

OUTPUT

```
Found: Phelps, Frank     322-555-2284

Found: Guzman, Mario     804-555-9066
```

Listing 10.12 shows the `Searching` class. It contains two static searching algorithms.

In the `linearSearch` method, the `while` loop steps through the elements of the array, terminating either when the target is found or the end of the array is reached. The `boolean` variable `found` is initialized to false and is only changed to true if the target element is located.

Note that we'll have to examine every element before we can conclude that the target doesn't exist in the array. On average, the linear search approach will look through half the data before finding a target that is present in the array.

The `linearSearch` method uses the equals method to search for a target object, so it is not a requirement that the array be filled with `Comparable` objects. The only restriction is that the array elements and the target be the same type.

Binary Search

If the elements in an array are sorted, in either ascending or descending order, then our approach to searching can be much more efficient than the linear search algorithm. A *binary search* eliminates large parts of the search pool with each comparison by capitalizing on the fact that the search pool is ordered.

LISTING 10.12

```
//********************************************************************
//  Searching.java       Author: Lewis/Loftus
//
//  Demonstrates the linear search and binary search algorithms.
//********************************************************************

public class Searching<T>
{
   //-----------------------------------------------------------------
   //  Searches the specified array of objects for the target using
   //  a linear search. Returns a reference to the target object from
   //  the array if found, and null otherwise.
   //-----------------------------------------------------------------
   public T linearSearch(T[] list, T target)
   {
      int index = 0;
      boolean found = false;

      while (!found && index < list.length)
      {
         if (list[index].equals(target))
            found = true;
         else
            index++;
      }

      if (found)
         return list[index];
      else
         return null;
   }

   //-----------------------------------------------------------------
   //  Searches the specified array of objects for the target using
   //  a binary search. Assumes the array is already sorted in
   //  ascending order when it is passed in. Returns a reference to
   //  the target object from the array if found, and null otherwise.
   //-----------------------------------------------------------------
   public Comparable<T> binarySearch(Comparable<T>[] list,
                                     Comparable<T> target)

   {
      int min = 0, max = list.length - 1, mid = 0;
      boolean found = false;
```

LISTING 10.12 *continued*

```
      while (!found && min <= max)
      {
         mid = (min+max) / 2;
         if (list[mid].equals(target))
            found = true;
         else
            if (target.compareTo((T)list[mid]) < 0)
               max = mid-1;
            else
               min = mid+1;
      }

      if (found)
         return list[mid];
      else
         return null;
   }
}
```

Consider the following sorted array of integers:

0	1	2	3	4	5	6	7	8	9	10	11	12	13	14
10	12	18	22	31	34	40	46	59	67	69	72	82	84	98

Suppose we were trying to determine if the number 67 is in this list. Initially, the target might be anywhere in the list, or not at all. That is, at first, all items in the search pool are *viable candidates*.

Instead of starting the search at one end or the other, a binary search begins in the middle of the sorted list. If the target element is not found at that middle element, then the search continues. The middle element of this list is 46, which is not our target, so we must search on. However, since the list is sorted, we know that if 67 is in the list, it will be in the later half of the array. All values at lower indexes are less than 46. Thus, with one comparison, we've taken half of the data out of consideration, and we are left with the following viable candidates:

Viable Candidates (indexes 8–14)

0	1	2	3	4	5	6	7	8	9	10	11	12	13	14
10	12	18	22	31	34	40	46	59	67	69	72	82	84	98

To search the remaining candidates, we once again examine the "middle" element. The middle element is 72, and thus we have still not found the target. But once again, we can eliminate half of the viable candidates (those greater than 72) and we are left with:

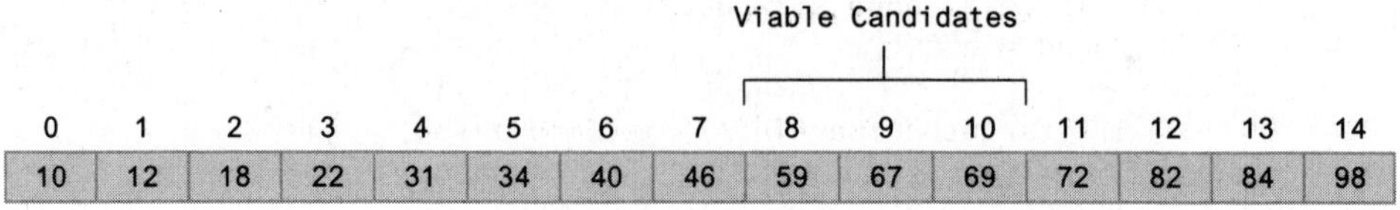

Employing the same approach again, we select the middle element, 67, and find the element we are seeking. If it had not been our target, we would have continued with this process until we either found the value or eliminated all possible data.

With each comparison, a binary search eliminates approximately half of the remaining data to be searched (it also eliminates the middle element as well). That is, a binary search eliminates half of the data with the first comparison, another quarter of the data with the second comparison, another eighth of the data with the third comparison, and so on. The binary search approach is pictured in Figure 10.5.

The `binarySearch` method from the `Searching` class performs a binary search by looping until the target element is found or until all viable candidates are eliminated. Two integer indexes, `min` and `max`, are used to define the portion of the array that is still considered viable. When `min` becomes greater than `max`, then the viable candidates have been exhausted.

On each iteration of the loop, the midpoint is calculated by dividing the sum of `min` and `max` by two. If there are currently an even number of viable candidates, and thus two "middle" values, this calculation discards the fractional remainder and picks the first of the two.

If the target element is not found, the value of `min` or `max` is modified to eliminate the appropriate half of the viable candidates. Then the search continues.

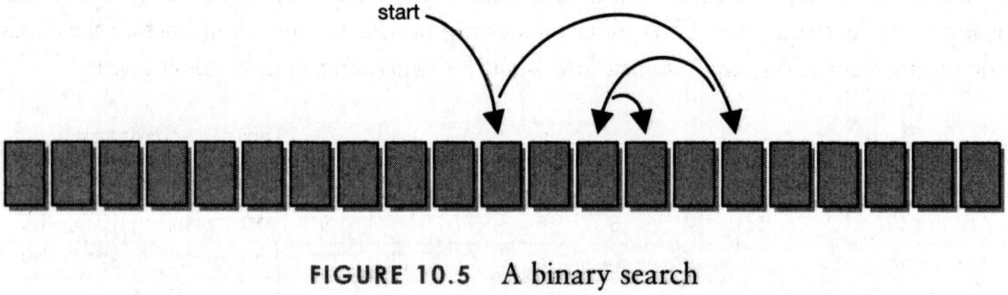

FIGURE 10.5 A binary search

Comparing Searches

As far as the search algorithms go, there is no doubt that the binary search approach is far more efficient than the linear search. However, the binary search requires that the data be sorted. So once again, the algorithm to choose depends on the situation.

If it's relatively easy to keep the data sorted, or if there will be a lot of searching, it will likely be more appropriate to use a binary search. On the other hand, a linear search is quite simple to implement and may be the best choice when long-term efficiency is not an issue.

SELF-REVIEW QUESTIONS *(see answers in Appendix L)*

SR 10.17 Given the following list of numbers, how many elements of the list would be examined by the linear search algorithm to determine if each of the indicated target elements are on the list?

`15 21 4 17 8 27 1 22 43 57 25 7 53 12 16`

a. 17
b. 15
c. 16
d. 45

SR 10.18 Describe the general concept of a binary search.

SR 10.19 Given the following list of numbers, how many elements of the list would be examined by the binary search algorithm to determine if each of the indicated target elements are on the list?

`1 4 7 8 12 15 16 17 21 22 25 27 43 53 57`

a. 17
b. 15
c. 57
d. 45

10.6 Designing for Polymorphism

We've been evolving the concepts underlying good software design throughout this book. For every aspect of object-oriented software, we should make decisions, consciously and carefully, that lead to well-structured, flexible, and elegant code. We want to define appropriate classes and objects, with proper encapsulation. We want to define appropriate relationships among the classes and objects, including leveraging the powerful aspects of inheritance when possible. Now we can add polymorphism to our set of intellectual tools for thinking about software design.

KEY CONCEPT
Polymorphism allows us to apply a consistent approach to inconsistent behaviors.

Polymorphism provides a means to create elegant versatility in our software. It allows us to apply a consistent approach to inconsistent but related behaviors. We should try to find opportunities in our software systems that lend themselves to polymorphic solutions. We should seek them out, actively and deliberately, before we begin to write code.

Whenever you find situations in which different types of objects perform the same type of behavior, there is an opportunity for a polymorphic solution. The more experience you get, the easier it will be to detect such situations. See if you recognize the opportunity for polymorphism in the following situations:

- Different types of vehicles move in different ways.
- All business transactions for a company must be logged.
- All products produced by a company must meet certain quality standards.
- A hotel needs to plan their remodeling efforts for every room.
- A casino wants to analyze the profit margin for their games.
- A dispatcher must schedule moving vans and personnel based on the job size.

KEY CONCEPT
We should hone our design senses to identify situations that lend themselves to polymorphic solutions.

The common theme in these examples is that the same basic behavior applies to multiple objects, and those behaviors are accomplished differently depending on the specific type of object. Every circle is drawn using the same basic techniques and information, which is different from the information needed and the steps taken to draw a rectangle. Yet both types of shapes get drawn. Different, but similar. Polymorphic.

Once a polymorphic situation is identified, the specifics of the design can be addressed. In particular, should you use inheritance or interfaces as the mechanism to define polymorphic references? The answer to that question lies in the relationships among the different types of objects involved. If those objects can be related naturally by inheritance, with true is-a relationships, then polymorphism via inheritance is probably the way to go. But if the main thing the objects have in common is their need to be processed in a particular way, then perhaps using an interface to create the polymorphic references is the better solution.

SELF-REVIEW QUESTIONS *(see answers in Appendix L)*

SR 10.20 Suppose you are designing classes for a banking-related system. Both checking accounts and savings accounts require deposit and withdraw operations. You decide to provide these behaviors using polymorphism. Which polymorphic mechanism (inheritance or interfaces) is best suited for this situation? Provide support for your choice.

SR 10.21 Suppose you are designing classes to help create aquarium-based screen savers. At times, you will want some aquarium objects to "float" from wherever they are to the top of the tank. You decide to provide this behavior using polymorphism. Which polymorphic mechanism (inheritance or interfaces) is best suited for this situation? Provide support for your choice.

SR 10.22 Suppose you are designing classes to support the modeling of rain forest environments. Animal objects, such as butterflies and monkeys, need to grow older periodically. You decide to provide this behavior using polymorphism. Which polymorphic mechanism (inheritance or interfaces) is best suited for this situation? Provide support for your choice.

10.7 Properties

A JavaFX *property* is an object that holds a value, similar to a wrapper class. But a property is *observable*, which means the property value can be monitored and changed as needed. Many JavaFX classes store properties rather than regular instance data. For instance, instead of storing an int primitive or even an `Integer` object, a JavaFX class might store an `IntegerProperty` object.

A key benefit to using properties is the concept of *property binding*. A property can be bound to another property, so that when the value of one property changes, the other is automatically updated. For example, the radius of the `Circle` class is represented by a `DoubleProperty` object, which could be bound to the property that represents the width of a `Scene`, so that the circle size changes automatically as the window is resized.

KEY CONCEPT
Many values in JavaFX classes are managed as properties, which can be bound to other properties.

The program in Listing 10.13 displays a small circle in the center of the scene, as well as two `Text` objects in the upper left corner that display the height and width of the scene. All of these elements are bound to the width and height of the scene in various ways such that, as the window (and therefore the scene) is resized, the position of the circle and the displayed text change automatically.

LISTING 10.13

```
import javafx.application.Application;
import javafx.beans.property.SimpleStringProperty;
import javafx.beans.property.StringProperty;
import javafx.scene.Group;
```

LISTING 10.13 *continued*

```
import javafx.scene.Scene;
import javafx.scene.paint.Color;
import javafx.scene.shape.Circle;
import javafx.scene.text.Text;
import javafx.stage.Stage;

//************************************************************************
//  PropertyBindingDemo.java       Author: Lewis/Loftus
//
//  Demonstrates the ability to bind one property to another.
//************************************************************************

public class PropertyBindingDemo extends Application
{
   //---------------------------------------------------------------------
   //  Displays the width and height of the scene, as well as a circle
   //  in the center of the scene. The scene is updated using property
   //  bindings as the window is resized.
   //---------------------------------------------------------------------
   public void start(Stage primaryStage)
   {
      Group root = new Group();
      Scene scene = new Scene(root, 300, 200, Color.SKYBLUE);

      Circle center = new Circle(6);
      center.centerXProperty().bind(scene.widthProperty().divide(2));
      center.centerYProperty().bind(scene.heightProperty().divide(2));

      StringProperty width = new SimpleStringProperty("Width: ");
      StringProperty height = new SimpleStringProperty("Height: ");

      Text widthText = new Text(20, 30, "");
      widthText.textProperty().bind(width.concat(scene.widthProperty()));

      Text heightText = new Text(20, 60, "");
      heightText.textProperty().bind(height.concat(scene.heightProperty()));

      root.getChildren().addAll(center, widthText, heightText);

      primaryStage.setTitle("Property Binding Demo");
      primaryStage.setScene(scene);
      primaryStage.show();
   }
}
```

LISTING 10.13 *continued*

DISPLAY

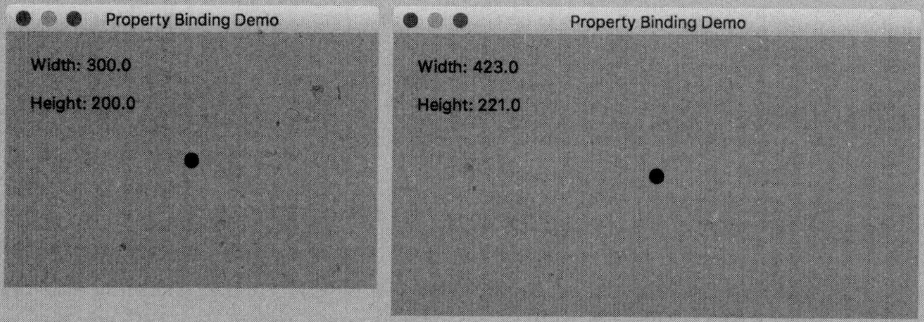

The properties that represent the x and y coordinates of the circle's center are bound to the properties that represent the width and height of the scene, respectively. The x coordinate is always kept at one-half the value of the width property, and the y coordinate is kept at one-half of the height property. So the circle stays in the center of the window as the window is resized.

The `centerXProperty` method returns the `DoubleProperty` object that represents the x coordinate of the circle. It is bound, using a call to the `bind` method of the property, to the property returned by the `widthProperty` method of the scene. That value is divided in half by a call to the `divide` method (properties are objects, so you can use regular arithmetic operators on them). A similar relationship is set up for the y coordinate and the height.

The text displayed by a `Text` object is stored as a `StringProperty` object. In this program, two additional `StringProperty` objects are created to bind them to (a property can only be bound to another property).

The text property displaying the width is bound to a string property containing `"Width: "` concatenated to the width of the scene. A similar relationship is set up for the height text.

Note that no explicit event handlers were set up for this program. Property binding is taking care of all dynamic updates to the elements in the scene.

KEY CONCEPT
Property bindings are used specifically to keep data in sync. They are not a replacement for event handlers in general.

However, it's important to recognize that a property binding cannot always be used in place of an event handler. Binding is used to keep data in sync, whereas an event handler is code executed when an event occurs to accomplish any desired effect. An event handler is, therefore, more versatile. Since we were only keeping data in sync in this program, property bindings were sufficient.

We've stated that a property is observable. To be more precise, a property implements the `ObservableValue` interface (or, more likely, one of its descendants). The `bind` method creates a `Binding` object to keep a particular value in sync with one or more sources. Methods such as `divide` also create bindings.

Change Listeners

A property can have a *change listener*, which is similar to an event handler in that it is set up to run whatever specific code you'd like. You would use a change listener if you wanted to respond to a property value changing and needed to do something other than keep two data values in sync.

Properties have an `addListener` method that can be used to set up a change listener for that property. You can specify the listener method as you would with an event handler convenience method:

```
myProperty.addListener(this::processChange);
```

A change listener method receives three parameters: the `ObservableValue` object (the property) whose value changed, the old value, and the new value. The types of the old and new values depend on the type of the value that the property holds. For example, here's a listener method that handles the changes to a `StringProperty` object:

```
public void processChange(ObservableValue<? extends String> val,
    String oldValue, String newValue)
{
    // whatever
}
```

As with event handling methods, the method name can be anything desired. Similarly, here's a change listener method that handles changes to an `IntegerProperty` object:

```
public void processChange(ObservableValue<? extends Integer> val,
    Integer oldValue, Integer newValue)
{
    // whatever
}
```

Listing 10.14 shows a program that is functionally equivalent to the `PropertyBindingDemo` program, but uses a change listener instead of property binding.

LISTING 10.14

```
import javafx.application.Application;
import javafx.beans.value.ObservableValue;
import javafx.scene.Group;
import javafx.scene.Scene;
import javafx.scene.paint.Color;
import javafx.scene.shape.Circle;
import javafx.scene.text.Text;
import javafx.stage.Stage;

//************************************************************************
//  ChangeListenerDemo.java       Author: Lewis/Loftus
//
//  Demonstrates the ability to respond to property changes using
//  change listeners. Functionally equivalent to PropertyBindingDemo.
//************************************************************************

public class ChangeListenerDemo extends Application
{
   private Scene scene;
   private Circle center;
   private Text widthText, heightText;

   //--------------------------------------------------------------------
   //  Displays the width and height of the scene, as well as a circle
   //  in the center of the scene. The scene is updated using a change
   //  listener as the window is resized.
   //--------------------------------------------------------------------
   public void start(Stage primaryStage)
   {
      Group root = new Group();

      scene = new Scene(root, 300, 200, Color.SKYBLUE);
      scene.widthProperty().addListener(this::processResize);
      scene.heightProperty().addListener(this::processResize);

      center = new Circle(6);
      center.setCenterX(scene.getWidth() / 2);
      center.setCenterY(scene.getHeight() / 2);
```

LISTING 10.14 *continued*

```
        widthText = new Text(20, 30, "Width: " + scene.getWidth());
        heightText = new Text(20, 60, "Height: " + scene.getHeight());

        root.getChildren().addAll(center, widthText, heightText);

        primaryStage.setTitle("Change Listener Demo");
        primaryStage.setScene(scene);
        primaryStage.show();
    }

    //--------------------------------------------------------------------
    //  Updates the position of the circle and the displayed width and
    //  height when the window is resized.
    //--------------------------------------------------------------------
    public void processResize(ObservableValue<? extends Number> property,
        Object oldValue, Object newValue)
    {
        center.setCenterX(scene.getWidth() / 2);
        center.setCenterY(scene.getHeight() / 2);
        widthText.setText("Width: " + scene.getWidth());
        heightText.setText("Height: " + scene.getHeight());
    }
}
```

In this version of the program, the scene, circle, and text objects are declared at the class level so that they can be accessed by the listener method. The same listener is used for changes in both the width and height of the scene.

The new property value could have been obtained from the parameters to the listener method, but then we would have had to have a separate listener for the width and height (so we'd know which property to set) and there would have been a lot of casting involved. Instead, the method parameters are ignored and the new values are taken directly from the scene object.

SELF-REVIEW QUESTIONS *(see answers in Appendix L)*

SR 10.23 What is a JavaFX property?

SR 10.24 What is the result of property binding?

SR 10.25 How do you perform mathematical operations on numeric properties?

SR 10.26 What is a change listener?

10.8 Sliders

A *slider* is a GUI control that allows the user to specify a numeric value within a bounded range. It's displayed as a track along which the slider *knob* can be dragged. A slider can be presented either vertically or horizontally and can have optional tick marks and labels indicating the range of values.

KEY CONCEPT

A slider allows the user to specify a numeric value within a bounded range.

The program shown in Listing 10.15 displays an ellipse and allows the user to control the shape of that ellipse using two sliders. The horizontal slider determines the value of the radius along the x axis of the ellipse and the vertical slider determines the value of the radius along the y axis.

LISTING 10.15

```
import javafx.application.Application;
import javafx.geometry.Insets;
import javafx.geometry.Orientation;
import javafx.scene.Scene;
import javafx.scene.control.Slider;
import javafx.scene.layout.BorderPane;
import javafx.scene.paint.Color;
import javafx.scene.shape.Ellipse;
import javafx.stage.Stage;

//************************************************************************
//  EllipseSliders.java       Author: Lewis/Loftus
//
//  Demonstrates the use of slider controls and property binding.
//************************************************************************

public class EllipseSliders extends Application
{
   private Ellipse ellipse;
   private Slider xSlider, ySlider;

   //--------------------------------------------------------------------
   //  Displays an ellipse with sliders that control the width and
   //  height of the ellipse.
   //--------------------------------------------------------------------
   public void start(Stage primaryStage)
   {
      ellipse = new Ellipse(250, 150, 150, 75);
      ellipse.setFill(Color.SALMON);
```

LISTING 10.15 *continued*

```
        xSlider = new Slider(0, 200, 150);
        xSlider.setShowTickMarks(true);
        xSlider.setPadding(new Insets(0, 20, 20, 80));

        ellipse.radiusXProperty().bind(xSlider.valueProperty());

        ySlider = new Slider(0, 100, 75);
        ySlider.setOrientation(Orientation.VERTICAL);
        ySlider.setShowTickMarks(true);
        ySlider.setPadding(new Insets(20, 0, 0, 30));

        ellipse.radiusYProperty().bind(ySlider.valueProperty());

        BorderPane pane = new BorderPane();
        pane.setLeft(ySlider);
        pane.setBottom(xSlider);
        pane.setCenter(ellipse);
        pane.setStyle("-fx-background-color: grey");

        Scene scene = new Scene(pane, 500, 300);

        primaryStage.setTitle("Ellipse Sliders");
        primaryStage.setScene(scene);
        primaryStage.show();
    }
}
```

DISPLAY

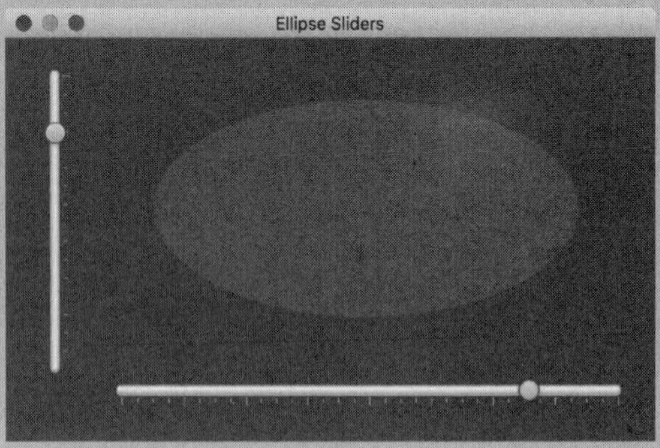

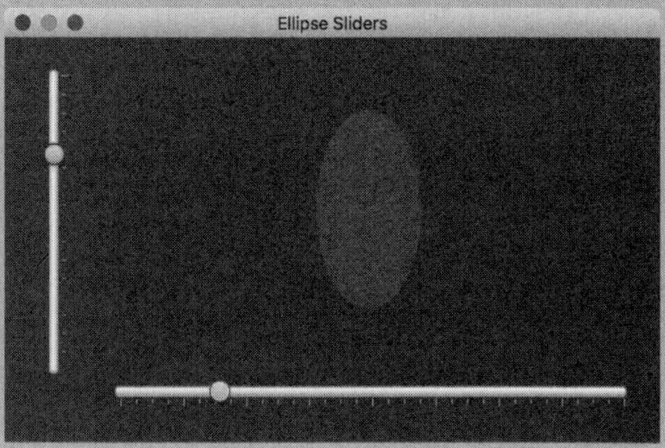

A slider is presented horizontally unless you explicitly set it to vertical using its `setOrientation` method. The `setShowTickMarks` method accepts a boolean value and is used to set whether tick marks should be displayed next to the slider bar. The `setPadding` method determines the spacing around the slider when it is displayed. The `Slider` class has additional methods that can be used to tailor the look and behavior of a slider.

The changes made to the ellipse are done through property bindings, which are discussed in Section 10.7. There are no explicit event handlers written for this program. The property representing the x radius of the ellipse is bound (using the `bind` method) to the value of the horizontal slider. Likewise, the property representing the y radius of the ellipse is bound to the value of the vertical slider. If property binding is not used, the value of a slider can also be obtained explicitly using the `getValue` method, or a change listener can be set up to react to the slider movement.

SELF-REVIEW QUESTIONS *(see answers in Appendix L)*

SR 10.27 What does a slider allow the user to do?

SR 10.28 How do you access the value that a slider represents?

10.9 Spinners

A *spinner* is a JavaFX control that allows the user to select a value from a list of predefined values arranged in a sequence. The current value is shown in a text field, and the user steps through the options using a pair of arrow buttons displayed next to, on either side of, or above and below the text field.

The options of a spinner are never displayed in a list, like they are with a drop-down choice box or combo box. In a spinner, only one value, the currently selected value, is displayed at a time. A spinner may be preferred so that the options won't obscure other elements in the GUI.

KEY CONCEPT
A spinner lets the user select a value from a list of predefined options using arrow buttons.

The program in Listing 10.16 presents two spinners, one that provides numeric options 1 through 10, and another that allows the user to select from a sequence of strings. The current values of the spinners are reflected in a `Text` object shown below them.

LISTING 10.16

```
import javafx.application.Application;
import javafx.beans.property.SimpleStringProperty;
import javafx.beans.property.StringProperty;
import javafx.collections.FXCollections;
```

LISTING 10.16 *continued*

```
import javafx.collections.ObservableList;
import javafx.geometry.Pos;
import javafx.scene.Scene;
import javafx.scene.control.Spinner;
import javafx.scene.control.SpinnerValueFactory.IntegerSpinnerValueFactory;
import javafx.scene.layout.VBox;
import javafx.scene.text.Font;
import javafx.scene.text.Text;
import javafx.stage.Stage;

//************************************************************************
//  SpinnerDemo.java        Author: Lewis/Loftus
//
//  Demonstrates the use of spinner controls and property binding.
//************************************************************************

public class SpinnerDemo extends Application
{
   private Spinner<Integer> intSpinner;
   private Spinner<String> stringSpinner;
   private Text text;

   //---------------------------------------------------------------------
   //  Presents an integer spinner and a string spinner, updating some
   //  text when either value changes.
   //---------------------------------------------------------------------
   public void start(Stage primaryStage)
   {
      IntegerSpinnerValueFactory svf =
         new IntegerSpinnerValueFactory(1, 10, 5);
      intSpinner = new Spinner<Integer>(svf);

      ObservableList<String> list = FXCollections.observableArrayList();
      list.addAll("Grumpy", "Happy", "Sneezy", "Sleepy", "Dopey",
         "Bashful", "Doc");
      stringSpinner = new Spinner<String>(list);
      stringSpinner.getStyleClass().add(
         Spinner.STYLE_CLASS_SPLIT_ARROWS_VERTICAL);

      StringProperty textString = new SimpleStringProperty("");

      text = new Text();
      text.setFont(new Font("Helvetica", 24));
```

LISTING 10.16 *continued*

```
        text.textProperty().bind(textString.concat(
            intSpinner.valueProperty()).concat(" and ").concat(
            stringSpinner.valueProperty()));

        VBox pane = new VBox(intSpinner, stringSpinner, text);
        pane.setStyle("-fx-background-color: skyblue");
        pane.setAlignment(Pos.CENTER);
        pane.setSpacing(25);

        Scene scene = new Scene(pane, 300, 250);

        primaryStage.setTitle("Spinner Demo");
        primaryStage.setScene(scene);
        primaryStage.show();
    }
}
```

DISPLAY

The set of spinner options is defined by a `SpinnerValueFactory`. In this example, the integer spinner is made by creating a `IntegerSpinnerValueFactory` with a minimum value of 1, a maximum value of 10, and an initial value of 5. The value factory is passed to the `Spinner` constructor.

For the string spinner, an `ObservableList` object serves as the value factory. It is filled with the strings representing the options, then used to create the spinner itself.

By default, the arrows of a spinner appear on the right side of the text field, pointing up and down (vertical). This is how the arrows appear on the integer spinner in the example. For the string spinner, they are explicitly set to appear above and below the text field by adding a particular spinner style class to the spinner. The `Spinner` class contains several constants that represent different arrow positions.

The `Text` object displayed at the bottom of the window is updated automatically whenever either spinner is updated. A property binding is set up to keep the displayed text in sync with the spinner values. Property bindings are discussed in Section 10.7.

SELF-REVIEW QUESTIONS *(see answers in Appendix L)*

SR 10.29 How does the user interact with a spinner?

SR 10.30 Why might a program designer opt to use a spinner rather than a choice box?

SR 10.31 What is a spinner value factory?

Summary of Key Concepts

- A polymorphic reference can refer to different types of objects over time.
- The binding of a method invocation to its definition is performed at run time for a polymorphic reference.
- A reference variable can refer to any object created from any class related to it by inheritance.
- The type of the object, not the type of the reference, is used to determine which version of a method to invoke.
- An interface name can be used to declare an object reference variable.
- An interface reference can refer to any object of any class that implements that interface.
- A parameter to a method can be polymorphic, giving the method flexible control of its arguments.
- Implementing a sort algorithm polymorphically allows it to sort any comparable set of objects.
- Polymorphism allows us to apply a consistent approach to inconsistent behaviors.
- We should hone our design senses to identify situations that lend themselves to polymorphic solutions.
- Many values in JavaFX classes are managed as properties, which can be bound to other properties.
- Property bindings are used specifically to keep data in sync. They are not a replacement for event handlers in general.
- A slider allows the user to specify a numeric value within a bounded range.
- A spinner lets the user select a value from a list of predefined options using arrow buttons.

Exercises

EX 10.1 Draw and annotate a class hierarchy that represents various types of documents, such as Word, PDF, TXT, and HTML. Each document should share a common structure consisting of the text of the document and a few basic formatting options. Explain how polymorphism could play a role in the process of displaying each document.

EX 10.2 Draw and annotate a class hierarchy that represents various cases of crime that are presented in a court. Show what characteristics would be represented in the various classes of the hierarchy. Explain how polymorphism could play a role in determining the sentences for the different types of crime.

EX 10.3 Draw and annotate a class hierarchy that represents various types of sales transactions in a store (cash, credit, etc.). Show what characteristics would be represented in the various classes of the hierarchy. Explain how polymorphism could play a role in the payment process.

EX 10.4 What would happen if the `pay` method were not defined as an abstract method in the `StaffMember` class of the `Firm` program?

EX 10.5 Describe a property binding that you could set up other than the examples used in this chapter.

EX 10.6 Write a statement that would bind the property representing the radius of a `Circle` object to the property representing the value in a slider.

Programming Projects

VideoNote
Developing a solution of PP 10.1.

PP 10.1 Modify the `Firm` example from this chapter such that it accomplishes its polymorphism using an interface called `Payable`.

PP 10.2 Define a class called `Planet` that represents a planet in our solar system. The `Planet` class should have a planet's name, mass in kilograms, diameter, distance from the sun, atmospheric conditions, and number of moons. Define a class called `ExoPlanet` that extends the `Planet` class to include the name of the star around which the exoplanet revolves. Modify the `toString` method of `ExoPlanet` to return the additional information. Write a driver program to display a few of these planets and exoplanets.

PP 10.3 Implement the `Speaker` interface described in Section 10.3, and create three classes that implement `Speaker` in various ways. Create a driver class whose `main` method instantiates some of these objects and tests their abilities.

PP 10.4 Rewrite the `Sorting` class so that both sorting algorithms put the values in descending order. Create a driver class with a `main` method to exercise the modifications.

PP 10.5 Write a program that stores a list of planets as defined in PP 10.2 in an `ArrayList`. Print the list of planets in the ascending order of mass.

PP 10.6 Create a new version of the `EllipseSliders` program from this chapter that uses change listeners instead of property binding to achieve the same functionality.

PP 10.7 Write a JavaFX application that displays a spinner with the options listing a number of different shapes, such as squares, circles, and arcs. When the user selects a shape, display the selected shape. Use a change listener to add this functionality.

PP 10.8 Write a JavaFX application that displays a `Text` object and a slider that controls the font size of the text.

PP 10.9 Create a new version of the `QuoteOptions` program from Chapter 5 that uses a spinner to pick the quote category rather than a set of radio buttons.

11

Exceptions

CHAPTER OBJECTIVES

- Discuss the purpose of exceptions.
- Examine exception messages and the call stack trace.
- Examine the `try-catch` statement for handling exceptions.
- Explore the concept of exception propagation.
- Describe the exception class hierarchy in the Java standard class library.
- Explore I/O exceptions and the ability to write text files.
- Enhance GUIs using tool tips and disabled components
- Explore additional GUI controls and containers.

Exception handling is an important part of an object-oriented software system. Exceptions represent problems or unusual situations that may occur in a program. Java provides various ways to handle exceptions when they occur. We explore the class hierarchy from the Java standard library used to define exceptions, as well as the ability to define our own exception objects. This chapter also discusses the use of exceptions when dealing with input and output, and examines an example that writes a text file. The Graphics Track sections of this chapter explore some GUI details that can improve the user experience, as well as some additional controls and containers.

11.1 Exception Handling

As we've discussed briefly in other parts of the text, problems that arise in a Java program may generate exceptions or errors. An *exception* is an object that defines an unusual or erroneous situation. An exception is thrown by a program or the run-time environment and can be caught and handled appropriately if desired. An *error* is similar to an exception except that an error generally represents an unrecoverable situation and should not be caught. Java has a predefined set of exceptions and errors that may occur during the execution of a program.

KEY CONCEPT
Errors and exceptions are objects that represent unusual or invalid processing.

Problem situations represented by exceptions and errors can have various kinds of root causes. Here are some situations that cause exceptions to be thrown:

- Attempting to divide by zero.
- An array index that is out of bounds.
- A specified file that could not be found.
- A requested I/O operation that could not be completed normally.
- An attempt was made to follow a null reference.
- An attempt was made to execute an operation that violates some kind of security measure.

These are just a few examples. There are dozens of others that address very specific situations.

As many of these examples show, an exception can represent a truly erroneous situation. But as the name implies, they may simply represent an exceptional situation. That is, an exception may represent a situation that won't occur under usual conditions. Exception handling is set up to be an efficient way to deal with such situations, especially given that they don't happen too often.

We have several options when it comes to dealing with exceptions. A program can be designed to process an exception in one of three ways. It can:

- not handle the exception at all,
- handle the exception where it occurs, or
- handle the exception at another point in the program.

We explore each of these approaches in the following sections.

SELF-REVIEW QUESTIONS *(see answers in Appendix L)*

SR 11.1 What is the difference between an error and an exception?

SR 11.2 In what ways might a thrown exception be handled?

11.2 Uncaught Exceptions

If a program does not handle the exception at all, it will terminate abnormally and produce a message that describes what exception occurred and where it was produced. The information associated with an exception is often helpful in tracking down the cause of a problem.

Let's look at the output of an exception. The program shown in Listing 11.1 throws an `ArithmeticException` when an invalid arithmetic operation is attempted. In this case, the program attempts to divide by zero.

Because there is no code in this program to handle the exception explicitly, it terminates when the exception occurs, printing specific information about the exception. Note that the last `println` statement in the program never executes, because the exception occurs first.

LISTING 11.1

```
//********************************************************************
//  Zero.java       Author: Lewis/Loftus
//
//  Demonstrates an uncaught exception.
//********************************************************************

public class Zero
{
   //-----------------------------------------------------------------
   //  Deliberately divides by zero to produce an exception.
   //-----------------------------------------------------------------
   public static void main(String[] args)
   {
      int numerator = 10;
      int denominator = 0;

      System.out.println(numerator / denominator);

      System.out.println("This text will not be printed.");
   }
}
```

OUTPUT

```
Exception in thread "main" java.lang.ArithmeticException: / by zero
        at Zero.main(Zero.java:17)
```

KEY CONCEPT
The messages printed when an exception is thrown provide a method call stack trace.

The first line of the exception output indicates which exception was thrown and provides some information about why it was thrown. The remaining lines are the *call stack trace*; they indicate where the exception occurred. In this case, there is only one line in the call stack trace, but there may be several depending on where the exception originated. The first trace line indicates the method, file, and line number where the exception occurred. The other trace lines, if present, indicate the methods that were called to get to the method that produced the exception. In this program, there is only one method, and it produced the exception; therefore, there is only one line in the trace.

The call stack trace information is also available by calling methods of the exception class that is being thrown. The method `getMessage` returns a string explaining the reason the exception was thrown. The method `printStackTrace` prints the call stack trace.

SELF-REVIEW QUESTIONS *(see answer in Appendix L)*

SR 11.3 True or False. Explain.

a. An exception and an error are the same thing.
b. An attempt to divide by zero will cause an exception to be thrown.
c. If a program does not handle a raised exception, the exception is ignored and nothing happens.
d. If a program does not handle an exception, a message related to the exception will be produced.
e. A call stack trace shows the sequence of method calls that led to the code where an exception occurred.

11.3 The `try-catch` Statement

Let's now examine how we catch and handle an exception when it is thrown. The *try-catchstatement* identifies a block of statements that may throw an exception. A *catch clause*, which follows a `try` block, defines how a particular kind of exception is handled. A `try` block can have several `catch` clauses associated with it. Each `catch` clause is called an *exception handler*.

When a `try` statement is executed, the statements in the `try` block are executed. If no exception is thrown during the execution of the `try` block, processing continues with the statement following the `try` statement (after all of the `catch` clauses). This situation is the normal execution flow and should occur most of the time.

If an exception is thrown at any point during the execution of the `try` block, control is immediately transferred to the appropriate catch handler if it is present. That is, control transfers to the first `catch` clause whose exception class corresponds to the exception that was thrown. After executing the statements in the `catch` clause, control transfers to the statement after the entire `try-catch` statement.

KEY CONCEPT

Each `catch` clause handles a particular kind of exception that may be thrown within the `try` block.

Let's look at an example. Suppose a hypothetical company uses codes to represent its various products. A product code includes, among other information, a character in the 10th position that represents the zone from which that product was made, and a four-digit integer in positions 4 through 7 that represents the district in which it will be sold. Due to some reorganization, products from zone R are banned from being sold in districts with a designation of 2000 or higher. The program shown in Listing 11.2 reads product codes from the user and counts the number of banned codes entered.

Try Statement

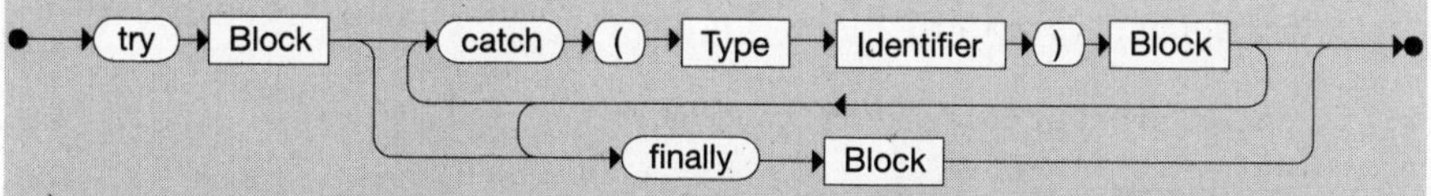

A `try` statement contains a block of code followed by one or more `catch` clauses. If an exception occurs in the `try` block, the code of the corresponding `catch` clause is executed. The `finally` clause, if present, is executed no matter how the `try` block is exited.

Example:

```
try
{
   System.out.println(Integer.parseInt(numString));
}
catch (NumberFormatException exception)
{
   System.out.println("Caught an exception.");
}
finally
{
   System.out.println("Done.");
}
```

LISTING 11.2

```
//********************************************************************
//  ProductCodes.java       Author: Lewis/Loftus
//
//  Demonstrates the use of a try-catch block.
//********************************************************************

import java.util.Scanner;

public class ProductCodes
{
   //-----------------------------------------------------------------
   //  Counts the number of product codes that are entered with a
   //  zone of R and and district greater than 2000.
   //-----------------------------------------------------------------
   public static void main(String[] args)
   {
      String code;
      char zone;
      int district, valid = 0, banned = 0;

      Scanner scan = new Scanner(System.in);

      System.out.print("Enter product code (XXX to quit): ");
      code = scan.nextLine();

      while (!code.equals("XXX"))
      {
         try
         {
            zone = code.charAt(9);
            district = Integer.parseInt(code.substring(3, 7));
            valid++;
            if (zone == 'R' && district > 2000)
               banned++;
         }
         catch (StringIndexOutOfBoundsException exception)
         {
            System.out.println("Improper code length: " + code);
         }
         catch (NumberFormatException exception)
         {
            System.out.println("District is not numeric: " + code);
         }
```

LISTING 11.2 *continued*

```
            System.out.print("Enter product code (XXX to quit): ");
            code = scan.nextLine();
        }

        System.out.println("# of valid codes entered: " + valid);
        System.out.println("# of banned codes entered: " + banned);
    }
}
```

OUTPUT

```
Enter product code (XXX to quit): TRV2475A5R-14
Enter product code (XXX to quit): TRD1704A7R-12
Enter product code (XXX to quit): TRL2k74A5R-11
District is not numeric: TRL2k74A5R-11
Enter product code (XXX to quit): TRQ2949A6M-04
Enter product code (XXX to quit): TRV2105A2
Improper code length: TRV2105A2
Enter product code (XXX to quit): TRQ2778A7R-19
Enter product code (XXX to quit): XXX
# of valid codes entered: 4
# of banned codes entered: 2
```

The programming statements in the `try` block attempt to pull out the zone and district information, and then determine whether it represents a banned product code. If there is any problem extracting the zone and district information, the product code is considered to be invalid and is not processed further. For example, a `StringIndexOutOfBoundsException` could be thrown by either the `charAt` or `substring` methods. Furthermore, a `NumberFormatException` could be thrown by the `parseInt` method if the substring does not contain a valid integer. A particular message is printed depending on which exception is thrown. In either case, since the exception is caught and handled, processing continues normally.

Note that, for each code examined, the integer `valid` is incremented only if no exception is thrown. If an exception is thrown, control transfers immediately to the appropriate `catch` clause. Likewise, the zone and district are tested by the `if` statement only if no exception is thrown.

The `finally` Clause

KEY CONCEPT

The `finally` clause is executed whether the `try` block is exited normally or because of a thrown exception.

A `try-catch` statement can have an optional *finally clause*. The `finally` clause defines a section of code that is executed no matter how the `try` block is exited. Most often, a `finally` clause is used to manage resources or to guarantee that particular parts of an algorithm are executed.

If no exception is generated, the statements in the `finally` clause are executed after the `try` block is complete. If an exception is generated in the `try` block, control first transfers to the appropriate `catch` clause. After executing the exception-handling code, control transfers to the `finally` clause and its statements are executed. A `finally` clause, if present, must be listed following the `catch` clauses.

Note that a `try` block does not need to have a `catch` clause at all. If there are no `catch` clauses, a `finally` clause may used by itself if that is appropriate for the situation.

SELF-REVIEW QUESTIONS *(see answers in Appendix L)*

SR 11.4 What is a `catch` clause?

SR 11.5 What is a `finally` clause?

SR 11.6 What output is produced by the following code fragment under each of the stated conditions?

```
try
{
   review.question();
}
catch (Exception1 exception)
{
   System.out.println("one caught");
}
catch (Exception2 exception)
{
   System.out.println("two caught");
}
finally
{
   System.out.println("finally");
}
System.out.println("the end");
```

a. No exception is thrown by the `review.question()` method.

b. An `Exception1` exception is thrown by the `review.question()` method.
c. An `Exception2` exception is thrown by the `review.question()` method.
d. An `Exception3` exception is thrown by the `review.question()` method.

11.4 Exception Propagation

If an exception is not caught and handled where it occurs, control is immediately returned to the method that invoked the method that produced the exception. We can design our software so that the exception is caught and handled at this outer level. If it isn't caught there, control returns to the method that called it. This process is called *propagating the exception.* This propagation continues until the exception is caught and handled or until it is passed out of the `main` method, which terminates the program and produces an exception message. To catch an exception at an outer level, the method that produces the exception must be invoked inside a `try` block that has `catch` clauses to handle it.

KEY CONCEPT
If an exception is not caught and handled where it occurs, it is propagated to the calling method.

The `Propagation` program shown in Listing 11.3 succinctly demonstrates the process of exception propagation. The `main` method invokes method `level1` in the `ExceptionScope` class (see Listing 11.4), which invokes `level2`, which invokes `level3`, which produces an exception. Method `level3` does not catch and handle the exception, so control is transferred back to `level2`. The `level2` method does not catch and handle the exception either, so control is transferred back to `level1`. Because the invocation of `level2` is made inside a `try` block (in method `level1`), the exception is caught and handled at that point.

Note that the output does not include the messages indicating that the methods `level3` and `level2` are ending. These `println` statements are never executed, because an exception occurred and had not yet been caught. However, after method `level1` handles the exception, processing continues normally from that point, printing the messages indicating that method `level1` and the program are ending.

VideoNote
Proper exception handling.

Note also that the `catch` clause that handles the exception uses the `getMessage` and `printStackTrace` methods to output that information. The stack trace shows the methods that were called when the exception occurred.

LISTING 11.3

```
//********************************************************************
//  Propagation.java       Author: Lewis/Loftus
//
//  Demonstrates exception propagation.
//********************************************************************

public class Propagation
{
   //-----------------------------------------------------------------
   //  Invokes the level1 method to begin the exception demonstration.
   //-----------------------------------------------------------------
   public static void main(String[] args)
   {
      ExceptionScope demo = new ExceptionScope();

      System.out.println("Program beginning.");
      demo.level1();
      System.out.println("Program ending.");
   }
}
```

OUTPUT

```
Program beginning.
Level 1 beginning.
Level 2 beginning.
Level 3 beginning.

The exception message is: / by zero

The call stack trace:
java.lang.ArithmeticException: / by zero
        at ExceptionScope.level3(ExceptionScope.java:54)
        at ExceptionScope.level2(ExceptionScope.java:41)
        at ExceptionScope.level1(ExceptionScope.java:18)
        at Propagation.main(Propagation.java:17)

Level 1 ending.
Program ending.
```

LISTING 11.4

```
//********************************************************************
//  ExceptionScope.java       Author: Lewis/Loftus
//
//  Demonstrates exception propagation.
//********************************************************************

public class ExceptionScope
{
   //-----------------------------------------------------------------
   // Catches and handles the exception that is thrown in level3.
   //-----------------------------------------------------------------
   public void level1()
   {
      System.out.println("Level 1 beginning.");

      try
      {
         level2();
      }
      catch (ArithmeticException problem)
      {
         System.out.println();
         System.out.println("The exception message is: " +
                             problem.getMessage());
         System.out.println();
         System.out.println("The call stack trace:");
         problem.printStackTrace();
         System.out.println();
      }

      System.out.println("Level 1 ending.");
   }

   //-----------------------------------------------------------------
   //  Serves as an intermediate level. The exception propagates
   //  through this method back to level1.
   //-----------------------------------------------------------------
   public void level2()
   {
      System.out.println("Level 2 beginning.");
      level3();
      System.out.println("Level 2 ending.");
   }
```

LISTING 11.4 *continued*

```
   //-----------------------------------------------------------------
   // Performs a calculation to produce an exception. It is not
   // caught and handled at this level.
   //-----------------------------------------------------------------
   public void level3()
   {
      int numerator = 10, denominator = 0;

      System.out.println("Level 3 beginning.");
      int result = numerator / denominator;
      System.out.println("Level 3 ending.");
   }
}
```

KEY CONCEPT

A programmer must carefully consider how and where exceptions should be handled, if at all.

A programmer must pick the most appropriate level at which to catch and handle an exception. There is no single best answer as to how to do this. It depends on the situation and the design of the system. Sometimes the right approach will be not to catch an exception at all and let the program terminate.

SELF-REVIEW QUESTIONS *(see answers in Appendix L)*

SR 11.7 What happens if an exception is not caught?

SR 11.8 How would the result of the `Propagation` program change if the following code fragment was placed in the `level2` method just before the call to the `level3` method?

```
int num = 10, den = 0;
int res = num / den;
```

SR 11.9 How would the result of the `Propagation` program change if the following code fragment was placed in the `level2` method just after the call to the `level3` method?

```
int num = 10, den = 0;
int res = num / den;
```

11.5 The Exception Class Hierarchy

The classes that define various exceptions are related by inheritance, creating a class hierarchy that is shown in part in Figure 11.1.

The `Throwable` class is the parent of both the `Error` class and the `Exception` class. Many types of exceptions are derived from the `Exception` class, and these classes also have many children. Though these high-level classes are defined in the `java.lang` package, many child classes that define specific exceptions are part of several other packages. Inheritance relationships can span package boundaries.

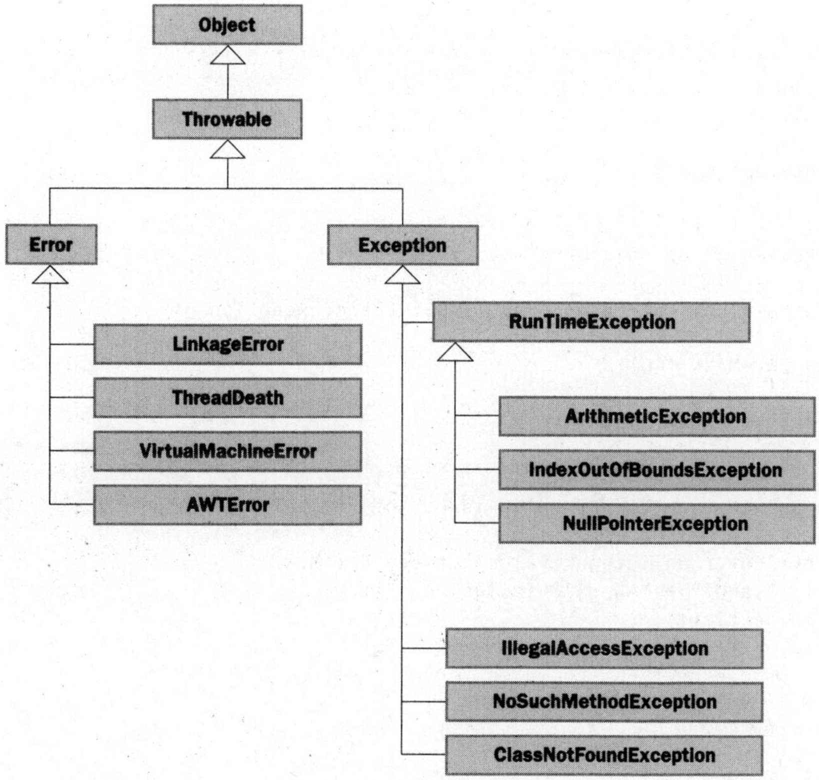

FIGURE 11.1 Part of the `Error` and `Exception` class hierarchy

We can define our own exceptions by deriving a new class from `Exception` or one of its descendants. The class we choose as the parent depends on what situation or condition the new exception represents.

KEY CONCEPT
A new exception is defined by deriving a new class from the `Exception` class or one of its descendants.

The program in Listing 11.5 instantiates an exception object and throws it. The exception is created from the `OutOfRangeException` class, which is shown in Listing 11.6. Note that this exception is not part of the Java standard class library. It was created to represent the situation in which a value is outside a particular valid range.

LISTING 11.5

```
//********************************************************************
//  CreatingExceptions.java       Author: Lewis/Loftus
//
//  Demonstrates the ability to define an exception via inheritance.
//********************************************************************

import java.util.Scanner;

public class CreatingExceptions
{
   //-----------------------------------------------------------------
   // Creates an exception object and possibly throws it.
   //-----------------------------------------------------------------
   public static void main(String[] args) throws OutOfRangeException
   {
      final int MIN = 25, MAX = 40;

      Scanner scan = new Scanner(System.in);

      OutOfRangeException problem =
         new OutOfRangeException("Input value is out of range.");

      System.out.print("Enter an integer value between " + MIN +
                       " and " + MAX + ", inclusive: ");
      int value = scan.nextInt();

      //  Determine if the exception should be thrown
      if (value < MIN || value > MAX)
         throw problem;

      System.out.println("End of main method.");   // may never reach
   }
}
```

LISTING 11.5 *continued*

OUTPUT

```
Enter an integer value between 25 and 40, inclusive: 69
Exception in thread "main" OutOfRangeException:
   Input value is out of range.
   at CreatingExceptions.main(CreatingExceptions.java:20)
```

After reading in an input value, the `main` method evaluates it to see whether it is in the valid range. If not, the *throw statement* is executed. A `throw` statement is used to begin exception propagation. Because the `main` method does not catch and handle the exception, the program will terminate if the exception is thrown, printing the message associated with the exception.

We create the `OutOfRangeException` class by extending the `Exception` class. Often, a new exception is nothing more than what you see in this example: an extension of some existing exception class that stores a particular message describing the situation it represents. The important point is that the class is ultimately

LISTING 11.6

```
//********************************************************************
//  OutOfRangeException.java       Author: Lewis/Loftus
//
//  Represents an exceptional condition in which a value is out of
//  some particular range.
//********************************************************************

public class OutOfRangeException extends Exception
{
   //-----------------------------------------------------------------
   // Sets up the exception object with a particular message.
   //-----------------------------------------------------------------
   OutOfRangeException(String message)
   {
      super(message);
   }
}
```

a descendant of the `Exception` class and the `Throwable` class, which gives it the ability to be thrown using a `throw` statement.

The type of situation handled by this program, in which a value is out of range, does not need to be represented as an exception. We've previously handled such situations using conditionals or loops. Whether you handle a situation using an exception or whether you take care of it in the normal flow of your program is an important design decision.

Checked and Unchecked Exceptions

Some exceptions are checked, whereas others are unchecked. A *checked exception* must either be caught by a method or it must be listed in the *throws clause* of any method that may throw or propagate it. A `throws` clause is appended to the header of a method definition to formally acknowledge that the method will throw or propagate a particular exception if it occurs. An *unchecked exception* requires no `throws` clause.

KEY CONCEPT
The `throws` clause on a method header must be included for checked exceptions that are not caught and handled in the method.

The only unchecked exceptions in Java are objects of type `RuntimeException` or any of its descendants. All other exceptions are considered checked exceptions. The `main` method of the `CreatingExceptions` program has a `throws` clause, indicating that it may throw an `OutOfRangeException`. This `throws` clause is required because the `OutOfRangeException` was derived from the `Exception` class, making it a checked exception.

SELF-REVIEW QUESTIONS *(see answers in Appendix L)*

SR 11.10 What is a checked exception?

SR 11.11 True or False? Explain.

a. An `ArithmeticException` is an `Exception`.
b. An `ArithmeticException` is `Throwable`.
c. An `ArithmeticException` is a checked exception.
d. A `NoSuchMethodException` is a checked exception.
e. We can create our own exceptions by extending the `Exception` class.
f. A `throws` clause must be appended to the header of a method definition if the method may potentially throw an `ArithmeticException`.

SR 11.12 What happens if the input to the `CreatingExceptions` program is 42? What if it is −3?

11.6 I/O Exceptions

Processing input and output is a task that often produces unforeseeable situations, leading to exceptions being thrown. Let's explore some I/O issues and the problems that may arise.

A *stream* is an ordered sequence of bytes. The term stream comes from the analogy that as we read and write information, the data flows from a source to a destination (or *sink*) as water flows down a stream. The source of the information is like a spring filling the stream, and the destination is like a cave into which the stream flows.

> **KEY CONCEPT**
> A stream is a sequential sequence of bytes; it can be used as a source of input or a destination for output.

In a program, we treat a stream as either an *input stream*, from which we read information, or as an *output stream*, to which we write information. A program can deal with multiple input and output streams at one time. A particular store of data, such as a file, can serve either as an input stream or as an output stream to a program, but it generally cannot be both at the same time.

There are three streams that are referred to as the *standard I/O streams*. They are listed in Figure 11.2. The `System` class contains three object variables (`in`, `out`, and `err`) that represent the three standard I/O streams. These references are declared as both public and static, which allows them to be accessed directly through the `System` class.

> **KEY CONCEPT**
> Three public reference variables in the `System` class represent the standard I/O streams.

Throughout this book we've been using the standard output stream, with calls to `System.out.println` for instance. We've also used the standard input stream to create a `Scanner` object when we want to process input read interactively from the user. The `Scanner` class manages the input read from the standard input stream in various ways that makes our programming tasks easier. It also processes various I/O exceptions internally, creating an `InputMismatchException` when needed.

The standard I/O streams, by default, represent particular I/O devices. `System.in` typically represents keyboard input, whereas `System.out` and `System.err`

Standard I/O Stream	Description
`System.in`	Standard input stream.
`System.out`	Standard output stream.
`System.err`	Standard error stream (output for error messages)

FIGURE 11.2 Standard I/O streams

typically represent a particular window on the monitor screen. The `System.out` and `System.err` streams write output to the same window by default, though they could be set up to write to different places. The `System.err` stream is usually where error messages are sent.

In addition to the standard input streams, the `java.io` package of the Java API provides many classes that let us define streams with particular characteristics. Some of the classes deal with files, others with memory, and others with strings. Some classes assume that the data they handle consists of characters, whereas others assume the data consists of raw bytes of binary information. Some classes provide the means to manipulate the data in the stream in some way, such as buffering the information or numbering it. By combining classes in appropriate ways, we can create objects that represent a stream of information that has the exact characteristics we want for a particular situation.

KEY CONCEPT
The Java class library contains many classes for defining I/O streams with various characteristics.

The broad topic of Java I/O, along with the sheer number of classes in the `java.io` package, prohibits us from covering it in detail in this book. Our focus for the moment is on I/O exceptions.

Many operations performed by I/O classes can potentially throw an `IOException`. The `IOException` class is the parent of several exception classes that represent problems when trying to perform I/O.

An `IOException` is a checked exception. As described earlier in this chapter, that means that either the exception must be caught, or all methods that propagate it must list it in a `throws` clause of the method header.

Because I/O often deals with external resources, many problems can arise in programs that attempt to perform I/O operations. For example, a file from which we want to read might not exist; when we attempt to open the file, an exception will be thrown, because that file can't be found. In general, we should try to design programs to be as robust as possible when dealing with potential problems.

We've seen in previous examples how we can use the `Scanner` class to read and process input read from a text file. Now let's explore an example that writes data to a text output file.

Suppose we want to test a program we are writing, but don't have the real data available. We could write a program that generates a test data file that contains random values. The program shown in Listing 11.7 generates a file that contains random integer values within a particular range. It also writes one line of standard output, confirming that the data file has been written.

LISTING 11.7

```
//********************************************************************
//  TestData.java       Author: Lewis/Loftus
//
//  Demonstrates I/O exceptions and the use of a character file
//  output stream.
//********************************************************************

import java.util.Random;
import java.io.*;

public class TestData
{
   //-----------------------------------------------------------------
   //  Creates a file of test data that consists of ten lines each
   //  containing ten integer values in the range 10 to 99.
   //-----------------------------------------------------------------
   public static void main(String[] args) throws IOException
   {
      final int MAX = 10;

      int value;
      String fileName = "test.txt";

      PrintWriter outFile = new PrintWriter(fileName);

      Random rand = new Random();

      for (int line=1; line <= MAX; line++)
      {
         for (int num=1; num <= MAX; num++)
         {
            value = rand.nextInt (90) + 10;
            outFile.print (value + "   ");
         }
         outFile.println ();
      }
```

LISTING 11.7 *continued*

```
        outFile.close();
        System.out.println("Output file has been created: " + fileName);
    }
}
```

OUTPUT

```
Output file has been created: test.txt
```

The constructor of the `PrintWriter` class accepts a string representing a file name to be opened as a text output stream. Like the `System.out` object, a `PrintWriter` object has `print` and `println` methods that can be used to write the data to the file.

The data that is contained in the file `test.txt` after the `TestData` program is run might look like this:

85	90	93	15	82	79	52	71	70	98
74	57	41	66	22	16	67	65	24	84
86	61	91	79	18	81	64	41	68	81
98	47	28	40	69	10	85	82	64	41
23	61	27	10	59	89	88	26	24	76
33	89	73	36	54	91	42	73	95	58
19	41	18	14	63	80	96	30	17	28
24	37	40	64	94	23	98	10	78	50
89	28	64	54	59	23	61	15	80	88
51	28	44	48	73	21	41	52	35	38

Note that in the `TestData` program, we have eliminated explicit exception handling. That is, if something goes wrong, we simply allow the program to terminate instead of specifically catching and handling the problem. Because all `IOExceptions` are checked exceptions, we must include the `throws` clause on the method header to indicate that they may be thrown. For each program, we must carefully consider how best to handle the exceptions that may be thrown. This requirement is especially important when dealing with I/O, which is fraught with potential problems that cannot always be foreseen.

The `TestData` program uses nested `for` loops to compute random values and write them to the output file. After all values are printed, the file is closed. Output files must be closed explicitly to ensure that the data is retained. In general, it is good practice to close all file streams explicitly when they are no longer needed.

SELF-REVIEW QUESTIONS *(see answers in Appendix L)*

SR 11.13 What is a stream?

SR 11.14 What are the standard I/O streams?

SR 11.15 What `Stream` class object have we been using explicitly throughout this book?

SR 11.16 An I/O exception, the `InputMismatchException`, will occur during the `main` method of the `CreatingExceptions` program (see Listing 11.5) if the user enters an alphabetic character. Why doesn't the `main` method definition include a throws `InputMismatchException` clause?

SR 11.17 An I/O exception, the `FileNotFoundException`, will occur during the `main` method of the `TestData` program if the `test.txt` is not writable. Why doesn't the `main` method definition include a throws `FileNotFoundException` clause?

SR 11.18 What is the purpose of the `close` method of the `PrintWriter` class?

11.7 Tool Tips and Disabling Controls

Paying attention to details when designing a graphical user interface (GUI) can often be the difference between a good user experience and a bad one. This section describes two such details: tool tips and the ability to disable controls.

A *tool tip* is a short line of text that appears when the mouse pointer is paused momentarily over a control or other GUI element. Tool tips are usually used to provide a hint to the user about the control, such as the purpose of a button. They are especially helpful with buttons that display icons instead of text.

KEY CONCEPT
A tool tip provides a hint to the user about the purpose of a control.

A tool tip is represented by the `ToolTip` class, and can be applied to any node in a scene graph. Tool tips are most often applied to controls, which have a convenience method called `setToolTip` for setting them up:

```
myButton.setToolTip(new ToolTip("Update the total cost"));
```

Another helpful practice when designing a GUI is to *disable* a control if it should not be used or currently has no effect. For example, you might disable a slider controlling the volume of the background music until the user checks the check box that indicates background music should be played.

KEY CONCEPT
Controls should be disabled when their use is inappropriate.

A disabled control appears "greyed out" and doesn't respond to any user attempt to interact with it. Disabled components not only convey to the user which actions are appropriate and which aren't, they may also prevent erroneous situations from occurring.

Controls are enabled by default. To disable a control, call it's `setDisable` method, passing in the boolean value `true`:

```
myButton.setDisable(true);
```

To re-enable the control, call `setDisable` again, passing in `false`.

The program in Listing 11.8 uses both tool tips and disabled controls. The scene displays the image of a light bulb and two buttons. The buttons control whether the light bulb is "on" or "off".

LISTING 11.8

```
import javafx.application.Application;
import javafx.event.ActionEvent;
import javafx.geometry.Pos;
import javafx.geometry.Rectangle2D;
import javafx.scene.Scene;
import javafx.scene.control.Button;
import javafx.scene.control.Tooltip;
import javafx.scene.image.Image;
import javafx.scene.image.ImageView;
import javafx.scene.layout.HBox;
import javafx.scene.layout.VBox;
import javafx.stage.Stage;

//************************************************************************
//  LightBulb.java       Author: Lewis/Loftus
//
//  Demonstrates the use of tool tips and disabled controls.
//************************************************************************

public class LightBulb extends Application
{
   private Button onButton, offButton;
   private ImageView bulbView;

   //--------------------------------------------------------------------
   //  Displays an image of a light bulb that can be turned on and off
   //  using enabled buttons with tool tips set.
   //--------------------------------------------------------------------
   public void start(Stage primaryStage)
```

LISTING 11.8 *continued*

```
   {
      Image img = new Image("lightBulbs.png");
      bulbView = new ImageView(img);
      bulbView.setViewport(new Rectangle2D(0, 0, 125, 200));   // off

      onButton = new Button("On");
      onButton.setPrefWidth(70);
      onButton.setTooltip(new Tooltip("Turn me on!"));
      onButton.setOnAction(this::processButtonPress);

      offButton = new Button("Off");
      offButton.setPrefWidth(70);
      offButton.setTooltip(new Tooltip("Turn me off!"));
      offButton.setDisable(true);
      offButton.setOnAction(this::processButtonPress);

      HBox buttons = new HBox(onButton, offButton);
      buttons.setAlignment(Pos.CENTER);
      buttons.setSpacing(30);

      VBox root = new VBox(bulbView, buttons);
      root.setAlignment(Pos.CENTER);
      root.setStyle("-fx-background-color: black");
      root.setSpacing(20);

      Scene scene = new Scene(root, 250, 300);

      primaryStage.setTitle("Light Bulb");
      primaryStage.setScene(scene);
      primaryStage.show();
   }

   //--------------------------------------------------------------------
   //  Determines which button was pressed and sets the image viewport
   //  appropriately to show either the on or off bulb. Also swaps the
   //  disable state of both buttons.
   //--------------------------------------------------------------------
   public void processButtonPress(ActionEvent event)
   {
      if (event.getSource() == onButton)
      {
         bulbView.setViewport(new Rectangle2D(143, 0, 125, 200));  // on
         onButton.setDisable(true);
         offButton.setDisable(false);
```

LISTING 11.8 *continued*

```
        }
        else
        {
            bulbView.setViewport(new Rectangle2D(0, 0, 125, 200));  // off
            offButton.setDisable(true);
            onButton.setDisable(false);
        }
    }
}
```

DISPLAY

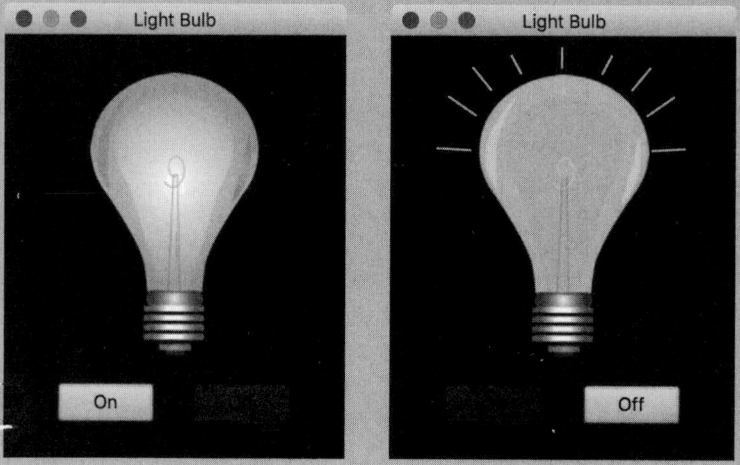

The two buttons are labeled On and Off. Both buttons have tool tips set, such that when the user rests the mouse pointer on top of either one, appropriate text appears explaining the purpose of the button.

The buttons are also set up so that only one of them is enabled at a time. Initially, the light bulb is off, so the Off button is disabled. That indicates to the user that the On button is the only appropriate action at that moment. When the user presses the On button, the image of the light bulb changes, the On button is disabled, and the Off button is enabled.

FIGURE 11.3 The image used in the `LightBulb` program.

There is actually only one image used in this program; it contains both the "off" and "on" versions of the light bulb side by side (see Figure 11.3). A viewport is used on the `ImageView` to display only one side or the other at any point. Viewports were introduced in Chapter 4.

One event handler method is used to process both buttons. That method determines which button was pressed, then changes the viewport and disabled status of the buttons accordingly.

SELF-REVIEW QUESTIONS *(see answers in Appendix L)*

SR 11.19 What is a tool tip?

SR 11.20 Why might you want to disable a control?

11.8 Scroll Panes

Sometimes we need to deal with images or information that is too large to fit in a reasonable area. A *scroll pane* is often helpful in these situations because it offers a limited view of the underlying node, and provides scroll bars that allow the user to change what section is visible.

KEY CONCEPT
A scroll pane is useful for viewing large images or large amounts of data.

The program in Listing 11.9 displays a scroll pane that contains a fairly large map of the United States. Only part of the map is visible, but the user can use the scroll bars along the right side and bottom of the pane to change which section of the map is visible.

The image is loaded into an `Image` object, which is used to create an `ImageView`. The image view is then passed to the `ScrollPane` constructor.

To view a different section of the map, the user can drag the knob of either scroll bar. Alternatively, the user can move the knob by clicking in the scroll bar itself, or by clicking the small arrows at either end of the scroll bar.

LISTING 11.9

```
import javafx.application.Application;
import javafx.scene.Scene;
import javafx.scene.control.ScrollPane;
import javafx.scene.image.Image;
import javafx.scene.image.ImageView;
import javafx.stage.Stage;

//************************************************************************
//  MapViewer.java       Author: Lewis/Loftus
//
//  Demonstrates the use of a scroll pane.
//************************************************************************

public class MapViewer extends Application
{
   //--------------------------------------------------------------------
   //  Presents a scroll pane that allows the user to determine which
   //  section of the underlying image (a map of the USA) is visible.
   //--------------------------------------------------------------------
   public void start(Stage primaryStage)
   {
      Image img = new Image("map.jpg");
      ImageView imgView = new ImageView(img);

      ScrollPane root = new ScrollPane(imgView);

      Scene scene = new Scene(root, 600, 400);

      primaryStage.setTitle("Map Viewer");
      primaryStage.setScene(scene);
      primaryStage.show();
   }
}
```

LISTING 11.9 *continued*

DISPLAY

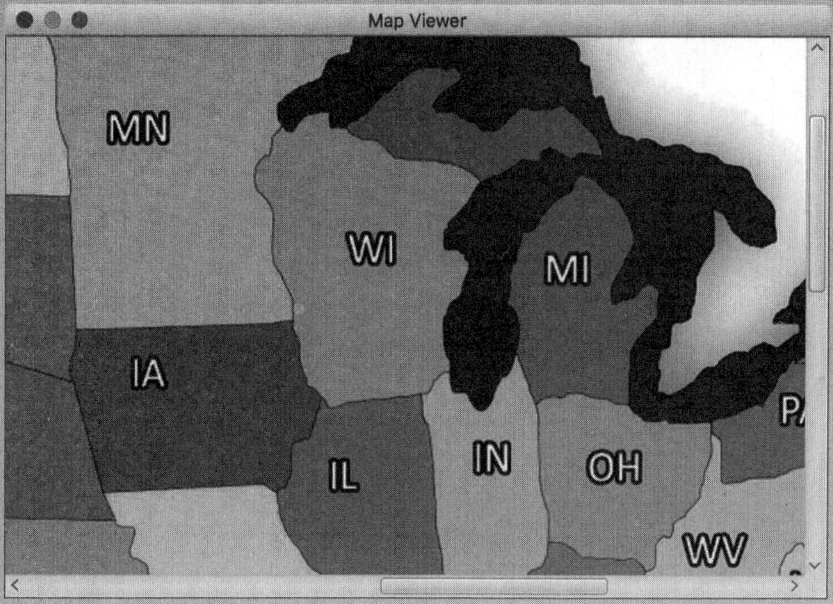

The programmer can specify whether the scroll bars in a scroll pane are always displayed, never displayed, or only when they are needed. Such decisions can be applied independently on the two scroll bars by specifying the `ScrollBarPolicy`. For example, the following line of code establishes that the horizontal bar of the scroll pane is always displayed:

```
myScrollPane.setHbarPolicy(ScrollBarPolicy.ALWAYS);
```

By default, both scroll bars of a scroll pane only appear if needed. If the window is resized, for instance, such that the full height of the image can be seen without scrolling, the scroll bar on the right side of the pane disappears. If the whole image can be seen, both scroll bars will vanish.

Note that no explicit event handlers need to be set up to use a scroll pane in this manner. The viewing area of the scroll pane is adjusted automatically as the scroll bars are used.

SELF-REVIEW QUESTIONS *(see answers in Appendix L)*

SR 11.21 What does a scroll pane do?

SR 11.22 What are the three ways the user can change the knob position on a scroll bar?

SR 11.23 What does the scroll bar policy determine?

11.9 Split Panes and List Views

KEY CONCEPT
A split pane displays two nodes side by side or one on top of the other.

A JavaFX *split pane* displays two (or more) GUI nodes, separated by a moveable divider bar. The divider bar can be dragged by the user, giving more space to one side and reducing the space in the other. The nodes are displayed side by side or one on top of the other, with a vertical or horizontal divider bar, respectively.

The program shown in Listing 11.10 displays a split pane with a vertical divider bar. A list of words (food items) is shown on the left side of the divider bar, and an image of the selected food item is shown on the right side. When the user selects a different item in the list, the image changes.

KEY CONCEPT
A list view displays a scrollable list of selectable options.

The list of food items is presented using a *list view*. Unlike a choice box, which presents a drop-down list when clicked, the options in a list view are always visible. If the number of options is too large to be completely visible, a scroll bar allows the user to move up and down the list. An item in a list view can be selected using a mouse click, or the user can scroll through the options using the arrow keys on the keyboard.

The items in a `ListView` are `Observable` values. In this program, an `ObservableList` object is created and filled with the food item names stored in an array of strings. Then the observable list is used to create the `ListView` object.

An array of `Image` objects is created by loading JPEG images from files that have the same name as the strings used in the list. An `ImageView` is displayed in a `StackPane` (to keep it centered), and the stack pane is displayed in the right side of the split pane. The image displayed in the image view is changed when a new item is selected from the list.

When the list view is set up, it's minimum width is set to 100 pixels. Similarly, the minimum width of the image view is set to 300. The split pane respects the minimum sizes of the nodes it displays, and will not allow the divider bar to be dragged beyond that point.

LISTING 11.10

```
import javafx.application.Application;
import javafx.beans.value.ObservableValue;
import javafx.collections.FXCollections;
import javafx.collections.ObservableList;
import javafx.scene.Scene;
import javafx.scene.control.ListView;
import javafx.scene.control.SplitPane;
import javafx.scene.image.Image;
import javafx.scene.image.ImageView;
import javafx.scene.layout.StackPane;
import javafx.stage.Stage;

//********************************************************************
//  FoodImages.java       Author: Lewis/Loftus
//
//  Demonstrates a split pane and a list view.
//********************************************************************

public class FoodImages extends Application
{
   private Image[] foodImages;
   private ImageView imgView;
   private ListView<String> listView;

   //-----------------------------------------------------------------
   //  Displays a split pane with a list of food items on the left
   //  and an image of the selected food item on the right.
   //-----------------------------------------------------------------
   public void start(Stage primaryStage)
   {
      String[] food = {"apples", "asparagus", "bacon", "bread",
          "carrots", "cheesecake", "eggs", "hamburger", "muffins",
          "onions", "oranges", "pancakes", "peanuts", "pizza",
          "potatoes", "pretzels", "spaghetti", "sushi", "watermelon"};

      foodImages = new Image[food.length];
      for (int i = 0; i < food.length; i++)
          foodImages[i] = new Image(food[i] + ".jpg");

      imgView = new ImageView(foodImages[0]);
      StackPane imgPane = new StackPane(imgView);
      imgPane.setMinWidth(300);

      imgView.setPreserveRatio(true);
      imgView.fitWidthProperty().bind(imgPane.widthProperty());
```

LISTING 11.10 *continued*

```
        ObservableList<String> list = FXCollections.observableArrayList();
        list.addAll(food);

        listView = new ListView<String>(list);
        listView.setMinWidth(100);
        listView.getSelectionModel().select(0);
        listView.getSelectionModel().selectedItemProperty().addListener(
            this::processListSelection);

        SplitPane root = new SplitPane();
        root.setDividerPositions(0.25);
        root.getItems().addAll(listView, imgPane);

        Scene scene = new Scene(root, 600, 350);

        primaryStage.setTitle("Food Images");
        primaryStage.setScene(scene);
        primaryStage.show();
    }

    //--------------------------------------------------------------------
    //  Processes a list view selection by getting the index of the
    //  selected item and displaying the corresponding image.
    //--------------------------------------------------------------------
    public void processListSelection(ObservableValue<? extends String> val,
            String oldValue, String newValue)
    {
        int index = listView.getSelectionModel().getSelectedIndex();
        imgView.setImage(foodImages[index]);
    }
}
```

LISTING 11.10 *continued*

DISPLAY

The initial selection of the list view is set by obtaining the selection model of the view and selecting the first element (at index 0). The selection model of a list view defaults to single selection mode, allowing only one item to be selected at a time, but the selection model could be set to allow the selection of multiple contiguous items at one time, or even allow any combination of items to be selected.

In this example, a property binding is used to keep the width of the image view in synch with the width of the stack pane, so that as the divider bar is moved, or as the window is resized, the image fills the right side of the split pane. Property bindings are discussed in Chapter 10.

A change listener is set up to handle the selection of a new food item. When an item in the list view is selected, the change listener method gets the index of the current selection from the selection model and then loads the corresponding image into the image view.

When the split pane is created in this program, two items are added to it, so the split pane is made up of two sections and a single divider bar. If more than two nodes are added to a split pane, each node will be separated from the next by a divider bar. The initial position of each divider bar can be set using a call to the `setDividerPositions` method. In this example, the divider bar's initial position is set to 0.25, giving 25% of the room to the left half and 75% to the right.

SELF-REVIEW QUESTIONS *(see answers in Appendix L)*

SR 11.24 Describe the role of the divider bar on a split pane.

SR 11.25 What is the difference between a choice box and a list view?

SR 11.26 What happens if more than two nodes are added to a split pane?

Summary of Key Concepts

- Errors and exceptions are objects that represent unusual or invalid processing.
- The messages printed when an exception is thrown provide a method call stack trace.
- Each `catch` clause handles a particular kind of exception that may be thrown within the `try` block.
- The `finally` clause is executed whether the `try` block is exited normally or because of a thrown exception.
- If an exception is not caught and handled where it occurs, it is propagated to the calling method.
- A programmer must carefully consider how and where exceptions should be handled, if at all.
- A new exception is defined by deriving a new class from the `Exception` class or one of its descendants.
- The `throws` clause on a method header must be included for checked exceptions that are not caught and handled in the method.
- A stream is a sequential sequence of bytes; it can be used as a source of input or a destination for output.
- Three public reference variables in the `System` class represent the standard I/O streams.
- Output file streams should be explicitly closed or they may not correctly retain the data written to them.
- The Java class library contains many classes for defining I/O streams with various characteristics.
- A tool tip provides a hint to the user about the purpose of a control.
- Controls should be disabled when their use is inappropriate.
- A scroll pane is useful for viewing large images or large amounts of data.
- A split pane displays two nodes side by side or one on top of the other.
- A list view displays a scrollable list of selectable options.

Exercises

EX 11.1 Create a UML class diagram showing the relationship among `RuntimeException`, `IndexOutOfBoundsException`, `ArrayIndexOutOfBoundsException`, and `StringIndexOutOfBoundsException`. Use the online Java API documentation to find information about these classes.

EX 11.2 What would happen if the `try` statement were removed from the `level1` method of the `ExceptionScope` class in the `Propagation` program?

EX 11.3 What is wrong with the following code? How can it be fixed?

```
try{
        System.out.println(Integer.parseInt(str.
        charAt(8)));
}catch(IndexOutOfBoundsException e){
        e.printStackTrace();
}catch(StringIndexOutOfBoundsException e){
        e.printStackTrace();
}catch(NumberFormatException e){
        e.printStackTrace();
}
```

EX 11.4 Look up the following exception classes in the online Java API documentation and describe their purpose:

a. `ArithmeticException`

b. `NullPointerException`

c. `NumberFormatException`

d. `PatternSyntaxException`

EX 11.5 Other than the examples discussed in this chapter, describe a situation in which you might disable control(s) to help guide user actions.

EX 11.6 Explain how the functionality of the `FoodImages` program would change if the property binding was removed.

VideoNote
Developing a solution of PP 11.1.

Programming Projects

PP 11.1 Write a program that creates an exception class called `StringTooLongException`, designed to be thrown when a string is discovered that has too many characters in it. In the `main` driver of the program, read strings from the user until the user enters `"DONE"`. If a string is entered that has too many characters (say 20), throw the exception. Allow the thrown exception to terminate the program.

PP 11.2 Modify the solution to PP 11.1 such that it catches and handles the exception if it is thrown. Handle the exception by printing an appropriate message, and then continue processing more strings.

PP 11.3 Suppose in a particular business all documents are given a two-character designation starting with either U, C, or P, standing for unclassified, confidential, or proprietary. Create an exception class called `InvalidDocumentCodeException`, designed to be thrown when an improper designation for a document is encountered during processing. If a document designation is encountered that doesn't fit that description, the exception is thrown. Create a driver program to test the exception, allowing it to terminate the program.

PP 11.4 Modify the solution to PP 11.3 such that it catches and handles the exception if it is thrown. Handle the exception by printing an appropriate message, and then continue processing.

PP 11.5 Write a JavaFX application that displays three pages of text, one page at a time. Add Next and Previous buttons to allow the user to navigate through the pages. Disable the buttons appropriately when they should not be used.

PP 11.6 Write a JavaFX application that uses a split pane to display a list of visual effects that can be applied to the objects on screen. Display some text on the right side of the split pane and the list on the left. As the user selects an effect, apply it to the text on the right.

PP 11.7 Write a JavaFX application based on the `DisplayFile` program from Chapter 9. In addition to opening and displaying a file, allow the user to modify the text in the text area. Provide a Save button that, when pressed, displays a dialog box that lets the user save the modifications to a file. Hint: use the `showSaveDialog` method of the `FileChooser` class and use a try-catch statement to handle any exceptions that occur during the process of writing the file.

12 Recursion

CHAPTER OBJECTIVES

- Explain the underlying concepts of recursion.
- Explore examples that promote recursive thinking.
- Examine recursive methods and unravel their processing steps.
- Define infinite recursion and discuss ways to avoid it.
- Explain when recursion should and should not be used.
- Demonstrate the use of recursion to solve problems.
- Explore the use of recursion in graphics-based programs.
- Explore fractals and their relationship to recursion.

Recursion is a powerful programming technique that provides elegant solutions to certain problems. This chapter provides an introduction to recursive processing. It contains an explanation of the basic concepts underlying recursion and then explores the use of recursion in programming. Several specific problems are solved using recursion, demonstrating its versatility, simplicity, and elegance.

12.1 Recursive Thinking

KEY CONCEPT
Recursion is a programming technique in which a method calls itself. The key to being able to program recursively is to be able to think recursively.

We've seen many times that one method can call another method to accomplish a goal. What we haven't seen yet, however, is that a method can call itself. *Recursion* is a programming technique in which a method calls itself in order to fulfill its purpose. But before we get into the details of how we use recursion in a program, we need to explore the general concept of recursion. The ability to think recursively is essential to being able to use recursion as a programming technique.

In general, recursion is the process of defining something in terms of itself. For example, consider the following definition of the word *decoration*:

`decoration`: n. any ornament or adornment used to decorate something

The word *decorate* is used to define the word *decoration*. You may recall your grade school teacher telling you to avoid such recursive definitions when explaining the meaning of a word. However, in some situations, recursion is an appropriate way to express an idea or definition. For example, suppose we wanted to formally define a list of one or more numbers, separated by commas. Such a list can be defined recursively as either a number or as a number followed by a comma followed by a list. This definition can be expressed as follows:

A *List* is a: `number`
or a: `number comma` *`List`*

This recursive definition of *List* defines each of the following lists of numbers:

```
24, 88, 40, 37
96, 43
14, 64, 21, 69, 32, 93, 47, 81, 28, 45, 81, 52, 69
70
```

No matter how long a list is, the recursive definition describes it. A list of one element, such as in the last example, is defined completely by the first (non-recursive) part of the definition. For any list longer than one element, the recursive part of the definition (the part which refers to itself) is used as many times as necessary until the last element is reached. The last element in the list is always defined by the non-recursive part of the definition. Figure 12.1 shows how one particular list of numbers corresponds to the recursive definition of *List*.

Infinite Recursion

Note that the definition of *List* contains one option that is recursive and one option that is not. The part of the definition that is not recursive is called the *base case*. If all options had a recursive component, the recursion would never end. For

```
LIST: number   comma   LIST
        24       ,     88,  40,  37
                       number   comma   LIST
                         88       ,     40,  37
                                        number   comma   LIST
                                          40       ,     37
                                                         number
                                                           37
```

FIGURE 12.1 Tracing the recursive definition of *List*

example, if the definition of *List* was simply "a number followed by a comma followed by a *List*," no list could ever end. This problem is called *infinite recursion.* It is similar to an infinite loop except that the "loop" occurs in the definition itself.

KEY CONCEPT
Any recursive definition must have a non-recursive part, called the base case, which permits the recursion to eventually end.

As in the infinite loop problem, a programmer must be careful to design algorithms so that they avoid infinite recursion. Any recursive definition must have a base case that does not result in a recursive option. The base case of the *List* definition is a single number that is not followed by anything. In other words, when the last number in the list is reached, the base case option terminates the recursive path.

Recursion in Math

Let's look at an example of recursion in mathematics. The value referred to as *N*! (pronounced *N factorial*) is defined for any positive integer *N* as the product of all integers between 1 and *N* inclusive. Therefore, 3! is defined as:

```
3! = 3*2*1 = 6
```

and 5! is defined as:

```
5! = 5*4*3*2*1 = 120.
```

Mathematical formulas are often expressed recursively. The definition of *N*! can be expressed recursively as:

```
1! = 1
N! = N * (N-1)! for N > 1
```

KEY CONCEPT
Mathematical problems and formulas are often expressed recursively.

The base case of this definition is 1!, which is defined as 1. All other values of $N!$ (for $N > 1$) are defined as N times the value $(N-1)!$. The factorial function is defined in terms of the factorial function. That's recursion.

Using this definition, 50! is equal to 50 * 49!. And 49! is equal to 49 * 48!. And 48! is equal to 48 * 47!. This process continues until we get to the base case of 1. Because $N!$ is defined only for positive integers, this definition is complete and will always conclude with the base case.

The next section describes how recursion is accomplished in programs.

SELF-REVIEW QUESTIONS *(see answers in Appendix L)*

SR 12.1 What is recursion?

SR 12.2 How many times is the recursive part of the definition of a *List* used to define a list of 10 numbers? How many times is the base case used?

SR 12.3 What is infinite recursion?

SR 12.4 When is a base case needed for recursive processing?

SR 12.5 Write a recursive definition of 5 * n (integer multiplication), where n > 0. Define the multiplication process in terms of integer addition. For example, 5 * 7 is equal to 5 added to itself 7 times.

12.2 Recursive Programming

Let's use a simple mathematical operation to demonstrate the concept of recursive programming. Consider the process of summing the values between 1 and N inclusive, where N is any positive integer. The sum of the values from 1 to N can be expressed as N plus the sum of the values from 1 to $N-1$. That sum can be expressed similarly, as shown in Figure 12.2.

$$\sum_{i=1}^{N} i = N + \sum_{i=1}^{N-1} i = N + N-1 + \sum_{i=1}^{N-2} i$$
$$= N + N-1 + N-2 + \sum_{i=1}^{N-3} i$$
$$\vdots$$
$$= N + N-1 + N-2 + \cdots + 2 + 1$$

FIGURE 12.2 The sum of the numbers 1 through N, defined recursively

For example, the sum of the values between 1 and 20 is equal to 20 plus the sum of the values between 1 and 19. Continuing this approach, the sum of the values between 1 and 19 is equal to 19 plus the sum of the values between 1 and 18. This may sound like a strange way to think about this problem, but it is a straightforward example that can be used to demonstrate how recursion is programmed.

As we mentioned earlier, in Java, as in many other programming languages, a method can call itself. Each call to the method creates a new environment in which to work. That is, all local variables and parameters are newly defined with their own unique data space every time the method is called. Each parameter is given an initial value based on the new call. Each time a method terminates, processing returns to the method that called it (which may be an earlier invocation of the same method). These rules are no different from those governing any "regular" method invocation.

KEY CONCEPT

Each recursive call to a method creates new local variables and parameters.

A recursive solution to the summation problem is defined by the following recursive method called `sum`:

```
// This method returns the sum of 1 to num
public int sum(int num)
{
    int result;
    if (num == 1)
        result = 1;
    else
        result = num + sum(num-1);
    return result;
}
```

Note that this method essentially embodies our recursive definition that the sum of the numbers between 1 and N is equal to N plus the sum of the numbers between 1 and $N-1$. The `sum` method is recursive, because `sum` calls itself. The parameter passed to `sum` is decremented each time `sum` is called until it reaches the base case of 1. Recursive methods invariably contain an `if-else` statement, with one of the branches, usually the first one, representing the base case, as in this example.

Suppose the `main` method calls `sum`, passing it an initial value of 1, which is stored in the parameter `num`. Since `num` is equal to 1, the result of 1 is returned to `main` and no recursion occurs.

Now let's trace the execution of the `sum` method when it is passed an initial value of 2. Since `num` does not equal 1, `sum` is called again with an argument of `num-1`, or 1. This is a new call to the method `sum`, with a new parameter `num` and a new local variable `result`. Since this `num` is equal to 1 in this invocation, the result of 1 is returned without further recursive calls. Control returns to the first

KEY CONCEPT
A careful trace of recursive processing can provide insight into the way it is used to solve a problem.

version of `sum` that was invoked. The return value of 1 is added to the initial value of `num` in that call to `sum`, which is 2. Therefore, `result` is assigned the value 3, which is returned to the `main` method. The method called from `main` correctly calculates the sum of the integers from 1 to 2 and returns the result of 3.

The base case in the summation example is when *N* equals 1, at which point no further recursive calls are made. The recursion begins to fold back into the earlier versions of the `sum` method, returning the appropriate value each time. Each return value contributes to the computation of the sum at the higher level. Without the base case, infinite recursion would result. Each call to a method requires additional memory space; therefore, infinite recursion often results in a run-time error indicating that memory has been exhausted.

Trace the `sum` function with different initial values of `num` until this processing becomes familiar. Figure 12.3 illustrates the recursive calls when `main` invokes `sum` to determine the sum of the integers from 1 to 4. Each box represents a copy of the method as it is invoked, indicating the allocation of space to store the formal parameters and any local variables. Invocations are shown as solid lines,

FIGURE 12.3 Recursive calls to the `sum` method

and returns as dotted lines. The return value `result` is shown at each step. The recursive path is followed completely until the base case is reached; the calls then begin to return their result up through the chain.

Recursion vs. Iteration

Of course, there is a non-recursive solution to the summation problem we just explored. A `for` loop can be used to compute the sum of the numbers between 1 and `num` inclusive iteratively as follows:

KEY CONCEPT
Recursion is the most elegant and appropriate way to solve some problems, but for others it is less intuitive than an iterative solution.

```
sum = 0;
for (int number = 1; number <= num; number++)
    sum += number;
```

This solution is certainly more straightforward than the recursive version. We used the summation problem to demonstrate recursion because it is simple, not because you would use recursion to solve it under normal conditions. Recursion has the overhead of multiple method invocations and, in this case, presents a more complicated solution than its iterative counterpart.

A programmer must learn when to use recursion and when not to use it. Determining which approach is best depends on the problem being solved. All problems can be solved in an iterative manner, but in some cases the iterative version is much more complicated. Recursion, for some problems, allows us to create relatively short, elegant programs.

Direct vs. Indirect Recursion

Direct recursion occurs when a method invokes itself, such as when `sum` calls `sum`. *Indirect recursion* occurs when a method invokes another method, eventually resulting in the original method being invoked again. For example, if method `m1` invokes method `m2`, and `m2` invokes method `m1`, we can say that `m1` is indirectly recursive. The amount of indirection could be several levels deep, as when `m1` invokes `m2`, which invokes `m3`, which invokes `m4`, which invokes `m1`. Figure 12.4 depicts a situation with indirect recursion. Method invocations are shown with solid lines, and returns are shown with dotted lines. The entire invocation path is followed, and then the recursion unravels following the return path.

Indirect recursion requires all of the same attention to base cases that direct recursion requires. Furthermore, indirect recursion can be more difficult to trace because of the intervening method calls. Therefore, extra care is warranted when designing or evaluating indirectly recursive methods. Ensure that the indirection is truly necessary and clearly explained in documentation.

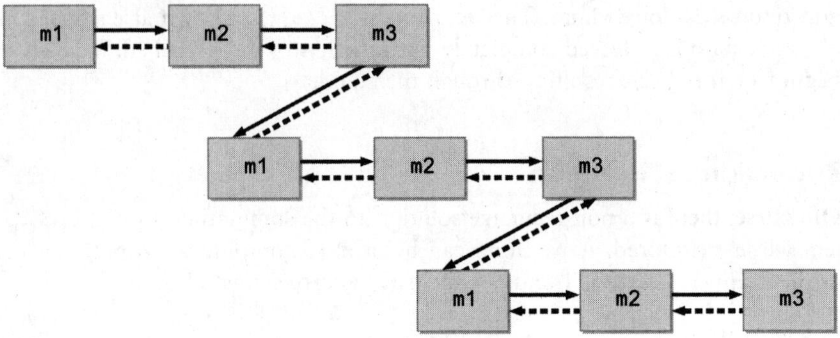

FIGURE 12.4 Indirect recursion

SELF-REVIEW QUESTIONS *(see answers in Appendix L)*

SR 12.6 Is recursion necessary?

SR 12.7 When should recursion be avoided?

SR 12.8 Describe what is returned by the following recursive method.

```
public int exercise(int n)
{
    if (n < 0)
        return -1;
    else
        if (n < 10)
            return 1;
        else
            return 1 + exercise(n/10);
}
```

SR 12.9 Write a recursive method that returns the value of 5 * n, where n > 0. See Self-Review Question 12.5. Explain why you would not normally use recursion to solve this problem.

SR 12.10 What is indirect recursion?

12.3 Using Recursion

Each of the following sections describes a particular recursive problem. For each one, we examine exactly how recursion plays a role in the solution and how a base case is used to terminate the recursion. As you examine these examples, consider how complicated a non-recursive solution for each problem would be.

Traversing a Maze

Solving a maze involves a great deal of trial and error: following a path, backtracking when you cannot go farther, and trying other untried options. Such activities often are handled nicely using recursion. The program shown in Listing 12.1 creates a `Maze` object and attempts to traverse it.

LISTING 12.1

```
//********************************************************************
//  MazeSearch.java       Author: Lewis/Loftus
//
//  Demonstrates recursion.
//********************************************************************
public class MazeSearch
{
   //-----------------------------------------------------------------
   //  Creates a new maze, prints its original form, attempts to
   //  solve it, and prints out its final form.
   //-----------------------------------------------------------------
   public static void main(String[] args)
   {
      Maze labyrinth = new Maze();

      System.out.println(labyrinth);

      if (labyrinth.traverse(0, 0))
         System.out.println("The maze was successfully traversed!");
      else
         System.out.println("There is no possible path.");

      System.out.println(labyrinth);
   }
}
```

OUTPUT

```
1110110001111
1011101111001
0000101010100
1110111010111
1010000111001
1011111101111
1000000000000
1111111111111
```

LISTING 12.1 *continued*

```
The maze was successfully traversed!

7770110001111
3077707771001
0000707070300
7770777070333
7070000773003
7077777703333
7000000000000
7777777777777
```

The Maze class shown in Listing 12.2 uses a two-dimensional array of integers to represent the maze. The goal is to move from the top-left corner (the entry point) to the bottom-right corner (the exit point). Initially, a 1 indicates a clear path and a 0 indicates a blocked path. As the maze is solved, these array elements are changed to other values to indicate attempted paths and ultimately a successful path through the maze if one exists.

LISTING 12.2

```
//********************************************************************
//  Maze.java        Author: Lewis/Loftus
//
//  Represents a maze of characters. The goal is to get from the
//  top left corner to the bottom right, following a path of 1s.
//********************************************************************

public class Maze
{
   private final int TRIED = 3;
   private final int PATH = 7;

   private int[][] grid = { {1,1,1,0,1,1,0,0,0,1,1,1,1},
                            {1,0,1,1,1,0,1,1,1,1,0,0,1},
                            {0,0,0,0,1,0,1,0,1,0,1,0,0},
                            {1,1,1,0,1,1,1,0,1,0,1,1,1},
```

LISTING 12.2 *continued*

```
                                {1,0,1,0,0,0,0,1,1,1,0,0,1},
                                {1,0,1,1,1,1,1,1,0,1,1,1,1},
                                {1,0,0,0,0,0,0,0,0,0,0,0,0},
                                {1,1,1,1,1,1,1,1,1,1,1,1,1} };

   //-----------------------------------------------------------------
   //  Attempts to recursively traverse the maze. Inserts special
   //  characters indicating locations that have been tried and that
   //  eventually become part of the solution.
   //-----------------------------------------------------------------
   public boolean traverse(int row, int column)
   {
      boolean done = false;

      if (valid(row, column))
      {
         grid[row][column] = TRIED;   // this cell has been tried

         if (row == grid.length-1 && column == grid[0].length-1)

            done = true;   // the maze is solved
         else
         {
            done = traverse(row+1, column);      // down
            if (!done)
               done = traverse(row, column+1);   // right
            if (!done)
               done = traverse(row-1, column);   // up
            if (!done)
               done = traverse(row, column-1);   // left
         }

         if (done)  // this location is part of the final path
            grid[row][column] = PATH;
      }
      return done;
   }

   //-----------------------------------------------------------------
   //  Determines if a specific location is valid.
   //-----------------------------------------------------------------
   private boolean valid(int row, int column)
   {
      boolean result = false;
```

LISTING 12.2 *continued*

```
      // check if cell is in the bounds of the matrix
      if (row >= 0 && row < grid.length &&
          column >= 0 && column < grid[row].length)

      // check if cell is not blocked and not previously tried
      if (grid[row][column] == 1)
          result = true;

      return result;
   }

   //-----------------------------------------------------------------
   //  Returns the maze as a string.
   //-----------------------------------------------------------------
   public String toString()
   {
      String result = "\n";
      for (int row=0; row < grid.length; row++)
      {
         for (int column=0; column < grid[row].length; column++)
            result += grid[row][column] + "";
         result += "\n";
      }

      return result;
   }
}
```

VideoNote
Tracing the `MazeSearch` program.

The only valid moves through the maze are in the four primary directions: down, right, up, and left. No diagonal moves are allowed. In this example, the maze is 8 rows by 13 columns, although the code is designed to handle a maze of any size.

Let's think this through recursively. The maze can be traversed successfully if it can be traversed successfully from position (0, 0). Therefore, the maze can be traversed successfully if it can be traversed successfully from any positions adjacent to (0, 0), namely position (1, 0), position (0, 1), position (–1, 0), or position (0, –1). Picking a potential next step, say (1, 0), we find ourselves in the same type of situation we did before. To successfully traverse the maze from the new current position, we must successfully traverse it from an adjacent position. At any point, some of the adjacent positions may be invalid, may be blocked, or may represent a possible successful path. We continue this process recursively. If the base case, position (7, 12) is reached, the maze has been traversed successfully.

The recursive method in the `Maze` class is called `traverse`. It returns a boolean value that indicates whether a solution was found. First, the method determines whether a move to the specified row and column is valid. A move is considered valid if it stays within the grid boundaries and if the grid contains a 1 in that location, indicating that a move in that direction is not blocked. The initial call to `traverse` passes in the upper-left location (0, 0).

If the move is valid, the grid entry is changed from a 1 to a 3, marking this location as visited so that later we don't retrace our steps. The `traverse` method then determines whether the maze has been completed by having reached the bottom-right location. Therefore, there are actually three possibilities of the base case for this problem that will terminate any particular recursive path:

- an invalid move because the move is out of bounds
- an invalid move because the move has been tried before
- a move that arrives at the final location

If the current location is not the bottom-right corner, we search for a solution in each of the primary directions, if necessary. First, we look down by recursively calling the `traverse` method and passing in the new location. The logic of the `traverse` method starts all over again using this new position. A solution is either ultimately found by first attempting to move down from the current location, or it's not found. If it's not found, we try moving right. If that fails, we try up. Finally, if no other direction has yielded a correct path, we try left. If no direction from the current location yields a correct solution, then there is no path from this location, and `traverse` returns false.

If a solution is found from the current location, the grid entry is changed to a 7. The first 7 is placed in the bottom-right corner. The next 7 is placed in the location that led to the bottom-right corner, and so on until the final 7 is placed in the upper-left corner. Therefore, when the final maze is printed, the zeros still indicate a blocked path, a 1 indicates an open path that was never tried, a 3 indicates a path that was tried but failed to yield a correct solution, and a 7 indicates a part of the final solution of the maze.

Note that there are several opportunities for recursion in each call to the `traverse` method. Any or all of them might be followed, depending on the maze configuration. Although there may be many paths through the maze, the recursion terminates when a path is found. Carefully trace the execution of this code while following the maze array to see how the recursion solves the problem. Then consider the difficulty of producing a non-recursive solution.

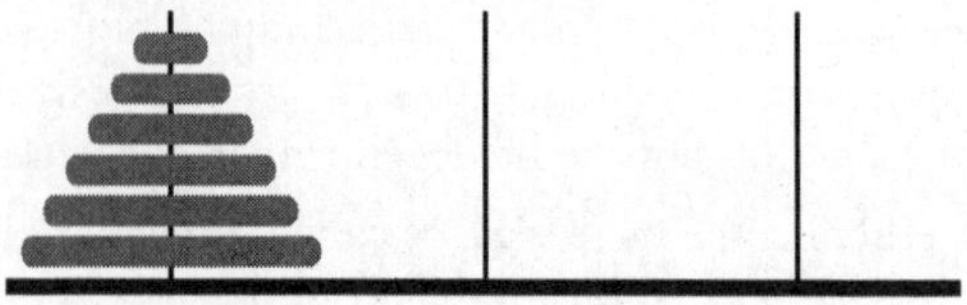

FIGURE 12.5 The Towers of Hanoi puzzle

The Towers of Hanoi

The *Towers of Hanoi* puzzle was invented in the 1880s by Edouard Lucas, a French mathematician. It has become a favorite among computer scientists, because its solution is an excellent demonstration of recursive elegance.

The puzzle consists of three upright pegs and a set of disks with holes in the middle so that they slide onto the pegs. Each disk has a different diameter. Initially, all of the disks are stacked on one peg in order of size such that the largest disk is on the bottom, as shown in Figure 12.5.

The goal of the puzzle is to move all of the disks from their original (first) peg to the destination (third) peg. We can use the "extra" peg as a temporary place to put disks, but we must obey the following three rules:

- We can move only one disk at a time.
- We cannot place a larger disk on top of a smaller disk.
- All disks must be on some peg except for the disk in transit between pegs.

These rules imply that we must move smaller disks "out of the way" in order to move a larger disk from one peg to another. Figure 12.6 shows the step-by-step solution for the Towers of Hanoi puzzle using three disks. In order to ultimately move all three disks from the first peg to the third peg, we first have to get to the point where the smaller two disks are out of the way on the second peg so that the largest disk can be moved from the first peg to the third peg.

The first three moves shown in Figure 12.6 can be thought of as moving the smaller disks out of the way. The fourth move puts the largest disk in its final place. The last three moves then put the smaller disks to their final place on top of the largest one.

Let's use this idea to form a general strategy. To move a stack of *N* disks from the original peg to the destination peg:

- Move the topmost $N-1$ disks from the original peg to the extra peg.
- Move the largest disk from the original peg to the destination peg.
- Move the $N-1$ disks from the extra peg to the destination peg.

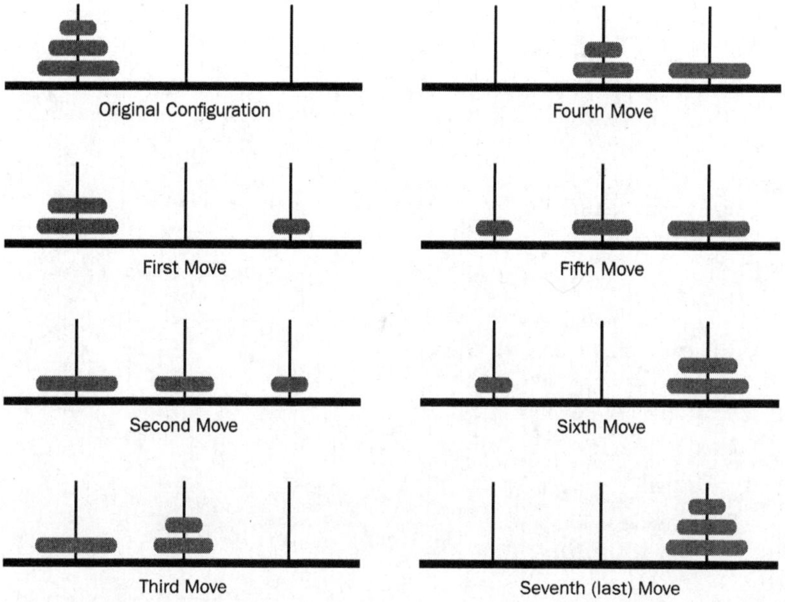

FIGURE 12.6 A solution to the three-disk Towers of Hanoi puzzle

This strategy lends itself nicely to a recursive solution. The step to move the $N-1$ disks out of the way is the same problem all over again: moving a stack of disks. For this subtask, though, there is one less disk, and our destination peg is what we were originally calling the extra peg. An analogous situation occurs after we've moved the largest disk and we have to move the original $N-1$ disks again.

The base case for this problem occurs when we want to move a "stack" that consists of only one disk. That step can be accomplished directly and without recursion.

The program in Listing 12.3 creates a `TowersOfHanoi` object and invokes its `solve` method. The output is a step-by-step list of instructions that describe how the disks should be moved to solve the puzzle. This example uses four disks, which is specified by a parameter to the `TowersOfHanoi` constructor.

The `TowersOfHanoi` class shown in Listing 12.4 uses the `solve` method to make an initial call to `moveTower`, the recursive method. The initial call indicates that all of the disks should be moved from peg 1 to peg 3, using peg 2 as the extra position.

VideoNote
Exploring the Towers of Hanoi.

The `moveTower` method first considers the base case (a "stack" of one disk). When that occurs, it calls the `moveOneDisk` method that prints a single line

LISTING 12.3

```
//********************************************************************
//  SolveTowers.java       Author: Lewis/Loftus
//
//  Demonstrates recursion.
//********************************************************************

public class SolveTowers
{
   //-----------------------------------------------------------------
   // Creates a TowersOfHanoi puzzle and solves it.
   //-----------------------------------------------------------------
   public static void main(String[] args)
   {
      TowersOfHanoi towers = new TowersOfHanoi(4);

      towers.solve();
   }
}
```

OUTPUT

```
Move one disk from 1 to 2
Move one disk from 1 to 3
Move one disk from 2 to 3
Move one disk from 1 to 2
Move one disk from 3 to 1
Move one disk from 3 to 2
Move one disk from 1 to 2
Move one disk from 1 to 3
Move one disk from 2 to 3
Move one disk from 2 to 1
Move one disk from 3 to 1
Move one disk from 2 to 3
Move one disk from 1 to 2
Move one disk from 1 to 3
Move one disk from 2 to 3
```

describing that particular move. If the stack contains more than one disk, we call `moveTower` again to get the *N*–1 disks out of the way, then move the largest disk, then move the *N*–1 disks to their final destination with yet another call to `moveTower`.

LISTING 12.4

```
//********************************************************************
//  TowersOfHanoi.java       Author: Lewis/Loftus
//
//  Represents the classic Towers of Hanoi puzzle.
//********************************************************************

public class TowersOfHanoi
{
   private int totalDisks;

   //-----------------------------------------------------------------
   //  Sets up the puzzle with the specified number of disks.
   //-----------------------------------------------------------------
   public TowersOfHanoi(int disks)
   {
      totalDisks = disks;
   }

   //-----------------------------------------------------------------
   //  Performs the initial call to moveTower to solve the puzzle.
   //  Moves the disks from tower 1 to tower 3 using tower 2.
   //-----------------------------------------------------------------
   public void solve()
   {
      moveTower(totalDisks, 1, 3, 2);
   }

   //-----------------------------------------------------------------
   //  Moves the specified number of disks from one tower to another
   //  by moving a subtower of n-1 disks out of the way, moving one
   //  disk, then moving the subtower back. Base case of 1 disk.
   //-----------------------------------------------------------------
   private void moveTower(int numDisks, int start, int end, int temp)
   {
      if (numDisks == 1)
         moveOneDisk(start, end);
      else
      {
         moveTower(numDisks-1, start, temp, end);
         moveOneDisk(start, end);
         moveTower(numDisks-1, temp, end, start);
      }
   }
```

LISTING 12.4 *continued*

```
   //-----------------------------------------------------------------
   //  Prints instructions to move one disk from the specified start
   //  tower to the specified end tower.
   //-----------------------------------------------------------------
   private void moveOneDisk(int start, int end)
   {
      System.out.println("Move one disk from " + start + " to " +
                         end);
   }
}
```

Note that the parameters to `moveTower` describing the pegs are switched around as needed to move the partial stacks. This code follows our general strategy and uses the `moveTower` method to move all partial stacks. Trace the code carefully for a stack of three disks to understand the processing. Compare the processing steps to Figure 12.6.

KEY CONCEPT
The Towers of Hanoi solution has exponential complexity, which is very inefficient. Yet the implementation of the solution is incredibly short and elegant.

Unfortunately, despite its short and elegant implementation, the solution to the Towers of Hanoi puzzle is terribly inefficient. To solve the puzzle with a stack of N disks, we have to make 2^N-1 individual disk moves. This situation is an example of *exponential complexity*. As the number of disks increases, the number of required moves increases exponentially.

Legend has it that priests of Brahma are working on this puzzle in a temple at the center of the world. They are using 64 gold disks, moving them between pegs of pure diamond. The downside is that when the priests finish the puzzle, the world will end. The upside is that even if they move one disk every second of every day, it will take them over 584 billion years to complete it. That's with a puzzle of only 64 disks! It is certainly an indication of just how intractable exponential algorithmic complexity is.

SELF-REVIEW QUESTIONS *(see answers in Appendix L)*

SR 12.11 Under what conditions does the recursion stop in the `MazeSearch` program?

SR 12.12 Identify where in the `MazeSearch` program each of the following is provided.

a. The original maze is defined.
b. A test to see if we have arrived at the goal occurs.
c. A location is marked as having been tried.
d. A test to see if we already tried a location occurs.

SR 12.13 Trace the `MazeSearch` program to determine the series of calls to the method `valid` (including the values of the parameters that are passed) that would occur if the original maze is as shown.

a.	b.	c.
1 1	0 0	1 1
1 1	0 0	1 0

SR 12.14 Explain the general approach to solving the Towers of Hanoi puzzle. How does it relate to recursion?

SR 12.15 Trace the `SolveTowers` code for an initial stack of 1 disk. How many calls to the `moveTower` method are made? How many calls are made for an initial stack of 2 disks? How many for 3 disks? Describe a pattern related to the number of calls made to the `moveTower` method as the number of disks increases.

12.4 Tiled Images

Let's explore an example that uses recursion to present graphical elements. Carefully examine the display for the `TiledImages` program shown in Listing 12.5. The entire area is divided into four equal quadrants. A full color picture of a young girl is shown in the bottom-right quadrant. The same image is shown in monochrome in the bottom-left quadrant, and in sepia tone in the top-right quadrant.

The interesting part of the display is in the top-left quadrant. It contains a copy of the entire collage, including itself. In this smaller version you can see the three main images in their quadrants. And again, in the top-left corner, the collage is repeated (including itself). This repetition occurs for several levels. It is similar to the effect you can create when looking at a mirror in the reflection of another mirror.

LISTING 12.5

```
import javafx.application.Application;
import javafx.scene.Group;
import javafx.scene.Scene;
```

LISTING 12.5 *continued*

```
import javafx.scene.effect.ColorAdjust;
import javafx.scene.effect.SepiaTone;
import javafx.scene.image.Image;
import javafx.scene.image.ImageView;
import javafx.scene.paint.Color;
import javafx.stage.Stage;

//**********************************************************************
//  TiledImages.java       Author: Lewis/Loftus
//
//  Demonstrates the use of recursion.
//**********************************************************************

public class TiledImages extends Application
{
   private final static int MIN = 20;

   private Image image;
   private ColorAdjust monochrome;
   private SepiaTone sepia;
   private Group root;

   //-----------------------------------------------------------------
   //  Sets up the display of a series of tiled images.
   //-----------------------------------------------------------------
   public void start(Stage primaryStage)
   {
      image = new Image("girl.jpg");

      monochrome = new ColorAdjust(0, -1, 0, 0);
      sepia = new SepiaTone();

      root = new Group();
      addPictures(300);

      Scene scene = new Scene(root, 600, 600, Color.WHITE);

      primaryStage.setTitle("Tiled Images");
```

LISTING 12.5 *continued*

```
      primaryStage.setScene(scene);
      primaryStage.show();
   }

   //-----------------------------------------------------------------
   //  Uses the parameter to specify the size and position of an image.
   //  Displays the image in full color, monochrome, and sepia tone,
   //  then repeats the display recursively in the upper left quadrant.
   //-----------------------------------------------------------------
   private void addPictures(double size)
   {
      ImageView colorView = new ImageView(image);
      colorView.setFitWidth(size);
      colorView.setFitHeight(size);
      colorView.setX(size);
      colorView.setY(size);

      ImageView monochromeView = new ImageView(image);
      monochromeView.setEffect(monochrome);
      monochromeView.setFitWidth(size);
      monochromeView.setFitHeight(size);
      monochromeView.setX(0);
      monochromeView.setY(size);

      ImageView sepiaView = new ImageView(image);
      sepiaView.setEffect(sepia);
      sepiaView.setFitWidth(size);
      sepiaView.setFitHeight(size);
      sepiaView.setX(size);
      sepiaView.setY(0);

      root.getChildren().addAll(sepiaView, colorView, monochromeView);

      if (size > MIN)
         addPictures(size / 2);
   }
}
```

LISTING 12.5 *continued*

DISPLAY

The `start` method of the program loads the image file and sets up the scene. The `start` method makes an initial call to the `addPictures` method, which recursively puts all of the different versions of the picture into the collage.

The `addPictures` method accepts a parameter representing the size at which the image should be displayed. This value also helps determine where the image should be positioned within the collage.

Each time it is called, the `addPictures` method creates three `ImageView` objects. Every copy of the picture in the collage is presented in its own `ImageView` object. The first image view presents the image in full color. The second and third image view have an *effect* applied to them using the `setEffect` method. As the name implies, the `SepiaTone` effect applies a sepia tone to the image, similar to the look of antique photographs. The monochrome effect applied to the other image view is accomplished using a `ColorAdjust` effect with the appropriate constructor parameters.

The size of each `ImageView` is accomplished using calls to the `setFitWidth` and `setFitHeight` methods. The position of each `ImageView` is accomplished using calls to the `setX` and `setY` methods, which determines the location of the upper-left corner of the image.

After the three main image views are added to the root of the scene, the `addPictures` method is called again recursively, with a size value that is half of the current value. That recursive call is responsible for the entire upper-left quadrant at each level of the collage.

The base case for the recursion occurs when the `size` value is too small (somewhat arbitrarily set at 20). Because the size is decreased each time `addPictures` is called, the base case is eventually reached and the recursion stops. That's why a tiny square of white is visible in the upper-left corner of the collage; no call to `addPictures` was made in that last level to fill in that quadrant.

SELF-REVIEW QUESTIONS *(see answers in Appendix L)*

SR 12.16 Where does recursion occur in the `TiledImages` program? What does it accomplish?

SR 12.17 How many `Image` objects are created in the `TiledImages` program? How many `ImageView` objects?

SR 12.18 What is the base case of the recursion in the `TiledImages` program?

12.5 Fractals

A *fractal* is a geometric shape that can be made up of the same pattern repeated at different scales and orientations. The nature of a fractal lends itself to a recursive definition.

Interest in fractals has grown immensely in recent years, largely due to Benoit Mandelbrot, a Polish mathematician born in 1924. He demonstrated that fractals occur in many places in mathematics and nature. Computers have made fractals much easier to generate and investigate.

KEY CONCEPT

A fractal is a geometric shape with repeated patterns that can be described recursively.

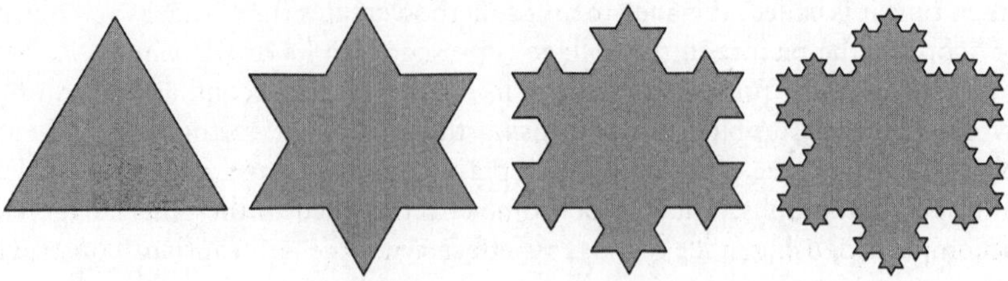

FIGURE 12.7 The first four orders of the Koch snowflake

One particular example of a fractal is called the *Koch snowflake*, named after Helge von Koch, a Swedish mathematician. It begins with an equilateral triangle, which is considered to be the Koch fractal of order 1. Koch fractals of higher orders are constructed by modifying all of the line segments in the shape in the same way.

To create the next higher order Koch fractal, each line segment in the shape is modified by replacing its middle third with a sharp protrusion made of two line segments, each having the same length as the replaced part. Relative to the entire shape, the protrusion on any line segment points outward. Figure 12.7 shows the first few orders of the Koch fractal. As the order increases, the fractal begins to resemble a snowflake.

The program shown in Listing 12.6 displays a Koch snowflake of several different orders. The buttons at the top of the window allow the user to increase and decrease the order of the fractal. Each time a button is pressed, the fractal image is updated.

LISTING 12.6

```
import javafx.application.Application;
import javafx.event.ActionEvent;
import javafx.geometry.Pos;
import javafx.scene.Scene;
import javafx.scene.control.Button;
import javafx.scene.image.Image;
import javafx.scene.image.ImageView;
import javafx.scene.layout.HBox;
import javafx.scene.layout.VBox;
import javafx.scene.text.Text;
import javafx.stage.Stage;
```

LISTING 12.6 *continued*

```
//********************************************************************
//  KochSnowflake.java       Author: Lewis/Loftus
//
//  Demonstrates the use of recursion to draw a fractal.
//********************************************************************

public class KochSnowflake extends Application
{
   private final static int MIN_ORDER = 1;
   private final static int MAX_ORDER = 6;

   private int order;
   private Button up, down;
   private Text orderText;
   private KochPane fractalPane;

   //-----------------------------------------------------------------
   //  Displays two buttons that control the order of the fractal
   //  shown in the pane below the buttons.
   //-----------------------------------------------------------------
   public void start(Stage primaryStage)
   {
      Image upImage = new Image("up.png");
      up = new Button();
      up.setGraphic(new ImageView(upImage));
      up.setOnAction(this::processUpButtonPress);

      Image downImage = new Image("down.png");
      down = new Button();
      down.setGraphic(new ImageView(downImage));
      down.setOnAction(this::processDownButtonPress);
      down.setDisable(true);

      order = 1;
      orderText = new Text("Order: 1");

      HBox toolbar = new HBox();
      toolbar.setStyle("-fx-background-color: darksalmon");
      toolbar.setAlignment(Pos.CENTER);
      toolbar.setPrefHeight(50);
      toolbar.setSpacing(40);
      toolbar.getChildren().addAll(up, orderText, down);
```

LISTING 12.6 *continued*

```
        fractalPane = new KochPane();

        VBox root = new VBox();
        root.setStyle("-fx-background-color: white");
        root.getChildren().addAll(toolbar, fractalPane);

        Scene scene = new Scene(root, 400, 450);

        primaryStage.setTitle("Koch Snowflake");
        primaryStage.setScene(scene);
        primaryStage.show();
    }

    //-----------------------------------------------------------------
    //  Increments the fractal order when the up button is pressed.
    //  Disables the up button if the maximum order is reached.
    //-----------------------------------------------------------------
    public void processUpButtonPress(ActionEvent event)
    {
        order++;
        orderText.setText("Order: " + order);
        fractalPane.makeFractal(order);

        down.setDisable(false);
        if (order == MAX_ORDER)
            up.setDisable(true);
    }

    //-----------------------------------------------------------------
    //  Decrements the fractal order when the down button is pressed.
    //  Disables the down button if the minimum order is reached.
    //-----------------------------------------------------------------
    public void processDownButtonPress(ActionEvent event)
    {
        order--;
        orderText.setText("Order: " + order);
        fractalPane.makeFractal(order);

        up.setDisable(false);
        if (order == MIN_ORDER)
            down.setDisable(true);
    }
}
```

LISTING 12.6 *continued*

DISPLAY

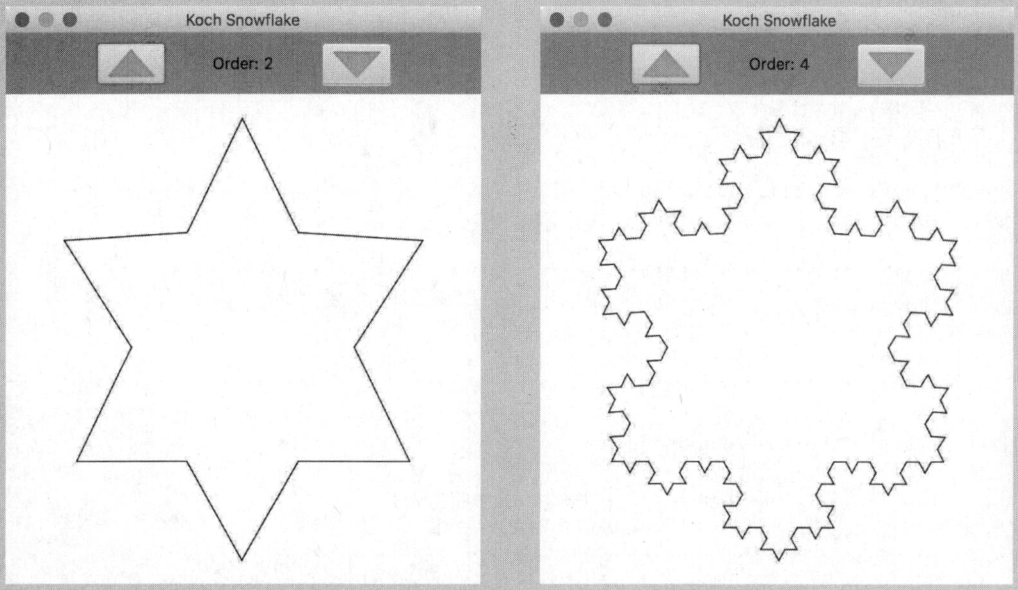

The `start` method in Listing 12.6 sets up the GUI, with the two `Button` objects and a `Text` object displayed along the top. The two buttons are labeled with up and down arrow images, respectively, instead of text. The `Text` object displays the current order of the fractal. The fractal itself is presented in its own `Pane` below the buttons.

There are two methods handling the action events that occur when a button is pressed. When the up button is pressed, the order value is increased and the fractal is redrawn. Similar processing occurs in the method handling the down button.

The minimum and maximum order allowed by this program are set as constants. The buttons controlling the order of the fractal are disabled when these levels are reached. The minimum order (1) is a natural limit. There is no natural limit to the maximum order, but there is a practical limit. Given the initial size of the line segments, the details of this fractal at an order greater than 6 or so become hard to see and can take a large amount of time to compute.

The pane in which the fractal is displayed is defined by a separate class called `KochPane`, shown in Listing 12.7, that extends the `Pane` class. The `KochPane` constructor makes a call to the `makeFractal` method, passing in an order of 1. Therefore, when the program is run, the lowest order fractal (a triangle) is displayed initially.

LISTING 12.7

```
import javafx.scene.layout.Pane;
import javafx.scene.shape.Line;

//************************************************************************
//  KochPane.java       Author: Lewis/Loftus
//
//  Represents the pane in which the Koch Snowflake fractal is presented.
//************************************************************************

public class KochPane extends Pane
{
   public final static double SQ = Math.sqrt(3) / 6;

   //---------------------------------------------------------------------
   //  Makes an initial fractal of order 1 (a triangle) when the pane
   //  is first created.
   //---------------------------------------------------------------------
   public KochPane()
   {
      makeFractal(1);
   }

   //---------------------------------------------------------------------
   //  Draws the fractal by clearing the pane and then adding three
   //  lines of the specified order between three predetermined points.
   //---------------------------------------------------------------------
   public void makeFractal(int order)
   {
      getChildren().clear();
      addLine(order, 200, 20, 60, 300);
      addLine(order, 60, 300, 340, 300);
      addLine(order, 340, 300, 200, 20);
   }
```

LISTING 12.7 *continued*

```
    //-----------------------------------------------------------------
    //  Recursively adds a line of the specified order to the fractal.
    //  The base case is a straight line between the given points.
    //  Otherwise, three intermediate points are computed and four line
    //  segments are added as a fractal of decremented order.
    //-----------------------------------------------------------------
    public void addLine(int order, double x1, double y1, double x5,
        double y5)
    {
        double deltaX, deltaY, x2, y2, x3, y3, x4, y4;

        if (order == 1)
        {
            getChildren().add(new Line(x1, y1, x5, y5));
        }
        else
        {
            deltaX = x5 - x1;    // distance between the end points
            deltaY = y5 - y1;

            x2 = x1 + deltaX / 3;    // one third
            y2 = y1 + deltaY / 3;

            x3 = (x1 + x5) / 2 + SQ * (y1 - y5);    // projection
            y3 = (y1 + y5) / 2 + SQ * (x5 - x1);

            x4 = x1 + deltaX * 2 / 3;    // two thirds
            y4 = y1 + deltaY * 2 / 3;

            addLine(order - 1, x1, y1, x2, y2);
            addLine(order - 1, x2, y2, x3, y3);
            addLine(order - 1, x3, y3, x4, y4);
            addLine(order - 1, x4, y4, x5, y5);
        }
    }
}
```

The `makeFractal` method is called whenever the fractal is updated (when either button is pressed). It actually creates the fractal of the new order from scratch each time it is called. It removes all line segments from the pane and makes three initial calls to the `addLine` method, passing in the order of the fractal and the (x, y)

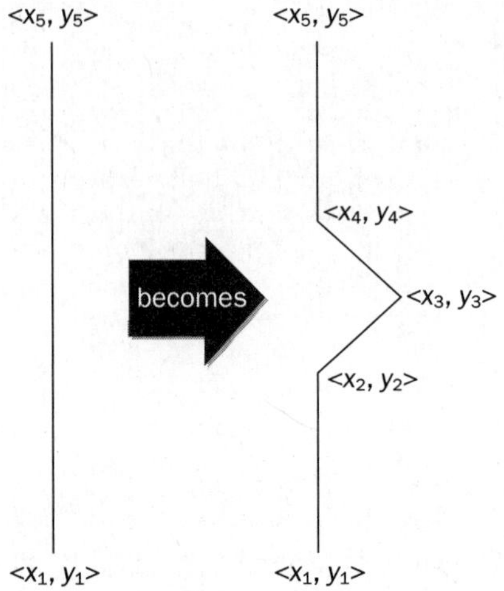

FIGURE 12.8 The transformation of each line of a Koch snowflake

coordinates of the endpoints of three line segments that make a Koch snowflake of order 1 (a triangle).

In the `addLine` method, if the order is one, a single line segment is drawn between the two points passed as parameters. Otherwise (because the order is greater than one), three intermediate points are calculated and appropriate line segments are added between them at an order one less than the current level. Figure 12.8 shows the transformation.

Based on the position of the two end points passed as parameters, a point one-third of the way and a point two-thirds of the way between them are computed. The calculation of (x_3, y_3), the point at the tip of the protrusion, is more complicated and uses a simplifying constant that incorporates multiple geometric relationships. The calculations to determine the three new points have nothing to do with the recursive technique used to draw the fractal.

KEY CONCEPT
A Koch snowflake has a finite area but an infinite perimeter.

The recursion in this program occurs when the `addLine` method calls itself (four times). Each recursive call decrements the fractal order value by one. The base case is an order value of 1.

An interesting mathematical feature of a Koch snowflake is that it has an infinite perimeter but a finite area. As the order of the fractal increases, the perimeter grows exponentially larger, with a mathematical limit of infinity. However, a rectangle large enough to surround the second-order fractal of the Koch snowflake is large enough to contain all higher-level fractals. The shape is restricted forever in area, but its perimeter gets infinitely longer.

SELF-REVIEW QUESTIONS *(see answers in Appendix L)*

SR 12.19 What is a fractal? What does it have to do with recursion?

SR 12.20 Why does the program impose an upper limit on the order of the Koch snowflake fractal?

SR 12.21 Describe how each line segment of a Koch snowflake is changed when going to the next higher order fractal.

Summary of Key Concepts

- Recursion is a programming technique in which a method calls itself. A key to being able to program recursively is to be able to think recursively.
- Any recursive definition must have a non-recursive part, called the base case, which permits the recursion to eventually end.
- Mathematical problems and formulas are often expressed recursively.
- Each recursive call to a method creates new local variables and parameters.
- A careful trace of recursive processing can provide insight into the way it is used to solve a problem.
- Recursion is the most elegant and appropriate way to solve some problems, but for others it is less intuitive than an iterative solution.
- The Towers of Hanoi solution has exponential complexity, which is very inefficient. Yet the implementation of the solution is incredibly short and elegant.
- A fractal is a geometric shape with repeated patterns that can be described recursively.
- A Koch snowflake has a finite area but an infinite perimeter.

Exercises

EX 12.1 Write a recursive definition of a valid Java identifier (see Chapter 1).

EX 12.2 Write a recursive definition of xy (x raised to the power y), where x and y are integers and $y > 0$.

EX 12.3 The Collatz conjecture starts with a positive integer n, and if n is even, it is divided by 2 to obtain the next term. Otherwise, the next term is calculated as $3n + 1$. The process is repeated for each subsequent term. The conjecture is that the sequence will always converge to 1. Write a Java method that accepts an integer n and prints the sequence of integers from n to 1 using recursion.

EX 12.4 The Hofstadter Q sequence is defined by $Q(n) = Q(n - Q(n - 1)) + Q(n - Q(n - 2))$. The first two values in the sequence are given as 1, 1. That is, $Q(1) = 1$, $Q(2) = 1$. Write a recursive method that accepts a positive integer n and finds the nth Hofstadter number.

EX 12.5 Modify the method that calculates the sum of the integers between 1 and N shown in this chapter. Have the new version match the following recursive definition: The sum of 1 to N is the sum of 1 to $(N/2)$ plus the sum of $(N/2 + 1)$ to N. Trace your solution using an N of 7.

EX 12.6 Write a recursive method that returns the value of $N!$ (N factorial) using the definition given in this chapter. Explain why you would not normally use recursion to solve this problem.

EX 12.7 Write a recursive method to reverse a string. Explain why you would not normally use recursion to solve this problem.

EX 12.8 Design or generate a new maze for the `MazeSearch` program in this chapter and rerun the program. Explain the processing in terms of your new maze, giving examples of a path that was tried but failed, a path that was never tried, and the ultimate solution.

EX 12.9 Annotate the lines of output of the `SolveTowers` program in this chapter to show the recursive steps.

EX 12.10 Produce a chart showing the number of moves required to solve the Towers of Hanoi puzzle using the following number of disks: 2, 3, 4, 5, 6, 7, 8, 9, 10, 15, 20, and 25.

EX 12.11 How many line segments are used to construct a Koch snowflake of order N? Produce a chart showing the number of line segments that make up a Koch snowflake for orders 1 through 9.

Programming Projects

PP 12.1 Design and implement a recursive version of the `PalindromeTester` program from Chapter 5.

VideoNote

Developing a solution of PP 12.1.

PP 12.2 A `Bag` is a data structure that can be defined as: A `Bag` may be empty, or a `Bag` may contain an `Object` and a `Bag`. Identify the base case and the recursive case in this definition. Write a Java class that implements the `Bag` structure. Include a method to add items to the `Bag`. Some helper methods may include `size()`, which returns the number of elements in the `Bag`, and `isEmpty()`, which returns true if the `Bag` is empty. Use recursion to write a `toString` method that returns a string in the form "(1, (2, (3, EMPTY)))", which describes a `Bag` containing the integers 1, 2, and 3. Write a driver program to test the functionality of the `Bag`.

PP 12.3 Modify the `Maze` class so that it prints out the path of the final solution as it is discovered without storing it.

PP 12.4 Design and implement a program that traverses a 3D maze.

PP 12.5 Design and implement a recursive program that solves the Non-Attacking Queens problem, which determines all ways in which eight queens can be positioned on an eight-by-eight chessboard so that none of them are in the same row, column, or diagonal as any other queen. There are no other chess pieces on the board.

PP 12.6 Modify the `Bag` class described in PP 12.2 to include a `contains(obj)` method that returns true if `obj` is contained in the `Bag` and false otherwise.

PP 12.7 Modify the `Bag` class described in PP 12.2 to include a `parse()` method that accepts a string representing a `Bag`. Parse the string and create a new `Bag` from the string. If the string is not a valid `Bag`, then throw a `ParseException`.

PP 12.8 Consider an array of size n containing integers. We now define a left child and a right child for each element of the array as follows:

```
left(i)  = 2i
right(i)  = 2i + 1
```

Here, `i` is the index of the array + 1. For example, consider the following array:

```
[24, 16, 22, 8, 12, 20, 14, 3, 1, 10]
```

Since left(1) is $2 \times 1 = 2$, the left child of `24` is `16`. And, since right(1) is $2 \times 1 + 1 = 3$, the right child of `24` is `22`.

Note that left(6) is $2 \times 6 = 12$, which is beyond the bounds of the array, so `20` has no left child.

Write a recursive method that will accept an array and an index, and print the array in the order: left child, element, right child. For example, the array above will be printed in the order: `3, 8, 1, 16, 10, 12, 24, 20, 22, 14`. That is, `3, 8, 1` is the left child of `16`, and `10, 12` is the right child of `16`. `3, 8, 1, 16, 10, 12` is then the left child of `24`, and so on.

PP 12.9 Design and implement a recursive version of a binary search. An iterative binary search algorithm was introduced in Chapter 10. For the recursive version, instead of using a loop to repeatedly loop for the target value, allow each call to a recursive method check one value. If the value is not the target, refine the search space and call the method again. The indexes that define the range of viable candidates can be passed to the method. The base case is either finding the target value or running out of data to search. Design the program to work for on an array of sorted `String` objects.

PP 12.10 Create a new version of the `TiledImages` program from this chapter that displays the repeated images in the lower-right quadrant instead of the upper-left.

PP 12.11 Write a JavaFX application similar to the `KochSnowflake` program from this chapter that presents various orders of the *C-Curve fractal.* A C-Curve fractal of order 1 is a straight vertical line segment. Each successive order is created by replacing all line segments by two line segments, both half of the size of the original, which meet at a right angle. Specifically, a C-Curve line segment from (x_1, y_1) to (x_3, y_3) is replaced by two line segments from (x_1, y_1) to (x_2, y_2) and from (x_2, y_2) to (x_3, y_3), where:

- $x_2 = (x_1 + x_3 + y_1 - y_3) / 2$
- $y_2 = (x_3 + y_1 + y_3 - x_1) / 2$

Impose a maximum order of 15 on the C-Curve fractal.

PP 12.12 Write a JavaFX application similar to the `KochSnowflake` program from this chapter that presents various orders of the *Sierpinski Triangle* fractal. A Sierpinski Triangle of order 1 is a single triangle. Each successive order is created by replacing each triangle with three smaller triangles made using the midpoint of each segment of the original. Here are Sierpinski Triangles of order 1, 2, and 5:

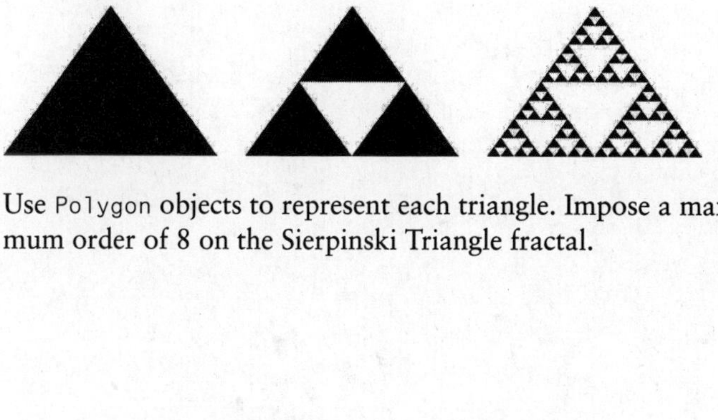

Use `Polygon` objects to represent each triangle. Impose a maximum order of 8 on the Sierpinski Triangle fractal.

13 Collections

CHAPTER OBJECTIVES

- Explore the concept of a collection.
- Stress the importance of separating the interface from the implementation.
- Examine the difference between fixed and dynamic implementations.
- Define and use dynamically linked lists.
- Introduce classic linear data such as queues and stacks.
- Introduce classic non-linear data structures such as trees and graphs.
- Discuss the Java Collections API.
- Define the use of generic types and their use in collection classes.

Problem solving often requires techniques for organizing and managing information. This chapter explores objects that store information, called collections, as well as various ways to implement them. You've already seen an example of a collection, `ArrayList`, introduced in Chapter 5. Many collections have been developed over the years, and some of them have become classics. This chapter explains how collections can be implemented using references to link one object to another.

13.1 Collections and Data Structures

A *collection* is an object that serves as a repository for other objects. It is a general term that can be applied to many situations, but we usually use it when discussing an object whose specific role is to provide services to add, remove, and otherwise manage the elements that are contained within. For example, the `ArrayList` class (discussed in Chapter 5) represents a collection. It provides methods to add elements to the end of a list or to a particular location in the list based on an index value. It provides methods to remove specific elements as needed.

Some collections maintain their elements in a specific order, while others do not. All collection classes in Java are generic, so you specify the type of objects that the collection manages when you create the collection object. For example, you can create an `ArrayList<String>` that holds character strings, or an `ArrayList<Book>` that holds `Book` objects.

Separating Interface from Implementation

A crucial aspect of collections is that they can be implemented in a variety of ways. That is, the underlying *data structure* that stores the objects can be implemented using various techniques. The `ArrayList` class from the Java standard library, for instance, is implemented using an array (hence the name). All operations on an `ArrayList` are accomplished by invoking methods that perform the appropriate operations on the underlying array. The `LinkedList` class also represents a list collection, but it's underlying implementation does not use an array. Its implementation relies on a data structure called a linked list (again, appropriately named), which is discussed in the next section.

An *abstract data type* (ADT) is a collection of data and the particular operations that are allowed on that data. An ADT has a name, a domain of values, and a set of operations that can be performed. An ADT is considered abstract, because the operations you can perform on it are separated from the underlying implementation. That is, the details of how an ADT stores its data and accomplishes its methods are separate from the concept that it embodies. Essentially, the terms *collection* and *abstract data type* are interchangeable.

Objects are perfectly suited for defining collections. An object, by definition, has a well-defined interface whose implementation is hidden in the class. The way the data is represented, and the operations that manage the data, are encapsulated inside the object. This type of object is reusable and reliable, because its interaction with the rest of the system is controlled.

KEY CONCEPT
An object, with its well-defined interface, is a perfect mechanism for implementing a collection.

SELF-REVIEW QUESTIONS *(see answers in Appendix L)*

SR 13.1 What is a collection?

SR 13.2 What's the difference between a collection and a data structure?

SR 13.3 Why are objects particularly well suited for implementing abstract data types?

13.2 Dynamic Representations

Arrays are limited in one key way: they have a fixed size throughout their existence. Sometimes we don't know how big to make an array, because we don't know how much information we will store. The `ArrayList` class handles this by creating a larger array and copying everything over whenever necessary. This is not always an efficient implementation.

A *dynamic data structure* is implemented using links. Using references as links between objects, we can create whatever type of structure is appropriate for the situation. If implemented carefully, the structure can be quite efficient to search and modify. Structures created this way are considered to be dynamic, because their size is determined dynamically, as they are used, and not by their declaration.

KEY CONCEPT

The size of a dynamic data structure grows and shrinks as needed.

Dynamic Structures

Recall that the variable used to keep track of an object is actually a reference to the object, meaning that it stores the address of the object. A declaration such as

```
House home = new House("602 Greenbriar Court");
```

actually accomplishes two things: it declares `home` to be a reference to a `House` object, and it instantiates an object of class `House`. Now consider an object that contains a reference to another object of the same type. For example:

```
class Node
{
    int info;
    Node next;
}
```

Two objects of this class can be instantiated and chained together by having the `next` reference of one `Node` object refer to the other `Node` object. The second

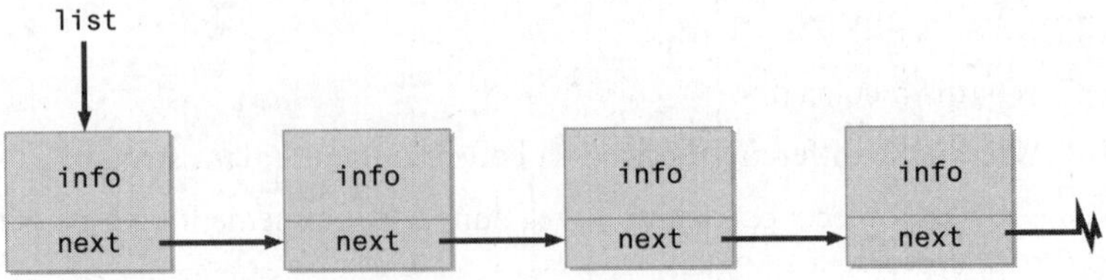

FIGURE 13.1 A linked list

> **KEY CONCEPT**
> A dynamically linked list is managed by storing and updating references to objects.

object's `next` reference can refer to a third `Node` object, and so on, creating a *linked list*. The first node in the list could be referenced using a separate variable. The last node in the list would have a `next` reference that is `null`, indicating the end of the list. Figure 13.1 depicts this situation.

In this example, the information stored in each `Node` class is a simple integer, but keep in mind that we could define a class to contain any amount of information of any type.

A Dynamically Linked List

The program in Listing 13.1 sets up a list of `Magazine` objects and then prints the list. The list of magazines is encapsulated inside the `MagazineList` class shown in Listing 13.2 and is maintained as a dynamically linked list.

The `MagazineList` class represents the list of magazines. From outside of the class (an external view), we do not focus on how the list is implemented. We don't know, for instance, whether the list of magazines is stored in an array or in a linked list. The `MagazineList` class provides a set of methods that allows the user to maintain the list of magazines. That set of methods, specifically `add` and `toString`, defines the operations to the `MagazineList` interface.

VideoNote
Example using a linked list.

The `MagazineList` class uses an inner class called `MagazineNode` to represent a node in the linked list. Each node contains a reference to one magazine and a reference to the next node in the list. Because `MagazineNode` is an inner class, it is reasonable to allow the data values in the class to be public. Therefore, the code in the `MagazineList` class refers to those data values directly.

The `Magazine` class shown in Listing 13.3 is well encapsulated, with all data declared as `private` and methods provided to accomplish any updates necessary. Note that because we use a separate class to represent a node in the list, the `Magazine` class itself does not need to contain a link to the next `Magazine` in the list. That allows the `Magazine` class to be free of any issues regarding its containment in a list.

LISTING 13.1

```
//********************************************************************
//  MagazineRack.java       Author: Lewis/Loftus
//
//  Driver to exercise the MagazineList collection.
//********************************************************************

public class MagazineRack
{
   //-----------------------------------------------------------------
   //  Creates a MagazineList object, adds several magazines to the
   //  list, then prints it.
   //-----------------------------------------------------------------
   public static void main(String[] args)
   {
      MagazineList rack = new MagazineList();

      rack.add(new Magazine("Time"));
      rack.add(new Magazine("Woodworking Today"));
      rack.add(new Magazine("Communications of the ACM"));
      rack.add(new Magazine("House and Garden"));
      rack.add(new Magazine("GQ"));

      System.out.println(rack);
   }
}
```

OUTPUT

```
Time
Woodworking Today
Communications of the ACM
House and Garden
GQ
```

Other methods could be included in the `MagazineList` class. For example, in addition to the `add` method provided, which always adds a new magazine to the end of the list, another method called `insert` could be defined to add a node anywhere in the list (to keep it sorted, for instance). A parameter to `insert` could indicate the value of the node after which the new node should be inserted. Figure 13.2 shows how the references would be updated to insert a new node.

KEY CONCEPT

Insert and delete operations can be implemented by carefully manipulating object references.

LISTING 13.2

```
//********************************************************************
//  MagazineList.java       Author: Lewis/Loftus
//
//  Represents a collection of magazines.
//********************************************************************

public class MagazineList
{
   private MagazineNode list;

   //----------------------------------------------------------------
   //  Sets up an initially empty list of magazines.
   //----------------------------------------------------------------
   public MagazineList()
   {
      list = null;
   }

   //----------------------------------------------------------------
   //  Creates a new MagazineNode object and adds it to the end of
   //  the linked list.
   //----------------------------------------------------------------
   public void add(Magazine mag)
   {

      MagazineNode node = new MagazineNode(mag);
      MagazineNode current;

      if (list == null)
         list = node;
      else
      {
         current = list;
         while (current.next != null)
            current = current.next;
         current.next = node;
      }
   }

//----------------------------------------------------------------
//  Returns this list of magazines as a string.
//----------------------------------------------------------------
public String toString()
```

LISTING 13.2 *continued*

```
   {
      String result = "";

      MagazineNode current = list;

      while (current != null)
      {
         result += current.magazine + "\n";
         current = current.next;
      }

      return result;
   }

   //*****************************************************************
   //  An inner class that represents a node in the magazine list.
   //  The public variables are accessed by the MagazineList class.
   //*****************************************************************
   private class MagazineNode
   {
      public Magazine magazine;
      public MagazineNode next;

      //--------------------------------------------------------------
      // Sets up the node
      //--------------------------------------------------------------
      public MagazineNode(Magazine mag)
      {
         magazine = mag;
         next = null;
      }
   }
}
```

LISTING 13.3

```
//********************************************************************
//  Magazine.java        Author: Lewis/Loftus
//
//  Represents a single magazine.
//********************************************************************

public class Magazine
{
   private String title;

   //-----------------------------------------------------------------
   //  Sets up the new magazine with its title.
   //-----------------------------------------------------------------
   public Magazine(String newTitle)
   {
      title = newTitle;
   }

   //-----------------------------------------------------------------
   //  Returns this magazine as a string.
   //-----------------------------------------------------------------
   public String toString()
   {
      return title;
   }
}
```

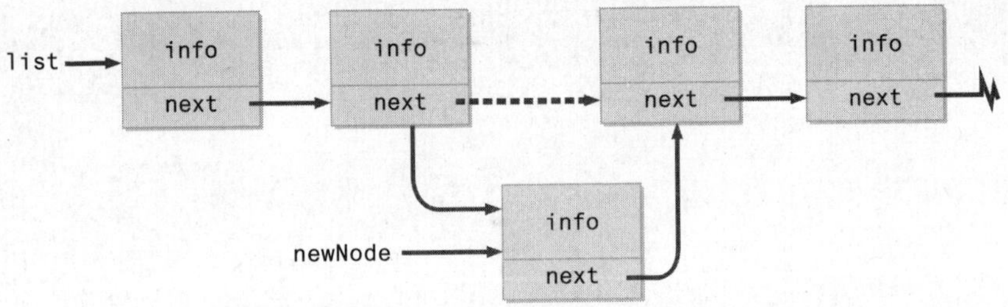

FIGURE 13.2 Inserting a node into the middle of a list

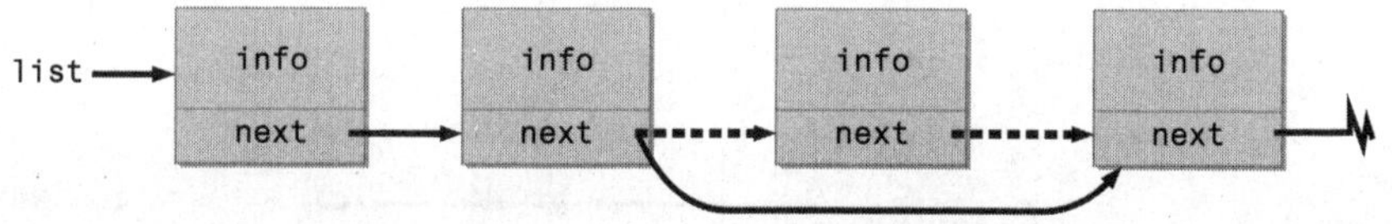

FIGURE 13.3 Deleting a node from a list

Another operation that would be helpful in the list interface would be a `delete` method to remove a particular node. Recall from our discussion in Chapter 3 that by removing all references to an object, it becomes a candidate for garbage collection. Figure 13.3 shows how references would be updated to delete a node from a list. Care must be taken to accomplish the modifications to the references in the proper order to ensure that other nodes are not lost and that references continue to refer to valid, appropriate nodes in the list.

Other Dynamic List Representations

You can use different list implementations, depending on the specific needs of the program you are designing. For example, in some situations it may make processing easier to implement a *doubly linked list* in which each node has not only a reference to the next node in the list but another reference to the previous node in the list. Our generic `Node` class might be declared as follows:

KEY CONCEPT
Many variations on the implementation of dynamically linked lists can be defined.

```
class Node
{
   int info;
   Node next, prev;
}
```

Figure 13.4 shows a doubly linked list. Note that, like a single linked list, the `next` reference of the last node is `null`. Similarly, the previous node of the first node is `null` since there is no node that comes before the first one. This type of structure makes it easy to move back and forth between nodes in the list but requires more effort to set up and modify.

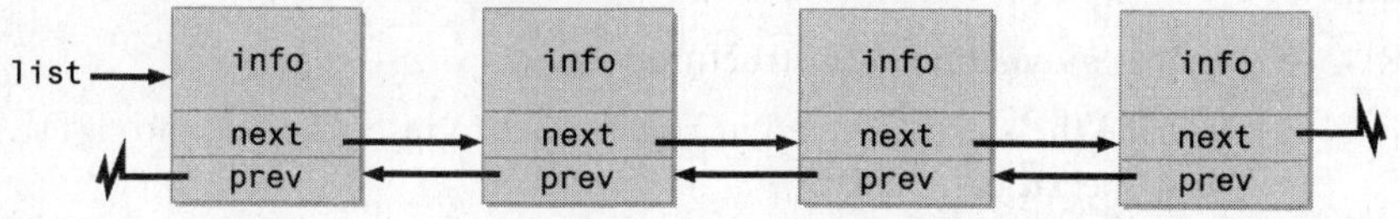

FIGURE 13.4 A doubly linked list

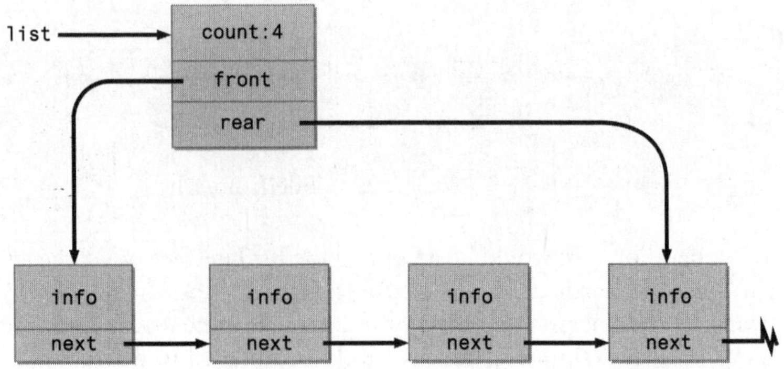

FIGURE 13.5 A list with front and rear references

Another implementation of a linked list could include a *header node* for the list that has a reference to the front of the list and another reference to the rear of the list. A rear reference makes it easier to add new nodes to the end of the list. The header node could contain other information, such as a count of the number of nodes currently in the list. The declaration of the header node would be similar to the following:

```
class ListHeader
{
    int count;
    Node front, rear;
}
```

Note that the header node is not of the same class as the `Node` class to which it refers. Figure 13.5 depicts a linked list that is implemented using a header node.

Still other linked list implementations can be created. For instance, the use of a header can be combined with a doubly linked list, or the list can be maintained in sorted order. The implementation should cater to the type of processing that is required. Some extra effort to maintain a more complex data structure may be worthwhile if it makes common operations on the structure more efficient.

SELF-REVIEW QUESTIONS *(see answers in Appendix L)*

SR 13.4 What is a dynamic data structure?

SR 13.5 Describe the steps depicted in Figure 13.2 to insert a node into a list. What special cases exist?

SR 13.6 Describe the steps depicted in Figure 13.3 to delete a node from a list. What special cases exist?

SR 13.7 Suppose `first` is a reference to a `Node` object, and that it refers to the first node in a linked list. Show, in pseudocode, the steps that would count and return the number of nodes on the list.

SR 13.8 What is a doubly linked list?

SR 13.9 What is a header node for a linked list?

13.3 Linear Collections

In addition to lists, some collections have become classic in that they represent important generic situations that commonly occur in computing. Like lists, a queue and a stack are *linear collections*, meaning that the data they represent is organized in a linear fashion. This section explores some linear collections in more detail.

Queues

A *queue* is similar to a list except that it has restrictions on the way you put items in and take items out. Specifically, a queue uses *first-in, first-out* (FIFO) processing. That is, the first item put in the list is the first item that comes out of the list. Figure 13.6 depicts the FIFO processing of a queue.

KEY CONCEPT
A queue is a linear collection that manages data in a first-in, first-out manner.

Any waiting line is a queue. Think about a line of people waiting for a teller at a bank. A customer enters the queue at the back and moves forward as earlier customers are serviced. Eventually, each customer comes to the front of the queue to be processed.

Note that the processing of a queue is conceptual. We may speak in terms of people moving forward until they reach the front of the queue, but the reality might be that the front of the queue moves as elements come off. That is, we are

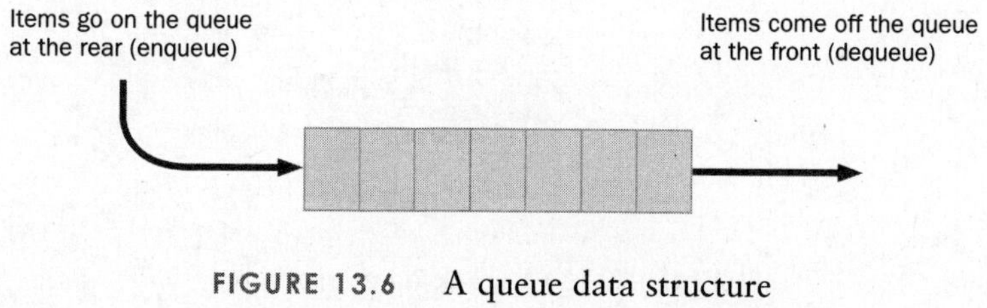

FIGURE 13.6 A queue data structure

not concerned at this point with whether the queue of customers moves toward the teller, or remains stationary as the teller moves when customers are serviced.

VideoNote
Implementing a queue.

A queue data structure typically has the following operations:

- enqueue—adds an item to the rear of the queue
- dequeue—removes an item from the front of the queue
- empty—returns true if the queue is empty

Stacks

KEY CONCEPT
A stack is a linear collection that manages data in a last-in, first-out manner.

A *stack* is similar to a queue except that its elements go on and come off at the same end. The last item to go on a stack is the first item to come off, like a stack of plates in the cupboard or a stack of hay bales in the barn. A stack, therefore, processes information in a *last-in, first-out* (LIFO) manner, as shown in Figure 13.7.

A typical stack ADT contains the following operations:

- push—pushes an item onto the top of the stack
- pop—removes an item from the top of the stack
- peek—retrieves information from the top item of the stack without removing it
- empty—returns true if the stack is empty

The `java.util` package of the API contains a class called `Stack` that implements a stack data structure. It contains methods that correspond to the standard stack operations, plus a method that searches for a particular object in the stack.

The `Stack` class has a `search` method that returns an integer corresponding to the position in the stack of the particular object. This type of searching is not usually considered to be part of the classic stack collection.

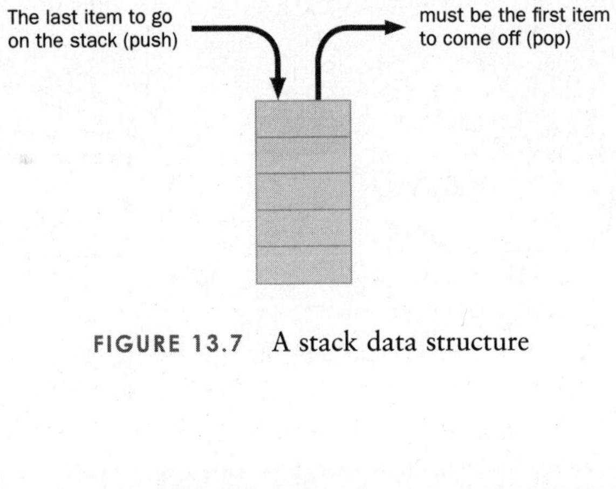

FIGURE 13.7 A stack data structure

Like `ArrayList`, `Stack` is a generic class. You specify the type of object that will go on the stack when you create the `Stack` object.

Let's look at an example that uses a stack to solve a problem. The program in Listing 13.4 accepts a string of characters that represents a secret message. The program decodes and prints the message.

LISTING 13.4

```
//********************************************************************
//  Decode.java          Author: Lewis/Loftus
//
//  Demonstrates the use of the Stack class.
//********************************************************************

import java.util.*;

public class Decode
{
   //-----------------------------------------------------------------
   //  Decodes a message by reversing each word in a string.
   //-----------------------------------------------------------------
   public static void main(String[] args)
   {
      Scanner scan = new Scanner(System.in);

      Stack<Character> word = new Stack<Character>();

      String message;
      int index = 0;

      System.out.println("Enter the coded message:");
      message = scan.nextLine();
      System.out.println("The decoded message is:");

      while (index < message.length())
      {
         // Push word onto stack
         while (index < message.length() && message.charAt(index) != ' ')
         {
            word.push(message.charAt(index));
            index++;
         }
```

LISTING 13.4 *continued*

```
            // Print word in reverse
            while (!word.empty())
               System.out.print(word.pop());
            System.out.print(" ");
            index++;
         }

         System.out.println();
      }
   }
```

OUTPUT

```
Enter the coded message:
artxE eseehc esaelp
The decoded message is:
Extra cheese please
```

A message that has been encoded has each individual word in the message reversed. Words in the message are separated by a single space. The program uses the `Stack` class to push the characters of each word on the stack. When an entire word has been read, each character is popped off the stack and printed.

SELF-REVIEW QUESTIONS *(see answers in Appendix L)*

SR 13.10 How is a queue different from a list?

SR 13.11 Show the contents of a queue after the following operations are performed. Assume the queue is initially empty.

```
enqueue(5);
enqueue(21);
dequeue();
enqueue(72);
enqueue(37);
enqueue(15);
dequeue();
```

SR 13.12 What is a stack?

SR 13.13 Show the contents of a stack after the following operations are performed. Assume the stack is initially empty.

```
push(5);
push(21);
pop();
push(72);
push(37);
push(15);
pop();
```

SR 13.14 What is the `Stack` class?

13.4 Non-Linear Data Structures

Linear collections such as lists, stacks, and queues are appropriately managed by linear data structures such as an array or linked list. Collections whose elements are not inherently linear, however, may be better implemented using a *non-linear data structure*. This section examines two types of non-linear structures: trees and graphs.

Trees

A *tree* is a non-linear data structure that consists of a *root node* and potentially many levels of additional nodes that form a hierarchy. All nodes other than the root are called *internal nodes*. Nodes that have no children are called *leaf nodes*. Figure 13.8 depicts a tree. Note that we draw a tree "upside down," with the root at the top and the leaves at the bottom.

KEY CONCEPT

A tree is a non-linear data structure that organizes data into a hierarchy.

In a general tree like the one in Figure 13.8, each node could have many child nodes. As we mentioned in Chapter 9, the inheritance relationships among classes can be depicted using a general tree structure.

In a *binary tree*, each node can have no more than two child nodes. Binary trees are useful in various programming situations and usually are easier to implement than general trees. Technically, binary trees are a subset of general trees, but they are so important in the computing world that they usually are thought of as their own data structure.

The operations on trees and binary trees vary, but minimally include adding and removing nodes from the tree or binary tree. Because of their non-linear nature, trees and binary trees are implemented nicely using references as dynamic links. However, it is possible to implement a tree data structure using a fixed representation such as an array.

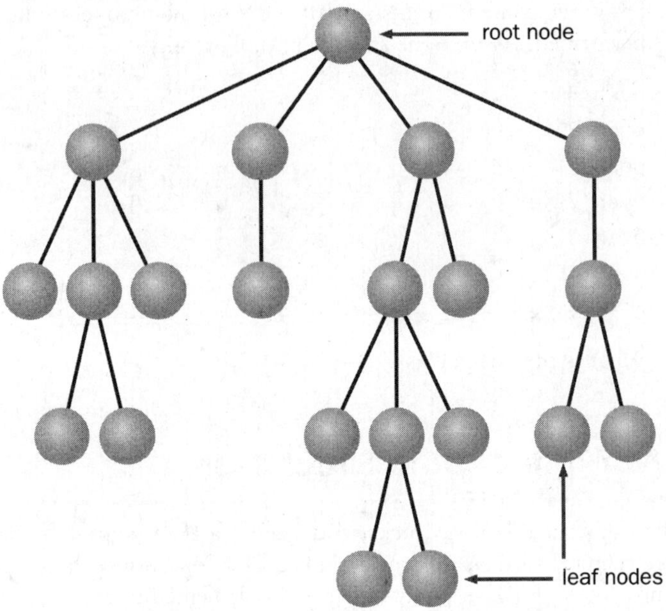

FIGURE 13.8 A tree data structure

Graphs

KEY CONCEPT
A graph is a non-linear data structure that connects nodes using generic edges.

Like a tree, a *graph* is a non-linear data structure. Unlike a tree, a graph does not have a primary entry point like the tree's root node. In a graph, a node is linked to another node by a connection called an *edge*. Generally, there are no restrictions on the number of edges that can be made between nodes in a graph. Figure 13.9 presents a graph data structure.

Graphs are useful when representing relationships for which linear paths and strict hierarchies do not suffice. For instance, the highway system connecting cities on a map and airline connections between airports are better represented as graphs than by any other data structure discussed so far.

In a general graph, the edges are bi-directional, meaning that the edge connecting nodes A and B can be followed from A to B and also from B to A. In a *directed graph*, or *digraph*, each edge has a specific direction. Figure 13.10 shows a digraph, in which each edge indicates the direction using an arrowhead.

A digraph might be used, for instance, to represent airline flights between airports. Unlike highway systems, which are in almost all cases bi-directional, having a flight from one city to another does not necessarily mean there is a

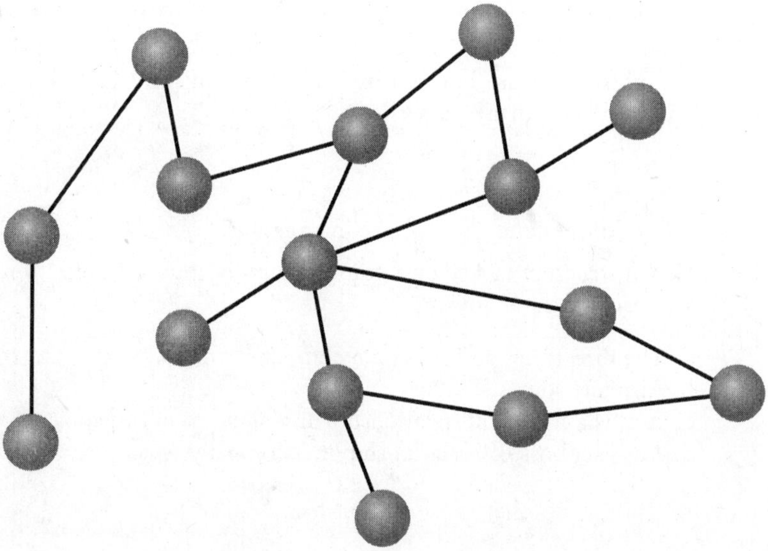

FIGURE 13.9 A graph data structure

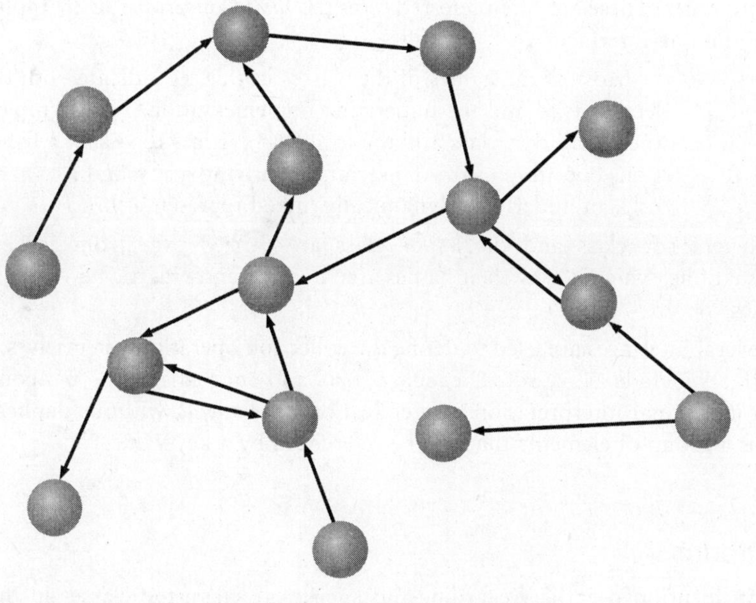

FIGURE 13.10 A directed graph

corresponding flight going the other way. Or, if there is, we may want to associate different information with it, such as cost.

Like trees, graphs often are implemented using dynamic links, although they can be implemented using arrays as well.

SELF-REVIEW QUESTIONS *(see answers in Appendix L)*

SR 13.15 What do trees and graphs have in common?

SR 13.16 Which structure (a tree or a graph) would be a good choice to represent each of the following.

a. The directories and files on a computer system.
b. Airplane routes.
c. An "is a friend of" relationship among a group of people.
d. An "is a boss of" relationship in a company.

13.5 The Java Collections API

The Java standard class library contains several classes that represent collections of various types. These are often referred to as the *Java Collections API* (Application Programming Interface).

KEY CONCEPT
The Java Collections API defines several collection classes implemented in various ways.

Most of the names of the classes in this set indicate both the collection type and the underlying implementation. For example, both the `ArrayList` class and the `LinkedList` class represent a list collection, but an `ArrayList` uses an underlying array and a `LinkedList` uses an underlying dynamically linked representation.

The `Vector` class and the `Stack` class are carried over from earlier Java incarnations, which is why their names aren't consistent with the newer collection classes.

Several interfaces are used to define the collection operations themselves. These interfaces include `List`, `Set`, `SortedSet`, `Map`, and `SortedMap`. A `Set` is consistent with its normal interpretation as a collection of elements without duplicates. A `Map` is a group of elements that can be referenced by a key value.

Generics

As we mentioned earlier regarding the `ArrayList` class, the classes in the Java Collections API are implemented as *generic types*, meaning that the type of object that the collection manages can be established when an object of that collection type is instantiated.

> **KEY CONCEPT**
> The classes of the Java Collections API are implemented as generic types.

For example, to create a `LinkedList` of `String` objects, we would instantiate a collection object in the following way:

```
LinkedList<String> myStringList = new LinkedList<String>();
```

Similarly, to create a `LinkedList` of `Book` objects, we would instantiate the collection as follows:

```
LinkedList<Book> myBookList = new LinkedList<Book>();
```

By specifying the type stored in the collection, we gain two advantages:

- Only objects of the appropriate type can be added to the collection.
- When an object is removed from the collection, its type is already established, avoiding the need to cast it to an appropriate type.

> **KEY CONCEPT**
> Generic classes ensure type compatibility among the objects stored by the collection.

The `myStringList` object can store only `String` objects, and the `myBookList` collection can store only `Book` objects. Keep in mind that these include objects related to the specified type by inheritance. For example, if a `Dictionary` class is derived from `Book`, then we could store a `Dictionary` object in the `myBookList` collection. After all, if we're using inheritance correctly, a `Dictionary` is a `Book`.

If no specific type is specified when the collection object is created, the collection is defined as containing references of the `Object` class, which means they can store any type of object. This makes the use of the collections classes consistent with earlier versions of Java that did not include generic specifications.

The details of the collection classes and the techniques for defining a generic class go beyond the scope of this book and so are not explored further here.

SELF-REVIEW QUESTIONS *(see answers in Appendix L)*

SR 13.17 What is the Java Collections API?

SR 13.18 What is a generic type, and how does it relate to the Java Collections API?

Summary of Key Concepts

- An object, with its well-defined interface, is a perfect mechanism for implementing a collection.
- The size of a dynamic data structure grows and shrinks as needed.
- A dynamically linked list is managed by storing and updating references to objects.
- Insert and delete operations can be implemented by carefully manipulating object references.
- Many variations on the implementation of dynamically linked lists can be defined.
- A queue is a linear collection that manages data in a first-in, first-out manner.
- A stack is a linear collection that manages data in a last-in, first-out manner.
- A tree is a non-linear data structure that organizes data into a hierarchy.
- A graph is a non-linear data structure that connects nodes using generic edges.
- The Java Collections API defines several collection classes implemented in various ways.
- The classes of the Java Collections API are implemented as generic types.
- Generic classes ensure type compatibility among the objects stored by the collection.

Exercises

EX 13.1 Suppose `current` is a reference to a `Node` object and that it currently refers to a specific node in a linked list. Show, in pseudocode, the steps that would delete the node following `current` from the list. Carefully consider the cases in which `current` is referring to the first and last nodes in the list.

EX 13.2 Modify your answer to Exercise 13.1 assuming that the list was set up as a doubly linked list, with both `next` and `prev` references.

EX 13.3 Suppose `current` and `newNode` are references to `Node` objects. Assume `current` currently refers to a specific node in a linked list and `newNode` refers to an unattached `Node` object. Show, in pseudocode, the steps that would insert `newNode` behind `current` in the list. Carefully consider the cases in which `current` is referring to the first and last nodes in the list.

EX 13.4 Modify your answer to Exercise 13.3 assuming that the list was set up as a doubly linked list, with both `next` and `prev` references.

EX 13.5 Would the front and rear references in the header node of a linked list ever refer to the same node? Would they ever both be null? Would one ever be null if the other was not? Explain your answers using examples.

EX 13.6 Consider a queue with values 2,7,4,6,3,2,8,9,1. Show the contents of the queue after the following operations are performed.

```
enqueue(4);
enqueue(6);
enqueue(5);
enqueue(3);
dequeue();
dequeue();
dequeue();
enqueue(7);
enqueue(11);
enqueue(10);
enqueue(13);
dequeue();
dequeue();
dequeue();
```

EX 13.7 In terms of the final state of a queue, does it matter how dequeue operations are intermixed with enqueue operations? Does it matter how the enqueue operations are intermixed among themselves? Explain using examples.

EX 13.8 Consider a stack with values 1,2,3,4,5. Show the contents of the stack after the following operations are performed.

```
pop();
pop();
pop();
push(5);
push(4);
push(3);
pop();
push(6);
push(8);
pop();
push(7);
pop();
pop();
```

EX 13.9 In terms of the final state of a stack, does it matter how the pop operations are intermixed with the push operations? Does it matter how the push operations are intermixed among themselves? Explain using examples.

EX 13.10 Would a tree data structure be a good choice to represent a family tree that shows lineage? Why or why not? Would a binary tree be a better choice? Why or why not?

EX 13.11 What data structure would be a good choice to represent the links between various Web sites? Give an example.

Programming Projects

PP 13.1 Design and implement a class called `CalendarEvent` that represents events on a calendar. Each event should contain a title, a date, a start time, and a duration. Write a program that creates a list of `CalendarEvents` and prints the list.

PP 13.2 Modify the `CalendarEvent` class defined in PP 13.1 by implementing the `Comparable` interface. Create a new class called `Calendar` that consists of a collection of `CalendarEvents`. The `Calendar` class should have methods to add and delete `CalendarEvents`. Write a program that creates a `Calendar` with a collection of `CalendarEvents` and prints the collection in sorted order.

PP 13.3 Design and implement a version of selection sort (from Chapter 10) that operates on a linked list of nodes that each contain an integer.

PP 13.4 Design and implement a version of insertion sort (from Chapter 10) that operates on a linked list of nodes that each contain an integer.

VideoNote
Developing a solution of PP 13.3.

PP 13.5 Design and implement an application that simulates cars at a traffic signal. Use a queue data structure to represent the line of cars. As cars arrive at the signal, they are put at the end of the queue. When the light is green, car objects are removed from the front of the queue with a dequeue operation. Randomly determine when new cars arrive at the signal, and change the light from green to red at fixed intervals. Print a message each time an operation occurs during the simulation.

PP 13.6 Modify the solution to PP 13.5 so that it runs several different simulations with different values. You can increase or decrease the traffic-light timing, or increase or decrease the number of cars arriving at the signal. At the end of each simulation, print a summary of the simulation, including the number of cars in the queue and how long it took on average for each car to move through the queue.

PP 13.7 Design and implement an application that evaluates a postfix expression that operates on integer operands using the arithmetic operators +, −, *, /, and %. We are already familiar with infix expressions, in which an operator is positioned between its two operands. A *postfix expression* puts the operators after its operands. Keep in mind that an operand could be the result of another operation. This eliminates the need for parentheses to force precedence. For example, the following infix expression:

```
(5 + 2) * (8 – 5)
```

is equivalent to the following postfix expression:

```
5 2 + 8 5 – *
```

The evaluation of a postfix expression is facilitated by using a stack. As you process a postfix expression from left to right, you encounter operands and operators. If you encounter an operand, push it on the stack. If you encounter an operator, pop two operands off the stack, perform the operation, and push the result back on the stack. When you have processed the entire expression, there will be one value on the stack, which is the result of the entire expression.

You may want to use a `StringTokenizer` object to assist in the parsing of the expression. You can assume the expression will be in valid postfix form.

PP 13.8 Design and implement a program that prompts the user to enter a string and then performs two palindrome tests. The first should use a single stack to test whether the string is a palindrome. The second should use two stacks to test whether the string is a palindrome when capitalization, spaces, punctuation, and other non-alphanumeric characters are ignored. The program should print the results of both tests.

PP 13.9 Design and implement a class named `StringTree`, a binary tree for storing `String` objects in alphabetic order. Each node in the tree should be represented by a `Node` class, which stores the string value and pointers to the right and left child nodes. For any node value in the tree, the value of its left child should come before that value, and the value of its right child should come after that value. The `StringTree` class should contain both a method for adding strings to the tree and a method for printing the tree's value in alphabetic order. Write a driver program that reads strings from a file (one per line) and adds them to the tree. After processing the input, print the tree values.

Glossary

A

abstract—A Java reserved word that serves as a modifier for classes, interfaces, and methods.

abstract class—A class used in the design of an inheritance hierarchy to specify undefined functionality that must be defined by its descendants. An abstract class cannot be instantiated.

abstract data type (ADT)—A collection of data and the operations that are defined on that data.

abstract method—A method header with no body. The code of an abstract method is defined by the implementing class.

Abstract Windowing Toolkit (AWT)—A graphics package in the Java API that, along with the Swing package, has been replaced by the JavaFX package.

abstraction—The concept of hiding details. If the right details are hidden at the right times, abstraction can significantly help control complexity and focus attention on appropriate issues.

access—The ability to reference a variable or invoke a method from outside the class in which it is declared. Controlled by the visibility modifier used to declare the variable or method. *See also* visibility modifier.

access modifier—*See* visibility modifier.

action event—A type of event that indicates the user took some action. An action event is generated by several GUI controls, such as a button when it is pushed.

actual parameter—The value passed to a method as a parameter. *See also* formal parameter.

address—(1) A numeric value that uniquely identifies a particular memory location in a computer's main memory. (2) A designation that uniquely identifies a computer among all others on a network.

ADT—*See* abstract data type.

aggregate object—An object that contains variables that are references to other objects. *See also* has-a relationship.

alert—A simplified dialog box in JavaFX. There are several types of predefined alerts.

algorithm—A step-by-step process for solving a problem. A program is based on one or more algorithms.

alias—A reference to an object that is currently also referred to by another reference. Each reference is an alias of the other.

analog—A representation that is in direct proportion to the source of the information. *See also* digital.

anchor pane—A JavaFX layout pane in which nodes can be anchored to the top, bottom, left side, right side, or center of the pane.

animation—A series of images or drawings that give the appearance of movement when displayed in order at a particular speed.

API—*See* Application Programming Interface.

applet—A Java program that is linked into an HTML document, then retrieved and executed using a Web browser. JavaFX technology has generally replaced applets.

application—(1) A generic term for any program. (2) A Java program that can be run without the use of a Web browser, as opposed to a Java applet.

Application Programming Interface (API)—A set of classes that defines services for a programmer. Not part of the language itself, but often relied on to perform even basic tasks. *See also* class library.

arc—A JavaFX shape that is defined as a portion of an ellipse.

arc type—The type of a JavaFX arc, which may be open, chord, or round.

architectural design—A high-level design that identifies the large portions of a software system and key data structures. *See also* detailed design.

architecture—*See* computer architecture.

architecture neutral—Not specific to any particular hardware platform. Java code is considered architecture neutral because it is compiled into bytecode and then interpreted on any machine with a Java interpreter.

arithmetic operator—An operator that performs a basic arithmetic computation, such as addition or multiplication.

arithmetic promotion—The act of promoting the type of a numeric operand to be consistent with the other operand.

array—A programming language construct used to store an ordered list of primitive values or objects. Each element in the array is referenced using a numerical index from 0 to *N*–1, where *N* is the size of the array.

array element—A value or object that is stored in an array.

array element type—The type of the values or objects that are stored in an array.

ASCII—A popular character set used by many programming languages. ASCII stands for American Standard Code for Information Interchange. It is a subset of the Unicode character set, which is used by Java.

assembly language—A low-level language that uses mnemonics to represent program commands.

assert—A Java reserved word used to establish an assertion about a program for testing purposes.

assignment conversion—Some data types can be converted to another in an assignment statement. *See* widening conversion.

assignment operator—An operator that results in an assignment to a variable. The = operator performs basic assignment. Many other assignment operators perform additional operations prior to the assignment, such as the *= operator.

association—A relationship between two classes in which one uses the other or relates to it in some way. *See also* operator association, use relationship.

autoboxing—The automatic conversion from a primitive value to a corresponding wrapper object. The reverse process is called unboxing.

AWT—*See* Abstract Windowing Toolkit.

base—The numerical value on which a particular number system is based. It determines the number of digits available in that number system and the place value of each digit in a number. *See also* binary, decimal, hexadecimal, octal, place value.

base 2—*See* binary.

base 8—*See* octal.

base 10—*See* decimal.

base 16—*See* hexadecimal.

base case—The condition that terminates recursive processing, allowing the active recursive methods to begin returning to their point of invocation.

base class—*See* superclass.

behavior—The functional characteristics of an object, defined by its methods. *See also* identity, state.

binary—The base-2 number system. Modern computer systems store information as strings of binary digits (bits).

binary operator—An operator that uses two operands.

binary search—A searching algorithm that requires that the list be sorted. It repetitively compares the middle element of the list to the target value, narrowing the scope of the search each time. *See also* linear search.

binary string—A series of binary digits (bits).

binary tree—A tree data structure in which each node can have no more than two child nodes.

binding—The process of associating an identifier with the construct that it represents. For example, the process of binding a method name to the specific definition that it invokes.

bit—A binary digit, either 0 or 1.

bit shifting—The act of shifting the bits of a data value to the left or right, losing bits on one end and inserting bits on the other.

bits per second (bps)—A measurement rate for data transfer devices.

bitwise operator—An operator that manipulates individual bits of a value, either by calculation or by shifting.

black-box testing—Producing and evaluating test cases based on the input and expected output of a software component. The test cases focus on covering the equivalence categories and boundary values of the input. *See also* white-box testing.

block—A group of programming statements and declarations enclosed in braces ({}).

boolean—A Java reserved word representing a logical primitive data type that can only take the values `true` or `false`.

boolean expression—An expression that evaluates to a true or false result, primarily used as conditions in selection and repetition statements.

boolean operator—Any of the bitwise operators AND (&), OR (|), or XOR (^) when applied to `boolean` operands. The results are equivalent to their logical counterparts, except that boolean operators are not short-circuited.

border pane—A JavaFX layout pane that organizes its nodes into five regions: top, bottom, left, right, and center.

boundary values—The input values corresponding to the edges of equivalence categories. Used in black-box testing.

bounds checking—The process of determining whether an array index is in bounds, given the size of the array. Java performs automatic bounds checking.

bps—*See* bits per second.

break—A Java reserved word used to interrupt the flow of control by breaking out of the current loop or `switch` statement.

browser—A program that retrieves HTML documents and other resources across a network and formats them for viewing. A browser is the primary vehicle for accessing the World Wide Web.

bug—A slang term for a defect or error in a computer program.

build-and-fix approach—An unwise approach to software development in which a program is created without any significant planning or design, then modified until it reaches some level of acceptance.

bus—A group of wires in the computer that carry data between components such as the CPU and main memory.

button—A GUI control that allows the user to initiate an action with a mouse click. *See also* check box, radio button.

byte—(1) A unit of binary storage equal to eight bits. (2) A Java reserved word that represents a primitive integer type, stored using eight bits in two's complement format.

byte stream—An I/O stream that manages 8-bit bytes of raw binary data. *See also* character stream.

bytecode—The low-level format into which the Java compiler translates Java source code. The bytecodes are interpreted and executed by the Java interpreter, perhaps after transportation over the Internet.

capacity—*See* storage capacity.

Cascading Style Sheets (CSS)—A language used to describe the way content looks when presented. CSS is used to format web pages, and is also used in JavaFX to style nodes.

case—(1) A Java reserved word that is used to identify each unique option in a `switch` statement. (2) The orientation of an alphabetic character (uppercase or lowercase).

case sensitive—Differentiating between the uppercase and lowercase versions of an alphabetic letter. Java is case sensitive; therefore the identifier `total` and the identifier `Total` are considered to be different identifiers.

cast—A Java operation expressed using a type or class name in parentheses to explicitly convert and return a value of one data type into another.

catch—A Java reserved word that is used to specify an exception handler, defined after a `try` block.

CD-Recordable (CD-R)—A compact disc on which information can be stored once using a home computer with an appropriate drive. *See also* CD-Rewritable, CD-ROM.

CD-ROM—An optical secondary memory medium that stores binary information in a manner similar to a musical compact disc.

central processing unit (CPU)—The hardware component that controls the main activity of a computer, including the flow of information and the execution of commands.

change listener—An object that is set up to respond when an observable value, such as a JavaFX property, is changed.

char—A Java reserved word that represents the primitive character type. All Java characters are members of the Unicode character set and are stored using 16 bits.

character set—An ordered list of characters, such as the ASCII or Unicode character sets. Each character corresponds to a specific, unique numeric value within a given character set. A programming language adopts a particular character set to use for character representation and management.

character stream—An I/O stream that manages 16-bit Unicode characters. *See also* byte stream.

character string—A series of ordered characters. Represented in Java using the `String` class and string literals such as `"hello"`.

check box—A GUI control that allows the user to set a boolean condition with a mouse click. A check box can be used alone or independently among other check boxes. *See also* radio button.

checked exception—A Java exception that must be either caught or explicitly thrown to the calling method. *See also* unchecked exception.

child class—*See* subclass.

choice box—A GUI control that allows the user to select one of several options from a drop down menu. A choice box displays the most recent selection. *See also* combo box.

class—(1) A Java reserved word used to define a class. (2) The blueprint of an object—the model that defines the variables and methods an object will contain when instantiated.

class diagram—A diagram that shows the relationships between classes, including inheritance and use relationships. *See also* Unified Modeling Language.

class hierarchy—A tree-like structure created when classes are derived from other classes through inheritance. *See also* interface hierarchy.

class library—A set of classes that define useful services for a programmer. *See also* Application Programming Interface.

class method—A method that can be invoked using only the class name. An instantiated object is not required as it is with instance methods. Defined in a Java program using the `static` reserved word.

class variable—A variable that is shared among all objects of a class. It can also be referenced through the class name, without instantiating any object of that class. Defined in a Java program using the `static` reserved word.

CLASSPATH—An operating system setting that determines where the Java interpreter searches for class files.

client–server model—A manner in which to construct a software design based on objects (clients) making use of the services provided by other objects (servers).

coding guidelines—A series of conventions that describe how programs should be constructed. They make programs easier to read, exchange, and integrate. Sometimes referred to as coding standards, especially when they are enforced.

coding standard—*See* coding guidelines.

cohesion—The strength of the relationship among the parts within a software component. *See also* coupling.

collision—The process of two hash values producing the same hash code. *See also* hash code, hashing.

color picker—A JavaFX GUI control that lets the user select a color. A color picker appears as a single field that displays a drop-down palette of colors when clicked.

combo box—A GUI control that allows the user to select one of several options from a drop down list. A combo box displays the most recent selection. *See also* choice box.

command-line arguments—The values that follow the program name on the command line. Accessed within a Java program through the `String` array parameter to the main method.

comment—A programming language construct that allows a programmer to embed human-readable annotations into the source code. *See also* documentation.

compiler—A program that translates code from one language to equivalent code in another language. The Java compiler translates Java source code into Java bytecode. *See also* interpreter.

compile-time error—Any error that occurs during the compilation process, often indicating that a program does not conform to the language syntax or that an operation was attempted on an inappropriate data type. *See also* logical error, run-time error, syntax error.

computer architecture—The structure and interaction of the hardware components of a computer.

concatenation—*See* string concatenation.

condition—A `boolean` expression used to determine whether the body of a selection or repetition statement should be executed.

conditional coverage—A strategy used in white-box testing in which all conditions in a program are executed, producing both `true` and `false` results. *See also* statement coverage.

conditional operator—A Java ternary operator that evaluates one of two expressions based on a condition.

conditional statement—*See* selection statement.

const—A Java reserved word that is not currently used.

constant—An identifier that contains a value that cannot be modified. Used to make code more readable and to facilitate changes. Defined in Java using the `final` modifier.

constructor—A special method in a class that is invoked when an object is instantiated from the class. Used to initialize the object.

container—A Java graphical user interface component that can hold other components. *See also* containment hierarchy.

containment hierarchy—The relationships among graphical components of a user interface. *See also* container.

control—A JavaFX GUI element, such as a button, slider, or text field, that allows the user to interact with a program.

control characters—*See* nonprintable characters.

controller—Hardware devices that control the interaction between a computer system and a particular kind of peripheral.

coupling—The strength of the relationship between two software components. *See also* cohesion.

CPU—*See* central processing unit.

data stream—An I/O stream that represents a particular source or destination for data, such as a file. *See also* processing stream.

data structure—A programming construct used to organize data into a format to facilitate access and processing. Arrays, linked lists, and trees can all be considered data structures.

data type—A designation that specifies a set of values (which may be infinite). Each Java variable has a data type that specifies the kinds of values that can be stored in it.

data transfer device—A hardware component that allows information to be sent between computers, such as a modem.

date picker—A JavaFX GUI control that lets the user select a calendar date. A date picker appears as a single field that displays a drop-down calendar when clicked.

debugger—A software tool that allows a programmer to step through an executing program and examine the value of variables at any point. *See also* jdb.

decimal—The base-10 number system, which humans use in everyday life. *See also* binary.

default—A Java reserved word that is used to indicate the default case of a `switch` statement, used if no other cases match. Also used to specify the default implementation of an interface method.

default visibility—The level of access designated when no explicit visibility modifier is used to declare a class, interface, method, or variable. Sometimes referred to as package visibility. Anything declared with default visibility is visible only to classes in the same package.

defect testing—Testing designed to uncover errors in a program.

delimiter—Any symbol or word used to set the boundaries of a programming language construct, such as the braces (`{}`) used to define a Java block statement, method body, or class content.

deprecated—Something, such as a particular method in the Java API, that is considered out-of-favor and should not be used.

derived class—*See* subclass.

design—(1) The plan for implementing a program, which includes a specification of the classes and objects used and an expression of the important program algorithms. (2) The process of creating a program design.

desk check—A type of review in which a developer carefully examines a design or program to find errors.

detailed design—(1) The low-level algorithmic steps of a method. (2) The development stage at which low-level algorithmic steps are determined.

development stage—The software life-cycle stage in which a software system is first created, preceding use, maintenance, and eventual retirement.

dialog box—A graphical window that pops up to allow brief, specific user interaction.

digital—A representation that breaks information down into pieces, which are in turn represented as numbers. All modern computer systems are digital.

digitize—The act of converting an analog representation into a digital one by breaking it down into pieces.

digraph—A graph data structure in which each edge has a specific direction.

dimension—The number of index levels of an array.

direct recursion—The process of a method invoking itself. *See also* indirect recursion.

disable—Make a GUI control inactive so that it cannot be used.

DNS—*See* Domain Name System.

do—A Java reserved word that represents a repetition construct. A `do` statement is executed one or more times. *See also* for, while.

documentation—Supplemental information about a program, including comments in a program's source code and printed reports such as a user's guide.

domain name—The portion of an Internet address that specifies the organization to which the computer belongs.

Domain Name System (DNS)—Software that translates an Internet address into an IP address using a domain server.

domain server—A file server that maintains a list of Internet addresses and their corresponding IP addresses.

double—A Java reserved word that represents a primitive floating point numeric type, stored using 64 bits in IEEE 754 format.

doubly linked list—A linked list with two references in each node: one that refers to the next node in the list and one that refers to the previous node in the list.

dynamic binding—The process of associating an identifier with its definition during run time. *See also* binding.

dynamic data structure—A set of objects that are linked using references, which can be modified as needed during program execution.

editor—A software tool that allows the user to enter and store a file of characters on a computer. Often used by programmers to enter the source code of a program.

efficiency—The characteristic of an algorithm that specifies the required number of a particular operation in order to complete its task. For example, the efficiency of a sort can be measured by the number of comparisons required to sort a list. *See also* order.

element—A value or object stored in another object such as an array.

element type—*See* array element type.

else—A Java reserved word that designates the portion of code in an `if` statement that will be executed if the condition is false.

encapsulation—The characteristic of an object that limits access to the variables and methods contained in it. All interaction with an object occurs through a well-defined interface that supports a modular design.

enumerated type—A programmer-defined data type that lists all possible values of that type and possibly defines operations on those values.

equality operator—One of two Java operators that returns a boolean result based on whether two values are equal (==) or not equal (!=).

equivalence category—A range of functionally equivalent input values as specified by the requirements of the software component. Used when developing black-box test cases.

error—Any defect in a design or program. *See also* compile-time error, exception, logical error, runtime error, syntax error.

escape sequence—In Java, a sequence of characters beginning with the backslash character (\), used to indicate a special situation when printing values.

For example, the escape sequence `\t` specifies that a horizontal tab should be printed.

exception—(1) A situation that arises during program execution that is erroneous or out of the ordinary. (2) An object that can be thrown and processed by special `catch` blocks. *See also* error.

exception handler—The code in a `catch` clause of a `try` statement, executed when a particular type of exception is thrown.

exception propagation—The process that occurs when an exception is thrown: control returns to each calling method in the stack trace until the exception is caught and handled or until the exception is thrown from the main method, terminating the program.

exponent—The portion of a floating point value's internal representation that specifies how far the decimal point is shifted. *See also* mantissa.

expression—A combination of operators and operands that produce a result.

extends—A Java reserved word used to specify the parent class in the definition of a child class.

event—(1) A user action, such as a mouse click or key press. (2) An object that represents a user action, to which the program can respond. *See also* event-driven programming.

event-driven programming—An approach to software development in which the program is designed to acknowledge that an event has occurred and to act accordingly. *See also* event.

event handler—An object set up to respond to an event when it occurs.

false—A Java reserved word that serves as one of the two boolean literals (`true` and `false`).

fetch-decode-execute—The cycle through which the CPU continually obtains instructions from main memory and executes them.

FIFO—*See* first-in, first-out.

file—A named collection of data stored on a secondary storage device such as a disk. *See also* text file.

file chooser—A specialized dialog box that allows the user to select a file from a storage device.

file server—A computer in a network, usually with a large secondary storage capacity, that is dedicated to storing software needed by many network users.

fill—The interior area of a shape. In JavaFX, the fill color can be set explicitly. *See also* stroke.

filtering stream—*See* processing stream.

final—A Java reserved word that serves as a modifier for classes, methods, and variables. A `final` class cannot be used to derive a new class. A `final` method cannot be overridden. A `final` variable is a constant.

finalize—A Java method defined in the `Object` class that can be overridden in any other class. It is called after the object becomes a candidate for garbage collection and before it is destroyed. It is used to perform "clean-up" activity that is not performed automatically by the garbage collector.

finally—A Java reserved word that designates a block of code to be executed when an exception is thrown, after any appropriate catch handler is processed.

first-in, first-out (FIFO)—A data management technique in which the first value that is stored in a data structure is the first value that comes out. *See also* last-in, first-out; queue.

float—A Java reserved word that represents a primitive floating point numeric type, stored using 32 bits in IEEE 754 format.

flow pane—A JavaFX layout pane that arranges its nodes horizontally in rows, fitting as many in a row as the width of the container allows. A flow plan can also display nodes vertically in columns.

flushing—The process of forcing the contents of the output buffer to be displayed on the output device.

font—A specification that describes how characters are displayed visually.

font family—A consistent font design for a group of characters. Examples of font families are Arial and Helvetica.

font posture—A specification of whether a character is displayed in italic or not.

font size—The size of a character when displayed, expressed in units called points.

font weight—The specification of how bold a character is when displayed.

for—A Java reserved word that represents a repetition construct. A `for` statement is executed zero or more times and is usually used when a precise number of iterations is known.

formal parameter—An identifier that serves as a parameter name in a method. It receives its initial value from the actual parameter passed to it. *See also* actual parameter.

fourth-generation language—A high-level language that provides built-in functionality such as automatic report generation or database management, beyond that of traditional high-level languages.

fractal—A geometric shape made up of the same pattern repeated at different scales and orientations. A fractal can be generated using recursion.

function—A named group of declarations and programming statements that can be invoked (executed) when needed. A function that is part of a class is called a method. Java has no functions because all code is part of a class.

functional interface—An interface that contains a single abstract method, used for defining lambda expressions in Java.

garbage—(1) An unspecified or uninitialized value in a memory location. (2) An object that cannot be accessed anymore because all references to it have been lost.

garbage collection—The process of reclaiming unneeded, dynamically allocated memory. Java performs automatic garbage collection of objects that no longer have any valid references to them.

gigabyte (GB)—A unit of binary storage, equal to 2^{30} (approximately 1 billion) bytes.

goto—(1) A Java reserved word that is not currently used. (2) An unconditional branch.

grammar—A representation of language syntax that specifies how reserved words, symbols, and identifiers can be combined into valid programs.

graph—A nonlinear data structure made up of nodes and edges that connect the nodes. *See also* digraph.

graphical user interface (GUI)—Software that allows the user to interact with a program using mouse-driven controls, such as buttons, sliders, and text fields.

grid pane—A JavaFX layout pane that arranges its nodes in a flexible grid of rows and columns. *See also* tile pane.

group—A JavaFX node that contains other nodes.

hardware—The tangible components of a computer system, such as the keyboard, monitor, and circuit boards.

has-a relationship—The relationship between two objects in which one is composed, at least in part, of one or more of the other. *See also* aggregate object, is-a relationship.

hash code—An integer value calculated from any given data value or object, used to determine where a value should be stored in a hash table. Also called a hash value. *See also* hashing.

hash method—A method that calculates a hash code from a data value or object. The same data value or object will always produce the same hash code. Also called a hash function. *See also* hashing.

hash table—A data structure in which values are stored for efficient retrieval. *See also* hashing.

hashing—A technique for storing items so that they can be found efficiently. Items are stored in a hash table at a position specified by a calculated hash code. *See also* hash method.

HBox—A JavaFX layout pane that arranges its nodes in a single row horizontally.

hexadecimal—The base-16 number system, often used as an abbreviated representation of binary strings.

hierarchy—An organizational technique in which items are layered or grouped to reduce complexity.

high-level language—A programming language in which each statement represents many machine-level instructions.

HTML—*See* HyperText Markup Language.

hybrid object-oriented language—A programming language that can be used to implement a program in a procedural manner or an object-oriented manner, at the programmer's discretion. *See also* pure object-oriented language.

hypermedia—The concept of hypertext extended to include other media types such as graphics, audio, video, and programs.

hypertext—A document representation that allows a user to navigate through it in a nonlinear fashion. Links to other parts of the document are embedded at the appropriate places to allow the user to jump from one part of the document to another. *See also* hypermedia.

HyperText Markup Language (HTML)—The notation used to define Web pages. *See also* browser, World Wide Web.

icon—A small, fixed-sized picture, often used to decorate a graphical interface.

identifier—Any name that a programmer makes up to use in a program, such as a class name or variable name.

identity—The designation of an object, which, in Java, is an object's reference name. *See also* state, behavior.

IEEE 754—A standard for representing floating point values. Used by Java to represent `float` and `double` data types.

if—A Java reserved word that specifies a simple conditional construct. *See also* else.

image—A picture, often specified using the GIF, JPEG, or PING formats.

image view—A JavaFX node used to display an image.

immutable—The characteristic of an object whose instance data cannot be changed once the object is created. For example, the contents of a `String` object are immutable once the string has been defined.

implementation—(1) The process of translating a design into source code. (2) The source code that defines a method, class, abstract data type, or other programming entity.

implements—A Java reserved word that is used in a class declaration to specify that the class implements the methods specified in a particular interface.

import—A Java reserved word that is used to specify the packages and classes that are used in a particular Java source code file.

index—The integer value used to specify a particular element in an array.

index operator—The brackets (`[]`) in which an array index is specified.

indirect recursion—The process of a method invoking another method, which eventually results in the original method being invoked again. *See also* direct recursion.

infinite loop—A loop that does not terminate because the condition controlling the loop never becomes false.

infinite recursion—A recursive series of invocations that does not terminate because the base case is never reached.

infix expression—An expression in which the operators are positioned between the operands on which they work. *See also* postfix expression.

inheritance—The ability to derive a new class from an existing one. Inherited variables and methods of the original (parent) class are available in the new (child) class as if they were declared locally.

initialize—To give an initial value to a variable.

initializer list—A comma-separated list of values, delimited by braces ({}), used to initialize and specify the size of an array.

inline documentation—Comments that are included in the source code of a program.

inner class—A nonstatic, nested class.

input/output buffer—A storage location for data on its way from the user to the computer (input buffer) or from the computer to the user (output buffer).

input/output devices—Hardware components that allow the human user to interact with the computer, such as a keyboard, mouse, and monitor.

input/output stream—A sequence of bytes that represents a source of data (input stream) or a destination for data (output stream).

input validation—Examining user input to make sure it meets certain criteria before allowing processing to continue.

insertion sort—A sorting algorithm in which each value, one at a time, is inserted into a sorted subset of the entire list. *See also* selection sort.

inspection—*See* walkthrough.

instance—An object created from a class. Multiple objects can be instantiated from a single class.

instance method—A method that must be invoked through a particular instance of a class, as opposed to a class method.

instance variable—A variable that must be referenced through a particular instance of a class, as opposed to a class variable.

instanceof—A Java reserved word that is also an operator, used to determine the class or type of a variable.

instantiation—The act of creating an object from a class.

int—A Java reserved word that represents a primitive integer type, stored using 32 bits in two's complement format.

integration test—The process of testing software components that are made up of other interacting components. Stresses the communication between components rather than the functionality of individual components.

interface—(1) A Java reserved word that is used to define a set of abstract methods that will be implemented by particular classes. (2) The set of messages to which an object responds, defined by the methods that can be invoked from outside of the object. (3) The techniques through which a human user interacts with a program, often graphically. *See also* graphical user interface.

interface hierarchy—A tree-like structure created when interfaces are derived from other interfaces through inheritance. *See also* class hierarchy.

interpreter—A program that translates and executes code on a particular machine. The Java interpreter translates and executes Java bytecode. *See also* compiler.

Internet—The most pervasive wide-area network in the world; it has become the primary vehicle for computer-to-computer communication.

Internet address—A designation that uniquely identifies a particular computer or device on the Internet.

invocation—*See* method invocation.

I/O devices—*See* input/output devices.

IP address—A series of several integer values, separated by periods (.), that uniquely identifies a particular computer or device on the Internet. Each Internet address has a corresponding IP address.

is-a relationship—The relationship created through properly derived classes via inheritance. The subclass *is-a* more specific version of the superclass. *See also* has-a relationship.

ISO-Latin-1—A 128-character extension to the ASCII character set defined by the International Standards Organization (ISO). The characters correspond to the numeric values 128 through 255 in both ASCII and Unicode.

iteration—(1) One execution of the body of a repetition statement. (2) One pass through a cyclic process, such as an iterative development process.

iteration statement—*See* repetition statement.

iterative development process—A step-by-step approach for creating software, which contains a series of stages that are performed repetitively.

iterator—An object that has methods that allow you to process a collection of items one at a time.

java—The Java command-line interpreter, which translates and executes Java bytecode. Part of the Java Development Kit.

Java—The programming language used throughout this text to demonstrate software development concepts. Described by its developers as object oriented, robust, secure, architecture neutral, portable, high-performance, interpreted, threaded, and dynamic.

Java API—*See* Application Programming Interface.

Java Development Kit (JDK)—A collection of basic software tools, including a compiler and interpreter, for developing Java software. *See also* Software Development Kit.

Java Virtual Machine (JVM)—The conceptual device, implemented in software, on which Java bytecode is executed. Bytecode, which is architecture neutral, does not run on a particular hardware platform; instead, it runs on the JVM.

javac—The Java command-line compiler, which translates Java source code into Java bytecode. Part of the Java Development Kit.

javadoc—A software tool that creates external documentation in HTML format about the contents and structure of a Java software system. Part of the Java Development Kit.

JavaFX—The preferred package for developing graphics and graphical user interfaces in Java. Replaces the AWT and Swing packages.

javah—A software tool that generates C header and source files, used for implementing `native` methods. Part of the Java Development Kit.

javap—A software tool that disassembles a Java class file, containing unreadable bytecode, into a human-readable version. Part of the Java Development Kit.

jdb—The Java command-line debugger. Part of the Java Development Kit.

JDK—*See* Java Development Kit.

JVM—*See* Java Virtual Machine.

key event—The set of events generated when the user uses the keyboard. Examples of key events are key pressed and key released.

keyboard focus—The JavaFX node that is set to receive input.

kilobit (Kb)—A unit of binary storage, equal to 2^{10}, or 1024 bits.

kilobyte (K or KB)—A unit of binary storage, equal to 2^{10}, or 1024 bytes.

Koch snowflake—A fractal named after Swedish mathematician Helge von Koch.

label—(1) A graphical user interface component that displays text, an image, or both. (2) An identifier in Java used to specify a particular line of code. The `break` and `continue` statements can jump to a specific, labeled line in the program.

lambda expression—A block of code that can be passed as a parameter or returned from a method to be executed later.

LAN—*See* local-area network.

last-in, first-out (LIFO)—A data management technique in which the last value that is stored in a data structure is the first value that comes out. *See also* first-in, first-out; stack.

layout pane—A JavaFX container that governs how its contents are arranged and presented visually. Examples include stack panes and flow panes.

lexicographic ordering—The ordering of characters and strings based on a particular character set such as Unicode.

life cycle—The stages through which a software product is developed and used.

LIFO—*See* last-in, first-out.

linear search—A search algorithm in which each item in the list is compared to the target value until the target is found or the list is exhausted. *See also* binary search.

link—(1) A designation in a hypertext document that allows the user to "jump" to another document. (2) An object reference used to connect two objects in a dynamically linked structure such as a linked list.

linked list—A dynamic data structure in which objects are chained together using references.

list—A collection that keeps its elements in a specific order.

list view—A JavaFX control that allows the user to select from a displayed list of options.

listener—An object that is set up to respond to an event when it occurs. A listener is similar to an event handler.

literal—A primitive value used explicitly in a program, such as the numeric literal `147` or the string literal `"hello"`.

local-area network (LAN)—A computer network designed to span short distances and connect a relatively small number of computers. *See also* wide-area network.

local variable—A variable defined within a method, which does not exist except during the execution of the method.

logical error—A problem stemming from inappropriate processing in the code. It does not cause an abnormal termination of the program, but it produces incorrect results. *See also* compile-time error, run-time error, syntax error.

logical line of code—A logical programming statement in a source code program, which may extend over multiple physical lines. *See also* physical line of code.

logical operator—One of the operators that perform a logical NOT (`!`), AND (`&&`), or OR (`||`), returning a boolean result. The logical operators are short-circuited, meaning that if their left operand is sufficient to determine the result, the right operand is not evaluated.

long—A Java reserved word that represents a primitive integer type, stored using 64 bits in two's complement format.

loop—*See* repetition statement.

loop control variable—A variable whose value specifically determines how many times a loop body is executed.

low-level language—Either machine language or assembly language, which are not as convenient to construct software in as high-level languages are.

machine language—The native language of a particular CPU.

main memory—The volatile hardware storage device where programs and data are held when they are actively needed by the CPU. *See also* secondary memory.

maintenance—(1) The process of fixing errors in or making enhancements to a released software product. (2) The software life-cycle phase in which the software is in use and changes are made to it as needed.

mantissa—The portion of a floating point value's internal representation that specifies the magnitude of the number. *See also* exponent.

megabyte (MB)—A unit of binary storage, equal to 2^{20} (approximately 1 million) bytes.

member—A variable or method in an object or class.

memory—Hardware devices that store programs and data. *See also* main memory, secondary memory.

memory location—An individual, addressable cell inside main memory into which data can be stored.

memory management—The process of controlling dynamically allocated portions of main memory, especially the act of returning allocated memory when it is no longer required. *See also* garbage collection.

method—A named group of declarations and programming statements that can be invoked (executed) when needed. A method is part of a class.

method call conversion—The automatic widening conversion that can occur when a value of one type is passed to a formal parameter of another type.

method definition—The specification of the code that gets executed when the method is invoked. The definition includes declarations of local variables and formal parameters.

method invocation—A line of code that causes a method to be executed. It specifies any values that are passed to the method as parameters.

method overloading—*See* overloading.

method reference—A compact lambda expression that specifies a particular method.

mnemonic—(1) A word or identifier that specifies a command or data value in an assembly language. (2) A keyboard character used as a alternative means to activate a GUI control such as a button.

modal—Having multiple modes (such as a dialog box).

modem—An old-fashioned data transfer device that allows information to be sent along a telephone line.

modifier—A designation used in a Java declaration that specifies particular characteristics to the construct being declared.

monitor—The screen in the computer system that serves as an output device.

mouse event—The set of events generated when the user operates the mouse. Examples of mouse events are mouse clicked and mouse dragged.

multidimensional array—An array that uses more than one index to specify a value stored in it.

multiple inheritance—Deriving a class from more than one parent, inheriting methods and variables from each. Multiple inheritance is not supported in Java.

multiplicity—The numeric relationship between two objects, often shown in class diagrams.

NaN—An abbreviation that stands for "not a number," which is the designation for an inappropriate or undefined numeric value.

narrowing conversion—A conversion between two values of different but compatible data types. Narrowing conversions could lose information because the converted type usually has an internal representation smaller than the original storage space. *See also* widening conversion.

native—A Java reserved word that serves as a modifier for methods. A native method is implemented in another programming language.

natural language—A language that humans use to communicate, such as English or French.

negative infinity—A special floating point value that represents the "lowest possible" value. *See also* positive infinity.

nested class—A class declared within another class in order to facilitate implementation and restrict access.

nested if statement—An `if` statement that has as its body another `if` statement.

network—Two or more computers connected together so that they can exchange data and share resources.

network address—*See* address.

new—A Java reserved word that is also an operator, used to instantiate an object from a class.

newline character—A nonprintable character that indicates the end of a line.

node—(1) An element in a JavaFX graphical user interface. (2) An element of a data structure such as a linked list or a tree.

nonprintable characters—Any character, such as escape or newline, that does not have a symbolic representation that can be displayed on a monitor or printed by a printer. *See also* printable characters.

nonvolatile—The characteristic of a memory device that retains its stored information even after the power supply is turned off. Secondary memory devices are nonvolatile. *See also* volatile.

null—A Java reserved word that is a reference literal, used to indicate that no object is being referenced.

number system—A set of values and operations defined by a particular base value that determines the number of digits available and the place value of each digit.

object—(1) The primary software construct in the object-oriented paradigm. (2) An encapsulated collection of data variables and methods. (3) An instance of a class.

object diagram—A visual representation of the objects in a program at a given point in time, often showing the status of instance data.

object-oriented programming—An approach to software design and implementation that is centered around objects and classes. *See also* procedural programming.

octal—The base-8 number system, sometimes used to abbreviate binary strings. *See also* binary, hexadecimal.

off-by-one error—An error caused by a calculation or condition being off by one, such as when a loop is set up to access one too many array elements.

operand—A value on which an operator performs its function. For example, in the expression 5 + 2, the values 5 and 2 are operands.

operating system—The collection of programs that provide the primary user interface to a computer and manage its resources, such as memory and the CPU.

operator—A symbol that represents a particular operation in a programming language, such as the addition operator (+).

operator association—The order in which operators within the same precedence level are evaluated, either right to left or left to right. *See also* operator precedence.

operator overloading—Assigning additional meaning to an operator. Operator overloading is not supported in Java, though method overloading is.

operator precedence—The order in which operators are evaluated in an expression as specified by a well-defined hierarchy.

order—The dominant term in an equation that specifies the efficiency of an algorithm. For example, selection sort is of order n^2.

ordinal value—An integer associated with a value in an enumerated type.

overflow—A problem that occurs when a data value grows too large for its storage size, which can result in inaccurate arithmetic processing. *See also* underflow.

overloading—Assigning additional meaning to a programming language construct, such as a method or operator. Method overloading is supported by Java, but operator overloading is not.

overriding—The process of modifying the definition of an inherited method to suit the purposes of the subclass. *See also* shadowing variables.

package—A Java reserved word that is used to specify a group of related classes.

package visibility—*See* default visibility.

parameter—(1) A value passed from a method invocation to its definition. (2) The identifier in a method definition that accepts the value passed to it when the method is invoked. *See also* actual parameter, formal parameter.

parameter list—The list of actual or formal parameters to a method.

parent class—*See* superclass.

pass by reference—The process of passing a reference to a value into a method as the parameter. In Java, all objects are managed using references, so an object's formal parameter is an alias to the original. *See also* pass by value.

pass by value—The process of making a copy of a value and passing the copy into a method. Therefore, any change made to the value inside the method is not reflected in the original value. All Java primitive types are passed by value.

PDL—*See* Program Design Language.

peripheral—Any hardware device other than the CPU or main memory.

persistence—The ability of an object to stay in existence after the executing program that creates it terminates. *See also* serialize.

physical line of code—A line in a source code file, terminated by a newline or similar character. *See also* logical line of code.

pixel—A picture element. A digitized picture is made up of many pixels.

place value—The value of each digit position in a number, which determines the overall contribution of that digit to the value. *See also* number system.

pointer—A variable that can hold a memory address. Instead of pointers, Java uses references, which provide essentially the same functionality as pointers but without the need for explicit dereferencing.

point-to-point connection—The link between two networked devices that are connected directly by a wire.

polygon—A JavaFX multisided shape defined by a series of vertex points.

polyline—A JavaFX shape made up of a series of connected line segments. A polyline is similar to a polygon, but the shape is not closed.

polymorphism—An object-oriented technique by which a reference that is used to invoke a method can result in different methods being invoked at different times. All Java method invocations are potentially polymorphic in that they invoke the method of the object type, not the reference type.

portability—The ability of a program to be moved from one hardware platform to another without having to change it. Because Java bytecode is not related to any particular hardware environment, Java programs are considered portable. *See also* architecture neutral.

positive infinity—A special floating point value that represents the "highest possible" value. *See also* negative infinity.

postfix expression—An expression in which an operator is positioned after the operands on which it works. *See also* infix expression.

postfix operator—In Java, an operator that is positioned behind its single operand, whose evaluation yields the value prior to the operation being performed. Both the increment (++) and decrement (– –) operators can be applied postfix. *See also* prefix operator.

precedence—*See* operator precedence.

prefix operator—In Java, an operator that is positioned in front of its single operand, whose evaluation yields the value after the operation has been performed. Both the increment (++) and decrement (– –) operators can be applied prefix. *See also* postfix operator.

primitive data type—A data type that is predefined in a programming language.

printable characters—Any character that has a symbolic representation that can be displayed on a monitor or printed by a printer. *See also* nonprintable characters.

private—A Java reserved word that serves as a visibility modifier for inner classes as well as methods and variables. A private inner class is accessible only to members of the class in which it is declared. Private methods and variables are visible only in the class in which they are declared.

procedural programming—An approach to software design and implementation that is centered around procedures (or functions) and their interaction. *See also* object-oriented programming.

processing stream—An I/O stream that performs some type of manipulation on the data in the stream. Sometimes called a filtering stream. *See also* data stream.

program—A series of instructions executed by hardware, one after another.

Program Design Language (PDL)—A language in which a program's design and algorithms are expressed. *See also* pseudocode.

programming language—A specification of the syntax and semantics of the statements used to create a program.

programming language statement—An individual instruction in a given programming language.

prompt—A message or symbol used to request information from the user.

propagation—*See* exception propagation.

property—A JavaFX object that holds an observable value which can be monitored and changed as needed.

property binding—A relationship established between two JavaFX properties, such that when one changes the other is automatically updated.

protected—A Java reserved word that serves as a visibility modifier for inner classes as well as methods and variables. A protected inner class is visible to classes in the same package and to all classes in other packages that extend the class in which it is declared. Protected methods and variables are visible to all classes in the same package and to classes outside the package that extend the class.

prototype—A program used to explore an idea or prove the feasibility of a particular approach.

pseudocode—Structured and abbreviated natural language used to express the algorithmic steps of a program. *See also* Program Design Language.

pseudorandom number—A value generated by software that performs extensive calculations based on an initial seed value. The result is not truly random because it is based on a calculation, but it is usually random enough for most purposes.

public—A Java reserved word that serves as a visibility modifier for classes, interfaces, methods, and variables. Anything declared public is visible to all classes.

pure object-oriented language—A programming language that enforces, to some degree, software development using an object-oriented approach. *See also* hybrid object-oriented language.

queue—A collection that manages information in a first-in, first-out manner.

radio button—A GUI control that allows the user choose one of a set of options with a mouse click. A radio button is useful only as part of a group of other radio buttons. *See also* check box.

RAM—*See* random access memory.

random access device—A memory device whose information can be directly accessed. *See also* random access memory, sequential access device.

random access memory (RAM)—A term basically interchangeable with main memory. Should probably be called read-write memory, to distinguish it from read-only memory.

random number generator—Software that produces a pseudorandom number, generated by calculations based on a seed value.

read-only memory (ROM)—Any memory device whose stored information is stored permanently when the device is created. It can be read from, but not written to.

recursion—The process of a method invoking itself, either directly or indirectly. Recursive algorithms often provide elegant, though perhaps inefficient, solutions to a problem. *See also* recursion.

reference—A variable that holds the address of an object. In Java, a reference can be used to interact with an object, but its numeric address cannot be accessed, set, or operated on directly.

register—A small area of storage in the CPU of the computer.

relational operator—One of several operators that determine the ordering relationship between two values: less than (<), less than or equal to (<=), greater than (>), and greater than or equal to (>=). *See also* equality operator.

release—A version of a software product that is made available to the customer.

repetition statement—A programming construct that allows a set of statements to be executed repetitively as long as a particular condition is true. The body of the repetition statement should eventually make the condition false. Also called an iteration statement or loop. *See also* do, for, while.

requirements—(1) The specification of what a program must and must not do. (2) An early phase of the software development process in which the program requirements are established.

reserved word—A word that has special meaning in a programming language and cannot be used for any other purpose.

retirement—The phase of a program's life cycle in which the program is taken out of active use.

return—A Java reserved word that causes the flow of program execution to return from a method to the point of invocation.

return type—The type of value returned from a method, specified before the method name in the method declaration. Could be `void`, which indicates that no value is returned.

reuse—Using existing software components to create new ones.

review—The process of critically examining a design or program to discover errors. There are many types of review. *See also* desk check, walkthrough.

RGB value—A collection of three values that define a color. Each value represents the contribution of the colors red, green, and blue.

ROM—*See* read-only memory.

root node—(1) A JavaFX node that serves as the container of all other nodes in a scene. (2) The node in a tree from which all other nodes branch.

rotation—Causing a graphical node to appear at an angle, rotated around a given point.

rubberbanding—The graphical effect caused when a shape seems to resize itself as the mouse is dragged.

running sum—A sum of numeric values calculated as each value is read or encountered.

runtime error—A problem that occurs during program execution that causes the program to terminate abnormally. *See also* compile-time error, logical error, syntax error.

scaling—(1) Causing a graphical node to appear larger or smaller in size. (2) The ability of a problem solution to handle to a large increase in input.

scene—A JavaFX container that is used to display GUI nodes such as shapes and controls on a stage (window).

scope—The areas within a program in which an identifier, such as a variable, can be referenced. *See also* access.

scroll pane—A JavaFX control that offers a limited view of a large image or other node and provides horizontal and/or vertical scroll bars to change that view.

SDK—*See* Software Development Kit.

searching—The process of determining the existence or location of a target value within a list of values. *See also* binary search, linear search.

secondary memory—Hardware storage devices, such as magnetic disks, which store information in a relatively permanent manner. *See also* main memory.

seed value—A value used by a random number generator as a base for the calculations that produce a pseudo-random number.

selection sort—A sorting algorithm in which each value, one at a time, is placed in its final, sorted position. *See also* insertion sort.

selection statement—A programming construct that allows a set of statements to be executed if a particular condition is true. *See also* if, switch.

semantics—The interpretation of a program or programming construct.

sentinel value—A specific value used to indicate a special condition, such as the end of input.

serialize—The process of converting an object into a linear series of bytes so it can be saved to a file or sent across a network. *See also* persistence.

service methods—Methods in an object that are declared with public visibility and define a service that the object's client can invoke.

shadowing variables—The process of defining a variable in a subclass that supersedes an inherited version.

shearing—Distorting the appearance of a graphical node by rotating one axis so that the x and y axes are no longer perpendicular.

short—A Java reserved word that represents a primitive integer type, stored using 16 bits in two's complement format.

sibling—Two items in a tree or hierarchy, such as a class inheritance hierarchy, that have the same parent.

sign bit—A bit in a numeric value that represents the sign (positive or negative) of that value.

signed numeric value—A value that stores a sign (positive or negative). All Java numeric values are signed. A Java character is stored as an unsigned value.

signature—The number, types, and order of the parameters of a method. Overloaded methods must each have a unique signature.

slider—A JavaFX control that allows the user to specify a numeric value within a bounded range by moving a knob to the appropriate place in the range.

software—(1) Programs and data. (2) The intangible components of a computer system.

software component—*See* component.

Software Development Kit (SDK)—A collection of software tools that assist in the development of software. The Java Software Development Kit is another name for the Java Development Kit.

software engineering—The discipline within computer science that addresses the process of developing high-quality software within practical constraints.

sorting—The process of putting a list of values into a well-defined order. *See also* insertion sort, selection sort.

spinner—A JavaFX control that allows the user to select a value from a list of predefined values arranged in a sequence. A spinner only displays one value and uses arrow buttons to control the selection.

split pane—A JavaFX control that displays two or more nodes, either side by side or one on top of the other, separated by a moveable divider bar.

stack—A collection that manages data in a last-in, first-out manner.

stack pane—A JavaFX layout pane that stacks its contents on top of each other in the center of the pane.

stack trace—The series of methods called to reach a certain point in a program. The stack trace can be analyzed when an exception is thrown to assist the programmer in tracking down the problem.

stage—A JavaFX window used to display a scene of nodes.

standard I/O stream—One of three common I/O streams representing standard input (usually the keyboard), standard output (usually the monitor screen), and standard error (also usually the monitor). *See also* stream.

state—The state of being of an object, defined by the values of its data. *See also* behavior, identity.

statement—*See* programming language statement.

statement coverage—A strategy used in white-box testing in which all statements in a program are executed. *See also* condition coverage.

static—A Java reserved word that serves as a modifier for methods and variables. A static method is also called a class method and can be referenced without an instance of the class. A static variable is also called a class variable and is common to all instances of the class.

static data structure—A data structure that has a fixed size and cannot grow and shrink as needed. *See also* dynamic data structure.

storage capacity—The total number of bytes that can be stored in a particular memory device.

stream—A source of input or a destination for output.

strictfp—A Java reserved word that is used to control certain aspects of floating point arithmetic.

string—*See* character string.

string concatenation—The process of attaching the beginning of one character string to the end of another, resulting in one longer string.

stroke—A shape's outline. In JavaFX, the stroke's color and width can be set explicitly. *See also* fill.

strongly typed language—A programming language in which each variable is associated with a particular data type for the duration of its existence. Variables are not allowed to take on values or be used in operations that are inconsistent with their type.

structured programming—An approach to program development in which each software component has one entry and exit point and in which the flow of control does not cross unnecessarily.

stub—A method that simulates the functionality of a particular software component. Often used during unit testing.

subclass—A class derived from another class via inheritance. Also called a derived class or child class. *See also* superclass.

subscript—*See* index.

super—A Java reserved word that is a reference to the parent class of the object making the reference. Often used to invoke a parent's constructor.

super reference—*See* super.

superclass—The class from which another class is derived via inheritance. Also called a base class or parent class. *See also* subclass.

support methods—Methods in an object that are not intended for use outside the class. They provide support functionality for service methods. As such, they are usually not declared with public visibility.

swapping—The process of exchanging the values of two variables.

swing—A graphics package in the Java API that, along with the AWT package, has been replaced by the preferred JavaFX package.

switch—A Java reserved word that specifies a compound conditional construct.

synchronization—The process of ensuring that data shared among multiple threads cannot be accessed by more than one thread at a time. *See also* synchronized.

synchronized—A Java reserved word that serves as a modifier for methods. Separate threads of a process can execute concurrently in a method, unless the method is synchronized, making it a mutually exclusive resource. Methods that access shared data should be synchronized.

syntax error—An error produced by the compiler because a program did not conform to the syntax of the programming language. Syntax errors are a subset of compile-time errors. *See also* compile-time error, logical error, run-time error, syntax rules.

syntax rules—The set of specifications that govern how the elements of a programming language can be put together to form valid statements.

tab pane—A JavaFX control that allows the user to switch between a set of tabs that each display a node or layout container. Only one tab is visible at a time.

target value—The value that is sought when performing a search on a collection of data.

TCP/IP—Software that controls the movement of messages across the Internet. The acronym stands for Transmission Control Protocol/Internet Protocol.

terabyte (TB)—A unit of binary storage, equal to 2^{40} (approximately 1 trillion) bytes.

termination—The point at which a program stops executing.

ternary operator—An operator that uses three operands.

test case—A set of input values and user actions, along with a specification of the expected output, used to find errors in a system.

testing—(1) The process of running a program with various test cases in order to discover problems. (2) The process of critically evaluating a design or program.

text area—A GUI control that displays, or allows the user to enter, multiple lines of data.

text field—A GUI control that displays, or allows the user to enter, a single line of data.

text file—A file that contains data formatted as ASCII or Unicode characters.

this—A Java reserved word that is a reference to the object executing the code making the reference.

thread—An independent process executing within a program. A Java program can have multiple threads running in a program at one time.

throw—A Java reserved word that is used to start an exception propagation.

throws—A Java reserved word that specifies that a method may throw a particular type of exception.

tile pane—A JavaFX layout pane in which nodes are organized in a rectangular gird. Each cell, or tile, of the grid is the same size. *See also* grid pane.

timer—An object that generates an event at regular intervals.

token—A portion of a string defined by a set of delimiters.

tool tip—A short line of text that appears when the mouse pointer pauses on top of a particular component. Usually, tool tips are used to inform the user of the component's purpose.

top-level domain—The last part of a network domain name, such as edu or com.

Towers of Hanoi—A classic peg-and-disk puzzle. Its solution is an elegant example of recursion.

transformation—A JavaFX effect applied to a node that changes how it is presented, such as translating the node along an axis or scaling its size.

transient—A Java reserved word that serves as a modifier for variables. A transient variable does not contribute to the object's persistent state and therefore does not need to be saved. *See also* serialize.

translation—To shift the position of a shape or other graphical node along an axis.

tree—A nonlinear data structure that forms a hierarchy stemming from a single root node.

true—A Java reserved word that serves as one of the two boolean literals (`true` and `false`).

truth table—A complete enumeration of all permutations of values involved in a boolean expression, as well as the computed result.

try—A Java reserved word that is used to define the context in which certain exceptions will be handled if they are thrown.

two-dimensional array—An array that uses two indices to specify the location of an element. The two dimensions are often thought of as the rows and columns of a table. *See also* multidimensional array.

two's complement—A technique for representing numeric binary data. Used by all Java integer primitive types (`byte`, `short`, `int`, `long`).

type—*See* data type.

UML—*See* Unified Modeling Language.

unary operator—An operator that uses only one operand.

unchecked exception—A Java exception that does not need to be caught or dealt with if the programmer so chooses.

underflow—A problem that occurs when a floating point value becomes too small for its storage size, which can result in inaccurate arithmetic processing. *See also* overflow.

Unicode—The international character set used to define valid Java characters. Each character is represented using a 16-bit unsigned numeric value.

Unified Modeling Language (UML)—A graphical notation for visualizing relationships among classes and objects. Abbreviated UML. There are many types of UML diagrams. *See also* class diagrams.

uniform resource locator (URL)—A designation for a resource that can be located through a World Wide Web browser.

unit test—The process of testing an individual software component. May require the creation of stub modules to simulate other system components.

unsigned numeric value—A value that does not store a sign (positive or negative). The bit usually reserved to represent the sign is included in the value, doubling the magnitude of the number that can be stored. Java characters are stored as unsigned numeric values, but there are no primitive numeric types that are unsigned.

URL—*See* uniform resource locator.

use relationship—A relationship between two classes, often shown in a class diagram, that establishes that one class uses another in some way, such as relying on its services. *See also* association.

user interface—The manner in which the user interacts with a software system, which is often graphical. *See also* graphical user interface.

variable—An identifier in a program that represents a memory location in which a data value is stored.

VBox—A JavaFX layout pane that arranges its nodes in a single column vertically.

viewport—A rectangular area used to restrict the pixels displayed in an image view.

visibility modifier—A Java modifier that defines the scope in which a construct can be accessed. The Java visibility modifiers are `public`, `protected`, `private`, and `default` (no modifier used).

void—A Java reserved word that can be used as a return value for a method, indicating that no value is returned.

volatile—(1) A Java reserved word that serves as a modifier for variables. A volatile variable might be changed asynchronously and therefore indicates that the compiler should not attempt optimizations on it. (2) The characteristic of a memory device that loses stored information when the power supply is interrupted. Main memory is a volatile storage device. *See also* nonvolatile.

von Neumann architecture—The computer architecture named after John von Neumann, in which programs and data are stored together in the same memory devices.

walkthrough—A form of review in which a group of developers, managers, and quality assurance personnel examine a design or program in order to find errors. Sometimes referred to as an inspection. *See also* desk check.

WAN—*See* wide-area network.

waterfall model—One of the earliest software development process models. It defines a basically linear interaction between the requirements, design, implementation, and testing stages.

Web—*See* World Wide Web.

while—A Java reserved word that represents a repetition construct. A `while` statement is executed zero or more times. *See also* do, for.

white-box testing—Producing and evaluating test cases based on the interior logic of a software component. The test cases focus on stressing decision points and ensuring coverage. *See also* black-box testing, condition coverage, statement coverage.

white space—Spaces, tabs, and blank lines that are used to set off sections of source code to make programs more readable.

wide-area network (WAN)—A computer network that connects two or more local area networks, usually across long geographic distances. *See also* local-area network.

widening conversion—A conversion between two values of different but compatible data types. Widening conversions usually leave the data value intact because the converted type has an internal representation equal to or larger than the original storage space. *See also* narrowing conversion.

word—A unit of binary storage. The size of a word varies by computer, and is usually two, four, or eight bytes. The word size indicates the amount of information that can be moved through the machine at one time.

World Wide Web (WWW or Web)—Software that makes the exchange of information across a network easier by providing a common user interface for multiple types of information. Web browsers are used to retrieve and format HTML documents.

wrapper class—A class designed to store a primitive type in an object. Usually used when an object reference is needed and a primitive type would not suffice.

WWW—*See* World Wide Web.

Number Systems

B

This appendix contains a detailed introduction to number systems and their underlying characteristics. The particular focus is on the binary number system, its use in computers, and its similarities to other number systems. This introduction also covers conversions between bases.

In our everyday lives, we use the *decimal number system* to represent values, to count, and to perform arithmetic. The decimal system is also referred to as the *base-10 number system*. We use 10 digits (0 through 9) to represent values in the decimal system.

Computers use the *binary number system* to store and manage information. The binary system, also called the *base-2 number system*, has only two digits (0 and 1). Each 0 and 1 is called a *bit*, short for binary digit. A series of bits is called a *binary string*.

There is nothing particularly special about either the binary or decimal systems. Long ago, humans adopted the decimal number system probably because we have 10 fingers on our hands. If humans had 12 fingers, we would probably be using a base-12 number system regularly and find it as easy to deal with as we do the decimal system now. It all depends on what you get used to. As you explore the binary system, it will become more familiar and natural.

Binary is used for computer processing because the devices used to manage and store information are less expensive and more reliable if they only have to represent two possible values. Computers have been made that use the decimal system, but they are not as convenient.

There are an infinite number of number systems, and they all follow the same basic rules. You already know how the binary number system works, but you might not be aware that you do. It all goes back to the basic rules of arithmetic.

Place Value

In decimal, we represent the values of 0 through 9 using only one digit. To represent any value higher than 9, we must use more than one digit. The position of each digit has a *place value* that indicates the amount it contributes to the overall

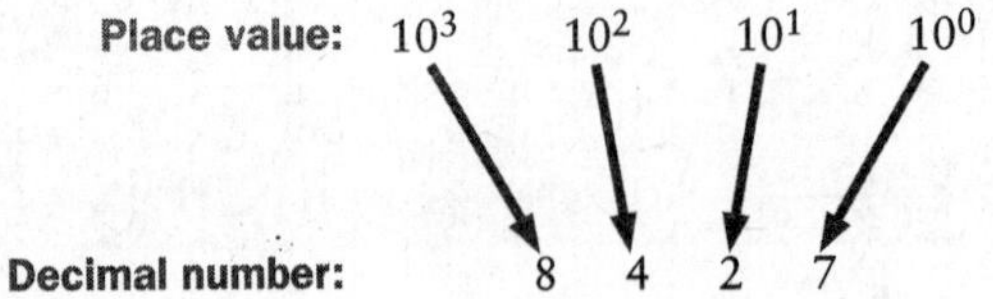

Decimal number: $8 * 10^3 + 4 * 10^2 + 2 * 10^1 + 7 * 10^0 =$

$8 * 1000 + 4 * 100 + 2 * 10 + 7 * 1 = 8427$

FIGURE B.1 Place values in the decimal system

value. In decimal, we refer to the one's column, the ten's column, the hundred's column, and so on.

Each place value is determined by the *base* of the number system, raised to increasing powers as we move from right to left. In the decimal number system, the place value of the digit furthest to the right is 10^0, or 1. The place value of the next digit is 10^1, or 10. The place value of the third digit from the right is 10^2, or 100, and so on. Figure B.1 shows how each digit in a decimal number contributes to the value.

The binary system works the same way except that we exhaust the available digits much sooner. We can represent 0 and 1 with a single bit, but to represent any value higher than 1, we must use multiple bits.

The place values in binary are determined by increasing powers of the base as we move right to left, just as they are in the decimal system. However, in binary, the base value is 2. Therefore, the place value of the bit furthest to the right is 2^0, or 1. The place value of the next bit is 2^1, or 2. The place value of the third bit from the right is 2^2, or 4, and so on. Figure B.2 shows a binary number and its place values.

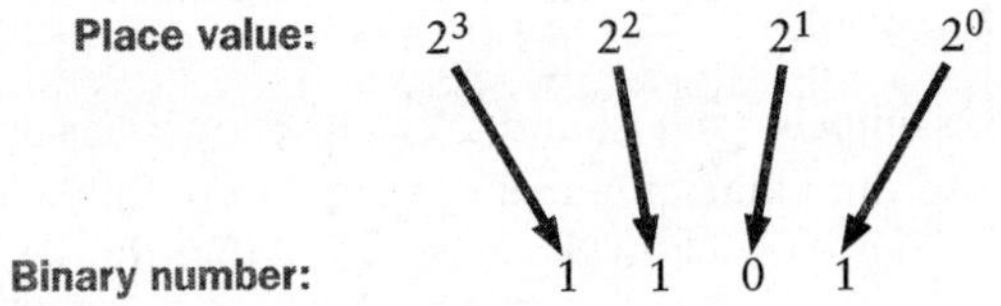

Decimal number: $1 * 2^3 + 1 * 2^2 + 0 * 2^1 + 1 * 2^0 =$

$1 * 8 + 1 * 4 + 0 * 2 + 1 * 1 = 13$

FIGURE B.2 Place values in the binary system

The number 1101 is a valid binary number, but it is also a valid decimal number as well. Sometimes to make it clear which number system is being used, the base value is appended as a subscript to the end of a number. Therefore, you can distinguish between 1101_2, which is equivalent to 13 in decimal, and 1101_{10} (one thousand, one hundred and one), which in binary is represented as 10001001101_2.

A number system with base *N* has *N* digits (0 through *N*–1). As we have seen, the decimal system has 10 digits (0 through 9), and the binary system has two digits (0 and 1). They all work the same way. For instance, the base-5 number system has five digits (0 to 4).

Note that, in any number system, the place value of the digit furthest to the right is 1, since any base raised to the zero power is 1. Also notice that the value 10, which we refer to as "ten" in the decimal system, always represents the base value in any number system. In base 10, 10 is one 10 and zero 1's. In base 2, 10 is one 2 and zero 1's. In base 5, 10 is one 5 and zero 1's.

Bases Higher Than 10

Since all number systems with base *N* have *N* digits, then base 16 has 16 digits. But what are they? We are used to the digits 0 through 9, but in bases higher than 10, we need a single digit, a single symbol, that represents the decimal value 10. In fact, in *base 16*, which is also called *hexadecimal*, we need digits that represent the decimal values 10 through 15.

For number systems higher than 10, we use alphabetic characters as single digits for values greater than 9. The hexadecimal digits are 0 through F, where 0 through 9 represent the first 10 digits, and A represents the decimal value 10, B represents 11, C represents 12, D represents 13, E represents 14, and F represents 15.

Therefore, the number 2A8E is a valid hexadecimal number. The place values are determined as they are for decimal and binary, using increasing powers of the base. So in hexadecimal, the place values are powers of 16. Figure B.3 shows how the place values of the hexadecimal number 2A8E contribute to the overall value.

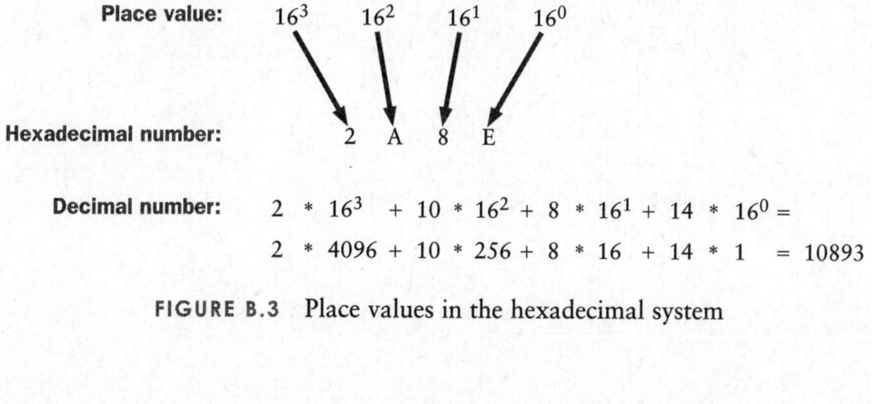

FIGURE B.3 Place values in the hexadecimal system

All number systems with bases greater than 10 use letters as digits. For example, base 12 has the digits 0 through B and base 19 has the digits 0 through I. However, beyond having a different set of digits and a different base, the rules governing each number system are the same.

Keep in mind that when we change number systems, we are simply changing the way we represent values, not the values themselves. If you have 18_{10} pencils, it may be written as 10010 in binary or as 12 in hexadecimal, but it is still the same number of pencils.

Figure B.4 shows the representations of the decimal values 0 through 20 in several bases, including *base 8*, which is also called *octal*. Note that the larger the base, the higher the value that can be represented in a single digit.

Binary (base 2)	Octal (base 8)	Decimal (base 10)	Hexadecimal (base 16)
0	0	0	0
1	1	1	1
10	2	2	2
11	3	3	3
100	4	4	4
101	5	5	5
110	6	6	6
111	7	7	7
1000	10	8	8
1001	11	9	9
1010	12	10	A
1011	13	11	B
1100	14	12	C
1101	15	13	D
1110	16	14	E
1111	17	15	F
10000	20	16	10
10001	21	17	11
10010	22	18	12
10011	23	19	13
10100	24	20	14

FIGURE B.4 Counting in various number systems

Conversions

We've already seen how a number in another base is converted to decimal by determining the place value of each digit and computing the result. This process can be used to convert any number in any base to its equivalent value in base 10.

Now let's reverse the process, converting a base-10 value to another base. First, find the highest place value in the new number system that is less than or equal to the original value. Then divide the original number by that place value to determine the digit that belongs in that position. The remainder is the value that must be represented in the remaining digit positions. Continue this process, position by position, until the entire value is represented.

For example, Figure B.5 shows the process of converting the decimal value 180 into binary. The highest place value in binary that is less than or equal to 180 is 128 (or 2^7), which is the eighth bit position from the right. Dividing 180 by 128 yields 1 with 52 remaining. Therefore, the first bit is 1, and the decimal value 52 must be represented in the remaining seven bits. Dividing 52 by 64, which is the next place value (2^6), yields 0 with 52 remaining. So the second bit is 0. Dividing 52 by 32 yields 1 with 20 remaining. So the third bit is 1, and the remaining five bits must represent the value 20. Dividing 20 by 16 yields 1 with 4 remaining. Dividing 4 by 8 yields 0 with 4 remaining. Dividing 4 by 4 yields 1 with 0 remaining.

Since the number has been completely represented, the rest of the bits are zero. Therefore, 180_{10} is equivalent to 10110100 in binary. This can be confirmed by converting the new binary number back to decimal to make sure we get the original value.

Place value	Number	Digit
128	180	1
64	52	0
32	52	1
16	20	1
8	4	0
4	4	1
2	0	0
1	0	0

$$180_{10} = 10110100_2$$

FIGURE B.5 Converting a decimal value into binary

Place value	Number	Digit	
256	1967	7	
16	175	A	$1967_{10} = 7AF_{16}$
1	15	F	

FIGURE B.6 Converting a decimal value into hexadecimal

This process works to convert any decimal value to any target base. For each target base, the place values and possible digits change. If you start with the correct place value, each division operation will yield a valid digit in the new base.

In the example in Figure B.5, the only digits that could have resulted from each division operation would have been 1 or 0, since we were converting to binary. However, when we are converting to other bases, any valid digit in the new base could result. For example, Figure B.6 shows the process of converting the decimal value 1967 into hexadecimal.

The place value of 256, which is 16^2, is the highest place value less than or equal to the original number, since the next highest place value is 16^3 or 4096. Dividing 1967 by 256 yields 7 with 175 remaining. Dividing 175 by 16 yields 10 with 15 remaining. Remember that 10 in decimal can be represented as the single digit A in hexadecimal. The 15 remaining can be represented as the digit F. Therefore 1967_{10} is equivalent to 7AF in hexadecimal.

Shortcut Conversions

We have established techniques for converting any value in any base to its equivalent representation in base 10, and from base 10 to any other base. Therefore, you can now convert a number in any base to any other base by going through base 10. However, an interesting relationship exists between the bases that are powers of 2, such as binary, octal, and hexadecimal, which allows very quick conversions between them.

To convert from binary to hexadecimal, for instance, you can simply group the bits of the original value into groups of four, starting from the right, then convert each group of four into a single hexadecimal digit. The example in Figure B.7 demonstrates this process.

To go from hexadecimal to binary, we reverse this process, expanding each hexadecimal digit into four binary digits. Note that you may have to add leading zeros to the binary version of each expanded hexadecimal digit if necessary to make four binary digits. Figure B.8 shows the conversion of the hexadecimal value 40C6 to binary.

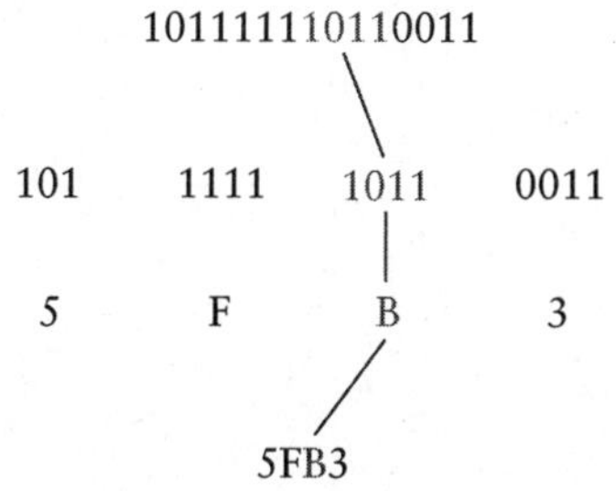

$$101111110110011_2 = 5FB3_{16}$$

FIGURE B.7 Shortcut conversion from binary to hexadecimal

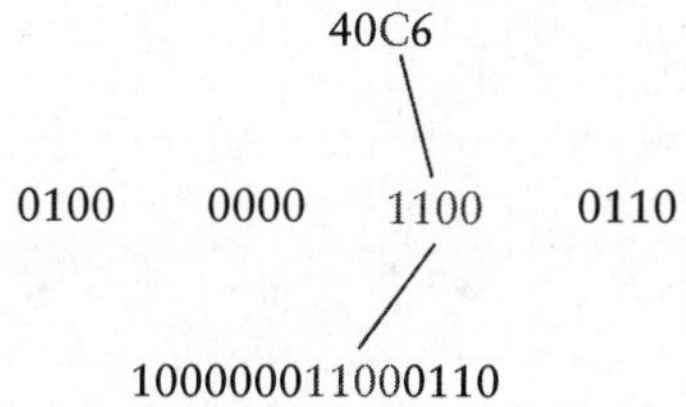

$$40C6_{16} = 100000011000110_2$$

FIGURE B.8 Shortcut conversion from hexadecimal to binary

Why do we section the bits into groups of four when converting from binary to hexadecimal? The shortcut conversions work between binary and any base that is a power of 2. We section the bits into groups of that power. Since $2^4 = 16$, we section the bits in groups of four.

Converting from binary to octal is the same process except that the bits are sectioned into groups of three, since $2^3 = 8$. Likewise, when converting from octal to binary, we expand each octal digit into three bits.

To convert between, say, hexadecimal and octal is now a process of doing two shortcut conversions. First convert from hexadecimal to binary, then take that result and perform a shortcut conversion from binary to octal.

By the way, these types of shortcut conversions can be performed between any base B and any base that is a power of B. For example, conversions between base 3 and base 9 can be accomplished using the shortcut grouping technique, sectioning or expanding digits into groups of two, since $3^2 = 9$.

The Unicode Character Set

C

The Java programming language uses the Unicode character set for managing text. A *character set* is simply an ordered list of characters, each corresponding to a particular numeric value. Unicode is an international character set that contains letters, symbols, and ideograms for languages all over the world. Each character is represented as a 16-bit unsigned numeric value. Unicode, therefore, can support over 65,000 unique characters. When even that many characters proved insufficient, a strategy for extending the encoding was developed to represent supplmentary characters.

Some programming languages still use the ASCII character set. ASCII stands for the American Standard Code for Information Interchange. The 8-bit extended ASCII set is quite small, so the developers of Java opted to use Unicode in order to support international users. However, ASCII is essentially a subset of Unicode, including corresponding numeric values, so programmers used to ASCII should have no problems with Unicode.

Figure C.1 shows a list of commonly used characters and their Unicode numeric values. These characters also happen to be ASCII characters. All of the characters in Figure C.1 are called *printable characters* because they have a symbolic representation that can be displayed on a monitor or printed by a printer. Other characters are called *nonprintable characters* because they have no such symbolic representation. Note that the space character (numeric value 32) is considered a printable character, even though no symbol is printed when it is displayed. Nonprintable characters are sometimes called *control characters* because many of them can be generated by holding down the control key on a keyboard and pressing another key.

The Unicode characters with numeric values 0 through 31 are nonprintable characters. Also, the delete character, with numeric value 127, is a nonprintable character. All of these characters are ASCII characters as well. Many of them have fairly common and well-defined uses, while others are more general. The table in Figure C.2 lists a small sample of the nonprintable characters.

Value	Char	Value	Char	Value	Char	Value	Char	Value	Char
32	*space*	51	3	70	F	89	Y	108	l
33	!	52	4	71	G	90	Z	109	m
34	"	53	5	72	H	91	[	110	n
35	#	54	6	73	I	92	\\	111	o
36	$	55	7	74	J	93	]	112	p
37	%	56	8	75	K	94	^	113	q
38	&	57	9	76	L	95	–	114	r
39	'	58	:	77	M	96	,	115	s
40	(	59	;	78	N	97	a	116	t
41	)	60	<	79	O	98	b	117	u
42	*	61	=	80	P	99	c	118	v
43	+	62	>	81	Q	100	d	119	w
44	'	63	?	82	R	101	e	120	x
45	–	64	@	83	S	102	f	121	y
46	.	65	A	84	T	103	g	122	z
47	/	66	B	85	U	104	h	123	{
48	0	67	C	86	V	105	i	124	|
49	1	68	D	87	W	106	j	125	}
50	2	69	E	88	X	107	k	126	~

FIGURE C.1 A small portion of the Unicode character set

Nonprintable characters are used in many situations to represent special conditions. For example, certain nonprintable characters can be stored in a text document to indicate, among other things, the beginning of a new line. An editor will process these characters by starting the text that follows it on a new line, instead of printing a symbol to the screen. Various types of computer systems use different nonprintable characters to represent particular situations.

Except for having no visible representation, nonprintable characters are essentially equivalent to printable characters. They can be stored in a Java character variable and be part of a character string. They are stored using 16 bits, can be converted to their numeric value, and can be compared using relational operators.

Value	Character
0	*null*
7	*bell*
8	*backspace*
9	*tab*
10	*line feed*
12	*form feed*
13	*carriage return*
27	*escape*
127	*delete*

FIGURE C.2 Some nonprintable characters in the Unicode character set

The first 128 characters of the Unicode character set correspond to the common ASCII character set. The first 256 characters correspond to the ISO-Latin-1 extended ASCII character set. Most operating systems and Web browsers will handle these characters, but they may not be able to print the other Unicode characters.

The Unicode character set contains most alphabets in use today, including Greek, Hebrew, Cyrillic, and various Asian ideographs. It also includes Braille, and several sets of symbols used in mathematics and music. Figure C.3 shows a few characters from non-Western alphabets.

Value	Character	Source
1071	Я	Russian (Cyrillic)
3593	ฉ	Thai
5098	Ꮺ	Cherokee
8478	℞	Letterlike Symbols
8652	⇌	Arrows
10287	⠯	Braille
13407	㑟	Chinese/Japanese/Korean (Common)

FIGURE C.3 Some non-Western characters in the Unicode character set

Java Operators

D

Java operators are evaluated according to the precedence hierarchy shown in Figure D.1. Operators at low precedence levels are evaluated before operators at higher levels. Operators within the same precedence level are evaluated according to the specified association, either right to left (R to L) or left to right (L to R). Operators at the same precedence level are not listed in any particular order.

The order of operator evaluation can always be forced by the use of parentheses. It is sometimes a good idea to use parentheses even when they are not required, to make it explicitly clear to a human reader how an expression is evaluated.

For some operators, the operand types determine which operation is carried out. For instance, if the + operator is used on two strings, string concatenation is performed, but if it is applied to two numeric types, they are added in the arithmetic sense. If only one of the operands is a string, the other is converted to a string, and string concatenation is performed. Similarly, the operators `&`, `^`, and `|` perform bitwise operations on numeric operands but boolean operations on boolean operands.

The boolean operators `&` and `|` differ from the logical operators `&&` and `||` in a subtle way. The logical operators are "short-circuited" in that if the result of an expression can be determined by evaluating only the left operand, the right operand is not evaluated. The boolean versions always evaluate both sides of the expression. There is no logical operator that performs an exclusive OR (XOR) operation.

Java Bitwise Operators

The Java *bitwise operators* operate on individual bits within a primitive value. They are defined only for integers and characters. They are unique among all Java operators, because they let us work at the lowest level of binary storage. Figure D.2 lists the Java bitwise operators.

Three of the bitwise operators are similar to the logical operators `!`, `&&`, and `||`. The bitwise NOT, AND, and OR operations work basically the same way

<table>
<tr><th>Precedence Level</th><th>Operator</th><th>Operation</th><th>Associates</th></tr>
<tr><td>1</td><td>[]
.
(parameters)
++
--</td><td>array indexing
object member reference
parameter evaluation and method invocation
postfix increment
postfix decrement</td><td>L to R</td></tr>
<tr><td>2</td><td>++
--
+
-
~
!</td><td>prefix increment
prefix decrement
unary plus
unary minus
bitwise NOT
logical NOT</td><td>R to L</td></tr>
<tr><td>3</td><td>new
(type)</td><td>object instantiation
cast</td><td>R to L</td></tr>
<tr><td>4</td><td>*
/
%</td><td>multiplication
division
remainder</td><td>L to R</td></tr>
<tr><td>5</td><td>+
+
-</td><td>addition
string concatenation
subtraction</td><td>L to R</td></tr>
<tr><td>6</td><td><<
>>
>>></td><td>left shift
right shift with sign
right shift with zero</td><td>L to R</td></tr>
<tr><td>7</td><td><
<=
>
>=
instanceof</td><td>less than
less than or equal
greater than
greater than or equal
type comparison</td><td>L to R</td></tr>
<tr><td>8</td><td>==
!=</td><td>equal
not equal</td><td>L to R</td></tr>
<tr><td>9</td><td>&
&</td><td>bitwise AND
boolean AND</td><td>L to R</td></tr>
<tr><td>10</td><td>^
^</td><td>bitwise XOR
boolean XOR</td><td>L to R</td></tr>
<tr><td>11</td><td>|
|</td><td>bitwise OR
boolean OR</td><td>L to R</td></tr>
<tr><td>12</td><td>&&</td><td>logical AND</td><td>L to R</td></tr>
<tr><td>13</td><td>||</td><td>logical OR</td><td>L to R</td></tr>
</table>

FIGURE D.1 Java operator precedence

Precedence Level	Operator	Operation	Associates
14	?:	conditional operator	R to L
15	=	assignment	R to L
	+=	addition, then assignment	
	+=	string concatenation, then assignment	
	−=	subtraction, then assignment	
	*=	multiplication, then assignment	
	/=	division, then assignment	
	%=	remainder, then assignment	
	<<=	left shift, then assignment	
	>>=	right shift (sign), then assignment	
	>>>=	right shift (zero), then assignment	
	&=	bitwise AND, then assignment	
	&=	boolean AND, then assignment	
	^=	bitwise XOR, then assignment	
	^=	boolean XOR, then assignment	
	|=	bitwise OR, then assignment	
	|=	boolean OR, then assignment	
16	->	lambda expression	R to L

FIGURE D.1 Java operator precedence, continued

as their logical counterparts, except they work on individual bits of a value. The rules are essentially the same. Figure D.3 shows the results of bitwise operators on all combinations of two bits. Compare this chart to the truth tables for the logical operators in Chapter 5 to see the similarities.

The bitwise operators include the XOR operator, which stands for *exclusive OR*. The logical `||` operator is an *inclusive OR* operation, which means it returns true if both operands are true. The `|` bitwise operator is also inclusive and yields a

Operator	Description
~	bitwise NOT
&	bitwise AND
|	bitwise OR
^	bitwise XOR
<<	left shift
>>	right shift with sign
>>>	right shift with zero fill

FIGURE D.2 Java bitwise operators

a	b	~ a	a & b	a | b	a ^ b
0	0	1	0	0	0
0	1	1	0	1	1
1	0	0	0	1	1
1	1	0	1	1	0

FIGURE D.3 Bitwise operations on individual bits

1 if both corresponding bits are 1. However, the exclusive OR operator (^) yields a 0 if both operands are 1. There is no logical exclusive OR operator in Java.

When the bitwise operators are applied to integer values, the operation is performed individually on each bit in the value. For example, suppose the integer variable `number` is declared to be of type `byte` and currently holds the value 45. Stored as an 8-bit byte, it is represented in binary as `00101101`. When the bitwise complement operator (~) is applied to `number`, each bit in the value is inverted, yielding `11010010`. Since integers are stored using two's complement representation, the value represented is now negative, specifically –46.

Similarly, for all bitwise operators, the operations are applied bit by bit, which is where the term "bitwise" comes from. For binary operators (with two operands), the operations are applied to corresponding bits in each operand. For example, assume `num1` and `num2` are `byte` integers, `num1` holds the value 45, and `num2` holds the value 14. Figure D.4 shows the results of several bitwise operations.

The operators `&`, `|`, and `^` can also be applied to boolean values, and they have basically the same meaning as their logical counterparts. When used with boolean values, they are called boolean operators. However, unlike the operators `&&` and `||`, which are "short-circuited," the boolean operators are not short-circuited. Both sides of the expression are evaluated every time.

num1 & num2	num1 | num2	num1 ^ num2
00101101	00101101	00101101
& 00001110	| 00001110	^ 00001110
= 00001100	= 00101111	= 00100011

FIGURE D.4 Bitwise operations on bytes

Like the other bitwise operators, the three bitwise shift operators manipulate the individual bits of an integer value. They all take two operands. The left operand is the value whose bits are shifted; the right operand specifies how many positions they should move. Prior to performing a shift, `byte` and `short` values are promoted to `int` for all shift operators. Furthermore, if either of the operands is `long`, the other operand is promoted to `long`. For readability, we use 16 bits in the examples in this section, but the concepts are the same when carried out to 32- or 64-bit strings.

When bits are shifted, some bits are lost off one end, and others need to be filled in on the other. The *left-shift* operator (<<) shifts bits to the left, filling the right bits with zeros. For example, if the integer variable `number` currently has the value 13, then the statement

```
number = number << 2;
```

stores the value 52 into `number`. Initially, `number` contains the bit string 0000000000001101. When shifted to the left, the value becomes 0000000000110100, or 52. Notice that for each position shifted to the left, the original value is multiplied by 2.

The sign bit of a number is shifted along with all of the others. Therefore, the sign of the value could change if enough bits are shifted to change the sign bit. For example, the value −8 is stored in binary two's complement form as 1111111111111000. When shifted left two positions, it becomes 1111111111100000, which is −32. However, if enough positions are shifted, a negative number can become positive and vice versa.

There are two forms of the right-shift operator: one that preserves the sign of the original value (>>) and one that fills the leftmost bits with zeros (>>>).

Let's examine two examples of the *right-shift-with-sign-fill* operator. If the `int` variable `number` currently has the value 39, the expression `(number >> 2)` results in the value 9. The original bit string stored in `number` is 0000000000100111, and the result of a right shift two positions is 0000000000001001. The leftmost sign bit, which in this case is a zero, is used to fill from the left.

If `number` has an original value of −16, or 1111111111110000, the right-shift (with sign fill) expression `(number >> 3)` results in the binary string 1111111111111110, or −2. The leftmost sign bit is a 1 in this case and is used to fill in the new left bits, maintaining the sign.

If maintaining the sign is not desirable, the *right-shift-with-zero-fill* operator (>>>) can be used. It operates similarly to the >> operator but fills with zero no matter what the sign of the original value is.

Java Modifiers

E

This appendix summarizes the modifiers that give particular characteristics to Java classes, interfaces, methods, and variables. For discussion purposes, the set of all Java modifiers is divided into two groups: visibility modifiers and all others.

Java Visibility Modifiers

The table in Figure E.1 describes the effect of Java visibility modifiers on various constructs. Visibility modifiers operate in the same way on classes and interfaces and in the same way on methods and variables.

Default visibility means that no visibility modifier was explicitly used. Default visibility is sometimes called *package visibility*, but you cannot use the reserved word `package` as a modifier.

Note that only inner classes can have private or protected visibility.

Modifier	Classes and interfaces	Methods and variables
default (no modifier)	Visible in its package.	Visible to any class in the same package as its class.
`public`	Visible anywhere.	Visible anywhere.
`protected`	Can only be applied to inner classes. Visible in its package and to classes that extend the class in which it is declared.	Visible to any class in the same package and to any derived classes.
`private`	Can only be applied to inner classes. Visible to the enclosing class only.	Not visible by any other class.

FIGURE E.1 Java visibility modifiers

A Visibility Example

Consider the highly contrived situation depicted in the Figure E.2 Class `P` is the parent class that is used to derive child classes `C1` and `C2`. Class `C1` is in the same package as `P`, but `C2` is not. Class `P` contains four methods, each with different visibility modifiers. One object has been instantiated from each of these classes.

The `public` method `a()` has been inherited by `C1` and `C2`, and any code with access to object `x` can invoke `x.a()`. The `private` method `d()` is not visible to `C1` or `C2`, so objects `y` and `z` have no such method available to them. Furthermore, `d()` is fully encapsulated and can be invoked only from within object `x`.

The `protected` method `b()` is visible in both `C1` and `C2`. A method in `y` could invoke `x.b()`, but a method in `z` could not. Furthermore, an object of any class in package `One` could invoke `x.b()`, even those that are not related to class `P` by inheritance, such as an object created from class `Another1`.

Method `c()` has `default` visibility, since no visibility modifier was used to declare it. Therefore object `y` can refer to the method `c()` as if it were declared locally, but object `z` cannot. Object `y` can invoke `x.c()`, as can an object instantiated from any class in package `One`, such as `Another1`. Object `z` cannot invoke `x.c()`.

These rules generalize in the same way for variables. The visibility rules may appear complicated initially, but they can be mastered with a little effort.

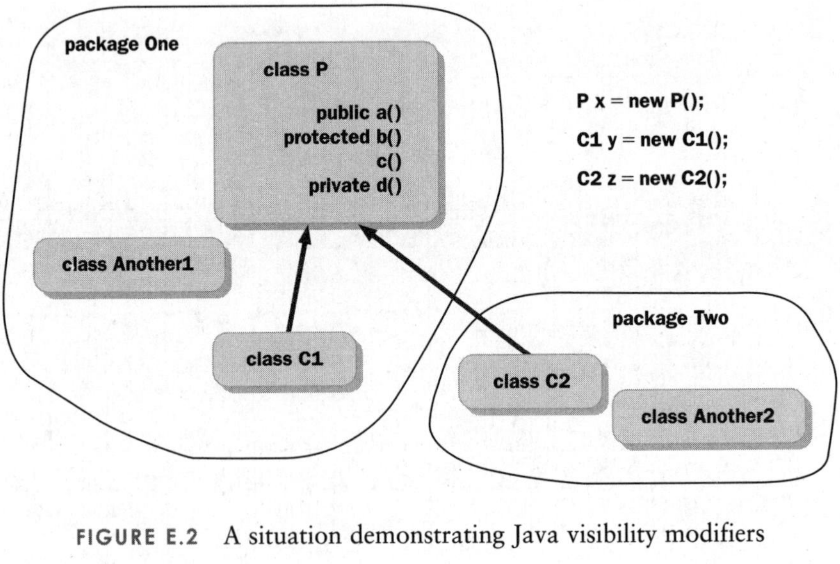

FIGURE E.2 A situation demonstrating Java visibility modifiers

Other Java Modifiers

Figure E.3 summarizes the rest of the Java modifiers, which address a variety of issues. Furthermore, a modifier has different effects on classes, interfaces, methods, and variables. Some modifiers cannot be used with certain constructs and therefore are listed as not applicable (N/A).

The `transient` modifier is used to indicate data that need not be stored in a persistent (serialized) object. That is, when an object is written to a serialized stream, the object representation will include all data that is not specified as transient.

Modifier	Class	Interface	Method	Variable
`abstract`	The class may contain abstract methods. It cannot be instantiated.	All interfaces are inherently abstract. The modifier is optional.	No method body is defined. The method requires implementation when inherited.	N/A
`default`	N/A	N/A	Specifies the default implementation of an interface method. Cannot be applied to methods in classes.	N/A
`final`	The class cannot be used to drive new classes.	N/A	The method cannot be overridden.	The variable is a constant, whose value cannot be changed once initially set.
`native`	N/A	N/A	No method body is necessary since implementation is in another language.	N/A
`static`	N/A	N/A	Defines a class method. It does not require an instantiated object to be invoked. It cannot reference non-static methods or variables. It is implicitly final.	Defines a class variable. It does not require an instantiated object to be referenced. It is shared (common memory space) among all instances of the class.
`synchronized`	N/A	N/A	The execution of the method is mutually exclusive among all threads.	N/A
`transient`	N/A	N/A	N/A	The variable will not be serialized.
`volatile`	N/A	N/A	N/A	The variable is changed asynchronously. The compiler should not perform optimizations on it.

FIGURE E.3 The rest of the Java modifiers

Java Coding Guidelines

F

This appendix contains a series of guidelines that describe how to organize and format Java source code. They are designed to make programs easier to read and maintain. Some guidelines can be attributed to personal preferences and could be modified. However, it is important to have a standard set of practices that make sense and to follow them carefully. The guidelines presented here are followed in the example code throughout this text and are consistent with the Java naming conventions.

Consistency is half the battle. If you follow the same rules throughout a program and follow them from one program to another, you make the effort of reading and understanding your code easier for yourself and others. It is not unusual for a programmer to develop software that seems straightforward at the time, only to revisit it months later and have difficulty remembering how it works. If you follow consistent development guidelines, you reduce this problem considerably.

When an organization adopts a coding standard, it is easier for people to work together. A software product is often created by a team of cooperating developers, each responsible for a piece of the system. If they all follow the same development guidelines, they facilitate the process of integrating the separate pieces into one cohesive entity.

You may have to make tradeoffs between some guidelines. For example, you should make all of your identifiers easy to read yet keep them to a reasonably short length. Use common sense on a case-by-case basis to embrace the spirit of all guidelines as much as possible.

You may choose, or be asked, to follow this set of guidelines or some variation. If changes or additions are made, make sure they are clear and that they represent a conscious effort to use good programming practices. Most of these issues are discussed further in appropriate areas of the text but are presented succinctly here, without elaboration.

Design Guidelines

A. Design Preparation

1. The ultimate guideline is to develop a clean design. Think before you start coding. A working program is not necessarily a good program.
2. Express and document your design with consistent, clear notation.

B. Structured Programming

1. Do not use the `continue` statement.
2. Use the `break` statement only to terminate cases of a `switch` statement.
3. Have only one `return` statement in a method as the last line, unless it unnecessarily complicates the method.

C. Classes and Packages

1. Do not have additional methods in the class that contains the `main` method.
2. Define the class that contains the `main` method at the top of the file it is in, followed by other classes if appropriate.
3. If only one class is used from an imported package, import that class by name. If two or more are imported, you may use the * symbol.

D. Modifiers

1. Do not declare variables with `public` visibility.
2. Do not use modifiers inside an interface.
3. Always use the most appropriate modifiers for each situation. For example, if a variable is used as a constant, explicitly declare it as a constant using the `final` modifier.

E. Exceptions

1. Use exception handling only for truly exceptional conditions, such as terminating errors, or for significantly unusual or important situations.
2. Do not use exceptions to disguise or hide inappropriate processing.
3. Handle each exception at the appropriate level of design.

F. Miscellaneous

1. Use constants instead of literals whenever reasonable.
2. Design methods so that they perform one logical function. As such, the length of a method will tend to be no longer than 50 lines of code, and often much shorter.
3. Keep the physical lines of a source code file to less than 80 characters in length.
4. Extend a logical line of code over two or more physical lines only when necessary. Divide the line at a logical place.

Style Guidelines

A. Identifier Naming

1. Give identifiers semantic meaning. For example, do not use single letter names such as `a` or `i` unless the single letter has semantic meaning.
2. Make identifiers easy to read. For example, use `currentValue` instead of `curval`.
3. Keep identifiers to a reasonably short length.
4. Use the underscore character to separate words of a constant.

B. Identifier Case

1. Use `UPPERCASE` for constants, with the underscore character (_) separating words.
2. Use `TitleCase` for class, package, and interface names.
3. Use `lowercase` for variable and method names, except for the first letter of each word other than the first word. For example, `minTaxRate`. Note that all reserved words must be lowercase.

C. Indentation

1. Indent the code in any block by three or four spaces (be consistent).
2. If the body of a loop, `if` statement, or `else` clause is a single statement (not a block), indent the statement three spaces on its own line.
3. Put the left brace ({) starting each new block on a new line. Line up the terminating right brace (}) with the opening left brace. For example:

```
while (value < 25)
{
   value += 5;
   System.out.println ("The value is " + value);
}
```

4. In a `switch` statement, indent each `case` label three spaces. Indent all code associated with a `case` three additional spaces.

D. Spacing

1. Carefully use white space to draw attention to appropriate features of a program.
2. Put one space after each comma in a parameter list.
3. Put one space on either side of a binary operator.
4. Do not put spaces immediately after a left parenthesis or before a right parenthesis.
5. Do not put spaces before a semicolon.
6. Put one space before a left parenthesis, except before an empty parameter list.

7. When declaring arrays, associate the brackets with the element type, as opposed to the array name, so that it applies to all variables on that line. For example:

```
int[30] list1, list2;
```

8. When referring to the type of an array, do not put any spaces between the element type and the square brackets, such as `int[]`.

E. Messages and Prompts

1. Do not condescend.
2. Do not attempt to be humorous.
3. Be informative, but succinct.
4. Define specific input options in prompts when appropriate.
5. Specify default selections in prompts when appropriate.

F. Output

1. Label all output clearly.
2. Present information to the user in a consistent manner.

Documentation Guidelines

A. The Reader

1. Write all documentation as though the reader is computer literate and basically familiar with the Java language.
2. Assume the reader knows almost nothing about what the program is supposed to do.
3. Remember that a section of code that seems intuitive to you when you write it might not seem so to another reader or to yourself later. Document accordingly.

B. Content

1. Make sure comments are accurate.
2. Keep comments updated as changes are made to the code.
3. Be concise but thorough.

C. Header Blocks

1. Every source code file should contain a header block of documentation providing basic information about the contents and the author.
2. Each class and interface, and each method in a class, should have a small header block that describes its role.

3. Each header block of documentation should have a distinct delimiter on the top and bottom so that the reader can visually scan from one construct to the next easily. For example:

```
//*******************************************
//          header block
//*******************************************
```

D. In-Line Comments

1. Use in-line documentation as appropriate to clearly describe interesting processing.
2. Put a comment on the same line with code only if the comment applies to one line of code and can fit conveniently on that line. Otherwise, put the comment on a separate line above the line or section of code to which it applies.

E. Miscellaneous

1. Avoid the use of the /* */ style of comment except to conform to the java-doc (/** */) commenting convention.
2. Don't wait until a program is finished to insert documentation. As pieces of your system are completed, comment them appropriately.

Appendix G: JavaFX Layout Panes

A *layout pane* is a JavaFX container that visibly displays its nodes according to specific layout rules. This appendix provides an overview of several classes in the JavaFX API that represent predefined layout panes:

- `FlowPane`
- `TilePane`
- `StackPane`
- `HBox`
- `VBox`
- `AnchorPane`
- `BorderPane`
- `GridPane`

Several of these classes are used in examples throughout the Graphics Track sections of the book.

All layout panes are derived from the `Pane` class, which can also be used to display nodes. However, the `Pane` class does not apply any particular layout rules. The position of all nodes in a `Pane` would need to be set explicitly, as they are with a `Group`. The difference between a group and a pane is that a `Group` takes on the size of the nodes it contains and a `Pane` takes on the size of the container it is in. In many situations a group and a pane could be used interchangeably.

Layout panes can be nested within each other. A `VBox`, for instance, could be used to lay out a flow pane of buttons above a stack pane displaying an image.

Note that scroll panes, split panes, and tab panes are all considered to be controls, not layout panes, because they have built-in functionality that can be used without custom event handlers. Scroll panes have scroll bars, split panes have moveable divider bars, and tab panes have selectable tabs. The nodes added to these controls, however, could be layout panes.

Flow Pane

The nodes added to a *flow pane* are displayed horizontally (the default) or vertically in the order in which they are added to the pane. The nodes wrap when the pane's width or height cannot accommodate the next node. Rows or columns are created as needed to display all nodes.

The following code creates five buttons and adds them to a flow pane using the `FlowPane` constructor:

```
Button b1 = new Button("Push Me!");
Button b2 = new Button("No, Push ME!");
Button b3 = new Button("I'm the BEST! Push Me!");
Button b4 = new Button("Smart people push me!");
Button b5 = new Button("I'm here, too.");

FlowPane pane = new FlowPane(b1, b2, b3, b4, b5);
pane.setStyle("-fx-background-color: cyan");
pane.setAlignment(Pos.CENTER_LEFT);
pane.setHgap(10);
pane.setVgap(5);
```

As shown in the following figure, the first three buttons added to the pane are displayed in the first row. The width of the pane won't accommodate the fourth button, so a new row is started for the other two buttons.

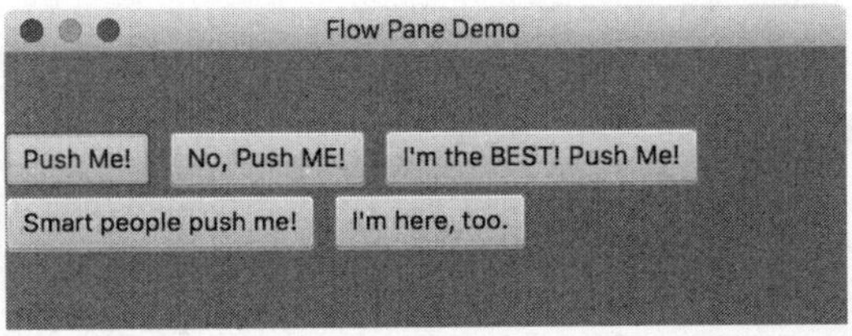

The layout rules of a pane are consulted and automatically adjust its contents accordingly as the pane is resized. So if this window, and therefore the scene and pane it contains, is widened enough to accommodate the fourth button, it will automatically pop up to the first row.

In this example, the horizontal gap between nodes in a row is set to 10 pixels. The vertical gap between rows is set to five pixels.

The alignment of the nodes within the pane is set to be centered vertically and to the left horizontally. The `Pos` enumerated type contains several values for specifying vertical and horizontal positioning and alignment. If the alignment had been set to `Pos.CENTER`, the nodes would be centered both vertically and horizontally like this:

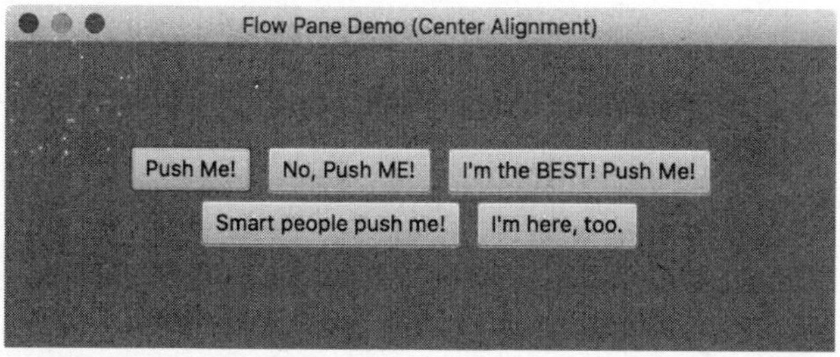

Tile Pane

A *tile pane* is similar to a flow pane except that the nodes are laid out in fixed-sized tiles (or cells). The size of the tile is set to accommodate the largest node in the pane.

Like flow pane, the nodes in a tile pane wrap at the pane boundaries. Since all nodes take up the same amount of space, this creates a grid of tiles.

A tile pane used to display the same buttons created in the flow pane example above could be set up with almost identical code:

```
TilePane pane = new TilePane(b1, b2, b3, b4, b5);
pane.setStyle("-fx-background-color: cyan");
pane.setAlignment(Pos.CENTER_LEFT);
pane.setHgap(10);
pane.setVgap(5);
```

When laid out, the space used to display each button is the size needed to display the widest (third) button:

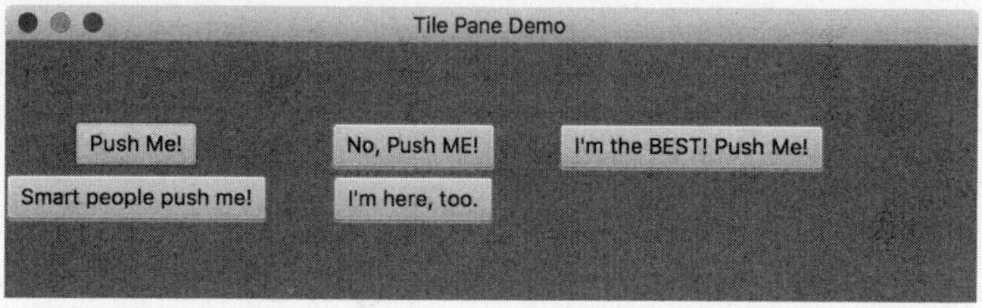

Stack Pane

As the name implies, a *stack pane* stacks its nodes on top of each other in the order they are added to the pane. By default, the nodes are centered both vertically and horizontally, though the alignment can be changed if desired.

Adding a node to a stack pane is a simple way to keep the node centered in its display area. Stack panes are also useful for overlaying shapes, text, and images to create a more complex result. The following code adds an image view and a rectangle to a stack pane:

```
ImageView imageView = new ImageView(new Image("tiger.jpg"));
Rectangle rect = new Rectangle(350, 300, null);
rect.setStroke(Color.ORANGE);
rect.setStrokeWidth(6);

StackPane imagePane = new StackPane(imageView, rect);
imagePane.setStyle("-fx-background-color: beige");
```

Note that the width and height of the rectangle are set when it is created, but its position is not. Both the image view and the rectangle are centered in the stack pane, making the rectangle serve as a frame of the image:

If the window (and thus the scene and pane) is resized, the stack pane will keep the image and rectangle centered in the window.

HBox and VBox

The HBox class represents a layout pane that arranges a series of nodes horizontally in one row. Similarly, a VBox arranges its nodes vertically in one column. Unlike a flow layout, the nodes do not wrap when they reach a pane boundary.

The padding around the entire series of nodes can be set explicitly, either through a call to the `setPadding` method or using CSS styling. The spacing between the nodes in the row or column can be set using a call to the `setSpacing` method.

The following code adds three radio buttons, a separator, a label, and a color picker to a `VBox`:

```
RadioButton sepiaButton = new RadioButton("Sepia");
RadioButton monoButton = new RadioButton("Monochrome");
RadioButton colorButton = new RadioButton("Full Color");

Separator sep = new Separator();
Label colorLabel = new Label("Frame:");
ColorPicker colorPicker = new ColorPicker(Color.ORANGE);

VBox colorControls = new VBox(sepiaButton, monoButton, colorButton,
     sep, colorLabel, colorPicker);
colorControls.setStyle("-fx-background-color: skyblue");
colorControls.setPadding(new Insets(20, 10, 20, 10));
colorControls.setSpacing(10);
```

Using an `Insets` object, the padding around the entire column is set so that there is a buffer of 20 pixels above and below the column, and 10 pixels on either side. The spacing between each node in the column is set to 10 pixels.

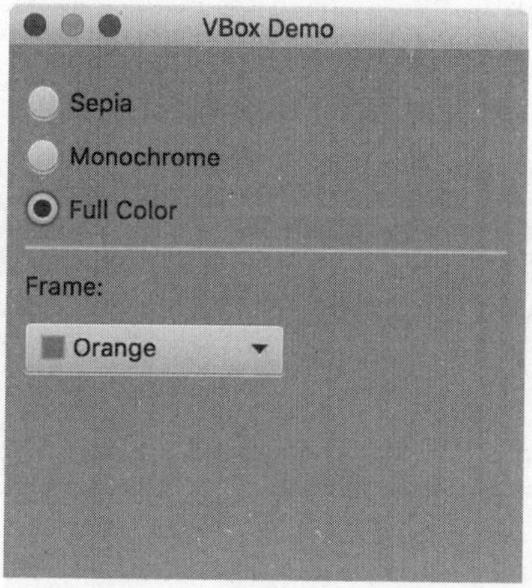

By default, the nodes in an `HBox` and `VBox` are left aligned, although the alignment can be changed using a method called `setAlignment`.

Anchor Pane

An *anchor pane* is a layout pane that allows you to anchor a node along the top, bottom, left side, or right side of the pane. As the pane is resized, it maintains the relative position of each anchored node.

The following code creates two `Button` objects and anchors them in an `AnchorPane`:

```
Button prev = new Button("Prev");
Button next = new Button("Next");

AnchorPane navPane = new AnchorPane(prev, next);
navPane.setStyle("-fx-background-color: black");
navPane.setPrefHeight(70);

AnchorPane.setBottomAnchor(prev, 20.0);
AnchorPane.setLeftAnchor(prev, 30.0);
AnchorPane.setBottomAnchor(next, 20.0);
AnchorPane.setRightAnchor(next, 30.0);
```

The anchors are set using calls to static methods such as `setBottomAnchor` and `setLeftAnchor`, which take as parameters the node being anchored and the spacing that should be maintained between the edge of the pane and the node.

A node can be anchored to more than one position. In this example, the Prev button is anchored to the bottom and left side, and the Next button is anchored to the bottom and right side. The effect is that the two buttons stay in the two bottom corners of the pane no matter how it is resized.

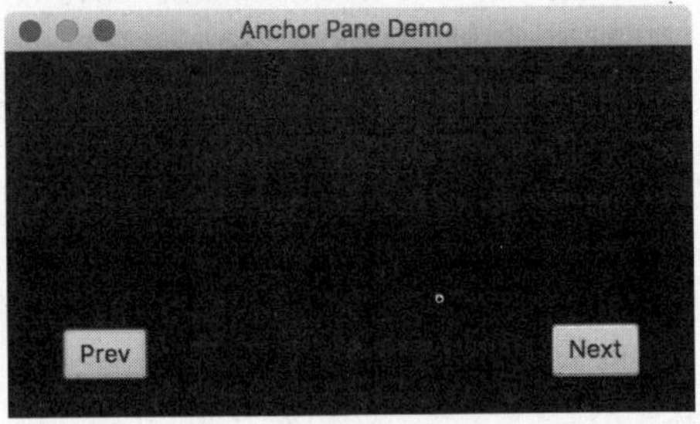

Multiple nodes can be anchored to the same edge of the pane, if desired.

Border Pane

A border pane displays nodes in five areas designated—Top, Bottom, Left, Right, and Center:

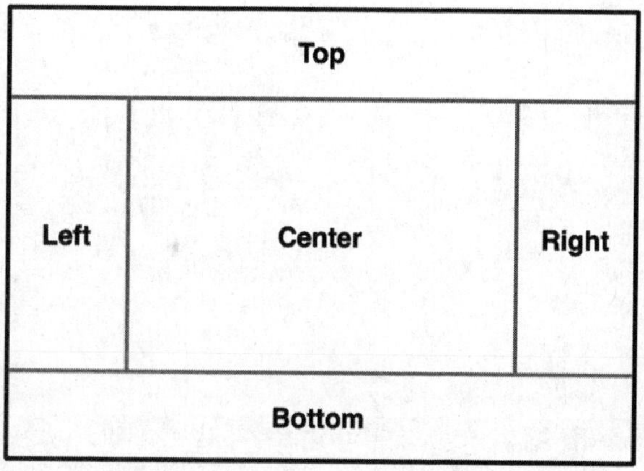

The areas of a border pane grow and shrink as needed. If you don't put anything in a particular area, it takes up no space and the other areas grow accordingly. A node is added to a particular area using the methods `setTop`, `setBottom`, `setLeft`, `setRight`, and `setCenter`. The border pane will display its contents at their preferred size if possible.

The following code creates a border pane and adds other panes (most from previous examples) to four of the five areas:

```
BorderPane borderPane = new BorderPane();
borderPane.setTop(titlePane);
borderPane.setLeft(colorControls);
borderPane.setCenter(imagePane);
borderPane.setBottom(navPane);
```

Since the Right area did not get a node to display, it takes up no space. A new stack pane containing a label is put in the Top area.

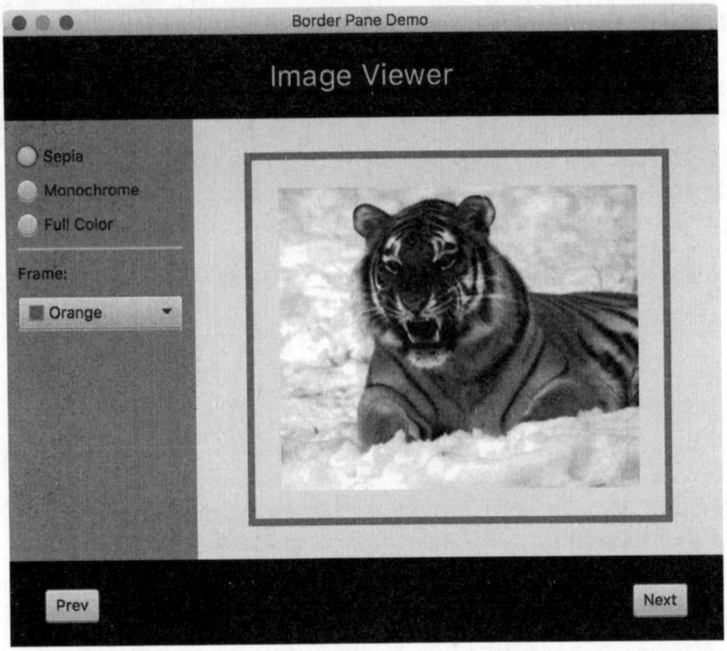

As the window is resized, the nested layout panes govern their respective areas accordingly. So, for instance, the image stays centered in the Center area, and the navigation buttons are kept in the corners of the Bottom area.

If the border pane is larger than needed to display the contents of each area, the extra space is allocated to the Center area.

Grid Pane

A *grid pane* organizes nodes into a flexible grid of rows and columns. A node is added to a particular cell in the grid, and can span multiple rows and/or columns. The width of a column is set to accommodate the widest node in that column, and the height of a row is set to accommodate the tallest node in that row. The size of the gaps between rows and columns can be set to provide spacing between the nodes.

The `add` method of a `GridPane` is overloaded. The following call adds the specified button to the cell in column 0 and row 0 (the upper left corner):

```
myGridPane.add(myButton, 0, 0);
```

The add method can also accept two additional parameters specifying the number of columns and rows the added node should span. The following line adds a slider to the cell in column two and row four, allowing it to span two columns and three rows:

```
myGridPane.add(mySlider, 2, 4, 2 3);
```

Let's look at a larger example. The following code creates and loads a grid pane with a variety of elements:

```
GridPane gridPane = new GridPane();
gridPane.setStyle("-fx-background-color: lemonchiffon");
gridPane.setAlignment(Pos.CENTER);
gridPane.setHgap(20);
gridPane.setVgap(10);
//  gridPane.setGridLinesVisible(true);

ImageView logo = new ImageView(new Image("mascot.png"));
gridPane.add(logo, 0, 0, 1, 3);

Text title = new Text("Welcome to Emotiful!");
title.setFont(new Font(24));
gridPane.add(title, 1, 0, 2, 1);

Label userLabel = new Label("User name:");
userLabel.setFont(new Font(18));
GridPane.setHalignment(userLabel, HPos.RIGHT);
gridPane.add(userLabel, 1, 1);

TextField userName = new TextField();
gridPane.add(userName, 2, 1);

Label pwLabel = new Label("Password:");
pwLabel.setFont(new Font(18));
GridPane.setHalignment(pwLabel, HPos.RIGHT);
gridPane.add(pwLabel, 1, 2);

TextField password = new TextField();
gridPane.add(password, 2, 2);

Text greeting = new Text("Have an emotiful day!");
greeting.setFont(new Font(18));
GridPane.setHalignment(greeting, HPos.CENTER);
gridPane.add(greeting, 0, 3, 3, 1);
```

There is no need to specify the overall size of the grid (the number of columns and rows). The grid pane will expand to accommodate the content. In this example, the content is spread out across three columns and four rows.

Since some nodes span rows and columns, and nodes can be aligned in various ways within a cell, it can be difficult to see how the underlying grid is being used to lay out the nodes. A call to the `setGridLinesVisible` method displays grid lines, which are especially helpful when you're initially designing the layout. Here's the same GUI with the grid lines visible:

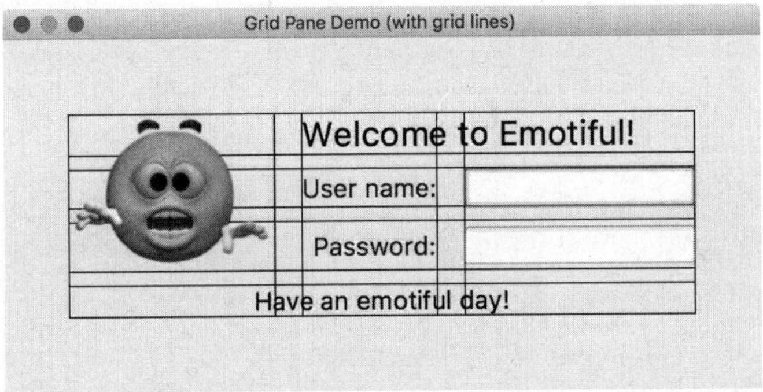

Remember that there are three columns and four rows in this layout; the gaps between the rows and columns are shown as well.

H JavaFX Scene Builder

The graphics and GUI examples developed throughout this book were done "by hand" in the sense that the controls and layout containers were created through explicit calls in the code. One of the advantages of JavaFX is that GUIs can also be defined easily and efficiently using a separate program called JavaFX Scene Builder. This appendix provides an overview and some examples using this tool.

JavaFX Scene Builder enables you to create GUIs by dragging and dropping components onto a central design area. You then modify and style the components as desired. When complete, the GUI is saved in an XML-based representation called FXML. Your development environment, such as NetBeans or Eclipse, uses the FXML representation to generate the GUI automatically.

When developing a GUI by hand, it can be difficult to get the layout and styling just right. With JavaFX Scene Builder, you don't write the GUI code at all.

JavaFX Scene Builder is a standalone application. In order to capitalize on it, the IDE you use has to support the generation of the GUI code from FXML. For example, the Eclipse and NetBeans IDEs both support FXML. We use NetBeans for the examples in this appendix.

Hello Moon

The first example we'll develop using JavaFX Scene Builder is called `HelloMoon` (a variation on the `HelloWorld` starter program). The program simply displays a label and an image—there is no user interaction. But it demonstrates key aspects of the drag-and-drop GUI building approach.

When the program runs, it will display a window similar to the one shown in Figure H.1.

When you open NetBeans, a start page is displayed that includes links to recently opened projects as well as links to the NetBeans documentation.

FIGURE H.1 A JavaFX program with a GUI generated by JavaFX Scene Builder

An application in NetBeans is defined as a project, which is a group of all files that pertain the project. These include source code files, images, and the FXML file that represents the GUI. To create a new project, select File > New Project. in the File menu or click the button on the toolbar. This will display the New Project dialog box, as shown in Figure H.2. Choose JavaFX project under Categories and a JavaFX FXML Application under Projects. Then click the Next > button.

Next, in the New JavaFX Application window, you specify the project name (HelloMoon), the project location, the FXML file name (which doesn't have to be the same as the project name, but could be), and the application class name. If the Create Application Class checkbox is checked, NetBeans will create a class with the specified name containing the program's main method. When this information is set, click the Finish button to create the project.

When NetBeans creates a JavaFX project, it creates some initial files for you. In the upper left corner of the NetBeans window, you'll see the Projects tab, where you can access all of the files in your project. Click on the HelloMoon entry, and then Source Packages, and finally <default package> to expand each node. The Projects tab should appear similar to the one shown in Figure H.3.

When we created the project, we didn't specify a package name, so our source files are in the default package. If you specify a package name, your files will be listed under that package.

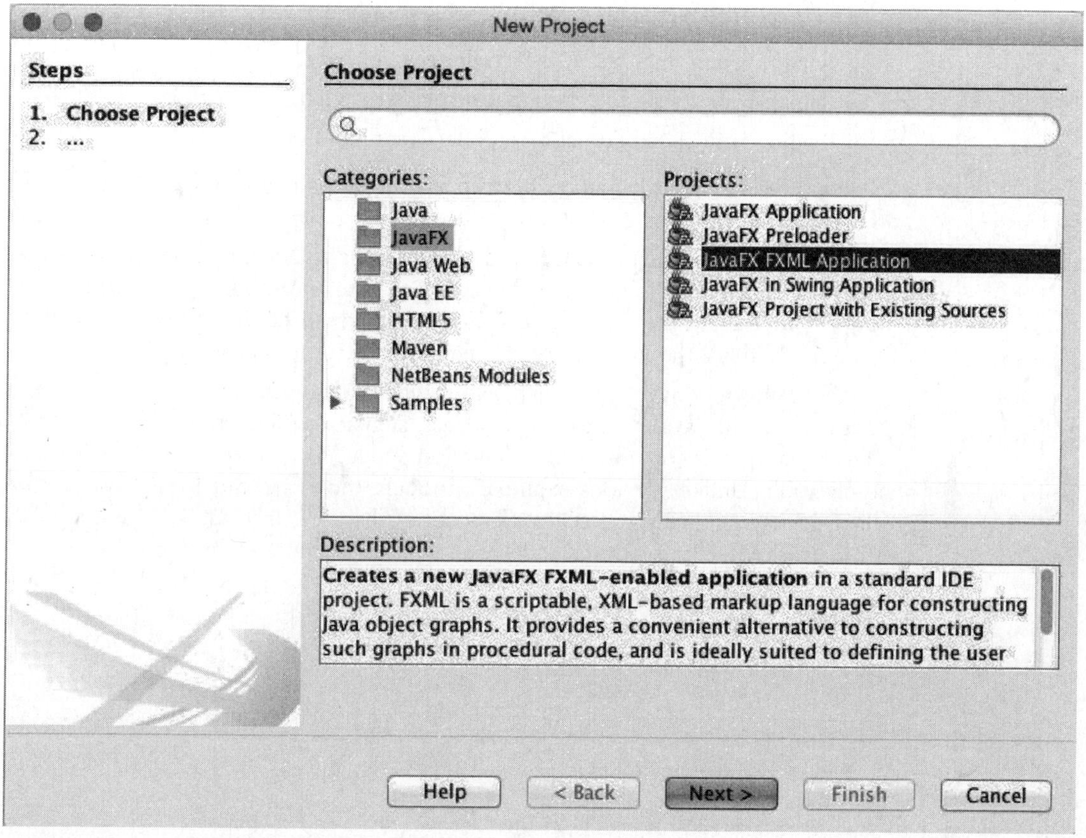

FIGURE H.2 The NetBeans New Project window

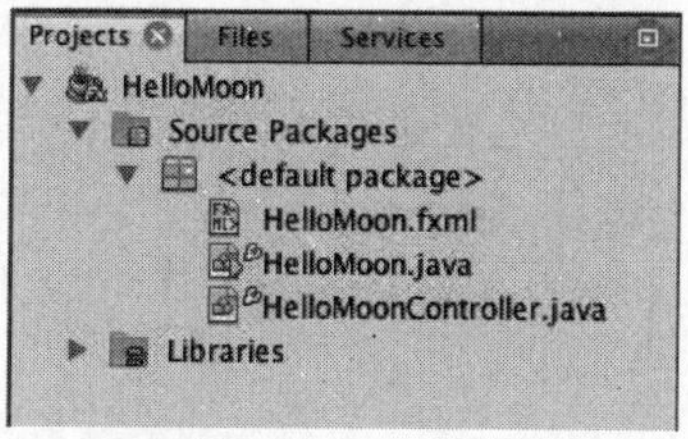

FIGURE H.3 The Projects tab in the NetBeans window

The three files NetBeans created for this project are:

- HelloMoon.fxml—the FXML representation of the GUI
- HelloMoon.java—the class that displays the GUI
- HelloMoonController.java—the class that handles user events

Double-clicking a file name will open that file in an editing tab in the center of the NetBeans window. Take a look at each one.

Remember, the FXML file is not Java code—it is an XML representation of the GUI. The default GUI contains a label and a button. Although we could change this file by editing the text of the FXML, that would be defeating the purpose. Instead, we'll use the JavaFX Scene Builder application to change it.

The HelloMoon.java file, shown below without documentation, contains a class that extends the JavaFX `Application` class, similar to those created in any hand-coded example. It contains a `start` method and a `main` method that launches the application. Unlike previous examples, though, the `start` method in `HelloMoon` class doesn't explicitly create the elements of the GUI. Instead, it loads the GUI from its FXML representation as a `Parent` object. Then the scene and stage are set.

```
import javafx.application.Application;
import javafx.fxml.FXMLLoader;
import javafx.scene.Parent;
import javafx.scene.Scene;
import javafx.stage.Stage;

public class HelloMoon extends Application
{
    public void start(Stage stage) throws Exception
    {
        Parent root = FXMLLoader.load(
            getClass().getResource("HelloMoon.fxml"));

        Scene scene = new Scene(root);

        stage.setScene(scene);
        stage.show();
    }

    public static void main(String[] args)
    {
        launch(args);
    }
}
```

Except for updating the documentation, we don't have to change the `HelloMoon` class at all. In fact, for this example we don't have to write any Java code explicitly to create the `HelloMoon` application. All the changes can be made to the GUI through the JavaFX Scene Builder.

The `HelloMoonController` class is used to handle events as the user interacts with the GUI. In `HelloMoon`, there is no user interaction, so this file is not needed at all in this application. You can right-click on the file name in the Projects tab and select delete to remove it. We'll see the use of this file in our next example.

Before modifying the GUI, add the image of the moon to the project by dragging the image file (moon.jpg) to the default package in the Projects tab. You could also add the image to the package by copying it into the src folder where the project is stored.

Now we get to the heart of the matter—updating the GUI using the standalone, drag-and-drop application called JavaFX Scene Builder. To launch Scene Builder directly from NetBeans, right-click the HelloMoon.fxml file and select Open.

The JavaFX Scene Builder window is shown in Figure H.4. The middle section shows a visual representation of the GUI. The Library section (top left) contains the various elements you may want to include in your GUI. The Document section (bottom left) lists the elements that are currently in your GUI.

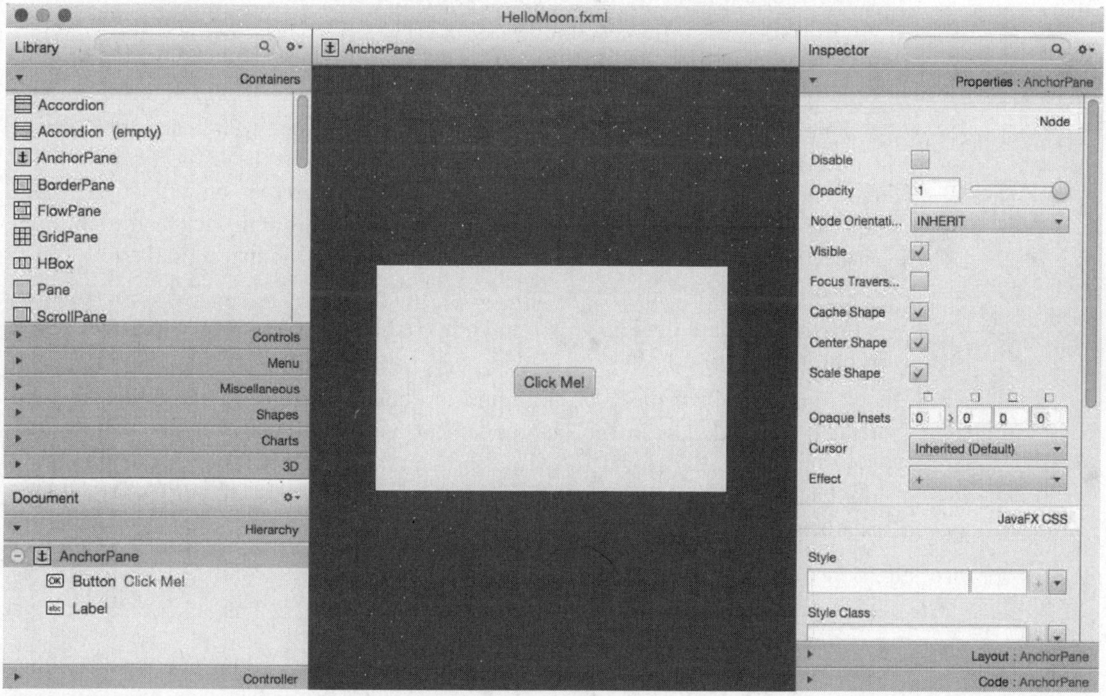

FIGURE H.4 JavaFX Scene Builder

(The default GUI file created by NetBeans contains a Button and a Label on an AnchorPane.) The Inspector section (right) allows you to tailor the characteristics of the selected element.

To create the GUI for HelloMoon, we'll first delete the controls provided in the default file. In the Hierarchy tab of the Document section, click on the Button element to select it. Then press the Delete or Backspace key to remove it. You'll be asked to confirm that you want to delete it. Repeat the process for the Label.

Instead of using the provided AnchorPane, we'll use a VBox layout container, which organizes its nodes in a vertical column. To make this change, drag a VBox from the Containers tab of the Library onto the central panel. Then use the Select > Trim Document to Selection menu option, which will remove the AnchorPane.

Before adding any elements to the VBox, let's modify some of its characteristics. First, select the VBox in the Document Hierarchy. Then, in the Inspector Properties tab, set its Alignment to CENTER, which will center its contents horizontally. Under Style, set the –fx-background-color property to #000, which will make the background of the entire VBox black. Finally, in the Inspector Layout tab, set the VBox Preferred Width and Height to be 400 and 325, respectively.

Now, add a label to the VBox by dragging a Label from the Library Controls tab to the central panel. In the Inspector Preferences tab, set the text of the label to "Hello, Moon!," change the color (Text Fill) to white, and change the Font to be bold and 36 point.

Finally, we'll add the moon image. Drag an ImageView from the Library Controls tab onto the central panel below the label. In the Inspector Properties tab, click the ellipses (. . .) button next to Image property which will let you select the file to be displayed. You can also set the Fit Width and Fit Height values in Inspector Layout tab to 0 to have the image displayed in its original size.

That completes the GUI setup. Save your changes in JavaFX Scene Builder, which will update the FXML file in your NetBeans project. You can now run the program in NetBeans.

Note that all of the GUI configuration could have been accomplished using regular method calls in the Java code. But using the JavaFX Scene Builder tool may make it easier to get the visual presentation correct faster. By representing the GUI in a standard XML file, the automated translation from FXML to Java is efficient and accurate.

Handling Events in JavaFX Scene Builder

The HelloMoon program displayed a label and an image, but the user couldn't interact with it. Let's look at an example that uses controls that the user can manipulate.

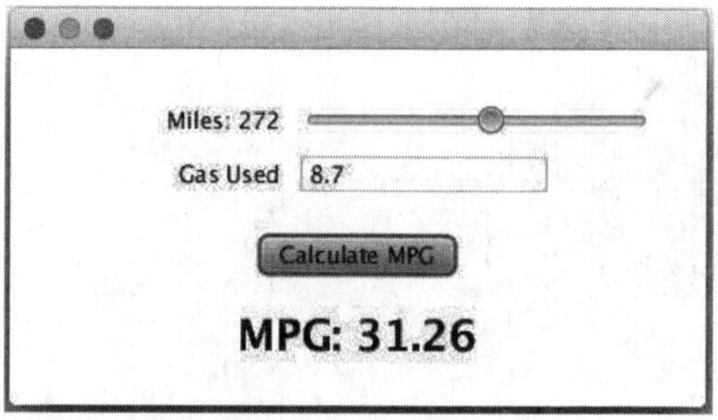

FIGURE H.5 A JavaFX program that computes miles per gallon

Figure H.5 displays an application that computes miles per gallon given the number of miles driven and the gallons of gas consumed. The user sets the miles value using a slider. The gallons are set using a value typed into a text field. When the user presses the Calculate MPG button, the result is displayed in a label at the bottom of the window.

As with the `HelloMoon` example, we will use JavaFX Scene Builder to develop the GUI. Unlike `HelloMoon`, the `MilesPerGallon` program will rely on a controller class to handle user events.

Create a new project in NetBeans as you did with the `HelloMoon` example. The MilesPerGallon.java file, containing the main class, will once again be used as generated. All changes to the GUI will be accomplished through JavaFX Scene Builder.

Open the FXML file in Scene Builder by right-clicking the file and selecting Open. Remove the default controls. As with `HelloMoon`, add a `VBox` as the root element of the GUI.

The top element in the `VBox` will be another layout container, a `GridPane` object, which allows elements to be laid out in a grid. We'll use a 2×2 GridPane to display the top two rows of elements in the GUI. The left column will display the labels for the miles and gas used, while the right column will display the slider and the text field.

Drag a `GridPane` from the Library Containers tab onto the central design area. It defaults to a 2×3 grid, as shown in Figure H.6. To remove the unneeded row, select the third row and press Backspace or Delete. Now drag two `Label` objects from Library Controls into each cell of the left column (column 0). Then drag a horizontal `Slider` into the top cell of the right column, and a `TextField` into the bottom cell of the right column.

Before we configure the look of these elements, add the remaining elements to the GUI. Drag a `Button` to the `VBox` (not in the `GridPane`, under it). Then add another label under the button to display the results.

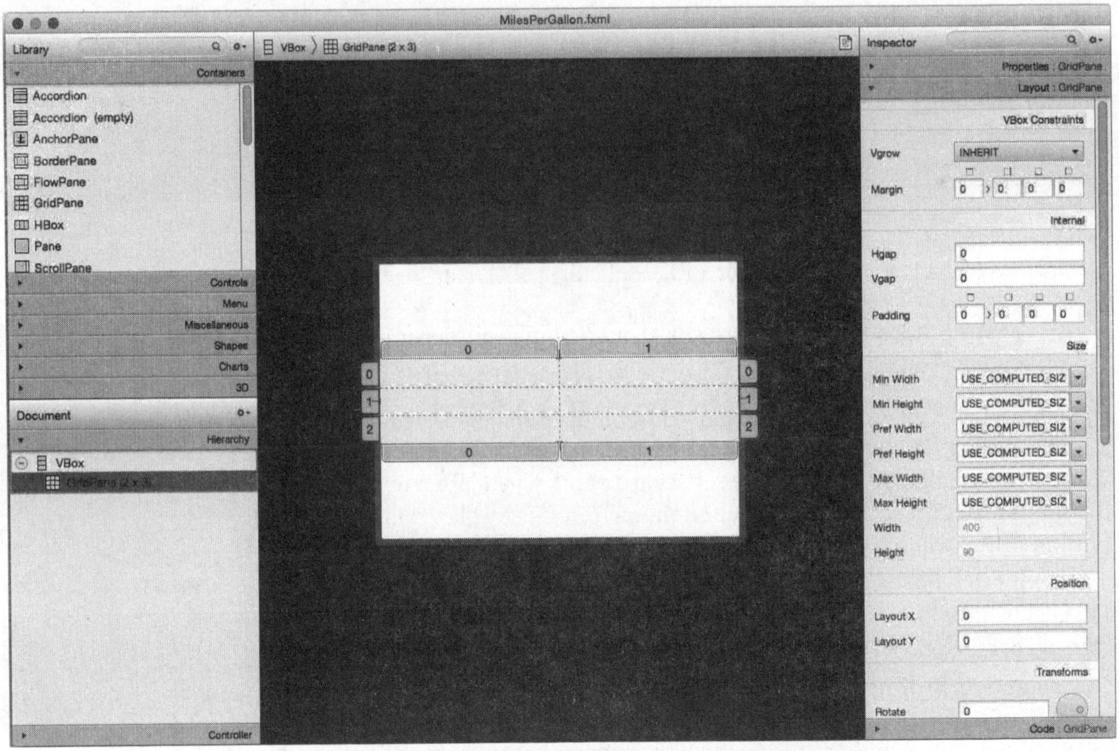

FIGURE H.6 A GridPane in JavaFX Scene Builder

At this point, all the pieces are in place, but they don't look like we want. Select each component in turn and use the Inspector to tailor its characteristics. For example, set the text of the labels and the button. Set the left column of the `GridPane` to be right aligned. Set the size of the slider and text field.

In the Inspector Properties of the `Slider`, set its Min and Max values to 0 and 500, respectively. Set its default Value to 100. Set the results label to display "---" initially, since no value for gas consumed has been entered.

With the initial design of the GUI established, we can turn our attention to handling user interaction. Each node that we need to reference in the code must be given an fx:id using Scene Builder. For example, select the `Slider`, then in the Inspector Code tab set its fx:id to `milesSlider`. This corresponds to the variable name used in the Java code to refer to this slider.

The `MilesPerGallonController` class handles the events generated when the user slides the slider or presses the button. The variables labeled with the `@FXL` annotation correspond to the fx:id property of key components. Some components, like the "Gas Used" label, does not need to be referred to in the code and therefore doesn't need an fx:id.

Here's the final version of the `MilesPerGallonController` class:

```
import javafx.beans.value.ChangeListener;
import javafx.beans.value.ObservableValue;
import javafx.event.ActionEvent;
import javafx.fxml.FXML;
import javafx.fxml.Initializable;
import javafx.scene.control.Button;
import javafx.scene.control.Label;
import javafx.scene.control.Slider;
import javafx.scene.control.TextField;

public class MilesPerGallonController
{
    private int milesTraveled = 100;

    @FXML
    private Label milesLabel;

    @FXML
    private Slider milesSlider;

    @FXML
    private TextField gasTextField;

    @FXML
    private Button calculateButton;

    @FXML
    private Label resultLabel;

    @FXML
    private void calculateMPG(ActionEvent event)
    {
        double gasUsed = Double.parseDouble (gasTextField.getText());
        double mpg = milesTraveled / gasUsed;
        resultLabel.setText(String.format("MPG: %.2f", mpg));
    }

    public void initialize()
    {
        milesSlider.valueProperty().addListener (new SliderListener());
    }

    // An inner class that serves as the listener for the slider.
    private class SliderListener implements ChangeListener<Number>
    {
        @Override
```

```
            public void changed(ObservableValue<? extends Number> ov,
                    Number oldValue, Number newValue)
            {
                milesTraveled = newValue.intValue();
                milesLabel.setText("Miles: " + milesTraveled);
            }
        }
    }
```

The `calculateMPG` method calculates the miles per gallon and updates the result label. We want this method to be executed whenever the button is pressed in the GUI. In JavaFX Scene Builder, select the button asnd open the Inspector Code tab. In the drop-down menu for the On Action event, choose the `calculateMPG` method.

The `initialize` method is called when the GUI is loaded and can be used to set up the controller. In this case, a `SliderListener` object is created and added to the slider. The `SliderListener` class is defined as an inner class and updates the miles traveled (and the value displayed) as the slider is changed.

This example shows the relationship between the settings in JavaFX Scene Builder and the Java code that handles user interaction. By letting Scene Builder handle the majority of the GUI design, we can focus on the underlying calculations in the program itself.

Regular Expressions

Throughout the book, we've used the `Scanner` class to read interactive input from the user and parse strings into individual tokens such as words. In Chapter 5, we also used it to read input from a data file. Usually, we used the default whitespace delimiters for tokens in the scanner input.

The `Scanner` class can also be used to parse its input according to a *regular expression,* which is a character string that represents a pattern. A regular expression can be used to set the delimiters used when extracting tokens, or it can be used in methods like `findInLine` to match a particular string.

Some of the general rules for constructing regular expressions include:

- The dot (.) character matches any single character.
- The * character matches zero or more characters.
- A string of characters in square brackets ([ ]) matches any single character in the string.
- The \ character followed by a character matches the pattern specified by that character.

For example, the regular expression `B.b*` matches `Bob`, `Bubba`, and `Baby`. The regular expression `T[aei]*ing` matches `Taking`, `Tickling`, and `Telling`.

Figure I.1 specifies some of the patterns that can be matched in a Java regular expression, although this list is not comprehensive. See the online documentation for the `Pattern` class for a complete list.

Regular Expression	Matches
`x`	The character x
`.`	Any character
`[ abc]`	a, b, or c
`[^abc]`	Any character except a, b, or c (negation)
`[a-z][A-Z]`	a through z or A through Z, inclusive (range)
`[a-d[m-p]]`	a through d or m through p (union)
`[a-z&&[ def]]`	d, e, or f (intersection)
`[a-z&&[ ^bc]]`	a through z, except for b and c (subtraction)
`[a-z&&[ ^m-p]]`	a through z but not m through p (subtraction)
`\d`	A digit: [0–9]
`\D`	A non-digit: [^0–9]
`\s`	A whitespace character
`\S`	A non-whitespace character
`^`	The beginning of a line
`$`	The end of a line

FIGURE I.1 Some patterns that can be matched in a Java regular expression

Javadoc Documentation Generator

J

Javadoc is a tool for creating documentation in HTML format from Java source code. The utility examines the source code, extracts specially marked information in the documentation, and then produces Web pages that summarize the software.

Documentation comments, also referred to as doc comments, are processed by the javadoc tool. Special labels called *tags* specify particular kinds of information about the code. For instance, the `@author` tag is used to specify the author of the code. The Javadoc tool parses the doc comments and the tags and generates the HTML pages that document the code.

Javadoc comes as a standard part of the Java Software Development Kit (SDK). The tool executable, javadoc.exe, resides in the bin folder of the installation directory along with the javac compiler and java execution tool. Therefore, if you are able to compile and execute your code using the command line, javadoc should also work.

Using javadoc is simple in its plain form; it is very much like compiling a java source file. For example:

```
javadoc myfile.java
```

The javadoc command may also specify options and package names. The source file name must contain the .java extension (similar to the javac compiler command).

Doc Comments

The document comments are subdivided into descriptions and tags. Descriptions should provide an overview of the functionality of the explained code. Tags address the specifics of the functionality such as code version (for classes or interfaces) or return types (for methods).

Javadoc processes code comments placed between /** and */. The comments are allowed to span multiple lines where each line begins with a * character, which are, along with any white space before them, discarded by the tool. These comments are allowed to contain HTML tags. For example:

```
/**
 *     This is an <strong>example</strong> document comment.
 */
```

Comment placement should be considered carefully. The javadoc tool automatically copies the first sentence from each doc to a summary at the top of the HTML document. The sentence begins after any white space following the * character and ends at the first period. The description that follows should be concise and complete. Document comments are recognized only if they are placed immediately before a class, constructor, method, interface, or field declaration.

The use of HTML inside the description should be limited to proper comment separation and display rather than styling.

Tags

Tags are included in a doc comment. Each tag must start on a separate line, hence it must be preceded by the * character. Tags are case sensitive and begin with the @ symbol.

Certain tags are required in some situations. The @param tag must be supplied for every parameter and is used to describe the purpose of the parameter. The @return tag must be supplied for every method that returns anything other than void, to describe what the method returns. The @author class and the @version tags are required for classes and interfaces only.

Figure J.1 lists the various tags used in javadoc comments.

Note the two different types of tags listed in Figure J.1. The *block tags,* which begin with the @ symbol (e.g., @author), must be placed in the tag section following the main description. The *inline tags,* enclosed in the { and } delimiters, can be placed anywhere in the description section or in the comments for block tags. For example:

```
/**
 * This is an <strong>example</strong> document comment.
 * The {@link Glossary} provides definitions of types used.
 *
 * @author Sebastian Niezgoda
 */
```

Tag Name	Description
@author	Inserts an "Author" entry with the specified text.
{ @code}	Same as <code>{@literal}</code>.
@deprecated	Inserts a bold "Deprecated" entry with the specified text.
{ @docRoot}	Relative link to the root of the document.
@exception	See @throws.
{ @inheritDoc}	Copies documentation from the closest inherited class or implemented interface where used allowing for more general comments of hierarchically higher classes to be reused.
{ @link}	Inserts a hyperlink to an HTML document. Use: {@link name url}.
{ @linkPlain}	Same as {@link} but is displayed as plain text. Use: {@linkPlain link label}.
{ @literal}	Text enclosed in the tag is denoted literally, as containing any HTML. For example, {@literal <td> TouchDown} would be displayed as <td> TouchDown (<td> not interpreted as a table cell).
@param	Inserts a "Parameters" section, which lists and describes parameters for a particular constructor/method.
@return	Inserts a "Returns" section, which lists and describes any return values for a particular constructor/method. Use: @return description. An error will be thrown if included in a comment of a method with the void return type.
@see	Included a "See Also" comment with a link pointing to a document with more information. Use: @see link.
@serial	Used for a serializable field. Use: @serial text.
@serialData	Used to document used to describe data written by the writeObject, readObject, writeExternal, and readExternal methods. Use: @serialdata text.
@serialField	Used to comment on the ObjectStreamField. Use: @serialField name type description.
@since	Inserts a new "Since" heading that is used to denote when particular features were first introduced. Use: @since text.
@throws	Includes a "Throws" heading. Use: @throws name description.
{ @value}	Returns the value of a code element it refers to. Use: @value code-member label.
@version	Add a "Version" heading when the -version command–line option is used. Use: @version text.

FIGURE J.1 Various tags used in javadoc comments

Files Generated

The javadoc tool analyzes a java source file or package and produces a three-part HTML document for each class. The HTML file is often referred to as a documentation file. It contains cleanly organized information about the class file derived from the doc comments included in the code.

The first part of the document contains an overall description of the class. The class name appears first followed by a graphical representation of the inheritance relationships. A general description is displayed next, which is extracted from the first sentence of each doc comment entity (as discussed previously).

Next, a list of constructors and methods is provided. The signatures of all the constructors and methods included in the source file are listed along with one-sentence descriptions. The name of the constructor/method is a hyperlink to a more detailed description in the third part of the document.

Finally, complete descriptions of the methods are provided. Again, the signature is provided first followed by an explanation of the entity, but this time without the one-sentence limit, which is obtained from the doc comments. If applicable, a list of parameters and return values, along with their descriptions, is provided in the respective sections.

The HTML document makes extensive use of hyperlinks to provide necessary additional information, using the `@see` tag for example, and for navigational purposes. The header and the footer of the page are navigation bars, with the following links:

- *Package* provides a list of classes included in the package along with a short purpose and description of each class.
- *Tree* presents a visual hierarchy of the classes within the package. Each class name is a link to the appropriate documentation HTML file.
- *Deprecated* lists functionality that is considered deprecated that is used in any of the class files contained in the package.
- *Index* provides an alphabetical listing of classes, constructors, and methods in the package. The class name is also associated with a short purpose and description of the class. Each appearance of the class name is a link to the appropriate HTML documentation. The signature of every constructor and method is a link to the appropriate detailed description. A one-sentence description presented next to the signature listing associates the constructor/method with the appropriate class.
- *Help* loads a help page with how-to instructions for using and navigating the HTML documentation.

All pages could be viewed with or without frames. Each class summary has links that can be used to quickly access any of the parts of the document.

The output content could be tailored by command-line options used when executing the javadoc tool. By default, if no options are specified, the output returned is equivalent to using the `-protected` option. The options include:

- `private` shows all classes, methods, and variables.
- `public` shows only public classes, methods, and variables.
- `protected` shows only protected and public classes, methods, and variables.
- `help` presents the online help.
- `keywords` includes HTML meta tags to the output file generated to assist with searching.

K Java Syntax

This appendix contains syntax diagrams that collectively describe the way in which Java language elements can be constructed. Rectangles indicate something that is further defined in another syntax diagram, and ovals indicate a literal word or character.

Compilation Unit

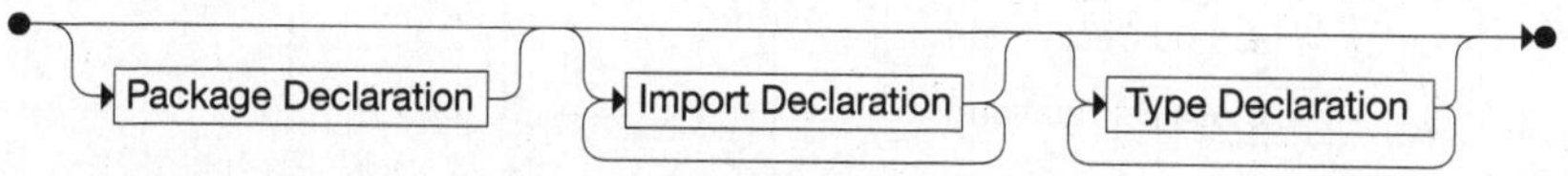

Package Declaration

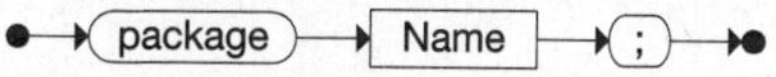

Import Declaration

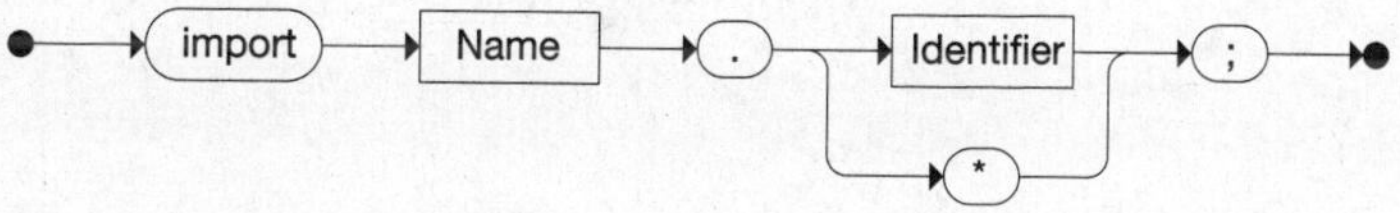

Type Declaration

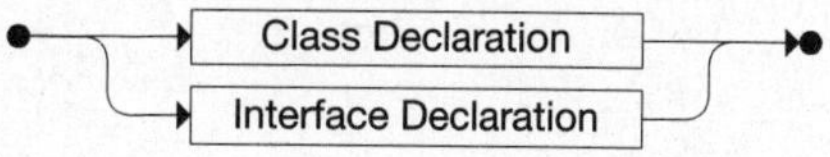

Class Declaration

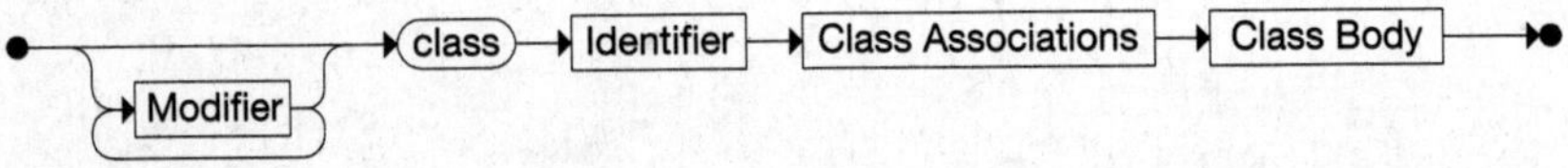

Class Associations

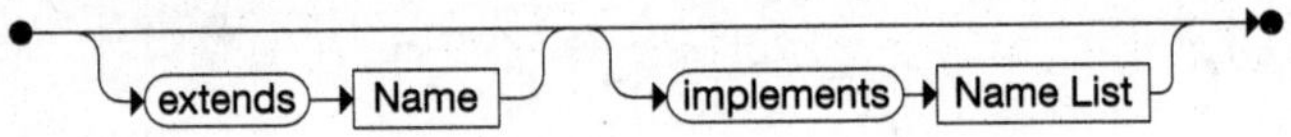

Class Body

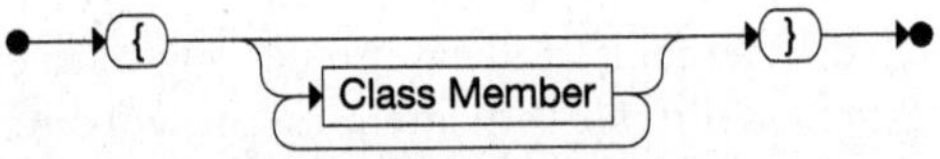

Class Member

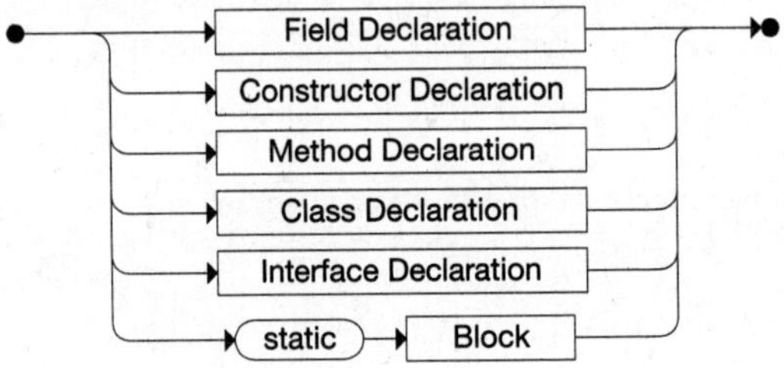

Interface Declaration

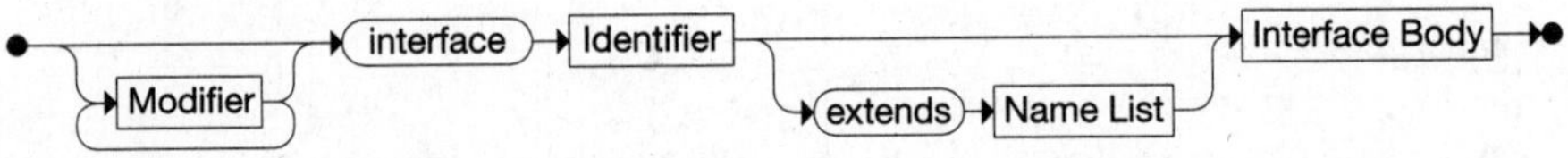

Interface Body

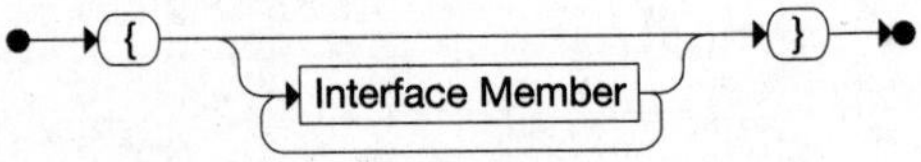

Interface Member

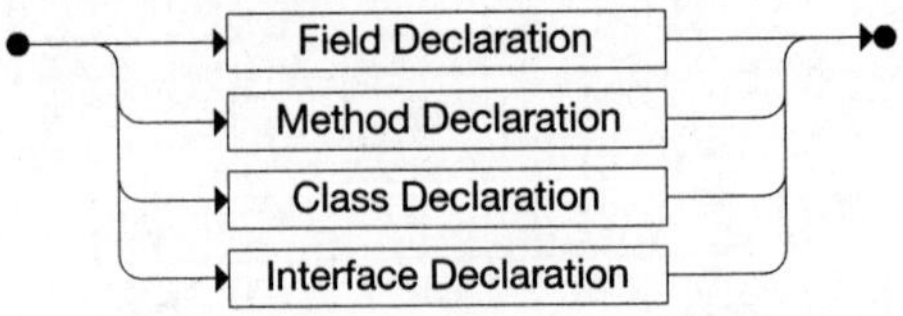

Field Declaration

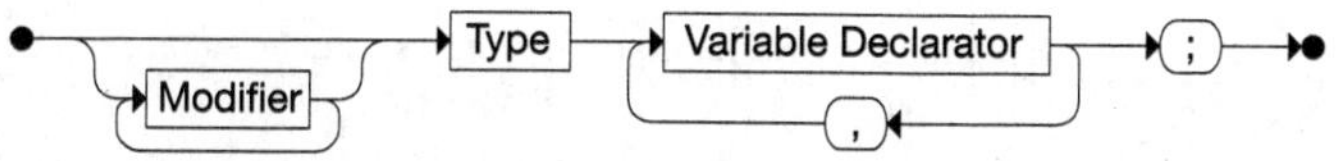

Variable Declarator

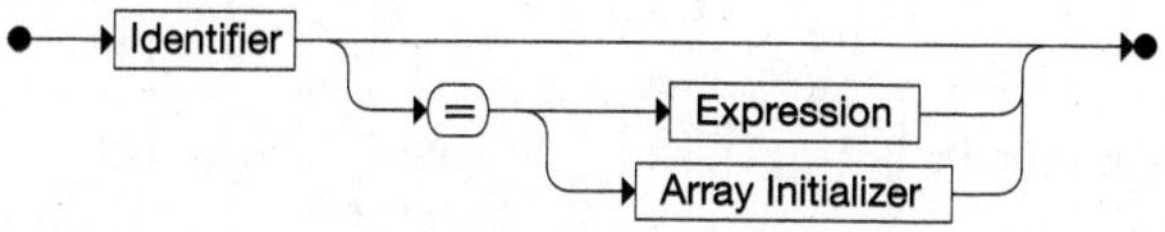

Type

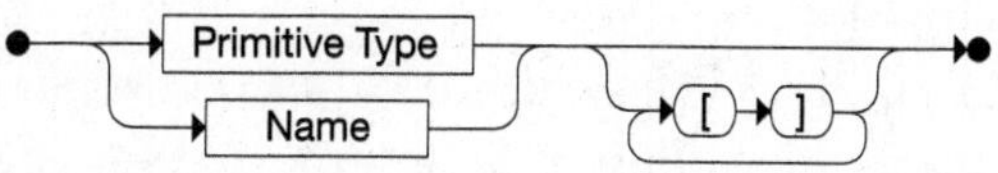

Modifier

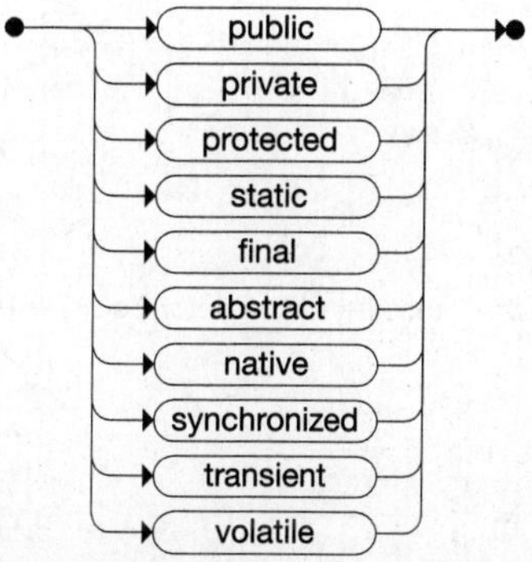

Primitive Type

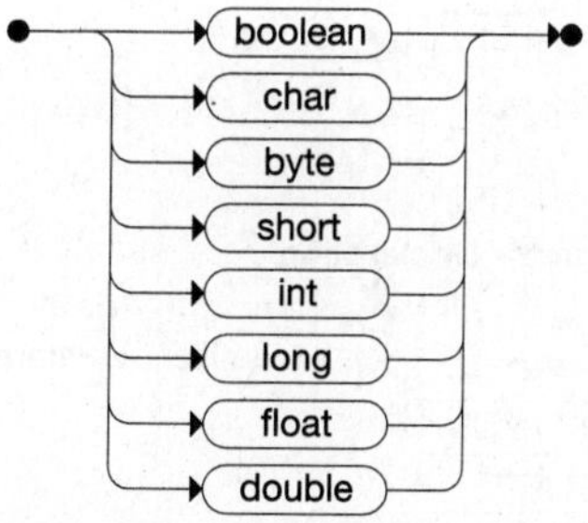

Array Initializer

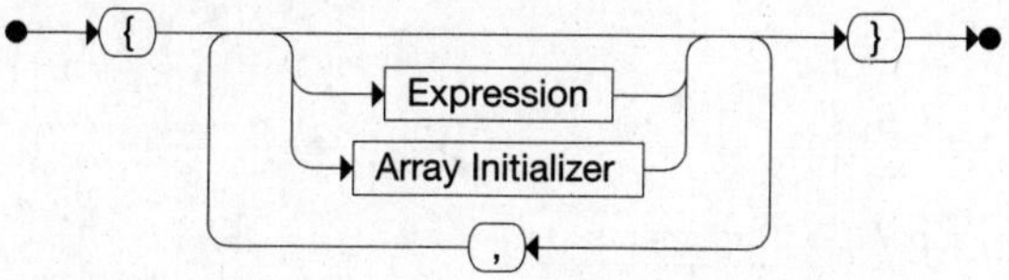

Name

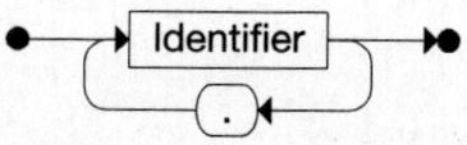

Name List

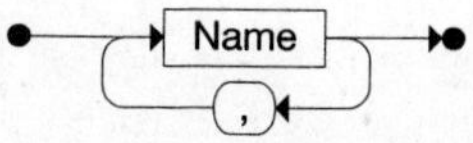

Method Declaration

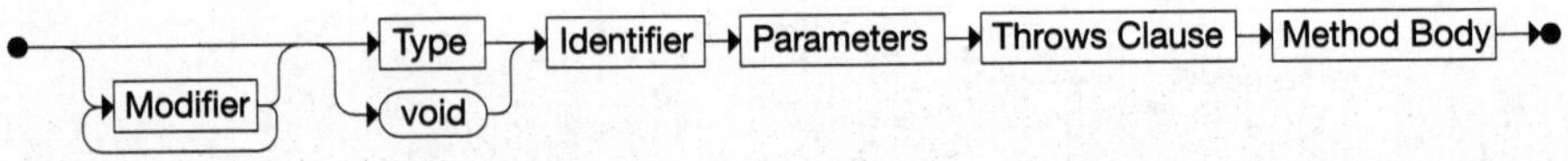

Parameters

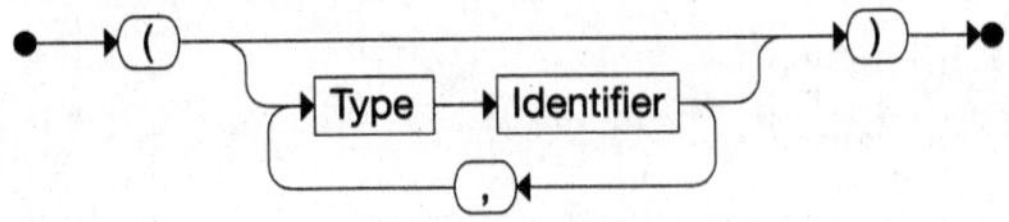

Throws Clause

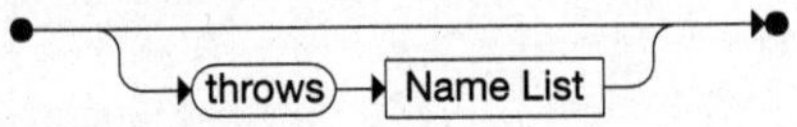

Method Body

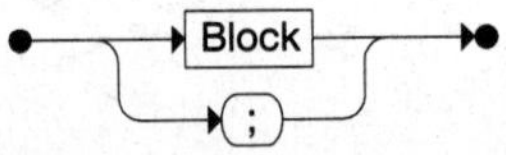

Constructor Declaration

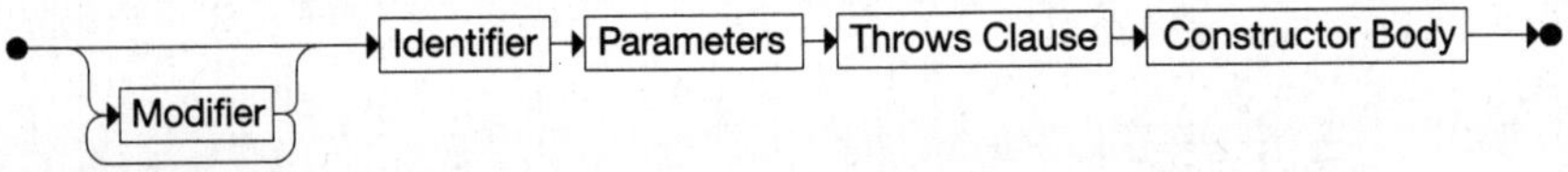

Constructor Body

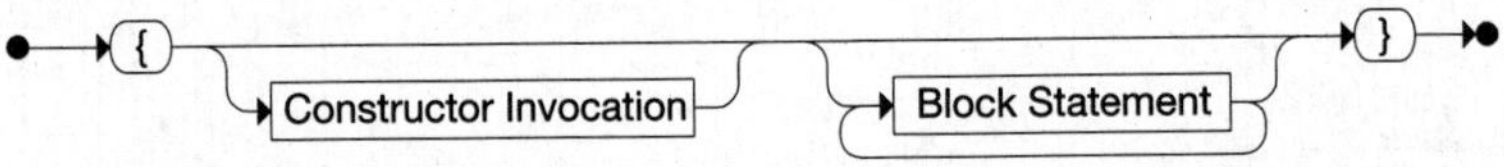

Constructor Invocation

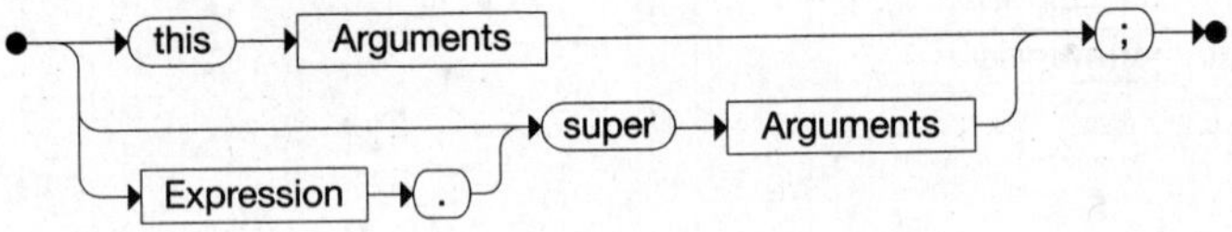

Block

Block Statement

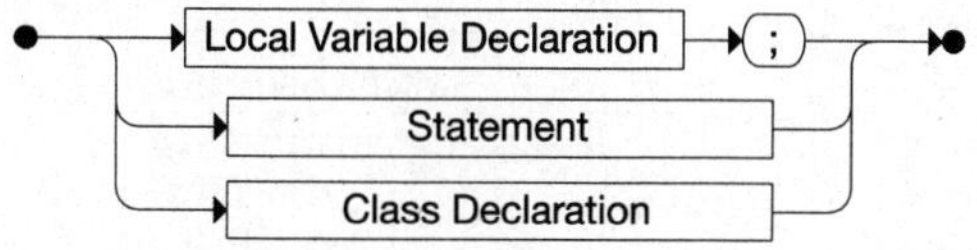

Local Variable Declaration

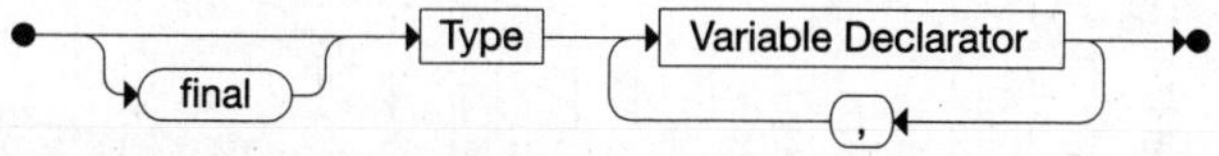

Statement

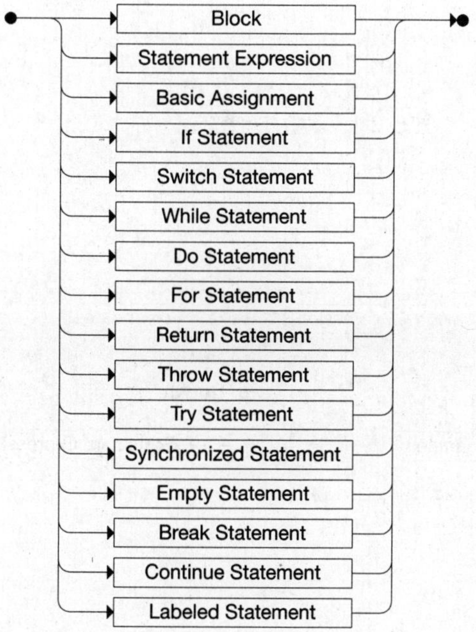

If Statement

Switch Statement

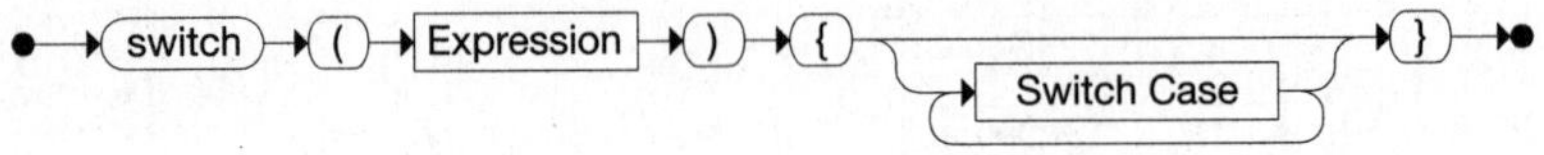

Switch Case

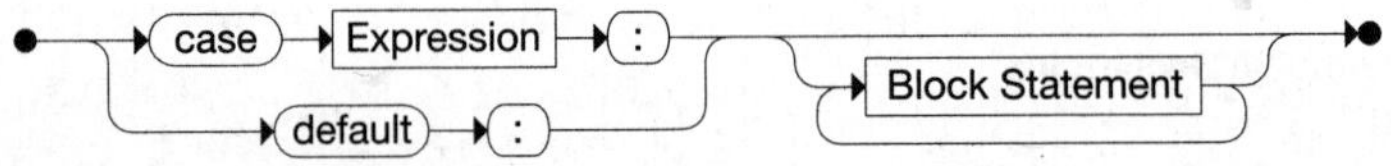

While Statement

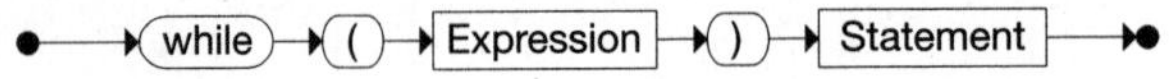

Do Statement

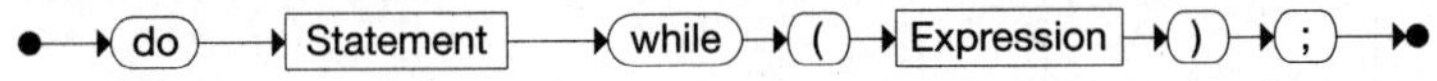

For Statement

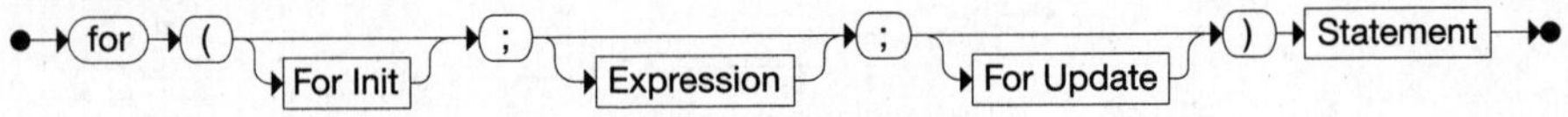

For Init

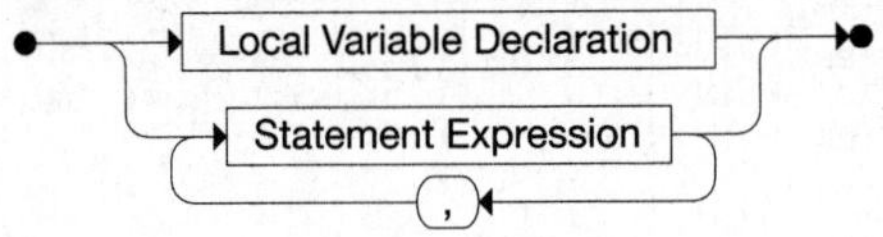

For Update

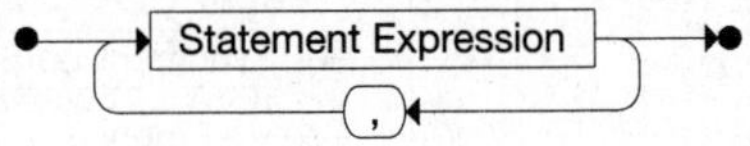

Basic Assignment

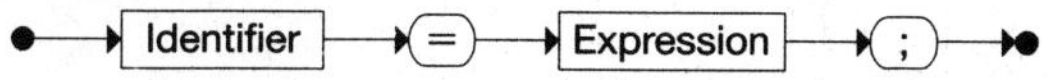

Return Statement

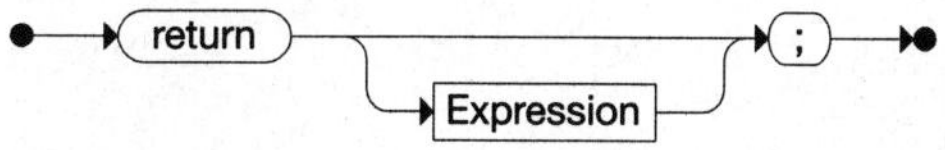

Throw Statement

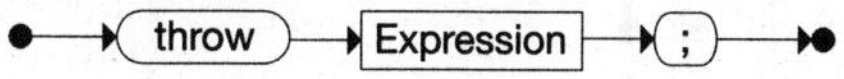

Try Statement

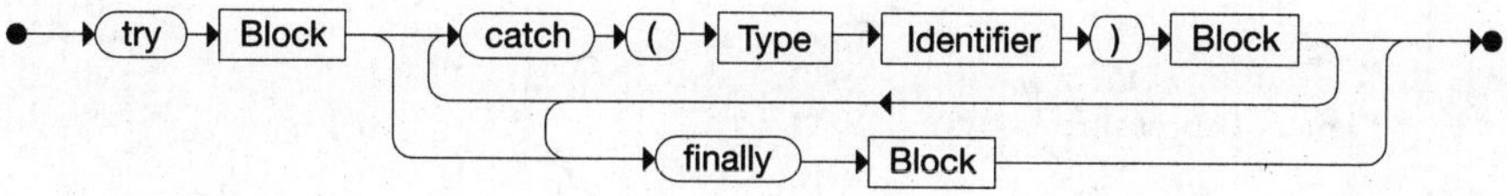

Synchronized Statement

Empty Statement

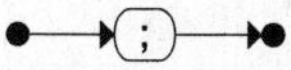

Break Statement

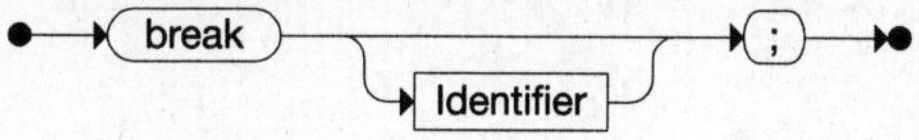

Continue Statement

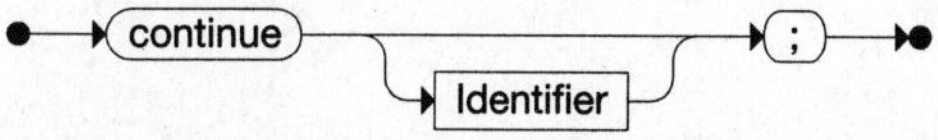

Labeled Statement

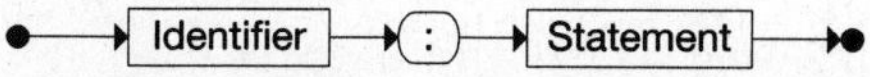

Expression

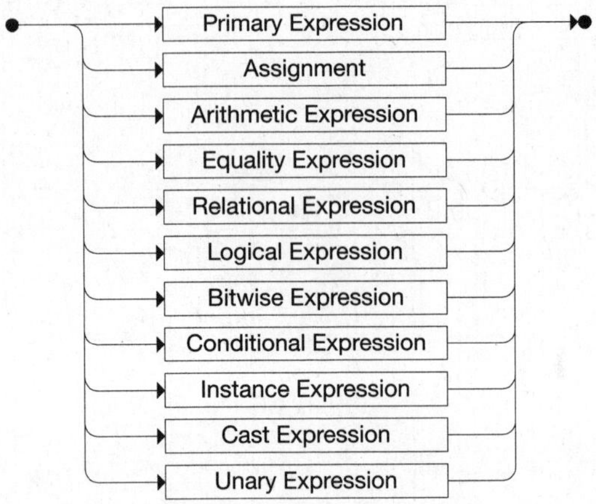

Primary Expression

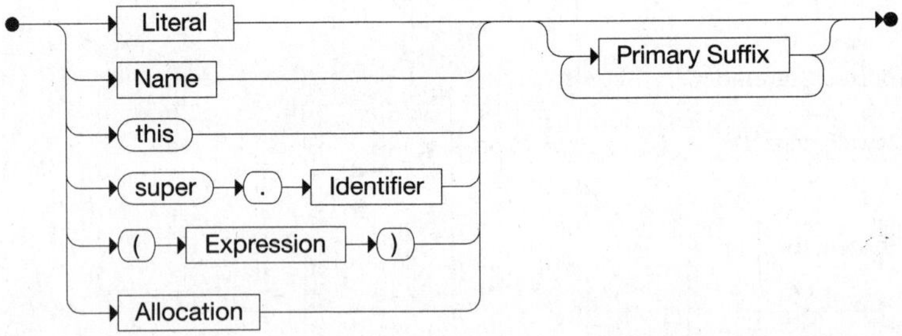

Primary Suffix

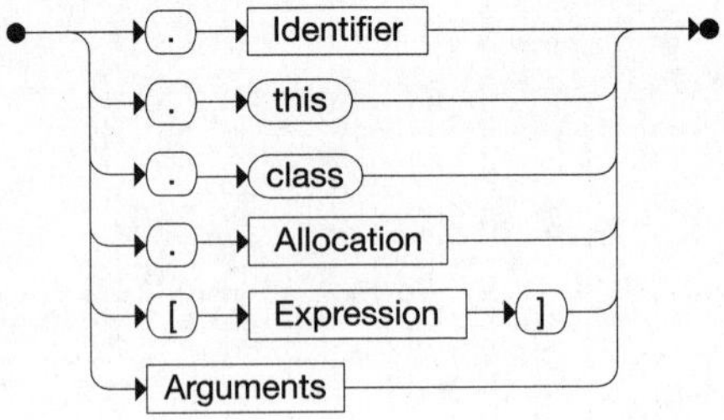

Arguments

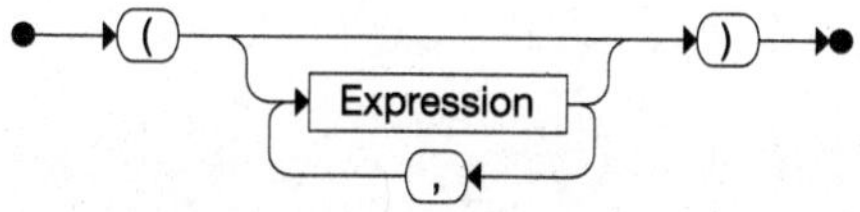

Allocation

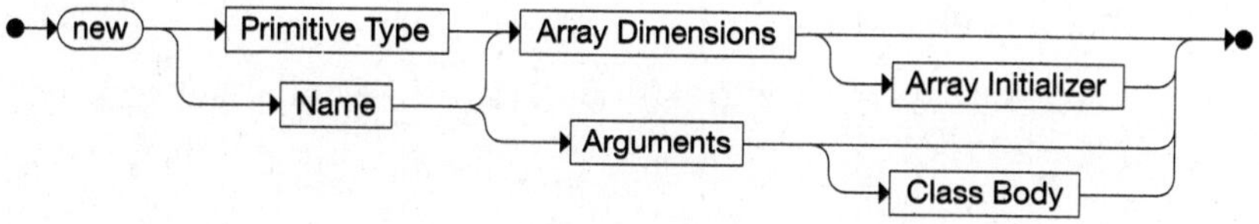

Array Dimensions

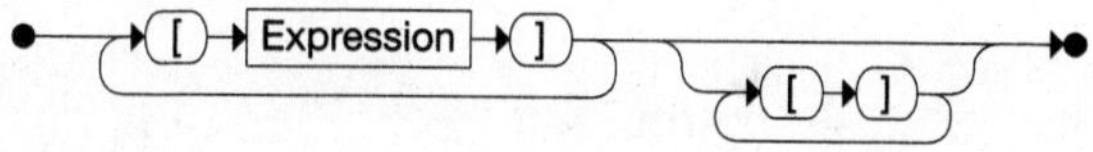

Statement Expression

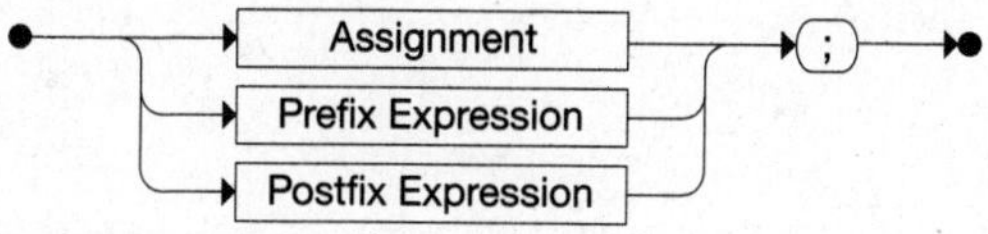

Assignment

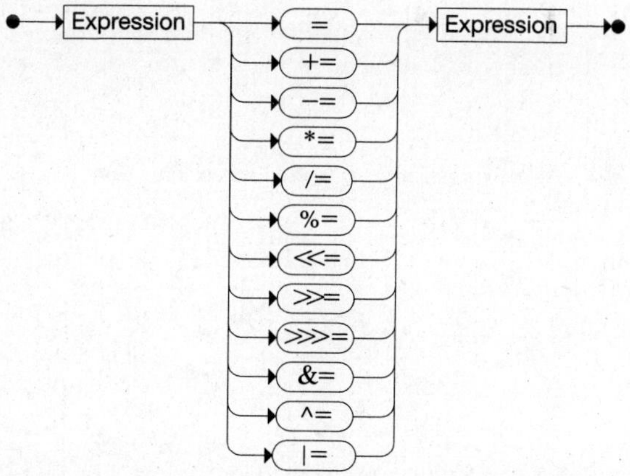

Arithmetic Expression

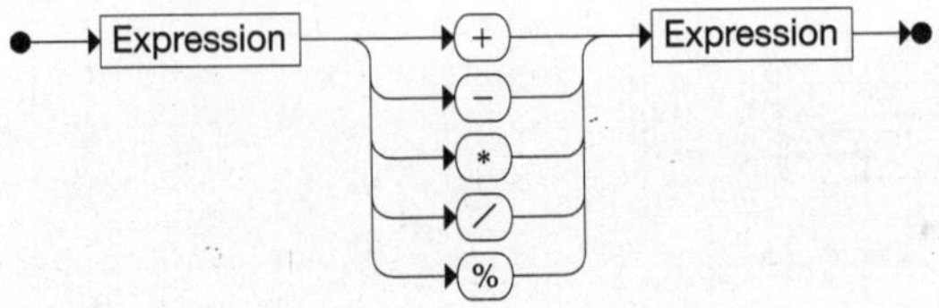

Equality Expression

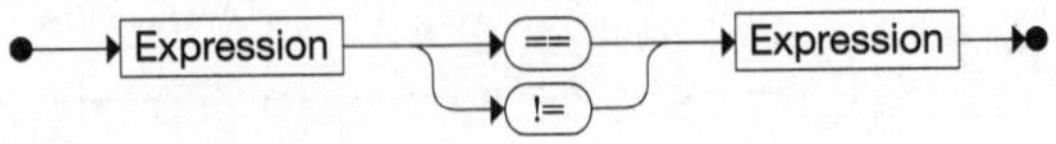

Relational Expression

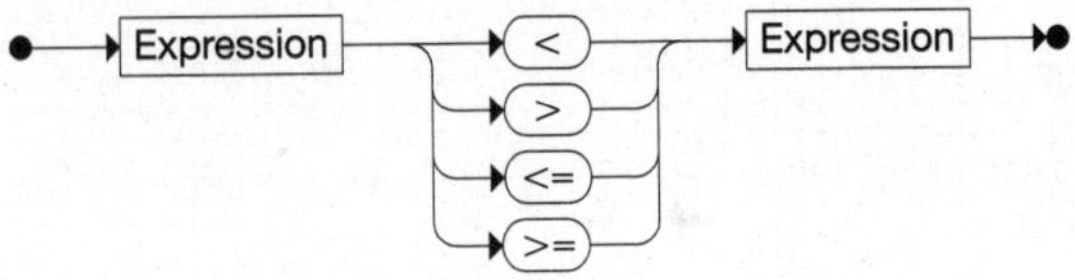

Logical Expression

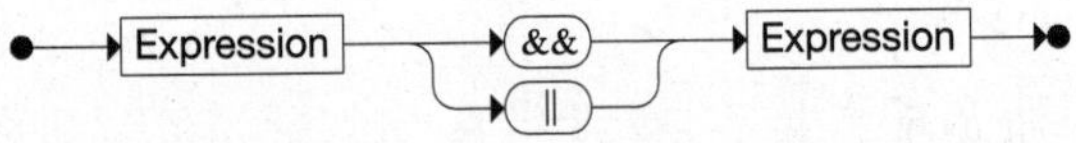

Bitwise Expression

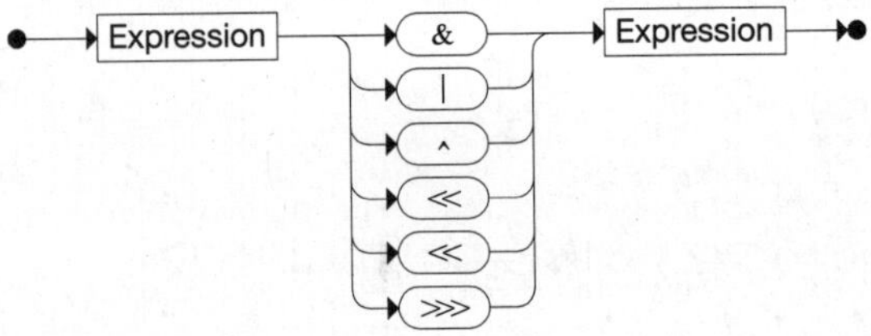

Conditional Expression

Instance Expression

Cast Expression

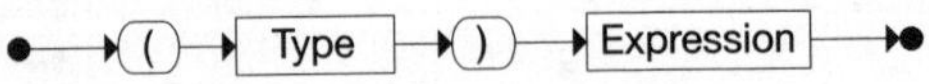

Unary Expression

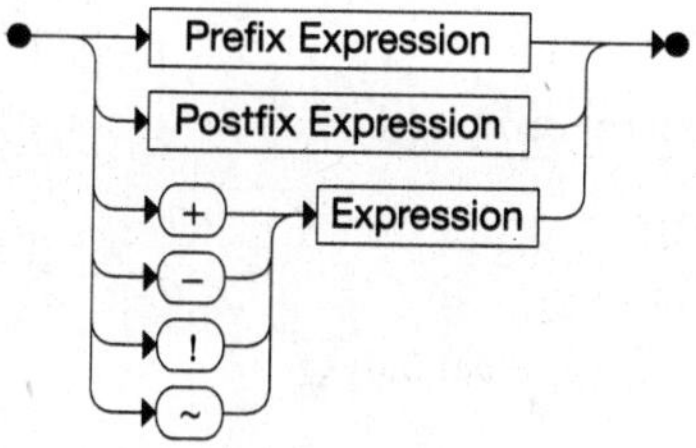

Prefix Expression

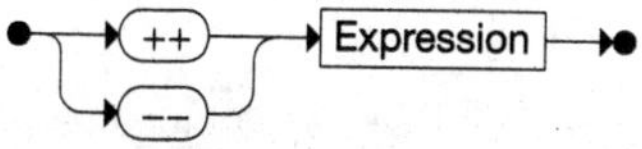

Postfix Expression

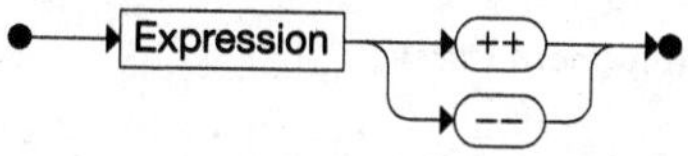

Literal

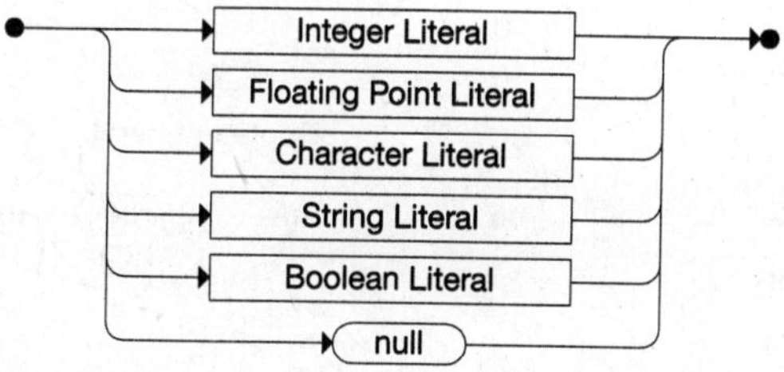

Integer Literal

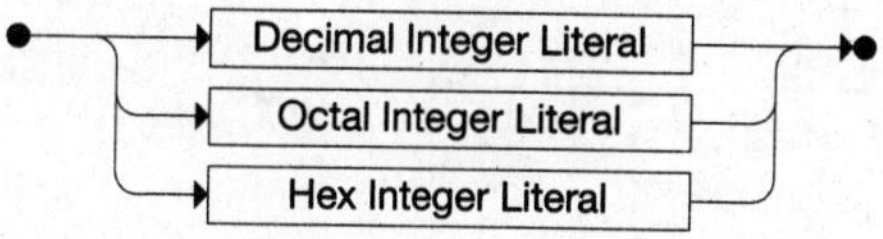

Decimal Integer Literal

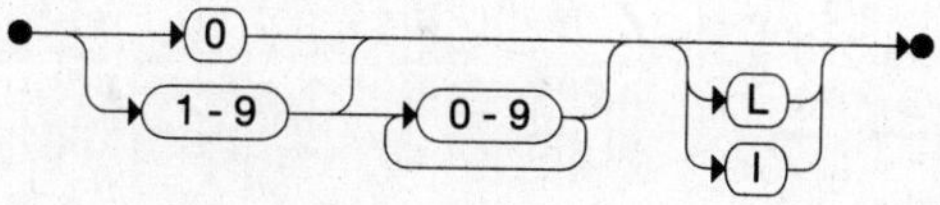

Octal Integer Literal

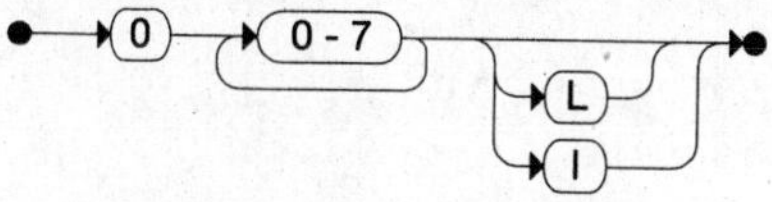

Hex Digit

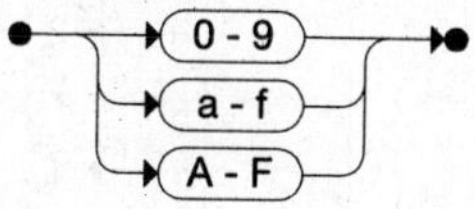

Hex Integer Literal

Floating Point Literal

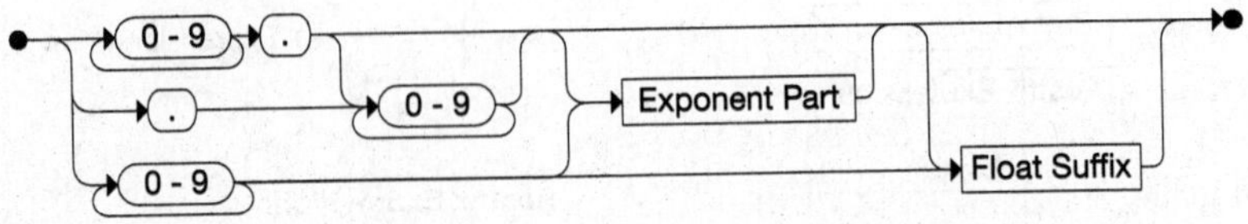

Exponent Part

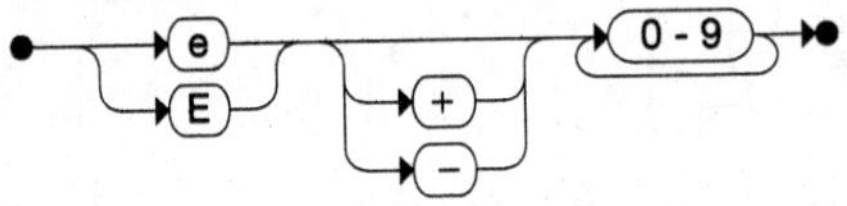

Float Suffix

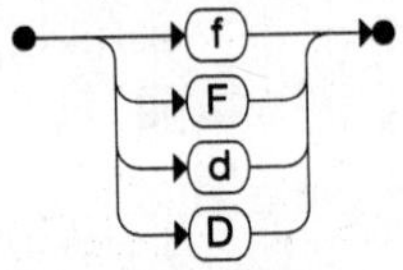

Character Literal

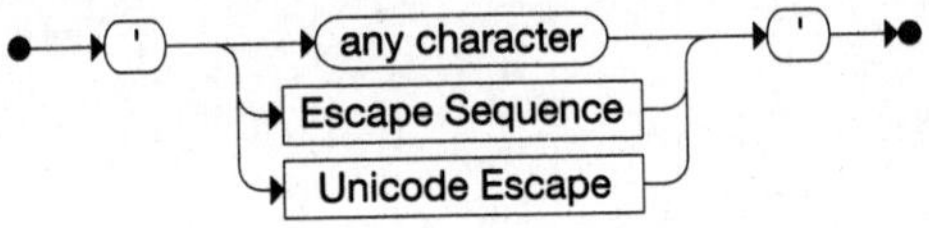

Boolean Literal

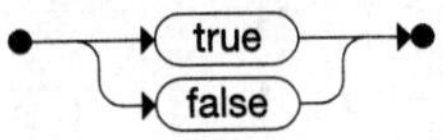

String Literal

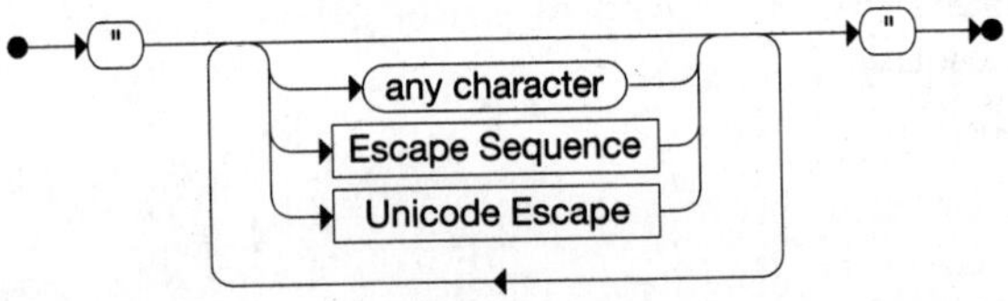

Escape Sequence

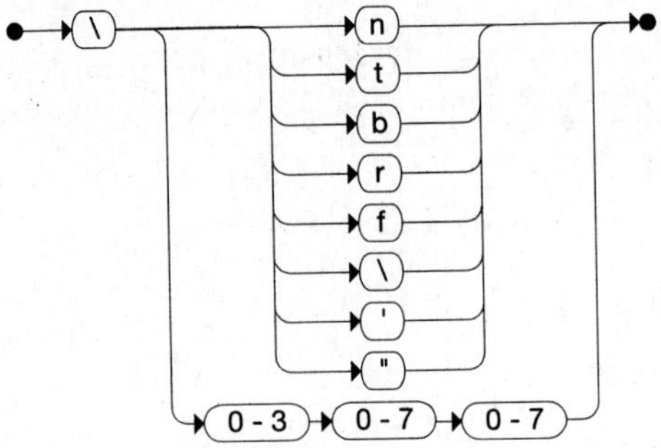

Identifier

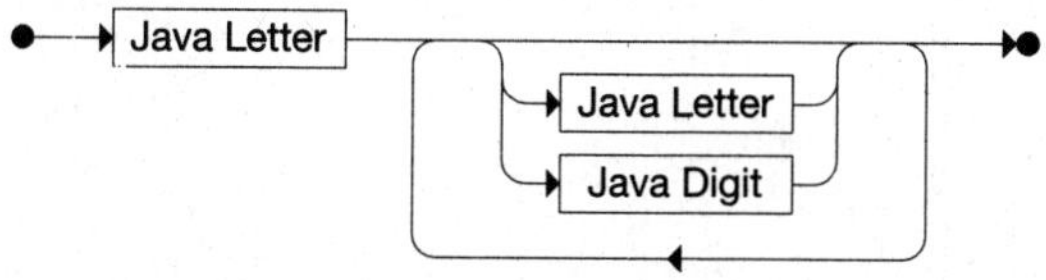

Java Letter

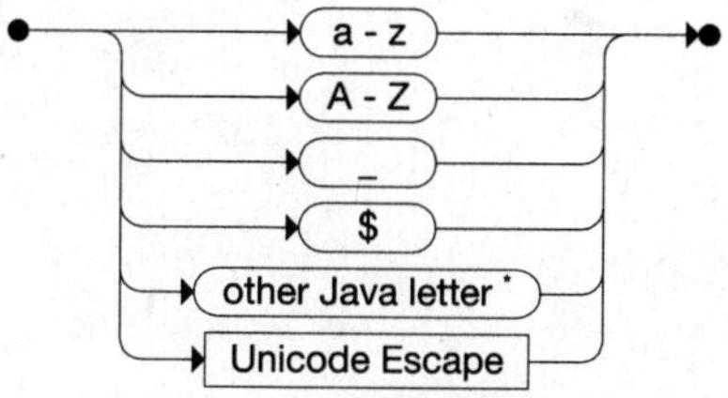

* The "other Java letter" category includes letters from many languages other than English.

Java Digit

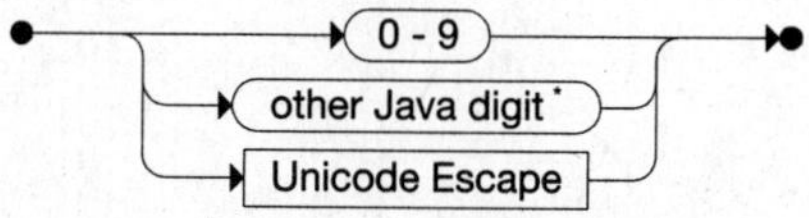

* The "other Java digit" category includes additional digits defined in Unicode.

Unicode Escape*

* In some contexts, the character represented by a Unicode Escape is restricted.

Answers to Self-Review Questions

L

Chapter 1 Introduction

1.1 Computer Processing

SR 1.1 The hardware of a computer system consists of its physical components such as a circuit board, monitor, or keyboard. Computer software consists of the programs that are executed by the hardware and the data that those programs use. Hardware is tangible, whereas software is intangible.

SR 1.2 The operating system provides a user interface and efficiently coordinates the use of resources such as main memory and the CPU.

SR 1.3 It takes 7,200,000 numbers for a three-minute song ($40{,}000 \times 60 \times 3$) and 144,000,000 numbers for one hour of music ($40{,}000 \times 60 \times 60$).

SR 1.4 The information is broken into pieces, and those pieces are represented as numbers.

SR 1.5 In general, N bits can represent 2^N unique items. Therefore:

a. 2 bits can represent 4 items because $2^2 = 4$.
b. 4 bits can represent 16 items because $2^4 = 16$.
c. 5 bits can represent 32 items because $2^5 = 32$.
d. 7 bits can represent 128 items because $2^7 = 128$.

SR 1.6 It would take 6 bits to represent each of the 50 states. Five bits is not enough because $2^5 = 32$ but six bits would be enough because $2^6 = 64$.

1.2 Hardware Components

SR 1.7 A kilobyte (KB) is $2^{10} = 1{,}024$ bytes, a megabyte (MB) is $2^{20} = 1{,}048{,}576$ bytes, and a gigabyte (GB) is $2^{30} = 1{,}073{,}741{,}824$ bytes. Therefore:

a. 3 KB = 3 * 1,024 bytes = 3,072 bytes = approximately 3 thousand bytes
b. 2 MB = 2 * 1,048,576 bytes = 2,097,152 bytes = approximately 2.1 million bytes
c. 4 GB = 4 * 1,073,741,824 bytes = 4,294,967,296 bytes = approximately 4.3 billion bytes

SR 1.8 There are eight bits in a byte. Therefore:

a. 8 bytes = 8 * 8 bits = 64 bits
b. 2 KB = 2 * 1,024 bytes = 2,048 bytes = 2,048 * 8 bits = 16,384 bits
c. 4 MB = 4 * 1,048,576 bytes = 4,194,304 bytes = 4,194,304 * 8 bits = 33,554,432 bits

SR 1.9 Under the stated conditions, one hour of music would require 288,000,000 bytes (40,000 × 60 × 60 × 2). Dividing this number by the number of bytes in a megabyte (1,048,576 bytes) gives approximately 275 MB. Note that a typical audio CD has a capacity of about 650 MB and can store about 70 minutes of music. This coincides with an actual sampling rate of 41,000 measurements per second, two bytes of storage space per measurement, and the need to store two streams of music to produce a stereo effect.

SR 1.10 The two primary hardware components are main memory and the CPU. Main memory holds the currently active programs and data. The CPU retrieves individual program instructions from main memory, one at a time, and executes them.

SR 1.11 A memory address is a number that uniquely identifies a particular memory location in which a value is stored.

SR 1.12 Main memory is volatile, which means the information that is stored in it will be lost if the power supply to the computer is turned off. Secondary memory devices are nonvolatile; therefore, the information that is stored on them is retained even if the power goes off.

SR 1.13 The word that best matches is

a. peripheral b. controller c. modem d. main or RAM
e. secondary or ROM f. RAM g. CPU

1.3 Networks

SR 1.14 A file server is a network computer that is dedicated to storing and providing programs and data that are needed by many network users.

SR 1.15 Counting the number of unique connections in Figure 1.16, there are 10 communication lines needed to fully connect a point-to-point network of five computers. Adding a sixth computer to the network will require that it be connected to the original five, bringing the total to 15 communication lines.

SR 1.16 Having computers on a network share a communication line is cost effective because it cuts down on the number of connections needed and it also makes it easier to add a new computer to the network. Sharing lines, however, can mean delays in communication if the network is busy.

SR 1.17 The word Internet comes from the word internetworking, a concept related to wide-area networks (WANs). An internetwork connects one network to another. The Internet is a WAN.

SR 1.18 TCP stands for *Transmission Control Protocol.* IP stands for *Internet Protocol.* A protocol is a set of rules that govern how two things communicate.

SR 1.19 Breaking down the parts of each URL:

a. `duke` is the name of a computer within the `csc` subdomain (the Department of Computing Sciences) of the `villanova.edu` domain, which represents Villanova University. The `edu` top-level domain indicates that it is an educational organization. This URL is requesting a file called `examples.html` from within a subdirectory called `jss`.

b. `java` is the name of a computer (Web server) at the `sun.com` domain, which represents Sun Microsystems, Inc. The `com` top-level domain indicates that it is a commercial business. This URL is requesting a file called `index.html` from within a subdirectory called `products`.

1.4 The Java Programming Language

SR 1.20 The Java programming language was developed in the early 1990s by James Gosling at Sun Microsystems. It was introduced to the public in 1995.

SR 1.21 The processing of a Java application begins with the `main` method.

SR 1.22 The characters "Hello" will be printed on the computer screen.

SR 1.23 The entire line of code is a comment, so there is no result.

SR 1.24 All of the identifiers shown are valid except `12345` (since an identifier cannot begin with a digit) and `black&white` (since an identifier cannot contain the character &). The identifiers `RESULT` and `result` are both valid, but should not be used together in a program because they differ only by case. The underscore character (as in `answer_7`) is a valid part of an identifier.

SR 1.25 Although any of the listed names *could* be used as the required identifier, the only "good" choice is `scoreSum`. The identifier `x` is not descriptive and is meaningless, the identifier `sumOfTheTestScoresOfTheStudents` is unnecessarily long, and the identifier `smTstScr` is unclear.

SR 1.26 White space is a term that refers to the spaces, tabs, and newline characters that separate words and symbols in a program. The compiler ignores extra white space; therefore, it doesn't affect execution. However, it is crucial to use white space appropriately to make a program readable to humans.

1.5 Program Development

SR 1.27 At the lowest level, a computer's instructions perform only simple tasks, such as copying a value or comparing two numbers. However, by putting together millions of these simple instructions every second, a computer can perform complex tasks.

SR 1.28 High-level languages allow a programmer to express a series of program instructions in English-like terms that are relatively easy to read and use. However, in order to execute, a program must be expressed in a particular computer's machine language, which consists of a series of bits that are basically unreadable by humans. A high-level language program must be translated into machine language before it can be run.

SR 1.29 Java bytecode is a low-level representation of a Java source code program. The Java compiler translates the source code into bytecode, which can then be executed using the Java interpreter. The bytecode might be transported across the Web before being executed by a Java interpreter that is part of a Web browser.

SR 1.30 The word that best matches is

a. machine b. assembly c. high-level d. high-level
e. compiler f. interpreter

SR 1.31 Syntax rules define how the symbols and words of a programming language can be put together. The semantics of a programming language instruction determine what will happen when that instruction is executed.

SR 1.32 a. Compile-time error b. Run-time error (you cannot divide by zero) c. Logical error

1.6 Object-Oriented Programming

SR 1.33 1. Understand the problem.
2. Design a solution.
3. Consider alternatives and refinements to the solution.
4. Implement the solution.
5. Test the solution.

SR 1.34 The first solution to a problem that we think of may not be a good one. By considering alternative solutions before expending too much energy implementing our first idea, we can often save overall time and effort.

SR 1.35 The primary elements that support object-oriented programming are objects, classes, encapsulation, and inheritance. An object is defined by a class, which contains methods that define the operations on those objects (the services that they perform). Objects are encapsulated such that they store and manage their own data. Inheritance is a reuse technique in which one class can be derived from another.

Chapter 2 Data and Expressions

2.1 Character Strings

SR 2.1 A string literal is a sequence of characters delimited by double quotes.

SR 2.2 Both the `print` and `println` methods of the `System.out` object write a string of characters to the monitor screen. The difference is that, after printing the characters, the `println` performs a carriage return so that whatever's printed next appears on the next line. The `print` method allows subsequent output to appear on the same line.

SR 2.3 A parameter is data that is passed into a method when it is invoked. The method usually uses that data to accomplish the service that it provides. For example, the parameter to the `println` method indicates what characters should be printed.

SR 2.4 The output produced by the code fragment is

```
One
Two Three
```

SR 2.5 The output produced by the code fragment is

```
Ready
Set

Go
```

SR 2.6 The output produced by the statement is

```
It is good to be 10
```

The + operator in the sub-expression `(5 + 5)` represents integer addition, since both of its operands are integers. If the inner parentheses are removed, the + operators represent string concatenation and the output produced is

```
It is good to be 55
```

SR 2.7 An escape sequence is a series of characters that begins with the backslash (\) and that implies that the following characters should be treated in some special way. Examples: `\n` represents the newline character, `\t` represents the tab character, and `\"` represents the quotation character (as opposed to using it to terminate a string).

SR 2.8

```
System.out.println("\"I made this letter longer than "
+ "usual because I lack the time to\nmake it short.\""
+ "\n\tBlaise Pascal");
```

2.2 Variables and Assignment

SR 2.9 A variable declaration establishes the name of a variable and the type of data that it can contain. A declaration may also have an optional initialization, which gives the variable an initial value.

SR 2.10 Given those variable declarations, the answers are:

a. Five variables are declared: `count`, `value`, `total`, `MAX_VALUE`, and `myValue`.
b. They are all of type `int`.
c. `count`, `MAX_VALUE`, and `myValue` are each given an initial value.
d. Yes, it is valid. `myValue` is a variable of type `int` and 100 is an `int` literal.
e. No, it is not valid. `MAX_VALUE` is declared as a `final` variable and therefore it cannot be assigned a value other than its initial value.

SR 2.11 The variable name you choose should reflect the purpose of the variable. For example:

```
int numCDs = 0;
```

SR 2.12 The variable name you choose should reflect the purpose of the variable. Since the number of feet in a mile will not change, it is a good idea to declare a constant. For example:

```
final int FT_PER_MILE = 5280;
```

SR 2.13 First, by carefully choosing the name of the constant, you can make your program more understandable than if you just use the literal value. Second, using a constant ensures that the literal value represented by the variable will not be inadvertently changed somewhere in the program. Third, if you ever do have to rewrite the program using a different literal value, you will only need to change that value once, as the initial value of the constant, rather than many places throughout the program.

2.3 Primitive Data Types

SR 2.14 Primitive data are basic values such as numbers or characters. Objects are more complex entities that usually contain primitive data that help define them.

SR 2.15 An integer variable can store only one value at a time. When a new value is assigned to it, the old one is overwritten and lost.

SR 2.16 The four integer data types in Java are `byte`, `short`, `int`, and `long`. They differ in how much memory space is allocated for each and therefore how large a number they can hold.

SR 2.17 Java automatically assigns an integer literal the data type `int`. If you append an L or an l on the end of an integer literal, for example `1234L`, Java will assign it the type `long`.

SR 2.18 Java automatically assigns a floating point literal the data type `double`. If you append an F or an f on the end of a floating point literal, for example `12.34f`, Java will assign it the type `float`.

SR 2.19 A character set is a list of characters in a particular order. A character set defines the valid characters that a particular type of computer or programming language will support. Java uses the Unicode character set.

SR 2.20 The original ASCII character set supports $2^7 = 128$ characters, the extended ASCII character set supports $2^8 = 256$ characters, and the UNICODE character set supports $2^{16} = 65{,}536$ characters.

2.4 Expressions

SR 2.21 The result of `19%5` in a Java expression is 4. The remainder operator `%` returns the remainder after dividing the second operand into the first. The remainder when dividing 19 by 5 is 4.

SR 2.22 The result of `13/4` in a Java expression is 3 (not 3.25). The result is an integer because both operands are integers. Therefore, the / operator performs integer division, and the fractional part of the result is truncated.

SR 2.23 After executing the statement, `diameter` holds the value 20. First, the current value of `diameter` (5) is multiplied by 4, and then the result is stored back in `diameter`.

SR 2.24 Operator precedence is the set of rules that dictates the order in which operators are evaluated in an expression.

SR 2.25 The evaluations of the expressions are

```
a. 15 + 7 * 3             = 15 + 21       = 36
b. (15 + 7) * 3           = 22 * 3        = 66
c. 3 * 6 + 10 / 5 + 5     = 18 + 2 + 5    = 25
d. 27 % 5 + 7 % 3         = 2 + 1         = 3
e. 100 / 2 / 2 / 2        = 50 / 2 / 2    = 25 / 2   = 12
f. 100 / ( 2 / 2) / 2     = 100 / 1 / 2   = 100 / 2  = 50
```

SR 2.26 Expression a is valid. Expression b is invalid because there are two open parentheses but only one close parenthesis. Similarly with expression c, where there are two open parentheses but no close parenthesis. Expression d might be a valid algebraic expression in an algebra book, but it is not a valid expression in Java. There is no operator between the operands 2 and (4).

SR 2.27 After the sequence of statements, the value in `result` is 8.

SR 2.28 After the sequence of statements, the value in `result` is 8. Note that even though `result` was set to `base + 3`, changing the value of `base` to 7 does not retroactively change the value of `result`.

SR 2.29 An assignment operator combines an operation with assignment. For example, the += operator performs an addition, then stores the value back into the variable on the left-hand side.

SR 2.30 After executing the statement, `weight` holds the value 83. The assignment operator -= modifies `weight` by first subtracting 17 from the current value (100), then storing the result back into `weight`.

2.5 Data Conversion

SR 2.31 A widening conversion tends to go from a small data value, in terms of the amount of space used to store it, to a larger one. A narrowing conversion does the opposite. Information is more likely to be lost in a narrowing conversion, which is why narrowing conversions are considered to be less safe than widening ones.

SR 2.32 The conversions are: a. widening, b. narrowing, c. widening, d. widening, e. widening.

SR 2.33 During the execution of the statement, the `value` stored in value is read and transformed into a `float` as it is being copied into the memory location represented by `result`. But the `value` variable itself is not changed, so `value` will remain an `int` variable after the assignment statement.

SR 2.34 During the execution of the statement, the value stored in `result` is read and then transformed into an `int` as it is being copied into the memory location represented by `value`. But the `result` variable itself is not changed, so it remains equal to 27.32, whereas `value` becomes 27.

SR 2.35 The results stored are

a. 3 integer division is used since both operands are integers.
b. 3.0 integer division is used since both operands are integers, but then assignment conversion converts the result of 3 to 3.0.
c. 2.4 floating point division is used since one of the operands is a floating point.
d. 3.4 `num1` is first cast as a `double`; therefore, floating point division is used since one of the operands is a floating point.
e. 2 `val1` is first cast as an `int`; therefore, integer division is used since both operands are integers.

2.6 Interactive Programs

SR 2.36 The corresponding lines of the `GasMileage` program are

a. `import java.util.Scanner;`
b. `Scanner scan = new Scanner(System.in);`
c. `Scanner scan = new Scanner(System.in);`
d. `miles = scan.nextInt();`

SR 2.37 Under the stated assumptions, the following code will ask users to enter their age and store their response in value.

```
System.out.print("Enter your age in years: ");
value = myScanner.nextInt();
```

Chapter 3 Using Classes and Objects

3.1 Creating Objects

SR 3.1 A null reference is a reference that does not refer to any object. The reserved word `null` can be used to check for null references before following them.

SR 3.2 The `new` operator creates a new instance (an object) of the specified class. The constructor of the class is then invoked to help set up the newly created object.

SR 3.3 The following declaration creates a String variable called `author` and initializes it:

```
String author = new String("Fred Brooks");
```

For strings, this declaration could have been abbreviated as follows:

```
String author = "Fred Brooks";
```

This object reference variable and its value can be depicted as follows:

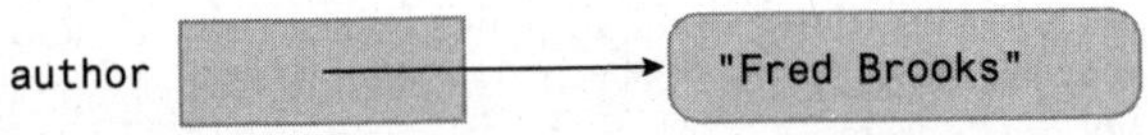

SR 3.4 To set an integer variable `size` to the length of a `String` object called `name`, you code:

```
size = name.length();
```

SR 3.5 Two references are aliases of each other if they refer to the same object. Changing the state of the object through one reference changes it for the other because there is actually only one object. An object is marked for garbage collection only when there are no valid references to it.

3.2 The `String` Class

SR 3.6 Strings are immutable. The only way to change the value of a `String` variable is to reassign it a new object. Therefore, the variables changed by the statements are: a. none, b. `s1`, c. none, d. `s3`.

SR 3.7 The output produced is:

```
o
Found
11
5
```

SR 3.8 The following statement prints the value of a `String` object in all uppercase letters:

```
System.out.println(title.toUpperCase());
```

SR 3.9 The following declaration creates a `String` object and sets it equal to the first 10 characters of the `String` description;

```
String front = description.substring(0, 10);
```

3.3 Packages

SR 3.10 A Java package is a collection of related classes. The Java standard class library is a group of packages that support common programming tasks.

SR 3.11 Each package contains a set of classes that support particular programming activities. The classes in the `java.net` package support network communication and the classes in the `javafx.scene.shape` package represent shapes such as circles and rectangles.

SR 3.12 The `Scanner` class and the `Random` class are part of the `java.util` package. The `String` and `Math` classes are part of the `java.lang` package.

SR 3.13 The `Point` class, according to the online Java API documentation, represents a location with coordinates (x, y) in two-dimensional space.

SR 3.14 An `import` statement establishes the fact that a program uses a particular class, specifying what package that class is a part of. This allows the programmer to use the class name (such as `Random`) without having to fully qualify the reference (such as `java.util.Random`) every time.

SR 3.15 The `String` class is part of the `java.lang` package, which is automatically imported into any Java program. Therefore, no separate import declaration is needed.

3.4 The Random Class

SR 3.16 A call to the `nextInt` method of a `Random` object returns a random integer in the range of all possible `int` values, both positive and negative.

SR 3.17 Passing a positive integer parameter x to the `nextInt` method of a `Random` object returns a random number in the range of 0 to $x-1$. So a call to `nextInt(20)` will return a random number in the range 0 to 19, inclusive.

SR 3.18 The ranges of the expressions are:

a. From 0 to 49 b. From 10 to 14 c. From 5 to 14
e. From –25 to 24

SR 3.19 The expressions to generate the given ranges are:

```
a. generator.nextInt(31);         // range is 0 to 30
b. generator.nextInt(10) + 10;    // range is 10 to 19
c. generator.nextInt(11) - 5;     // range is -5 to 5
```

3.5 The Math Class

SR 3.20 A class or static method can be invoked through the name of the class that contains it, such as `Math.abs`. If a method is not static, it can be executed only through an instance (an object) of the class.

SR 3.21 The values of the expressions are:

a. 20 b. 16.0 c. 16.0 d. 243.0 e. 125.0 f. 4.0

SR 3.22 The following statement prints the sine of an angle measuring 1.23 radians:

```
System.out.println(Math.sin(1.23));
```

SR 3.23 The following declaration creates a `double` variable and initializes it to 5 raised to the power 2.5:

```
double result = Math.pow(5, 2.5);
```

SR 3.24 Examples of methods that are not listed in Figure 3.5 include:

```
static int min(int a, int b)
static float max(long a, long b)
static long round(double a)
```

3.6 Formatting Output

SR 3.25 To obtain a `NumberFormat` object for use within a program, you request an object using one of the static methods provided by the `NumberFormat` class. The method you invoke depends upon your intended use of the object. For example, if you intend to use it for formatting percentages, you might code:

```
NumberFormat fmt = NumberFormat.getPercentInstance();
```

SR 3.26 a. The statement is:

```
NumberFormat moneyFormat = NumberFormat.getCurrencyInstance();
```

Do not forget, you also must import `java.text.NumberFormat` into your program.

b. The statement is:

```
System.out.println(moneyFormat.format(cost));
```

c. If the locale is the United States, the output will be `$54.89`. If the locale is the United Kingdom, the output will be `£54.89`.

SR 3.27 To output a floating point value as a percentage, you first obtain a `NumberFormat` object using a call to the static method `getPercentageInstance` of the `NumberFormat` class. Then, you pass the value to be formatted to the `format` method of the formatter object, which returns a properly formatted string. For example:

```
NumberFormat fmt = NumberFormat.getPercentageInstance();
System.out.println(fmt.format(value));
```

SR 3.28 The following code will prompt for and read in a `double` value from the user and then print the result of taking the square root of the absolute value of the input value to two decimal places:

```
Scanner scan = new Scanner(System.in);
DecimalFormat fmt = new DecimalFormat("0.00");
double value, result;
System.out.print("Enter a double value: ");
value = scan.nextDouble();
result = Math.sqrt(Math.abs(value));
System.out.println(fmt.format(result));
```

3.7 Enumerated Types

SR 3.29 The following is a declaration of an enumerated type for movie ratings:

```
enum Ratings {G, PG, PG13, R, NC17}
```

SR 3.30 Under the listed assumptions, the output is:

```
clubs
hearts
0
2
```

SR 3.31 By using an enumerated type, you guarantee that variables of that type will only take on the enumerated values.

3.8 Wrapper Classes

SR 3.32 A wrapper class is defined in the Java standard class library for each primitive type. In situations where objects are called for, an object created from a wrapper class may suffice.

SR 3.33 The corresponding wrapper classes are `Byte`, `Integer`, `Double`, `Character`, and `Boolean`.

SR 3.34 One approach is to use the constructor of `Integer`, as follows:

```
holdNumber = new Integer(number);
```

Another approach is to take advantage of autoboxing, as follows:

```
holdNumber = number;
```

SR 3.35 The following statement uses the `MAX_VALUE` constant of the `Integer` class to print the largest possible `int` value:

```
System.out.println(Integer.MAX_VALUE);
```

3.9 Introduction to JavaFX

SR 3.36 If the IDE you're using will automatically launch a JavaFX application, no `main` method is needed. Otherwise, a one-line `main` method calling the `launch` method is required.

SR 3.37 A JavaFX stage is a window in which a scene is displayed. The primary stage of a JavaFX application is automatically created and passed into the `start` method.

SR 3.38 The root node of a scene contains all nodes displayed in the scene.

SR 3.39 The point (20, 50) is 20 pixels from the left edge of the scene and 50 pixels down from the top edge of the scene. All visible pixels in the Java coordinate system have positive coordinate values.

3.10 Basic Shapes

SR 3.40 Shapes are drawn in the order they are added to a container such as a group or pane. So, to make one shape appear in front of another, it should be added after it.

SR 3.41 The following declarations create a `Rectangle` that is 100 pixels wide, 200 pixels high, with its upper-left corner positioned at point (30, 20):

```
Rectangle myRect = new Rectangle(30, 20, 100, 200);
```

SR 3.42 The last two parameters to the `Ellipse` constructor specify the horizontal radius and the vertical radius, respectively. So that ellipse is taller than it is wide.

SR 3.43 If the value `null` is passed to the `setFill` method of a `Circle` object, its fill color will be fully transparent. Any shapes behind the circle will be visible through the circle.

SR 3.44 By grouping a set of nodes in a scene, you can apply transformations such as rotations and position shifts (translation) to the entire group at once.

3.11 Representing Colors

SR 3.45 An RGB value is a set of three integer values that represent a color by specifying the relative contributions of the colors red, green, and blue.

SR 3.46 The following statement creates a `Color` object equivalent to `Color.PINK`:

```
Color myPink = Color.rgb(255, 165, 0);
```

SR 3.47 The following statement creates a `Color` object equivalent to `Color.YELLOW`, which is defined by a full contribution of red and green, and no contribution of blue:

```
Color myYellow = Color.color(1.0, 1.0, 0.0);
```

Chapter 4 Writing Classes

4.1 Classes and Objects Revisited

SR 4.1 An attribute is a data value stored in an object and defines a particular characteristic of that object. For example, one attribute of a `Student` object might be that student's current grade point average. Collectively, the values of an object's attributes determine that object's current state.

SR 4.2 An operation is a function that can be done to or done by an object. For example, one operation of a `Student` object might be to compute that student's current grade point average. Collectively, an object's operations are referred to as the object's behaviors.

SR 4.3 Some attributes and operations that might be defined for a class called `Book` that represents a book in a library are:

Attributes	Operations
`idNumber`	`checkOut`
`onShelfStatus`	`checkIn`
`readingLevel`	`isAvailable`
`dueDate`	`placeOnHold`
	`setStatus`

SR 4.4 The answers are:

a. False—Identifying classes to help us solve a problem is a key step in object-oriented programming. In addition to identifying classes that already exist, we also identify, design, and implement new classes, as needed.
b. True—We call such operations mutators.
c. True—The result of many operations depends on the current state of the object on which they are operating.
d. False—In Java, the state of an object is represented by its instance data.

4.2 Anatomy of a Class

SR 4.5 A class is the blueprint of an object. It defines the variables and methods that will be a part of every object that is instantiated from it. But a class reserves no memory space for variables. Each object has its own data space and, therefore, its own state.

SR 4.6 The instance data of the `Die` class are `MAX`, an integer constant equal to 6 that represents the number of faces on the die and therefore the maximum value of the die, and `faceValue`, an integer variable that represents the current "up" or face value of the die.

SR 4.7 The methods defined for the `Die` class that can change the state of a `Die` object are `roll` and `setFaceValue`.

SR 4.8 When you pass an object to a `print` or `println` method, the `toString` method of the object is called automatically to obtain a string description of the object. If no `toString` method is defined for the object, then a default string is used. Therefore, it is usually a good idea to define a `toString` method when defining classes.

SR 4.9 The scope of a variable is the area within a program in which the variable can be referenced. An instance variable, declared at the class level, can be referenced in any method of the class. Local variables, including the formal parameters, declared within a particular method, can be referenced only in that method.

SR 4.10 A UML diagram helps us visualize the entities (classes and objects) in a program as well as the relationships among them. UML diagrams are tools that help us capture the design of a program prior to writing it.

4.3 Encapsulation

SR 4.11 A self-governing object is one that controls the values of its own data. Encapsulated objects, which don't allow an external client to reach in and change its data, are self-governing.

SR 4.12 An object's interface is the set of public operations (methods) defined on it. That is, the interface establishes the set of services the object will perform for the rest of the system.

SR 4.13 A modifier is a Java reserved word that can be used in the definition of a variable or method and that specifically defines certain characteristics of its use. For example, by declaring a variable with private visibility, the variable cannot be directly accessed outside of the object in which it is defined.

SR 4.14 A constant can be declared with public visibility because that would not violate encapsulation. Since the value of a constant cannot be changed, it is not generally a problem for another object to access it directly.

SR 4.15 The modifiers affect the methods and variables in the following ways:

a. A public method is called a service method for an object because it defines a service that the object provides.
b. A private method is called a support method because it cannot be invoked from outside the object and is used to support the activities of other methods in the class.
c. A public variable is a variable that can be directly accessed and modified by a client. This explicitly violates the principle of encapsulation and therefore should be avoided.
d. A private variable is a variable that can be accessed and modified only from within the class. Variables almost always are declared with private visibility.

4.4 Anatomy of a Method

SR 4.16 Although a method is defined in a class, it is invoked through a particular object to indicate which object of that class is being affected. For example, the `Student` class may define the operation that computes the grade point average (GPA) of a student, but the operation is invoked through a particular `Student` object to compute the GPA for that student. The exception to this rule is the invocation of a static method (see Chapter 3), which is executed through the class name and does not affect any particular object.

SR 4.17 An invoked method may return a value, which means it computes a value and provides that value to the calling method. The calling method usually uses the invocation and thus its return value, as part of a larger expression.

SR 4.18 An explicit `return` statement is used to specify the value that is returned from a method. The type of the return value must match the return type specified in the method definition.

SR 4.19 A `return` statement is required in methods that have a return type other than void. A method that does not return a value could use a `return` statement without an expression, but it is not necessary.

SR 4.20 An actual parameter is a value sent to a method when it is invoked. A formal parameter is the corresponding variable in the header of the method declaration; it takes on the value of the actual parameter so that it can be used inside the method.

SR 4.21 The following code implements the requested `getFaceDown` method:

```
//-----------------------------------------------------------------
// Face down value accessor.
//-----------------------------------------------------------------
public int getFaceDown()
{
   return (MAX + 1) - faceValue;
}
```

SR 4.22 In the `Transactions` program

a. Three `Account` objects are created.
b. Two arguments (actual parameters) are passed to the `withdraw` method when it is invoked on the `acct2` object.
c. No arguments (actual parameters) are passed to the `addInterest` method when it is invoked on the `acct3` object.

SR 4.23 The method `getBalance` is a classic accessor method. One can also classify the `toString` method as an accessor, since it returns information about the object. The `deposit`, `withdraw`, and `addInterest` methods all provide both mutator and accessor capabilities, because they can be used to change the account balance and also return the value of the balance after the change is made. All of the methods mentioned above are service methods—they all have public visibility and provide a service to the client.

4.5 Constructors Revisited

SR 4.24 Constructors are special methods in an object that are used to initialize the object when it is instantiated.

SR 4.25 A constructor has the same name as its class, and it does not return a value.

4.6 Arcs

SR 4.26 An arc is defined as a portion of an ellipse using a start angle (where the arc begins) and a length angle (how long the arc is along the ellipse edge).

SR 4.27 `ArcType.ROUND` specifies an arc that includes the portion between the rounded ellipse edge and the center point of the ellipse, forming a "pie" shape. `ArcType.OPEN` specifies an arc that is only made up of the curve along the ellipse edge.

SR 4.28 A start angle of 180 degrees and an arc length of 180 degrees specify the entire bottom half of the underlying ellipse. The same arc could be defined using a start angle of 0 degree and an arc length of –180 degrees.

4.7 Images

SR 4.29 An `Image` object represents the image itself. An `ImageView` object is a JavaFX node that allows an `Image` to be displayed.

SR 4.30 A layout pane is a JavaFX node that organizes the visual presentation of its contents according to particular rules.

SR 4.31 Style properties for JavaFX nodes can be set using a call to the `setStyle` method, passing in a string that contains property name/value pairs in Cascading Style Sheet (CSS) notation.

4.8 Graphical User Interfaces

SR 4.32 A GUI control generates an event, typically when the user interacts with the control. A programmer sets up an event handler to execute certain code when an event occurs.

SR 4.33 A `Button` object generates an action event when the user pushes it.

SR 4.34 A JavaFX event handler can be defined using (1) a method reference, which specifies which method will be invoked when the event occurs, (2) a full class that implements the appropriate event handler interface, or (3) a lambda expression that defines the code to be executed right in the call to set the event handler. These are all notational variations of the same approach.

SR 4.35 A `FlowPane` is a layout pane that organizes its nodes into a row or column that wraps when it reaches a pane boundary.

4.9 Text Fields

SR 4.36 When the user presses Return while the cursor is in a text field, the text field generates an action event (which may be processed by an event handler).

SR 4.37 The rows and columns of a `GridPane` are numbered starting at 0. So, the upper left cell in a `GridPane` is at column 0 and row 0. Likewise, the cell that is three over and two down from the upper left corner is at column 2 and row 1.

Chapter 5 Conditionals and Loops

5.1 Boolean Expressions

SR 5.1 The flow of control through a program determines the program statements that will be executed on a given run of the program.

SR 5.2 Each conditional and loop is based on a boolean condition that evaluates to either true or false.

SR 5.3 The equality operators are equal (==) and not equal (`!=`). The relational operators are less than (<), less than or equal to (<=), greater than (>), and greater than or equal to (>=). The logical operators are not (`!`), and (&&), and or (`||`).

SR 5.4 Assuming the given declarations, the values are: a. true, b. true, c. false, d. true, e. true, f. true, g. true, h. false, i. true, j. true

SR 5.5 A truth table is a table that shows all possible results of a boolean expression, given all possible combinations of variables and conditions.

SR 5.6 The truth table is:

`value > 0`	`done`	`!done`	`(value > 0) || !done`
`true`	`true`	`false`	`true`
`true`	`false`	`true`	`true`
`false`	`true`	`false`	`false`
`false`	`false`	`true`	`true`

SR 5.7 The truth table is:

c1	c2	!c1	!c2	c1 && !c2	!c1 && c2	c1 && !c2 || !c1 && c2
true	true	false	false	false	false	false
true	false	false	true	true	false	true
false	true	true	false	false	true	true
false	false	true	true	false	false	false

5.2 The `if` Statement

SR 5.8 Based on the given assumptions, the output would be:

a. `red white yellow`
b. `blue yellow`
c. `blue yellow`

SR 5.9 A block statement groups several statements together. We use them to define the body of an `if` statement or loop when we want to do multiple things based on the boolean condition.

SR 5.10 A nested `if` occurs when the statement inside an `if` or `else` clause is an `if` statement. A nested `if` lets the programmer make a series of decisions. Similarly, a nested loop is a loop within a loop.

SR 5.11 Based on the given assumptions, the output would be:

a. `red orange white yellow`
b. `black blue green`
c. `yellow green`

SR 5.12

```
if (temperature <= 50)
{
    System.out.println("It is cool.");
    System.out.println("Dress warmly.");
}
else
    if (temperature > 80)
    {
        System.out.println("It is warm.");
        System.out.println("Dress cooly.");
    }
    else
```

```
{
    System.out.println("It is pleasant.");
    System.out.println("Dress pleasantly.");
}
```

5.3 Comparing Data

SR 5.13 Because they are stored internally as binary numbers, comparing floating point values for exact equality will be true only if they are the same bit-by-bit. It's better to use a reasonable tolerance value and consider the difference between the two values.

SR 5.14 We compare strings for equality using the `equals` method of the `String` class, which returns a boolean result. The `compareTo` method of the `String` class can also be used to compare strings. It returns a positive, 0, or negative integer result depending on the relationship between the two strings.

SR 5.15
```
//-----------------------------------------------------------------
// Returns true if this Die equals die, otherwise
// returns false.
//-----------------------------------------------------------------
public boolean equals(Die die)
{
    return (this.faceValue == die.faceValue);
}
```

SR 5.16
```
if (s1.compareTo(s2) < 0)
    System.out.println(s1 + "\n" + s2);
else
    System.out.println(s2 + "\n" + s1);
```

5.4 The `while` Statement

SR 5.17 An infinite loop is a repetition statement that never terminates. Specifically, the body of the loop never causes the condition to become false.

SR 5.18 The output is the integers 0 through 9, printed one integer per line.

SR 5.19 The loop is not entered, so there is no output.

SR 5.20 Since the value of `high` always remains larger than the value of `low`, the code loops continuously, producing many lines of zeros, until the program is terminated.

SR 5.21 The output is:

```
0 1 2 3 4 5 6 7 8 9 10
1 2 3 4 5 6 7 8 9 10
2 3 4 5 6 7 8 9 10
3 4 5 6 7 8 9 10
4 5 6 7 8 9 10
5 6 7 8 9 10
6 7 8 9 10
7 8 9 10
8 9 10
9 10
10
```

SR 5.22

```
int count = 1;
System.out.print("divisors of " + value + ":");
while (count <= value)
{
    if ((value % count) == 0)
        System.out.print(" " + count);
    count++;
}
```

SR 5.23

```
int count1 = 1, count2;
while (count1 <= value)
{
    System.out.print("divisors of " + count1 + ":");
    count2 = 1;
    while (count2 <= count1)
    {
        if ((count1 % count2) == 0)
            System.out.print(" " + count2);
        count2++;
    }
    System.out.println();
    count1++;
}
```

5.5 Iterators

SR 5.24 a. `Scanner user = new Scanner(System.in);`
b. `Scanner infoFileScan = new Scanner(new File("info.dat"));`
c. `Scanner infoStringScan = new Scanner(infoString);`

SR 5.25 The following code prints out the average number of characters per line:

```
int numChars = 0;
int numLines = 0;
String holdLine;

// Read and process each line of the file
while (fileScan.hasNext())
{
   numLines++;
   holdLine = fileScan.nextLine();
   numChars += holdLine.length();
}
System.out.println ((double)numChars/numLines);
```

5.6 The ArrayList Class

SR 5.26 An `ArrayList` stores and manages multiple objects at one time. It allows you to access the objects by a numeric index and keeps the indexes of its objects continuous as they are added and removed. An `ArrayList` dynamically increases its capacity as needed.

SR 5.27 An `ArrayList` generally holds references to the `Object` class, which means that it can hold any type of object at all (this is discussed further in Chapter 8). A specific type of element can and should be specified in the `ArrayList` declaration to restrict the type of objects that can be added and eliminate the need to cast the type when extracted.

SR 5.28 `ArrayList<Die> dice = new ArrayList<Die>();`

SR 5.29 `[Andy, Don, Betty]`

5.7 Determining Event Sources

SR 5.30 To set up an event handler that will process events from multiple sources, you call the appropriate convenience method (such as `setOnAction`) for each source, specifying the same event handler method. Then, when any of the sources generate the event, the common event handler method is called.

SR 5.31 Calling the `getSource` method on event object that is passed to the event handler method returns the control that generated the event.

5.8 Managing Fonts

SR 5.32 If you only need to specify a font family and font size, a `Font` object can be created with the `new` operator:

```
Font myFont = new Font("Courier", 24);
```

If you want to specify the font weight and/or font posture, you can use the static `font` method:

```
Font yourFont = Font.font("Arial", FontWeight.BOLD,
    FontPosture.ITALIC, 18);
```

SR 5.33 A `Font` object represents the font family, the font size, the font weight (how bold it is), and the font posture (whether it is shown in italic or not).

SR 5.34 In addition to the characteristics of the `Font` used, the appearance of text is affected by its fill and stroke color, as well as whether the text is underlined or shown with the "strike through" effect.

5.9 Check Boxes

SR 5.35 (a) and (d) could be reasonably determined using check boxes, since they involve a combination of multiple items. (b) could also be done with (a single) check box, because it's a boolean option. However, (c) and (e) are not appropriate for check boxes, since only one of them should be checked at a time.

SR 5.36 You can call the `isSelected` method of a check box, which returns a boolean result, to determine if it is currently checked.

SR 5.37 An `HBox` arranges its nodes into a single horizontal row, and a `VBox` arranges its nodes into a single vertical column.

5.10 Radio Buttons

SR 5.38 Since radio buttons provide mutually exclusive options, they would not be appropriate for (a) or (d), which must allow multiple selections. A single radio button could be used for (b), but a check box would probably be a better choice. Radio buttons would serve well for (c) or (e), which require a single answer from several choices.

SR 5.39 The primary difference between check boxes and radio buttons is that check boxes work together as a group to provide a set of mutually exclusive options. Check boxes work independently.

SR 5.40 To specify a set of mutually exclusive radio buttons, you call the `setToggleGroup` method of each button in the set, passing in the same `ToggleGroup` object.

Chapter 6 More Conditionals and Loops

6.1 The `switch` Statement

SR 6.1 When a Java program is running, if the expression evaluated for a `switch` statement does not match any of the case values associated with the statement, execution continues with the `default` case. If no `default` case exists, processing continues with the statement following the `switch` statement.

SR 6.2 If a case does not end with a `break` statement, processing continues into the statements of the next case. We usually want to use `break` statements in order to jump to the end of the `switch`.

SR 6.3 If the user enters 72, the output is: `That grade is average.` If the user enters 46, the output is: `That grade is not passing.` If the user enters 123, the output is: `That grade is not passing.`

SR 6.4 An equivalent `switch` statement is:

```
switch (num1)
{
    case 5:
        myChar = 'W';
        break;
    case 6:
        myChar = 'X';
        break;
    case 7:
        myChar = 'Y';
        break;
    default:
        myChar = 'Z';
}
```

6.2 The Conditional Operator

SR 6.5 The conditional operator is a trinary operator that evaluates a condition and produces one of two possible results. A conditional statement, such as the `if` and `switch` statements, is a category of statements that allow conditions to be evaluated and the appropriate statements executed as a result.

SR 6.6 `char id = (first) ? 'A': 'B';`

SR 6.7
```
System.out.println("The value is " + ((val <= 10) ? "not " : "")
+ "greater than 10.");
```

6.3 The do Statement

SR 6.8 A `while` loop evaluates the condition first. If it is true, it executes the loop body. The `do` loop executes the body first and then evaluates the condition. Therefore, the body of a `while` loop is executed zero or more times, and the body of a `do` loop is executed one or more times.

SR 6.9 The output is the integers 0 through 9, printed one integer per line.

SR 6.10 The code contains an infinite loop. The numbers 10, 11, 12, and so on will be printed until the program is terminated or until the number gets too large to be held by the `int` variable `low`.

SR 6.11

```
Scanner scan = new Scanner(System.in);
int num, sum = 0;
do
{
    System.out.print("enter next number (0 to quit) > ");
    num = scan.nextInt();
    sum += num;
} while (num != 0);
System.out.println(sum);
```

6.4 The for Statement

SR 6.12 A `for` loop is usually used when we know, or can calculate, how many times we want to iterate through the loop body. A `while` loop handles a more generic situation.

SR 6.13 The output is: `100`

SR 6.14 The output is: `60`

SR 6.15 The output is:

```
     *
    ***
   *****
  *******
 *********
***********
```

SR 6.16

```
final int NUMROLLS = 100;
int sum = 0;
for (int i = 1; i <= NUMROLLS; i++)
{
    sum += die.roll();
}
System.out.println((double)sum/NUMROLLS);
```

6.5 Using Loops and Conditionals with Graphics

SR 6.17 To modify the `Bullseye` program so that it has a 10-ring target, you'd need to change the `for` loop header to iterate 10 times, and you'd need to decrease the amount that the radius was reduced for each circle (say, from 20 to 16).

SR 6.18 To modify the `Boxes` program so that boxes that are neither narrow nor short are filled with white, you only need to change the default value of the variable `fill`. Instead of setting `fill` to `null` before the `if` statement, you'd set it to `Color.WHITE`.

6.6 Graphic Transformations

SR 6.19 To shift the position of a `Circle` named `ring` 100 pixels lower:

```
ring.setTranslateY(100);
```

SR 6.20 To display an `ImageView` named `view` at twice its original size:

```
view.setScaleX(2.0);
view.setScaleY(2.0);
```

SR 6.21 If you scale a node by a different factor along the x and y axes, the appearance of the node will be distorted. For example, if you scale an `ImageView` by 2.0 on the x-axis and 0.5 on the y-axis, the image will be twice as wide and half as tall.

SR 6.22 To rotate an `Ellipse` named `oval` 40 degrees clockwise:

```
oval.setRotate(20);
```

To rotate it 10 degrees counterclockwise:

```
oval.setRotate(-10);
```

Chapter 7 Object-Oriented Design

7.1 Software Development Activities

SR 7.1 The four basic activities in software development are requirements analysis (deciding what the program should do), design (deciding how to do it), implementation (writing the solution in source code), and testing (validating the implementation).

SR 7.2 Typically, the client provides an initial set of requirements or a description of a problem they would like to have solved. It is the responsibility of the software developer to work with the client to make sure the requirements or problem statement is correct and unambiguous.

SR 7.3 Software development is a problem-solving activity. Therefore, it is not surprising that the four basic development activities presented in this section are essentially the same as the five general problem-solving steps presented in Section 1.6. "Establishing the requirements" directly corresponds to "understanding the problem." "Designing a solution" and "considering alternative designs" taken together correspond to "creating a design"—in the case of software, the design is the solution. Finally, in both approaches we include "implementation" and "testing" stages.

7.2 Identifying Classes and Objects

SR 7.4 Identifying the nouns in a problem specification can help you identify potential classes to use when developing an object-oriented solution to a problem. The nouns in the specification often correspond to objects that should be represented in the solution.

SR 7.5 It is not crucial to identify and define all the methods that a class will contain during the early stages of problem solution design. It is often sufficient to just identify those methods that provide the primary responsibilities of the class. Additional methods can be added to a class as needed, when you evolve and add detail to your design.

7.3 Static Class Members

SR 7.6 Memory space for an instance variable is created for each object that is instantiated from a class. A static variable is shared among all objects of a class.

SR 7.7 Assuming you decide to use the identifier `totalBalance`, the declaration is:

```
private static int totalBalance = 0;
```

SR 7.8 Assuming that the minimum required is 100 and you decide to use the identifier `MIN_BALANCE`, the declaration is:

```
public static final int MIN_BALANCE = 100;
```

SR 7.9 The `main` method of any program is static, and can refer only to static or local variables. Therefore, a `main` method could not refer to instance variables declared at the class level.

7.4 Class Relationships

SR 7.10 A dependency relationship between two classes occurs when one class relies on the functionality of the other. It is often referred to as a "uses" relationship.

SR 7.11 A method executed through an object might take as a parameter another object created from the same class. For example, the `concat` method of the `String` class is executed through one `String` object and takes another `String` object as a parameter.

SR 7.12 An aggregate object is an object that has other objects as instance data. That is, an aggregate object is one that is made up of other objects.

SR 7.13 The `this` reference always refers to the currently executing object. A non-static method of a class is written generically for all objects of the class, but it is invoked through a particular object. The `this` reference, therefore, refers to the object through which that method is currently being executed.

7.5 Interfaces

SR 7.14 A class can be instantiated; an interface cannot. An interface contains a set of abstract methods for which a class provides the implementation.

SR 7.15

```
public interface Nameable
{
   public void setName(String name);
   public String getName();
}
```

SR 7.16 a. False—An interface can also include constants.
b. True—There is no body of code defined for an abstract method.
c. True—An interface is a collection of constants and abstract methods.
d. False—Although the class must define the methods that are included in the interface, the class can also define additional methods.
e. True—As long as each of the implementing classes provides the required methods.
f. True—As long as the class provides the required methods for each interface it implements.
g. False—Although the signatures of the methods must be the same, the implementations of the methods can be different.

7.6 Enumerated Types Revisited

SR 7.17 Using the enumerated type `Season`, the output is

```
winter
summer
0
June through August
```

7.7 Method Design

SR 7.18 Method decomposition is the process of dividing a complex method into several support methods to get the job done. This simplifies and facilitates the design of the program.

SR 7.19 Based on the `PigLatinTranslator` class:

a. The service provided by the class, namely to translate a string into Pig Latin, is accessed through a static method. Therefore, there is no need to create an object of the class. It follows that there is no need for a constructor.

b. The methods defined as private methods do not provide services directly to clients of the class. Instead, they are used to support the public method `translate`.

c. The `Scanner` object declared in the `translate` method is used to scan the string `sentence`, which is passed to the method by the client.

SR 7.20 The sequence of calls is:

a. `translate – translateWord – beginsWithVowel`

b. `translate – translateWord – beginsWithVowel – beginsWithBlend`

c. `translate – translateWord – beginsWithVowel – beginsWithBlend – translateWord – beginsWithVowel – translateWord – beginsWithVowel – beginsWithBlend – translateWord – beginsWithVowel – beginsWithBlend`

SR 7.21 Objects are passed to methods by copying the reference to the object (its address). Therefore, the actual and formal parameters of a method become aliases of each other.

7.8 Method Overloading

SR 7.22 Overloaded methods are distinguished by having a unique signature, which includes the number, order, and type of the parameters. The return type is not part of the signature.

SR 7.23 a. They are distinct.

b. They are not distinct. The return type of a method is not part of its signature.

c. They are not distinct. The names of a method's parameters are not part of its signature.

d. They are distinct.

SR 7.24
```
//-----------------------------------------------------------------
// Sets up the new Num object, storing a default value
// of 0.
//-----------------------------------------------------------------
public Num()
{
    value = 0;
}
```

7.9 Testing

SR 7.25 The word that best matches is

a. regression	b. review	c. walkthrough	d. defects
e. test case	f. test suite	g. black-box	h. white-box

7.10 GUI Design

SR 7.26 The general guidelines for GUI design include: know the needs and characteristics of the user, prevent user errors when possible, optimize user abilities by providing shortcuts and other redundant means to accomplish a task, and be consistent in GUI layout and coloring schemes.

SR 7.27 A good user interface design is important because, to the user, the interface *is* the program. Since it is the only way the user interacts with the program, in the user's mind the interface represents the entire program.

7.11 Mouse Events

SR 7.28 When a mouse button is clicked, it generates a mouse-pressed event, a mouse-released event, and a mouse-clicked event. The programmer can choose which events the program should respond to.

SR 7.29 When a mouse is moved, it generates multiple mouse-moved events in rapid succession. The location of the mouse pointer can be obtained from the event object.

SR 7.30 The location of the mouse when an event occurs can be obtained by calling the `getX` and `getY` methods on the event object passed to the event handler method

7.12 Key Events

SR 7.31 When a key is typed on the keyboard, it generates a key pressed event, a key released event, and a key typed event. The programmer can choose which events the program should respond to.

SR 7.32 To determine which keyboard key has been pressed when a key event occurs, you can call the `getCode` method on the `KeyEvent` object and compare it to the codes listed in the `KeyCode` enumerated type.

SR 7.33 When a keyboard key is pressed in the `AlienDirection` program, the event handler determines if the key pressed is an arrow key and, if so, updates the position of the alien image accordingly. If any key other than an arrow key is pressed, it is ignored.

Chapter 8 Arrays

8.1 Array Elements

SR 8.1 An array is an object that stores a list of values. The entire list can be referenced by its name, and each element in the list can be referenced individually based on its position in the array.

SR 8.2 Each element in an array can be referenced by its numeric position, called an index, in the array. In Java, all array indexes begin at zero. Square brackets are used to specify the index. For example, `nums[5]` refers to the sixth element in the array called `nums`.

SR 8.3 a. 61, b. 139, c. 73, d. 79, e. 74, f. 11

8.2 Declaring and Using Arrays

SR 8.4 An array's element type is the type of values that the array can hold. All values in a particular array have the same type, or are at least of compatible types. So we might have an array of integers, or an array of `boolean` values, or an array of `Dog` objects, etc.

SR 8.5 Arrays are objects. Therefore, as with all objects, to create an array we first create a reference to the array (its name). We then instantiate the array itself, which reserves memory space to store the array elements. The only difference between a regular object instantiation and an array instantiation is the bracket syntax.

SR 8.6
```
int[] ages = new int[100];
```

SR 8.7 `int[] faceCounts = new int[6];`

SR 8.8 Whenever a reference is made to a particular array element, the index operator (the brackets that enclose the subscript) ensures that the value of the index is greater than or equal to zero and less than the size of the array. If it is not within the valid range, an `ArrayIndexOutOfBoundsException` is thrown.

SR 8.9 An off-by-one error occurs when a program's logic exceeds the boundary of an array (or similar structure) by one. These errors include forgetting to process a boundary element as well as attempting to process a nonexistent element. Array processing is susceptible to off-by-one errors because their indexes begin at zero and run to one less than the size of the array.

SR 8.10
```
for (int index = 0; index < values.length; index++)
{
    values[index]++;
}
```

SR 8.11
```
int sum = 0;
for (int index = 0; index < values.length; index++)
{
    sum += values[index];
}
System.out.println(sum);
```

SR 8.12 An array initializer list is used in the declaration of an array to set up the initial values of its elements. An initializer list instantiates the array object, so the `new` operator is not needed.

SR 8.13 An entire array can be passed as a parameter. Specifically, because an array is an object, a reference to the array is passed to the method. Any changes made to the array elements will be reflected outside of the method.

8.3 Arrays of Objects

SR 8.14 An array of objects is really an array of object references. The array itself must be instantiated, and the objects that are stored in the array must be created separately.

SR 8.15 a. `String[] team = new String[6];`

b.
```
String[] team = {"Amanda", "Clare", "Emily", "Julie",
                 "Katie", "Maria"};
```

SR 8.16 a. `Book[] library = new Book[10];`

b. `library[0] = new Book("Starship Troopers", 208);`

8.4 Command-Line Arguments

SR 8.17 A command-line argument is data that is included on the command line when the interpreter is invoked to execute the program. Command-line arguments are another way to provide input to a program. They are accessed using the array of strings that is passed into the `main` method as a parameter.

SR 8.18
```
//-----------------------------------------------------
// Prints the sum of the string lengths of the first
// two command line arguments.
//-----------------------------------------------------
public static void main(String[] args)
{
   System.out.println(args[0].length() +
   args[1].length());
}
```

SR 8.19
```
//-----------------------------------------------------
// Prints the sum of the first two command line
// arguments, assuming they are integers.
//-----------------------------------------------------
public static void main(String[] args)
{
   System.out.println(Integer.parseInt(args[0])
                        + Integer.parseInt(args[1]));
}
```

8.5 Variable Length Parameter Lists

SR 8.20 A Java method can be defined to accept a variable number of parameters by using ellipses (...) in the formal parameter list. When a set of values is passed to the method, they are automatically converted to an array. This allows the method to be written in terms of array processing without forcing the calling method to create the array.

SR 8.21
```
public int distance(int ... legs)
{
   int sum = 0;
   for (int leg : legs)
   {
      sum += leg;
   }
   return sum;
}
```

SR 8.22
```
double travelTime(int speed,  int ... legs)
{
    int sum = 0;
    for (int leg : legs)
    {
        sum += leg;
    }
    return (double)sum/speed;
}
```

8.6 Two-Dimensional Arrays

SR 8.23 A multidimensional array is implemented in Java as an array of array objects. The arrays that are elements of the outer array could also contain arrays as elements. This nesting process could continue for as many levels as needed.

SR 8.24
```
int high = scores[0][0];
int low = high;
for (int row = 0; row < scores.length; row++)
    for (int col = 0; col < scores[row].length; col++)
    {
        if (scores[row][col] < low)
            low = scores[row][col];
        if (scores[row][col] > high)
            high = scores[row][col];
    }
System.out.println(high - low);
```

8.7 Polygons and Polylines

SR 8.25 A polyline is a shape made up of multiple line segments connected end to end. A `PolyLine` object is specified by a series of values representing the (x, y) coordinates of the line segment vertices.

SR 8.26 A polygon is a closed shape, whereas a polyline may be open. The first and last points of a polygon are automatically connected, which is not the case for a polyline.

SR 8.27 Coordinate values in JavaFX are stored as `double` values so that they may be calculated using floating-point operations to increase accuracy.

8.8 An Array of Color Objects

SR 8.28 To determine if the user has double-clicked the mouse button, you can call the `getClickCount` method of the `MouseEvent` object passed to the event handler method.

SR 8.29 The color of a dot is determined by cycling through an array holding six `Color` objects. After 12 dots have been drawn, the array has been cycled through exactly twice. So the next dot color would be red, the first color in the array.

SR 8.30 The only modification to the `Dots` program that would be necessary to add more dot colors would be to add `Color` objects to the `colorList` array. All processing is done in terms of the length of that array.

8.9 Choice Boxes

SR 8.31 A choice box is a JavaFX control that allows the user to select an option from a drop-down menu of choices.

SR 8.32 There are two action event handlers in the `JukeBox` program. One handles a change in the song selected using the choice box. The other handles the user pressing either the Play or Stop buttons.

SR 8.33 The `JukeBox` program relies on fact that the index of the song name, the related audio clip, and the choice box selection all corresponding to a particular song. The choice box is loaded with strings from an array of song names, which correspond to the array of audio clips. When the user makes a selection, the index of that selection dictates which audio clip to play.

Chapter 9 Inheritance

9.1 Creating Subclasses

SR 9.1 A child class is derived from a parent class using inheritance. The methods and variables of the parent class automatically become a part of the child class, subject to the rules of the visibility modifiers used to declare them.

SR 9.2 Because a new class can be derived from an existing class, the characteristics of the parent class can be reused without the error-prone process of copying and modifying code.

SR 9.3 Each inheritance derivation should represent an *is-a* relationship: the child *is-a* more specific version of the parent. If this relationship does not hold, then inheritance is being used improperly.

SR 9.4 The `protected` modifier establishes a visibility level (like public and private) that takes inheritance into account. A variable or method declared with protected visibility can be referenced by name in the derived class, while retaining some level of encapsulation. Protected visibility allows access from any class in the same package.

SR 9.5 The `super` reference can be used to call the parent's constructor, which cannot be invoked directly by name. It can also be used to invoke the parent's version of an overridden method.

SR 9.6
```
public class SchoolBook2 extends Book2
{
   private int ageLevel;
   //-----------------------------------------------------------------
   // Constructor: Sets up the schoolbook with the
   // specified number of pages and age level (assumed
   // to be between 4 and 16 inclusive).
   //-----------------------------------------------------------------
   public SchoolBook2(int numPages, int age)
   {
      super(numPages);
      ageLevel = age;
   }
   //-----------------------------------------------------------------
   // Returns a string that describes the age level.
   //-----------------------------------------------------------------
   public String level()
   {
      if (ageLevel <= 6)
         return "Pre-school";
      else
         if (ageLevel <= 9)
            return "Early";
         else
            if (ageLevel <= 12)
               return "Middle";
            else
               return "Upper";
   }
}
```

SR 9.7 With single inheritance, a class is derived from only one parent, whereas with multiple inheritance, a class can be derived from multiple parents, inheriting the properties of each. The problem with multiple inheritance is that collisions must be resolved in the cases when two or more parents contribute an attribute or method with the same name. Java supports only single inheritance.

9.2 Overriding Methods

SR 9.8 A child class may prefer its own definition of a method in favor of the definition provided for it by its parent. In this case, the child overrides (redefines) the parent's definition with its own.

SR 9.9 The answers are:

a. True—The child "overrides" the parent's definition of the method if both methods have the same signature.
b. False—A constructor is a special method with no return type which has the same name as its class. If you tried to override the parent's constructor, you would create a syntax error since all methods except constructors must have a return type.
c. False—A `final` method cannot be overridden (that's why it is "final").
d. False—On the contrary, the need to override methods of a parent class occurs often when using inheritance.
e. True—Such a variable is called a *shadow* variable. You can do this, but it may lead to confusing situations and its use is discouraged.

9.3 Class Hierarchies

SR 9.10 There are many potential answers to this problem.

SR 9.11 All classes in Java are derived, directly or indirectly, from the `Object` class. Therefore, all public methods of the `Object` class, such as `equals` and `toString`, are available to every object.

SR 9.12 The only Java class that does not have a parent class is the `Object` class. As mentioned in the previous answer, all other classes are derived from `Object` either directly or indirectly. `Object` is the root of the Java inheritance tree.

SR 9.13 An abstract class is a representation of a general concept. Common characteristics and method signatures can be defined in an abstract class so that they are inherited by child classes derived from it.

SR 9.14 It is a contradiction to define an abstract class as `final`. An abstract class cannot be instantiated and often contains abstract methods. Typically the definitions of these methods are completed by one or more classes that extend the abstract class. But a `final` class cannot be extended, so there would be no way to complete its definition.

SR 9.15 A new interface can be derived from an existing interface using inheritance, just as a new class can be derived from an existing class.

9.4 Visibility

SR 9.16 A class member is not inherited if it has private visibility, meaning that it cannot be referenced by name in the child class. However, such members do exist for the child and can be referenced indirectly.

SR 9.17 The `Pizza` class can refer to the variable servings explicitly, because it is declared with `protected` visibility. It cannot, however, refer to the `calories` method explicitly, because the `calories` method is declared as `private`.

9.5 Designing for Inheritance

SR 9.18 An inheritance derivation represents an "is-a" relationship when the child class represents a more specific version of the parent class. For example, a dictionary is a type of book, so if a `Dictionary` class extends a `Book` class, the inheritance represents an "is-a" relationship.

SR 9.19 Common features of classes should appear as high as possible in a class hierarchy, as long as it is appropriate for the features to be at the level where they are defined. This approach supports understandability, consistency, and reuse.

SR 9.20 You can define a class with multiple roles by having the class implement more than one interface.

SR 9.21 You should override the `toString` method of a parent in its child class, even when the method is not invoked through the child by your current applications, to avoid problems at a later time. Someone who later uses the class directly or extends the class may assume the existence of a valid `toString` method.

SR 9.22 The `final` modifier can be applied to a particular method, which keeps that method from being overridden in a child class. It can also be applied to an entire class, which keeps that class from being extended at all.

9.6 Inheritance in JavaFX

SR 9.23 The `Shape` class serves as the parent of all geometrical shapes such as `Circle` and `Rectangle`. Properties common to all shapes are defined in the `Shape` class, such as the stroke and fill of a shape.

SR 9.24 `Ellipse` is derived from `Shape`, and `Shape` is derived from `Node`. So an ellipse is a shape, and all shapes are nodes.

SR 9.25 The `Label` class is a descendent of `Node` through the following inheritance path: `Node` > `Parent` > `Region` > `Control` > `Labeled` > `Label`. So a `Label` is a `Node`, and there are also several intermediate classes that are used to establish particular characteristics of a `Label` object. For example, only `Parent` objects can have other nodes added to them. So a `Label` is a `Parent`, but a `Shape`, for instance, is not.

SR 9.26 An object of any class derived from the `Parent` class can serve as a root node of a `Scene`. So, for instance, any control can be the root node, but a shape cannot.

9.7 Color and Date Pickers

SR 9.27 A `ColorPicker` allows the user to pick a color from a drop-down palette of colors, or from a more complex selection pane, or by specifying a color using an RGB value or another representation model.

SR 9.28 The `getValue` method of a date picker returns a `LocalDate` object. The `getValue` method of a color picker returns a `Color` object.

9.8 Dialog Boxes

SR 9.29 A dialog box is a window that appears on top of the current window, designed to provide a brief, specific interaction with the user. For example, a dialog box may inform the user that an error occurred or get a key piece of input.

SR 9.30 The `Alert` class is designed to generate several basic types of dialog boxes. In addition, the `TextInputDialog` and the `ChoiceDialog` classes can be used to create dialog boxes that get user input of a specific type.

SR 9.31 A file chooser is a specialized dialog box that allows the user to select a file from a hard drive or other storage medium. Users often encounter file chooses when opening or saving a file within an application.

Chapter 10 Polymorphism

10.1 Late Binding

SR 10.1 Polymorphism is the ability of a reference variable to refer to objects of various types at different times. A method invoked through such a reference is bound to different method definitions at different times, depending on the type of the object referenced.

SR 10.2 Compile time binding is considered more efficient than dynamic binding. Compile time binding occurs before the program is executed and therefore does not delay the execution progress of the program. Dynamic binding occurs while the program is running and therefore does affect the runtime efficiency of the program.

10.2 Polymorphism via Inheritance

SR 10.3 In Java, a reference variable declared using a parent class can be used to refer to an object of the child class. If both classes contain a method with the same signature, the parent reference can be polymorphic.

SR 10.4 Yes, the statements are valid. Since a `CDPlayer` is a `MusicPlayer`, it is legal to assign an object of class `CDPlayer` to a variable of class `MusicPlayer`.

SR 10.5 No, the third statement is not valid. A `MusicPlayer` is not necessarily a `CDPlayer`. It is not legal to perform `cdplayer = mplayer` without using an explicit `cast` operation. Consider that the `mplayer` variable could potentially represent many different kinds of music players: CD players, record players, mp3 players, etc. Suppose at the time of the assignment statement, it represents an mp3 player. Then, you would be assigning an mp3 player object to a `CDPlayer` variable. That, most likely, doesn't make sense and would cause problems if it was allowed to happen.

SR 10.6 When a child class overrides the definition of a parent's method, two versions of that method exist. If a polymorphic reference is used to invoke the method, the version of the method that is invoked is determined by the type of the object being referred to, not by the type of the reference variable.

SR 10.7 The `StaffMember` class is abstract because it is not intended to be instantiated. It serves as a placeholder in the inheritance hierarchy to help organize and manage the objects polymorphically.

SR 10.8 The `pay` method has no meaning at the `StaffMember` level, so is declared as abstract. But by declaring it there we guarantee that every object of its children will have a `pay` method. This allows us to create an array of `StaffMember` objects, which is actually filled with various types of staff members, and pay each one. The details of being paid are determined by each class as appropriate.

SR 10.9 It depends. The `pay` method invocation is polymorphic. The actual method that is invoked is determined at run time and is based on the class of the object referenced by the current (according to the value of `count`) element of the staff list.

10.3 Polymorphism via Interfaces

SR 10.10 An interface name can be used as the type of a reference. Such a reference variable can refer to any object of any class that implements that interface. Because all classes implement the same interface, they have methods with common signatures, which can be dynamically bound.

SR 10.11
a. Invalid—`Speaker` is an interface and interfaces do not have constructors.
b. Valid—the `Dog` class implements `Speaker`.
c. Valid—note that all the classes involved implement `Speaker`.
d. Valid—`Philosopher` implements `Speaker`, so it is legal to assign a philosopher object to a speaker variable.
e. Invalid—`first` is declared to be a `Speaker`, so we cannot invoke the `Philosopher` method `pontificate` through `first`.

10.4 Sorting

SR 10.12 The `Comparable<T>` interface contains a single method called `compareTo`, which should return an integer that is less than zero, equal to zero, or greater than zero if the executing object is less than, equal to, or greater than the object to which it is being compared, respectively.

SR 10.13 The sequence of changes the selection sort algorithm makes to the list of numbers is:

```
5  7  1  8  2  4  3
1  7  5  8  2  4  3
1  2  5  8  7  4  3
1  2  3  8  7  4  5
1  2  3  4  7  8  5
1  2  3  4  5  8  7
1  2  3  4  5  7  8
```

SR 10.14 The sequence of changes the insertion sort algorithm makes to the list of numbers is:

```
5  7  1  8  2  4  3
5  7  1  8  2  4  3
1  5  7  8  2  4  3
1  5  7  8  2  4  3
1  2  5  7  8  4  3
1  2  4  5  7  8  3
1  2  3  4  5  7  8
```

SR 10.15 The sorting methods in this chapter all operate on an array of `Comparable` objects. So the sorting method doesn't really "know" what the objects are, other than that they are comparable and therefore have a `compareTo` method that can be invoked.

SR 10.16 Selection sort and insertion sort are generally equivalent in efficiency, because they both take about n^2 number of comparisons to sort a list of n numbers. Selection sort, though, generally makes fewer swaps. Several sorting algorithms are more efficient than either of these.

10.5 Searching

SR 10.17 a. 4, b. 1, c. 15, e. 15

SR 10.18 A binary search assumes that the search pool is already sorted and begins by examining the middle element. Assuming the target is not found, approximately half of the data is eliminated as viable candidates. Then, the middle element of the remaining candidates is examined, eliminating another quarter of the data. This process continues until the element is found or all viable data has been examined.

SR 10.19 a. 1, b. 3, c. 4, d. 4

10.6 Designing for Polymorphism

SR 10.20–SR 10.22 For the questions in this section, reasonable arguments can be made for using either inheritance or interfaces in each of the situations described. The point of the questions is to think about choices, consider alternative approaches, and practice making technical arguments to support their decisions.

10.7 Properties

SR 10.23 A JavaFX property is an object that holds a value that is observable, meaning the property can be monitored and changed as needed.

SR 10.24 Property binding allows the value of one property to be bound to another, so that when the value of one property changes, the other is automatically updated.

SR 10.25 Numeric properties can't be part of regular arithmetic expressions that use built-in operators such as + and –. Instead, numeric properties have methods such as `add` and `subtract` to perform such operations.

SR 10.26 A change listener is similar to an event handler, defining code that is executed when an observable property value is changed.

10.8 Sliders

SR 10.27 A slider allows the user to specify a numeric value on a bounded range by sliding a knob along the slider track between a minimum and maximum value.

SR 10.28 The current value of a slider, which is represented as a JavaFX property, is obtained using a call to the slider's `valueProperty` method.

10.9 Spinners

SR 10.29 The user interacts with a spinner by clicking on one of a pair of arrows next to the spinner field, which causes the next or previous value in the spinner to be selected (and displayed).

SR 10.30 A spinner may be preferred over a choice box in situations where the drop-down menu of a choice box would obscure important elements in the GUI.

SR 10.31 A spinner value factory is an object that serves as the underlying model for the options provided by a spinner.

Chapter 11 Exceptions

11.1 Exception Handling

SR 11.1 An exception is an object that defines an unusual or erroneous situation. An error is similar, except that an error generally represents an unrecoverable situation and should not be caught.

SR 11.2 A thrown exception can be handled in one of three ways: it can be ignored, which will cause a program to terminate; it can be handled where it occurs using a `try` statement; or it can be caught and handled higher in the method calling hierarchy.

11.2 Uncaught Exceptions

SR 11.3
a. False—Exceptions and errors are related but are not always the same thing.
b. True—Division by zero is invalid, so an exception is thrown.
c. False—An exception must be either handled or thrown.
d. True—If the exception is not handled, the program will terminate and display a message.
e. True—That is the purpose of the call stack trace.

11.3 The `try-catch` Statement

SR 11.4 A `catch` phrase of a `try` statement defines the code that will handle a particular type of exception.

SR 11.5 The `finally` clause of a `try` statement is executed no matter how the `try` block is exited. If no exception is thrown, the `finally` clause is executed after the `try` block is complete. If an exception is thrown, the appropriate `catch` clause is executed; then the `finally` clause is executed.

SR 11.6 The output produced is:

a.
```
finally
the end
```
b.
```
one caught
finally
the end
```
c.
```
two caught
finally
the end
```
d.
```
finally
```

11.4 Exception Propagation

SR 11.7 If an exception is not caught immediately when thrown, it begins to propagate up through the methods that were called to get to the point where it was generated. The exception can be caught and handled at any point during that propagation. If it propagates out of the `main` method, the program terminates.

SR 11.8 If the exception generating code was added to the `level2` method, just before the call to the `level3` method, then the output would not include any mention of "Level 3"—this is because the call to level 3 does not occur since the exception is raised before the call is made.

SR 11.9 There is no change. The exception is still raised in level 3. The new code in level 2 does not get executed.

11.5 The Exception Class Hierarchy

SR 11.10 A checked exception is an exception that must be either (1) caught and handled or (2) listed in the `throws` clause of any method that may throw or propagate it. This establishes a set of exceptions that must be formally acknowledged in the program one way or another. Unchecked exceptions can be ignored completely in the code if desired.

SR 11.11 a. True—It inherits from `RunTimeException` which inherits from `Exception`.
b. True—It inherits from `Throwable` through `RunTimeException` and `Exception`.
c. False—It inherits from `RunTimeException` so it is unchecked.
d. True—It does not inherit from `RunTimeException`.
e. True—See, for example, the `OutOfRangeException` defined in this section.
f. False—The `ArithmeticException` is unchecked.

SR 11.12 If the input is `42`, the program defined `OutOfRangeException` is thrown in `main`, the message "Input value is out of range." is printed along with the stack trace that consists of just information about `CreatingExceptions.main`, and the program terminates. If the input is `–3`, the same thing happens. If the input is the string "thirty," then a library defined `InputMismatchException` is thrown, a stack trace that consists of information about five methods is printed, and the program terminates. I/O exceptions are the topic of the next section of this textbook.

11.6 I/O Exceptions

SR 11.13 A stream is a sequential series of bytes that serves as a source of input or a destination for output.

SR 11.14 The standard I/O streams in Java are `System.in`, the standard input stream; `System.out`, the standard output stream; and `System.err`, the standard error stream. Usually, standard input comes from the keyboard and standard output and error go to a default window on the monitor screen.

SR 11.15 The `Stream` object we have been using explicitly throughout this book is the `System.out` object. We have used it when printing output from our programs. Sometimes we have also used the `System.in` object, to create `Scanner` objects for reading input from the user.

SR 11.16 The `main` method definition of the `CreatingExceptions` program does not include a `throws InputMismatchException` clause, because the `Scanner` class takes care of that—there is no need to repeat code in the `main` method when it is already included in a helper class.

SR 11.17 The `main` method definition of the `TestData` program does not include a `throws FileNotFoundException` clause, because the `FileWriter` class takes care of that—there is no need to repeat code in the `main` method when it is already included in a helper class.

SR 11.18 If the `PrintWriter` constructor of the `TestDate` class is passed the `fw` object instead of the `bw` object, the program still works. The only difference is that the program does not use the buffering capabilities of the `BufferedWriter` class and therefore the processing may not be as efficient.

11.7 Tool Tips and Disabling Controls

SR 11.19 A tool tip is a short line of text that appears when the user pauses the mouse pointer on top of a control or other GUI element. They are typically used to explain the role of an icon button or similar control whose purpose is not obvious.

SR 11.20 A programmer might disable a control when using that control is not valid. It's a technique for guiding the user to proper actions and eliminates the need for event handlers to handle inappropriate situations.

11.8 Scroll Panes

SR 11.21 A scroll pane provides a restricted viewing area of an image or other GUI element that is too large to display fully in the space allotted. Scroll bars on the side and bottom of the scroll pane allow the user to change the viewable area.

SR 11.22 To change the knob position on a scroll bar, the user can (1) drag the knob, (2) click on the scroll bar itself on either side of the knob, or (3) click the small arrows at either end of the scroll bar.

SR 11.23 The scroll bar policy of a scroll pane determines whether the scroll bars are always displayed, never displayed, or only displayed when they are needed to be able to access other areas of the underlying GUI node.

11.9 Split Panes and List Views

SR 11.24 A divider bar separates two nodes in a split pane. A divider bar can be dragged by the user to change the relative space given to the two nodes.

SR 11.25 The options of a choice box are only visible when the user clicks on it to produce the drop-down menu of options. The options of a list view, on the other hand, are always displayed, with a scroll bar if necessary to access a long list options.

SR 11.26 A split pane can contain more than two nodes. For each additional node added, an additional divider bar is added as well to separate it from the last node added.

Chapter 12 Recursion

12.1 Recursive Thinking

SR 12.1 Recursion is a programming technique in which a method calls itself, solving a smaller version of the problem each time, until the terminating condition is reached.

SR 12.2 The recursive part of the definition of a List is used 9 times to define a list of 10 numbers. The base case is used once.

SR 12.3 Infinite recursion occurs when there is no base case that serves as a terminating condition or when the base case is improperly specified. The recursive path is followed forever. In a recursive program, infinite recursion will often result in an error that indicates that available memory has been exhausted.

SR 12.4 A base case is always required to terminate recursion and begin the process of returning through the calling hierarchy. Without the base case, infinite recursion results.

SR 12.5 $5 * n = 5$ if $n = 1$, $5 * n = 5 + (5 * (n - 1))$ if $n > 1$

12.2 Recursive Programming

SR 12.6 Recursion is not necessary. Every recursive algorithm can be written in an iterative manner. However, some problem solutions are much more elegant and straightforward when written recursively.

SR 12.7 Avoid recursion when the iterative solution is simpler and more easily understood and programmed. Recursion has the overhead of multiple method calls and is not always intuitive.

SR 12.8 If n < 0 a –1 is returned; otherwise the number of digits in the integer n is returned.

SR 12.9 The recursive solution below is more complicated than the iterative version, so it normally would not be done in this way.

```
// Returns 5 * num, assumes num > 0
public int multByFive(int num)
{
    int result = 5;   // when num == 1
    if (num > 1)
        result = 5 + multByFive(num - 1);
    return result;
}
```

SR 12.10 Indirect recursion occurs when a method calls another method, which calls another method, and so on until one of the called methods invokes the original. Indirect recursion is usually more difficult to trace than direct recursion, in which a method calls itself.

12.3 Using Recursion

SR 12.11 The `MazeSearch` program recursively processes each of the four positions adjacent to the "current" one unless either (1) the current position is outside of the playing grid or (2) the final destination position is reached.

SR 12.12 a. The original maze is defined when the `grid` array is declared and initialized.

b. A test to see if we have arrived at the goal occurs at the second `if` statement in the `traverse` method.

c. A location is marked as having been tried in the first statement in the first `if` block of the `traverse` method.

d. A test to see if we already tried a location occurs in the second `if` statement of the `valid` method.

SR 12.13 a. `valid 0,0 valid 1,0 valid 2,0 valid 1,1`

b. `valid 0,0`

c. `valid 0,0 valid 1,0 valid 2,0 valid 1,1 valid 0,0 valid 1,-1 valid 0,1 valid 1,1 valid 0,2 valid -1,1 valid 0,0 valid -1,0 valid 0,-1`

SR 12.14 The Towers of Hanoi puzzle of *N* disks is solved by moving *N*–1 disks out of the way onto an extra peg, moving the largest disk to its destination, then moving the *N*–1 disks from the extra peg to the destination. This solution is inherently recursive because, to move the substack of *N*–1 disks, we can use the same process.

SR 12.15 For an initial stack of one disk, there is one call to the `moveTower` method. For an initial stack of two disks, there are three calls. For three disks, there are seven calls. For every disk added, the number of calls increases by double the previous number, plus one.

12.4 Tiled Images

SR 12.16 In the `TiledImages` program, recursion occurs in the last line of the `addPictures` method when it calls itself. Each call to the `addPictures` method displays three differently colored versions of an image. The recursion causes that process to be repeated in the upper left corner within a smaller area.

SR 12.17 There is only one `Image` object created in the `TiledImages` program. That image is displayed in 15 different `ImageView` objects. The image is displayed three times at each level of the recursion, which occurs five times in this program before the base case is reached.

SR 12.18 The base case of the recursion in the `TiledImages` program is the value of the parameter `size` dropping below a threshold of 20 pixels. As long as the size, which is cut in half with each recursive call, is greater than that minimum value, the recursive call is made.

12.5 Fractals

SR 12.19 A fractal is a geometric shape that is made up of the same pattern repeated at different scales and orientations. The algorithm used to generate a fractal is often easiest to define recursively.

SR 12.20 In the example program, a maximum order is set for the Koch snowflake fractal because the details of the fractal at an order greater than six or so become hard to see and can take a large amount of time to compute. Conceptually, the fractal continues for an infinite number of levels.

SR 12.21 At each level of the Koch snowflake fractal, every line segment is transformed by replacing its middle third with a sharp protrusion made up of two line segments. In the example program, the two endpoints of an existing line segment are used to compute three intermediate points, and the corresponding four new line segments replaces the original.

Chapter 13 Collections

13.1 Collections and Data Structures

SR 13.1 A collection is an object whose purpose is to store and organize primitive data or other objects. Some collections are helpful in particular problem-solving situations.

SR 13.2 A collection is a conceptual organization of elements that often can be implemented using different underlying data structures. For example, the Java API has two classes that represent a List collection: `ArrayList` and `LinkedList`.

SR 13.3 An abstract data type (ADT) is a collection of data and the operations that can be performed on that data. An object is essentially the same thing in that we encapsulate related variables and methods in an object. The object hides the underlying implementation of the ADT, separating the interface from the underlying implementation, permitting the implementation to be changed without affecting the interface.

13.2 Dynamic Representations

SR 13.4 A dynamic data structure is constructed using references to link various objects together into a particular organization. It is dynamic in that it can grow and shrink as needed. New objects can be added to the structure, and obsolete objects can be removed from the structure at run time by adjusting references between objects in the structure.

SR 13.5 To insert a node into a list, first find the node that comes before the new node (let's call it `beforeNode`). Then, set the new node's `next` pointer equal to `beforeNode`'s `next` pointer. Then, set `beforeNode`'s `next` pointer to the new node. A special case exists when inserting a node at the beginning of the list.

SR 13.6 To delete a node from a list, first find the node that comes before the node to be deleted (let's call it `beforeNode`). Then, set `beforeNode`'s `next` pointer to the deleted node's `next` pointer. A special case exists when deleting the first node of the list.

SR 13.7

```
set count = 0;
current = first;
while current != null
    count++;
    current = current.next;
return count;
```

SR 13.8 Each node in a doubly linked list has references to both the node that comes before it in the list and the node that comes after it in the list. This organization allows for easy movement forward and backward in the list and simplifies some operations.

SR 13.9 A header node for a linked list is a special node that holds information about the list, such as references to the front and rear of the list and an integer to keep track of how many nodes are currently in the list.

13.3 Linear Collections

SR 13.10 A queue is a linear collection like a list, but it has more constraints on its use. A general list can be modified by inserting or deleting nodes anywhere in the list, but a queue only adds nodes to one end (enqueue) and takes them off of the other (dequeue). Thus, a queue uses a first-in, first-out (FIFO) approach.

SR 13.11 The contents of the queue from front to rear are: `72 37 15`

SR 13.12 A stack is a linear collection that adds (pushes) and removes (pops) nodes from one end. It manages information using a last-in, first-out (LIFO) approach.

SR 13.13 The contents of the stack from top to bottom are: `37 72 5`

SR 13.14 The `Stack` class is defined in the `java.util` package of the Java standard class library. It represents a stack collection whose elements are specified using a generic type `T`.

13.4 Non-Linear Data Structures

SR 13.15 Trees and graphs are both non-linear data structures, meaning that the data they store is not organized in a linear fashion. Trees create a hierarchy of nodes. The nodes in a graph are connected using general edges.

SR 13.16 a. tree, b. graph, c. graph, d. tree

13.5 The Java Collections API

SR 13.17 The Java Collections API is a set of classes in the Java standard class library that represents collections of various types, such as `ArrayList` and `LinkedList`.

SR 13.18 A generic type is a collection object that is implemented such that the type of objects it manages can be established when the collection is created. This allows some compile-time control over the types of objects that are added to the collection and eliminates the need to cast the objects when they are removed from the collection. All collections in the Java Collections API have been implemented as generic types.

Index

:: operator, 206
== operator, 221, 238
–– (decrement operator), 106–107
' ' (single quotes for character literals), 99
– (subtraction operator), 101
!== (equal to operator), 221–222
($) dollar sign, 59
%= (remainder assignment operator), 107–108
% (remainder operator), 101
('&') ampersand, 99
& (AND bitwise operator), 663
( ) (parentheses), 88–89, 111–112, 129
  arithmetic expressions, 103–104
  boolean expressions, 225
  casting data conversion, 111–112
  invoking methods, 129
  operator precedence using, 88–89, 103–104
| bitwise operator, 663
{} (braces for if statements), 233, 237
( ) cast operator, 111–112
/ (division operator), 101
++ (increment operator), 106–107
*– (multiplication assignment operator), 107
* (multiplication operator), 101
. (dot operator for accessing methods), 129
/ (division operator), 101–102
/* and */ (multiple line comments), 58
/** and */ (external comments), 58
(//) comments, 57
/= (division assignment operator), 107
?: (conditional operator), 288
[] (square brackets for arrays), 384, 388
\' (single quote escape sequence), 89
\" (double quote escape sequence), 89
\\ (backslash escape sequence), 89, 99, 101
\b (backspace escape sequence), 89
\n (newline escape sequence), 89
\r (carriage return escape sequence), 89
\t (tab escape sequence), 89
^ (XOR bitwise operator), 663
(_) underscore character, 59
('|') vertical bar, 99
"0.###", 149
{ } (class definition), 56
{} (braces for if statements), 233, 237
| (NOT logical operator), 222–224
| (OR bitwise operator), 663
|| (OR logical operator), 222–224
~ (NOT bitwise operator), 663
+ (plus symbol), 86, 88
  addition operator, 101
  string concatenation, 86, 88
++ (increment operator), 106–107
+= (addition assignment operator), 107
< (less than relational operator), 221
<< (left-shift bitwise operator), 665
<= (less than or equal to relational operator), 221
–= (subtraction assignment operator), 107
== (not equal to operator), 221–222
> (greater than relational operator), 221–222
>= (greater than or equal to relational operator), 221–222
>> (right-shift bitwise operator), 665
>>> (right-shift with zeros bitwise operator), 665

A

abstract classes, 453–454
abstract data type (ADT), 602
abstract method, 208, 339, 343, 453–455
abstract modifier, 453, 669
Abstract Windowing Toolkit (AWT), 158
accessor methods, encapsulation, 186–187, 397
action events, 206–207, 266, 273, 426, 465, 591
actual parameters, 191
add method, 209, 605, 684–685
Addition program, 88
Address class, 333, 335
addresses, 41
  Internet address, 51
  IP address, 51
  memory, 41
Advanced Research Projects Agency (ARPA), 50

Advanced Research Projects Agency (ARPA) network (ARAPNET), 50
aggregate object, 333
aggregation, 332–336
alerts, 466
algorithms, 348–349
aliases, 130–132
American Standard Code for Information Interchange, 99
analog information, 33
analog signals, 36
AND bitwise operator (&), 663
applets, 55
application programming interfaces, 136–138
applyPattern method, 149
arc length, 198
arc type, 199
architecture, computer hardware functions, 39–40
arcs, 198–201
args identifier, 59, 406
arguments, 191
arithmetic operators, 101–102
arithmetic/logic unit, 45
ArrayList class, 257–258
ArrayList object, 257
arrays
  appropriate counter, 390
  bounds checking, 388–393
  choice boxes, 423–427
  of color objects, 420–423
  command-line arguments, 406–407
  declaration, 385–396
  of double values, 419
  element type of, 386
  elements, 384–385
  execution of BasicArray program, 387
  four-dimensional, 416
  initializer list, 393–394
  instantiation using new operator, 385, 387, 397
  iterator version of for loop, 387–388
  length of, 388
  lists as, 384
  multidimensional, 416–417
  of objects, 396–405
  one-dimensional, 412
  as parameters, 394
  polygons drawn using, 417–420
  polylines drawn using, 417–420
  ragged, 417
  of String objects, 406
  syntax, 393
  two-dimensional, 412–417
  variable-length parameter lists, 408–411
ASCII character set, 99–100, 657
assembly language, 64–65
assignment
  /= (division assignment operator), 107
  *– (multiplication assignment operator, 107
  %= (remainder assignment operator), 107–108
  –= (subtraction assignment operator), 107
  data values and, 93–95
  evaluation of a particular expression, 104
  Java defined operations, 106–107
  operator (=), 93
  operators (=), 104
  statement, 93–95
  variables and, 93–95
assignment conversion, 111
  between primitive types and object types, 157
asterisk (*), 139
autoboxing, 157

B

background color, 160, 203, 260, 262
band, 258
bar code readers, 40
base class, 437
base value, 35
base-2 number system, 649
base-10 number system, 649
binary numbers, 35–38
binary search, 507–510
binary string, 649
binary tree, 615
BIOS (basic input/output system), 44
bit(s), 35–37, 97, 649
bitwise operations, 661–665
black-box testing, 363
block statement, 231–235
blueprint, 74
boolean expressions, 220–224
  conditionals and loops, 220–221
  equality operators, 221–222
  if statement, 220, 224–228
  if-else statement, 220, 228–231
  logical operators, 222–224
  println statement, 220
  relational operators, 221–222
  switch statement, 220
boolean integer data type, 155
boolean literals, 100
boolean operators, 664
boolean primitive data types, 100, 111, 155
boolean values, 111
boolean variable, 100

boundaries, 363–364
  equivalence categories for, 363–364
bounds checking, 388–393
  automatic, 388
  off-by-one errors, 388
break statement, 251, 284–285
browser, 52
bus, 39
Button object, 206
buttons
  check boxes, 265–269
  event sources, 260–262
  Play or Stop button, 423, 427
  radio, 269–273
  toggle, 265
  tool tips, 552–553
by value parameter passing, 354
byte integer data type, 97, 110, 155
bytecode, 67
bytes, 42

C

C and C++, 69
cache, 43
call stack trace, 532
called method, 188
calling method, 188
cameras, 41
casting data conversion, 111–112
catch clause, 532
CD-Recordable (CD-R) disk, 44
central processing unit (CPU), 30, 39–40, 45–46
  arithmetic/logic unit, 45
  components and main memory, 45
  control unit, 45
  fetch–decode–execute cycle, 45–46
  instruction register, 45
  machine language instruction, 64
  microprocessor, 46
  program counter, 45
  system clock, 46
  von Neumann architecture, 45
change listener, 516–518
char character data type, 100, 110–111
char integer data type, 110, 155
character strings, 57, 89
  data comparison, 240–241
  escape sequences, 89
  if statements for, 240–241
  object data and, 86–89, 240–241
  print and println methods for, 84–85
  string concatenation, 86–89
  string literals, 84, 86
  Unicode relationships, 240–241
characters
  ASCII character set, 99–100
  assignment conversion for, 111
  bounds checking, 388–393
  char character data type, 100, 110–111
  comparing, 239
  control, 99, 657
  conversion of, 109–112
  if statements for, 239
  literals, 99
  narrowing conversions for, 110
  nonprintable, 657–659
  primitive data as, 99
  printable, 657
  set, 99–100, 657
  underscore character (_), 59
  Unicode character set, 100, 657–659
check boxes, 265–269
checked exceptions, 544
child class, 451
choice boxes, 423–427
CircleStats program, 149
class, 436
  abstract, 453–454
  aggregation, 332–336
  anatomy of, 178–184
  assigning responsibilities to, 321
  attributes and operations, 176–177
  DecimalFormat class, 148–149
  dependency, 326–332
  encapsulation, 185–188
  enumerated types, 152–154, 345–348
  instance data, 183
  Math class, 143–144
  members of, 179–180
  NumberFormat class, 146–147
  objects and, 74
  packages, 136–140
  polymorphism and, 453–454
  Random class, 140–141
  relationships, 326–338
  software design. *See* software design
  static members, 321–325
  subclasses. *See* subclasses
  this reference, 336–338
  UML diagrams, 183–184
  visibility modifiers, 186–187
  wrapper class, 155–157
  writing, 175–211
class definition { }, 56

class hierarchies, 450–455
abstract classes, 453–454
child class and, 451
interface hierarchy, 455
Object class, 452–453
organizing animals, 451
UML class diagram, 450
class library, 136
class methods, 322
class variable, 322
client, 318
clock speed, 46
collections
abstract data type (ADT), 602
data structures for, 602
dynamic representations, 603–610
generic types, 618–619
graphs, 616–618
implementation of, 602–603, 609–610
interfaces for, 602
Java Collections API, 618–619
linear, 611–614
linked list, 602, 604–610
list representations, 609–610
non-linear data, 615–618
queues, 611–612
stacks, 612–614
trees, 615–616
Color class, 169
Color object, 168
color picker, 462–465
color representation, Java graphics, 168–169
combo box, 427
command-line arguments, 406–407
comments, 57–58
double slash (//) symbols, 58
inline documentation, 57–58
javadoc. *See* javadoc
javadoc (/** and */) symbols for, 58
multiple line (/* and */) symbols for, 58
newline character, 58
tags, 700–701
Comparable interface, 500, 502
compilers, 66–68, 91, 96
compile-time error, 70
complement operator (), 664
computer error, 69
computer systems, 29–76
architecture, 39–40
central processing unit (CPU), 30, 45–46
development environments, 68
errors, 69–70
input/output (I/O) devices, 30, 40–41
memory, 30, 41–45
object-oriented (OO) programming, 71–76
processing, 30–38
programming languages. *See* programming languages
semantics, 68–69
software. *See* software
syntax, 68–69
wide area network (WAN), 50
World Wide Web, 52
conditional statements, 220
block statement, 231–235
boolean expressions for, 220–224
comparison of loop statements, 298
conditional operator, 288–289
data comparison using, 238–241
determining event sources, 260–262
do statement, 221, 289–292
flow of control, 220
if statement, 225–228
if-else statement, 220, 228–231
iterators, 253–256
nested if statement, 235–237
for statement, 221
switch statement, 220, 284–287
using graphics, 299–303
while statement, 242–251
constants, 95–96
coding errors and, 96
reasons to use, 96
constructors, 113, 488–489
Arc, 198
Button, 206
child class, 445
Circle, 162
Coin, 231
ColorPicker, 465
for creating shapes, 161
DatePicker, 465
DecimalFormat class, 148–149
default, 197–198
Die, 180, 191
DVDCollection, 404
eliminating, 130
Ellipse, 162
FahrenheitPane, 209
Font, 264
FoodItem, 456
Grade, 397
image, 203
inherited, 441

initialization of instantiated object, 197, 443
invoking, 129, 346
JavaFX shape classes, 161–162
overloading of, 361
parameters of, 338, 409, 411
Polygon, 419
Polyline, 419
Rectangle, 162
regular method and, 197
Scanner, 256
of Scene class, 160
of Slogan increments, 324
for some JavaFX shape classes, 161
super(), 445
this reference, 338
VBox, 269
of wrapper classes, 155
Contact class, 500
Contact object, 500
continue statement, 251
continuous fetch–decode–execute cycle, 45–46
control characters, 99, 657
control flow statements, 364
control unit, 45
controllers, 40
conversions
assignment, 111
casting, 111–112
data, 109–112
narrowing, 110
number system, 653–654
promotion, 111
reverse, 157
coordinate systems, Java, 160
Countdown program, 85

D

data
assignment statement, 93–95
boolean primitive data types, 100, 111, 155
char character data type, 100, 110–111
character strings, 86–89, 240–241
comparison of types, 240–241
constants, 95–96
constructors, 113–115
enumerated types, 152–154, 345–348
escape sequences, 89
expressions, 101–108
floating points, 97–98
instance, 183
integers, 97–98
local, 191–192
parameters, 408–411
Unicode relationships, 240–241
variable-length parameter lists, 408–411
data conversion, 109–112
assignment, 111
casting, 111–112
narrowing, 110–111
via promotion, 111
widening, 109–110
data structures
collections and, 602–603
dynamic, 602–611
generic types, 618–619
graphs, 616–618
header nodes, 610
implementation of, 602–603, 609–610
interfaces for, 602
linear, 611–614
linked list, 602, 604–610
list representations, 609–610
non-linear data, 615–618
queues, 611–612
stacks, 612–614
trees, 615–616
date picker, 462–465
debugging, 69
decimal number system, 649
decimal values, 35
DecimalFormat class, 148–149
DecimalFormat constructor, 149
declaration
arrays, 385–396
asterisk (*), 139
boolean variable, 100
bounds checking, 388–393
character variable, 100
constants, 95–96
constructors. *See* constructors
import declaration, 138–139
instance data, 183
java.util package, 138–139
local data, 191–192
method, 188
numeric variable, 98
polymorphism and, 481–493
reference variables, 481–493
square brackets [] used for, 385–388, 393
String methods for, 128–130, 396–405
syntax and, 393
of variables, 91, 93, 128
decorate, 566

decoration, 566
default constructor, 197–198
default modifier (reserved word), 669
default visibility, 667
defect testing, 362–364
delimiters, 115
derived classes, 75
dialog box, 466–472
  file choosers, 469–472
  polymorphism used for, 469–472
digital computers, 33–38
  binary values, 35–38
  digitized process, 34–35
  sampling rate, 33–35
  signals, 34–38
digital signal, 36
digraph, 616
direct access, 44
direct access device, 43
direct recursion, 571
directed graph, 616
disabled control, 549–553
divide-by-zero error, 245
do statement, 221, 289–292
  logic of, 290
  termination conditions, 292
  while clause for, 290
documentation, 55
  API, 137–138
  coding guidelines, 671–675
  comments, 57–58, 699
  guidelines, 674–675
  inline, 57–58
  javadoc document comments, 699–700
  tags, 700–701
dollar sign ($), 59
domain name, 51
Domain Name System (DNS), 51
domain server, 51
doubly linked list, 609
drawing
  arrays of color objects, 420–423
  arrays used for, 417–420
  background color, 160, 203, 260, 262
  Circle class, 513
  pixels, 41, 160–161, 203, 301, 310, 374, 556, 678, 681
  polygons, 417–420
  polylines, 417–420
  recursion used for, 583–594
  RGB (red-green-blue) values, 168
  viewports, 203–204
DVD, 44
DVDCollection class, 402
dynamic data structures, 602–611

E

Eclipse, 68
edge, 616
editors, 66
else clause, 235, 237
encapsulated object, 75
encapsulation, 185–188
  accessor method, 186–187
  effects of public and private visibility, 186–187
  inheritance and, 439–441
  mutator methods, 186–187
  service (support) methods, 186
  visibility modifiers, 186, 439–441
equality operators, 221–222
equivalence category, 363
errors, 69–70
  black-box testing, 363
  coding, 96
  compile-time, 70
  computer, 69
  defect testing, 362–364
  divide-by-zero, 245
  exceptions and, 530
  logical, 70
  off-by-one, 388
  run-time, 70, 530
  syntax, 70
event, 204
event handler methods, 204, 371, 426, 553
  date picker and color picker, 465
  determining event sources, 260–262
  exceptions, 553
  in JavaFX scene builder, 692–696
  managing fonts, 262–265
  using check boxes, 265–269
  using radio buttons, 269–273
event-driven programs
  action events, 206–207, 266, 273, 426, 465, 591
  buttons, 260–262
  graphical user interfaces (GUIs) as, 204
  handling events in scene builder, 692–696
  key events, 371–374
  list selection events, 556–560
  mouse events, 366–371
  split panes, 556–560
EventHandler interface, 207–208

exceptions
call stack trace, 532
catch clause, 532
checked, 544
class hierarchy, 541–544
disabled control, 549–553
Error and Exception class hierarchy, 541
errors and, 530
finally clause, 536
handling, 530, 532
input/output (I/O), 545–549
list views, 556–560
propagation, 537–540
run-time errors, 530
scroll panes, 553–556
split panes, 556–560
streams, 545
throws clause, 544
tool tips and, 549–553
try blocks, 532–535
try-catch statements, 532–535
uncaught, 531–532
unchecked, 544
exponential complexity, 582
expressions, 101–108
arithmetic operators, 101–102
assignment operators, 107–108
decrement (−) operator, 106–107
increment (++) operator, 106–107
lambda, 207–208
logical operators, 222–224
operator precedence, 102–106
postfix form of the operator, 106–107
prefix form of the operator, 106–107
regular, 117
relational operators, 221–222
tree, 103
extends clause, 452, 460

F

Facts program, 86
FahrenheitPane constructor, 209
false boolean value, 100
fetch–decode–execute cycle, 45–46
file chooser dialog box, 469–472
file server, 48
final modifier, 186, 322, 343, 449, 459–460, 669
finally clause, 536
first-in, first-out (FIFO) processing, 611
floating point literals, 98
floating-point data types
assignment conversion, 111
casting data conversion, 111–112
conversions, 109–112
data comparison, 240–241
if statement for, 238–241
flow of control, 220
Font constructor, 264
font family, 263
Font object, 264
font posture, 263
font size, 263
font weight, 263
for statement, 221, 293–298, 347, 390, 502
comparison of loop statements, 298
for-each version, 296–298
header of, 293
increment code for, 293–295
initialization of, 293–295
iterators and, 297–298
logic of, 293
nested, 412
repetition of, 293–295
using graphics, 301–303
formal parameters, 191
formatting output
DecimalFormat class, 148–149
NumberFormat class, 146–147
printf method, 149–151
fourth-generation language (4GLs), 66
fractals, 587–594
functional interface, 208
functional specification, 318

G

garbage, 131
GasMileage program, 115–116
getCount method, 323–324
getFaceValue method, 190
getSource method, 262
getters, 187
getText method, 211
gigabyte (GB), 42
glass-box testing, 364
goggles, 41
Google search engine, 53
Gosling, James, 54
graphic transformations, 304–310
applying on groups, 307–310
rotation, 305–306
scaling, 304–305
shearing, 306
translation, 304

graphical user interface (GUI), 32–33, 136, 204–208, 260, 591
:: operator, 206
Abstract Windowing Toolkit (AWT), 158
action events, 206–207, 266, 273, 426, 465, 591
buttons, 273
check box, 266
choice box, 423
control, 204
design, 365–366
dialog boxes in, 466
event, 204. *See also* event
event handler, 204, 207–208. *See also* event handler methods
event-driven, 204. *See also* event-driven programs
Java SDK, 68
key events, 371–374
method reference, 206, 208
mouse events, 366–371
sliders, 519–521
spinners, 521
split panes, 556
text field, 208
`this` reference, 206
tool tips and disable controls, 549
user events, 260
graphics, 41, 52, 55
color representation, 168–169
drawing. *See* drawing
fractals, 587–594
on groups, 307–310
Java's support of, 157–158
rotation, 305–306
scaling, 304–305
shearing, 306
tiled images, 583–587
transformations, 304–310
translation, 304
using loops and conditionals with, 299–303
Graphics Track, 157
graphs, 616–618
greater than, 221
greater than or equal to, 221
`Group` object, 166–167

H

hard disks, 43
hardware components, 38–47
bus, 39
central processing unit (CPU), 39–40, 45–46
computer architecture, 39–40
controllers, 40
input/output (I/O) devices, 40–41
main memory, 41–45
peripherals, 40
secondary memory, 41–45
has-a relationship, 332
`hasNext` method, 253
header node, 610
high-level languages, 65–66
horizontal slider, 519
hypermedia, 52
hypertext, 52
HyperText Markup Language (HTML), 52
HyperText Transfer Protocol, 53

I

`IceCream program`, 153
`idChar`, 284
identifiers, 58–61
abbreviations for, 60
case sensitivity of, 60, 673
coding guidelines, 673
naming, 60, 673
reserved words, 58–61
title case for, 60
`if` statement, 220–221, 224–228, 284, 422
braces {} used in, 233, 237
character data comparisons, 239
data comparison using, 238–241
floating-point data comparisons, 238–239
flowchart of, 226
indentation, 226, 233, 237
infinite loop, 247
nested, 235–237
object comparisons, 240–241
using graphics, 301
`if-else` statement, 220, 228–231, 288–289, 569
block statements, 233, 235
conditional (ternary) operators as, 288–289
nested, 237
true/false conditions of, 228
`Image` object, 201
`ImageDisplay` program, 203
images
arrays of color objects, 420–423
color picker, 462–465
fractals, 587–594
pixels, 41, 160–161, 203, 301, 310, 374, 556, 678, 681
recursion used for, 583–594

tiled images, 583–587
viewports, 203–204
ImageView, 201
ImageView objects, 305
implementation
of collections, 602–603, 609–610
of data structures, 602–603, 609–610
software design, 319
import declaration, 138–139
import statement, 115
inclusive OR operation, 663
index values
of an ArrayList, 257
array elements, 393
bounds checking, 388–393
collection and, 602
initializer list, 393–94
integer, 257
indirect recursion, 571
infinite recursion, 566–567
information storage and management, 33–38, 41–45
analog, 33
binary values, 35–38
bits, 35–37
capacity of devices, 42–45
digital, 34–38
main memory, 30, 41–45
sampling rate, 33–35
secondary memory, 30, 41–45
signals, 34–38
inheritance, 75, 436, 619
abstract classes, 453–454
alternative hierarchy for organizing animals, 451
child class, 450–451
class hierarchies, 450–455
class hierarchy and, 541
color and date pickers, 462–465
designing for, 458–460
dialog box, 466–472
file choosers, 469–472
final modifier, 459–460
interface hierarchies, 455
is-a relationship, 437
issues, 459
in JavaFX, 460–462
multiple, 445–446
Object class, 452–453
object-oriented concept of, 158
overriding methods, 447–450
parent (base) class, 450–451
polymorphic reference in Java using, 481–493, 495, 511–512
protected modifier, 439–441
relationships between interfaces, 455
restricting, 459–460
shadow variables, 449–450
single, 445
subclasses, 436–446
super reference, 442–445
transformations, 310
trees and, 615
visibility and, 455–458
visibility modifiers, 186
initializer list, 393–394
input stream, 545
input/output (I/O) devices, 30, 40–41
exceptions, 545–549
insertion sort algorithm, 503–504
instance data, 183
instance variable, 322
instantiation, 129, 155
objects, 129
using new operator, 385, 387, 394, 397
instruction register, 45
int integer data type, 385–386
array declaration using, 385–386, 412
autoboxing, 157
conversion for, 110–111
primitive data, as, 97–98
square brackets ([]) for, 385–386, 412
variable value declaration using, 91–93
wrapper classes for, 155–156
Integer class, 155–156
integer data types
assignment conversion, 111
bounds checking, 388–393
casting conversion, 111–112
literals, 98
narrowing conversion, 110
primitive data, as, 97–98
promotion conversion, 111
widening conversion for, 110
integer index value, 257
integer literals, 98
integrated development environments (IDEs), 68
Intel Dual Core i7 processor, 46
interactive programs, 113–117
interface hierarchy, 455
interfaces, 207, 338–345
abstract method, 339
Comparable interface, 343–344
compareTo method, 344

interfaces *(continued)*
- Complexity interface, 339, 341
- graphical user interface (GUI), 32–33
- hasNext method, 345
- implements, 339
- inheritance and, 455
- Iterator interface, 344–345
- point-and-click interfaces, 32
- polymorphism via, 494–496
- reference variables for, 494–496
- remove method, 345
- software design, 338–345

internal nodes, 615
Internet
- address, 51
- Advanced Research Projects Agency (ARPA) network (ARAPNET), 50
- domain name, 51
- domain server, 51
- hypertext, 52
- IP address, 51
- search engines, 53
- subdomains, 51
- Transmission Control Protocol (TCP), 51
- Uniform Resource Locator (URL), 53
- World Wide Web, 52

interpreter, 68
invoking methods, 129
IP address, 51
is-a relationship, 437
isSelected method, 269
iterators, 253–256
- conditional statements and, 254–256
- delimiters, 256
- hasNext method, 253
- path separation (/), 256
- reading text files using, 254–256
- recursion *vs*, 571
- Scanner class for, 254, 256

J

Java bitwise operators, 661–665
Java Collections API, 618–619
Java programming language, 52, 54–63
- // symbols, 55
- API documentation, 137–138
- architecture neutral, 68
- attributes of object, 176
- automatic bounds checking, 388
- automatic garbage collection, 132
- BlueJ, 68
- boolean variable declarations in, 100
- bytecode, 67
- case sensitivity, 60
- casting conversions, 111–112
- character strings (" "), 57, 89
- character variable declarations in, 100
- class definition (), 56
- class library, 136
- coding guidelines, 671–675
- color in, 168–169
- comments, 57–58
- compilers, 66–67, 91
- conditional operator, 288–289
- conditional statements in, 220
- constants, 95
- debugger, 68
- deprecated, 55
- design guidelines, 672
- documentation, 55
- documentation guidelines, 674–675
- dollar sign ($), 59
- DrJava, 68
- Eclipse, 68
- enumerated type, 152–153
- escape sequences, 89
- exceptions, 70
- floating point literals, 98
- identifiers, 58–61
- identifiers and reserved words, 58–61
- import declaration, 138–139
- inline documentation, 55
- integer literals, 98
- interpreter, 68
- iterator object in, 253
- Java API, 55
- Java coordinate system, 160
- Java Development Kit (JDK), 68
- Java Software Development Kit (SDK), 68
- Java Standard Edition, 54
- Java Virtual Machine (JVM), 68
- java.lang package, 138–139, 155, 452, 460, 541
- java.util package, 138–139, 612
- jEdit, 68
- jGRASP, 68
- main method, 56
- modifiers, 669
- multiple inheritance, 446
- narrowing conversions, 110
- numeric primitive types, 97
- numeric variable declarations in, 98
- object, 71

object-oriented programming language, 55
overriding methods, 447–450
packages, 136–138
primitive data types in, 97–100
`printf` method, 149–151
`println` method, 57
"regular" method invocation, 569
relational operators, 221–222
reserved words, 59–61
run-time environment, 406
semantics, 68–69
source code, 68
standard class library, 55
strongly typed, 95
style guidelines, 673–674
syntax rules, 68–69
terminates, 56
underscore character (_), 59
white space, 61–63
widening conversions, 109–110
wrapper classes, 155–156
Java regular expressions, 697–698
Java standard class library, 57, 128
classes of, 136, 143, 176, 253, 343, 618
`DecimalFormat` class, 148–149
interfaces, 343–344
`java.lang package of`, 143, 452
`java.util package of`, 257
`NumberFormat` class, 146–147
javadoc, 58
compiling a code, 699
deprecated, 702
document comments, 699–700
files generated, 702–703
help, 702
index, 702
javadoc command, 699
output content, 703
package, 702
tags, 700–701
tree, 702
JavaFX API, 157–161
alerts, 466
arcs, 198–201
change listener, 516–518
color and date pickers, 462–465
dialog boxes, 466–472
`DirectoryChooser`, 472
graphic transformations, 304–310
graphical user interface in, 204–208
handling events in scene builder, 692–696
`HelloMoon` program, 687–692
images, 201–204
inheritance, 460–462
key events, 371
`launch` method, 159
layout pane, 677–686
list views, 556–560
mouse events, 366
`Node` class hierarchy in, 461
polygon, 417
properties, 513–518
`RadioButton` class, 270
scene builder, 687–696
scroll panes, 553–556
shapes in, 161–167
spinners, 521–524
split panes, 556–560
style property, 203

K

key events, 371–374
key typed event, 372
keyboard key, 374
keyboard focus, 374
kilobyte (KB), 42

L

labels, 207, 519, 693–694, 699
lambda expression, 207–208
languages. *See* programming languages
last-in, first-out (LIFO) processing, 612
late binding, 480
layout panes, 203, 677–686
leaf nodes, 615
left-shift operator (<<), 665
legacy system, 151
`legnth` method, 129
less than, 221
lexicographic ordering, 241
`Lincoln` program, 58, 61–62, 84
linear collections, 611–614
linear search, 505–507
linked list, 602
list views, 556–560
listeners, change, 516–518, 521, 560
literals
boolean, 100
characters, 99
floating point, 98
integer, 98
string, 84, 86

local data, 191–192
logical || operator, 663
logical complement, 222
logical error, 70
logical NOT operation, 222
logical operators, 222–224
long integer data type, 97–98, 110, 155, 338
loops, 221
  boolean expressions for, 220–221
  comparison of, 298
  do statement, 221, 289–292
  for-each statements, 296–298
  infinite, 246–247
  nested, 248–251
  for statement, 221, 293–298, 347, 390, 502
  while statement, 221, 242–251, 289–292
low-level languages, 65

M

Mac OS, 32
machine language, 64
main memory, 30, 41–45
main method, 56–57, 188, 220, 333
MAX_VALUE, 156
megabyte (MB), 42
memory, 30–31, 41–45
  address, 41
  bytes, 42
  capacity, 42–45
  computer hardware functions, 30–31, 41–45
  direct access devices, 43–44
  locations, 41–42
  magnetic devices, 43–44
  main, 30–31, 41–45
  random access memory (RAM), 44
  read-only memory (ROM), 44
  secondary, 30, 41–45
  sequential access device, 44
  storage capacity of a device, 42
  volatility of, 42
method, 59, 64, 69, 74, 132, 135–136, 149, 153, 156, 158–160, 166, 168, 182–187, 360, 364, 369, 374, 394, 397, 404, 455, 469, 472, 476, 480–483, 489, 495–496, 500, 502–503, 507, 515–516, 518, 521, 532, 537, 544, 546, 569–571, 577, 579, 586–587, 591, 593, 602, 604, 609
  abstract, 208, 339, 343, 453–455
  accessor, 187, 397
  add, 209, 605, 684–685
  algorithms for, 348–349
  anatomy of, 188–196
  applyPattern, 149
  bank account example, 192–196
  called, 188
  calling, 188
  class, 322
  constructor as, 129
  constructors as, 129, 180, 197
  declaration, 180, 188
  decomposition, 349–353
  event handler. *See* event handler methods
  flow of control following method invocations, 189
  getCount, 323–324
  getFaceValue, 190
  getSource, 262
  getText, 211
  hasNext, 253
  inheritance and, 447–450
  invoking, 129
  isSelected, 269
  launch, 159
  legnth, 129
  local data, 191–192
  main, 56–57, 178–179, 188, 220, 333
  mutator, 187, 397
  nextDouble, 115
  nextFloat, 141
  nextInt, 115, 140–141
  nextLine, 115
  object's, 69, 74–75
  overloading, 359–361
  overriding, 447–450
  parameters, 84, 191, 354–358
  parseInt, 211
  print and println, 84–85
  printf, 149–151
  println, 57, 93, 128, 180, 258, 333, 548
  recursion, 566–568
  reference, 206, 208
  remove, 345
  return statement, 190–191
  rgb, 168
  roll, 187
  Scanner class, 113–115
  service (support), 186
  signature, 360
  static, 143, 168–169, 176, 322–324, 347, 349, 393, 454, 465
  String, 84, 128–130, 133, 137, 396–405
  visibility, 668–669
microphones, 40
microprocessor, 46

MIN_VALUE, 156
mnemonics, 64
modifiers, 669
abstract, 453
final, 186, 322, 343, 449, 459–460
protected, 439–441
static, 321, 324
transient, 669
visibility, 186–187, 439–441, 455–458
modulus operator, 101
Mosaic, 52
mouse events, 366–371
mouse dragged events, 366
mouse entered events, 366
mouse moved events, 366
rubberbanding, 369
multidimensional arrays, 416–417
mutator methods, 187, 397

N

narrowing conversions, 110–111
native modifier (reserved word), 669
natural languages, 69
negative integers, 363
Nelson, Ted, 52
nested for loop, 412
nested if statement, 220, 224–228, 235–237, 287
processRadioButtonAction method, 273
using graphics, 303
nested loops, 248–251
nested statements
boolean expressions, 220, 224–228
indentation for, 237
palindrome example, 248–251
parentheses for, 103
for statement, 221, 293–298, 347, 390, 502
two-dimensional arrays using, 412–416
while statement, 221, 242–251, 289–292
networks, 47–53
connections, 48–49
Internet, 50–52
local-area network (LAN), 49–50
network address, 48
point-to-point connection, 48–49
protocol, 51
Uniform Resource Locators (URL), 53, 256
WAN, 50
wide-area network (WAN), 50
World Wide Web, 52
new operator, 113, 115, 128–130, 146, 148, 180, 385, 387, 394, 397
newline character (n), 163
nextDouble method, 115
nextFloat method, 141
nextInt method, 115, 140–141
nextLine method, 115
nonnegative integers, 363
nonprintable characters, 657–659
NOT bitwise operator (~), 663
number system
base-2, 649
base-10, 649
bases higher than 10, 651–652
conversions, 653–654
decimal, 649
place value, 649–651
shortcut conversions, 654–655
NumberFormat class, 146–147

O

Object class, 452–453
object-oriented (OO) programming, 71–76, 179
aggregation and, 332–336
assigning responsibilities, 321
characteristics of, 72
classes, 75
classes and, 319–321
concept of an enumerated type, 345–348
dependency and, 326–332
GUI design, 365–366
inheritance, 75
interfaces, 338–345
key events, 371–374
method design, 348–358
mouse events, 366–371
overloading methods, 359–361
polymorphism, 76
problem solving, 72–73
software design, 318–319. *See* software design
software principles, 73–76
static class members, 321–325
testing, 361–364
this reference, 336–338
UML class diagram, 336–337, 341, 344
objects, 176
aggregate, 332–336
aliases of, 130–132
ArrayList object, 257
arrays of, 396–406
arrays of color objects, 420–423
attributes associated with, 176

objects *(continued)*
behaviors of, 176
Button object, 206
character strings and, 86–89, 240–241
class and, 74
classifying groups of, 436
comparison of, 240–241
constructors and, 129, 197, 443
creating, 128–132
declarations of variables, 128
dependencies among, 326–332
of a derived class, 455
dot (.) operator for accessing methods, 129
encapsulated, 75
encapsulation, 185–188
event-driven programs, 204–208
Font object, 264
garbage, 131–132
Group object, 166–167
identifying, 319–321
Image object, 201
ImageView objects, 305
immutable, 132
instantiation, 129
method, 69, 74–75
new operator, 113, 115, 128–130, 146, 148, 180, 385, 387, 394, 397
Object class, 452–453
operations associated with, 176
ordinal values, 152–153
parentheses ( ) for invoking methods, 129
pointers, 129
reference variables, 128–130
returned values, 129–130
RobotFace objects, 308, 310
self-governing, 185
Stage object, 160
state of, 176
string literals, 84, 86, 99, 240
String object, 130, 132, 240
text fields, 208–211
Text object, 163, 263, 270
this reference, 336–338
ToggleGroup object, 270
wrapper class, 155–157
observable property, 513
off-by-one errors, 388
operations, object behavior and, 176–177
operators
. (dot operator for accessing methods), 129
:: operator, 206
?: operator, 288
= = operator, 221, 239
| bitwise, 663
() cast, 111–112
–– (decrement operator), 106–107
– (decrement) operator, 106–107
/= (division assignment operator), 107
/ (division operator), 101
!== (equal to operator), 221–222
++ (increment) operator, 106–107
++ (increment operator), 106–107
*– (multiplication assignment operator, 107
* (multiplication operator), 101
== (not equal to operator), 221–222
| (NOT logical operator), 222–224
!= operator, 221
+ operator, 86, 88
|| (OR logical operator), 222–224
%= (remainder assignment operator), 107–108
% (remainder operator), 101
–= (subtraction assignment operator), 107
– (subtraction operator), 101
arithmetic, 101–102
assignment, 107–108
AND bitwise operator (&), 663
boolean, 664
complement operator (), 664
conditional, 288–289
decrement (–) operator, 106–107
equality, 221–222
increment (++) operator, 106–107
Java bitwise, 661–665
left-shift, 665
logical, 222–224
logical || operator, 663
modulus, 101
new operator, 113, 115, 128–130, 146, 148, 180, 385, 387, 394, 397
postfix form, 106–107
prefix form, 106–107
relational, 221–222
string concatenation, 86–89, 661
ternary (conditional), 288
unary, 223
OR bitwise operator (|), 663
Oracle, 54
ordinal method, 153
ordinal values, 152
Otlet, Paul, 52
output data
DecimalFormat class, 148–149
Java standard class library, 146–149
NumberFormat class, 146–147

print and println methods, 84–85
printf method, 149–151
output stream, 545
overloading methods, 359–361
overriding methods, 447–450

P

packages, 136–139
packets, 49
palindromes, 248–249
panes
exceptions used for, 553–556
layout, 203, 677–686
scroll, 553–556
split, 556–560
parameter list, 191
Parametermodifier object, 354, 356
parameters, 191
actual, 191
args identifier, 59, 406
arguments, 191
arrays as, 394
character strings as, 84
of constructors, 338, 409, 411
data, 408–411
formal, 191
method, 84, 191, 354–358
by value parameter passing, 354
variable-length parameter lists, 408–411
ParameterTester class, 354
parent class, 437
parseInt, 156
parseInt method, 211
path separation (/), 256
petabyte (PB), 42
PianoKeys program, 91, 93
PigLatin program, 349–354
pixels, 41, 160–161, 203, 301, 310, 374, 556, 678, 681
plotters, 41
polymorphism, 76
class and, 453–454
declaration and, 481–493
designing for, 511–512
late (dynamic) binding, 480
method overriding and, 449
object-oriented (OO) programming, 76
polymorphic reference in Java using inheritance, 481–493, 495, 511–512
properties, 513–518
searching and, 505–511
sliders and, 519–521
sorting, 496–504
spinners and, 521–524
used for dialog box, 469–472
via inheritance, 481–493
via interfaces, 494–496
primitive data types, 97–100
assignment conversion, 111
autoboxing, 157
boolean, 100
bounds checking, 388–393
casting data conversion, 111–112
characters, 99–100
data values as, 97–101
double, 97–98
false, 100
float, 97–98
floating point, 97–98
int, 385–386
integers, 97–98
long, 97–98, 110, 155, 338
narrowing conversions, 110
promotion conversion, 111
short, 97–98, 110, 155
true, 100
wrapper class, 155–157
print method, 180
printable characters, 657
printf method, 149–151
println method, 57, 93, 128, 180, 258, 333, 548
println statement, 89, 220, 248
private method, 186
private modifier, 186, 667
private (reserved word), 186
private visibility, 186–187, 456
processButtonPress, 208
processCheckBoxAction method, 266
processColorButton method, 262
processMouseClick method, 369
processRadioButtonAction method, 273
processReturn method, 211
program counter, 45
programming languages, 64–66
assembly language, 64–65
compilers, 66–67, 91
debugging, 69
development environments, 68
editors, 66–68
errors, 69–70
fourth-generation languages, 64, 66
high-level languages, 65–66

programming languages *(continued)*
  interpreters, 67
  machine language, 64
  semantics, 68–69
  software tools, 66–68
  syntax rules, 68–69
programs
  class definition (), 56
  comments, 57–58
  compilers, 66–68
  computer hardware and, 30
  debuggers, 68
  development environments, 68
  documentation, 57
  editors, 66
  errors, 69–70
  interpreters, 67–68
  invoking (calling) methods, 57
  object-oriented (OO), 71–76
  semantics, 69
  terminating, 56
propagating the exception, 537–540
property binding, 513, 516–517, 521, 524
`protected` modifier, 439–441, 667
protocol, 51
pseudocode, 349
pseudorandom number generator, 140
`public` modifier, 58–59, 186, 667
`public` (reserved word), 182, 186
`public static` variable, 346
public visibility, 186–187
`PushCounter` program, 207–208

Q

quadratic formula, 143
`Quadratic` program, 143
`Question` class, 339
queues, 611–612

R

radio buttons, 269–273
ragged arrays, 417
random access, 44
random access memory (RAM), 44
`Random` class, 140–141
read-only memory (ROM), 44
rear reference, 610
recursion
  definition, 566
  direct *vs* indirect, 571–572
  fractals and, 587–594
  infinite, 566–567
  in math, 567–568
  programming, 568–572
  `sum` method, 569–570
  tiled images, 583–587
  Towers of Hanoi puzzle, 578–582
  traversing a maze, 573–577
  using, 572–582
  vs iteration, 571
reference to a `String object`, 128
reference variables
  garbage, 131
  for interfaces, 494–496
  object aliases for, 130–132
  objects, 128–130
  polymorphic reference, 481–493, 495, 511–512
  string methods, 128–130
registers, 45
regression testing, 362
regular expressions, 117
relational operators, 221–222
remainder operator (%), 101
repetition statement, 221
reserved words, 58–61
  `abstract` modifier, 453, 669
  `boolean`, 100
  `class`, 58–59
  constants declared using, 95–96
  `extend`, 437
  `false`, 100
  `final` modifier, 186, 322, 343, 449, 459–460, 669
  identifiers, 58–61
  `implement`, 339, 343
  `private` modifier, 186, 667
  `private` (reserved word), 186
  `protected` modifier, 439–441, 667
  `public`, 182, 186
  `public` modifier, 58–59, 186, 667
  `return`, 190–191
  `static` modifier, 321, 324, 669
  `super` reference, 442–445
  `this` reference, 336–338
  `true`, 100
  visibility modifiers, 186, 439–441
  `void`, 58–59, 155, 190, 197, 700
restricting inheritance, 459–460
return statement, 190–191
returned values
  `Math` class, 143–144
  `Random` class, 140–141
  `String` class, 84, 129, 132–136, 239–241
review, code evaluation by, 362

rgb method, 168
RGB (red-green-blue) values, 168
right-shift-with-sign-fill (>>) operator, 665
right-shift-with-zero-fill (>>>) operator, 665
robust programs, 70
roll method, 187
RollingDice class, 178–180, 182, 184, 190
root node, 615
rotation transformation, 305–306
rubberbanding, 369
running sum, 245
run-time errors, 70, 530

S

sampling rate, 34–35
scaling transformation, 304–305
Scanner class, 113–117, 128, 697
Scanner object, 113, 115, 117, 128, 254, 256
scanners, 40
scope of a variable, 183
scroll bars, 553–556
scroll panes, 553–556
search engines, 53
searching
  binary, 507–510
  comparison of approaches, 511
  linear, 505–507
  polyphormism and, 505–511
secondary memory, 30, 41–45
  direct access device, 43
  nonvolatility of, 42
  random access memory (RAM), 44
  read-only memory (ROM), 44
  sequential access device, 44
  storage capacity of a device, 42
seed value, 140
selection sort algorithm, 497
selection statement, 220
sentinel value, 243, 245
sequential access device, 44
service methods, 186
setFaceValue method, 180, 187, 191–192
setFill method, 162
setRotate, 167
setScale methods, 304
setStroke method, 162
setters, 187
setTranslate methods, 304
setTranslateX, 166
shearing transformation, 306
short integer data type, 97–98, 110, 155
siblings, 451
sign bit of a number, 665
signals
  analog, 36
  digital, 34–38
  sampling rate, 34–35
signature, method invocation and, 360
Simula, 72
sink, 545
slider knob, 519
SliderListener class, 696
sliders, 519–521
Slogan class, 323–324
software
  application, 32
  buttons, 32
  checkboxes, 32
  development environments, 68
  graphical user interface (GUI), 32–33
  hardware components and, 31
  icons, 32
  menus, 32
  operating system, 31–32
  point-and-click interfaces, 32
  program development tools, 66–68
  radio buttons, 32
  reuse, 75
  sliders, 32
  user interface, 31
  windows, 32
software design, 318–319
  aggregation and, 332–336
  client, 318
  defect testing, 362–364
  dependency and, 326–332
  design review, 362
  development activities, 318–319
  enumerated types, 345–348
  functional specification, 318
  GUI design, 365–366
  identifying classes and objects, 319–321
  implementation, 319
  interfaces, 338–345
  key events, 371–374
  method design, 348–358
  method overloading, 359–361
  mouse events, 366–371
  parameter passing, 354–358
  static class members, 321–325
  static methods, 322–324
  static variables, 322
  testing programs for, 319, 361–364
  this reference, 336–338

software failure
  2003 Northeast Blackout, 380–381
  Ariane 5 Flight 501, 477–478
  Denver Airport Baggage Handling System, 217–218
  LA Air Traffic Control, 433–434
  NASA Mars Climate Orbiter and Polar Lander, 124–125
  Therac-25, 281–282
software reuse, 75, 436
sorting, 496–504
  comparison of approaches, 504
  insertion, 503–504
  polymorphism and, 496–502
  selection, 497–502
source code, 68
span variable, 346
speakers, 41
spinners, 521–524
split panes, 556–560
stack ADT, 612
StackPane class, 203
stacks, 612–614
Stage object, 160
standard I/O streams, 115, 545
start angle of the arc, 198
statement coverage, 364
static class members, 321–325
  methods, 322–325
  static modifier, 321, 324, 669
  variables, 322
static methods, 143, 168–169, 176, 322–324, 347, 349, 393, 454, 465
static modifier (reserved word), 321, 324, 669
static variables, 322
storage capacity of a device, 42
streams, 545–546
String class, 84, 129, 132–136, 239–241
string concatenation, 86–89, 661
  operator plus sign (+), 86, 88
string literals, 84, 86, 99, 240
String methods, 129–130
String objects, 130, 132, 240
  args identifier, 59, 406
  arrays of, 406
  immutable objects in, 132
  index of characters, 132
  instantiation using, 396–397
  new operator, 128–130, 146, 148, 180, 385, 387, 394, 397
  parameters as, 406
  reference to, 128–129
  returned values, 129–130
string property, 515
StringMutation program, 132
stroke, 162
StudentBody program, 333, 336
subclasses, 436–446
  base class, 437
  extends reserved word used, 437
  multiple inheritance, 445–446
  overriding methods, 447–450
  parent class, 437
  protected modifier, 439–441
  shadow variables, 449–450
  super reference, 442–445
  UML class diagram, 438, 441
subdomains, 51
Sun Microsystems, 54
super reference, 442–445
superclass, 437
support methods, 186
swapping, 502
switch statement, 220, 284–287, 374
  break statement and, 284–285
  data types for, 285
  default case, 284
  equal conditions of, 286–287
  implicit boolean condition of, 286
  single value cases of, 284
synchronized modifier (reserved word), 669
syntax error, 70
System class, 84, 128, 136, 149, 545
system clock, 46
System.err standard I/O stream, 545–546
System.in object, 115
System.in standard I/O stream, 545–546
System.out object, 85
System.out standard I/O stream, 545–546

T

tags, 700–701
target language, 68
terabyte (TB), 42
ternary (conditional) operator, 288
ternary operator, 288
test case, 363
test suite, 363
testing programs
  black-box testing, 363
  boundaries, 363–364
  defect testing, 362–364
  equivalence category, 363

glass-box testing, 364
regression testing, 362
statement coverage, 364
test case, 363
test suite, 363
walkthrough, 362
white-box testing, 364
text area, 472
text fields, 208–211
Text object, 163, 263, 270
this reference, 336–338
throw statement, 543–544
throws clause, 544
tiled images, 583–587
toggle buttons, 265
ToggleGroup object, 270
tokens, 115
tool tips and, GUI programs for, 549–553
top-level domain (TLD), 51
toString method, 180, 182, 190, 192, 333
touch screens, 41
toUpperCase method, 135
Towers of Hanoi puzzle, 578–582
transient modifier (reserved word), 669
translate method, 353
translation transformation, 304
Transmission Control Protocol (TCP), 51
traversing a maze, 573–577
trees, 615–616
binary, 615
collections, 615–616
data structures, 615–616
expressions, 103
inheritance and, 615
javadoc, 702
true boolean value, 100
truth tables, 222–224, 663
try block, 532–533, 535–536
try-catch statements, 532–535
two-dimensional arrays, 412–417

U

unary operator, 223
unboxing, 157
unchecked exceptions, 544
underscore character (_), 59
Unicode character set, 100, 657–659
Unified Modeling Language (UML) diagrams, 183–184, 186, 336, 404
class hierarchies, 450
class hierarchy, 450
inheritance relationship, 438, 441
for the MiniQuiz program, 344
object-oriented (OO) programming, 336–337, 341, 344
Uniform Resource Locators (URL), 53, 256
USB flash drives, 30, 43
useDelimiter method, 256
user interface, 31

V

variable-length parameter lists, 408–411
variables, 91–93
assignment and, 93–95
boolean, 100
character, 100
class, 322
declaration of, 91, 93, 128
enumerated types, 152–154, 345–348
inheritance and, 449–450, 481–482
initializer lists, 393–394
instance, 183, 322
int value declaration, 91–93, 129, 385–387, 393, 396
interfaces for, 494–496
late binding, 480
local data, 191–192
new operator, 129–130
null value setting, 129
numeric, 98
ordinal values, 152
reference, 481–493
scope of, 183
shadow, 449–450
span, 346
static, 322
static class members, 322
variable declaration, 91, 93
viewports, 203–204
virtual reality devices, 40
visibility modifiers, 186, 439–441, 455–458
default, 667
effects of public and private visibility, 186–187
encapsulation and, 186
example, 668
inheritance and, 455–458
Java, 667–669
package, 667
private modifier, 186, 667
protected modifier, 439–441, 667
public modifier, 186, 667
Void class, 155

void integer data type, 58–59, 155, 190, 197, 700
void modifier, 56, 58–59, 155
  Java programming use of, 56, 58–59, 155, 197
  return statement and, 190–191, 197
  wrapper class for, 155
volatile modifier (reserved word), 669
von Neumann, John, 45
von Neumann architecture of computer design, 45

W

walkthrough, 362
Web server, 52
while clause for do statement, 290
while statement, 221, 242–251, 289–292
  body of, 242
  break statement, 251
  continue statement, 251
  divide-by-zero error, 245
  infinite loops, 246–247
  input validation, 245
  iteration using, 251, 256
  logic of, 242
  nested loops, 248–251
  repetition of, 243
  sentinel values, 243, 245
white space, 61–63, 115
white-box testing, 364
wide area network (WAN), 50
widening conversions, 109–110
World Wide Web, 52
wrapper class, 155–157
writing classes, 127–169

X

XOR bitwise operator (^), 663